# American Literary Scholarship

## 1982

# American Literary Scholarship

## *An Annual* / 1982

*Edited by* J. Albert Robbins

*Essays by* Wendell Glick, Rita K. Gollin, Donald B. Stauffer, Robert Milder, Jerome Loving, Louis J. Budd, Robert L. Gale, Hugh Witemeyer, Karl F. Zender, Scott Donaldson, William J. Scheick, George Hendrick, John J. Murphy, Louis Owens, Jerome Klinkowitz, Richard Crowder, Lee Bartlett, Walter J. Meserve, John M. Reilly, Michael J. Hoffman, F. Lyra, Marc Chenetier, Rolf Meyn, Hiroko Sata, Mona Pers, Gaetano Prampolini

*Duke University Press,* Durham North Carolina, 1984

© 1984, Duke University Press. Library of Congress Catalogue Card number 65–19450. I.S.B.N. 0–8223–0601–8. Printed in the United States of America by Heritage Printers, Inc.

6/15/84 *Pur.* 37.75

# Foreword

To this year's volume we welcome six new contributors, and say welcome back to a seventh (former) member. Professor Rita Gollin of State University College, Geneseo, New York, succeeds David Kesterson in the Hawthorne chapter. The pair who have covered Pound and Eliot for us (George J. Bornstein and Stuart McDougal, the University of Michigan) have been succeeded by Professor Hugh Witemeyer of the University of New Mexico. Replacing Kermit Vanderbilt in the chapter on 19th-Century Literature for a one-year assignment is George Hendrick, the University of Illinois. With the departure of Jack Salzman, Fiction: 1930s to 1950s is being covered by Louis Owens, California State University, Northridge. With Jonathan Morse's resignation from Themes, Topics, Criticism, we are fortunate to have back the former "tenant" of chap. 20, Michael J. Hoffman, University of California, Davis. In the chapter on Foreign Scholarship, German Contributions, recently covered by Professor Hans Galinsky, are now being assessed by Professor Rolf Meyn, the University of Hamburg.

As he announced in last year's volume, James Woodress has resigned as editor. Next year's volume—*ALS 1983*, which Woodress normally would have edited—will be handled by our new co-editor, Professor Warren G. French (Department of English, Indiana University–Purdue University at Indianapolis, Indianapolis, Indiana 46202). Though he has surrendered formal editorial duties, Jim Woodress, I am delighted to say, is still available for consultation when we need him.

Warren French is hardly a newcomer to *ALS*. For nine years beginning with *ALS 1966*, he authored Fiction: 1900 to the 1930s, plus three years (*ALS* for 1974, 1975, and 1976) covering 19th-Century Literature. And, as American scholars know, he is a valued and seasoned editor.

*ALS 1983* will have six new names in the roster of contributors. They are Kent P. Ljungquist (Worcester Polytechnic Institute), chap. 3, Poe; Robert A. Weisbuch (University of Michigan), chap. 5, Whitman and Dickinson; Linda W. Wagner (Michigan State University), chap. 9, Faulkner; Jackson R. Bryer (University of Maryland), chap. 10, Fitzgerald and Hemingway; David Nordloh (Indiana University), chap. 12, 19th-Century Literature; and James Guimond (Rider College), chap. 16, Poetry: 1900 to the 1940s. Many will recognize the names of Linda Wagner and Jackson Bryer as former contributors. These and the other chapter authors for *ALS 1983* are already at work. We urge those with essays and notes published in 1983 to send offprints to Warren French or to me or directly to the appropriate contributor.

What must be a record for *ALS* longevity is held by Richard Crowder—a total of 13 volumes. Our older readers have come to associate his name with Poetry: 1900 to the 1930s (later redefined as 1900 to the 1940s). He began his long tenure with *ALS 1969*—missing only *ALS 1972* while on sabbatical leave—and terminates service with the present volume.

We feel lucky indeed that our contributors stay with us as long as they do before the needs of their own research or sheer fatigue impel them to give up their demanding *ALS* duties. We thank those departing for splendid service and welcome the newcomers and the pair of returning veterans.

J. Albert Robbins

*Indiana University*

# Table of Contents

# Key to Abbreviations

## Festschriften, Essay Collections, and Books Discussed in More Than One Chapter

*The Afro-American Novel* / Peter Bruck and Wolfgang Karrer, eds., *The Afro-American Novel Since 1960* (Amsterdam: B. R. Grüner)

*Les Américains et les Autres* / *Les Américains et les autres* Actes de GRENA, 1981 (Aix: Université de Provence)

*American Literature in Context, II* / Brian Harding, *American Literature in Context, II, 1830–1865* (Methuen)

*American Literature in Context, IV* / Ann Massa, *American Literature in Context, IV, 1900–1930* (Methuen)

*American Novelists Revisited* / Fritz Fleischmann, ed., *American Novelists Revisited: Essays in Feminist Criticism* (Hall)

*American Realism* / Eric J. Sundquist, ed., *American Realism: New Essays* (Hopkins)

*American Visionary Poetry* / Hyatt H. Waggoner, *American Visionary Poetry* (LSU)

*Apocalyptic Vision* / Lois Parkington Zamora, ed., *The Apocalyptic Vision in America: Interdisciplinary Essays on Myth and Culture* (Popular Press)

*The Artist and Political Vision* / Benjamin R. Barber and Michael J. Gargas McGrath, eds., *The Artist and Political Vision* (Transaction)

*Autobiographical Occasions* / Albert E. Stone, *Autobiographical Occasions and Original Acts: Versions of American Identity from Henry Adams to Nate Shaw* (Penn.)

*The Avatars* / Ernest Lee Tuveson, *The Avatars of Thrice Great Hermes: An Approach to Romanticism* (Bucknell)

*British Influence* / Linden Peach, *British Influence on the Birth of American Literature* (St. Martin's)

*The Businessman in American Literature* / Emily Stipes Watts, *The Businessman in American Literature* (Georgia)

*Closure in the Novel* / Marianna Torgovnick, *Closure in the Novel* (Princeton, 1981)

*Confidence Man in American Literature* / Gary Lindberg, *The Confidence Man in American Literature* (Oxford)

*Early American Literature* / A. Owen Aldridge, *Early American Literature: A Comparatist Approach* (Princeton)

*Edwardian Fiction* / Jefferson Hunter, *Edwardian Fiction* (Harvard)

*Fifty Western Writers* / Fred Erisman and Richard W. Etulain, eds., *Fifty Western Writers: A Bio-Bibliographical Source Book* (Greenwood)

*From Cooper to Philip Roth* / Jon Bakker and D. R. M. Wilkinson, eds., *From Cooper to Philip Roth: Essays on American Literature Presented to J. G. Riewald on the Occasion of His Seventieth Birthday* (Costerus 26) (Rodopi, 1980)

*From DuBois to Van Vechten* / Chidi Ikonné, *From DuBois to Van Vechten: The Early New Negro Literature* (Greenwood, 1981)

*Group Portrait* / Nicholas Delbanco, *Group Portrait: Joseph Conrad, Stephen Crane, Ford Madox Ford, Henry James, and H. G. Wells* (Morrow)

*Haas Festschrift* / Rudolf Claus Uhlig and Volker Bischoff, eds., *Die Amerikanische Literatur in der Weltliteratur: Themen und Aspekte—Festschrift zum 60. Geburtstag, von Rudolf Haas* (Berlin: E. Schmidt)

*Hawthorne Essays* / A. Robert Lee, ed., *Nathaniel Hawthorne: New Critical Essays* (Vision Press)

*Interpretive Conventions* / Steven Mailloux, *Interpretive Conventions: The Reader in the Study of American Fiction* (Cornell)

*Kessel Festschrift* / Manfred Schlenke, ed., *Festschrift fur Eberhard Kessel zum 75. Geburtstag* (Munich: Fink)

*Longfellow Conference* / *Papers Presented at the Longfellow Commemorative Conference, April 1–3, 1982* (Washington, D.C.: U.S. Government Printing Office)

*The Mind of the Novel* / Bruce F. Kawin, *The Mind of the Novel: Reflexive Fiction and the Ineffable* (Princeton)

*Mississippi Writers Talking* / John Griffin Jones, *Mississippi Writers Talking: Interviews with Eudora Welty, Shelby Foote, Elizabeth Spencer, Barry Hannah, Beth Henley*, vol. I (Miss.)

*Narration and Discourse* / Janet H. McKay, *Narration and Discourse in American Realistic Fiction* (Penn.)

*New Americans* / Glen A. Love, *New Americans: The Westerner and the Modern Experience in the American Novel* (Bucknell, 1981)

*New England Heritage* / James Nagel and Richard Astro, eds., *American Literature: The New England Heritage* (Garland, 1981)

*The Nightingale's Burden* / Cheryl Walker, *The Nightingale's Burden: Women Poets and American Culture before 1900* (Indiana)

*Paradoxical Resolutions* / Craig Hansen Werner, *Paradoxical Resolutions: American Fiction Since James Joyce* (Illinois)

*Philosophy in Literature* / Konstantin Kolenda, *Philosophy in Literature: Metaphysical Darkness and Ethical Light* (Barnes and Noble)

*Regulated Children* / Barbara Finkelstein, ed., *Regulated Children, Liberated Children: Education in Psychohistorical Perspective* (New York: Psychohistory Press, 1979)

*The Romantic Heroic Ideal* / James D. Wilson, *The Romantic Heroic Ideal* (LSU)

*Savages and Naturals* / John R. Cooley, *Savages and Naturals: Black Portraits by White Writers* (Delaware)

*The Seventh of Joyce* / Bernard Benstock, ed., *The Seventh of Joyce* (Indiana)

*Stories* / Jackson R. Bryer, ed., *The Short Stories of F. Scott Fitzgerald: New Approaches in Criticism* (Wis.)

*The Teller and the Tale* / Wendell M. Aycock, ed., *The Teller and the Tale: Aspects of the Short Story* (Texas Tech)

*Through the Custom-House* / John Carlos Rowe, *Through the Custom-House: Nineteenth-Century American Fiction and Modern Theory* (Hopkins)

*The Twenties* / *The Twenties*: Actes du GRENA, *1980* (Aix en Provence: Université de Provence)

*Twentieth-Century American Literary Naturalism* / Donald Pizer, *Twentieth-Century American Literary Naturalism: An Interpretation* (So. Ill.)

*Ultimately Fiction* / Dennis W. Petrie, *Ultimately Fiction: Design in Modern American Literary Biography* (Purdue, 1981)

*Visages de l'Harmonie / Visages de
l'Harmonie dans la Litterature
Anglo-Americaine* (Reims:
Faculté des Lettres et Sciences
Humaines)
*Vision and Refuge* / Virginia Faulkner
and Frederick C. Luebke, eds.,
*Vision and Refuge: Essays on the
Literature of the Great Plains*
(Nebraska)

*The War Within* / Daniel Joseph
Singal, *The War Within: From
Victorian to Modernist Thought in
the South, 1919–1945* (N.C.)
*Women and Western American Litera-
ture* / Helen W. Stauffer and
Susan J. Rosowski, eds., *Women
and Western American Literature*
(Whitston)

## Periodicals, Annuals, Series

*AASt / Anglo-American Studies*
(Salamanca, Spain)
*AAus / Americana-Austriaca: Beitrage
zur Amerikakunde*
*ABBW / AB Bookman's Weekly*
(from merger of *Antiquarian
Bookman* and *Bookman's Weekly*)
*AEB / Analytical & Enumerative
Bibliography*
*AFLSHN / Annales de la Faculté
des lettres et sciences humaines
de Nice*
*Agenda*
*AL / American Literature*
*Allt om Böcker*
*ALR / American Literary Realism*
*ALS / American Literary Scholarship*
*AmerS / American Studies*
*AmerSS / American Studies in
Scandinavia*
*Amst / Amerikastudien*
*AN&Q / American Notes and Queries*
*Antæus*
*AntigR / Antigonish Review*
*APR / American Poetry Review*
*AQ / American Quarterly*
*AR / Antioch Review*
*ArAA / Arbeiten aus Anglistik und
Amerikanistik*
*ArielE / Ariel: A Review of Inter-
national English Literature*
*ArQ / Arizona Quarterly*
*AS / American Speech*
*ASch / American Scholar*
*ASW / American Studies* (Warsaw)
*AtM / Atlantic Monthly*
*ATQ / American Transcendental
Quarterly*

*AULFL / Acta Universitatis Lodzien-
sis Folia Litteraria*
*BB / Bulletin of Bibliography*
*BC / Book Collector*
*BForum / Book Forum*
*Biography: An Interdisciplinary
Quarterly*
*BMMLA / Bulletin of the Midwest
Modern Language Association*
*Boundary / Boundary 2: A Journal
of Post-Modern Literature*
*BR / Bennington Review* (Benning-
ton, Vt.)
*BRH / Bulletin of Research in the
Humanities*
*BRMMLA / Rocky Mountain Review
of Language and Literature*
*BSUF / Ball State University Forum*
*BuR / Bucknell Review*
*Callaloo: A Black South Journal of
Arts and Letters*
*C&L / Christianity and Literature*
*CB / Classical Bulletin*
*CEA / CEA Critic*
*CE&S / Commonwealth Essays and
Studies* (Pau, France)
*CentR / The Centennial Review*
*Chasqui*
*ChiR / Chicago Review*
*Cithara: Essays in the Judaeo-
Christian Tradition*
*CL / Comparative Literature*
*CLAJ / College Language Association
Journal*
*CLQ / Colby Library Quarterly*
*CLS / Comparative Literature Studies*
*CMHS / Collections of the Mas-
sachusetts Historical Society*

# Key to Abbreviations

CollL / College Literature

CompD / Comparative Drama

Conjunctions (New York)

ConL / Contemporary Literature

ConP / Contemporary Poetry: A
Journal of Criticism

ContempR / Contemporary Review
(London)

CP / Concerning Poetry

CQ / The Cambridge Quarterly

CR / Critical Review (Australia)

CRAA / Centre de Recherches sur
l'Amerique Anglophone

CRCL / Canadian Review of Comparative Literature

Credences: A Journal of Twentieth-
Century Poetry and Poetics
(Buffalo, N.Y.)

CRevAS / Canadian Review of
American Studies

Crit / Critique: Studies in Modern
Fiction

CritI / Critical Inquiry

Criticism: A Quarterly for Literature
and the Arts (Detroit)

CritQ / Critical Quarterly

CS / Concord Saunterer

DAI / Dissertation Abstracts
International

DeltaES / Delta: Revue du Centre
d'Etudes et de Recherche sur les
Ecrivains du Sud aux Etats-Unis
(Montpellier, France)

DicS / Dickinson Studies (formerly
Emily Dickinson Bulletin)

DLB / Dictionary of Literary
Biography

DQ / Denver Quarterly

DrN / Dreiser Newsletter

DSN / Dickens Studies Newsletter

EA / Etudes Anglaises

EAL / Early American Literature

EAS / Essays in Arts and Science

Edda: Nordisk Tidsskrift for
Litteraturforskning

EGN / Ellen Glasgow Newsletter

EIC / Essays in Criticism

EigoS / Eigo Seinen: The Rising
Generation (Tokyo)

EIHC / Essex Institute Historical
Collections

Eire / Eire-Ireland: A Journal of
Irish Studies

EJ / English Journal

ELH / English Literary History
(formerly Journal of English Literary History)

ELN / English Language Notes

ELT / English Literature in Transition
(1880–1920)

ELWIU / Essays in Literature
(Western Ill. Univ.)

EngR / English Record

EON / Eugene O'Neill Newsletter

ES / English Studies

ESC / English Studies in Canada
(Toronto)

ESQ: A Journal of the American
Renaissance

EurH / Europäisch Hochschul-
schriften: Publications Universi-
taire Européennes (European University Studies)

EuWN / Eudora Welty Newsletter

Expl / Explicator

FInt / Fiction International

FN / Filologicheskie Nauki

FR / French Review

FSt / Feminist Studies

GaR / Georgia Review

Gothic (Baton Rouge, La.)

GPQ / Great Plains Quarterly

GRENA / Groupe d'Etudes et de
Recherches Nord-Américaines
(Aix: Université de Provence)

GrLR / Great Lakes Review

HC / Hollins Critic

HCN / Hart Crane Newsletter (now
called The Visionary Company)

HemR / Hemingway Review (Ada,
Ohio)

HJ / Higginson Journal (formerly
Higginson Journal of Poetry)

HJR / Henry James Review

HK / Heritage of the Great Plains
(was Heritage of Kansas)

HLB / Harvard Library Bulletin

HLQ / Huntington Library Quarterly

HN / Hemingway Notes

Horisont (Malmoe, Sweden)

HSE / Hungarian Studies in English

HSL / Hartford Studies in Literature

HSN / *Hawthorne Society Newsletter*
HTR / *Harvard Theological Review*
HudR / *Hudson Review*
ICarbS (Carbondale, Ill.)
InL / *Inostrannaya Literatura*
*Interpretations*
IowaR / *Iowa Review*
JAC / *Journal of American Culture*
JAmS / *Journal of American Studies*
JBlS / *Journal of Black Studies*
JEGP / *Journal of English &*
*Germanic Philology*
JGE: *The Journal of General*
*Education*
JIS / *Journal of Indian Studies*
JLN / *Jack London Newsletter*
JML / *Journal of Modern Literature*
JNT / *Journal of Narrative Technique*
JOHJ / *John O'Hara Journal*
JPC / *Journal of Popular Culture*
KanQ / *Kansas Quarterly*
KR / *Kenyon Review*
Kvin / *Kvinnovetenskaplig Tidskrift*
(Lund, Sweden)
L&P / *Literature and Psychology*
Lang&S / *Language and Style*
*Laurels*
LC / *Library Chronicle* (Univ. of
Penn.)
LFQ / *Literature / Film Quarterly*
LGJ / *Lost Generation Journal*
LiLi: *Zeitschrift für Literaturwis-*
*senschaft und Linguistik*
LiNQ: (*Literature in North Queens-*
*land*)
LitR / *Literary Review* (Fairleigh
Dickinson Univ.)
LJGG / *Literaturwissenschaftliches*
*Jahrbuch im Auftrage der Görres-*
*Gesellschaft*
LO / *Literaturnoe Obozrenie*
LU / *Literaturnaya Ucheba*
LWU / *Literatur in Wissenschaft*
*und Unterricht* (Kiel)
MarkhamR / *Markham Review*
MD / *Modern Drama*
*Meanjin*
MELUS: *Journal of the Society for*
*the Study of the Multi-Ethnic*
*Literature of the United States*
*Menckeniana*

*Metromedicine* (Dordrecht, Nether-
lands)
MFS / *Modern Fiction Studies*
MidAmerica: *The Yearbook of the*
*Society for the Study of Mid-*
*western Literature*
Midstream: *A Quarterly Jewish*
*Review*
MinnR / *Minnesota Review*
MissQ / *Mississippi Quarterly*
MissR / *Missouri Review*
MLN / *Modern Language Notes*
MLQ / *Modern Language Quarterly*
MLS / *Modern Language Studies*
ModA / *Modern Age*
Mosaic: *A Journal for the Comparative*
*Study of Literature and Ideas*
MP / *Modern Philology*
MPS / *Modern Poetry Studies*
MQ / *Midwest Quarterly*
MQR / *Michigan Quarterly Review*
MR / *Massachusetts Review*
MSE / *Massachusetts Studies in*
*English*
MSEx / *Melville Society Extracts*
MSpr / *Moderna Språk* (Stockholm)
MTJ / *Mark Twain Journal*
N&Q / *Notes and Queries*
NCF / *Nineteenth-Century Fiction*
NConL / *Notes on Contemporary*
*Literature*
NCTR / *Nineteenth Century Theatre*
*Research*
NDEJ / *Notre Dame English Journal*
NDQ / *North Dakota Quarterly*
NEQ / *New England Quarterly*
NewL / *New Letters*
NewRep / *New Republic*
NLH / *New Literary History*
NMAL / *Notes on Modern American*
*Literature*
NMW / *Notes on Mississippi Writers*
NOR / *New Orleans Review*
Novel: *A Forum on Fiction*
NYFQ / *New York Folk Quarterly*
Obsidian: *Black Literature in Review*
(Fredonia, N.Y.)
OhR / *Ohio Review*
OL / *Orbis Litterarum: International*
*Review of Literary Studies*
ON / *Old Northwest*

OntarioR / Ontario Review
PAAS / Proceedings of the American
   Antiquarian Society
Paideuma: A Journal Devoted to
   Ezra Pound Scholarship
ParisR / Paris Review
Parnassus: Poetry in Review
PBSA / Papers of the Bibliographical
   Society of America
PerfAJ / Performing Arts Journal
PHum / Przegląd Humanistyezny
PLL / Papers on Language and
   Literature
PMHB / Pennsylvania Magazine of
   History and Biography
PMLA: Publications of the Modern
   Language Association
PNotes / Pynchon Notes
PoeS / Poe Studies
Poetry
PoT / Poetics Today (Tel Aviv)
PQ / Philological Quarterly
PR / Partisan Review
Prospects: An Annual of American
   Cultural Studies
QJLC / Quarterly Journal of the
   Library of Congress
RALS / Resources for American
   Literary Study
RANAM / Recherches Anglaises et
   Américaines (Strasbourg)
Raritan: A Quarterly Review (New
   Brunswick, N.J.)
Renascence: Essays on Value in
   Literature
RES / Review of English Studies
RFEA / Revue Française d'Etudes
   Americaines (Paris)
RJN / Robinson Jeffers Newsletter
RLMC / Rivista di Letterature
   Moderne e Comparate (Firenze)
Russell: The Journal of Bertrand
   Russell Archives (Hamilton, Ont.)
SA / Studi Americani
SAB / South Atlantic Review
SAF / Studies in American Fiction
Sagetrieb (Orono, Me.)
SAJL / Studies in American Jewish
   Literature
SALit / Studies in American Lit-
   erature (Kyoto)
Salmagundi

SAmH / Studies in American Humor
SAP / Studia Anglica Posnaniensia:
   An International Review of English
   Studies
SAQ / South Atlantic Quarterly
SAR / Studies in the American
   Renaissance
SB / Studies in Bibliography
SBL / Studies in Black Literature
Scan / Scandinavica: An International
   Journal of Scandinavian Studies
SCB / South Central Bulletin
SCR / South Carolina Review
SDR / South Dakota Review
Seahorse: The Anaïs Nin/Henry Miller
   Journal (Columbus, Ohio)
SECC / Studies in Eighteenth-Century
   Culture
SHR / Southern Humanities Review
SIR / Studies in Romanticism
SLJ / Southern Literary Journal
SN / Studia Neophilologica
SNNTS / Studies in the Novel (North
   Texas State Univ.)
SoQ / Southern Quarterly
SoR / Southern Review
SoRA / Southern Review (Australia)
SoSt / Southern Studies: An Inter-
   disciplinary Journal of the South
   (formerly LaS)
Sphinx, A Magazine of Literature and
   Society
Sprachkunst: Beiträge zur
   Literaturwissenschaft
SR / Sewanee Review
SSF / Studies in Short Fiction
StHum / Studies in the Humanities
StQ / Steinbeck Quarterly
Sulfur
SWR / Southwest Review
TCL / Twentieth-Century Literature
Thalia: Studies in Literary Humor
Thought: A Review of Culture and
   Idea
ThQ / Thoreau Quarterly (formerly
   Thoreau Journal Quarterly)
TJ / Theatre Journal (formerly
   Educational Theatre Journal)
TSE: Tulane Studies in English
TSL / Tennessee Studies in Literature
TSLL / Texas Studies in Literature
   and Language

TUSAS / Twayne United States
Authors Series
TW / Theatre Work
TWN / Thomas Wolfe Review (for-
merly Thomas Wolfe Newsletter)
TWNew / Tennessee Williams
Newsletter
UMSE / Univ. of Mississippi Studies
in English
USP / Under the Sign of Pisces:
Anaïs Nin and Her Circle
UTQ / University of Toronto
Quarterly
UZTU / Uchenie Zapiski Tartasrkogo
Universitets: Trudy po Romano-
Germanskoi Filologii
VLit / Voprosy Literatury
VMHB / Virginia Magazine of History
and Biography
VN / Victorian Newsletter
VQR / Virginia Quarterly Review
WAL / Western American Literature
WE / The Winesburg Eagle: The

Official Publication of the Sher-
wood Anderson Society
WiF / William Faulkner: Materials,
Studies, and Criticism (Tokyo)
WLT / World Literature Today
WMQ / William and Mary Quarterly
WS / Women's Studies
WSJour / Wallace Stevens Journal
WWR / Walt Whitman Review
WWS / Western Writers Series
(Boise State Univ.)
YER / Yeats Eliot Review (formerly
T. S. Eliot Review)
YR / Yale Review
YREAL / Yearbook of Research in
English and American Literature
(Berlin)
YULG / Yale University Library
Gazette
ZAA / Zeitschrift für Anglistik und
Amerikanistik
ZAL:A&E / Zeitgenössische Ameri-
kanische Literatur: Anglistik &
Englischunterricht

## Publishers

AHM / Arlington Heights, Ill.: AHM
Publishing Corp. (now Harlan
Davidson, Inc.)
Alabama / University: Univ. of
Alabama Press
Archon / Hamden, Conn.: Archon
Books
Arno / New York: Arno Press
Barnes and Noble / Totowa, N.J.:
Barnes and Noble
Basic Books / New York: Basic Books
Beacon / Boston: Beacon Press
Belknap / Cambridge, Mass.: Belknap
Press of Harvard Univ. Press
Bilingual / Ypsilanti, Mich.:
Bilingual Press
Black Sparrow / Santa Barbara, Calif.:
Black Sparrow Press
Borgo Press / San Bernardino, Calif.:
Borgo Press
Bowker / New York: R. R. Bowker Co.
Bowling Green / Bowling Green,
Ohio: Bowling Green State Univ.,
Popular Press

Brigham Young / Provo, Utah: Brig-
ham Young Univ. Press
Brown / Providence, R. I.: Brown
Univ. Press
Bucknell / Lewisburg, Pa.: Bucknell
Univ. Press
Burt Franklin / New York: Burt
Franklin & Co.
Calif. / Berkeley: Univ. of California
Press
Cambridge / Cambridge, Eng.:
Cambridge Univ. Press
Chicago / Chicago: Univ. of Chicago
Press
Chronicle Books / San Francisco:
Chronicle Books
Columbia / New York: Columbia
Univ. Press
Continuum / New York: Continuum
Cornell / Ithaca, N.Y.: Cornell Univ.
Press
Crowell / New York: Thomas Y.
Crowell
Delacorte / New York: Delacorte
Press

Delaware / Newark, Del.: Univ. of
Delaware Press

Dial / New York: Dial Press

Dodd Mead / New York: Dodd,
Mead and Co.

Duke / Durham, N.C.: Duke
Univ. Press

Elsevier / Utrecht, Netherlands:
Elsevier

Empire Books / New York: Empire
Books

Europa / Budapest: Europa

Fairleigh Dickinson / Madison, N.J.:
Fairleigh Dickinson Univ. Press

Florida / Gainesville: Univ. Press of
Florida

Fordham / Bronx, N.Y.: Fordham
Univ. Press

Gale / Detroit: Gale Research Co.

Gallimard / Paris: Gallimard

Garland / New York: Garland
Publishing Co.

Georgetown / Washington, D.C.:
Georgetown Univ. Press

Georgia / Athens: Univ. of Georgia
Press

Gordian / Staten Island, N.Y.:
Gordian Press

Greenwood / Westport, Conn.:
Greenwood Press

Grey Fox / San Francisco: Grey Fox
Press

Grove / New York: Grove Press

Hall / Boston: G. K. Hall and Co.

Harper / New York: Harper & Row

Harvard / Cambridge, Mass.: Harvard
Univ. Press

Harvester / Sussex: Harvester Press

Holy Cow! / Minneapolis: Holy Cow!
Press

Hopkins / Baltimore: Johns Hopkins
Univ. Press

Humanities Press / Atlantic Highlands, N.J.: Humanities Press

Illinois / Urbana: Univ. of Illinois
Press

Indiana / Bloomington: Indiana Univ.
Press

Kennikat / Port Washington, N.Y.:
Kennikat Press

Kent State / Kent, Ohio: Kent State
Univ. Press

Kentucky / Lexington: Univ. Press of
Kentucky

Knopf / New York: Alfred A. Knopf

Library of America / New York:
Library of America (Viking)

Little, Brown / Boston: Little, Brown

Longman / New York: Longman

LSU / Baton Rouge: Louisiana State
Univ. Press

McFarland / Jefferson, N.C.:
McFarland & Co.

Macmillan / London: Macmillan Press

Mass. / Amherst: Univ. of Massachusetts Press

Methuen / London: Methuen

Michigan / Ann Arbor: Univ. of
Michigan Press

Miss. / Jackson: Univ. Press of
Mississippi

Missouri / Columbia: Univ. of
Missouri Press

MLA / New York: Modern Language
Association

Morrow / New York: William Morrow
& Co.

Nebraska / Lincoln: Univ. of
Nebraska Press

N.C. / Chapel Hill: Univ. of North
Carolina Press

Nelson-Hall / Chicago: Nelson-Hall

New Directions / New York: New
Directions Publishing Corp.

New England / Hanover, N.H.: Univ.
Press of New England

N. Mex. / Albuquerque: Univ. of
New Mexico Press

North Point / San Francisco: North
Point Press

Northwood / Midland, Mich.: Northwood Institute Press

Norton / New York: W. W. Norton
& Co.

NYU / New York: New York Univ.
Press

Ohio / Athens: Ohio Univ. Press

Ohio State / Columbus: Ohio State
Univ. Press

Oxford / New York: Oxford Univ.
Press

Penn. / Philadelphia: Univ. of
Pennsylvania Press

Penn. State / University Park: Pennsylvania State Univ. Press
Performing Arts Network / Beverly Hills, Calif.: Performing Arts Network
Persephone / Watertown, Mass.: Persephone Press
Pittsburgh / Pittsburgh: Univ. of Pittsburgh Press
Popular Press / Bowling Green, Ohio: Bowling Green State Univ., Popular Press
Prentice-Hall / Englewood Cliffs, N.J.: Prentice-Hall
Princeton / Princeton, N.J.: Princeton Univ. Press
Prometheus / Buffalo, N.Y.: Prometheus Press
Purdue / West Lafayette, Ind.: Purdue Univ. Press
Random House / New York: Random House
Rodopi / Amsterdam: Rodopi N.V.
Routledge / London: Routledge and Kegan Paul
Rowan and Littlefield / Totowa, N.J.: Rowan and Littlefield
Rutgers / New Brunswick, N.J.: Rutgers Univ. Press
St. Martin's / New York: St. Martin's Press
San Diego / San Diego: San Diego State Univ. Press
Scarecrow / Metuchen, N.J.: Scarecrow Press
Simon and Schuster / New York: Simon and Schuster
So. Ill. / Carbondale: Southern Illinois Univ. Press
Stein and Day / Briarcliff Manor, N.Y.: Stein and Day
Sterling / New York: Sterling Publishing Co.

SUNY / Albany: State Univ. of New York Press
Swallow / Athens, Ohio: Swallow Press
Syracuse / Syracuse, N.Y.: Syracuse Univ. Press
Temple / Philadelphia: Temple Univ. Press
Tenn. / Knoxville: Univ. of Tennessee Press
Texas / Austin: Univ. of Texas Press
Texas Tech / Lubbock: Texas Tech Press
Times Books / New York: Times Books
Transaction / New Brunswick, N.J.: Transaction Books
TUSAS / Twayne United States Authors Series
Twayne / Boston: Twayne Publishers
Ungar / New York: Frederick Ungar Publishing Co.
Univ. Microfilms / Ann Arbor, Mich.: University Microfilms International
Univ. Press / Washington, D.C.: University Press of America
Univ. Publications / Frederick, Md.: University Publications of America
Viking / New York: Viking Press
Virginia / Charlottesville: Univ. Press of Virginia
Vision Press / London: Vision Press
Ward Schori / Evanston, Ill.: Ward Schori
Wash. Square / New York: Washington Square Press (Div. of Simon & Schuster)
Whitston / Troy, N.Y.: Whitston Publishing Co.
Wis. / Madison: Univ. of Wisconsin Press
Yale / New Haven, Conn.: Yale Univ. Press

*Part I*

Part E

# 1. Emerson, Thoreau, and Transcendentalism

## Wendell Glick

This year was *Annus Mirabilis* for Emerson, the centenary of Emerson's death, and scholars rose with alacrity to the occasion with contributions appropriate to Emerson's influence on American literature and thought. The preeminent accomplishment, in a galaxy of contributions of high order, was the issuance by the Belknap Press of the two final volumes of *The Journals and Miscellaneous Notebooks of Ralph Waldo Emerson*, making 16 in all—a consummation achieved after more than 20 years of dedicated collaboration by 15 editors and in spite of the ignorant sniping of Edmund Wilson. The importance to scholars of the availability of this reservoir of original material cannot be overestimated; many important studies already have profited from it. The year's Thoreau scholarship, if less voluminous than that of Emerson, was also considerable. My search during the year has yielded 11 volumes that I have classified below under the loose rubric of "Bibliographies, Edited Texts, General Studies." It has produced seven new volumes of Emerson studies, five books in whole or in part on Thoreau, and a long intellectual biography that traces the ontological and epistemological circumlocutions of Bronson Alcott. And it has yielded as well a copious harvest of essays: my files contain more than 50 articles that merit at least passing mention. I come away from reading the accumulated scholarship of the year on American Transcendentalism and the Transcendentalists with the feeling that our profession is in pretty good shape.

### i. Bibliographies, Edited Texts, General Studies

Bibliographies of the two major figures of American Transcendentalism appeared during the year in the Pittsburgh Series in Bibliography:

Again this year I acknowledge the aid of Mara Smith in helping me to locate the periodical criticism, and of Roger Lips for his comments on the Emerson scholarship.—W.G.

*Ralph Waldo Emerson: A Descriptive Bibliography*, compiled by
Joel Myerson, and *Henry David Thoreau: A Descriptive Bibliography*, compiled by Raymond R. Borst. I erred in my report on the
publication of the Emerson bibliography in my 1981 *ALS* essay,
mentioning there my inability to secure a copy of it; having now
held a copy of the 800-page volume in my hands, I am amazed at the
comprehensiveness of the reference matter it contains and the effort
that must have been expended in its compilation. All scholars are by
now familiar with the Pittsburgh format for this series, which begins
with the listing and description of the separate publications of the
author, followed by the collected editions in sequence, and other
categories of data. The listing, description, and reproduction of title
pages of Emerson's separate publications alone comprise more than
500 pages; and the proportion of items, many of them very rare, that
Myerson has been able to locate, examine, and describe is very high.
All of the information in the Pittsburgh bibliographies is organized
for ready accessibility, and despite its enormous size the Emerson
volume is no exception. The 45-page index locates each item. Raymond A. Borst's Thoreau bibliography, organized similarly to the
Emerson, is a more slender volume also attractively illustrated by
reproductions of the title pages of all Thoreau first editions and of
shelves of standard Thoreau works. Both of these volumes are essential tools, supplanting their predecessors, and every respectable academic library will have to have them.

A less essential aid to the study of Emerson, but useful nonetheless, is Mary Alice Ihrig's *Emerson's Transcendental Vocabulary: A
Concordance* (Garland), which identifies in the Centenary Edition
the location of nine "word-clusters" which in Ihrig's judgment are
"the key words in the published prose of Emerson" (p. vii). The root
words in the clusters are (in the order of listing in the concordance): "Beauty," "Culture," "Fate," "Genius," "Greatness-Heroism,"
"Nature," "Prudence," "Soul-Spirit," and "Wealth-riches." Ihrig's
printing of full sentences in which the key word appears makes her
book interesting to leaf through, but those using it as a concordance
will no doubt quibble with her choices of "word-clusters." Another
compiler might have deemed as just as central to Emerson's thought
such words as "truth," "reason," "understanding," "experience," and
many others. *Critical Essays on American Transcendentalism*, ed.
Philip F. Gura and Joel Myerson (Hall), is more than an anthology

of interpretations of the Transcendental movement, though it runs the gamut of studies from the earliest contemporary analyses by Theodore Parker and Charles Dickens through Perry Miller, Lawrence Buell, Joel Porte, and George Hochfield to Myerson and Gura themselves. The long introduction categorizing the selections serves also as an important historical and bibliographical aid. Gura and Myerson discuss the critical literature under such general rubrics as the philosophical underpinnings of Transcendentalism; the Transcendentalists and social movements; French, German, Oriental, and Italian influences upon American Transcendentalism; Transcendental journalism, and others. No other volume that I know of gives as full a sense of the ebb and flow of the dialectic of American Transcendentalism as does this one.

Volumes 15 and 16 of *The Journals and Miscellaneous Notebooks of Ralph Waldo Emerson* (Belknap) conclude this monumental editorial and publishing venture. Edited by Linda Allardt, David W. Hall, and Ruth Bennett, volume 15 covers the period from 1860 to 1866. During these Civil War years in which Emerson was lecturing extensively both Thoreau and Hawthorne died; and into his own journal Emerson copied extensively from that of Thoreau, which Thoreau's sister, Sophia, lent him, preparatory to editing the small Thoreau volume, *Letters to Various Persons*. Emerson's feelings toward the deceased friend at this period are mixed: (e.g., p. 487) "I see the Thoreau poison working today in many valuable lives, in some for good, in some for harm." Volume 16, which continues the entries from 1866 to Emerson's death in 1882, is increasingly episodic, and the journal entries terminate altogether in 1875, though the record of Emerson's lectures, travels, and other activities can be followed in his pocket diaries, here included, until 1880. Until 1872 Emerson continued to lecture. After the burning of his house in July of that year he visited England, southern Europe, and Egypt with Ellen, and one can trace in his brief comments his meetings with many of the most distinguished persons of his day. Both of these volumes, as with the others in the series, are supplied with full indexes.

We were provided this year with another glimpse into the daily life of the Ralph Waldo Emerson family with the publication of *The Letters of Ellen Tucker Emerson*, ed. Edith E. W. Gregg (2 vols., Kent State). Born in 1839, Ellen wrote voluminously of the day-to-day affairs of the family from 1846, the date of the first published letter, until her death in 1909. These letters will be useful chiefly for the information they supply about the comings and goings of the distinguished visitors to the Emerson home; in themselves they have little literary value. Ellen Emerson was a chronicler of facts who made few distinctions between the most trivial event and the most significant, and the reader of these letters is quickly submerged in anecdotal detail. A typical entry: "This is baking-day. The fifty pies are on the way" (1:623). Hawthorne is mentioned but three times—his death and funeral not at all—and there is almost no new information on Thoreau as one might have hoped, since Ellen was a child while Thoreau lived with the family. Thoreau's death elicits no comment. Ellen Tucker Emerson's biography of her mother (*ALS 1980*, pp. 8–9) yields a much fuller sense of life in the Emerson family.

Joel Myerson's *Studies in the American Renaissance* (Twayne) continues to publish valuable bibliographical aids and hitherto unpublished primary material. "Bronson Alcott's 'Journal for 1837' (Part Two)," ed. Larry A. Carlson (pp. 53–167) resumes Alcott's 1837 entries where they were terminated in *SAR 1981* (with the week of 30 April–6 May) and concludes with Alcott's comment on a visit to Orestes Brownson on 27 and 28 December. Many of these entries deal with Alcott's attempts to stem the decline in the fortunes of the Temple School and to counter the assaults on his reputation. They reflect his increasing psychological and economic reliance on Emerson. Carlson's footnotes are copious and helpful. Phyllis Cole's "Jones Very's 'Epistles to the Unborn'" (*SAR*, pp. 169–83) prints for the first time three essays ("epistles") sent by Very to Emerson and found in Emerson's papers upon his death. Emerson chose not to publish them, but Cole views them as "documentation of a personal pathology" that provides "a crucial text for understanding Very's highly personal pietism and obsessive interest in the language of the Bible." Titles of the epistles are, respectively, "An Epistle on Birth," "An Epistle on Prayer," and "An Epistle on Miracles." David A. Zonderman's "George Ripley's Unpublished Lecture on Charles Fourier" (*SAR*, pp. 185–208) "by Ripley's own description, was intended as an introduction to the life and thought of Fourier." The lecture summarizes the life of Fourier and states the fundamental assumptions of the French reformer's philosophy. Zonderman suggests that Ripley may have intended the lecture to drum up sympathy and support for Brook Farm as well as to acquaint lay people with the principles of associationism. Guy R. Woodall's "The Journals of Convers Francis (Part Two)" (*SAR*, pp. 227–84) continues and concludes publication of this rather desultory material begun in *SAR 1981*, beginning with the 1825 entries, and terminating with Francis' death in 1863. Acquainted with Emerson, Francis attended many of Emerson's lectures, though the responses entered in his journal are not perceptive. In his entry for 16 February 1837, for example, Francis wrote: "Went to Boston, in the evening to hear one of Mr. Emerson's course of lectures. The subject was 'Ethics.' It was distinguished by all his usual peculiarities of beautiful thought and expression" (p. 247). A very useful tool is "A Calendar of the Correspondence of Henry D. Thoreau" (*SAR*, pp. 325–99), compiled by Carolyn Kappes, Walter Harding, Randy F. Nelson, and Elizabeth Witherell. It incorporates discoveries of letters to and from Thoreau since 1958 when the standard edition of the correspondence was published by Walter Harding and Carl Bode; it lists place and date of composition and present manuscript location of 763 separate items as a "preliminary report on the new edition of the correspondence" (p. 325) now being prepared as a part of the Princeton Edition. Publication of the checklist follows an arduous search by the Princeton editors for unpublished letters. And finally, Leonard Neufeldt in "James Freeman Clarke: Notes Toward a Comprehensive Bibliography" (*SAR*, pp. 209–26) has "attempted to compile a comprehensive survey of Clarke manuscripts and inventory of primary and secondary works," present inventories being inaccurate and incomplete. Neufeldt provides no item-by-item list of Clarke manuscripts, which continue to show up; but he summarizes the holdings in the major collections of the Houghton Library, the Massachusetts Historical Society, the Andover-Harvard Theological Library, the Huntington Library, the Unitarian Universalist Association, and the Boston Public Library. With its permanent format, *SAR* is an appropriate repository for reference material of the sort I have been describing.

Peter Carafiol's *Transcendent Reason: James Marsh and the Forms of Romantic Thought* (Florida) is an examination of the struggle of a New England minister, uncomfortable with both the authoritarian orthodoxy of the past and the rationalistic Unitarianism of his time, to discover premises supportive of his Christian belief. Marsh was "trapped," Carafiol believes, in what Perry Miller has called "the dilemma of a rational New England mind caught in shifting connota-

tions of the word reason" (p. 36). What set him off from many others
who found themselves in the same "trap" was his resort to Coleridge
to find answers to his epistemological dilemma. In his introduction
to *Aids to Reflection*, Carafiol argues, Marsh "Americanized" Coleridge, applying his thought to uniquely American intellectual problems with a slant that made Coleridge for the first time understand-
able and palatable to the American mind. Unwittingly therefore,
though no Transcendentalist himself, Marsh supplied in Coleridge
"the spiritual epistemology that could make Transcendentalist assumptions active and communicable" (p. 96), failing to comprehend
the full implications of Coleridgean doctrine. This is an engaging
and, to me, a convincing book, though the documentation is sometimes scant.

Brian Harding's *American Literature in Context II: 1830–1865*
(Methuen) contains worthwhile biographical and critical essays on
William Ellery Channing, Emerson, Orestes A. Brownson, and Thoreau, Herbert S. Bailey, Jr., in "On Publishing Thoreau" (*ThQ* 14:33–
37) summarizes Thoreau's experiences with his publishers and nar-
rates the events leading to the Princeton University Press's decision
to publish the CEAA-approved edition of *Walden*. Wendell Glick's
edition of *The Great Short Works of Henry David Thoreau* (Harper)
contains a new introduction to Thoreau (also published in *ThQ* 14:
28–32), and reprints, wherever they are available, the definitive
Princeton texts.

### ii. Emerson

*a.* **Life and Thought.** Leonard Neufeldt's *The House of Emerson*
(Nebraska) may be the most original of the critical studies written
on Emerson during the year. Taking his cue from Emerson's statement in *Nature* that "Every spirit builds itself a house; and beyond
its house, a world; and beyond its world, a heaven," Neufeldt attempts to mold a book out of previously published essays on Emerson's views of science, Webster, Thoreau, epistemology, and other
subjects, to which Neufeldt has added a leaven of new material. The
integrating principle—the "figure" that unites these separate insights
and coagulates "Emerson's view of man and the world," Neufeldt
alleges, is "metamorphosis," and "the term that takes us to the center
of his view of any creative activity . . . is 'metaphor'" (p. 17). But

this book as a whole lacks the vitality and unity of some of its parts; it is in some of its meaty chapters that the book's virtues (and they are many) chiefly lie. Neufeldt pursues his "figure" too swiftly through too great a number of Emerson pieces—his discussion of *Nature* excluded—to probe them as deeply as he is capable of doing. But these are lucid essays by one of the most astute critics of Emerson we now have. *Emerson Centenary Essays*, ed. Joel Myerson (So. Ill.), is a collection of 11 essays on a variety of subjects, chronologically arranged, reflecting in their choice the high standards of the editor. Most are clear and orderly and thus easy to read. They make careful use of previous criticism and of primary source material, and they focus sharply upon single issues. Evelyn Barish in "The Moonless Night: Emerson's Crisis of Health, 1825–1827" (pp. 1–16) has done some interesting medical sleuthing in analyzing Emerson's early symptoms in the light of modern medical knowledge. Wesley T. Mott in "'Christ Crucified': Christology, Identity, and Emerson's Sermon No. 5" (pp. 17–40) views this sermon as a milestone in Emerson's evolution from religious orthodoxy to Transcendentalism. Jerome Loving in "Emerson's Foreground" (pp. 41–64) cursorily summarizes what is known of the period from 10 October 1826 to Emerson's resignation from the pulpit of the Second Church in September 1832. Glen M. Johnson in "Emerson on 'Making' in Literature: His Problem of Professionalism, 1836–1841" (pp. 65–73) treats (too briefly) "Emerson's need to develop a theory of creation consistent with the demands of writing for a vocation" (p. 65). David Robinson examines in "*The Method of Nature* and Emerson's Period of Crisis" (pp. 74–92) "the process by which Emerson [in 1841] came to place heavier and heavier stress on momentary illumination, as opposed to purposeful self-culture, as the means of affirming the value of the soul" (p. 91). Richard Lee Francis' "The Poet and Experience: *Essays: Second Series*" (pp. 93–106) follows up Robinson's analysis of Emerson's 1841 crisis with a survey of Emerson's evolution toward a sense of his vocation of "poet." David W. Hill in "Emerson's Eumenides: Textual Evidence and the Interpretation of 'Experience'" (pp. 107–21) sees in the seven lords of life of this essay "steps toward a usable self," each a "momentary stay against confusion" (p. 109). One notes in many of these essays the view that Emerson's works, individually, grow out of his own needs and tensions. "Emerson's Shakespeare: From Scorn to Apotheosis" by Sanford E. Marovitz (pp. 122–55) traces the evolution in Emerson's judgment of the dramatist "through a series of subtle modulations according to the circumstances of his [Emerson's] life at the time" (p. 153). Robert E. Burkholder speculates in "The Contemporary Reception of *English Traits*" (pp. 156–72) on why the book was more favorably reviewed and received in America than in England; and Ronald A. Sudol's slight " 'The Adirondacs' and Technology" (pp. 173–79) views this poem as Emerson's coming to terms with the news of the laying of the transatlantic cable. Merton M. Sealts, Jr., concludes the collection with "Emerson as Teacher" (pp. 180–90), suggesting that our understanding of Emerson is increased if we think of him in such a role; Emerson's almost 1,500 lecture engagements lend support to Sealts's label. On the whole this is a stimulating book to which the chronology of the essays gives coherence. Important questions are raised, and thoughtful answers given.

The same may be said of *Emerson: Prospect and Retrospect*, ed. Joel Porte (Harvard). As the title states, Porte has selected essays that "suggest not only how extensively Emerson is linked to the present but also how firmly he was rooted in America's past and in the history of his own time" (p. vi). The initial essay, Phyllis Cole's "The Advantage of Loneliness: Mary Moody Emerson's Almanacks, 1802–1855" (pp. 1–23) is tangential to the main purpose of the collection, perhaps, since it examines the writings of Emerson's aunt that record *her* personal search for an epistemology among the 18th-century remnants and the 19th-century romantic impulses then current. Cole finds in her "an awareness that must be called prophetic" (p. 32). Kenneth Marc Harris in "Emerson's Second Nature" (pp. 33–48) sees in the essay "Nature" (1844) an answer to the question posed in the "Introduction" to *Nature* (1836) as to "whether the 'human mind' is or is not a part of nature" (p. 40). The answer is affirmative, Harris believes; as Emerson wrote in 1844, "Nature, who made the mason, made the house" (p. 43). In "Emerson on History" (pp. 49–64) by Robert D. Richardson, Jr. the Porte collection brings us yet another analysis of Emerson's views of the relation between the individual and history, a central problem in Emerson exegesis as the outpouring year by year of scholarly essays on the subject attests. Enough substantial interpretations of Emerson's view of history now exist to form a book-length collection. According to Richardson, Emerson believed that "the motor of history, the driving, shaping force, was the human mind itself" (p. 64). "Emerson and the Persistence of the Commodity" by Michael T. Gilmore (pp. 65–84) treats Emerson's ambivalence toward commerce, "his delight in as well as his disdain for the marketplace" (p. 67n), and traces his shift away from the "antimarket bias" (p. 83) of Thoreau. In "Interpreting the Self: Emerson and the Unconscious" (pp. 85–104) Jeffrey Steele links Emerson with Schlegel, Coleridge, Heidegger, and Jung in his [Emerson's] locating "divinity in the unconscious" (p. 89). Joseph Jones's "Thought's New-Found Path and the Wilderness: 'The Adirondacs' " (pp. 105–19) may be compared to Ronald A. Sudol's essay on "The Adirondacs" in Myerson's *Emerson's Centenary Essays*; Jones's is the more subtle of the two, demonstrating that by 1858 Emerson was siding firmly "with the improvers, the civilizers" (p. 118) and was in opposition to the partisans of wilderness conservation such as Thoreau. Of all the essays in this fine collection, my choice for the most informative is Michael Lopez's "Transcendental Failure: 'The Palace of Spiritual Power' " (pp. 121–53), which examines Emerson's "philosophy of power in relation to the similar views of such near contemporaries as Carlyle, Nietzsche, Fichte, Santayana, Henry James, William Ellery Channing, and others. Compared to Lopez's astringent essay, Stuart Levine's "Emerson and Modern Social Concepts" is a bland, discursive commentary on Emerson's anticipation of later social, cultural, and technological transformations, and particularly of specialization. The final essay in the volume, Ronald Bush's "T. S. Eliot: Singing the Emerson Blues" (pp. 179–97) suggests that in spite of Eliot's aversion to Emerson, "Emerson becomes a surprisingly good measure of the complexities of Eliot's inner biography" (p. 181). At a time, Bush believes, "when an understanding of Emerson might have helped him recognize the contours of his [personal] predicament, he became more hardened than ever against any Emerson-like doctrine" (p. 193).

In *Emerson in His Journals* (Belknap) Joel Porte has given us, as it were, an autobiography of a man who declined to write one. The man revealed by Porte's judicious selection from the newly edited journals is much more a flesh and blood person than Emerson's more formal published works reveal him to be. We see him here making candid judgments of people and events, making resolutions for the future, and reacting to Lidian and the children. We experience his enthusiasms, his gripes, his insecurities; we enjoy his fine sense of humor. The reflections of this brilliant renaissance man range through

aphoristic philosophy, natural observation, reactions to social encounters, judgments of famous authors and historical figures, domestic details and gossip, travel experiences, and many other issues. Each
of the nine segments into which he has divided Emerson's life Porte
has prefaced with a succinct introduction, and the illustrations he
provides are attractive and illuminating. Porte has rendered us in this
book a fine balance of the many facets of Emerson's life and thought.

Whereas Merton Sealts views Emerson as teacher, David Robinson in *Apostle of Culture: Emerson as Preacher and Lecturer* (Penn.)
views him as Unitarian preacher who perpetuated the legacy of
Unitarian theology throughout his life. Robinson's general point
seems to be that one who ignores Emerson's Unitarian background
cannot satisfactorily explain Emerson's lifelong commitment to "self-
culture," an essential tenet of the Unitarians. Emerson built upon
Unitarian premises, Robinson believes, "extending their own assumptions" (p. 185). Robinson's knowledge of Unitarianism is deeper
than that of most Emerson scholars, but his grasp of Emerson is less
comprehensive than that of some; and the division of his book into
31 short, discrete, self-contained essays detracts from its continuity
and raises questions, in my mind at least, whether ideas can be so
rigidly compartmentalized without distortion. Should the sharp focus
on the influence of Unitarianism on Emerson, moreover, exclude the
Calvinistic concern with "culture" of the self which lay back of Unitarianism? Is there a place in a book on Emerson "as preacher and
lecturer" for the traditions of rhetoric and pulpit oratory to which
Emerson's church-going and his Harvard years exposed him? Robinson's point surely needed to be made, but not so completely di-
vorced from its broader context.

Since *Ralph Waldo Emerson* by Donald Yannella (TUSAS 414)
was written "not for specialists in the literature of nineteenth-century
America but for general readers," I will say little about it in this essay.
It is a reliable summary of what is generally known of Emerson, based
on recent scholarship. Who the audience of "general readers" is that
would read this book is not clear to me, but the graduate student
seeking an entree to Emerson would find more interesting and more
profitable an expedition through the journals with Joel Porte as his
mature and perceptive guide. Like Neufeldt's *House of Emerson*,
B. L. Packer's *Emerson's Fall: A New Interpretation of the Major
Essays* (Continuum) posits an organizing principle that is alleged

to give Emerson's major works a new unity, and, like Neufeldt, Packer begins with a core of previously published essays. The two books are interesting to read one after the other, since the lenses through which Emerson is viewed are totally different. As her title suggests, Packer argues that "no sooner has Emerson freed himself from what he regarded as the inadequate biblical myth of origin [*sic*] sin than he found himself forced to fabricate his own fables in explanation of the fallenness of the world." Packer discovers "four chief fables" for "explaining the Fall in the years that begin with *Nature* and end with *Representative Men*" which she denominates "*contraction*," "*dislocation*," "*ossification*," and "*reflection*" (pp. x–xi). The system formed by these fables was "as useful to Emerson as Genesis had been to his Puritan ancestors" (ibid). But as Packer makes her way through Emerson's works, commenting briefly on each, she at times loses sight of her thesis that Emerson created his own personal mythology, and her idiosyncratic piling of assertion upon assertion makes her more difficult to follow than Emerson himself. There is no index. Gary Lindberg, through the legerdemain available to a critic whose knowledge of his author is limited, and whose broad net sweeps up nearly every famous American of the century, labels Emerson a confidence man (*The Confidence Man in American Literature*). "Man Tinkering is another face of Man Thinking," Lindberg informs us in "The Oversoul as Jack-of-All-Trades" (p. 157). Having made such an assertion, he admits that there may be a problem: "*Is* there any legitimate connection between the jack-of-all-trades and the concept of self-reliance?" he muses (p. 158). His answer is different from mine.

The perennial question of Emerson's ambivalence with respect to reform movements draws as always several essays. This year I have noted three. Len Gougeon's "Emerson and Abolition: The Silent Years, 1837–1844" (*AL* 54:560–75) duplicates many of the conclusions of its author's earlier essay "Emerson and Furness: Two Gentlemen of Abolition" (*ATQ* 41:17–31), in which Gougeon points to similarities in the initial coolness of both Furness and Emerson toward Garrisonian abolitionism. The reserve of the two during the 1840s Gougeon attributes to "the seminal influence of Unitarian social values and attitudes on both" and to the tilt of Unitarianism toward moral suasion rather than political activism as a method for effecting social change. The events of the '50s moved both men toward greater militancy. Gougeon goes on to suggest as an additional reason for Emerson's initial coolness toward abolitionism "his belief in the basic inferiority of the Negro" (p. 568). These essays offer little that is new. Moreover, the tension over reform methodology in Emerson had its parallels in the conflict waged in the columns of the *Liberator* at the same time among the abolitionists themselves over the relative efficacy of moral suasion and political action as instruments of reform —a conflict which in the early '40s split the abolitionist movement. The stated aim of Wendell Jackson's short essay "Emerson and the Burden of Slavery" (*CLAJ* 25:48–56) is to "weigh the impact of slavery upon Emerson's social point of view," the reverse of what Gougeon attempted. But Jackson begins his essay by speculating over the reasons for Emerson's early reserve toward organized abolitionism (he had poor health; he feared "dissipating his energies" [p. 50]) and ends it by raising again the old question of whether Emerson's late activism diminished "his earlier imaginative and critical powers." Jackson's diffuse speculations on these diverse issues are not very informative. I find Priscilla J. Brewer's "Emerson, Lane, and the Shakers: A Case of Converging Ideologies" (*NEQ* 55:254–75) no more convincing. Emerson's relationship with the Shakers was too tenuous to justify the claim implied by Brewer's title, and his early coolness toward the sect, which moderated as he learned more about it, Brewer fails to develop into a significant statement about Emerson or the Transcendental movement. Adding the unstable quantity of Charles Lane to the mix only muddies the issue further. Mary K. Cayton's essay " 'Sympathy's Electric Chain' and the American Democracy: Emerson's First Vocational Crisis" (*NEQ* 55:3–24) posits an initial period of role examination in Emerson from age 18 to his entering the Harvard Divinity School in 1825. Upset over the moral corruption of Boston, the young elitist sets out "in the tradition of Federalist social organicism . . . [to] uncover that which all people had in common and thereby show them how to walk in the path of virtue," developing in rural Roxbury a "solitude of soul" that would insulate him from Bostonian corruption and simultaneously send a "contagion" of virtue into society. Many youths before and since have had like impulses. The unstated purpose of Robert Loewenberg's "Emerson's Platonism and 'the terrific Jewish idea' " (*Mosaic* 15,ii:93–108) seems to be to reconcile Emerson to Harold Bloom; the greater part of the essay is an adumbration of Bloom's observation that "It is precisely the theme of self-reliance that ties Emerson's whimsy so infallibly to the Jews" (p. 105). Loewenberg takes no account of weightier studies of Emerson's Platonism by Gray, Carpenter, and others. During the year *The Concord Saunterer* (16:1–22) reprinted from the *New England Magazine* (Dec. 1890) Frank B. Sanborn's "Emerson and His Friends in Concord," which recreates the Concord environment that had such an impact on Emerson and Thoreau. Sanborn's judgments, unfortunately, do not improve with age. Nancy Craig Simmons' "The 'Autobiographical Sketch' of James Elliot Cabot" (*HLB* 30:117–52) adds a few facts to what we knew of Emerson's relationship at the end of his life to Cabot, who aided him (along with Ellen) in editing *Letters and Social Aims* (1875), who wrote the first authorized Emerson biography (1887), and who was named by Emerson in his last will as his "literary executor." The impression one gets from reading the Simmons essay and the "Sketch" of Cabot's life is that Emerson could hardly have chosen an executor more conscientious, responsible, and worthy of trust, or one who in his management of Emerson's literary remains was more firmly guided by the principle of doing "what 'Mr. Emerson' wanted" (p. 119).

I mention two essays that I overlooked in the past. Timothy Summerlin's "To Reconcile or to Submit: The Changing Face of Joy in Emerson's Poetry" (*ATQ* 49:5–20) contains some interesting explications of certain of Emerson's poems but is marred by its author's limited grasp of Emerson's aesthetics. Sheldon Liebman's essay "Poetry and Idealism: Emerson's Literary Theory, 1817–1826" (*ATQ* 49:35–53), spanning the same early period as the Cayton essay (above), establishes a foreground for Emerson's mature view of the poet as Divine Creator and hierophant, the commonly held view of the English romantics. Age 14 was early for Emerson to possess a consciously formulated poetic theory, but Liebman points out that during his youth Emerson read Thomas Jeffrey and Thomas Campbell and the popular British literary reviews and apparently accepted in most respects the critical theory of the Scotch philosophers as it was taught at Harvard. His remarks in the early journals place Emerson not far from Bryant and Longfellow: poetry, he believed, should be moral; it should provide an escape from ordinary life; it should both teach and give pleasure; and it was a means of "refining the taste, polishing manners, and deepening the affections." Liebman believes that Emerson's ideas from 1817 to 1826 amounted to "a representative and rather complete summary of popular literary ideas in the era immediately before the American Renaissance." William H. Gass in "Emerson and the Essay" (*YR* 71:321–62) gives us Gass speaking about himself *as* Emerson the essayist spoke about *himself*, the self of the essayist being, Gass believes, the essayist's only subject. This is more than an essay about Emerson's refinement of the essay as a literary form; it dramatizes Emerson as man thinking, man shaping the essay "into the narrative disclosure of a thought," coming to no conclusion, achieving unity in each essay by "a kind of reassociation of the sensibility" with that of the reader, the mind moving out from its "initiating center . . . in widening rings the way it does in Emerson's first great essay, 'Circles,' where the sentences surround their subject, and metaphors of form control the flow of feeling" (p. 348). Gass's remarkable achievement in this essay is that his own sentences "surround their subject" the while that he is telling us how Emerson's sentences surround theirs: to discuss Emerson's craft of writing essays, Gass employs Emerson's craft of writing essays. Reading Gass's essay is an "experience" as Gass claims Emerson intended reading his essays to be. Amy Schrager Lang examines in "Emerson and the Law" (*Prospects* 7:229–47) the social outcome of Emerson's philosophy, pointing out that Emerson's "appeal for self-trust was not a call to egotism, or to an arrogant disregard of social forms" but that instead "as each man looked to himself and found the perfect law written in his heart, he would be brought into hamony with all other men."

*b.* **Emerson and Other Writers.** The most ambitious of the comparative studies appearing this year was Jerome Loving's *Emerson, Whitman, and the American Muse* (N.C.), though much of Loving's book is a repetition of studies done elsewhere. His chapter 2, "Emerson—the Foreground," is a reprinting of "Emerson's Foreground" in Myerson's *Emerson's Centenary Essays*; and his "Whitman—The Foreground" is hardly more than a general summary of well-known facts. One result of reading this book is an awareness of the paucity of hard facts linking these two writers, and Loving has to struggle to set up his parallels between them. He concludes that both "cease to write at their best when they abandon language and its ability to clothe the invisible world with original and exotic tropes for the vernacular of the philosopher," when they take "the path from individualism to institutionalism" (pp. 189–90). But the same could be said of so many American writers—Archibald MacLeish, for example—so that drawing a parallel on this basis offers little that is unique in the Emerson-Whitman relationship. Beverley Wilson Palmer in "The American Identity and Europe: Views of Emerson and Sumner" (*HLB* 30:74–86) sees in the reactions of these two men to their European travels paradigms of two general American reactions to the uses to America of foreign cultures: Emerson reflects skepticism regarding their value; Sumner sees them as potentially civilizing forces in the new nation. Some of Palmer's conclusions about Emerson are disturbingly inclusive (e.g., "Emerson concluded that travel chiefly produced disillusionment)." James R. Saucerman attributes to Emerson's reading of Charles Lyell's *The Principles of Geology* Emerson's shift of his view of a cataclysmic origin of the universe to one of "steady geologic processes presently in operation" (p. 51 of "A Note on Emerson's Use of Lyell" [*AN&Q* 20:50–52]). Clarence O. Johnson in "Mr. Binks Read Emerson: Stephen Crane and Emerson's 'Nature'" (*ALR* 15:104–10) makes the startling observation that, though Crane was no Transcendentalist, "If we read Emerson without his transcendental underpinnings . . . we find him speaking of the same natural religion Crane describes." As have others, e.g., Martin Bickman (*ALS 1980*, p. 13) Steve Carter searches for parallels between Emerson and Jung. In contradistinction to the usual emphasis upon similarities between the two, however, Carter emphasizes the differences, particularly with respect to their uses of archetypal figures ("The Poetry of Mind: Differences Between Emerson and Jung" [*ATQ* 49:21–34]).

### iii. Thoreau

*a.* **Life and Thought.** Forays into the deeps of Thoreau's psyche continue, this year's premier probe being *Dark Thoreau* by Richard Bridgman (Nebraska). Thoreau's "Surely joy is the condition of life" rings plaintive and hollow against the thunder of Bridgman's massive assault; more typical of Thoreau's "doom-laden" imagination, Bridgman believes (p. 70), is his query in his journal of September 1851: "Is not disease the rule of existence?" (p. 255). "Morbidity and pessimism," Bridgman concludes after systematically combing Thoreau's works, "were consistent features of his mind" (p. 285). The Thoreau whom Bridgman mercilessly extracts from the works was preoccupied with slime, offal, stench, decay, blood, death, predation among animals, and muck; Thoreau was a superficial, inconsistent, prudish, passive, misanthropic, fearful, self-deceiving, moral posturer. Leon Edel is somewhere saying *Amen*. If Bridgman is correct (and his evidence is copious), a great many who in the past have read Thoreau for sustenance have had their blinders on. Edel's contribution this year to Thoreau iconoclasm is included in *The Stuff of Sleep and Dreams* (Harper), where he addresses what he calls "the 'mystery' of Walden Pond" (p. 47). Despite Thoreau's claims to the contrary, Edel argues, Thoreau was not in seclusion at Walden Pond. Consequently, he "lived one kind of life and fancied he lived another" (p. 52). Though Thoreau told us in *Walden* where he lived and what he lived for, Edel knows better. *Walden* "reflects Thoreau's profound dejection" (p. 58), despite the book's "half-truths" having become "impermeable myth" (p. 65). The new ways of reading and divining the "imaginings, fantasies, thoughts" of authors, Edel argues expansively—their stuff of sleep and dreams—"make it necessary for us to reexamine the nature of literary study" (p. 43).

An antidote to the "dark" Thoreau of Bridgman and Edel is supplied by William Howarth's two books: *Thoreau in the Mountains* (Farrar) and *The Book of Concord: Thoreau's Life As a Writer* (Viking). The former is an anthology of Thoreau's writings about the mountains he traversed in Massachusetts, Maine, Vermont, and New Hampshire, with commentary by Howarth, who in recent years has systematically followed Thoreau in his journeys. The latter is a far more substantial study, demonstrating that what Thoreau lived for was to write and that his journal, which Howarth has studied microscopically in manuscript, was "the private history of his imagination" (pp. xvi–xvii). Following the journal, and keying into the journal narrative Thoreau's published works as they emerged through the successive stages of his creative growth, Howarth weaves a coherent picture of Thoreau's ascent from journeyman writer in 1837 to mature artist in 1862. Howarth does not see as does Bridgman morbidity, pessimism, and vacillation as consistent dimensions of Thoreau's life and thought. Nor does he grant that Thoreau was the author of but one important book, from which he declined creatively during the final eight years of his life. "The Book of Concord [the Journal] was his main achievement, a place where art and life merged at the highest level" (p. 10). Gary Lindberg not unexpectedly finds an important role for Thoreau in his study of *The Confidence Man in American Literature*, joining him to the company of Emerson, Franklin, Poe, Melville, Whitman, Twain, Faulkner, and others. Thoreau qualifies ("A Solitary Performance at Walden Pond," pp. 167–80) by virtue of his linguistic legerdemain; Thoreau allegedly treats words as "covers in a shell game," thus punishing "opponents for being so literal" (p. 179). To Lindberg *Walden* is "a handbook on how to extricate oneself from a desperate and trivial world" (p. 179). If Bridgman is correct, Lindberg's escapist from desperation will quickly find himself neck-deep in offal, stench, and muck. Ronald Wesley Hoag's essay, "The Mark on the Wilderness: Thoreau's Contact with Ktaadn" (*TSLL* 24:22–46), challenges the usual interpretation of Thoreau's response to Mount Katahdin, Hoag arguing that Thoreau's highly charged response to the "savage and awful" mountaintop did not mean that Thoreau "identifies nature as the wellspring of evil" (p. 24) but instead that "Man is the evil in the Maine Woods" (p. 23) and "the experience that overwhelms Thoreau . . . is a breathtaking apprehension of the *sublime*," as the sublime is delineated by Edmund Burke (p. 33). Fritz Oehlschlaeger forges another link (a tenuous one) between Frost and Thoreau, connecting "A Drumlin Woodchuck" to Thoreau's thought on the authority of a pun between "burrow" and "thorough" ("Two Woodchucks, or Frost and Thoreau on the Art of the Burrow" [*CLQ* 7:214–19]). William Bronk ("The Actual and the Real in Thoreau" [*ThQ* 14:26–27]) and Sherman Paul ("Thinking with Thoreau" [*ThQ* 14:18–25]) describe sensitively their absorption of Thoreau into their own lives. One becomes aware in the reading of such testimonials that the definitive study of Thoreau's influence will never be written.

*b.* **Studies of Individual Works.** *A Week* continues to receive critical attention. David B. Suchoff in " 'A More Conscious Silence': Friendship and Language in Thoreau's *Week*" (*ELH* 49:673–88), building upon the recent studies of Paul David Johnson, Walter Hesford, Eric J. Sundquist, and others, argues that the "major theme" of *A Week* is the "rift between the abundant meaning inherent in Nature and the possibility of poetic access to it" (p. 673). Suchoff thus discerns in *A Week* the dilemma Thoreau later explicitly confronts in the "Conclusion" of *Walden*: his fear that his expression will be inadequate to the truth he yearns to reveal. "The relation between friends," Suchoff suggests—consciously a silent relation—"stands as a solution to the work's quest for an original language" (p. 685). John Carlos Rowe in *Through the Custom-House* chooses *A Week* as the first of six works which resist interpretation by conventional critical methods. As Stanley Cavell used Wittgenstein to interpret *Walden*, Rowe uses Heidegger to interpret *A Week*, "a wilder and less 'homely' " book, Rowe believes, than *Walden* (p. 33). The principle of organization of *A Week* Rowe discerns in its "reflection on language," which to him "seems lacking in *Walden*"; "*A Week* is a way of thinking the being of poetry as the poetry of being" (p. 51). "Unlike *Walden*, the text of *A Week* is not merely a metaphor for a fuller, more immediate experience of the divine, but the 'bringing into being' of the nature of such experience" (p. 49). Steven Fink in "Variations on the Self: Thoreau's Personae in *A Week on the Concord and Merrimack Rivers*" (*ESQ* 28:24–35) argues that whereas in *Walden* the persona is explicitly announced, Thoreau in *A Week* intentionally repressed "a clearly articulated persona . . . in order to present not a 'Transcendental man' experimenting with experience but the Transcendental experience itself, expressed through a multiplicity of voices" (p. 26). Fink's assignment of first-person roles seems arbitrary to me: he distinguishes the "I" as "literary excursionist" (p. 32), as "Romantic Traveller" (p. 32), as "gentleman amateur" (p. 32), and as "prophetic or visionary voice" (p. 33). "The voices all refer to 'Henry Thoreau,' just as all the voices in 'Song of Myself' refer to 'Walt Whitman' " (p. 34).

Barry Wood in "Thoreau's Narrative Art in 'Civil Disobedience' " (*PQ* 60:105–15) declines to examine Thoreau's essay as a political document, suggesting instead that the "narrative center" of the piece is not a scrap of adventitious biography thrown in but is a "key to the dual vision of the essay"—the section preceding the narrative symbolizing death to the moral and spiritual man whose life is in the state, and the section following effecting a "narrative synthesis" in which a new political perspective is gained through ascent to a "higher" view. To accuse Thoreau of political naiveté is thus to miss the point: Thoreau is not primarily a political thinker but an artist.

*Walden*, of course, is still the focus of critical attention among Thoreau scholars, and several of the recent essays are particularly noteworthy. Michael Ackland's "Thoreau's *Walden*: In Praise of Mental Perception" (*ATQ* 49:55–72) which I overlooked last year, is one such, as are John M. Dolan's "The Distant Drum in *Walden*" (*ThQ* 14:64–85) and John C. Broderick's "A Lifetime of *Waldens*" (*ThQ* 14:10–17). Ackland builds a case in opposition to the commentaries of Michael West and Richard Poirier "which postulate in *Walden* an 'excremental vision' arising from his [Thoreau's] psychological failure to overcome life's brute physicality." West and Poirier fail, Ackland argues, to recognize "the primacy of reflective awareness in Thoreau's conception of imaginative vision." Through a careful explication of passages from *Walden* Ackland argues for Thoreau's firm belief in the power of the imagination to enable man to escape "his self-engrossment" and to penetrate "beyond transient, sensory phenomena to nature's 'grandest laws.'" Dolan's article in some ways complements that of Ackland. Advising the reader of *Walden* to attend to Thoreau's instructions in "Reading" as to how books should be read, Dolan goes on to reflect as a philosopher on the struggle to understand *Walden* as a paradigm of the struggle to understand one's self. In much of his essay Dolan dwells upon the distinctions between reflected and unreflected judgment, citing in the process a wide range of literary persons and philosophers. "A very great force is needed," he concludes, "to break us out of our normalcy and thoughtlessness, our normal thoughtlessness. *Walden* is such a force." Broderick's essay combines a personal response to *Walden* with new insights into Thoreau's writing technique. Broderick calls attention to the "asides" in *Walden* that offer "personal glimpses of the author or his alter ego" and points out how these asides "humanize the book, its author, and its hero."

Each year when I write this essay I am struck by the number of writers on Thoreau who are engaged on an affective as well as an intellectual-critical level: Broderick's and Dolan's essays exemplify such an engagement, and this year there are several more written with a sense of intimacy with the persona of *Walden*. Rutherford Aris, a chemical engineer and ex-Yorkshireman introduced to Thoreau by Robert Bridges, sensitively develops in "The Intangible Tints of Dawn" (*ThQ* 14:52–60) the religious significance of Thoreau's dawn symbolism. Lewis Leary in "*Walden*: Refreshment and Amusement" testifies to the comic, catalytic force of the book in his 60 years of reading it: "It moves people out of themselves and into themselves also" (*ThQ* 14:61–63). In "Into History: Thoreau's Earliest 'Indian

Book' and His First Trip to Cape Cod" (*ESQ* 28:75–88) Linck C. Johnson examines with care the evidence which casts doubt on the generally accepted date of 1847 for Thoreau's compilation of his first "Indian Book." Johnson conjectures as to Thoreau's probable intentions for the material and suggests that the reason they never reached fruition was that by the time Thoreau began to write about Cape Cod his interests had shifted and the Indian material was no longer of use. In " 'Native to New England': Thoreau, 'Herald of Freedom,' and *A Week*" (*SB* 36:213–20) Johnson reviews Thoreau's interest in Nathaniel P. Rogers and his newspaper *The Herald of Freedom*, pointing out that Thoreau once intended to include his review of Rogers' paper in *A Week*, and questioning the inclusion of two revised manuscript paragraphs in the Princeton text of "Herald of Freedom." Gary Scharnhorst in "James T. Fields and Early Notices of *Walden*" (*NEQ* 55:114–17) calls attention to two prepublication notices of *Walden* in the *Boston Transcript* and the New York *Post* that antedate those in Horace Greeley's *Tribune*, hitherto assumed to be the first. For Mario L. D'Avanzo ("John Field's Well: The Biblical Context" [*MSE* 8:4–8]) the unusable well of Baker Farm recalls the "broken bowl" passage in Ecclesiastes and "betokens death and the destruction of the true aim of life."

### iv. Minor Transcendentalists

Frederick C. Dahlstrand has written the single book of the year dealing with a member of the diverse group on the periphery of American Transcendentalism. *Amos Bronson Alcott: An Intellectual Biography* (Fairleigh Dickinson) is impressive in the scope of its scholarship: Dahlstrand has studied not only the major Transcendentalists and contemporary reform movements but has examined the tens of thousands of pages of Alcott's manuscript journals and the 34 bound volumes of his correspondence at the Houghton Library. He has also gone through the diaries of Alcott's wife and daughters and the collections at Fruitlands Museum, the Boston Public Library, and the Massachusetts Historical Society. The record of his investigations is recorded in almost 1,000 footnotes to the 12 chapters that chronicle Alcott's erratic life. Read in tandem with Madelon Bedell's *The Alcotts: Biography of a Family* (see *ALS 1980*, p. 18) one gets an intimate sense of Emerson's "tedious archangel," that "pail without a bottom." But Dahlstrand has attempted to find the pail's bottom despite Emerson's warning and despite Alcott's taking on the ideological color of a succession of philosophies in the course of a long life. I confess to some tedium in following the convolutions of this chameleon; the question that arises for me is whether this book adds much that is new to Odell Shepard's *Pedlar's Progress: The Life of Bronson Alcott*, published in 1937, Alcott's educational innovations excluded. Dahlstrand claims, however, that out of Alcott's search for the answers to 19th-century problems "came something new and dynamic." David Robinson's "The Political Odyssey of William Henry Channing" (*AQ* 34:165–84) is a spinoff of his *Apostle of Culture: Emerson as Preacher and Lecturer*; he develops here more fully than in his book the Unitarian concept of "self-culture" which gave direction to Emerson's early thought. Robinson argues that Channing is "an appropriate focal point for an examination of transcendental politics" because in him the question takes shape as to "how self-culture was made supple enough not only to justify, but to inspire, the efforts at reform that transcendentalism spawned." It was when Channing reoriented self-culture "toward group action and organization" that he diverged from what he saw as "Emerson's excessive individualism." Perhaps so, but this divergence was not unique to Channing and Emerson. It divided reformers like a cleaver in the 1840s. A lecture delivered by Robinson at the Harvard Divinity School commemorating the bicentennial of Channing's birth, also focusing on Channing's belief in self-culture, was later published as "The Legacy of Channing: Culture as a Religious Category in New England Thought" (*HTR* 74:221–39). Linda Black's "Louisa May Alcott's 'Huckleberry Finn' " (*MTJ* 21:15–17) points out that Alcott's character Dan Kean "shares some intriguing similarities with Huck" and that Alcott has received less critical scrutiny than she deserves. Sarah I. Davis' "Margaret Fuller's 'Canova' and Hawthorne's 'Drowne's Wooden Image' " demonstrates that Hawthorne read Fuller's piece in the 1843 *Dial* before he wrote his story and cites internal evidence that Hawthorne used material from the Fuller essay (*ATQ* 49[1981]:73–78). Martha A. Fisher's "German Influence on Elizabeth Palmer Peabody: *The Spirit of Hebrew Poetry* in the *Aesthetic Papers*" (*CS* 16:7–15) reiterates that Peabody read Goethe, Herder, and other German writers but suggests also that Peabody derived from Herder's *The Spirit of Hebrew Poetry* her belief that the function of the artist is to serve his/her nation and culture, and that she chose the selections in *Aesthetic Papers* with this aim in mind. There is enough that is new in this essay to cause me to wonder whether the time is ripe for an Elizabeth Peabody biography. Persons less interesting and less significant have recently been deemed worthy.

*University of Minnesota, Duluth*

# 2. Hawthorne

*Rita K. Gollin*

This was another relatively uneventful year for Hawthorne studies. Much of the year's criticism seems twice-told or eccentric, but illuminating essays also appeared, using both new and traditional critical approaches. The only discernible trend is the increased attention paid by both biographical and textual critics to the writer himself. There was only one book-length study (written in Hungarian), two collections of essays, and one new edition. Of the 11 essays in *Nathaniel Hawthorne: New Critical Essays* (eight by British scholars, three by Americans), two are good, four are flawed, and five restate the familiar. The second collection, the January issue of the *Essex Institute Historical Collections*, includes seven of the papers presented at the Hawthorne Society's Concord Conference in 1980, all densely detailed biographical studies. The edition of *Tales and Sketches* should please both the general and the particular Hawthorne reader: one of four books issued by the Library of America, it is nicely printed, reasonably priced, and includes not only all of Hawthorne's collected stories but his two volumes of Greek myths retold for children and 16 uncollected tales. Other work proceeds as usual: the two annual issues of the *Hawthorne Society Newsletter* include short notes, abstracts of program papers, and current bibliography. Meanwhile, the Centenary Edition of the letters moves toward completion, as does the last volume of the *Nathaniel Hawthorne Journal*.

## i. Texts, Editions, Bibliography, Biography

*Tales and Sketches* (Library of America), the first of four projected volumes of Hawthorne's writing, includes in its nearly 1,500 pages *Twice-told Tales, Mosses from an Old Manse, The Snow-Image, A Wonder Book, Tanglewood Tales,* and 16 uncollected tales of certain authorship. Roy Harvey Pearce follows the Centenary Edition (correcting some typographical errors) and provides a clear chronology and textual notes. Some may be disconcerted by the chronological ordering even of tales Hawthorne never chose to collect and by the placement of the three prefaces after all the collected tales, but Pearce includes tables of contents of the three collections, and the sequence invites fresh attention to minor as well as important stories and a fresh consideration of Hawthorne's development as a literary artist.

In addition to Buford Jones's annotated "Current Hawthorne Bibliography" (*HSN* 8,i:11–14 and with Julia Tillman 8,ii:8–12), two useful bibliographies were published this year. Jeanetta Boswell in *Nathaniel Hawthorne and the Critics: a Checklist of Criticism 1900– 1978* (Scarecrow) lists over 2,800 items, including some relatively unknown publications and a few dating from the 19th century. Minor problems include reprints not noted as such and some double listing, and a bibliography ending in 1978 is already dated. But Boswell provides a handy index of coauthors, editors, and translators, and the subject index is useful if not entirely error-free. James C. Wilson's *The Hawthorne-Melville Relationship: An Annotated Bibliography* (*ATQ*; published also as issues 45 and 46 of *ATQ*) is another useful compilation. It begins by surveying patterns and changes in studies of the relationship, focusing on the issue of "estrangement," then it surveys studies of mutual influence (reflected in literary portraits of one another and parallels of character, theme, structure, and philosophy). Wilson summarizes major discussions of the relationship in his annotated bibliography, then lists "minor" discussions, including dissertations.

Two of the year's most interesting biographical essays examine Hawthorne's relationships with his family and their emergence in his fiction. Nina Baym in "Nathaniel Hawthorne and His Mother: A Biographical Speculation" (*AL* 54:1–27) asks why Hawthorne chose an isolated mother as the protagonist of *The Scarlet Letter*. She answers by calling attention to his emotional turmoil as he wrote the novel right after his mother's death, suggesting that the legend of a reclusive widow presented to Sophia during their courtship masked a deep attachment. Baym proposes Ebe as a model for Pearl and Mrs. Hawthorne as a model for the "socially stigmatized" Hester, stressing that Hawthorne's older sister Elizabeth was a seven months' child and that four years later Mrs. Hawthorne was a widow living with her own family rather than her husband's. But Baym builds too much on conjecture: Ebe was born in wedlock and there is no evidence that the Hawthornes scorned the young mother or that Hawthorne empathized with his mother's "guilt" and used this in formulating Hester's relationship to the Puritan community. Although Baym occasionally overstates, her conjectures demand attention.

Gloria C. Erlich in "Doctor Grimshawe and Other Secrets" (*EIHC* 118:49–58) finds in Hawthorne's unfinished manuscript a "disguised version of the family romance" containing "scarcely disguised materials" from his childhood which the author could not adequately assimilate. Through Doctor Grimshawe, Hawthorne tried to resolve his ambivalence about his chief father surrogate, his generous but authoritarian uncle Robert Manning. The contradictory characteristics of other older men in the romance also result from tangled memories of childhood enthrallment. In a more explicitly Freudian reading Erlich interprets the hero's longing for an old home as nostalgia for the fixed values of childhood, "a psychic drive for reunion with the lost mother and a fruitless search for the lost father." The study has important implications for Hawthorne's other narratives about young men dominated by older men of uncertain benevolence and by other quests for ancestral treasure.

Four of the papers in the special issue of the *Essex Institute Historical Collections* examine Hawthorne's relationship with his Concord neighbors, preceded by Rita K. Gollin's brief introductory account of his life and literary activities during the Concord years. James R. Mellow in "Literary Archaeology: Attempting to Reconstruct Certain Days and Nights in the Lives of the Hawthornes and Their Concord Friends and Neighbors" (*EIHC* 118:9–19) uses letters and journals of Hawthorne and his circle to reconstruct two episodes. Mellow begins with a summer day in 1842 when Margaret Fuller was in town and Hawthorne was an exuberantly happy newlywed, and ends with Hawthorne's funeral, effectively combining "scattered" quotations to create a sense of immediacy. Gay Wilson Allen in "Emerson and Hawthorne, Neighbors" (*EIHC* 118:20–30) examines the understandings and misunderstandings in the relationship, beginning with 1838 when Emerson recorded dislike of a Hawthorne sketch, and ending in 1864 when he mourned the death of an admired friend. The two men walked and talked together and in their journals recorded not only their critical judgments of each other's

writing, personality, and politics but also their affection for one
another. Frederick Wagner in "All Pie and Apple Orchard: Hawthorne and the Alcotts" (*EIHC* 118:31–41) looks at Hawthorne
through the eyes of his next-door neighbor Bronson Alcott, who had
sold him the Wayside in 1852 and supervised improvements of the
house and grounds in 1860. Although the families exchanged visits
and gifts, Alcott complained that Hawthorne restricted even casual
encounters and refused intimacy. In "Louisa May Alcott's 'Hawthorne'" (*EIHC* 118:42–48) Rita K. Gollin discusses the young writer's relationship to her "dark mysterious" neighbor and the admiring
poem she wrote him. "The Hawthorne" not only eulogizes him in
the figure of the long-blossoming tree but links him with Emerson
and Thoreau, the Concord writers she most admired.

Another paper in the same issue, "Nathaniel Hawthorne and
Emanuel Leutze" by Sterling Eisiminger and John L. Idol, Jr. (*EIHC*
118:67–71), examines Hawthorne's encounter with the painter of
his last portrait. During his trip to Washington in 1861 Hawthorne
admired the fresco Leutze was painting in the Capitol, and was easily
persuaded to sit for what would be his last portrait. He enjoyed
Leutze's cigars and champagne and the "blessed state of mutual
good-will."

Hawthorne's friendship with Longfellow is Rita K. Gollin's subject
in " 'Standing on the Green Sward': The Veiled Correspondence of
Nathaniel Hawthorne and Henry Wadsworth Longfellow" (*Longfellow Conference*). She concentrates on the changing self-dramati-
zations in Hawthorne's letters beginning in 1837, when he humbly
informed his former college classmate about his first published book.
The persona became more genial as Hawthorne became more famous
and wrote more as an equal, free to chide as well as to praise and to
confess his own professional anxieties.

## ii. General Studies

The one book-length general study is Csaba Tóth's *Hawthorne világa*
[*The World of Hawthorne*] (Budapest: Europa), written in Hungarian. Tóth examines Hawthorne's life and work in the context of
the socioeconomic developments of his time, saying that Hawthorne's
understanding of the Puritan past helped him understand the possibilities of American civilization. Praising Hawthorne as a literary

pioneer, Tóth examines his influence on his contemporaries (especially Melville) and on 20th-century writers.

Jeffrey L. Duncan's "The Design of Hawthorne's Fabrications" (*YR* 71:51–71) is a ruminative essay about Hawthorne's effort to be true to his ideas of "reality" and about his uncertainty whether reality is ideal or actual. Hawthorne's fiction sets conflicting definitions of aesthetic and moral truth against one another and thus poses problems for the reader. Duncan argues convincingly that the unanswered questions in Hawthorne's fictions are designed to express his dismay at seeking certainties he could not find.

Eric Mottram in "Power and Law in Hawthorne's Fictions" (*Hawthorne Essays*, pp. 187–228) has a good subject: statements about the forms and origins of repression (sexual, social, and political). But the essay is marred by disjunctions, inaccurate generalizations, and idiosyncratic diction. It is virtually impossible to follow such statements as "His writing necessity presses out from a vocabulary of law, witchcraft, judgement, science and medicine, and theology—towards the Sin the Passion could not redeem, the Sin which it is therefore not permitted to eradicate"; and quotations from such diverse sources as Marx, Todorov, and Robbe-Grillet more often take the reader off on tangents than into Hawthorne's fiction.

The two remaining general studies examine Hawthorne's writing in the context of American cultural and literary patterns. Lois Zamora's chapter on "The Myth of Apocalypse and the American Literary Imagination" in *The Apocalyptic Vision* (pp. 97–138) treats Hawthorne as a key figure. In *The Scarlet Letter*, *The Blithedale Romance*, and other fictions "we sense the end of American innocence"; they present ironic commentaries on the idea of America as a new Eden. There are a few factual errors, and Zamora does not address Hawthorne's complex ideas about time and eternity, but she places him clearly in the tradition she defines. James L. Machor in "Pastoralism and the American Urban Ideal: Hawthorne, Whitman, and the Literary Pattern" (*AL* 54:329–53) analyzes the ways Hawthorne and Whitman dramatized the complementarity of pastoral and urban ideals. Using "My Kinsman, Major Molineux" and *The Blithedale Romance* as examples, Machor discusses Hawthorne's balanced ironic treatments, but his terminology is often too loose. It is indeed naive of Robin to believe the city "will comport with his urban-pastoral image," but it is stretching the point to argue that the rebellious crowd enacts a conflicting "version of urban pastoralism." Similarly, although Coverdale can see only a limited version of the "urban-pastoral ideal" from his boardinghouse window, only incidentally do the old clothes worn at Blithedale show the incompatibility of city values and pastoral dreams.

### *iii.* Novels and Longer Works

As in 1981, most of the articles about novels treat individual works, primarily *The Scarlet Letter*. Eric Homberger's "Nathaniel Hawthorne and the Dream of Happiness" (*Hawthorne Essays*, pp. 171–86) is an exception, a study of the relationship of isolation to the "dream of happiness" in the completed novels (including *Fanshawe*), read as refractions of Hawthorne's experience. But analyses are often marred by misstatements, misemphases, and oversimplifications. Homberger argues clearly that the deep structure of the novels results from "Hawthorne's reserved and taciturn nature," but he is reductive and inconsistent in construing the "dream of happiness."

Most of the year's studies of *The Scarlet Letter* treat "The Custom-House" as an integral part, as does A. Robert Lee in " 'Like a Dream Behind Me': Hawthorne's 'The Custom-House' and *The Scarlet Letter*" (*Hawthorne Essays*, pp. 48–67). But Lee seems curiously unaware of recent scholarship, as when he says that attention to the novel "has almost invariably ignored, or at best skimped, Hawthorne's 'The Custom-House.' " Lee recognizes the crafty disingenuousness of the narrative personae and reads "The Custom-House" as a "pathway" into the novel, but others have done so before. The essay contains curious misapprehensions—that Hawthorne wrote the novel in the Old Manse, for example, or that he went to Europe because of a "need to break free" of New England. Nevertheless, Lee understands how the novel challenges rigid morality and invites the reader's complicity in reaching judgments. A complementary essay, Mark Kinkead-Weekes's "The Letter, the Picture, and the Mirror: Hawthorne's Framing of *The Scarlet Letter*" (*Hawthorne Essays*, pp. 68–87) also follows clues from "The Custom-House." Kinkead-Weekes evaluates Hawthorne's combination of "literalness" with "numinousness" and tries to explain the novel's main characters and symbols without offering either "exclusive interpretation" or the assertion of "deconstructive indecipherability." Although he does not always avoid the first danger, he comments sympathetically about the ways Hawthorne presents one realm of experience while intimating the existence of others.

In a study published last year ("Communal Theme and the Outer Frame of *The Scarlet Letter*" in *Closure in the Novel*) Marianna Torgovnick argues that the "outer frame" of the novel consists of "The Custom-House" and Hawthorne's final chapter, a frame that reveals Hawthorne's beliefs about our need for social order despite its spiritual constraints. She observes that Hawthorne carefully "rechannels" the reader's sympathy for Hester's passionate independence after the forest scene. Although Torgovnick slightly oversimplifies Hawthorne's ambivalence about Hester, her analysis of the novel's thematic closure is clear, fresh, and intelligent.

Millicent Bell in "The Obliquity of Signs: *The Scarlet Letter*" (*MR* 23:9–26) studies Hawthorne's "methodological indeterminacy." She reads the novel as "an essay in semiology," going from the question of what Hawthorne's signs mean to the more important question of what his use of signs signifies. The novel's "insistent ambiguity" expresses his skepticism about the possibility of reading the world as text; this explains why the narrator offers the reader alternative readings of particular symbols. Hawthorne "seeks spiritual meaning in the quotidian," Bell says, but with no certainty that it exists.

Two other ambitious essays are less successful. Michael Ragussis in "Family Discourse and Fiction in *The Scarlet Letter*" (*ELH* 49: 863–88) argues that "the ban of silence lies on everyone in *The Scarlet Letter*" because of the major characters' tangled family relationships. Silence is a form of "symbolic imprisonment." The premise is interesting, but analyses are uneven: it is not true that Pearl is not "allowed a human name," nor that she is "a counterfeit pearl, disowned by father and mother alike," though it is true that she needs and bestows identity. The essay explains that Dimmesdale confesses in the third person to distance himself, but does not establish that he is "the invisible self that we all share but fail to recognize." In the end the reader may be confused by equivocations, such as the interpretation of the *A* as standing for "Adultery at the beginning, for the impossibility of finding an unadulterated origin." In another ingenious exercise Andrew Hudgins' "Landscape and Movement in *The Scarlet Letter*" (*SDR* 19:5–17) examines "the literary geography" of the romance and proposes that it is structured in concentric circles with the scaffold as center. Despite some interesting comments on the scaffold as *axis mundi*, the study is overly schematized and distorting: for example, Hudgins says Hester must move outward from the scaffold, "which seems both to attract and repel her," but then return to it before she can move out further; and he does not recognize Hawthorne's ambivalence about Hester's discoveries in the moral wilderness.

Three essays offer widely varied hypotheses about individual characters in *The Scarlet Letter*. Dorena Allen Wright in "The Meeting at the Brook-Side: Beatrice, the Pearl-Maiden, and Pearl Prynne" (*ESQ* 28:112–20) suggests that Pearl's role as moral guide derives from Dante's Beatrice and the medieval Pearl. Wright meticulously places her study in the literary tradition, and she illuminates both the forest scene and Pearl's agency in Dimmesdale's conversion; but, in arguing that Pearl is "human rather than divine" and that she leads Dimmesdale to a purely secular conversion, she eliminates alternatives proposed by the author. Watson Branch in "From Allegory to Romance: Hawthorne's Transformation of *The Scarlet Letter*" (*MP* 80:145–60) speculates ingeniously that Chillingworth was only a "satanic physician-investigator" in Hawthorne's original story and became Hester's husband during the revision, which would explain such "flaws" as "the unnecessary repetition of information about Chillingworth in chapter 8," Chillingworth's failure to punish Hester, and Hester's failure to warn Dimmesdale about her husband. The question of how Hawthorne revised and expanded his first novel is fascinating; but Branch's essay has the unintended effect of proving how tightly it is plotted. Daniel Cottom in "Hawthorne versus Hester: The Ghostly Dialectic of Romance in *The Scarlet Letter*" (*TSLL* 24:47–67) takes another unusual approach, suggesting that, through his diffident persona as narrator of "The Custom-House" and "editor" of *The Scarlet Letter*, Hawthorne "opposes himself to Hester" and opposes his own "symbolic realm of romance" to Hester's "demonic realm of nature," where any woman must dwell who wants to transcend social judgment. Although Cottom is right in pointing out the power and range of Hawthorne's equivocal style, many of his arguments are marred by equivocations and non sequiturs. Hester cannot transcend "physicality" as the narrator can, but that is not a matter of sexual difference.

Richard Gray's "Hawthorne: A Problem" (*Hawthorne Essays,*

pp. 88–109) is a clear-minded essay for the general reader which accounts for the "personal note" in *The House of the Seven Gables* by relating it to Hawthorne's experiences and family traditions. Gray attributes tonal shifts to the influences of Dickens and Poe and (curiously) to a fear of being "caught at one particular pitch." Proposing the house as the novel's organizing principle, hardly a new idea, Gray interprets the final chapter as a "retreat" which precludes the need to choose between theories of history as recurrence or progressive change. In a version of what might be called the year's leitmotif he says Hawthorne "turns uncertainty itself into an art" in which conflicts are "resolved, if at all, by each reader."

All four essays on *The Blithedale Romance* discuss Coverdale's role as narrator. Keith Carabine's " 'Bitter Honey': Miles Coverdale as Narrator in *The Blithedale Romance*" (*Hawthorne Essays*, pp. 110–30) discusses Coverdale's "provisional status" as a writer distressed about his detachment from reality yet empowered by his role as observer. He is an "exhibitor" like Westervelt and a passive medium like Priscilla. But there are some inexact readings, and Carabine is only half right in saying the novel is "about the education of Coverdale into an acceptance of the role of the artist as sympathetic observer who misses out on life." It is because he misses out on life that he is a minor writer and not Hawthorne's ideal artist. For John Harmon McElroy and Edward L. McDonald in "The Coverdale Romance" (*SN* 14:1–16) Coverdale is pathetic and repulsive. Suggesting that he affected the action more directly than he acknowledged (probably telling Moodie how Zenobia mistreated Priscilla, for example), the authors propose the bizarre hypothesis that Coverdale strangled Zenobia "in a burst of dammed-up sexual frustration" after she spurned him, then sank her body in the river, thus punishing both the "fallen woman" and Hollingsworth but repressing memory of the traumatic events. The authors are right to mistrust Coverdale's confession of love for Priscilla and to recognize his attraction to Zenobia, but the circumstantial evidence they offer for his crime exceeds plausibility. Mary Suzanne Schriber in "Justice to Zenobia" (*NEQ* 55:61–78) has a different reason for doubting Coverdale's suggestion that Zenobia killed herself because of unrequited love. His views of women are conventionally sentimental, Schriber says. This accounts for his discomfort with Zenobia, while her responses to him ironically demonstrate how such conventional assumptions limit women.

Schriber argues effectively if not conclusively that since we can challenge Coverdale's hypotheses about what Zenobia thought drowning would be like, we can challenge his hypotheses about why she
drowned: perhaps it was an accident or perhaps she despaired about
her lot as a woman. Readers accept Coverdale's hypotheses because
they share his preconceptions, but that is unjust "to the character of
Zenobia and to the artistry of Hawthorne." In another carefully reasoned study, " 'Gifted Simplicity of Vision': Pastoral Expectations in
*The Blithedale Romance*" (*ESQ* 28:135–51), Judy Schaaf Anhorn
answers her question about "why and how Hawthorne manifests
himself in the novel" by firmly emplacing it in the traditions of literary pastoralism as modified by Coverdale's character and his problems as a writer, and by reading the natural "hieroglyphics" of grapes
and wine as symbols of the romantic artist's burden and harvest.
Anhorn discusses the ways Hawthorne's pastoral romance draws on
the author's experiences, anxieties, and aspirations, and on the ways
it "both celebrates and criticizes itself and its tradition."

Neither of the year's two essays on *The Marble Faun* illuminates
the novel. Graham Clarke in "To Transform and Transfigure: The
Aesthetic Play of Hawthorne's *The Marble Faun*" (*Hawthorne Essays*, pp. 131–47) concentrates on the interplay of art and life in the
novel and tries to distinguish between "transformation" and "transfiguration," but does not clearly make or apply the distinction. The
essay is not informed by previous criticism, and it is marred by misstatements and misreadings. In "God as Artist in *The Marble Faun*"
(*Renascence* 34:144–60) Robert Emmet Whelan offers a reading of
the novel as a psychomachia, with Miriam as Will, Hilda as Religious
Faith, and so on. Whelan reads the novel as "a Holy War between
Flesh and Spirit" behind which "there looms large the Artist of artists
—God the Old Master." The essay contains self-contradictions and
misinterpretations, but its main problem is distorting oversimplification.

By contrast, Arnold Goldman in "Hawthorne's Old Home" (*Hawthorne Essays*, pp. 148–70) perceptively examines the strategies and
structures of the separate essays in *Our Old Home*. Although Hawthorne could finish none of the last romances, in his last published
work he resolved troublesome questions about England, his vocation,
and his human responsibilities. Goldman shows the aesthetic unity
of the work while making new sense of particular episodes: only after

he wrote about caressing a loathsome workhouse child in the essay on English poverty could Hawthorne write "Civic Banquets" as "a man who has come through, who is at peace with himself and with the world."

## iv. Short Works

Three of this year's nearly two dozen studies of short works treat groups of stories. Brian Way in "Art and the Spirit of Anarchy: A Reading of Hawthorne's Short Stories" (*Hawthorne Essays*, pp. 11–30) argues that a subversive spirit underlies Hawthorne's "consistent decorum of tone," the result of a tension "between the wish to affirm and the impulse to deny." The forms of subversion include two familiar ones (the narrator's presentation of conflicting meanings and Hawthorne's use of "the anarchic power of laughter" to expose absurdity) and one that is only half true (Hawthorne's "tendency to attack what he values most," including art and artists). Some judgments are dubious, but the commentary is generally accurate. Kermit Vanderbilt offers an interesting pedagogical device in "Hawthorne's Ironic Mode: With Side-Trips into Emerson" (*Thalia* 4:40–45): he uses statements from Emerson as epigraphs for Hawthorne stories to give a "perspective of ironic relief." The epigraph for "Young Goodman Brown," for example, is "In the woods, we return to reason and faith." The witty and original "Hawthorne-Emerson dialogue" invites fresh understanding of the writers' ideological differences and a fresh appreciation of Hawthornean irony. The title of Carol Billman's "Nathaniel Hawthorne: 'Revolutionizer' of Children's Literature?" (*SAF* 10:107–14) announces her subject. Billman concludes that Hawthorne followed current didactic traditions, diverging only in his decision to retell classical Greek myths. Yet the quotations she uses to establish the moralizations and domestications of Hawthorne's narratives also demonstrate the ways he enlisted the imaginative collaboration of the "innocents" who read or heard them.

Each of the three studies of "Rappaccini's Daughter" takes a different critical approach. Steven Mailloux in a chapter entitled "Practical Criticism: The Reader in American Fiction" in his *Interpretive Conventions: The Reader in the Study of American Fiction* (Cornell, pp. 66–92) uses the story to demonstrate reader-response criticism "based on a social model of reading." Drawing on Barthes's categories, Mailloux patiently explains how the reader follows a hermeneutic code of enigma-solution and a proairetic code of plot-resolution, invited first to judge by appearances, then to question motives, and finally to reach moral judgments. Although it is an oversimplification to suggest that previous criticism neglected the temporal process of reading, Mailloux convincingly demonstrates how Hawthorne trains good readers to move toward trustworthy ethical judgments unavailable to the shallow Giovanni. In "The Language of Inflation in 'Rappaccini's Daughter' " (*TSLL* 24:1–22) John Franzosa relates the story's language to the inflated language of economic and political debate in the 1840s, which called "all values into question." Hawthorne shared his contemporaries' skeptical attitudes toward authority, toward the relation of token to value, and toward the relation of language to thought and thing, and therefore worried about his authority as a writer. The argument is learned if at times far-fetched. The third essay, Margaret Hallissy's "Hawthorne's Venomous Beatrice" (*SSF* 19:231–40) begins well by discussing the age-old tradition of the poisonous woman as a figure for sexual excess, stressing the idea Hawthorne encountered in Browne—that poison can become its own antidote. This Hallissy considers the reason for characterizing Beatrice as both "sexual seductress and spiritual savior" who dies because Giovanni and Baglioni understand only her physical being. Yet it seems unwarranted to criticize Giovanni on the grounds that "unconsummated love is itself a violation of chastity in that it is unproductive" or to suggest that the idea might have originated in an account Hawthorne might have heard about George Rapp's problems with celibacy in his commune. More important, although Beatrice is not evil, she is obviously poisonous; and although poison can create its own antidote, that does not prove Beatrice was "Giovanni's true antidote."

The three articles on "Young Goodman Brown" are as varied in methodology as those on "Rappaccini's Daughter." Elizabeth Wright in "The New Psychoanalysis and Literary Criticism: A Reading of Hawthorne and Melville" (*PoT* 3:89–105) uses the story to test poststructural approaches, especially those of Lacan and Derrida, concentrating on "nodal points" which "manifest a desire for lost meanings." Some of her readings are interesting: of the punning significations of the devil, for example. But many are questionable at best; for example, Brown fears Faith "will betray him as a mother, and that is why he fears the devil father-figure is coming to claim her." And there are factual misreadings; she believes "they carved no hopeful verse upon his tombstone" means that Brown like Oedipus is buried in an unmarked grave. Asking how a "text questions the meaning of meaning" can be productive; but although Lacan and Derrida help Wright understand "patterns which undermine the stable meaning of the text," her use of their approaches often deforms Hawthorne's text. In " 'My Faith is Gone!': 'Young Goodman Brown' and Puritan Conversion' " ( *C&L* 32:23–32 ) Jane Donahue Eberwein reads the story as an allegory about a crisis of faith "in the context of Calvinist conversion psychology," which questioned whether a sinner had been saved, whether he was in a state of grace, and whether he had attained redemptive faith. "The experience of faith would be an introduction to a long period of strenuous combat with sinfulness"; thus Brown's marriage to Faith was followed by spiritual crisis. In the end he is "still in an unconverted state, with a heightened conviction of sin" which he projects onto his community and thus "becomes that quintessential Puritan sinner: the hypocrite." Other stern Puritans in Hawthorne's fiction also suffered from "psychological pressures imposed by a schematically defined conversion theology," Eberwein says, noting that Brown's generation "accused the witches at Salem." Norman H. Hostetler in "Narrative Structure and Theme in 'Young Goodman Brown' " ( *JNT* 12:221–28) reads the story more traditionally as an illustration of the "consequences of psychological misjudgment concerning perception and reality," carefully distinguishing the narrator's point of view from Brown's. The ambiguities of the narrator's descriptions establish his credibility, while Brown's credibility is undermined by his "extreme Lockean" certainty about the ontological status of what he beholds: "seeking to cut himself off from the evil in the external world, Brown has committed himself to the evil of his own mind." There are a few self-contradictions, as when Hostetler says evil is only in Brown's mind yet also assumes ( as does the narrator) that the devil has separate existence; but the essay clearly differentiates the moral implications of the narrator's structured perceptions from Brown's.

Two critics offer new information about the background of "My Kinsman, Major Molineux." Robert C. Grayson in "The New England Sources of 'My Kinsman, Major Molineux' " ( *AL* 54:545–59) lucidly discusses Hawthorne's extensive borrowings from Snow and other

New England historians—information about pre-revolutionary Boston localities, social customs, and historic events—to give his story verisimilitude and develop his "democratic" theme. Hawthorne refers to such places as the scene of the Boston massacre, and models his fictional uprising on documented mob activities. Three historical figures might have helped shape Robin: the young Peter Faneuil, the revolutionary Major Molineux, and the Molineux who proposed to Locke the question of whether a man formerly blind could visually distinguish a cube from a sphere from his previous tactile experience (which Grayson compares to Robin's problem of perceiving his kinsman's true condition). Avoiding the dangers of oversimplifying Hawthorne's use of his sources, Grayson discusses the young writer's fusion of fact with imagination in creating his unified narrative. Jesse Bier's note on "Hawthorne's 'My Kinsman, Major Molineux'" (*Expl* 41: 28–30) proposes another origin for the story's patronym: an essay in "Rees' Encyclopedia" on "the 'Molinists,'" the liberal 16th-century religious sect that had given Hawthorne his philosophic cue for the story," but with spelling taken from the preceding item about a New Zealand bay called Molineux's Harbour.

Of the remaining articles four increase our appreciation of particular stories by inquiring into the facts and attitudes that informed them. June Howard in "The Watchmaker, the Artist, and the Iron Accents of History: Notes on Hawthorne's 'Artist of the Beautiful'" (*ESQ* 28:1–10) argues that the story is ambivalent rather than ambiguous. It must be understood in two contexts: Hawthorne's dilemma as a writer, and the problems of industrialization in the 1840s. Howard reads the tale as a statement of the human struggle to remake social conditions and (whether in fiction or any other creation) to "reconcile beauty and industry." In "Hawthorne's Pygmalion as William Rush" (*SSF* 19:343–49) Sarah I. Davis suggests that "Drowne's Wooden Image" originated in stories Hawthorne encountered in Dunlap and elsewhere which presented the Philadelphia sculptor as an artist who had the preternatural ability to "release" from wood a work with life of its own. Like Rush, Drowne is identified with the wood which is his medium; he is himself a wooden image, his latent creativity released only once. John F. Sears's "Hawthorne's 'Ambitious Guest' and the Significance of the Willey Disaster" (*AL* 54:354–67) draws on the facts of the 1826 avalanche which destroyed an entire family in the White Mountains and on the public response to it as a "cultural event." People felt challenged to understand the disaster as the work of divine providence, but it satisfied the American desire for ruins and a storied landscape and focused attention on the values of home and family. By introducing the character of the ambitious guest, Hawthorne challenged yet affirmed the cult of domesticity and also expressed ambivalence about his own professional ambitions. The fourth article also interprets one of Hawthorne's tales in the light of his self-definition as an author. Dennis Berthold in "Anti-Idealism in Hawthorne's 'The Snow-Image'" (*ArQ* 38:119–32) sees the tale as the epitome and confirmation of Hawthorne's shifts from the short story to the novel and from the ideal to the actual. It is true that the warmhearted if hardheaded Mr. Lindsey proves the snowmaiden incapable of human warmth; but this does not demonstrate Hawthorne's move from the ideal to the real, or account for his abandonment of the short story as "a vehicle suited only for childish fables." The tale is yet another instance of Hawthorne's attempts to conjoin actual and ideal in all his fictions.

Patrick Brancaccio in "'Chiefly About War Matters': Hawthorne's Reluctant Prophecy" (*EIHC* 118:59–66) reads Hawthorne's ruminative essay about the Civil War as a record of how his "own personal crisis as an artist and as an American is mirrored in the division in the nation." Unlike his Concord neighbors, Hawthorne did not admire John Brown; and he feared the war would bring no moral resolution, but only destruction and dehumanization. His prophecies express his "tortured vision of lost horizons," the end of the dream of America and "of a whole realm of experience where individual human action was meaningful."

The remaining four articles on Hawthorne's short works consider narrative strategies but differ widely in method, merit, and subject. Robert L. Chibka's "Hawthorne's Tale Told Twice: A Reading of 'Wakefield'" (*ESQ* 28:220–32), like several of the year's most intelligent essays, examines Hawthorne's treatment of the relationship of actual to imaginary and finds self-revelation beyond the narrator's explicit statements. Chibka reads the tale as twice-told in two senses: as the retelling of a newspaper story and as the narrator's speculative expansion of it. More than a cautionary tale about egotism, it is a study of the author as an isolated man whose worries about the moral imperatives of his self-appointed task emerge through the curious narrator's self-conscious attempts to understand a character who defies interpretation. Teresa Toulouse's "Spatial Relations in 'The Old Manse'" (*ESQ* 28:154–67) thoughtfully examines the structure of spatial movement in Hawthorne's preface. The initial walk through the landscape is a complex "act of memory," the trip down the Assabeth is a critical assessment of Transcendental idealism, and the return to the Manse reconciles actual and imaginary. The preface thus offers "a paradigm of the mind's relation to history and Nature" which resembles the strategies of the fictions and teaches how to read them. Harold Beaver's "Towards Romance: 'The Case of Roger Malvin's Burial'" (*Hawthorne Essays*, pp. 31–47) is more uneven. In a finicky but inexact reading of the story's opening paragraph Beaver confuses rather than explains how Hawthorne uses the word "naturally" (which he calls a "hiccup"), and most of his comments about the relation of nature to culture have little to do with the tale. There are errors of fact and interpretation as well as oddities of diction, such as using "art" and "fiction" for the unwilled flow of reverie. But Beaver is right about the psychological effects of concealment on Reuben and about Hawthorne's open rhetorical demands for "elaborate decipherment" even of what must remain inscrutable.

Finally, Douglas Robinson in "Narrative Balance in 'Alice Doane's Appeal'" (*ESQ* 28:213–19) offers a "holistic" reading to resolve disagreements about the tale's narrative structure. He distinguishes the story's "primary" narrator from the "recalled" narrator of the Alice Doane tale and from Leonard Doane (who confesses to murder but blames the wizard), and then contrasts this hierarchical narrative scheme with the simpler distancing from the historical narrative, arguing that in both segments Hawthorne insisted that imagination should interact with memory and emotion and that all explanations are provisional. The reader rightly wonders whether the wizard "really" manipulated Leonard; the Puritans wrongly leaped to conclusions about the witches. Perhaps granting Hawthorne too much conscious purpose, Robinson attributes the story's undermining "metafictional apparatus" to the author's rejection of "mind-deadening" absolutes and to indecision about his own narrative authority.

### v. Hawthorne and Others

Four of the year's essays explore Hawthorne's influence on later writers—Stephen Crane and Graham Greene as well as Melville and

Howells. (James C. Wright's Hawthorne-Melville bibliography and Rita K. Gollin's study of the Hawthorne-Longfellow relationship are discussed in part *i.*) But the question of literary indebtedness was not ignored. Joan F. Klingel's " 'Ethan Brand' as Hawthorne's *Faust*" (*SSF* 19:74–76) offers an interesting if slightly forced reading of Hawthorne's tale as an "inversion of Goethe's work" which shows "a man damned by his own will." Klingel compares and contrasts Hawthorne's Wandering Jew with Goethe's Devil, looks at the dog's role in both works, and argues that Faust's salvation by the Mater Gloriosa is inverted in Brand's farewell to Mother Earth. (Dorena Allen Wright's article on the influence of Dante and the Pearl Poet on "Rappaccini's Daughter" is discussed in part *iv.*)

Both Frederick Newberry in *"The Red Badge of Courage* and *The Scarlet Letter"* (*ArQ* 38:101–15) and Gretchen Graf Jordan in "Adultery and Its Fruit in *The Scarlet Letter* and *The Power and the Glory*: The Relation of Meaning and Form" (*YR* 71:72–87) support theories of influence by internal evidence. Newberry believes *"The Red Badge* owes a fairly substantial debt to *The Scarlet Letter."* Beyond the obvious parallels of the red emblems of both titles, the repeated use of the colors red, black, and green, and the symmetrical narrative organized in 24 chapters, both novels "present the question of guilt and remorse in nearly identical psychological fashion." Newberry compares Henry to both Dimmesdale and Hester as wearers of a badge of ambiguous meaning which generates self-division and isolates them from society. In a similar but denser study Jordan discusses the many ways Hawthorne's novel seems parallel to Greene's. She effectively analyzes both novels as literary constructs and as dramatizations of the writers' assumptions about individual responsibility to self, society, and God. Both examine the plight of priests who have fathered illegitimate daughters and whose final spiritual salvation remains open to question; both employ a "tone of ambiguity and irony" and set "symbolic action in a very real world" during a time of cultural change. "The metaphor of adultery and its fruit" served Hawthorne and Greene as it will probably serve no future writer, Jordan says—as cause and symbol of possible regeneration for both the sinner and his society.

The remaining two studies of Hawthorne's influence, both by Richard Brodhead, are lucid, perceptive, and instructive. Taking Melville as his particular example in "Hawthorne, Melville, and the

Fiction of Prophecy" (*Hawthorne Essays*, pp. 229–50), Brodhead effectively presents Hawthorne as the model for American writers who read him "in the light of their own ambitions," found he eluded them, but were then stimulated to practice their own art in new ways. After reading *Mosses from an Old Manse*, Melville developed his own notion of the writer as one who penetrates to the heart of reality and speaks the truth he finds. Revising *Moby-Dick* with Hawthorne as guide, he created Ahab, an inflexible figure like Hawthorne's obsessed men; but the obsessive projection took on "an oddly objective and authoritative status." Brodhead says that Melville challenged ethical norms as Hawthorne did, but moved further to condemn both the individual's and the world's truths as lies. Plinlimmon expresses Melville's "mystification at the secret of Hawthorne's poise," but Bartleby is the result of "rediscovering Hawthorne as an enigma" and using him as "the model for an art not of prophetic disclosure but of secrecy itself." In "Hawthorne Among the Realists: The Case of Howells" in *American Realism* (Johns Hopkins, pp. 25–41) Brodhead discusses Howells as one of the post–Civil War writers who "recanonized" Hawthorne as a novelist of "psychological analysis and moral irresolution." In *The Undiscovered Country* he reworked *The Blithedale Romance* by domesticating Hawthorne's potent "magic" and making power relationships benign. Hawthorne's influence is more crucial to *A Modern Instance*, which "lays claim to Hawthorne's artistic project . . . of disclosing through fiction the dynamics of the social and spiritual history of New England." The novel does not wholly solve its problem of determining the moral significance of ordinary reality because Hawthorne controlled Howells' imagination as "the master of uncertainty," suspicious of rigid ethical certainties. It is for such mastery that most of the year's studies praise Hawthorne.

*State University College of New York, Geneseo*

# 3. Poe

## Donald B. Stauffer

This is the tenth year that Edgar Poe has been accorded major-author status in *ALS*. In the 1973 volume editor James Woodress cautiously warned that he might be returned to chapter 11 in the following year, but so far he's holding his own—barely. This year the number of books dwindled to one, and there were only about 40 articles worth mentioning, some of these from previous years. Is the interest in Poe waning? I hope not. But there are some encouraging signs. One is the special issue of *UMSE*, entitled "Poe-Purri" [*sic*], with an introduction by Richard P. Benton; a survey by the editor, Benjamin Franklin Fisher IV, "A Ten-Year Shelf of Poe Books," that looks at Poe scholarship in the past, present, and future; and fine essays by Richard Wilbur, Kent Ljungquist, James Gargano, and others. The one book is Burton Pollin's word index, which will provide a new impetus to style studies. There were two fine essays on *Pym* by Douglas Robinson and Richard Kopley, and the colonial and federal scholar J. A. Leo Lemay is emerging as an important Poe critic, particularly in his groundbreaking study of "The Murders in the Rue Morgue." So it's a good year for quality.

### i. Biography, Bibliography, Reference

Biography receives more than the usual attention this year, with a general survey of the subject and discussions of several relatively minor points. In a useful and stimulating assessment of the field since Arthur Hobson Quinn's 1941 biography, Alexander Hammond in "On Poe Biography: A Review Essay" (*ESQ* 28:197–211) comes to a conclusion with which most of us would agree: that a good biography incorporating factual accuracy and critical acumen is sorely needed. His model would be Richard Sewall's two-volume *Life of Emily Dickinson*.

The need for more information about Poe's contemporaries is partially filled by an amusing and fact-filled account of his relations with the blustering English comic actor William E. Burton, whose literary pretensions led him to found his *Gentleman's Magazine* in 1837. He and Poe did not get along well, of course, and Dwight Thomas reproduces a number of letters and describes advertisements in *Burton's* and other magazines that help explain why. Of particular interest was an ambitious contest offering $1,000 in prizes to authors of winning manuscripts. The prizes were never awarded, and Poe had the unwelcome task of soothing some of the disappointed entrants ("William E. Burton and His Premium Scheme: New Light on Poe Biography," *UMSE* 3:68–80).

In two notes on William Duane, W. T. Bandy corrects a number of errors of biographical fact and clears up some minor textual matters. In one he positively identifies William Duane, Jr. (1808–82) as the person from whom Poe borrowed a volume of the *Southern Literary Messenger*. This volume was later sold to a bookseller by Mrs. Clemm without Poe's knowledge. In a second note Duane is identified as the pseudonymous UNEDA, who contributed to *American Notes & Queries* and became involved in a dispute with John Ingram over an alleged plagiarism of "The Gold-Bug." This accusation was circulated by one Francis Harold Duffee when the tale was first published ("Poe, Duane and Duffee," *UMSE* 3:81–95).

We all know Poe lived in poverty, but exact knowledge of his financial situation is scanty. John Ward Ostrom in "Edgar A. Poe: His Income as Literary Entrepreneur" (*PoeS* 15:1–7) uses primary and secondary sources in an attempt to establish an accurate accounting of Poe's financial struggles. He finds that Poe's income was above the equivalent of our 1981 national poverty level only once—when he was with *Graham's Magazine*. Ostrom calculates a lifetime earnings figure of about $6,200 (the dollar in 1840 was worth about nine times what it is today); he also provides a useful list of publications and what they paid contributors.

The only book this year is a reference tool that opens up the possibility of more accurate studies of Poe's prose style. Burton R. Pollin's *Word Index to Poe's Fiction* (Gordian), based on T. O. Mabbott's two-volume *Tales and Sketches* (Belknap Press) and Pollin's own Twayne edition of "Julius Rodman," *Pym*, and "Hans Pfaall," is a computer-generated index that lists every word in Poe's fiction. It includes frequencies of occurrence and keys to their location, a list of hyphenated words, and a word-frequency list. Because of space limitations actual citations furnishing the context of each word are not given; a location symbol keyed to one of the three volumes is used instead. And if a word occurs more than an arbitrarily decided 51 times, the locations are not cited. Thus, "nature," which occurs 229 times, is not keyed to locations, while "Nature," which occurs nine times, is. However, the entire original text of the index is available on magnetic tape or disk pack for those desiring completeness. Other scholarly activities by Pollin include a two-part article, "Edgar Allan Poe and His Illustrators," *ABC* N.S. 2(1981):3–17;34–40, surveying illustrations of Poe's works in publications all over the world, and a checklist. The latter is a continuation of a 1973 project in which Pollin added about 200 entries to supplement May Garrettson Evans' 1939 *Music and Edgar Allan Poe* (see *ALS* 1973, p. 37). In "Music and Edgar Allan Poe: A Second Annotated Check List" (*PoeS* 15:7–13) he has now assembled an additional checklist in three categories: compositions based on Poe's texts, music for TV and film productions, and a discography. On this same page of *Poe Studies* John L. Idol and Sterling K. Eisiminger provide a supplementary listing of performances of operas based on Poe's fiction.

*Poe Studies* continues its service to Poe scholarship with an updated annotated checklist entitled "Current Poe Bibliography" (15:13–18), compiled by J. Lasley Dameron, Thomas C. Carlson, John E. Reilly, and Benjamin Franklin Fisher, IV. Fisher has also compiled "Fugitive Poe References and Poe Reviews: A Bibliography" (*PoeS* 15:18–22) from 1960 on, that "do not focus on Poe but that discuss the author within a larger perspective or with a special angle of vision."

### *ii.* General Studies, Influences, Criticism

Two general studies look at various aspects of Poe's work. Richard Wilbur has long been admired for his ability to discover links between various images and themes in Poe's tales and poems. He demonstrates this ability once again in "Poe and the Art of Suggestion" (*UMSE* 3:1–13), where he discovers echoes of *Macbeth* in "The Tell-Tale Heart" (as does F. S. Frank—see below) and of the Episcopal burial service in "Annabel Lee," as well as repetitions of images and themes from one work to another. "I see no evidence that he meant his reader to elucidate one poem or story by reference to another," Wilbur writes of Poe. "Yet for us, as we struggle to understand him, cross-reference is an indispensable tool." In my Edgar Allan Poe Society lecture "The Merry Mood: Poe's Uses of Humor" (Baltimore: Poe Society and Enoch Pratt Free Library) I describe the aspect of play, both linguistic and thematic, in Poe's humorous writing, drawing upon the poetry, the criticism, the tales, and "Autography." I also defend "The Literary Life of Thingum Bob, Esq." as a mature piece of satire.

Comparative studies range from the influence of Cousin and Byron to comparisons with Fellini and Borges and his reputation in China. In a learned, detailed study, "Victor Cousin: Still Another Source of Poe's Aesthetic Theory?" (SAR pp. 1–27), Glen A. Omans offers a variety of reasons why Poe could have been influenced by Cousin's major work on aesthetics, a series of lectures on the true, the beautiful, and the good, published in 1836. Although Poe mentions Cousin only twice, Omans finds a number of striking correspondences between the thinking of the two writers about aesthetics, including the idea of the artist's search for ideal beauty, the concept of the act of creation as a "struggle" to combine elements reaching toward the ideal, the idea that poetry should not be useful or "true," and even the notion of art for art's sake. Omans finds it probable that Poe read Cousin in the original French and thus seemed to anticipate his ideas, which were not available to many American readers until a translation appeared in 1849, the year of Poe's death.

Katrina E. Bachinger in "Poe's Vote for Byron: The Problem of Its Duration" (Byron: Poetry and Politics, ed. Erwin A. Stürzl and James Hogg [Salzburg: Institut für Anglistik und Amerikanistik, 1981], pp. 301–22) disagrees with those who say that Poe abandoned his interest in Byron early in his career. She cites a number of reviews throughout his career that reflect a continuing concern with Byron, and also shows how several tales, including "Metzengerstein," "Some Words with a Mummy," and "The Assignation," reflect, often in a hoaxing way, his and his contemporaries' attitudes toward Byron.

In "Necessary Inadequacies: Poe's 'Tale of the Ragged Mountains' and Borges' South" (JNT 12:155–66) Reinhard H. Friederich shows the similarities between one of Poe's flawed tales and one of Borges' best. He argues that some of our irritation with Poe's tale for not living up to our expectations is typical of many of his tales, creating a tension between our expectations and our frustration that accounts for the varied responses of readers to his work.

Henri Peyre in "Edgar Allan Poe and Twentieth Century French Poetry: Paul Valéry" (*Laurels* 51, ii[1980]:73–87) stresses the importance of Poe's poetry and criticism as influences on major French writers, especially Valéry, who held Poe in lifelong respect and veneration. Michael H. Begnal in "Fellini and Poe: A Story With a Moral?", *LFQ* 10:130–33, analyzes "Toby Dammit," the third segment in the film *Spirits of the Dead*. He believes that Fellini "truly captured" the spirit of "Never Bet the Devil Your Head," with its subtitle, "A Tale With a Moral," by showing that the moral of the title is a ridiculous one.

In a chapter of *Anglo-American Encounters: England and the Rise of American Literature* (Cambridge Univ. Press, 1981), "Poe's England and the Divided Self" (pp. 69–96), Benjamin Lease takes up the questions of Poe's debts to and relationships with English writing and writers, and of his Americanness. The four sections of the chapter deal with the influence of *Blackwood's*, the English setting of "William Wilson," Poe and Dickens, and William Carlos Williams' essay on Poe. Each is well-written and factual, yet all are ultimately unsatisfying. Lease has assembled much material on each of these subjects, but he does not arrive at a coherent or original view. His section on Williams is most interesting when he moves into questions of Poe's literary nationalism and his role as journalist.

In the first Chinese study of Poe since the 1949 "Liberation" of China, Sheng Ning, assisted by Donald Stauffer, has uncovered substantial evidence that the most prominent writers in China in the 1920s and 1930s were deeply interested in Poe and strongly influenced by him, in spite of their later repudiation of him as a decadent writer ("The Influence of Edgar Allan Poe on Modern Chinese Literature," *UMSE* 3:155–82).

Three articles deal with Poe as a critic. In a previously overlooked 1980 essay on "Uses of the Daemon in Selected Works of Edgar Allan Poe" (*Interpretations* 12:31–39) Kent Ljungquist shows how Poe's concepts of the daemonic are related to power, awe, and knowledge, and how they are linked both to the experience of sublimity and to poetic inspiration. Daemons can be both malign and benign—as they are in "The Power of Words," a tale that gives expression to Poe's positive attitudes toward the daemonic. And Ljungquist shows how its opposite qualities are treated in "The Black Cat" and comically treated in "Loss of Breath."

R. E. Fount comes to the defense of Poe as a theorist of literary criticism against various detractors. Although he is not the first to point out Poe's important role as an influence on the New Criticism, Fount draws our attention to one noteworthy aspect of his theory, found in "Marginalia," where Poe writes of the desire of the poet to experience "those mere points of time where the confines of the waking world blend with those of the world of dreams." This "mystic" aspect connects him with the Symbolists and "qualifies Poe as America's first aesthetician of simultaneity" (*SAB* 46,ii[1981]:17–25).

In "Poe's Criticism of Women Writers" (*UMSE* 3:102–19) Ashby Bland Crowder responds to the charge that Poe was often gallant with the ladies and uncritical in his reviews of their work; he finds that this was not usually the case. Although Poe often made generalized statements of praise, he offset these by specific attacks on such elements as style, language, unity of effect, even in the case of such writers as Frances Sargent Osgood, with whom he had a strong personal relationship and thus had every reason to flatter.

### iii. Arthur Gordon Pym

Poe's only novel continues to be subjected to close scrutiny, and the three studies published this year are exceptionally good, although their approaches are quite different. In "The Hidden Journey of *Arthur Gordon Pym*" (*SAR*, pp. 29–51) Richard Kopley offers an original and even startling new reading. Based partly on Marie Bonaparte, partly on textual details, and partly on biographical scholarship, Kopley puts together a brief for seeing the central episode of the book as the death of Augustus on 1 August, the same date on which Poe's brother Henry had died. The novel thus becomes an effort on the part of Poe/Pym to come to terms with the death of his brother Henry/Augustus, "seeking, but never finding, the original moment of his brother's death so that he may die along with Henry. It is this impossible quest which is the hidden journey of *Arthur Gordon Pym*." Kopley also finds biographical and textual evidence to support the idea that the shrouded human figure represents Poe's mother as well as his brother, and that he is seeking a reunion with both. Although at times he asks too much of our credulity, as when he asserts that a figurehead exists on the *Penguin* but "is not described because Pym did not see it," there are still enough striking connections between the story and Poe's biography to force us to consider them seriously.

In an attempt to get away from the deadlock that the searches for meaning in the closing lines of *Pym* tend to produce Paul Rosenzweig continues to argue, as he did last year (see *ALS 1981*, p. 49), for ambiguity and inconclusiveness. He reasons persuasively that the novel as a whole—and the concluding editor's note in particular—is a conscious evasion of meaning. In " 'Dust Within the Rock': The Phantasm of Meaning in *The Narrative of Arthur Gordon Pym*" (*SNNTS* 14:137–51) he points out a continuing pattern of raising and then frustrating expectations in the reader, a pattern that works against closure and against any stable "meaning" that is not undercut by formal or thematic reversals. In particular he analyzes the position of the concluding note and its style to show how it—especially its cryptic pseudo-biblical conclusion—leaves the reader with the unsettling conclusion that nothing can be decided—or concluded.

Certainly one of the most entertaining and thought-provoking essays is Douglas Robinson's "Reading Poe's Novel: A Speculative Review of *Pym* Criticism, 1950–1980," *PoeS* 15:47–54. This lively survey traces *Pym* criticism through six stages, from the earliest, "the text's relation to its author," to the most recent, "the meaning of the problematic frame." Robinson finds that recent critics have curved this hierarchy into a circle, returning to a point where they combine close textual analysis with extratextual attention to problems of Poe's intentions and his beliefs about the world. This idea, he says, began with Lynen and was developed in various ways by Moldenhauer, Carlson, Ketterer, and others. In some ways this essay is a polemic in favor of what Robinson calls a visionary reading of the novel, but he is gracious enough to suggest that *Pym* criticism must continue to evolve, perhaps attempting to fuse Transcendental vision and Romantic irony in a holistic reading that would move toward a critical consensus. The article includes a checklist of Pym criticism of almost 100 items.

### iv. Tales, Sketches, "The Raven"

Jonathan Auerbach ("Poe's Other Double: The Reader in the Fiction," *Criticism* 24:341–61) looks at Poe's writing, particularly the later hoaxes, as responses to the external pressures of his audience and the popular magazine tradition of the times. In these tales, he says, Poe tried to come to grips with his distrust and fear of a mass readership by writing stories which treat his fear as an explicit theme. Auerbach looks at "The Man That Was Used Up," "The Premature Burial," "The Facts in the Case of M. Valdemar," and "Von Kempelen and His Discovery" as stages along the way toward an accommodation with a mass audience that would allow him to preserve his identity as a person: "to encode the self in a written form that would allow him to maintain control over his fiction" after it was exposed to the public.

David H. Hirsch in "Poe's 'Metzengerstein' as a Tale of the Subconscious" (*UMSE* 3:40–52) disagrees with those who read the tale as a hoax, preferring to read it as a serious tale concerned with body-soul dualism in which Poe uses metempsychosis as a metaphor to portray the relationship between the soul and beauty. Hirsch develops some interesting parallels between this tale and Plato's *Phaedrus* but, more important, he develops the idea of the figure of the horse and rider as the embodiment of a conflict of "potentially explosive and disruptive psychic energies" within the romantic artist's mind that sets Poe apart from other Romantics, such as Wordsworth and Emerson.

Christopher J. Forbes in "Satire of Irving's *A History of New York* in Poe's 'The Devil in the Belfry'" (*SAF* 10:93–100) points out the many parallels between Poe's tale and Irving's *History*. He states that Poe satirizes "Irving's" smugness and nostalgia; however, he never addresses the fact that Irving himself writes satire through the *persona* of Diedrich Knickerbocker.

The editor of a recent edition of Franklin's *Autobiography*, J. A. Leo Lemay, demonstrates that "The Business Man" is a satire of Franklin's famous work and that Poe had read it closely. Lemay points out a number of striking verbal and thematic parallels that show how Poe savagely attacked the idea of the self-made man; Lemay says it "should certainly be recognized as one of the cruelest burlesques of antebellum American materialism" ("Poe's 'The Business Man': Its Contexts and Satire of Franklin's *Autobiography*," *PoeS* 15:29–37).

And in an extraordinary and challenging new reading of "Rue Morgue" Lemay argues that symbolically and thematically the tale is about sexual repression and the need for reintegrating the opposing forces that exist in human beings. He bases his argument on three main premises: the underlying sexual content of much of the tale's language and imagery; the head-body dichotomy specifically referred to in the quotations and metaphors at the end of the tale; and the possibility (earlier suggested by Richard Wilbur) that the three pairs of characters (narrator/Dupin, Mme/Mlle Espanaye, and sailor/orangutan) are all doubles ("The Psychology of 'The Murders in the Rue Morgue,'" *AL* 54:165–88).

Kenneth V. Egan, Jr., in "Descent to an Ascent: Poe's Use of Perspective in 'A Descent Into the Maelstrom'" (*SSF* 19:157–62) finds the source of the mariner's insight is not ratiocination but an intuitive perception based on his having distanced himself from nature to the point where he can perceive the harmony underlying apparent chaos. Patricia H. Wheat's "The Mask of Indifference in 'The Masque of the Red Death'" (*SSF* 19:51–56) offers an extended summary and commentary on the tale to support her idea that Prince Prospero arms himself with indifference as a defense against his fear of death.

In "'The *language* of the cipher': Interpretation in 'The Gold-Bug'" (*AL* 53:646–60) Michael Williams sees "The Gold-Bug" as an exploration of referential language, in which "Jupiter and the narrator are entrapped in opposed but equally inadequate language strategies," while Legrand's awareness that relationships between word and referent are arbitrary enables him to solve the cryptogram and find the treasure.

F. S. Frank's "Neighborhood Gothic: Poe's 'Tell-Tale Heart'" (*Sphinx* 3[1981]:53–60) finds that Poe's "most Hawthornesque" tale anticipates the modern Gothic tale, "in which the irrational aspects of the unknown self supplant the monsters of Gothic fiction." Frank uses the term "neighborhood Gothic" to describe a modern type that uses familiarity rather than remoteness to achieve its effects of horror. "The Tell-Tale Heart" is of this type because it "urbanizes the Gothic hero-villain, minimizes the Gothic equipment, and normalizes the Gothic setting."

Of two articles on "Ligeia" one focuses on the narrator, the other

on the reader. In "The Multiple Murder in 'Ligeia': A New Look at
Poe's Narrator" (*CRevAS* 13:279–89) Terence J. Matheson applies
the unreliable narrator hypothesis to argue that he is the murderer
not only of Rowena but of Ligeia as well. Pointing out a number of
the discrepancies in the description of Ligeia familiar to readers of
the story, he sides with such literal readings of the tale as Roy Basler's
and makes some interesting and plausible points: that the marriage
was an incompatible one; that he murdered Ligeia, then suffered
guilt for his action; and in a futile attempt to atone for his act attempted to bring her back to life through a second, similar murder
of Rowena.

In a previously overlooked study Terry Heller ("Poe's 'Ligeia'
and the Pleasures of Terror," *Gothic* 2[1980]:39–48) uses a detailed
reading of the effects of the tale on the reader in order to explore the
idea that one reads a horror story because it is pleasurable to do so.
Heller studies the various interpretations of the tale and concludes
that it is finally incomprehensible—a reflection of the state of mind
of the narrator himself, who is confronted and thus terrified by the
meaninglessness of his own situation and, by extension, of the world.
The reader is also terrorized because Poe succeeds in removing aesthetic distance, thus threatening to involve the reader directly in the
narrator's own confusion: "Such a threat may stimulate still further
the reader's desire to know the unknowable narrator in order to
more fully understand the narrator's true relation to the reader. To
attempt such a knowing in this state is to prolong one's terror."
Reading horror fiction is thus a test of the reader's ability to "hold
together" psychologically in the face of a world which refuses to
surrender to one's powers of integration; and if one succeeds in keeping from falling apart, the effect is pleasurable.

There are also two articles on "The Fall of the House of Usher."
James W. Gargano (" 'The Fall of the House of Usher': An Apocalyptic Vision," *UMSE* 3:53–63) gives clear and persuasive reasons
why we should read the tale as a vision of the end of the world by a
narrator who not only is unwilling to believe the evidence of his
senses but is limited in his capacity to understand or interpret the
meaning of his prevision. "The central irony of Usher is nothing less
than the narrator's failure to understand that he is witnessing a revelation or preenactment of the end of the world and time." Gargano
builds skillfully on the readings of earlier critics, placing special

emphasis on the sentience of matter as reflecting a coming reorganization of the laws of nature.

This is probably the best place to mention Kent Ljungquist's "Poe and the Picturesque: Theory and Practice" (*UMSE* 3:25–39). The essay is both a comprehensive study of Poe's use of the term *picturesque* and an examination of his use of certain qualities of the picturesque in "Usher." Ljungquist skillfully points out that the term was widely used in the 1840s and 1850s, and that Poe placed it between the sublime on the one hand and beauty on the other; he used the term extensively in his critical writings, and, interestingly, in "Autography." In his study of the occurrence of the concept in "Usher" Ljungquist shows that Poe's opening descriptions of the landscape, of the house, and of Roderick "give subtle expression to picturesque theory," and that the rest of the tale develops various aspects of it.

Joan Dayan's "The Road to Landor's Cottage: Poe's Landscape of Effect" (*UMSE* 3:136–54) also deals with the picturesque, but only incidentally, in connection with her analysis of a seldom-regarded sketch. She sees "Landor's Cottage" as an exercise in ambiguity, in which the very style Poe uses renders his description more vague, while seeming to aim at exactness and specificity. The result is a composition that misleads the reader into looking for "content," while Poe's own elaborate manipulations of language derive from his interest in form. The argument is carefully buttressed with quotations from William Carlos Williams and references to the landscape gardening tradition, but I have the uneasy feeling that this is simply an effort to turn a piece of hackwork into an ingenious piece of veiled critical commentary, even though Dayan claims that here Poe is playing the reader's expectations off against his other journey narratives, such as "Usher" and *Pym*.

Jules Zanger in "Poe's American Garden: 'The Domain of Arnheim'" (*ATQ* 50[1981]:93–103) notes that in many ways Ellison is an atypical Poe hero, in his happiness and success. He ranges over a wide variety of topics, making connections between Poe's use of the garden and Christian and classical tradition, as well as connections to the theme of the garden in American cultural and intellectual history.

Finally, the sole essay on Poe's poetry. David Baguley in "Guiomar's Poetics of Death and 'The Raven'" (*PoeS* 15:38–40) describes Michael Guiomar's *Principles d'une esthétique de la mort* (1967), which works in the spirit of Gaston Bachelard to identify and categorize images and forms in literature and the arts that refer to death. Baguley than applies Guiomar's categories to a close analysis of "The Raven," leading to his conclusion that the bird is a harbinger of "irretrievable, even Diabolical or Infernal destruction."

*State University of New York at Albany*

# 4. Melville

*Robert Milder*

Among those writing on Melville who were most concerned with the direction of literary studies there was a common feeling, stated or implied, anxious or anticipatory, that the center cannot hold. The "wall (steel-reinforced concrete, not pasteboard) between scholarship and criticism" which Hershel Parker noted in 1975 remains as strong as ever, reminding us that for most Americanists the center was always bifurcated; now, however, Parker's wall seems an interior partition dividing members of a squabbling family who look uneasily through their windows at a troubling new neighbor outside. Books by Merton M. Sealts, Jr. (*Pursuing Melville, 1940–1980*), Milton R. Stern (*Critical Essays on Herman Melville's "Typee"*), and John Carlos Rowe (*Through the Custom-House*) recapitulate nearly the entire course of Melville studies from the laying of scholarly foundations through the proliferation of New Critical readings to the recent effort to deconstruct Melville's writings and dismantle an accumulated commentary which has come to seem oppressive. With *Moby-Dick*, particularly, the year's most prominent theme was the flight from rigidified culture and the return to origins, a theme which reflects the critic's situation vis-à-vis the academic tradition as much as it does Melville's within 19th-century America. Some of the newer critics were hostile toward even the best of the traditional scholarship and criticism; others like Bainard Cowan looked to a synthesis of New Critical formalism with the reconceived historicism offered by some of the Continental theorists. No Armageddon seems imminent, and more probable than a wrought synthesis is a slow percolation down of the new insights as they redefine our understanding of what a scholarly criticism involves. Meanwhile, the year produced some important work, though the distribution of the practical criticism was uneven: a good deal of writing on *Typee*, *Moby-Dick*, and *Billy Budd*, some notable contributions on *The Confidence-Man* and the stories, and almost nothing on anything else.

### i. Editions, Concordances, Bibliographies

After eleven years of silence the Northwestern-Newberry *Writings of Herman Melville* resumes with the publication of *Israel Potter*, its richest volume to date. Aside from providing an authoritative text, a relatively simple matter with *Israel Potter*, the edition contains a historical note by Walter E. Bezanson (at 60-odd pages, the longest by far in any Northwestern-Newberry volume), a note on the text by general editors Hayford, Parker, and Tanselle, and a photographic reproduction of Melville's major source, Henry Trumbull's *Life and Remarkable Adventures of Israel R. Potter*, prepared and introduced by R. D. Madison. Bezanson's historical note is a superb piece of scholarly criticism which traces the development of the manuscript as Melville broke loose from Trumbull's narrative and began to draw heavily upon other sources and upon his own imagination, though always (ostensibly) within the constraints of his promise to *Putnam's*: "Nothing of any sort to shock the fastidious," "very little reflective writing," "nothing weighty." In detailing the growth, publication, and reception of this "stepchild among Melville's books," Bezanson offers a rare and suggestive glimpse of the artist at work and of the writer-businessman of the mid-'50s trying (and sometimes perversely not trying) to reconcile the claims of his audience with his private inclinations. The materials Bezanson presents and the issues he raises should occupy critics for years to come and prompt the revaluation of a book "which gave scope for all but [Melville's] highest talents." Shrewd and discriminating, Bezanson's essay also goes far toward providing the "new consideration of Melville and his audience in the years following *Moby-Dick*" that Merton Sealts has said we urgently need.

An achievement of a different sort, the Library of America's *Typee, Omoo, Mardi*, ed. G. Thomas Tanselle, reprints the Northwestern-Newberry texts along with a "Chronology" of Melville's life and works, a "Note on the Texts," and eight pages of brief explanatory notes. While one applauds the Library of America project in general, it is hard to see whom, among academics, this particular volume will serve, since undergraduates reading only *Typee* will continue to use the cheaper mass-market paperbacks while advanced students will want the historical and textual apparatus of the Northwestern-Newberry editions. Perhaps the Library of America *Typee*,

*Omoo, Mardi* will bring the general reader to Melville. The attractions of the volume are its compactness and promise of continued availability; its drawbacks are its stately but uninspiring format and its omission of a good middle-length introduction aimed at the nonspecialist.

There were two Melville concordances published in 1982, both useful, neither definitive. At $250, and weighing close to 14 pounds, Eugene F. Irey's two-volume *Concordance to Herman Melville's "Moby-Dick"* (Garland) is not for everyone's shelf, but it is a convenient research tool notwithstanding the fact that it is keyed to a slightly corrected Mansfield-Vincent text based on the first American edition and does not consider the variants in the English edition. Most of Hershel Parker's objections to the Cohen-Calahan *Moby-Dick* concordance of 1978 apply to Irey's as well (see *ALS 1978*, pp. 44–45), but until the publication of a definitive *Moby-Dick* allows for a definitive concordance, Irey's, on most matters, will amply do. Jill B. Gidmark's *Melville Sea Dictionary* (Greenwood) is a more inventive project: a "Glossed Concordance" of sea words from Melville's first six books prefaced by a long technical analysis which sheds light on the idiosyncracies of Melville's diction (e.g., "Whenever *watery* is joined to a noun as an adjective, the resulting modification is strange and wonderful") and on his broader stylistic development from book to book. Gidmark's *Dictionary* is instructive and can even be fun, but readers should be warned that her concordance is not complete. A random flipping of pages took me to "Albicore," which lists one reference each for *Typee, Omoo,* and *Mardi* but not "See yon Albicore!" from "The Symphony." Nor does Gidmark explore Melville's use of sea vocabulary in landed works like *Pierre,* where sea images, though not plentiful, carry considerable weight.

Among the bibliographical studies James C. Wilson's "The Hawthorne-Melville Relationship: An Annotated Bibliography," a special issue of *ATQ* (Nos. 45–56[1981]; 79 pages), outlines the development of the scholarship and criticism under five headings which influence-hunters ought to memorize: "Biography," "Mutual Influence," "Literary Reflections of the Relationship," "Parallel Readings," and "Generic and Theoretical Approaches." Wilson's introductory essay is informed but noncommittal, as are most of his annotations, which might have been more helpful had they been evaluative. With Mary K. Madison's *Books on Melville, 1891–1981: A Checklist*

(Evanston, Ill.: Loose-Fish Press) the Melville Society continues its policy of distributing scholarly materials to its members free of charge. Madison includes 243 books dealing wholly or substantially with Melville or containing an important section on Melville, all of which are arranged chronologically by date of publication and indexed by author, editor, compiler, and/or translator. Madison also lists reprints and indicates which books are currently available. On the other side John Bryant previews what may soon be in print in "Trends in Melville Scholarship: Dissertations in the 1970s" (*MSEx* 50:12–14), an interim report on his project "to update and re-edit *Melville Dissertations: An Annotated Directory.*" Despite the languishing of graduate programs, Melville dissertations continue to appear at roughly double the rate of the 1960s, which doubled the rate of the '50s, and so on backward through every decade since the Melville revival. "The definitive treatment of a unique topic seems to be a thing of the past," Bryant observes, the current thesis being what he calls "an exercise in approach." In content the dissertations of the 1970s mirrored the interests of the published writing: "no single critical trend" was dominant; *Typee* "lost ground" while *The Confidence-Man* "grew in importance"; "the poetry attracted substantial interest"; "of least importance was *Israel Potter.*"

### ii. Biography, Scholarship, Source and Influence Studies

Biographical studies came to a virtual halt this year save for Stanton Garner's investigations in "Melville's Scout Toward Aldie" (*MSEx* 51:5–16) and "Melville's Scout Toward Aldie, Part 2: The Scout and the Poem" (*MSEx* 52:1–14). Working largely with Civil War letters, particularly those to and from Melville's cousin Col. Henry S. Gansevoort, Garner shows that Melville did not participate in the " 'mild adventure' " of a 14 April scout, as had been thought, but in the more elaborate and eventful operation of 18 April led by Col. Charles Russell Lowell, the episodes of which "so closely paralleled the action" in Melville's poem "that the differences between them become important in themselves."

Biographical in a more roundabout way is G. Thomas Tanselle's "Two Melville Association Copies: The Hubbard *Whale* and the Jones *Moby-Dick* (*BC* 31:170–86, 309–30), a fascinating piece of detective work which demonstrates how "the investigation of the immediate association" can lead to unexpected biographical and critical discoveries. In the case of the Hubbard *Whale* (a copy of the English edition of *Moby-Dick* presented by Melville to his former shipmate on the *Acushnet*, Henry Hubbard, and inscribed "March 23$^d$ 1853/Pittsfield"), Tanselle reports two finds: first, that Hubbard probably did not make an earlier visit to Melville in 1850 and thus (contrary to Leon Howard's conjecture) could not have given him a list of the *Acushnet*'s crewmen and their fate as he worked on *Moby-Dick*; and second, that an annotation in Hubbard's hand identifies Pip with one "Backus" and establishes the factual basis for at least one of Pip's leaps from the whaleboat. The Jones *Moby-Dick*, which seems once to have been owned by Allan Melville, has a lesser story to tell, but in following his leads through the bookshop world of 1880s and '90s New York Tanselle adds detail to the portraits we have of Melville's last years and of the cult of admirers who nourished his reputation in the 30 years between his death and the Melville revival. Alfred Kazin also evokes Melville's urban world in "New York from Melville to Mailer," *Contemporaries: From the 19th Century to the Present*, rev. ed. [New York: Horizon Press], pp. 400–412, the published version of a paper originally delivered in 1980 at the Rutgers University Conference on Literature and the Urban Experience. Kazin finds it strange that Melville had nothing to say about the human spectacle of New York which so impressed Walt Whitman and Stephen Crane. While Melville's silences do not afford Kazin much of a subject, they do remind us how little the outward world came to occupy Melville in his last years.

*Pursuing Melville, 1940–1980* (Wis.) by Merton M. Sealts, Jr., brings together articles, essays, introductions, and reviews covering most of a career—some of them acknowledged classics like "Melville's 'Geniality,'" other lesser-known pieces like "Melville's Burgundy Club Sketches"—to which Sealts adds a section from a seminar paper submitted to Stanley T. Williams in 1940; a chapter from his 1942 dissertation on Melville and ancient philosophy; a 60-page essay on his relationship with Charles Olson, part of which appeared in 1981 as "Olson, Melville, and the *New Republic* (ConL 22: 167–86; see *ALS 1981*, p. 58); and an important new essay, "Melville and the Platonic Tradition," which complements his earlier "Melville and Emerson's Rainbow" (also included in *Pursuing Melville*) and fulfills a scholarly ambition of 40 years. Those who know Sealts's writings separately should review them together as they are situated in his career by brief introductory notes and assessed in a closing "Letter to Henry A. Murray" which sets them within the opportunities and obligations felt by an entire generation of Melville students. "Melville and the Platonic Tradition" is one of the fullest expressions of Sealts's method—"sound basic scholarship as it passes over into biography and criticism"—and a major contribution to our understanding of the influences upon Melville's thought and writing. Drawing upon his work in "Melville and Emerson's Rainbow," Sealts demonstrates that "Melville's first-hand acquaintance with the Platonic dialogues antedated his knowledge of Emerson, beginning early in 1848 and constituting a major influence on both *Mardi* and *Moby-Dick*" and a lifelong source of interest following his temporary "revulsion against *all* faith and philosophy" in *Pierre.*

The practical difficulty of addressing several influences at once is exemplified by Sanford E. Marovitz in "Melville's Problematic '*Being*'" (*ESQ* 28:11–23), a learned and well-written article which sets out to illuminate Melville's "*Being* of the matter" remark to Hawthorne by surrounding it with scholarship. Marovitz's excursions into Plato and Platonism, Bayle, Browne, the great chain of being, Shakespeare, Milton, Coleridge, and Emerson, among others, bring forward much of the pertinent context, but the net result is the kind of suffocation one feels reading some of the more elaborate Mansfield-Vincent notes to *Moby-Dick*. Most of what Marovitz presents (very ably) we knew already, and he never performs the act of imagination that would bring his scholarship creatively to bear upon the passage itself.

There were two other influence studies in 1982, though I hesitate to include Linden Peach's "Man-out-of-clothes: Melville's Debt to Carlyle" (*British Influence*, pp. 138–61) in a section on scholarship because there is no scholarship visible in it, the entries from Peach's scant bibliography dating mostly from the 1920s, '30s, and '40s. The main achievement of Peach's section on *Moby-Dick* is to reduce the subtle and complicated work of influence study to the conjoining of texts through the word "like." A vastly better essay, Richard Brodhead's "Hawthorne, Melville, and the Fiction of Prophecy" (*Hawthorne Essays*, pp. 229–50) is plagued by similar problems. Brodhead's thesis is that Melville, like other American writers who responded deeply to Hawthorne, "misread" him, by which Brodhead means not a half-willful Bloomian "misprision" but an honest and fruitful mistake that led Melville to transform Hawthorne's "idea-possessed" or "daimonized" men—Ethan Brand, Aylmer, Reverend Hooper, Roderick Elliston—into a larger visionary "figure Hawthorne never drew: the heroic obsessive, or the monomaniac as superior man"—Ahab. Brodhead's major failing is to write as if Hawthorne's fiction constituted Melville's entire literary universe as he worked on *Moby-Dick,* so that if Ahab resembles yet differs from Hawthorne's obsessives, it must be because Melville was patterning himself after Hawthorne but misconceiving him. Moreover, Brodhead neglects the primary evidence (Melville's markings in his copies of Hawthorne's books) that would allow him to speak with authority on how Melville did respond to Hawthorne, and to trace with more precision the psychological and imaginative current that passed between author and source.

Melville himself was an influence upon a prominent 20th-century writer, Norman Mailer, Bernard Horn argues in "Ahab and Ishmael at War: The Presence of *Moby-Dick* in *The Naked and the Dead"* (*AQ* 34:379–95). Citing Mailer's acknowledgment of Melville in a 1963 interview, Horn describes Melville as an " 'ancestral' influence" who helped Mailer "exceed Hemingway's limitations" stylistically and metaphysically, and whose presence in Mailer's first novel was particularly formative. Last, in "A Possible Source for Melville's Goetic and Theurgic Magic" (*MSEx* 49:5–6) Douglas Robillard lends weight to the suspicion that Bulwer-Lytton's *Last Days of Pompeii* acquainted Melville with the terms that appear in his "Ego non baptiso" notation in a volume of Shakespeare. Melville may have known Bulwer-Lytton's book by the spring or summer of 1849, Robillard conjectures, for he seems to have "alluded to it in *Redburn.*"

### *iii.* General Studies

Broad thematic discussions of Melville formed a near-empty category in 1982. The lone exception was Gene Patterson-Black's "On Herman Melville" in *American Novelists Revisited* (pp. 107–42), a rambling essay which offers another version of the " 'father-wounded son' " searching for acceptance from other males and entangling himself in an emotional logic of expectation, disappointment, frustration, anger, hatred, and finally self-hatred. The turn Patterson-Black gives this familiar story is a dénouement of redemption which took place during or soon after Melville's visit to Europe and the Middle East in 1856–57 and which is recorded in the poem "Shelley's Vision," a parable of exorcism and one of several poems which show how "the repression of his earlier years" began to "lift under the influence of his self-forgiveness." This is a pleasant myth which leads Patterson-Black to some sympathetic commentary on the shorter poems and *Clarel*, but it has little to do with the biographical facts of Melville's later life—with the evidence of a domestic crisis in 1867, for example, or with the family legends of a withdrawn and irascible old man.

There is not much "context" to Brian Harding's chapter on Melville in *American Literature in Context, II* (pp. 182–201), but otherwise his discussion of *Moby-Dick* (Harding nods briefly to Melville's other works) is remarkably full and suggestive for a companion volume essay. Nearly everything is there, and in no discernible order. Too rich for most sophomores, Harding's lively chapter should stimulate more advanced students and is worth the attention of their teachers. Not so, "Melville's Withdrawal" (*New Yorker* 10 May:120–47) by John Updike, an oddly barren summary of the career which will disappoint those who have admired Updike's discerning literary essays in the *New Yorker*. Updike's writing is stylish as always, but whatever he was looking for in Melville he seems not to have found.

In a later section I will be noticing John Carlos Rowe's chapter on "Bartleby" from *Through the Custom-House*. Americanists should also read Rowe's Preface and "Introduction: The Modernity of Nineteenth-Century American Fiction" (pp. xi–xiii, 1–27)—a journey through structuralist and poststructuralist critical theory and an argument for how and why it should be brought to bear on 19th-century American texts. Rowe's argument rests on an analogy (Rowe calls it a homology) between the Modernist "desire to wipe out whatever came earlier, in the hope of reaching at last a point that could be called a true present" (Paul de Man's words), the poststructuralist notion of literary language as "defamiliarizing" or "subversive," and the general effort of 19th-century American writers to unburden themselves of the past and confront the world anew. Derrida is the dominant presence in *Through the Custom-House*, and in "the Derridean project of deconstruction" (as Rowe describes it) there is the possibility for a new and more sophisticated historicism "that would study the history-as-structure/structure-as-history of the various repressions at work in different cultural codes that promise a signified." Rowe, however, chooses to be ahistorical; he berates the traditional "formal and historical critics" who "conventionalize the work" by reintegrating it into its times, but he offers no revisionary historicism of his own and in effect abandons the effort "to *locate* the illusion of the signified as it operates within a given culture." The culture which interests Rowe is that of the present, not the past, and 19th-century texts are enlisted in the service of discovering "in a new sense the intelligibility of our own times."

### iv. Typee, Mardi

Aside from one article on *Mardi* the writing on Melville's first five books was restricted entirely to *Typee*. Milton R. Stern's *Critical Essays on Herman Melville's "Typee"* (Hall) reprints 18 selections of varying length and quality from the last 60-odd years along with a handful of familiar 19th-century responses, an introduction by Stern, a new essay by John Wenke, and an unannotated bibliography by Joseph Wenke which claims "to provide an accurate list of all the presently known English language materials that have contributed to the history of the critical reputation of *Typee*"—878 entries in all. Stern's valuable introduction surveys the development of the criticism from Melville's time to the present and assesses the current critical situation in a mood of near-despair. Though "*Typee* criticism has become distressingly repetitive," Stern says, the very quantity of published material precludes familiarity with it, which results in ever more repetition—a "vicious circle" in which Stern feels all academic criticism on major writers is caught.

Most of those who wrote on *Typee* came to terms with the superabundance of criticism by ignoring it. An exception is Kristin Herzog in "Melville, *Typee*, and Missions" (*Jour. of Presbyterian Hist.* 60: 161–79), an intelligent and well-researched article which covers the pertinent issues for a nonliterary audience but has little to teach specialists. Much less substantial is Gorman Beauchamp's "Melville and the Tradition of Primitive Utopia" (*JGE* 33[1981]:6–14), a poor relation of Beauchamp's "Melville, Montaigne, and the Cannibals" (*ArQ* 37:293–309; see *ALS 1981*, pp. 61–62) and a cautionary example of "contexting," or trotting forth oft-quoted passages and worn critical ideas under a new heading—in this case, Lewis Mumford's distinction between "utopias of reconstruction," which stress rational social organization and behavioral restraint, and "utopias of escape," which enact a daydream of gratification and "gentle, unthreatening anarchy." Denser but also redundant is John Wenke's "Melville's *Typee*: A Tale of Two Worlds" (*Critical Essays*, pp. 250–58), the last essay in Stern's collection and a compendium of themes from the 18 preceding articles.

The theme of cultural encounter continued to preoccupy *Typee*'s critics. "Melville's Cannibals and Christians" from Lee Clark Mitchell's *Witnesses to a Vanishing America* (Princeton [1981], pp. 189–212) is a fluent but undistinguished summary of the cultural attitudes expressed in Melville's writings (*Typee* especially), attitudes Mitchell characterizes as "tolerant, even open-ended" in their acceptance of cultural differences. For Mitchell it is the Typees themselves who prove the "cultural absolutists" in their insistence on tattooing Tommo, whose flight from their island is not a rejection of Marquesan life but an effort to keep the open independence of his cultural seas.

On the opposite side, two of the year's articles revise the usual account of Tommo-Melville's ambivalence toward Typee by faulting Tommo for his cultural inhibitions and positing an ironic distance between character and author. In Mitchell Breitwieser's "False Sympathy in Melville's *Typee*" (*AQ* 34:396–417) Tommo is a liberal individualist who romanticizes the natives in order to attack his own society, then recoils in horror when they depart from their assigned role of "noble primitives." T. Walter Herbert, Jr., argued this point at length in *Marquesan Encounters* (see *ALS 1980*, p.62), but where Herbert understood Tommo's (and Melville's) anthropological limitations as the common property of civilized Westerners, Breitwieser exempts Melville from the attitudinal structures of his time and maintains that "Melville deliberately made his narrator's sympathy eccentric, muddled, and indecisive, and by doing so obliged us to look for the self-interest underlying it." J. Kerry Grant takes a similar line in "The Failure of Language in Melville's *Typee*" (MLS 12,ii:61–68) except that for Grant the theme of Melville's book is the inadequacy of culturally bound language to accommodate the strange and enigmatic. Though Grant does not use the term, his subject is what Hayden White calls "troping," or the domestication of the unfamiliar through figuration. For Grant and Breitwieser both, Tommo is the source of *Typee*'s troping, and the sign of authorial irony is Tommo's awkwardness of language or hypergentility of response (to Marquesan nudity, for example). Neither asks whether a contemporary reader would have found Melville's language awkward, whether *Typee*'s labored chivalry on sexual matters might be assignable to the demands of Melville's audience or to his own uneasiness about sex, or whether the many quaintnesses of attitude and tone modern readers find in the book might derive from Melville's own provincialisms, his apprentice efforts at characterization and plot, his generic models, or his youthful sense of the posturings and vocabulary that genteel literature required.

A promised answer to this neglect of literary and historical context, Robert K. Martin's " 'Enviable Isles' : Melville's South Seas" (*MLS* 12,i:68–76) turns out to be an excellently illustrated restatement of the problem. "What concepts did [Melville] bring with him" to the Marquesas? "What did the South Seas mean in the 1840s, and how did these social meanings get integrated with Melville's personal experience? What kind of work did Melville finally create?" These are responsible questions, and Martin's appeal to the genre of travel narrative is a fine place to begin. But travel narrative for Martin means sensual escapism, which rapidly boils down to homosexuality. Though Martin forces his context upon *Typee*'s more general liberation of the instincts and senses, his essay is a perceptive and temperate one whose main defect is to ignore the initial questions it set for itself. A better antidote to the improbabilities of Breitwieser and Grant is "Melville's *Typee* and Frontier Travel Literature of the 1830s and 1840s" (*SDR* 19:46–64) by Robert Roripaugh, which compares *Typee*'s themes and narrative form to those in the Western writings of Irving, Parkman, Josiah Gregg, George Wilkins Kendall, and Lewis Garrard. While not on the order of Janet Giltrow's "Speaking Out: Travel and Structure in Herman Melville's Early Narratives" (see *ALS 1980*, pp. 62–63), Roripaugh's essay is a reminder that ambivalence toward the primitive and alternating past-tense narrative and present-tense commentary were "natural" features of the literature of cultural encounter, determined at once by the writer's own divided feelings and by the storytelling requirements of his genre.

Supplementing Jung's theory of archetypes with the work of Erich Neumann and Joseph Campbell, Julie M. Johnson in "Taji's Quest in Melville's *Mardi*: A Psychological Allegory in the Mythic Mode" (*CLQ* 18:220–30) reads Taji's story as an allegory of " 'the

process of individuation'" which has reference both to the development of the ego and to the cycle of the mythic hero. Jungian readings
often speak to the converted, but Johnson's essay should interest
nonbelievers as well, though critics who see Babbalanja as the main
presence in *Mardi* may feel that Johnson has neglected their book.

### v. Moby-Dick

A bountiful year. Reconceptions of allegory marked the longer discussions of *Moby-Dick*; among the shorter pieces there was an uncommon variety. In a section called "Traditional Conventions as
Prescriptive" from his book *Interpretive Conventions* (pp. 170–79)
Steven Mailloux notes the difference between the kinds (not the proportion) of praise and blame heaped upon *Moby-Dick* in England
and America and attributes the greater disgruntlement among British reviewers with *Moby-Dick's* erratic form to their application of
"*descriptive* knowledge [of literature] rigidified into *prescriptive*
rules." Though the absence of the Epilogue from *The Whale* helps
justify British complaints of authorial ineptitude, Mailloux acknowledges this variable and argues persuasively that the literary sophistication of "some" British reviewers produced "a built-in conservatism"
which hampered their response to "unprecedented masterpieces."

In "Ahab's Jonah-and-the-Whale Complex: The Fish Archetype
in *Moby-Dick*" (*ESQ* 28:167–82), a more detailed Jungian reading
than Johnson's of *Mardi*, Michael Vannoy Adams adduces some
striking parallels between Ahab's story and "what Jung variously
calls the 'Hero Myth' or 'Night Sea Journey' of Jonah." Adams is
knowledgeable about Jung and lucid in his presentation, but he is
more impressive on the outward correspondences between Ahab
and Jung's Jonah than he is on their psychological significance. Last
year in "'To Obey, Rebelling': The Quaker Dilemma in *Moby-Dick*"
(see *ALS 1981*, p. 63) Wynn M. Goering ascribed Starbuck's inaction
to his religious principles; this year in "'A Pantomime of Action':
Starbuck and American Whig Dissidence" (*NEQ* 55:432–39) James
Duban reads *Moby-Dick* in the political context of mid-19th-century
America and interprets Starbuck's hesitations as Melville's allegorical
treatment "of what many Americans came to regard as the impotent
and valor-ruined response of the Whig Party to President Polk's so-

called war of indemnity against Mexico." More loosely political, Nicolaus Mills's "The Crowd in Classic American Fiction" (*CentR* 26:61–
85) discusses Melville, Hawthorne, and Twain within the "paradigm"
of disenchantment with the American masses set by Cooper in the
Littlepage Trilogy. The "crowd" in *Moby-Dick* is the *Pequod*'s crew,
and Mills's remarks focus upon how Ahab mesmerizes this 30-man
ship of state "into a mob willing to hunt Moby Dick."

An original contribution to a much overworked subject, Philip
J. Egan's "Time and Ishmael's Character in 'The Town-Ho's Story'
of *Moby-Dick*" (*SNNTS* 14:337–47) addresses Ishmael's telling of
the story as it bears upon a problem with the "two Ishmaels" hypothesis, the unhinted development of Ishmael from the orphan of
the Epilogue to the exuberant and reflective narrator of *Moby-Dick*.
Set at some unspecified time between the *Pequod*'s voyage and the
writing of *Moby-Dick*, the scene at the Golden Inn is a revelation
of Ishmael's " 'intermediate self,' " an artist in words who "is able
to confront some of the awesome realities of the world but not yet
that of Moby Dick." Egan's evidence is slight (Ishmael's moment of
apparent faintness at the mention of Moby Dick) and his argument
depends upon imagining an extratextual life for Ishmael which Melville might easily have intimated if he had cared to. Nonetheless,
Egan provides a footbridge between the two Ishmaels for those who
want one, and he is particularly good on the "bachelor" environment
of the Golden Inn, which he correlates with the "bachelor phase" of
Ishmael's development. Describing Ishmael as "a 'secondary first-
person narrator' " who mediates between Ahab's world and our own,
Bruce F. Kawin in *The Mind of the Novel* (pp. 33–52) repeats the
earlier and better work of Walter L. Reed, Lawrence Buell, and
David L. Minter, none of which he lists in his "Selected Bibliography." Still more superfluous are James D. Wilson's pages on
*Moby-Dick* in *The Romantic Heroic Ideal* (LSU, pp. 88–95), which
announce that Ishmael is redeemed from the demoniac influence of
Ahab through the agency of Queequeg.

A want of originality can hardly be charged to Viola Sachs in *The
Game of Creation: The Primeval Unlettered Language of "Moby-
Dick; or, The Whale"* (Paris: Editions de la Maison des sciences de
l'homme). By "unlettered language" Sachs means an "intricate code"
of geometric shapes, sounds, puns, etymologies, colors, and (espe-

cially) numbers which, read aright, carry us beyond the "meaningless letters" of the text to "a mythic unique primordial tongue which existed before the confusion of languages occurred at the Tower of Babel." Its code broken, *Moby-Dick* reveals itself as an "inverted double of the Scriptures," the aim of which is a comprehensive dismantling of the Judeo-Christian heritage. This is scarcely news, but anyone who confines Sachs's novelty to mathematics will miss the significance of her reading. As Sachs presents it, *Moby-Dick* is the ultimate deconstructionist project, the deconstruction of deconstructionism, or the journey backward behind the labyrinth of words to the unfallen "pictorial and corporeal language of the savage" in which the instability of the signifier/signified relationship is obviated by a perfect in-touchness with things. What John Carlos Rowe described as the "modernity" of 19th-century American literature—its impulse to unburden itself of history and arrive at a " 'true present' "—comes full circle in Sachs's *Moby-Dick* as the modern finds its redemptive " 'point of origin' " in the archaic past.

Though Sachs's method is anomalous, her understanding of *Moby-Dick* as an effort to dissolve the encrustations of the past and repossess the living "body" of the world is shared by others who wrote on *Moby-Dick*, as is her premise that Melville's book is a systematic, if covert allegory. Both these ideas inform Bainard Cowan's *Exiled Waters: "Moby-Dick" and the Crisis of Allegory* (LSU), a thoughtful and allusive book that begins, significantly, not with the 19th-century crisis of allegory but with the present-day rift between old-line historical and New Critical approaches on one side and a sophisticated new historicism on the other, a rift Cowan proposes to heal by combining literary and cultural analysis in the manner of Walter Benjamin. Like Benjamin and others, Cowan defines allegory as "a cultural activity that arises at moments of crisis in the history of a literate people, when a text central to a people's identity can neither command belief any longer nor be entirely abandoned." The prototype for allegory's preservation by reinterpretation is Paul's rereading of the Old Testament, but by the Romantic age the Christian gospel had itself become "unreadable" and writers looked to nature to discover on its encoded body a renewed scripture. In *Moby-Dick* Ishmael reenacts the Romantic quest as "the distance gained from land on the 'exiled waters' of his voyage allows [him] to reenvision the

Western past and the natural present, freed from their enforced New England interpretation, as an allegory."

As Cowan develops his thesis through a reading of the five-part allegorical structure of *Moby-Dick*, his book recalls ambitious efforts like Paul Brodtkorb's *Ishmael's White World* (1965) or Robert Zoellner's *The Salt-Sea Mastodon* (1973). There is nothing facile or derivative about *Exiled Waters*, yet when Cowan invokes Benjamin or Bakhtin or writes (for example) that Ishmael "tropes the petrifying text of the city by turning away from it to the sea," readers may wonder if he is improving upon or even seriously modifying earlier readings, Zoellner's especially. Too often Cowan's apparatus of allegory seems to deliver up old wine in new and slightly bizarre bottles, and not even Melville's bottles, since despite his claim of historicism Cowan makes little effort to reconstruct the particulars of Melville's cultural world. An impressive book, nonetheless.

In Sharon Cameron's *The Corporeal Self: Allegories of the Body in Melville and Hawthorne* (Hopkins [1981]) "allegory" means something like anti-allegory, or an insistence on the literal meaning of the sign, which, because of Melville's obfuscations, is also a hidden meaning. When Cameron writes that "the fantasy in *Moby-Dick* is that human identities might be joined in a Siamese ligature, following which all men, fused, will be squeezed 'into each other,'" she means precisely what she says. Like the Freudian with his manifest and latent content, Cameron distinguishes between "the hermeneutic issues that comprise the novel's surface" and have occupied nearly every traditional critic to date "and the more primitive issues of identity to which that surface is forced to cede." Following Cameron requires a leap of faith, but the temptation becomes fairly strong when she remarks a characteristic fascination among American writers with bodily identity and speculates that American territorial expansion may have impressed itself upon the national mind in the form of a fixation upon extending the physical boundaries of the self. Here Cameron reminds us how outward facts may be internalized as constituent terms of perception, but she is too little the scholar to follow her thought to fruition.

David Simpson's *Fetishism and Imagination: Dickens, Melville, Conrad* (Hopkins), a companion to Simpson's *Wordsworth and the Figurings of the Real* (Macmillan, 1982), is an example of what John

Bryant euphemistically called "an exercise in approach," or a re-
grouping of oft-discussed themes under pseudocategories of the
author's inventing. All perception is apperception, or figuring, Simpson argues, and its ideal state is the fluidness of the "healthy imagination"; fetishism is an obsessed figuring which has lost sight of its
origins and become the slave of its own creations. In *Moby-Dick*
fetishism takes the form of "phallicism and narcissism," and the voyage of the *Pequod* is a quest "for the capture of what is lacking,"
which means "everything from abstract knowledge" down to Ahab's
missing leg and "another unmentioned member."

An overlooked essay from 1980, "Dante's Ulysses and Ahab's
Voyage: The Angelic Imagination in the Literal World" (*NDEJ*
12[1980]:141–74) by Thomas Werge anticipates this year's emphasis
upon the "world's body" but develops an almost antithetical perspective on *Moby-Dick*. Werge's subtitle comes from Allen Tate and refers to "a movement of spirit" which tries "to know and conquer all
the phenomena of experience while repudiating the literal world,
finiteness, and any guide except one's autonomous self," an impulse
Werge finds common to Dante's Augustinian Ulysses and Melville's
Ahab. Against Ahab's "atomistic Protestant Gnosticism" which de-
preciates the fallen world and would look upon God directly Werge
sets the sacramental vision Ishmael learns through Queequeg, "a
kind of literal and intercessory angel" who reconciles the worlds of
God and nature "through his adoration of limited forms as incarna-
tions of divinity." In "The Full Covenant: Father Mapple's Sermon
in Hebrew" (*ATQ* 50[1981]:105–16) Albert Waldinger contends
that *Moby-Dick* profits in its Hebrew translation, which gives Melville's "meaning a stability . . . substantially heightened by the original language of prophecy." Mapple's sermon does gain somewhat
from Waldinger's context, but Waldinger never explores its position
or authority in *Moby-Dick*, and his Judaic reading of Melville's book
is a fragment. Finally, in a note that bears upon several of the year's
interpretations, "The Chaldee Allusion in *Moby-Dick*: Its Antecedent and Its Implicit Skepticism" (*MSEx* 49:14–15), Jack Scherting
says it is "virtually certain" that Melville drew his meaning from the
1846 edition of Noah Webster's Dictionary (which he owned) and
that he intended Chaldee to be "associated with the proto-language
God supposedly bestowed upon Adam and Eve," a language "now
lost."

### vi. Pierre, The Confidence-Man

The best of the *Pierre* writing is Bainard Cowan's section from *Exiled Waters* (pp. 32–40), which offers Pierre as a failed allegorist who discovers the contradiction between Christianity and experience but cannot or will not deliteralize the biblical text. "More than a tour de force," *Pierre* for Cowan "is Melville's representation of the modern mind, nurtured in a tradition of Protestant appeal to the literal text but discovering that that text cannot be found written anywhere on the living body of the world." Delete Cowan's "not" and you have Thomas Werge's sacramental Melville. James D. Wilson's discussion of *Pierre* in *The Romantic Heroic Ideal* (pp. 161–67) is a flimsy performance which draws upon his 1973 article "Incest and American Romantic Fiction" (see *ALS 1973*, p. 77) and reads Melville's book as "a history of the romantic movement that serves to parody the strain of romantic optimism running from Wordsworth and Shelley to Melville's contemporaries Emerson and Thoreau." If Wilson has absorbed any of the relevant criticism of the last decade—Thomas F. Heffernan's "Melville and Wordsworth," for example (see *ALS 1977*, p. 52)—his discussion doesn't show it. The lone article on *Pierre*, "Antony as a Source for Pierre: The Saga of the Male Psyche" (*ATQ* 50[1981]:117–28) by Jeffrey M. Jeske, falls into this year's category of the source study manqué. After noting that "of the 491 total marks" Melville made in the edition of Shakespeare he purchased in 1849 "76, the greatest individual number, appear" in *Antony and Cleopatra*, Jeske ignores this wealth of material and offers a parallel reading of *Pierre* and Shakespeare's play founded upon their "common use of an archetypal pattern, much like that described by Jung, dealing with the maturation process of the male psyche." Separately, either work might profit from a Jungian reading, but the likenesses Jeske finds are labored and have little or no usefulness.

The *Confidence-Man* continued to draw appreciative attention. Tom Quirk's *Melville's Confidence Man: From Knave to Knight* (Missouri), the first book devoted wholly to *The Confidence-Man* and surely not the last, is "a genetic study" which begins with a model of how Melville worked (drawn from the Agatha letters) and argues that *The Confidence-Man* is a layered and partly overlaid book: it was conceived as a realistic social satire inspired by the exploits of

William Thompson, "the original confidence man," but encompassing "the general conditions of fraud and deceit" in mid-19th-century America; it evolved into a parody of "St. Paul's types of the faithful" from I Corinthians, a metamorphosis which required some addition and revision; and, with the appearance of Frank Goodman, it ultimately became a book of "deeply felt human sympathy" and gentle skepticism, its title character assuming the part of an "impractical knight-errant who attacks the ills of the world with a verbal lance." Informed, ably written, and winningly balanced in most of its judgments, *Melville's Confidence Man* is a book to be read for its many excellent parts. Over its thesis hangs a No TRUST sign. Cultivating the genetic to the neglect of the critical, Quirk assumes a narrow reading of the early chapters which he never puts to the test, posits a thematic division between the first encounters of the confidence man and those involving the Cosmopolitan, and then constructs a hypothesis on slim evidence to explain how and why this division may have come about.

Like Richard Boyd Hauck in his fine essay of last year (see *ALS 1981*, p. 67), Gerard W. Shepherd in "The Confidence Man as Drummond Light" (*ESQ* 28:83–96) shifts attention from the identity and motives of Melville's protagonist to "his function as a revealer of other characters in the book." Shepherd's main contribution is to apply his premise in detail to two representative encounters of the confidence man from the first half of the book (those with Henry Roberts and Pitch) and to show how the confidence man entangles his victims in a web of self-contradiction which betrays their professed philosophy of life. Shepherd makes a strong case for the unity of fictional intention which runs through the book's episodes. In Gary Lindberg's *The Confidence Man in American Literature* (Oxford, pp. 15–47) Melville's character is similarly a Drummond Light raying itself outward to illuminate others, but for Lindberg the moral or philosophical content of the confidence man's encounters is important only because his victims choose to stake their identity on their beliefs—as do most Americans, Lindberg argues, the fluidity of life in a sprawling democracy precluding any stable sense of self founded upon tradition, class, family, region, or occupation. Within Melville's book the confidence man is a tester of identities who "tricks his opponents into being themselves"; within Lindberg's more general thesis about American literature and culture he is a characteristically New World figure—half rogue, half hero—who manipulates the games of appearances by which Americans live and trades on the national "acceptance of promise."

"Melville's Masquerade and the Aesthetics of Self-Possession" (*ESQ* 28:233–42) by John Wenke shares Quirk's opinion that with the entrance of the Cosmopolitan *The Confidence-Man* takes a new turn. In the first half of the book, according to Wenke, the confidence man is an identic vampire who maintains his self-possession by robbing his victims of theirs; in the second half the "con man" is metamorphosed into a "good man" and "expresses his powers" by unmasking Charlie Noble and exposing the inhumaneness of Winsome and Egbert. In a related article, "No 'i' in Charlemont: A Cryptogrammic Name in *The Confidence-Man*" (*ELWIU* 9:269–76), Wenke returns to the theme of identity and makes an additional point: that the name Charlemont from the Cosmopolitan's story to Charlie Noble combines the words Charlie and Timon "in a suggestively coded form" which "points to major aspects of the novel," the "absent 'i' " directing us "to Melville's preoccupation with the problem of identity."

### vii. Stories, Poetry

John Carlos Rowe's "Ecliptic Voyaging: Orbits of the Sign in Melville's 'Bartleby the Scrivener' " (*Through the Custom-House*, pp. 111–38) should be read in the context of his "Introduction" (pp. 1–27; see "General Studies," above) with its theories of the "modernity of nineteenth-century American fiction" and the function of literary language in raising the culturally repressed. Rowe's "Bartleby" is a deconstructionist parable of the capacities of writing to center and decenter a culture. As a Master in Chancery, the narrator is the guardian of a "system of law" which establishes "a writing of pure repetition in order to control the subversive movement of signification that relies on the absence of a signified and thus denies any pure mastery or original authority." Enter Bartleby, the representative of Freud's "uncanny" or Derrida's "*différance*: the uncanny and vagrant property in language that motivates expression." Voyaging through "Bartleby," or Melville's canon, or American literature in general, Rowe works deftly within the hermetic world of his vocabulary and his theoretical premises; the question is whether poststructuralism is made to illuminate 19th-century fiction, or vice versa. For

Harold Schechter in "Bartleby the Chronometer" (*SSF* 19:359–66) Bartleby is an unsettler of a different sort, "a 'heavenly chronometer' sent down to remind the narrator . . . of the limitations" of horological behavior. Unlike those who read "Bartleby" as the narrator's unwitting confession, Schechter focuses upon the situation of the story and presents the narrator as an essentially good but not saintly man whose failure to save Bartleby testifies to our common human failure at unconditional charity. This reading was a refreshingly sane reprieve from critical overingenuity when Walter E. Anderson offered it last year in another *SSF* article (see *ALS 1981*, pp. 69–70), but aside from his framework of chronometricals and horologicals Schechter has nothing very new to add. A literate but vacuous essay, Ethel F. Cornwell's "Bartleby the Absurd" (*IFR* 9:93–99) shows no acquaintance whatever with the published criticism and divides its time between a description of Bartleby's socioeconomic sufferings and stylish plot summary; those looking for a discussion of Bartleby as "a metaphysical rebel exhibiting what Camus called 'an absurd sensitivity' " will not find it here. The only other writing on "Bartleby" is Merton M. Sealts, Jr.'s *Resources for Discussing Herman Melville's Tale, "Bartleby, the Scrivener"* (Madison: Wisconsin Humanities Committee, 22pp.). Prepared for lawyers attending an all-day seminar on "Bartleby," Sealts's pamphlet offers useful background for nonspecialists who will be teaching "Bartleby" and is a heartening example of how the study of literature can be presented to nonacademics without condescension toward the audience or violence to the author's work.

In "The Cocks of Melville's 'Cock-A-Doodle-Doo!' " (*ESQ* 28: 89–111) Allan Moore Emery takes up William Bysshe Stein's suggestion of 1959 that Melville's tale is a satiric response to Thoreau's essay "Walking" and elaborates it into a reading of the tale as a contrast between "two radically different individuals"—the narrator himself, a romantic naturalist whose moods are at the mercy of physiology; and Merrymusk, who like Socrates and St. Paul looks "beyond the confines" of his "wasted" body to "another, better life." Aside from "Walking," which Emery conjectures Melville may have read in a manuscript left with Hawthorne, Emery suggests as a possible source Frederick W. Shelton's "Letters from Up the River" published in the *Knickerbocker Magazine*. Emery is an energetic scholar with an instinct for where to hunt and an authoritative presentation but with an insensitivity to nuance and comic tone which lets his findings go unruled by the literary context. A second essay by Emery, "The Political Significance of Melville's Chimney" (*NEQ* 55:201–28), reads "I and My Chimney" as an allegory in which the narrator's house (nearly twice as wide as it is high) represents America; "his chimney, the federal Union"; the narrator himself— portly, rhetorical, and conservative—Daniel Webster; his wife, "the liberated females who participated in American abolitionism and who so vigorously persecuted . . . that political union so sacred to Websterian conservatives"; the mason Scribe, Garrison and Phillips but also "Southern theorists of disunion"; and the certificate the narrator extracts from Scribe, the Fugitive Slave Law. Objecting to the common autobiographical reading of "I and My Chimney," Emery observes rightly that the origins of the story should not be confused with its meaning, but his own evidence is thin and selective—for example, the narrator is associated with Webster largely on the basis of a reference to the Bunker Hill monument, which recalls for Emery Webster's famous Bunker Hill addresses of 1825 and 1843 but not Melville's recently completed book *Israel Potter*, which deals with a Bunker Hill veteran and is dedicated to the Bunker Hill monument.

In "The New Psychoanalysis and Literary Criticism" (*PoT* 3:89– 105) Elizabeth Wright presents herself as a woman of reason who is testing the literary value of Lacanian psychoanalysis by applying it to two stories which "have been much praised for their ambiguity": "Young Goodman Brown" and "Benito Cereno." The relationship of the new psychoanalysis to the old, as Wright explains it, is much like that of poststructuralism to New Criticism, the poststructuralist subverting the idea of a stable and determinate *conscious* meaning in the work, the new psychoanalyst of a stable and determinate *unconscious* meaning. In place of the New Critical myth of the literary artisan harmonizing the dissonance of experience through metaphor and organic structure Wright offers a new myth of the author or reader flying to fiction "in an attempt to reconstitute his lost wholeness, only to discover that language is the very thing which betrays him"; she also provides a new term, "structuration," for the dynamic activity of the text "producing itself" in the "breakdown" of its intended unity. As Wright applies her theories to "Benito Cereno" and "Young Goodman Brown," they yield the familiar doubleness which old (New) critics used to call "ambiguity" but which

Wright calls "ambivalence," the difference having mainly to do with Wright's assumption that multiple meanings in the text are evidence of the author's lack of control. Aside from privileging the critic over both author and text, it is hard to see what Wright's "Derridean and Lacanian" reading accomplishes. Wright puts the issue candidly when she says, "The new movement is not especially interested in the elucidation of individual works, except inasmuch as they can help validate its findings: that literature, far from presenting a unified consciousness, shows up the divisions of the self."

Also on "Benito Cereno," Robert J. Ward's "From Source to Achievement in 'Benito Cereno'" (AASt 2:233–40) reports that in adapting Amasa Delano's Narrative to his fictional purposes Melville made significant "omissions and additions concerning characterization," the results of which were to heighten Delano's innocence and Cereno's passive despair, to elevate Babo into the leader of the revolt, to "disengage the reader's possible sympathy for the slaves" by "increasing the cruelty and murderousness" of their behavior, and to mute the vengefulness of the Spanish sailors when the San Dominick is retaken. Though Ward's conclusions are generally similar to Rosalie Feltenstein's of 1947 (see "Melville's 'Benito Cereno,'" AL 19:245–55), their specificity makes it harder to argue that Melville intended his story as an attack upon slavery. In the note category Anthony Channell Hilfer's "The Philosophy of Clothes in Melville's 'Benito Cereno'" (PQ 61:220–26) uses Carlyle's Sartor Resartus to remark on appearance and reality, ironic role reversal, and the politics of naming in Melville's story. Hilfer's essay is another parallel reading dressed up as a source study but is worth reading so long as one ignores ascriptions of authorial intent implied in phrases like "Melville . . . seizes on the negative aspects of the clothes philosophy. . . ."

Among the writings on the poetry Shirley M. Dettlaff's "Ionian Form and Esau's Waste: Melville's View of Art in Clarel" (AL 54: 212–28) is a rich and thoughtful essay which takes up Melville's ambivalent response to 19th-century Hellenists, Arnold especially, and follows Melville's efforts to reconcile the classical ideal of human suffering transmuted by art into formal beauty and philosophic calm with his Hebraic metaphysics of vastness and terror and its accompanying aesthetics of the sublime. A slighter piece, Joseph Flibbert's "The Dream and Religious Faith in Herman Melville's Clarel" (ATQ

50[1981]:129–37) finds "an alternative to the anguish and nihilism of *Moby-Dick* and the dead ends of *The Confidence-Man*" in "the solemn dream-vision of Clarel, anchored in an accurate perception of the nature of reality and the limitations of human experience, inspired by the power of imagination, and meaningful only to himself." Aside from Stanton Garner's discussion of the backgrounds of "The Scout Toward Aldie" (see section *ii*), the only article on the shorter poetry is Robert E. Hogan's "Melville's Examination of Heroism in 'At the Cannon's Mouth'" (*BSUF* 23:69–72), which seems hard-pressed to define the exact shade of Melville's attitude toward this mystery of heroism.

### viii. Billy Budd, Sailor

*Billy Budd* replaced "Bartleby" as the most frequently addressed Melville work outside *Moby-Dick*, but except for essays by Robert Weisberg and James R. Hurtgen the writing was undistinguished. A courtroom aspect prevailed in several of the year's readings as critics dragged Vere to the dock, most of them to convict. The narrator joins Vere in Lyon Evans, Jr.'s "'Too Good to Be True': Subverting Christian Hope in *Billy Budd*" (*NEQ* 55:323–53), an inverted pyramid of "ifs" and "thens" whose Lawrance Thompsonian premise is that "Melville imitated the method of the Higher Critics in discrediting the four Gospels," Melville taking the role of Strauss to his credulous narrator's Matthew, Mark, Luke, and John. For Evans, Melville's narrator is an aging conservative blinded by romantic prejudices and deferential to authority who "forces the contradictory evidence to the Procrustean bed of Vere's dualistic interpretation"—Billy as innocent, Claggart as Satanic. Evans' Claggart may not be so bad at all, his Billy is a possible conspirator and nautical tough, and his Vere is "the central, organizing presence" in the narrative and the source of its doubtful mythologizing—this despite the fact that Vere did not become prominent in *Billy Budd* until a relatively late stage of composition when an innocent Billy and depraved Claggart were already in place. Vere is more darkly culpable in "Captain Vere and Upper-Class Mores in *Billy Budd*" (*SSF* 19:9–18) by Christopher Durer, who finds Vere's judgment of Billy "a deliberate act of a petty mind, held captive by the mores of an aristocratic civilization" which "dictate that a social inferior be punished for an offence against

his superior," regardless of his intent. Ignoring the complex historical, psychological, and mythic contexts of the story, Durer reads it
as Melville's attack on the "two sides . . . of contemporary English
civilization," Vere representing the "Tory landowner" and Claggart
(whom Durer finds associated with "the urbanized middle class")
the "Whig merchant." Where Durer sees a hidebound aristocrat,
Gail H. Coffler in a note on "Melville's *Billy Budd, Sailor*" (*Expl* 40:
2–3) finds an emperor and Stoic philosopher whom "Melville seems
to have admired greatly: Marcus Aurelius, whose surname was 'Ve-
rus,'" and whose effort to preserve the "peace and order" of his state
"at the cost of the sacrifice of Christians" reminds Coffler of Melville's
increasing valuation of "law and formal order" despite the repression
they bring.

A professor of law and former professor of literature, Robert
Weisberg in "How Judges Speak: Some Lessons on Adjudication in
*Billy Budd, Sailor*, with an Application to Justice Rehnquist" (*NYU
Law Review* 57:1–69) extends the arguments of C. B. Ives and others
and shows with lawyerly precision that Vere's handling of the trial
and execution of Billy ran counter to the procedures set down in
the Articles of War of 1749 or established by precedent, a fact Melville made known in a general way through the opinion of the surgeon. Vere's predispositions, not Naval law, required the sacrifice of
Billy, Vere's imposition of his judgment upon a reluctant court illustrating more broadly how judges can use their authority and verbal
skills to "give the force of seeming legality to drastic decisions the
law does not support." This is an old position newly and tightly
argued with near-definitive external evidence; its weak point is the
surgeon's testimony, which has the feel of an ironic modifier of the
main theme rather than a signpost pointing to it. On the question
of Vere's motives Weisberg is more controversial, casting Vere as a
would-be Nelson cursed with a prudent temperament and want of
genius who secretly envies and hates Billy, much as Claggart does,
for the "'frankness'" and valor he himself lacks. In Vere's mind Billy
*unwittingly stands in place of the envied, magnificently overt Ad-
miral Nelson*," so that when Billy strikes and kills Claggart, Vere
uses the opportunity to inflict a surrogate revenge. Weisberg's argument will never stand up in court, since "Vere's unarticulated resentment toward Nelson" is indeed unarticulated, even by the narrator.
Like Warner Berthoff's reading in *The Example of Melville*, how-

ever, Weisberg's speculation is an intriguing "maybe" of the sort *Billy Budd* seems calculated to produce. For James R. Hurtgen in "Melville: Billy Budd and the Context of Political Rule" (*The Artist and Political Vision*, pp. 245–65) Vere's behavior reflects Melville's "anguished" conviction "that the law must be served, however harsh and pitiless it may seem," a traditional reading renewed by Hurtgen through intelligence and subtlety and given a political turn. No "testament of acceptance," Hurtgen's *Billy Budd* is a rueful acknowledgment "that the human order is not only separate from the divine and the demonic . . . but *opposed* to the divine *no less* than to the demonic." Language, custom, and law are the channels through which men must regulate their affairs, and the "prepolitical" Billy has to die because his inarticulate and defenseless innocence is finally "as disruptive to society as the profound depravity of a Claggart." Fresher and more sophisticated than it sounds in summary, Hurtgen's judicious (not judicial) essay has the rare virtue of appealing to all levels of readers. In contrast, Konstantin Kolenda's "Innocence Sacrificed: Melville's *Billy Budd*" from *Philosophy in Literature* (pp. 61–74) seems aimed at the intelligent high school student who may or may not have read Melville's text. Superficially, Hurtgen and Kolenda appear to agree on many points, but Hurtgen is a subtle critic who refines and modifies a traditional reading, Kolenda a simple critic who reproduces it. Reinhard H. Friederich's "Comets, Stars, and Cynosure: *Billy Budd* in a Symbolist Context" (*ELWIU* 9:261–67) is a modest note about star references in *Billy Budd* encased within an overblown commentary on modern symbolism's precision of form and indeterminateness of meaning. Less pretentious but only marginally more useful, Alan C. Lupack's "The Merlin Allusions in *Billy Budd*" (*SSF* 19:277–78) suggests that the two references to the Dansker as an "old Merlin" associate Billy Budd with King Arthur, possibly Tennyson's King Arthur, whose tragedy, like Billy Budd's, "results from his being too good, too perfect for the real world."

*Washington University*

# 5. Whitman and Dickinson

## Jerome Loving

The life and poetry of Emily Dickinson may be more readily interesting to more people than the life and work of Walt Whitman, but
as in most years the critical interest in Whitman is preponderant this
year. This is measured not only by the greater number of studies of
Whitman but (also) by the death of the *Walt Whitman Review* (as
of June 1983). Like the famed phoenix, the *WWR*'s demise is marked
by the immediate birth of the *Walt Whitman Quarterly Review*. The
new journal, which will be published at the University of Iowa,
promises outside referees for submissions and an annual Charles E.
Feinberg prize of $250 for the most valuable essay on the poet.
Another benchmark of Whitman's staying power is the publication
of the sixth volume (with material remaining for another three or
four more) of Horace Traubel's *With Walt Whitman in Camden*.
The best work of the year is also on the Whitman side of this chapter:
Ernest Lee Tuveson's essay on the poet in *The Avatars of Thrice
Great Hermes*.

### i. Whitman

*a.* **Bibliography, Editing.**   Roberts W. French joins William White
in getting out part of the annual *WWR* checklist for this year, but
the big news in bibliography comes again from the reference-guide
mill at G. K. Hall. In *Walt Whitman, 1940–1975: A Reference Guide*
Donald Kummings continues the work of Scott Giantvalley (*ALS
1981*, p. 75). In this excellently annotated listing of 3,172 secondary
sources Kummings reflects the fact that the critical focus has shifted
since the 1940s from the poet's personality to his poetry. One can
easily imagine the reflection of the compiler of the volume beginning

Preparation of this chapter was facilitated by the research assistance of Susan
Roberson.—*J.L.*

with 1976. That checklist of, say, the last quarter of this century will reflect the end of a cycle of critical focus that began with the man, shifted to the poet, and concluded with the critic himself.

Those who still require Whitman's text, however, will be well served by Justin Kaplan's selection in *Walt Whitman: Complete Poetry and Collected Prose* (Library of America), which presents on acid-free paper both the 1855 and 1891/92 editions of *Leaves of Grass*, the complete prose works, and such supplementary prose pieces as the famous Emerson letter (in its original form). In most cases the copy-text for this volume is the NYU edition. For the intention in the Kaplan arrangement is not to replace *The Collected Writings* but to make accessible in one attractive and sturdy volume the salient parts of Whitman's poetry and prose. The most serious students of the poet will still need to consult the NYU series. And the history of that undertaking, once described by its general editor Gay Wilson Allen as "a million dollar project without a million dollars," is assessed by Ed Folsom in "The Whitman Project: A Review Essay" (*PQ* 61:369–94). Folsom notes that like the progress of Whitman's book between 1855 and 1881, the growth of the NYU project during the same period in this century "quickly gave way to a self-generating free form, one which is still evolving." The essay is evenhanded in its praise and criticism, but Folsom probably errs when he goes beyond its announced topic. Here his conclusions, especially with the Eitner and the Kaplan biography (see *ALS 1981*, p. 76, and *ALS 1980*, pp. 70–71), are of less value.

Herbert Bergman adds slightly to the Whitman early works in "A Hitherto Unknown Whitman Story and a Possible Early Poem" *WWR* 28:3–15. The tale, called "The Fireman's Dream: With the Story of His Strange Companion, A Tale of Fantasie," appears to be the first two chapters of a serialized novel. The fragment resembles "The Madman," the first part of another unfinished temperance novel begun after the publication of *Franklin Evans; Or the Inebriate* (1842). The poem apes Whitman's early verse but in fact may well be the work of another writer. The tale, on the other hand, is decidedly Whitman's and is interesting to the extent of its focus upon male relationships and boardinghouse life in New York City. In another discovery ("Whitman's Anthology of English Literature," *Duke Univ. Library Notes* 50:33–34) Kenneth M. Price identifies the source of Whitman clippings in the Trent Collection as Ludwig Herrig's *British Classical*

*Authors . . . from G. Chaucer to the Present Time* (1851). The clipped pages correspond to the missing section of the book in the Feinberg Collection (Library of Congress).

*b.* **Biography.** The reader of *With Walt Whitman in Camden, September 15, 1889–July 6, 1890* (So. Ill.) will encounter few surprises and generally a narrative that is of dubious biographical value. That is to say, the sixth volume of Horace Traubel's conversations with the aging poet, edited by Gertrude Traubel and William White, simply records the continuation of Whitman's "house-tied" days. In fact, the volume may do more for Traubel than it does for Whitman: it may redeem Traubel from the generally perceived role of budding socialist/poet in search of a vehicle for his populist platitudes. He does indeed appear in this volume to be consciously shaping his story—but around Whitman's life as a poet instead of as a political prophet. That Traubel is more of a biographer than a propagandist is also the conclusion of Tibbie E. Lynch in her examination of the first volume of the Traubel volumes ("Biographical Technique in Horace Traubel's *With Walt Whitman in Camden,*" *SAR,* pp. 433–44). Lynch sees the conversations and letters in the book as having a narrative quality instead of a fragmented one because Traubel provided "credible contexts" for the material. My reading of volume six may perhaps be influenced by the Lynch article, but this latest volume does appear to have a greater continuity than the others, suggesting that Traubel was getting better as a practitioner of the biographical art. We become involved as Whitman's 70th birthday party is planned and carried out as "Camden's Compliment" to the poet; wait with him for Thomas Harned and his next batch of homemade spirits; look back to 1855 and his friends' dislike for "Leaves of Grass" as the title for his first book of poetry, and forward with the planning of the mausoleum at Harleigh Cemetery in Camden. The effect is not that of the "years and hours" application Jay Leyda used on the lives of Melville and Dickinson. Here the editors are altogether upstaged by the poet's friend and admirer—one of the central players in the final act of Whitman's life.

Some of Whitman's acquaintances may have disapproved of the title of his first book, but many others objected to its content. One of the most severe detractors found only a "disgusting priapism" in *Leaves of Grass.* Until now his identity has been known to us only

as "Sigma"—though Whitman and his defender William Douglas
O'Connor suspected the author of the 1882 New York *Tribune* attack
to be Ainsworth Rand Spofford, then librarian of Congress. This
suspicion is now pretty much confirmed by Harold Aspiz in "Whitman's Literary Enemy: A. R. Spofford" (*WWR* 28:92–98). Aspiz's
careful research is well laid out, but his argument may outrun the
evidence when it suggests that Spofford's attitude was similar to that
of Ralph Waldo Emerson, his acquaintance. To the contrary, Spofford's views of Whitman were probably no more aligned with Emerson's than were those of the New Englander's many friends who
refused to believe that he was the author of the famous letter of
greeting to Whitman in 1855. Two other contemporary responses to
Whitman's book are discussed by Gary Scharnhorst in "D. A. Wasson
and W. R. Alger on the 1855 *Leaves of Grass*" (*WWR* 28:29–32).
The responses were confined to personal communications, but in a
good piece of detective work Scharnhorst speculates convincingly
that Alger may have written one of the anonymous condemnations
that Whitman reprinted in the appendix to his second edition.

*c.* **Criticism: General.** In his chapter on Whitman in *The Avatars*
(pp. 212–52) Ernest Lee Tuveson presents a most original and intriguing discussion of the tradition that may have influenced Whitman to insist upon the equality of body and soul. He sees Whitman
as the culmination of a worldview that has been vaguely (and er-
roneously) attributed to Neoplatonism. Whereas the Neoplatonic
tradition sees God as the creator of a world which is emblem instead
of essence, the doctrine of Hermes Trismegistus sees God in the
world. It is not pantheistic, however, because nature is defined as
"the manifestation, not the workmanship, of God." Since the world
in the hermetist conception emanates from divine intelligence, each
part of it is an essential component of God. No effort is made to
demonstrate that Whitman actually read the *Hermetica* (translated
by Ficino in the 15th century) because it is argued that by the poet's
day the ideas had been absorbed by Western culture—and confused
with Neoplatonism. Rather, he views Whitman as the democratic
or democratized beneficiary of a kind of gnosis that is (potentially)
common to "prophets en masse"—those who subscribe to the idea
that the physical does not die but rather scatters (as the poet himself
does at the end of "Song of Myself") because it is part of a constantly

changing nature. Interestingly, in volume 6 of Traubel (discussed above) Whitman describes death as going "along in the mist."

Jerome Loving's crisply written study *Emerson, Whitman, and the American Muse* (N.C.) analyzes with fresh insight the personal and literary connections of the two men. Several theses converge: by merging his homoerotic nature and Neoplatonic ideas Whitman discovered his universal character for which Emerson's essays provided a theory and language to idealize it as essentially American. Loving advances the date of Whitman's reading of Emerson's essays ten years before the summer of 1854, which Floyd Stovall concluded in 1974 (*ALS 1974*, pp. 62–63) was the time the thorough reading took place. The book's historical half is especially valuable, weighing the principal scholarship on this famous relationship. The careers of both men are perhaps too schematically drawn—"As I Ebb'd" is said to be Whitman's "farewell to the poetry of self-reliance as 'Experience' is Emerson's." Linguistic analysts will dispute the reading of "Experience" as "pessimistic" and "The Poet" as evidence of "exhaustion." Otherwise the book offers several original perceptions, notably linking Whitman's turn from politics toward poetry to the election of Franklin Pierce in 1852 and then asserting that in "Song of Myself" Whitman discovered the "hoax" of self-reliance in its isolating arrogance. This closely focused study of the subject is both provocative and indispensable. A separate chronology extracted from the narrative would be a welcome addition.[1]

Two studies by British scholars attempt with different results to assess Whitman's work. The chapter on the poet in Brian Harding's *American Literature in Context, II* (pp. 202–21) offers a stimulating and somewhat original discussion of the poet's celebration of body and soul. Noting Whitman's use of the metaphoric significance of "inspiration" (literally, "breathing in"), Harding suggests that the narrator in "Song of Myself" fuses the physical with the spiritual. In this sense Whitman responds to Emerson's theory of language (i.e., of its coming from things which are in turn emblems of the spirit): he imbibes the physical and turns it into words, which by the Emersonian progression are now a blend of the spiritual and the physical. Harding is almost as insightful and imaginative in his analyses of the later poetry, finding a more public poet in the 1860s. Indeed, for a chapter out of a literary survey its conclusions are both fresh and

1. The foregoing paragraph was written by David Porter.

profound. The same cannot be said, however, of the chapter on Whitman and Carlyle in Linden Peach's *British Influence* (pp. 162–93). First of all, their well-known exchange over the merits of democracy does not exactly coincide with the "birth" of American literature. And while Peach has his facts straight as to Whitman's reading of Carlyle's "Shooting Niagra," he overlooks a good deal of the Whitman biography in order to argue that the Wound Dresser "had a romantic view of the American Civil War in which he saw the first awakening of his idealised spiritual America." A reading of the poet's "The Eighteenth Presidency!" or his wartime letters and recorded conversations will quickly dispel such a notion, showing Whitman to have anticipated at least in part Carlyle's views on slavery and the black man. In general the chapter is weak in its use of both primary and secondary sources.

Four other studies take up the subject of Whitman and the American city. In "Pastoralism and the American Urban Ideal: Hawthorne, Whitman and the Literary Pattern" (*AL* 54:329–53) James L. Machor writes that the poet minimized the ostensible conflict between urban and pastoral impulses by internalizing and so idealizing the two to produce "urban pastoralism." In this aesthetic rather than cultural response the two seeming opposites become mirror images of each other. According to William Aarnes, however, Whitman's love of nature (as evidenced in *Specimen Days*) kept him from reconciling the two ("Withdrawal and Resumption: Whitman and Society in the Last Two Parts of *Specimen Days*," *SAR*, pp. 401–32). Rather, like Thoreau he "created a record of an excursion embodying the dual intention of criticizing, rejecting, society for lacking the virtues of Nature and of restoring society to those very virtues." In a more eloquent argument M. Wynn Thomas also finds Whitman rejecting the city, but only the postbellum one ("Walt Whitman and Mannahatta–New York," *AQ* 34:362–78). He attributes the falling off of Whitman's genius after 1860 to this disenchantment.

Of course, it was not only the "microcosm" that changed after the war but Whitman as well. And following the example of a number of critics (including himself in *American Poets* [*ALS 1968, passim*]), Hyatt H. Waggoner complains that Whitman wrote too consciously, too much as the prophet-poet. His argument in the chapter devoted to Whitman in *American Visionary Poetry* (LSU, pp. 25–65) occasionally wanders, but it is nevertheless fresh with insights into key poems from "Song of Myself" to "Out of the Cradle Endlessly Rocking." Whitman's vision, according to Waggoner, is that we are both "in and out of the game," neither objective observers of the world nor homeless in it. Less confident about the poet's acceptance of nature as "no saint" is Lawrence Lipking in *The Life of the Poet: Beginning and Ending Poetic Careers* (Chicago [1981]; pp. 114–30). He finds Whitman "deconstructing" his own book in the "Death-Bed Edition": "What one poem offers, the next takes back."

Whatever restraints the psyche encountered came from society and not from nature, according to Denise T. Askin in an essay whose discourse is often inflated or unsupported ("Whitman's Theory of Evil: A Clue to His Use of Paradox," *ESQ* 28:121–32). Whitman "liberates evil" from the taboos of civilization and "elevates it to its proper place in the divine procession." In a similar but more original thesis Andrew Hudgins writes that Whitman extended traditional epic conventions in order to transcend "the limited victories of culture-bound heroes like Ulysses and Aeneas" ("*Leaves of Grass* from the Perspective of Modern Epic Practice," *MQ* 23:380–90). In a related piece Hudgins finds in Whitman's shift from external to internal conflict the possibility that the American South represented the destructive, darker side of the national character he celebrated ("Walt Whitman and the South," *SLJ* 15:91–100).

Myrth Jimmie Killingsworth's "Whitman and Motherhood: A Historical View" (*AL* 54:28–43) attempts to explain Whitman's paradoxical position on women. In praising women as childbearers Whitman removed them as equals of men in physical and intellectual pursuits. "Whitman's difficulty," writes Killingsworth, "is decidedly Victorian. The mother as a physical being is unreal to him, and the only way he can successfully and consistently portray her is as a hopelessly untouchable, mysterious ideal." The focus of the essay blurs a bit, however, when he takes this historical evidence into a reading of "Out of the Cradle Endlessly Rocking." The argument that the sea is the mother object from which the "boy poet" cannot separate himself appears to ignore a good many other important thematic elements in the poem. Killingsworth does much better in his discussion of other poems that demonstrate Whitman's idealism towards women. Indeed, the general strength of the argument depends on its grasp of 19th-century American attitudes towards sexuality and the role of women. Also idealized by Whitman, according to Calvin Bedient in "Whitman: Overruled" (*Salmagundi* 58–59: 326–43), was the poet's homosexuality. He argues against Robert K. Martin (*ALS 1979*, p. 64) to say that Whitman's lovemaking was probably no more than vicarious.

**d. Criticism: Individual Works.**  In his foreword to William Everson's poetic rendering of the 1855 preface (*American Bard: The Original Preface to Leaves of Grass Arranged in Verse* [Viking, 1981]), James D. Hart remarks that Whitman probably did not consider the essay a preface because he never used it again except as reworked in fragments of poems. Also sometimes thought of as poetic fragments (as least in the shadow of "Song of Myself") are the "other" poems in Whitman's first book. But, for Ivan Marki in "The Last Eleven Poems in the 1855 *Leaves of Grass*" (*AL* 54:229–39), study of the formal structure of these so-called "cuttings" indicates that without them "the first edition would be incomplete, because its story would be unfinished and its drama unresolved." Unfortunately, the exact nature of the "story" is not clear enough—though a familiarity with Stephen Black's thesis (*ALS 1975*, pp. 86–87) helps us to see that by "story" he means a definable psychological movement in the book. Marki argues that the poet's "processes of consciousness" are begun in "Song of Myself" but concluded in the other 11 poems. The development of this position, however, is frequently undercut by the use of other equally tenuous statements as supporting evidence. More loosely subjective is William S. Haney II in " 'Song of Myself': The Touch of Consciousness" (*UMSE* 2[1981]:64–70), who ventures to say that the mystic unity celebrated in "Song of Myself" is "universally open to experience at any time and place by all men."

Also universally open to use and misuse, apparently, is Whitman's 1857 notation to himself about "The Great Construction of a New Bible," which he hoped to have ready by 1859. This very brief entry, which as far as I know was not repeated or reasserted elsewhere in Whitman's writings, has been treated frequently as the poet's last word on his position in world history. The latest to exaggerate and exploit Whitman's brief euphoria in the wake of the famous Emerson letter is Marilyn Teichert, who uses the statement as the basis for her argument that the "Children of Adam" poems are remarkably similar to the gospels in the sense that both repudiate "rigid and stultifying conventionalism" toward sex ("Children of Adam: Whitman's Gospel of Sexuality," *WWR* 28:25–29). M. Wynn Thomas is easily more interesting in his study of *Drum-Taps* ("Whitman's Obligation of Memory," *WWR* 28:43–54). In fact, no one in the past few years has written more extensively on these poems than Thomas. In this essay, whose summary obscures the depth of his observations, he argues that the Civil War was "artistically as well as personally important" to the poet, so much so that Whitman could claim retroactively in 1871 that "my book and the war are one." Another article that deals with the poet's wartime experiences is William Aarnes's, "'Almost Discover': The Spiritual Significance of Soldier Talk in Whitman's *Specimen Days*" (*WWR* 28:84–91). But its argument that the poet may have found some clue to the unknown in the "soldier talk" he records in *Specimen Days* is almost as arbitrary as the title of his essay is awkward. Aarnes is more original in "'Free Margins': Identity and Silence in *Specimen Days*" (*ESQ* 28:243–60). Here he is arbitrary only in his use of the "Great Construction" diary notation.

An essay that should not be ignored because of its critical approach is Mutlu Konuk Blasing's "Whitman's 'Lilacs' and the Grammars of Time" (*PMLA* 97:31–39). This structuralistic analysis of Whitman's great elegy to Lincoln demonstrates more clearly than before that it is not a consciously structured poem written in the convention of Milton's "Lycidas" or Shelley's "Adonais" but is instead the product of the same kind of language experiment that produced "Song of Myself": that of Emerson's endless seeker who cannot find sanctuary in any kind of religious affirmation but only in the reality of language itself. "When Lilacs Last in the Dooryard Bloom'd" has long been something of an anachronism to scholars because it was written relatively late in the poet's career (after the less-celebrated *Drum Taps*). Yet it has been considered by many one of the best, if not the very best, of his poems. What Blasing implicitly demonstrates is that Lincoln's sudden death led Whitman to "a new wakefulness of words"—a renaissance, as it were, of the spirit that kindled "Song of Myself," the Calamus sequence, "Out of the Cradle Endlessly Rocking," and "As I Ebb'd with the Ocean of Life." Other arguments for a stronger later Whitman can be found in Richard Pascal's "Whitman's 'Sparkles from the Wheel'" (*WWR* 28:20–24) and in

E. Dalgarno and K. Streibich's "Miracle Enough: The History of Whitman's Farewell Poem" (*WWR* 28:72–76). Both essays argue that their subjects have been unfairly neglected.

**e. Affinities and Influences.** For the poet who "absorbed" his country (and the world) more affectionately than it initially absorbed him, the list of affinities and influences is almost endless. The three most important influences were probably the Bible, the opera, and Emerson; but in the pluralistic spirit of the 1980s we can add just about anything—even the American pastime of baseball. This is the conclusion of Lowell Edwin Folsom (Ed Folsom) in "America's 'Hurrah Game': Baseball and Walt Whitman" (*IowaR* 11[1980]:68–80). Whitman had a long-standing interest in the game whose development, Folsom notes, coincides—both geographically and temporally —with the poet's adult life. He suggests that Whitman came to see baseball "as an essential metaphor for America."

Martin Bidney is more traditional but also highly abstract in his perception of parallels. In "Structure of Perception in Blake and Whitman: Creative Contraries, Cosmic Body, Fourfold Vision" (*ESQ* 28:36–47) Bidney finds in a well-worn literary coupling a similarity with regard to the two poets' "psychology of poetic creativity." And the French in Whitman is taken up by George Klawitter in "Early French Expectations of Walt Whitman" (*WWR* 28:54–63). He argues that the French acceptance of Whitman was slow because of that culture's preference for classic norms of prosody—a fact, he adds, that Betsy Erkkila overlooked in *Walt Whitman Among the French* (*ALS 1980*, p. 78).

Whitman's influence on other writers is the subject of two notes this year. In " 'Of War Times and Poetry and Democracy': A Final Visit with Whitman" (*WWR* 28:32–34) Robert J. Scholnick produces a letter which describes the last visit of Edmund Clarence Stedman to Whitman in Camden. It suggests that Stedman then got the idea for "W. W.," a poem he read at Whitman's funeral. That funeral, incidentally, was not Camden's final compliment to its Mickle-Street bard. In fact, disciples and admirers of the poet met every year to celebrate his life and work. Under the direction of Horace Traubel these meetings led to the formation of the Walt Whitman Fellowship, which lasted well into the 1920s. At the 1919 meeting in New York City Helen Keller revealed that of her three favorite writers (including Emerson and Thoreau) Whitman was her "best beloved." Her remarks are reprinted by Scott Giantvalley in "A Spirit Not 'Blind to His Vision, Deaf to his Message': Helen Keller on Walt Whitman" (*WWR* 28:63–66).

## ii. Dickinson

*a.* **Bibliography, Editing.** Thanks to the research of Karen Dandurand, we now know the number of poems published during Dickinson's lifetime to be eight instead of seven ("Another Dickinson Poem Published in Her Lifetime," *AL* 54:434–37). The poem is "Nobody Knows This Little Rose" (J. 35), which appeared in the Springfield *Republican* of 2 August 1858. Since that publication, of course, Dickinson's poetry has conquered Springfield, America, and the world. In *Emily Dickinson in Europe: Her Literary Reputation in Selected Countries* (Univ. Press, 1981) Ann Lilliedahl examines the poet's critical reception in Sweden, Norway, France, Germany, Austria, German-speaking Switzerland, and the former Danish colony of Iceland.

Other bibliographical tools now available are (1) Willis J. Buckingham, "Emily Dickinson: Annual Bibliography for 1980," *DicS* 44:28–41; (2) Buckingham and Martin A. Orzeck, "Index to *Dickinson Studies*, 1975–1980," *DicS* 40(1981):1–49; (3) Buckingham and Orzeck, "Index to the *Higginson Journal* 1972–1980," *DicS* 40(1981):50–70; and (4) Frederick L. Morey, "Emily Dickinson's Use of the Bible—a Checklist," *HJ* 33:39–41.

*b.* **Biography.** When Martin Wand and Richard B. Sewall published their *NEQ* article on Dickinson's eye problems (*ALS 1979*, p. 73), they stirred up a minor debate that is still in progress. After examining the extant images of Emily, her sister, and mother, they hypothesized that all three suffered from extropia, a disease in which one eye turns out. Now Mary Elizabeth Kromer Bernhard in "A Response to 'Eyes Be Blind, Heart Be Still' " (*NEQ* 55:112–14) calls into question this judgment by noting that the early daguerrotypes presented an image that was laterally reversed—a circumstance that may explain the appearance of extropia in the poet's right eye. More generally, Bernhard doubts that such a crude daguerrotype (and one taken long before the poet's eye treatments) can judiciously serve *ex post facto* "as the subject of an ophthalmologic examination."

James Guthrie, on the other hand, is more concerned about when the poet's malady began than he is about its exact nature. In " 'Before I got my eye put out': Dickinson's Illness and Its Effects on Her Poetry" (DicS 42:16–21) he suggests that Dickinson's eye trouble began earlier than the summers of 1864–65 when she was treated in Boston and that, rather than reducing her poetic output (as would seem to be the case in 1864–65), the earlier illness coincides with and may have been partly responsible for the great poetic outpouring of 1862, "for a decline of her vision could have been compensated for by a quickening of her poetic vision." For a handy survey of the scholarship relating to the poet's illnesses as well as to those many theories about her lover(s), see Frederick L. Morey, "The Esthetics of Emily Dickinson" (DicS 43:1–18). As the title suggests, Morey also attempts a discussion of the various "esthetic" approaches to Dickinson; but this part of the essay is loosely constructed and blandly executed.

c. Criticism: General.   The only book-length critical study of Dickinson this year is *Emily Dickinson: When a Writer Is a Daughter* (Indiana) by Barbara Antonina Clarke Mossberg. Mossberg argues that Dickinson, psychologically caught between childhood and adulthood because of her unfulfilled need for her father's recognition of her talents, approached all men and the world as the perpetual daughter in search of "a father-master-tutor-preceptor." Shut up in the "prose" of what men expected of her as a woman, she wrote as one "at odds with herself and her culture." Like recent feminist studies of Dickinson (and others) before her, Mossberg's study is preemptive in its implication that the feminine experience in all of its vital aspects is beyond the ken of the male critic. That is to say, the exclusive world of the female is more or less taken for granted and then used as evidence of Dickinson's alienation. Had Mossberg availed herself more of Margaret Homans' excellent analysis of Dickinson's referentiality (ALS 1980, pp. 83–84), her argument would have been less "exclusive" and certainly more palatable. As it is, this readable and comprehensive survey of how the poet's domestic situation might have affected her art fails to convince (me, at least) that the poet's gender was more than a minor player in the drama of making the poems.

A thesis at odds with Mossberg's is found in Rowena Revis Jones, "The Preparation of a Poet: Puritan Directions in Emily Dickinson's Education" (*SAR*, pp. 285–324). After a slow start it examines the poet's education (through family, church, school, and community) to argue that Dickinson was encouraged at every stage to develop her mind. "She was not, in short, as socially oppressed as some would make her out to be. Nor was the independence that marks the person and the poems necessarily a sign of rebellion or rage." But the essay waxes romantic as much in one direction as Mossberg sometimes does in the other: "To New Englanders of piety," Jones suggests, "especially those who looked upon women as made in the divine image, the cause of female education could well have presented itself as a religious cause, a way of advancing the kingdom of God." Taking the middle road between the two is Cheryl Walker, who admits that Dickinson's poetry "was inspirited in important ways by women" but maintains that her best work is much more than a logical extension of female conventions in American poetry up to that time (i.e., the themes of the forbidden lover and the secret sorrow). Walker's chapter on Dickinson in *The Nightingale's Burden* (pp. 87–116) concludes that after Dickinson's work became known, women poets in America could take *their* work seriously. If this survey of female poetry has a fault, it is in assuming that female poets could not—and cannot—take themselves seriously unless able to identify with some sort of gender-oriented corporation.

Two articles on Dickinson's referentiality this year turn out to be ellipses explaining ellipses. In "Terms and Golden Words: Alternatives of Control in Dickinson's Poetry" (*ESQ* 28:48–62) Cris Miller finds the poet's use of language falling into two categories: "terms," which stand for language with clearly established antecedents, and "words of Gold," which stand for language that transcends the quotidian through metaphor. The conclusion is that Dickinson never abandons one completely for the other. This is simply another way to say she occupies, like all good poets, that neutral territory between fact and fancy. Joan Burbick's announced aim is "to examine particular points in Dickinson's poetry where the direction and reference of words collapse and the reader is stopped precisely because the words cease to convey a sense of 'difference'" ("The Irony of Self-Reference: Emily Dickinson's Pronominal Language," *ELWIU*

9:83–95). She finds what similar studies before hers have found: that
the search for the source of what Whitman called the "Me myself"
always collapses into frustration and paradox.

Of course, the critic is nowhere today if he is not fashionably
murky. But unfortunately for Greg Johnson, the ambiguity allows
not for a disabling freedom in the pursuit of understanding but instead a demonstration of the critic's limited understanding of his
subjects—Emerson and Dickinson. In "Emily Dickinson: Perception and the Poet's Quest" (*Renascence* 35:2–15) he makes a lame
attempt to distinguish between the two poets' ways of seeing poeti-
cally. Dickinson rejects the Emersonian way of seeing transcendentally for the idea that "Truth must dazzle gradually." Transcendental
seeing is never clearly defined because that would undermine the
argument entirely and reveal its solipsistic method. "Every thing
looks permanent," Emerson writes in "Circles," "until its secret is
known. . . . Every ultimate fact is only the first of a new series."
Emerson and Dickinson both see "transcendentally"—as all great
poets do; in their cases, it is *what* they see that is dramatically different. Emerson's use as a straw man fails, it seems, to distract our
attention from the fact that this essay says nothing new and a few
old things wrong. The crutch for John M. Martin in "Nature and
Art: Two Undiscussed Poems by Emily Dickinson" (*DicS* 42:26–29)
is circular reasoning. He argues that Dickinson used nature as a
metaphor for her own art. Only slightly more reasonable is Susan R.
Van Dyne's impressionistic attempt to chart the continuity of "distinct" lyrical voices of our women poets beginning with Dickinson
("Double Monologues: Voice in American Women's Poetry" [*MR*
23:461–85]). Dickinson continues to "dazzle gradually"—despite
some of her critics.

**d. Criticism: Individual Works.** As we noted earlier, the critical
attention to Dickinson was relatively sparse this year. There were,
however, a number of *Explicator* items. In "Dickinson's 'I Like to
See It Lap the Miles' [J. 585]" (*Expl* 40:30–32) William Freedman
lumbers through a vaguely connected analysis to see the poem,
usually read as a description of a train, as an attempt to define
poetry—particularly its capacity to "traverse distances swiftly and
effortlessly." For Nicholas Ruddick, Dickinson used scientific images

in her poetry more often than has been thought—or more often than he thought ("Dickinson's 'Banish Air From Air' [J. 854]," *Expl* 40: 31–33). Peggy Anderson finds biblical imagery in her challenge to Charles R. Anderson's reading (in *Stairway of Surprise*, 1960) of the phrase "Son of None" in "Behind Me—Dips Eternity" (J. 721). "To anyone familiar with the Bible," she chides, "the phrase suggests 'Son of Nun' "—an allusion to Joshua in the Old Testament ("Dickinson's 'Son of None,'" *Expl* 41:32–33). (Charles Anderson's reading of another poem is also challenged by Eileen M. Donohoe in "Undeveloped Freight in Dickinson's 'I Read My Sentence—Steadily' [J. 412]," *CP* 15:43–48). Helene Knox handles her disagreement with Ruth Miller (*ALS 1968*, pp. 63–64) with more finesse. She sees a broader significance in the meaning of the word "Circumference" in the poem under discussion ("Dickinson's 'The Poets Light But Lamps' [J. 833]," *Expl* 41:31). And of more substance is Willis J. Buckingham's quarrel with Sharon Cameron's "pillar of salt" reading of J. 286. To her discussion of the narrator's awareness of death he counsels that its confrontation should not be confused with death itself—after which there is no conception to contemplate ("Dickinson's 'That After Horror—That 'Twas *Us*,'" *Expl* 40:34–35).

**e. Affinities and Influences.** Ralph Marcellino reports the sighting of an allusion to Virgil's *Aeneid* in "Emily Dickinson's 'Beware an Austrian' [J. 1694]" (*CB* 57:53–54). And Alice Hall Petry finds more than one source for "In Winter in My Room" (J. 1670). She finds two, which both come from the *Atlantic Monthly* and the pen of Oliver Wendell Holmes. The first is from the second installment of *Elsie Venner* (which concerns an offspring that is half-human, half-snake). The second source is from Paper #8 of *The Autocrat at the Breakfast Table* (where, as in Dickinson's poem, a worm is suspended by a string)—"The Ophidian Image in Holmes and Dickinson," *AL* 54:598–601. All this is possible, of course. We can also understand Petry's desire to see Dickinson's work "within the contexts of the contemporaneous nineteenth-century literature." But one could probably point to many other psychologically oriented, gothic pieces in the *Atlantic* that could have sparked the poet's imagination. Someone ought to examine this magazine more systematically in order to determine the extent of the poet's exposure to such macabre fiction.

If such a literary fare can be established as the reclusive Dickinson's more important windows to the literary world, we might better understand why publication in such a market was as foreign to her "as Firmament to Fin."

*Texas A&M University*

# 6. Mark Twain

## *Louis J. Budd*

*Adventures of Huckleberry Finn* had unwelcome exposure in 1982. My grazing in the local newspaper picked up three more proposed bannings from the curricula of secondary schools—none successful so far as I could tell. One came in Houston, Texas, and another in Davenport, Iowa, close to Mark Twain's boyhood ground. The most attention, heightened by editorials and letters of protest, was earned by the Mark Twain Junior High School in a suburb of Washington, D.C. The looming centennial of *Huckleberry Finn* may activate other censors who will have still poorer success.

The good news is that the *Mark Twain Journal* has transferred to the editorship of Thomas A. Tenney, in care of the College of Charleston. Cyril Clemens finished his reign as founding editor by, presumably out of carelessness, running in the Summer 1982 issue an article he had printed a year earlier. (How will future bibliographers figure that one out?) Tenney, who has elsewhere demonstrated his energy as well as his thoroughness, is preparing a fat catch-up issue that will pay off all promises, that is, will print articles accepted years ago in some cases. Tenney's standards will start to attract subscribers and more consistently sound articles; so we have to feel bullish about the future of the journal.

### *i.* Bibliographies

Tenney has continued both to recover older items that even he had not found yet and to annotate current items with "Mark Twain: A Reference Guide / Sixth Annual Supplement" (*ALR* 15:1–46). Unfortunately, because of a shift in timing, his survey for 1982 was not available when I wrote this chapter, and the *MLA International Bibliography* has not mastered its improvements enough to get back on its schedule. Therefore, I was especially grateful that Twain is

included in the annual "Checklist of Scholarship on Southern Literature" (*MissQ* 36,ii[1983]). Anybody who uses several checklists
soon realizes that none of them can catch everything because the
sources on Twain are too diverse. But the *Mississippi Quarterly*
group is casting a fine-meshed net under expert direction.

Among long-range projects the most impressive was *Mark Twain
International: A Bibliography and Interpretation of His Worldwide
Popularity* (Greenwood). Robert M. Rodney, its compiler, has spotted
over 5,000 reprintings of his work in 55 countries and 73 languages
and has analyzed their significance with both an introductory essay
and five sensibly conceived tables. Foreign scholars will doubtless
learn much about their own country's record, not just ours. Rodney's
research checks out against a regional listing in J. G. Reiwald and
J. Bakker's *The Critical Reception of American Literature in the
Netherlands, 1824–1900: A Documentary Conspectus from Contemporary Periodicals* (Rodopi), though they primarily and deftly sam-
ple reviews as a service to those trying to grasp Twain as he was
understood in his own time. Norman Kiell in his section on Twain in
*Psychoanalysis, Psychology, and Literature: A Bibliography* (Scarecrow) misses some relevant items while aiming to list everything,
but does interestingly devise more than 40 subheadings for Twain.
Distinctly useful too is Joe Weixlmann's *American Short-Fiction
Criticism and Scholarship, 1959–1977: A Checklist* (Ohio), which
includes any discussions "at least a full page" long. It gives 16 items
for "The Man That Corrupted Hadleyburg"; "The Private History
of a Campaign That Failed" runs a poor second with four.

#### ii. Editions

The facsimile holograph for *The Adventures of Tom Sawyer* (Univ.
Publications and Georgetown) is highly legible and is fascinatingly
usable because it reveals cruxes of gestation and revision. Close interpreters, who will keep consulting it, should persuade their nearest
library that the price ($125) is fair for two expensively produced
volumes. Because Paul Baender has brooded over the holograph for
decades, his introduction rings with quiet authority yet is suggestive
and poses stimulating questions. The Mark Twain Project itself produced no new volumes in either of its series, but a crammed history
of its progress is Hershel Parker's review of five volumes it produced

in 1979–80 (*JEGP* 81:596–604). He admiringly discusses its procedures for anybody who arrived late or has finally overcome a resistance toward textual editing.

Actually the Project and the University of California Press made a splash by issuing the first three titles in the Mark Twain Library: *No. 44, The Mysterious Stranger*; *The Adventures of Tom Sawyer*; and *Tom Sawyer Abroad* and *Tom Sawyer, Detective*. Ostensibly reprints, with much slimmed apparatus, of texts already established, the Tom Sawyer volumes are important on their own because they carry (admittedly minor) emendations of those texts and because they reproduce all the original illustrations. Their price in paperback adds a third virtue, making them triumphantly competitive with the fast-print houses. They will probably outsell also the *Mississippi Writings* volume (*Tom Sawyer*; *Life on the Mississippi*; *Huckleberry Finn*; *Pudd'nhead Wilson*) in the Library of America. By all reports, however, that enterprise is doing fine at bookstores, just as it deserves. Guy Cardwell's aids to the "best text now available"—meaning still the first edition for three of the *Mississippi Writings*—are as trustworthy as they are succinct. But we may as well shrug off *The Selected Letters of Mark Twain* (Harper), ed. Charles Neider, who further skews Albert Bigelow Paine's texts, as commerce.

Two or possibly three texts have turned up for future editors. Edgar M. Branch in "A New Clemens Footprint: Soleather Steps Forward" (*AL* 54:497–510) pretty well certifies a "humorous sketch, distinctly literary in intention," that appeared in a New Orleans newspaper in 1859. Given Branch's variety of evidence along with his reputation for measured judgment, few will doubt that we are watching Twain, while supposedly engrossed by piloting, follow a "profoundly rooted drive" toward writing. After my "Who Wants to Go to Hell? An Unsigned Sketch by Mark Twain?" (*SAmH* NS 1:6–16) was published, Robert H. Hirst, general editor of the Mark Twain Project, confirmed that its files hold a cryptically dated set of galleys for a raucous monologue printed by the *New York Sun* in 1885. A second-hand text is recovered in M. Thomas Inge's and George Munro's "Ten Minutes with Mark Twain: An Interview" (*ALR* 15:258–62). Inge and Munro managed to run down a Russian newspaper item that proves to be a reworking of two interviews in German, one of them evidently faked. Clearly, not all of Twain's published words have been located as yet.

### iii. Biography

When Jorge Luis Borges was recently invited to lecture in St. Louis, he accepted with the proviso that he get to visit Hannibal, where the blind Argentinian "expressed a long-time desire to actually touch the Mississippi River" (*Fence Painter* 2,ii). Twain's emotional presence obviously lives on. In *What Was Literature? Class Culture and Class Society* (Simon and Schuster) Leslie Fiedler keeps recalling his "bourgeois domesticity" as a warning point of comparison. The last member of it gets her own biography in Caroline Thomas Harnsberger, *Mark Twain's Clara, or What Became of the Clemens Family* (Ward Schori). Harnsberger, while loyal to her friend, is adequately objective about the Ashcroft-Lyon tangle and the dwindling end of Twain's descendants. His private secretary grows more comprehensible through Laurie Lentz, "Mark Twain in 1906: An Edition of Selected Extracts from Isabel V. Lyon's Journal" (*RALS* 11[1981]: 1–36). While agreeing with Hamlin Hill that the journal often lets Twain look ignoble, Lentz believes that Lyon's unflagging admiration should carry weight too.

Edgar M. Branch continues to ascertain facts that some of us supposed were washed away. "Sam Clemens, Steersman on the *John H. Dickey*" (*ALR* 15:195–208) fills in hard details of the river career in 1858 and retrieves three items of newspaper correspondence that probably came from Twain. Two of those items will also interest those who are evaluating his literary growth. In "Mark Twain, Business Man: The Margins of Profit" (*SAmH* NS 1:24–43) Alan Gribben synthesizes much information before analyzing what twists of plot and metaphor Twain borrowed from his scramble for riches. Despite regretting its effects, Gribben understandingly sets it within his legitimate need for income and within current attitudes, thus respecting complexities that, from a different angle, disappear in Kay Moser's "Mark Twain and Ulysses S. Grant," (*SAmH* NS 1:130–41). For her the puzzle of why Twain persisted in worshipping the tarnished ex-president is resolved by interpreting Grant as the approving father whom young Samuel Clemens had futilely longed for. Probably Freudian at heart also, two social scientists, Richard Weissbourd and Robert R. Sears, reason much more cautiously in "Mark Twain's Exhibitionism" (*Biography* 5:95–117) in order to connect his habit of seeking attention with the treatment of self-display in his fiction. Although a Twainian can pick flaws in their details, that does not destroy the tough subtlety of their conclusions, which should especially interest the critics who are searching texts for self-revelatory sets of mirrors.

The panache at Nook Farm seems a cinch for a spread in every magazine. This year it was Harold Holzer's "Mark Twain in Hartford: The Author's Exuberant Victorian Mansion" (*Architectural Digest* 39,vii:118–26). Towns such as Fredonia, New York, with any special ties to him may expect an eventual spotlight (*Mark Twain Soc. Bull.* 5,ii:1,3–7), and anybody, such as the author of *Mrs. Wiggs of the Cabbage Patch*, who sets down private impressions will be helped to go public (*Filson Club Hist. Quar.* 56:5–13). He was such a blazing phenomenon that focusing on his books, particularly just two or three, distorts the record, as I try to suggest through the selections for *Critical Essays on Mark Twain, 1867–1910* (Hall). Last and least, it may be helpful to predict that scholars will waver between a grade of negligible and untrustworthy for Nigey Lennon, *Mark Twain in California: The Turbulent California Years of Samuel Clemens* (Chronicle Books).

### iv. General Interpretations

As usual many a general book or article was happy to take notice of Twain. Reference guides likewise include him whenever it is plausible. Volume 11, "American Humorists," in the *Dictionary of Literary Biography* (Gale) naturally carries a long entry by Pascal Covici, Jr., who confronts Twain's practice in successive texts rather than imposing some master theory; he convincingly identifies the shifts in Twain's attitudes and techniques. For volume 12 of *DLB*, "American Realists and Naturalists," Hamlin Hill integrates the aptest criticism and soundest scholarship during recent years.

Both the latest book-length interpretations are succinct yet ambitious. Susan K. Harris in *Mark Twain's Escape from Time: A Study of Patterns and Images* (Missouri) perceives for him a third basic response besides humor and invective: aesthetic flight to a realm where suffering is avoidable. Except for needlessly invoking an outside theorist, she proceeds impressively. Her section "The Alienated Narrator and the Imagery of Respite" works particularly well with "No. 44, The Mysterious Stranger." The second section argues that Twain gradually "transformed his search for a resolution to his own alienation from an external to an internal one." Harris develops "My Platonic Sweetheart" as his firmest case for an "alternate, imperishable self."

Appropriately more aggressive in tone, James L. Johnson in *Mark Twain and the Limits of Power: Emerson's God in Ruins* (Tenn.) sets "some" of the "major and minor pieces" within a "short intellectual history" of the Romantic belief in and rush toward a mastery of experience. *Tom Sawyer* is expounded very sternly—the favorite approach these days—as dramatizing through Tom's callousness toward others the damages that such a belief can inflict on the self along with the community. *Huckleberry Finn* is presented more sternly still for its point that nobody, not even a marginal boy, can form comradely ties without ending up in some moral quandary, yet that Huck cannot back away from them without feeling indifferent to the claims of humanity. After a presently routine reading for *A Connecticut Yankee in King Arthur's Court,* Johnson, preferring the A. B. Paine text, carries Young Satan himself from exuberance into the limbo of solipsism; here the freshest point is the insistence that *The Mysterious Stranger* resulted from a lifelong tension between vitality and determinism instead of from the pressures of old age. Actually, Johnson has coped with only some of Twain's major books, but he teaches sophistication in considering Twain's optimisms, usually dismissed with sighs about American innocence.

Among broadly interpretive articles the quirkiest and yet most stimulating is Rolande Ballorain's "Mark Twain's Capers: A Chameleon in King Carnival's Court" in *American Novelists Revisited* (pp. 143–70). With bells and whistles she builds up to proclaiming Twain "one of the last truly European writers" because he joined the tradition of artists whose "vision of the world is 'carnivalesque.'" Beside her own dance of ideas Suzanne H. Uphaus in "Twain and Leacock: A Cross-Cultural View" (*CentR* 26:134–46) sounds downright sedate while deciding that Twain proved much tougher-minded and more rebellious than the Canadian humorist. My "Mark Twain and the Magazine World" (*UMSE* NS 2:35–42) notes that the quality monthlies offered a more discerning audience than the fans for his newspaper humor or the buyers of subscription books; I also survey his aborted plans to launch—for grand profits, of course—some kind of magazine.

## v. Individual Writings Before 1885

The leading article on Twain's first travel volume was Robert Regan's "The Reprobate Elect in *The Innocents Abroad*" (*AL* 54:240–57), which follows an artful reweaving of facts with a keen analysis of the result. Having charted Twain's restiveness toward the moral majority aboard the *Quaker City*, he proves that a highly conscious design intensified the attack on them in the reshaped book. Another sophisticated and persuasive essay, John Irwin Fischer's "How to Tell a Story: Mark Twain's Gloves and the Moral Example of Mr. Laurence Sterne" (*MTJ* 21,ii:17–21) may have been accepted by Cyril Clemens several years ago. It does not use Alan Gribben's major research or the Mark Twain Project edition for his notebooks. Nevertheless, Fischer skillfully argues that reading *A Sentimental Journey through France and Italy* influenced Twain's revision of the glove-buying episode. He ends by speculating that Sterne's openness to taking chances with strangers encouraged the best qualities of *The Innocents Abroad*. Modern readers will likewise learn from Richard F. Fleck's "The Complexities of Mark Twain's Near Eastern Stereotyping" (*MTJ* 21,ii:13–15), which emphasizes that a hungry journalist working both sides of any busy street played up to egalitarianism as much as to racial prejudices.

*The Gilded Age* hangs on like radioactive waste. In "Mark Twain's Unsentimental Heroine" (*SCR* 14,ii:22–32) Trygve Thoreson offers to rescue Laura Hawkins from the consensus that she helped it to end up as a disaster area. Allegedly, she has far more depth than the once reigning stereotypes and especially than her peers (if we agree that Twain cast her as a romantic lead). Also, supposedly unaware of the many seduction novels, *The Gilded Age* perceives and attacks a myth about the infallibility of the female heart in bestowing love. Still, Thoreson shrewdly deduces the effects of Laura's own reading before concluding challengingly: "Laura dies not because she has sinned, but because she placed her trust in precisely those things that Mark Twain the realist finds so uncertain as guides to conduct: sentimental ideals, the gospel of success, the promptings of the heart."

It's fair to guess that John Seelye will soon introduce some reprint with "What's in a Name? Sounding the Depths of *Tom Sawyer*" (*SR* 90:408–29). Strikingly inventive as usual, Seelye first centers on the "theatrical properties" of *Tom Sawyer*, then deserts current wisdom to hold that Tom "remains forever a boy," that his success guarantees his vision of "eternal play" which mocks final conformity with adulthood. He does much to justify a call to liberate *Tom Sawyer* from the shadow of *Huckleberry Finn*. Consciously modest in scope, Robert J. Coard in "Huck Finn and Two Sixteenth Century Lads" (*MQ* 23: 437–46) grants that the major parallels between *The Prince and the Pauper* and Twain's masterpiece have already been covered. After adding others which may qualify better as clichés of plot, he finishes with the worthwhile idea that struggling over historical dialogue must have sharpened Twain's delight in Huck's vernacular. Arthur Wrobel's "Mark Twain Baits the Masters: 'Some Thoughts on the Science of Onanism'" (*JPC* 15,iv:53–59) also savors a ridicule of stilted rhetoric. However, his strongest point shows that Twain's speech to the Stomach Club mocked the owlish moralizing and pseudomedical warnings about masturbation. Twain's relations with popular culture were always complex.

Horst H. Kruse in *Mark Twain and "Life on the Mississippi"* (Mass., 1981) reintroduces the practical-minded professional author. Updating a dissertation in German, he traces the genesis of an often maligned book to prove that it achieved what Twain had long intended: a "standard work" on the Mississippi Valley. Conversely, Twain did not try (and fail) to revisit his glory days as a pilot or to dramatize his past through such a persona. More specifically, Kruse attacks the charge of padding and even defends the relevance of the final chapters before conceding some patchwork. His conclusion reiterates that Twain's "attack on Southern backwardness and maudlin romanticism" was an "integral part" of his purpose "to serve as an instrument of social as well as political change." While never exciting, Kruse's own standard work is awesomely documented. Still, those cub-pilot chapters exert such charm that Kruse has to expect resistance. Meanwhile, Richard Lettis in "The Appendix of *Life on the Mississippi*" (*MTJ* 21,ii:10–12) outdoes Kruse, probably without convincing him. Praising all four addenda as vital organs, Lettis finds an ingenious rationale for Twain's grafting that Indian legend, "The Undying Head."

Panoramas of intellectual history feel obliged not only to display Twain but to treat *Huckleberry Finn* more solemnly each year. In doing so Gary Lindberg in *The Confidence Man in American Literature* (Oxford) cannot decide whether to demand ethical heroism from an outcast boy or to praise him as a genius at survival in a shifty world. The first-rate literary critic also feels that he or she must grapple with this masterpiece. Since Millicent Bell has too fine a mind to wrench a text for the sake of originality, her *"Huckleberry Finn*: Journey without End" (*VQR* 58:253–67) echoes those readings that find the hero rejecting society to escape the false identities forced upon him though she eloquently dignifies the final third as abandoning the "telic tendency" of plot "in favor of the idea that play is the essence of art." Ignoring any notion of play or humor, Cary Wall in "The Boomerang of Slavery: The Child, the Aristocrat, and Hidden White Identity in *Huck Finn*" (*SoSt* 21:208–21) likewise has Huck opting out of society, now because he comprehends the self-hatred that both the gentry and the "lower reaches" suffer from recognizing at some level of consciousness that the South has built upon injustice; Wall also can defend the Evasion sequence, now because Tom "takes over the role of aristocrat"—unadmirably of course. Although Forrest G. Robinson's "The Silences in *Huckleberry Finn*" (*NCF* 37:50–74) at first speaks just of "not a very happy book," his packed, far-ranging, and lucid analysis builds Huck's (and Twain's) burden of psychic wavering and guilt into a wish for oblivion; so Huck is finally relieved to die into a false identity as Tom Sawyer. Robinson reinforces those who keep us probing for the extent to which Huck is conceived in depth (Freudian or not) as a character.

I wish that a panel of such essayists could match tones against John Seelye for his "The Craft of Laughter: Abominable Showmanship and *Huckleberry Finn*." Encouraged by the preference of *Thalia* (4,i[1981]:19–25) for witty essays, Seelye juggles the argument that *Huckleberry Finn* abounds in practical jokes, ranged from the gross to the cerebral and typified by the King and the Duke though validated by Huck's trick of unfolding in the narrative present a plot he had already lived out. Among harder-ribbed essays the most obviously sound is Leland Krauth's "Mark Twain: The Victorian of Southwestern Humor" (*AL* 54:368–84). Starting from the "innate" propriety which softens Twain's handling of scenes like the camp meeting, Krauth convincingly shows that his reworking of episodes common to the native humorists avoided those involving adult sexuality and the "pastimes of manly backwoods living." Ultimately, by creating Huck as a truer gentleman than most persons he defers to and even leading him into the "cult of sensibility," Twain *"elevates the common* beyond itself." In a long chapter of *Narration and Discourse* Janet H. McKay sets up three linguistic relationships: Huck as narrator vs. himself as a character; Huck vs. Twain; and Huck vs. the other characters. Her schemata succeed best when she reveals how Twain covered his artfulness under Huck's seeming lack of it and how he let Huck favor writing indirect discourse without becoming rigid or obvious about it. After studying McKay we cannot help returning to the novel with a resharpened, line-to-line alertness, which can also rise after reading Barry A. Marks's "The Making of a Humorist: The Narrative Strategy of *Huckleberry Finn*" (*JNT* 12: 139–45). He expands that recently drawn line between Huck as a character and Huck as a narrator who knows about the lies once fed him. This allows room for the thesis that the "act of telling his story is appropriately seen as an effort to reevaluate the fundamental nature of truth and the possibility of open and sincere human relationships." Nobody has yet suggested that Huck composed the running heads too. However, Beverly R. David's "Mark Twain and the Legends for *Huckleberry Finn*" (*ALR* 15:155–65) joins fresh archival materials into a good case that the author supplied the punchlines for the illustrations after all, instead of carelessly letting his nephew color the tones of the original edition.

### *vi.* Individual Writings After 1885

*A Connecticut Yankee*, whether as a national landmark or a flea market, keeps attracting intellectual tourists. In *America and the Patterns of Chivalry* (Cambridge) the social historian John Fraser borrows Hank Morgan to keynote his critique of the knightly ideal that regenerated warm fealty during the 19th century. A self-breveted economist, Lorne Fienberg, in "Twain's Connecticut Yankee: The Entrepreneur as a Daimonic Hero" (*MFS* 28:155–67) decides that a "sophisticated sense of the process of economic growth and change" shapes Hank Morgan's career. If Twain did recognize that change operates through disruptive leaps and that each stage breeds its own jealous bureaucracy, he was more insightful than the social scientists of his era. With "Mark Twain: Technology, Social Change, and Political Power" (*The Artist and Political Vision*, pp. 267–89) two specialists in politics, Molly Lyndon Shanley and Peter G. Stillman, find that *A Connecticut Yankee* exposes the dangers of both the pastoral

and the industrialized utopia—especially the latter, which can arm
ideological coercion with the machine. Dismayingly, many of Hank's
casual if forceful jokes are extrapolated into coldhearted principles.
Those political scientists would have benefited from Allison R.
Ensor's Norton edition of *A Connecticut Yankee*, which supplements
a responsibly vetted text with a gallery of literary criticism. Already
included there, David Ketterer, with "Power Fantasy in the 'Science
Fiction' of Mark Twain" (pp. 130–41 in *Bridges to Fantasy*, ed.
George E. Slusser, et al. [So. Ill.]), returns to argue that Twain blazed
the way for novelists who weigh the abuses of wielding superior
technical knowledge. Probingly, Ketterer also intensifies the debate
over whether Twain's work always fits into the canonical genres.
David E. E. Sloane's "A Connecticut Yankee and Industrial America:
Mark Twain's Lesson" (*EAS* 10:197–205) lengthens the roll of contemporaries who venerated machines and took delight in the prospect of exporting American models. While repelled by the slaughter
of the knights, Sloane feels that Twain did not want the violence into
which his plot lured him.

   With a major, substantive, and precise study of the manuscripts,
Philip Cohen ("Aesthetic Anomalies in *Pudd'nhead Wilson*," *SAF*
10:55–69) establishes three main units in the order of their composition. This opens up dazzling insights; for example, because the beginning chapters were written last, they add complexities to Tom
and Roxy that dwindle away in the units already finished. Though
critics will have to grapple with Cohen on many counts, we can now
dismiss the old charge that Twain had lost interest in the serious
issues of the novel before he finished it. More ingenious than the
master but lacking his habit of humor, George E. Toles in "Mark and
*Pudd'nhead Wilson*: A House Divided" (*Novel* 16:55–75) accepts
the jagged fissures to contend, almost leisurely, that they reveal
Twain was struggling with ideas too painful to acknowledge, that
he verged on a horrifying insight only to pull back. In practice Toles
modifies the gaps between the depth and the superficiality of many
an incident into a planned, effective pattern. Similarly gliding past
the humor while admitting that the novel almost falls apart, Evan
Carton ("*Pudd'nhead Wilson* and the Fiction of Law and Custom"
in *American Realism*, pp. 82–94) believes that its "fundamental disunity" achieved the "repeated structural imitation of the dividedness
that its represented society covets." He gets much more said before

his reprise that in "illustrating the consubstantiality of its characters with its author and readers (its ultimate mimetic feat), Twain's novel implicates us in its community of disingenuousness and guilt." Carton has smoothly blended structuralist and reader-response criticism. Beginning with an old, narrowed problem, James E. Caron in "Pudd'nhead Wilson's Calendar: Tall Tales and a Tragic Figure" (*NCF* 36:452–70) tries to connect the epigraphs to the action in their chapters. Doing so, he asserts, can enthrone David Wilson as the central character, justify the term "tragedy" in the full title, and vindicate Twain as a literary "surgeon." Caron goes onward to broader perspectives like seeing the novel as a reflexively self-conscious narration that adapts the tall tale into an embodiment of communal dishonesty. He ends as sweepingly as Toles or Carton.

*Personal Recollections of Joan of Arc* pretty much rests in what James L. Johnson calls its "deserved obscurity" though he does briefly discuss its version of the "empowered Self in all the glory of its heavenly possibilities." Mirroring a section in her book, Susan K. Harris' "Narrative Structure in Mark Twain's *Joan of Arc*" (*JNT* 12:48–56) startlingly proposes that Sieur Louis de Conte ranks as the major character, whose sense of a lost idyll and whose "alienation" bring him close to functioning as Twain's surrogate, not merely spokesman. This refocusing still lets Harris admire the book totally.

Like *Following the Equator*, Twain's turn-of-the century journalism and fiction get no notice except for, unsurprisingly, the "Mysterious Stranger" manuscripts. Besides Johnson's and Harris' books, Robert E. Lowrey in "Imagination and Redemption: 44 in the Third Version of *The Mysterious Stranger*" (*SoR* 18:100–110) develops the hope that the mind, soaring above the workaday world, can reach an autonomy that cancels determinism. However, Lowrey narrows the "No. 44" text into a sort of Künstlerroman suggesting that "through art one may restructure the chaos of the visible world into patterns of imagery" that disclose an "infinite reality"—a position close to Harris'. Terence J. Matheson's "The Devil and Philip Traum: Twain's Satiric Purposes in *The Mysterious Stranger*" (*MarkhamR* 12:5–11) was overdue, at least in order to disturb a working assumption about "The Chronicle of Young Satan." He proposes that the authorial voice, ironic from the start, means for us to take Theodor as an unreliable narrator, transparently gullible and not capable of detecting Young Satan's casuistries. With *No. 44* (foreword and notes by John Tuckey) now affordable in the Mark Twain Library, that version will be taught more widely and therefore explicated more often.

Among Twain's fragmentary manuscripts the fantasies continue to attract the most study. Indeed, John H. Davis ("The Dream as Reality: Structure and Meaning in Mark Twain's 'The Great Dark,'" *MissQ* 35:407–26) finds that the best-known fragment is artistically and thematically coherent in its blurring of linear time to make the imaginary world genuine for the narrator. With less originality James C. Wilson ("'The Great Dark': Invisible Spheres Formed in Fright," *MQ* 23:229–43) interprets it as in the tradition of Poe's *Pym* and *Moby-Dick*. In "Mark Twain's Symbols of Despair: A Relevant Letter" (*ALR* 15:266–68) Daryl Jones refines his earlier clues (*ALS 1977*, pp. 96–97) about the source of "Everlasting Sunday" as an image. If Jones is right, he gives another surprising instance of the indelibility of Twain's emotive memory.

Because of the Mark Twain Library the Tom Sawyer texts will doubtless be assigned more often. Yet *Huckleberry Finn* will not only endure but prevail. Two volumes of original essays about it are in progress. Its centennial will bring symposia, exhibits in library foyers, and journalism at all levels. Television, that electronic Colonel Sellers, will surely horn in too.

*Duke University*

# 7. Henry James

## Robert L. Gale

Jamesian scholars and critics seem to be shifting much of their attention to Henry James as relevant modern and to ever more comparison studies. Only *The Princess Casamassima*, "The Turn of the Screw," *The Sacred Fount*, *The Ambassadors*, *The Golden Bowl*, and *The American Scene* were treated well and in detail by more than a critic each in 1982.

### i. Bibliography, Biography

*A Bibliography of Henry James*, 3rd. ed., ed. Leon Edel and Dan H. Laurence, aided by James Rambeau (Oxford), updates and thus makes even better the earlier Edel and Laurence editions. Details are added on collations, bindings, and James's transatlantic publishing history. Useful also is the partly descriptive bibliography of critical books, dissertations, and articles on James, 1978–81, in the "1981–1982 Annual Review" (*JML* 9:470–74). Of special value is the list of 19 recent Ph.D. dissertations on James.

In rollicking, rambling prose, with its support beams of historical knowledge partly sticking through, R. W. B. Lewis in "The Jameses' Irish Roots" (*NewRep*, 6–13 Jan: 30–37) traces the Irish strain in generations of pertinent and impertinent Jameses, including "the First William" (James's father's grandfather [1736–1822]), "William of Albany" (James's father's father [1778–1832]), "Henry James the Elder" (James's father [1811–82]), and Henry and Alice James. William of Albany arrived in America with little money but the genius to make millions, a little Latin but much familially contagious Celtic articulateness, and an anti-British desire to see American Revolutionary battlefields. "Henry James and Paradigms of Character" (*ModA* 26:1–7) by George A. Panichas rings like Bach in praise of James's character traits: loyalty, sympathy, control, and especially "dedication to his solitary profession." Dennis W. Petrie in a chapter analyzing Leon Edel's five-volume biography of Henry James in *Ultimately Fiction* considers the eight main criticisms of Edel's work: length, documentation, use of previous scholarship, form, amateur psychology, inward focus, interpretation of James, and concern not with James so much as with his imagination. Petrie himself faults Edel also for manufacturing climaxes in James's life, for rejecting "strict chronology in a 'retrospective' manner," and for reporting at a given moment something James could not then know. Petrie praises Edel for the organic quality of his biography, which also uses "particular structural units"—for example, vampirism, fraternal rivalry, and treachery.

## *ii.* Sources, Parallels, Influences

Adeline R. Tintner continues her interesting thesis that James reworked classics of literature by analogical plotting and verbal echoes. In "Henry James's *Hamlets*: 'A Free Rearrangement' " (*CLQ* 18: 168–82) she shows "the differences in the way James handled *Hamlet* in three fictional pieces." They are "Master Eustace" (Eustace Garnyer plays Hamlet to Claudius-like Mr. Cope and Gertrude-like widow Mrs. Garnyer), *The Princess Casamassima* (with its play within a play), and *The Ivory Tower* (Horty Vint calls Gray Fielder "a sort of 'happy Hamlet' "). Tintner in " 'Guest's Confession' and Shakespeare: Henry James's *Merchant of New York*" (*SSF* 19:65–69) sees James as borrowing character, plot, and diction elements from Shakespeare's *Merchant of Venice* for his own story of a miser and suitors in a city by water. And in "Henry James' Shakespearian Burlesques" (*ABBW* 29 Mar:2430, 2432, 2434, 2436, 2438, 2440, 2442) Tintner forces parodic parallels between *Antony and Cleopatra* and *Romeo and Juliet* on one side, and James's "Eugene Pickering" on the other. Immature Eugene cannot measure up as Antony to Madame Blumenthal's Cleopatra and so accepts Miss Vernor as an untragic Juliet.

Studies often compare James to 19th- and 20th-century British writers. For example, in the course of discussing the absence of frankness in 19th-century British fiction Ruth Bernard Yeazell in "Podsnappery, Sexuality, and the English Novel" (*CritI* 9:339–57) makes use of James's valuable critical precepts and artistic examples. Vivien Jones explains in "James and Trollope" (*RES* 33:278–

94) that he does not wish "to defend or excuse James's more waspish early comments, or the misrepresentations in the major essay [by James] of 1883" concerning Anthony Trollope, but instead "to explore . . . why they are there." James saw Trollope as the typical "unthinking mimetic novelist" and ignored "Trollope's relationship with his reader" in order to "make room for himself as novelist" while he was experimenting with "authorial consciousness" during the time "realism and modernism" were "intersect[ing]." At every turn Jones is too hard on James. "Henry James' Debt to George Meredith" (*ABBW* 20 Sept.:1811–12, 1814, 1816, 1818, 1820, 1822, 1824–27) by A. R. Tintner is really two essays on some of Meredith's influence on James. The first part is longer and less convincing, on James's "collag[ing]" of several elements from Meredith's *Egoist*. The second part is of major importance. It demonstrates James's theft from Meredith's *Emilia in England* (revised as *Sandra Belloni*) of words, character situations, plot ingredients, and even a character's name (Adela)—all for use in his short story "The Marriages." Tintner in "Pater in *The Portrait of a Lady* and *The Golden Bowl*, Including Some Unpublished Henry James Letters" (*HJR* 3:80–95) builds partly on and repeats insights from some of her previous Pater/ James studies to show that James echoes Pater's view of Da Vinci's *Mona Lisa* in his later fiction, echoes Pater's art-for-art's-sake aestheticism and his definition of success here and there, and even caricatures Pater's appearance in "Glasses." James also presents Adam Verver's active love of art (in *The Golden Bowl*) as a contrast to Pater. Tintner concludes that "James converted the *spectatorship* of art preached by Pater to the *doing* of art. . . ."

Kathryn C. Rentz in "The Question of James's Influence on Ford's *The Good Soldier*" (*ELT* 25:104–14, 129–30) points out that the main characters in Ford Madox Ford's novel are fundamentally different from several Jamesian ones whom they may resemble superficially. Ford's are more violent and amoral. Ironically, Ford evolved into the sort of novelist whom in his book on James he mistakenly defined the Master as being. It is curious that Alan W. Friedman in "Narrative Is to Death as Death Is to the Dying: Funerals and Stories" (*Mosaic* 15:65–76) incidentally brings in "The Beast in the Jungle" as dramatizing a nonliving analogue to John Dowell in *The Good Soldier*. *Group Portrait* by Nicholas Delbanco is different, refreshing, and magnificent. Concentrating on the five authors of the

subtitle (Conrad, Crane, Ford, James, and Wells) but also bringing
in others where appropriate, Delbanco shows how the big five were
unique but tolerant in their drive toward craftsmanship and col-
legiality, mostly in the years 1901–10. Of special value to Jamesians
is Delbanco's fine discussion of James and Wells; I find quite thrilling
Delbanco's step-by-step explication—occasionally using "anachrony"
—of one of the most curious unmating dances in Anglo-American
literary history. (The first chapter of *Group Portrait*, entitled "Figures in a Landscape," is also available in *Antaeus* [44:100–15].)
*Edwardian Fiction* by Jefferson Hunter mainly concerns techniques
and topics of various 1901–10 British writers. But Hunter includes
James in many apt spots.

James is often studied in connection with other American writers. The best such study this year is Cushing Strout's "Complimen-
tary Portraits: James's Lady and Wharton's Age" (*HudR* 35:405–
15), in which Edith Wharton's *Age of Innocence* is seen as complementing James's earlier *Portrait of a Lady* by doing precisely
what James himself says he did not do, that is, discuss males around
his central figure and dramatize social, even tribal consequences of
an awareness of marital corruption. Strout prefers James's Isabel
Archer's renunciation to Wharton's Newland Archer's costly terminal composure. Better still, Strout proves that comparing Wharton
to James need not be invidious to her. In "Hiding Behind James:
Roth's *Zuckerman Unbound*" (*Midstream* 28,iii:49–53) A. R. Tintner
first suggests that, just like Spencer Brydon, self-divided hero of
James's "Jolly Corner," Philip Roth's Nathan Zuckerman, hero of his
*Zuckerman Unbound*, is pursued by his alter ego, one Alvin Pepler.
So far, so good. But then Tintner wildly theorizes that fictive Zuckerman's book about onanism, plus other hints, should help us see that
the secret in the writings of Hugh Vereker, hero of James's "Figure
in the Carpet," also concerns onanism. And in "Henry James: Figure
of the Homosexual Artist in Bruce Elliot's *Village*, a Mass Market
Paperback" (*MarkhamR* 11:71–72) Tintner points out errors in the
characterization of the supposedly historical figure of Henry James
in Avon's huge family epic.

James is occasionally compared to writers using languages other
than English. In "Turgenev and James: Different Versions of the
Beast" (*RS* 50:69–78) Charles W. Mayer finds by internal evidence
alone in "The Beast in the Jungle" a connection between it and Ivan

Turgenev's story "Knock . . . Knock . . . Knock. . . ." Arthur Brakel
in "Ambiguity and Enigma in Art: The Case of Henry James and
Machado de Assis" (*CLS* 19:442–49) suggests that James's "Aspern
Papers" and *The Sacred Fount*, and *Dom Casmurro, Epitaph of a
Small Winner*, and "Midnight Mass" by Machado would be unread
today but for their "gaps, ambiguity, and open ended nature," combined with "an illusion of solubility." Brakel examines the activities
of narrators and readers which create problems of interpretation
and concludes that both authors go beyond "a totally empirical approach to life." The thesis here seems more profound and fruitful
than the sometimes superficially presented proofs. A. R. Tintner in
"Henry James's 'The Story in It' and Gabriele D'Annunzio" (*MFS*
28:201–14) proves that "James admired the genius of D'Annunzio to
the extent that his name, iconography, vocabulary, and attitude toward love and beauty inform one of his most ingenious short stories"
—namely, "The Story in It," which Tintner defines as "perhaps . . .
[James's] most sophisticated tale."

Fine insights concerning James, parallels, and influences abound
in William T. Stafford's *Books Speaking to Books: A Contextual Approach to American Fiction* (N.C., 1981), mostly but not wholly
when this wise, ranging critic relates first *The Wings of the Dove*,
*Moby-Dick*, and *Absalom, Absalom!* for containing similar symbols
of America—through physicality, ideas, traits (including suffering
and endurance), and techniques (including parable and trick)—
and second *The American* and the 1969 movie *Easy Rider* for dream
vision, onomastic symbolism, geographical direction, and outcome.
Both studies appeared earlier in journals (see *ALS 1974*, p. 94). Stafford in a definitively comprehensive Afterword discusses "The James
Family View of Emerson."

### *iii.* Criticism: General

Robert Weimann's "Realism, Ideology and the Novel in America
(1886–1896): Changing Perspectives in the Work of Mark Twain,
W. D. Howells, and Henry James" (*ZAA* 30,iii:197–212) is too general. Into his huge thesis that the formation of monopolies within
American capitalism began to occur at about the same time that
innovative and protesting American novelists found themselves rebelling against "accepted positions in social morality and ideology,"

largely inherited in the 1880s and early 1890s from New England idealism, agrarianism, and frontier democracy, Weiman fits Twain and Howells easily, but James less so.

Ralf Norrman's *The Insecure World of Henry James's Fiction: Intensity and Ambiguity* (St. Martin's) is Old World academic subtlety at its unremitting best. Norrman's master conclusion is that uncertainty characterizes James's world picture. Use of ambiguous pronouns suggests that uncertainty. Intersentence linking—that is, joining rheme (end part of sentence) and theme (beginning part of sentence)—concomitantly suggests an absence of finality in James's world. Intensity-creating, word-for-word repetitions by James's characters try to alleviate uncertainty, and these uneasy but articulate people half believe that if they can only find incantations magic enough, they can control reality. Given all this, it is proper for James to employ "chiastic inversion," oxymoron, and antithesis in diction, character development, and plot diagramming. Although Norrman sees James's chiasmus in his early fiction "in embryonic form," it is most pronounced in his later works. Norrman is patient in moving from pronouns in James to dialogical end-linking to "emphatic affirmation" to "the power of language over reality" to the climactic chapter (chap. 5) on chiasmus—thought to be "the most important key to the psychomorphology of James's thinking" by Norrman, who could have made his five main points adequately in a book half the size and 40 percent the price.

Observing that James "moves from the idea of endings as the reader's goal to the idea of endings as fundamentally artistic," Marianna Torgovnick in two chapters of her meticulously reasoned *Closure in the Novel* (Princeton, 1981) discusses his voluble discontent with 19th-century, especially Victorian, fictional endings, and then shows that James practiced what he preached in such representative works as "Osborne's Revenge," *The Portrait of a Lady, The Ambassadors,* and *The Golden Bowl.* The admittedly "cryptic" ending of the last-named work, Torgovnick shows, is an aesthetic and psychological delight if the reader develops "an interpretation that recognizes parallelism as the novel's closural pattern and explores concordances between the ending and the body of the novel—especially gestural patterns. . . ."

Fred G. See's "Henry James and the Art of Possession" (in *American Realism,* pp. 119–37) offers the fascinating theory that in the

1890s James created in fiction several young women, especially Fleda Vetch in *The Spoils of Poynton*, who seem possessed. See notes that "possession . . . for him [James] is sometimes erotic, sometimes materialistic, sometimes demonic, but always the dramatic struggle of one will to circumscribe and use another." Relating possession to various notions concerning divisive madness, See finds that using the theme enabled James "to represent not only the surface but the structure of reality," to subject ethical problems to an "inquisitorial understanding," and to present "literary signs" as objects for possession, even "a conflation in which opposite modes of reality interpenetrate one another." Briefly, Fleda becomes victim of Mona Brigstock, "an agent of possession," and loses Owen Gereth, a human spoil, not only to become an "unwilling parasite of Mrs. Gereth," a vampire, but also to muse with her on the burned (hence dispossessed) spoils, "the lost signs."

"James's Rhetoric of the Eye: Re-Marking the Impression" (*Criticism* 24:233–60) by John Carlos Rowe treats Jamesian "impressionism" in its mimetic and expressive "intentions," since an impression is regarded here as being "at once material and immaterial . . . violent act and superficial glance," momentary and enduring. Drawing on recent, controversial criticism, Rowe works eruditely through various examples to conclude that in James impressionism includes "a deceptive mimesis that denies temporal succession . . . or the spatialization of a certain temporality."

Stuart Hutchinson's *Henry James: An American as Modernist* (Vision Press) suggests that, though he was a late 19th-century American, James presents his characters—in the vacuum of a pre- and then an early 20th-century European aesthetic mode—with missing social, cultural, and philosophical underpinnings. Insisting both that America was "invented" only a short time before James started writing and that James misjudged European tradition as more stable than it was, Hutchinson interprets some of the best in James. Thus Dr. Austin Sloper (*Washington Square*) is to New York City what James was to America about 1880. Ralph Touchett commendably liberates Isabel Archer (*The Portrait of a Lady*), wrongly wishes to approve her subsequent conduct, and inaccurately evaluates much about her. "[D]isintegrating" late 19th-century Europe needed "new forces of vitality" just the way Madame de Vionnet needs Chad Newsome (*The Ambassadors*). Milly Theale (*The Wings of the*

*Dove*) does not surrender to Europe, is instead "complicitous" through seeking to turn it into a fool's paradise, and hence is not "a Christ-like martyr." James by the time of *The Golden Bowl* was as bleak as its four main characters, lost—all of them illustrative of "interchanging partnerships"—in "the . . . labyrinth of consciousness." Hutchinson's rather short book, which is oddly documented and incompletely indexed, is a model of coiled logic (but it overuses "it's").

Three general essays treat groups of short stories and plays. Brooke K. Horvath in "The Life of Art, the Art of Life: The Ascetic Aesthetics of Defeat in James's *Stories of Writers and Artists*" (*MFS* 28:93–107) takes the 11 stories reprinted by F. O. Matthiessen in James's *Stories of Artists and Writers* and elucidates the damning thesis that they all "show themselves informed by an aesthetics of defeat concocted to justify the artists' failure. A poetic equivocation [Horvath adds] mirrors failed life in failed artistic production, creating a wonderlessland of unfulfilled potentialities to which the characters surrender." In some pretty heady, mod verbiage Horvath discloses no less than 12 "artistic presumptions under which these vanquished artists [in James's stories] operate." In spite of protestations to the contrary, Horvath pontificates, but with great panache, in this major—if horrid—piece of Jamesian criticism. "The Turn of the Screw," "In the Cage," and "Covering End" are seen revisionally by Heath Moon in "More Royalist than the King: The Governess, the Telegraphist, and Mrs. Gracedew" (*Criticism* 24:16–35) as "rooted in his [James's] conception of a social order and not, as we often find in commentaries, in rarified gnostic cerebrations." Through a desire not to appear snobbish we often decline to see that Jamesian characters who are unmindful of conservative British class distinctions are "duly punished for violating the ethos of . . . [their] rank." Further, "disruption of the authority of the social order is . . . linked with the forces of sexual anarchy." The thesis of Susan Carlson Galenbeck's "British Comedy of Manners Distilled: Henry James's Edwardian Plays" (*HJR* 4:61–74) is that James's plays *The High Bid* and *The Outcry* are comedies of manners which attempt to be fine enough art and social commentary to help purify and save not only a delicate theatrical tradition but also a society. Galenbeck is especially to be commended for reminding us of the artistic and social virtues of *The High Bid*.

The valuable part of Charles Higgins' "Photographic Aperture: Coburn's Frontispieces to James's New York Edition" (*AL* 53:661–75) concerns A. L. Coburn's charming association with James, who was delighted to brief and otherwise help the young photographer find pictorial subjects for frontispieces to the 24 volumes of the New York Edition. But then Higgins repeatedly images these photographs as "emerg[ing] from the developing solution of fiction," and as "photographic palimpsest[s]" which are "not intratextual illustrations" of the fiction and yet are "paradoxically illustrative of it." When he adds that the photograph for volume 6 reveals a "phallic penetration of the Arc de Triomphe [the Princess Casamassima's circumscribed society] by a row of trees [Hyacinth Robinson]," can we take him seriously?

In an admirable preamble to his "Henry James, New and Old: The Vitality and Complexity of the Enterprise" (*ESQ* 28:261–77) Richard A. Hocks explains the prolific nature of 40 years of James criticism as due to James's Trollopean productivity combined with his Joycean intricacy. Hocks implicitly predicts (rightly, I feel) that the high cost of books on individual authors and "current genre-oriented studies" may mean fewer critical volumes on the Master all by himself.

Leon Edel continues to be prominent in Jamesian criticism. A remarkable essay is Daniel Mark Fogel's laudatory "Leon Edel and James Studies: A Survey and Evaluation" (*HJR* 4:3–30), in which Fogel offers a biographical sketch of Edel and analyzes his three areas of work on James: resources, editions, and introductions; minor critical items; and a massive biography—"the keystone of the arch." Fogel then honestly addresses adverse criticism of Edel's life of James but wrongly excuses much in Edel here on the grounds that he revised the five-volume life for its 1977 two-volume edition. The two best parts of Fogel's protracted essay are its praise of the stellar aspects of Edel's biography of James and Fogel's labor-of-love collation of Edel's five- and two-volume versions thereof. Fogel makes incidental use of a charming essay by Edel entitled "How I Came to Henry James" (*HJR* 3:160–64), in which he reports that, wanting to write a master's thesis on James Joyce, then still living, he was persuaded to do one instead on James, safely dead; went on to the Sorbonne in Paris; wrote his doctorate on James's plays; and obtained permission from James's nephew to edit them and to read unpublished James material. There he found a ghostly confirmation of his own previous insight that James's major-phase fiction owes much to techniques developed during his play-writing years. Fogel also used Edel's essay "Shaping and Telling: The Biographer at Work" ( *HJR* 3:165–75), in which fortunate James's fortunate biographer defines and illustrates his method of writing James's life as a series of dramatic episodes shaped by the biographer's artistic imagination. "A Bibliography of the Writings on Henry James by Leon Edel, With Some Annotations" ( *HJR* 3:176–99), compiled by Vivian Cadbury and William Laskowski, Jr., and annotated by A. R. Tintner, offers an astounding 193 items from 1930 through 1982.

### iv. Criticism: Individual Novels

Edward A. Geary's "*The Europeans*: A Centennial Essay" ( *HJR* 4: 31–49) is beautifully written. Quickly getting the obligatory survey of early reviews and thin criticism out of the way, Geary suggests that we should not locate "the thematic center" in any one character but rather at a point where lines drawn between pairs of characters intersect. Geary points out parallels and contrasts, notably involving Felix Young and Eugenia Münster, nature and art, garden and house, life as opportunity and life as discipline, sincerity and dissimulation, "New World naturalness and Old World richness," and pre- and post-lapsarian Eden. Less admirable is the survey of commentary on the various central characters, in the process of which Geary becomes harsh on Robert Acton.

Richard B. Hovey in "*Washington Square*: James and the Deeper Psychology" ( *HSL* 14:1–10) praises James's *Washington Square* for "its richness, its solid brilliance." His analysis of Dr. Sloper is rich and solid too. Hovey shows that Sloper's combination of rightness and wrongness results in sadomasochistic cruelty. But, hurt by deaths in his family, then by the inability of his daughter to replace his son, he both criticizes himself and transfers blame to his unconsciously hated daughter. Is Sloper a neurotic or a torturer?

D. R. M. Wilkinson's "A Complete Image: James's *The Bostonians*" (pp. 33–43 in *From Cooper to Philip Roth*) is a wise, unfrilly interpretation of *The Bostonians* as less a tract on feminism than a complex exploration of "the subtle and urgent workings of human love and fear, loyalty, treachery and hypocrisy, embodied in par-

ticular characters in dramatic situations." Wilkinson is especially
effective in discussing Verena Tarrant as a complex figure presented
in part comically, since James can "fuse wit and passion" from a perspective enabling him to juxtapose contradictions, and even reconcile
them.

Mark Seltzer's excellent essay "*The Princess Casamassima*: Realism and the Fantasy of Surveillance" (*American Realism*, pp. 95–
118) focuses on "the insistent continuity between secrecy and spectatorship, between the 'mysteries abysmal' of London and the urgent
solicitation to interpretation," to urge that the excellence of James's
"distinctly political novel" be seen to lie in its enactment of a narra-
tive-technique "power-play"—that is, police action—being equated
both with theatrical and allied entertainments and with "the prison
as a model for the city at large." Seltzer images James as panoptically
canny prison warden. The most abstruse essay of the year is Martha
Banta's exasperating "Beyond Post-Modernism: The Sense of History in *The Princess Casamassima*" (*HJR* 3:96–107). Instead of simply defining James's sense of history, Banta tests it, as revealed in
the story of Hyacinth Robinson, within the frame of Fredric Jameson's recently published studies of the Marxist view of history. So
she must first work through Jameson's discarding of "four [specified]
methods by which men have most frequently tried to deal with the
past" before she can suggest that both James and Jameson agree that
"there is no past . . . only representations of that past by means of
texts [and other artifacts?]." But then "James slips away from Jameson's position on two . . . important matters: the quality of the present
moment and the nature of the future." Even as they confront social
misery, both James and his hero Hyacinth savor life's rare sweetness;
and James posits a non-Marxist future as a viable center for continued consciousness in those who would go on striving and experimenting. What would James think if he were to learn that Jameson
was "a post-structuralist (a post post-modernist) against the structuralists (the post-modernists)"?

Paula Marantz Cohen's "Feats of Heroism in *The Spoils of
Poynton*" (*HJR* 3:108–16) defines Fleda Vetch as an economically
presented character who remains morally uncompromised though
demanding to retain her own space, not occupied by Mrs. Gereth or
her spoils, which Fleda appreciates as the beautiful record of a taste-
fully managed collector's life but which Mrs. Gereth wants to keep

hold of as objects of idolatry. The spoils thus define characters and catalyze their relationships. I laud Cohen for herself displaying, as does Fleda, heroinism (that is, feminine heroism).

J. C. Rowe's beautifully printed *Through the Custom-House: Nineteenth-Century American Fiction and Modern Theory* (Hopkins) seeks to "defamiliarize . . . critical conventions" by intertextually relating six works alleged here to be considered aberrant through their not plugging into "familiar critical mythologies" or even "revisionary" schools of interpretation. Jamesians need not directly concern themselves with Rowe and Thoreau/Heidegger, Hawthorne/Sartre, Poe/Freud, Melville/Derrida, and Twain/Nietzsche. But of interest is Rowe's first chapter, in which the critic justifies his conflating "literary text and philosophical pretext . . . to explore an idea of modernity related to the literary function of language." Of less interest here is Rowe's applying structural linguistics à la Ferdinand de Saussure and Emile Benveniste to "problems of narrative authority in James's *Sacred Fount*." This application partly negates the "phenomenological concept of intentionality and traditional notions of causality." Rowe's whole book, steadily technical and off-puttingly opinionated, invites dispute but may well become a path-finding classic. A much slighter effort is "James's Writer at the Sacred Fount" (*HJR* 3:117–28) by E. C. Curtsinger, who laboriously assigns allegorical roles to characters in *The Sacred Fount* in a sterile effort to squeeze the juiceless lemon which that novel is into "a whole and beautiful parable of the writer at work." At Newmarch, "the ideal realm," the narrator finds his muse (May Server) and produces a piece of "identifiable . . . art." If the reader will add dark Gilbert Long and bright Mrs. Briss, the sum will be harmonized art.

*A Unified Sensibility: A Study of Henry James'* The Ambassadors *and Its Scenario* (Tokyo: Hokuseido Press) is Jin Oshima's meticulously planned and composed study of the deviations between James's 20,000-word plan sent to the Harpers and the novel which grew out of it. Oshima tactfully notes that previous critics say little of value on the subject and that too many of them indiscriminately use James's scenario to support observations on the novel. Oshima shows that James did not closely follow his game plan but instead made Lambert, hero of *The Ambassadors,* more imaginative and more conscience-stricken, dramatically wrong concerning the nature of Chad Newsome's intimacy with Madame de Vionnet, and "betrayed" very much as heroines and other heroes in James are. The high point in *A Unified Sensibility* comes when its author discusses Madame de Vionnet and "the extreme greediness of her egotism." I feel that Oshima is on shaky ground when he implies that James had no right to redraw the lines of his scenario. The thesis of William Greenslade's long essay "The Power of Advertising: Chad Newsome and the Meaning of Paris in *The Ambassadors*" (*ELH* 49:99–122) is that "[t]o interpret Strether's reading of Chad . . . is to read the novel as in part an exploration of the uses of contemporary codes and strategies—the power which enables the arts of advertising to be effective." First Strether must confront Paris, "an endless promotion." Sadistic Chad "entertains [his sister] Sarah by . . . a piece of theatre which suffocates her." Chad is castigated as having had only his American monopolistic industrial dynamism nurtured by modern Paris, not his cultural potential by the immemorial city.

*Henry James's Ultimate Narrative: "The Golden Bowl"* (Brisbane: Univ. of Queensland Press, 1981) by R. B. J. Wilson is the most consummately wrought book-length study of a single work by James ever produced. It is the result of a 30-year labor of love, in which Wilson sees *The Golden Bowl* as James's most radiant, harmonious, and whole creation, which various critics of its structure, modes of characterization, and style may try to fragmentize but cannot. Wilson surveys previous pertinent scholarship, and then with a clarifying steadiness bordering on the hypnotic discusses centers of consciousness, authorial stance, the six main characters, and the final scene (with its multivalences and its plea for delayed reader judgment). An awesome achievement. Sarah B. Daugherty in *"The Golden Bowl*: Balzac, James, and the Rhetoric of Power" (*TSLL* 24: 68–82) urges us to read *The Golden Bowl* as a novel, not as a work of philosophy or ethics; further, to follow James's prefatory hint and not take it, as Daugherty puts it, "too seriously, or at any rate too moralistically," but instead to let our "sense of drama" be appealed to, as if the book were Balzacian in its powerful presentation of picturesque duplicity. A powerful essay. Carol J. Sklenicka opens her more modest "Henry James's Evasion of Ending in *The Golden Bowl*" (*HJR* 4:50–60) with a mind-boggling sentence: "The continuous expansion of Maggie Verver's moral experience in *The Golden Bowl* and her attempt to direct that experience—to, as she puts it, 'people [her scene] with serenities and dignities and decencies' rather than 'with terrors and shames and ruins'—are conflicting yet equally compelling motives that persist through this novel and that are held in precarious balance at its close." The rest of this high-density article shows that opposing the "desires [of the main characters] for a resolution is a narrative voice that insists . . . upon the impossibility of ending." Slighter still is David M. Craig's essay "The Indeterminacy of the End: Maggie Verver and the Limits of Imagination" (*HJR* 3:133–44), which begins with the obvious: that many critics have offered "contradictory interpretations" of the ending of *The Golden Bowl*. Extending R. B. Yeazell's insight that James's concern in this novel is with the "problem of knowing" (see *ALS 1976*, p. 100), Craig says that Maggie's vision is limited and hence this second "internal author" of only partly self-effacing narrator James's last great novel cannot "know" beyond the last-chapter action. This brings Craig to his explication of the final embrace by Maggie and her husband. Imaginative Maggie has already concluded that she cannot enter her husband's pagoda-like "marital demeanor" (Craig's words); so is it likely either that she will succeed later or that she will stop trying?

#### v. Criticism: Individual Tales

Frederick Newberry's naughty little note, called "A Note on the Horror in James's Revision of *Daisy Miller*" (*HJR* 3:229–32), suggests that when James in 1909 revised his 1878 "Daisy Miller" he added the word "horror" a couple of times to point up Winterbourne's view of Daisy in the Colosseum as a whore.

Stuart Hutchinson's radical but provocative essay "James's *In the Cage*: A New Interpretation" (*SSF* 19:19–25) discusses the limitations of critics whose seeing the telegraphist of "In the Cage" as caged by her reality away from outside experience prevents their praising Mudge (admittedly clumsy and blunt) for his force, taste, and even consideration.

Terence J. Matheson in "Did the Governess Smother Miles? A Note on James's *The Turn of the Screw*" (*SSF* 19:172–75) confesses that he may appear "flat-footed" when he concludes that "the frantic, raving governess" probably smothered Miles. Any disagreement?

In his brief but trenchant "Silence, Realism, and 'The Great Good Place'" (*HJR* 3:129–32) J. A. Ward observes that whereas the world of silence in James is usually occupied only temporarily and unsatisfactorily—and then for therapeutic reasons—in his short story "The Great Good Place" silence appeals the way "the infantile state and even . . . death" do, with their "premise that the consciousness of eternity through silence must accompany the obliteration of self-awareness."

### *vi.* Criticism: Specific Nonfictional Work

In 1980 A. R. Tintner bought an album of 46 photogaphs which James had gathered to use while writing *A Little Tour in France*. In "Photo Album Sheds Light on James' Book" (*ABBW*, 31 May: 4251, 4254, 4156, 4258–64) Tintner demonstrates conclusively that James wrote his book from the photographs in their album sequence, using their pictorial points of view and contents, and even becoming vague when he described locales for which he lacked camera back-up.

In "American Marginalia: James's *The American Scene*" (*TSLL* 24:83–101) Stuart Johnson argues that James in composing *The American Scene* maintained the paradoxical position of outsider drawn toward but resisting submersion in scenes he loved but had to handle objectively, and also of insider responding to scenes all around him. Complicating James's stance as observer-composer was his dual citizenship as knowledgeable native returning home and Europeanized visitor disturbed by much in America, including aliens. Related to James's stereoptican vision is his puzzlement over the blurring of distinctions between American public and private life. Perhaps more significant is Richard S. Lyons' " 'In Supreme Command': The Crisis of the Imagination in James's *The American Scene*" (*NEQ* 55:517–39). Lyons calls James's book on America brilliant, idiosyncratic, perverse, prejudiced, and snobbish, but also perceptive in "tracing the themes of American society and the American character that pervade his fiction." He finds, in the book, however, even more exciting "the drama of the inner life, the imagination at work upon experience": James, whose imagination is in command of the material, is here analyzed as making a character of himself witnessing his "nation's search for a cultural identity." New England as wintry Arcadia contrasts with menacing New York City; the South strikes James as "exotic," though ravaged by the railroad and the hotel. Home again in Lamb House, Rye, in England, James could "possess his reencounter with America only through his later expression of it" in *The American Scene.*

Leon Edel has provided an introduction for a new edition of James's *English Hours* (Oxford). (For coverage of Edel's commentary, see *ALS 1981*, p. 125.)

The sleeper essay of the year on James is Lauren T. Cowdery's "Henry James and the 'Transcendent Adventure': The Search for the Self in the Introduction to *The Tempest*" (*HJR* 3:145–53), the point of which is that in James's 1907 introduction to *The Tempest* "Shakespeare emerges . . . as an intriguing projection of . . . [James's] alter ego." James reverses his thesis (as expressed in "The Birthplace") that critics need not know about artists' lives by here not only deploring our lack of biographical data on Shakespeare but even imagining Shakespeare about to compose *The Tempest*; reverses his image that the writer looks out of "the house of fiction" from his unique window by imaging Shakespeare as looking at life through his window all right but then leaping out of it into the street, thus integrating "secret and public self"; reverses his indifference to music, by picturing Shakespeare as harpsichord improvisor; and reverses his mode of writing by positing Shakespeare's creativity as growing, not out of "encounters with *disponible* . . . at the level of 'the innermost friction of things' and without words," but out of "his wealth of figurative language . . . group[ing] . . . into points of view and thus inevitably into characters."

Millicent Bell in "Henry James and the Fiction of Autobiography" (*SoR* 18:463–79) theorizes that, although "his fiction is never confessional," James did deplore not making Strether of *The Ambassadors* more autobiographical and therefore sought to render his autobiographical volumes artistically like fiction by virtue of incidental discriminations so as to avoid the "inclusion and confusion" with which stupid life floods us. Bell sees James's *Autobiography* as dangerously "wandering, digressive . . . for . . . novelistic art," but as like "modern fiction" therefor. Without "ordinary plot," the volumes are free to expose "the developing spectatorial self" as their main theme, while tension results from James's desire to report both "being and doing" in his auto-fictive work.

*University of Pittsburgh*

# 8. Pound and Eliot

*Hugh Witemeyer*

### *i.* Pound

In "Date Line" (1934) Pound ranked "criticism in new composition" as the highest form of critical endeavor. Poets and translators the world over pay Pound this sort of homage every day of the year, but tributes in prose fiction are relatively rare. In Timothy Findley's novel *Famous Last Words* (Delacorte) a young American expatriate writer named Hugh Selwyn Mauberley is the protagonist, and Pound himself is an important minor character. Findley's presentation of a failed artist and his times builds upon Pound's, yet differs from it in subtle and imaginative ways. The novel has both delightful and disturbing resonances for readers familiar with Pound's career.

*a.* **Text, Biography, and Bibliography.** Among this year's more traditional biographical and textual studies the major contribution is Brita Lindberg-Seyersted's *Pound/Ford: The Story of a Literary Friendship* (New Directions). The friendship of Pound and Ford Madox Ford lasted from 1909 to 1939. This well-researched and carefully edited book reproduces and annotates the extant correspondence between them, their references to one another in letters to other people, and their writings about each other in essays and reviews. The book is a worthy companion to Forrest Read's *Pound/Joyce* (1967). A similar though much briefer record of such a friendship is "Ezra Pound and James Dickey: A Correspondence and a Kinship" by Lee Bartlett and Hugh Witemeyer (*Paideuma* 11:290–312).

Two poetic texts by Pound are published for the first time this year, one of them more responsibly edited than the other. "Fragment, 1944," ed. Christine Froula (*YR* 71:161–64), resembles the Pisan Cantos in tone, although it was composed in Rapallo shortly before the poet's arrest, as the editor carefully shows. "Translations from the Provençal and the Italian," ed. Charlotte Ward and introduced by James Laughlin (*Antaeus* 44:7–33), prints nine early versions of poems by Jaufre Rudel, Arnaut Daniel, Guido Cavalcanti, and Francesco Petrarch. The editor includes no textual note, however, to explain her dating of the translations or their relation to previously published translations by Pound of the same poets.

Two prose articles long out of print reappear this year. In "Pound's *Stretlets* Interview (1915)" (*Paideuma* 11:473–86) Archie Henderson, with the help of Nicolas Slonimsky, provides an English translation of and commentary upon Pound's interview with Zinaida A. Vengerova, originally published in Russian in a St. Petersburg miscellany sympathetic to the Futurists. Elsewhere, Pound's obituary essay on Harold Monro, first published in *The Criterion* for July 1932, is reprinted in full (*Agenda* 19,iv–20,i:121–31).

Several of this year's biographical memoirs of Pound contain previously unpublished letters from the poet. In "Gists and Piths: From the Letters of Pound and Williams" (*Poetry* 139:229–43, and Charlotte, N.C.: Windhover Press) James Laughlin prints excerpts from two important correspondences which he is editing for future publication. This memoir records the vivid reminiscences of a publisher whose place in literary history is assured. Other recollections and epistolary excerpts from the period 1935–50 appear in John J. Slocum's "Remembering Ezra Pound" (*YULG* 57:52–65). Eugenio Montale recalls Pound's Italian period in a 1972 memoir newly translated into English by Jonathan Galassi under the title "Voluntary Exile in Italy" (*Antaeus* 44:34–36). Six striking pictures of the poet taken in Italy between 1966 and 1972 appear together with a brief memoir in Ferdinando Carpanini's "Photographing Pound" (*London Magazine*, 22 July, pp. 50–54). Reno Odlin in "Pound at St. Elizabeths" (*AntigR* 51:39–48) recalls his conversations with Pound in Washington and quotes two passages of poetry which he says were intended for Cantos 95 and 100 but were cancelled before their publication. Finally, George Oppen remembers his only meeting with "Pound in the U.S.A., 1969" (*Sagetrieb* 1:119).

The purpose of Robert Schultz's "A Detailed Chronology of Ezra Pound's London Years, 1908–1920: Part One, 1908–1914" (*Paideuma* 11:456–72) remains obscure, since its compiler never articulates its principles of inclusion, its sources, or its intended uses. Leszek Engelking's "Ezra Pound in Poland" (*Paideuma* 11:105–31), on the other hand, clearly aims to document Pound's presence in Polish letters by providing a well-interpreted checklist of translations, criticism, and creative works from 1939 to 1981.

Pound's attitude toward Jews is the subject of "Ezra Pound's Anti-Semitism" by Ben D. Kimpel and T. C. Duncan Eaves (*SAQ* 81:56–69). The authors conclude that Pound was undeniably a vocal, anti-Semitic racist for at least 20 years of his life, from the mid-1930s to the mid-1950s. They also argue that Pound's anti-Semitism affects "only forty-five lines, less than" 2 percent of *The Cantos*, and therefore should not rule the poem out of court.

*b.* **General Studies and Relation to Other Writers.** Such a separation of political and literary judgments is unacceptable to a majority of the contributors to *Ezra Pound: Tactics for Reading*, ed. Ian F. A. Bell (Barnes and Noble). This collection of eight essays signals the emergence in Great Britain of a feisty group of young, linguistically sophisticated, leftist critics of Pound and of Anglo-American literary modernism in general. A common assumption of the pieces by Peter Brooker, David Murray, Martin Kayman, Bell, and Richard Godden is that "the relation of . . . poetic form to political ideology" in Pound's work is intimate and best comprehended by a neo-Marxist analysis. As Brooker puts it, "Pound's artistic method . . . is far from innocent: the moments of transcendent stillness which are so valued in the *Cantos'* putative formal unity collaborate in fact with a political ideology of mixed origin but of a decidedly fascistic tendency, in a logic also which bourgeois criticism has failed to pursue, just as it has failed, inevitably, to inspect the ideological bearing of its own aesthetic priorities." Evidently the prose of these essays is tough sledding in many places, and some of the writers wander very far from the subject of Pound. Eric Mottram's discussion of "Pound, Merleau-Ponty, and the Phenomenology of Poetry" and Joseph Riddel's deconstruction of Imagism (first published in *Boundary* 2,9–10 (1981):209–39) are especially trying. But the essays by Kayman, Godden, and Herbert Schneidau are lucid and cogent, and the book as a whole is substantive and challenging.

The art and politics of the major Modernist poets are also inseparable for Cairns Craig in *Yeats, Eliot, Pound and the Politics of Poetry: Richest to Richest* (Pittsburgh). Craig argues that the poets, working in the tradition of British associationism, formed an elitist theory of audience which eventually became an authoritarian theory of society. "The open poem demanded for its completion not the free mind of democratic man, but the rich mind of the privileged within a hierarchical society." Craig's thesis is interesting but incompletely documented and not entirely persuasive.

Apolitical approaches to Pound's poetics are taken by Laszlo K. Géfin in *Ideogram: History of a Poetic Method* (Texas) and John T. Gage in *In the Arresting Eye: The Rhetoric of Imagism* (LSU, 1981). These studies differ strikingly in the credence they accord the poet's aesthetic principles. For Géfin, the ideogrammic method is "a creative process isomorphic with natural processes." He fully accepts the ontological, epistemological, and linguistic assumptions governing the method because in his view they constitute a "sane and truly *humane* planetary consciousness." In contrast to Géfin's privileging of his subject John T. Gage's critical approach to imagism analyzes the movement's theory without taking it at face value. Gage argues that, despite its attacks upon rhetoric and its claim to present unmediated reality in the poems, imagism has a distinctive, mediating rhetoric of its own. Gage's skeptical approach tells us more about the theory and practice of the Imagist poets than Géfin's devout approach tells us about the work of Pound, the Objectivists, the Black Mountain poets, and the San Francisco poets.

The ideogrammic method may have its origins in Pound's college experience, Hugh Kenner suggests in "Poets at the Blackboard" (*YR* 71:173–84). Kenner draws an interesting parallel between the ambitions of American university curricula and those of Pound's poetry. Several other general essays this year emphasize origins of different sorts. In "Far Flung Vortices and Ezra's 'Hindoo' Yogi" (*Paideuma* 11:39–53) William French and Timothy Materer continue a vitriolic debate with Ian F. A. Bell and Eva Hesse over the sources of Pound's use of the term *vortex*. French and Materer contend that the term derives from the ancient Hindu concept of *Vritta*, meaning "a whirlpool or eddy in the mind." In another study of origins Matthew Little investigates "Pound's Use of the Word *Totalitarian*" (*Paideuma* 11: 147–56), concluding that Pound "argues primarily for awareness of and interest in totalities, not for total control by government."

The totality of Pound's own literary sensibility is at issue in several general studies this year. In "Doppelgänger: Ezra Pound in His Letters" (*Paideuma* 11:241–56) Timothy Materer contends that

Pound's letters reflect the same divided personality that Wyndham Lewis represented in a short story about the poet. Whereas Lewis and Materer assume a norm of unified sensibility, Sally M. Gall reminds us that a poet may do the police in different voices which need not mime a single persona. In "Domestic Monologues: The Problem of Voice in Contemporary American Poetry" (*MR* 23:489–503) Gall criticizes monotony of voice in recent dramatic monologues by citing examples of "many-tongued and multiple language" in poems by Pound and Eliot. In "Ezra Pound in Heaven" (*HudR* 35:73–86) Andrew J. Kappel reads Pound's later poetry as a quest to unite subject and object, perceiver and perceived in a paradise of "harmonious communion with everything else in the orderly cosmos." This unoriginal essay ends with a corny vision of Pound's ascension from "the swampy ground of San Michele" to a petal of "the heavenly rose."

Medieval distinctions of a firmer sort are the subject of Kevin Oderman's "'Calvalcanti': That the Body Is Not Evil" (*Paideuma* 11:257–79), one of the year's best studies of Pound's relationship to other writers. Oderman explores "Pound's use of Cavalcanti as a cipher for his own erotic mysticism." In "George Santayana and Ezra Pound" (*AL* 54:413–33) John McCormick presents a record of an acquaintance and correspondence that lasted from 1937 until 1952. McCormick attempts, none too successfully, to distinguish Santayana's Fascist sympathies and anti-Semitic prejudices from Pound's.

Pound's relation to Henry James is the subject of Robert Gregory's "On Not Going Home: Pound's Reading of James" (*Boundary* 10: 93–108) and, in part, of Brendan Jackson's "A Reluctant American: Pound's Response to Whitman, Whistler, and Henry James" (*Paideuma* 11:326–34). Jackson has little that is new to say about any of his artists, but Gregory argues that Pound creatively misread James in order to protect himself against the threat of a Jamesian "poetics of solipsism," of "endless relations in language" and mind. In an equally suggestive essay whose title reverses Gregory's, "Bringing It All Back Home: Derivations and Quotations in Robert Duncan and the Pound Tradition" (*Sagetrieb* 1:176–89), Michael André Bernstein reflects upon the constitution, function, and continuance of poetic tradition in the writings of Pound and his literary descendants. Finally, in "The Portrait of the Artist as Collage-Text: Pound's *Gaudier-Brzeska* and the 'Italic' Texts of John Cage" (*APR* 11,iii:19–

29) Marjorie Perloff continues her investigations of Pound's relationship to post-Modern writers and visual artists.

The most stimulating and far-reaching general essay of the year turns upon Pound's nonrelationship with another American poet. In "Pound/Stevens: Whose Era?" (*NLH* 13:485–514) Marjorie Perloff notes not only that Pound and Stevens had little use for each other, but also that critics who admire one tend to discount the other. These critics make profoundly different assumptions about the relation of poetic form and content, the nature of history and myth, and the persistence of romanticism. As a result, Perloff argues, "the division between Pound and Stevens continues to haunt our sense of Modernism." What definition of the term can comprehend both poets?

**c. The Shorter Poems.** Pound's earlier work attracted less attention than usual this year. The most significant essay is Fred C. Robinson's "'The Might of the North': Pound's Anglo-Saxon Studies and 'The Seafarer'" (*YR* 71:199–224). Robinson documents Pound's extensive college reading of Anglo-Saxon and his early translations and imitations. Robinson argues that many of Pound's emendations in "The Seafarer" imitate those of his textual source, the seventh edition of Sweet's *Anglo-Saxon Reader* (1898). Robinson concludes that Pound's translation conforms to "the scholarly dictates of his day" and is in no way an expressive persona or mask. Whether or not one accepts this conclusion, Robinson's essay moves the study of Pound's early dealings with Anglo-Saxon well beyond the stage at which it has rested for many years.

Personae also concern Adena Rosmarin in "The Historical Imagination: Browning to Pound" (*VN* 61:11–17). Rosmarin attempts to establish a formal distinction between the Victorian dramatic monologue of Browning and the Modernist "mask lyric" of Pound and Eliot. Unfortunately, the distinction is not well sustained by detailed discussions of relevant poems. A similar paucity of supporting evidence weakens G. Schmidt's claim, in "Pound's 'In Epitaphium Eius'" (*Expl* 40:44–45) that the anonymous troubadour commemorated in this early poem is Cino Polnesi. No less tenuous is Ian F. A. Bell's assertion in "'In a Station of the Metro' and Carpenterian Transformations" (*N&Q* 29:345–46) that Pound's famous haiku and his prose accounts of its origin are indebted to a passage in Edward Carpenter's *The Art of Creation* (1904). Somewhat more persuasive, by virtue of its accompanying photographic evidence, is the connection made by Peter Davidson in "Giulio Romano at the Spring Marriage" (*Paideuma* 11:503–10) between Pound's allusion to Romano in "Coitus" and Romano's fresco cycle in the Sala di Psiche of the Palazzo del Te at Mantua.

The only essay of the year on *Cathay*, Sanehide Kodama's "*Cathay* and Fenollosa's Notebooks" (*Paideuma* 11:207–40) reproduces the manuscript texts and notes of five *Cathay* poems and describes the tonal differences between the Chinese originals and Pound's translations. Elsewhere, two essays by Terri Brint Joseph emphasize indeterminacy of voice and meaning in two complex early poems. In " 'Near Perigord': A Perplexity of Voices" (*Paideuma* 11:93–98) Joseph argues from a study of manuscript drafts and published texts that Pound's revisions of the poem progressively "throw into doubt the identity of the speaker." In "The Decentered Center of Ezra Pound's *Hugh Selwyn Mauberley*" (*YREAL* 1:121–51) Joseph contends that the ambiguous voices and the unresolved "play between unity and disunity, continuity and discontinuity, and closure and anti-closure" in the structure of *Mauberley* express Pound's "sense of the 'openness' of language and reality itself."

The lower depths of Pound scholarship this year are plumbed by Ronald E. McFarland in "A Note on Monsieur Verog" (*Paideuma* 11:446–48). McFarland suggests that, because Victor Plarr was of French descent, the name *Verog* derives from *frog*.

*d.* **The Cantos.**   Pound's long poem attracts many capable studies of its genre, structure, and sources this year. In "Ezra Pound and the Menippean Tradition" (*Paideuma* 11:395–405) Max Nänny argues that the poem is not an epic but a satire in the tradition of Menippus, Lucian, Petronius, Rabelais, and Swift. To support his point Nänny adduces a number of formal characteristics which *The Cantos* have in common with such satire. Formal structures are the peculiar concern of Kay Davis in three articles. In "Ring Composition, Subject Rhyme, and Canto VI" (*Paideuma* 11:429–39) Davis identifies a structure of subject rhymes which recalls the ring composition (*ABCBA*) used in the oral poetry of Homer, *Beowulf*, and *La Chanson de Roland*. In "Fugue and Canto LXIII" (*Paideuma* 11:15–38) Davis finds the subject rhymes of an Adams canto organized into a pattern of theme, response, and countersubject which approximates the pattern of a traditional musical fugue. In "Eleusis and the Structure of the Adams Cantos" (*ConP* 5:45–55) Davis somewhat redundantly detects a "point-counterpoint of Eleusinian good and its negation" in other Adams cantos. For Jessica Prinz Pecorino, on the other hand, the best formal analogy with *The Cantos* is not music but the visual art of post-Cubist painters such as Robert Rauschenberg. In "Resurgent Icons: Pound's First Pisan Canto and the Visual Arts" (*JML* 9:159–74) Pecorino argues that "if Pound did not influence contemporary artists, he in the very least anticipated their methods." The sources of *The Cantos* continue to be investigated by a number of energetic scholars. Those indefatigable sleuths Ben D. Kimpel and T. C. Duncan Eaves add to our knowledge not only of "Pound's Research for the Malatesta Cantos" (*Paideuma* 11:406–19) but also of "Ezra Pound's Use of Sources as Illustrated by His Use of Nineteenth-Century French History" (*MP* 80:35–52). The second of these articles traces Pound's representation in Cantos 44–111 of French history from Napoleon to the Great War. In a related study of "Napoleon and Talleyrand in *The Cantos*" (*Paideuma* 11:55–78) Andrew J. Kappel traces the progress of these leaders from villains in the earlier cantos to "exemplary instances of the ideal emperor and his ideal minister" in the later cantos.

Paideuma this year contains explicatory notes on passages from Cantos 41, 45, 47, 80, 81, 84, 94, and 96. As this distribution suggests, the sources of the Pisan and post-Pisan cantos are attracting much attention. In " 'Saint Hilda,' Mr. Pound, and Rilke's Parisian Panther at Pisa" (*Paideuma* 11:79–87) William French suggests that Pound's image of himself at Pisa as a "caged panther" comes from Rilke's poem "Der Panther" (1907). Pound's use of Thomas Hart Benton's *Thirty Years' View* in Canto 88 is treated in Harold Schimmel's "Historical Grit and Epic Gestation" (*Sagetrieb* 1:220–54). In "Corpus Juris and Canto XCIV" (*Paideuma* 11:312–24) David Gordon gives the Latin text and an English translation of relevant passages of the *Corpus Civilis Juris* of Justinian I. In "What Ezra Pound Says We Owe to Edward VIII, Duke of Windsor" (*JML* 9:313–15) Andrew J. Kappel identifies Fritz Hesse's *Das Spiel in Deutschland* (1953) as the source of Pound's claim in Cantos 86 and 95 that Edward kept peace between England and Germany from 1936 to 1939. In "The Story of Abd-el-Melik's Money in Canto XCVI and XCVII" (*Paideuma* 11:420–28) Mohammad Y. Shaheen corrects the misconceptions of

Arabic history and culture which Pound took over from his source, Alexander Del Mar. Finally, when we finish hunting the sources of the later cantos, we may relax with A. D. Moody's sensitive close reading of selected passages in "*The Pisan Cantos*: Making Cosmos in the Wreckage of Europe" (*Paideuma* 11:135–46).

The post-Pisan cantos prompt the most recent statement in Donald Davie's rich, ongoing dialogue with the work of Pound, "*Res* and *Verba* in *Rock-Drill* and After" (*Paideuma* 11:382–94). Whereas Carol Helmstetter Cantrell argues in "Obscurity, Clarity, and Simplicity in the *Cantos* of Ezra Pound" (*MQ* 23:402–10) that the language of the poem is "deeply referential," Davie is not at all sure that the *verba* of the later cantos always point to *res*. "Pound moves often from signifier to signifier, leaving the signified to take care of itself." Reluctant to surrender the poem to the structuralists, however, Davie attempts to salvage its referentiality by arguing that its language is mimetic of a *forma mentis*, "a disposition of mind and feeling . . . which *precedes* the framing of propositions or the making of distinctions." Meanwhile, Davie's 1976 study of *Ezra Pound* reappears in a new paperback format (Chicago).

If critics like Davie are the antennae of the scholarly race, and if the work of Ian Bell's contributors, Robert Gregory, and Terri Brint Joseph represents a trend, we can probably expect more structuralist studies of Pound in the near future.

### *ii.* Eliot

The most imaginative criticism of Eliot in new composition this year is *Cats*, an English musical based on *Old Possum's Book of Practical Cats*. Andrew Lloyd Webber sets Eliot's poems to music, and Trevor Nunn and Richard Stilgoe add lyrics derived from Eliot's unpublished manuscripts and from his other poems. "Preludes," "Rhapsody on a Windy Night," and "The Dry Salvages" all contribute lines to the exuberant soundtrack (Geffen Records) of the spectacular Broadway production (*Newsweek*, 11 Oct.).

*a.* **Text, Biography, and Bibliography.** Excerpts from *Fireside* (1899), a magazine of 14 issues created by Eliot at the age of ten, appear in John J. Soldo's "Jovial Juvenilia: T. S. Eliot's First Magazine" (*Biography* 5:25–37). Soldo relates the contents of *Fireside* to

Eliot's later work, emphasizing the poet's sense of "writing as a form of play." An anonymous review of Émile Durkheim's *The Elementary Forms of the Religious Life*, trans. J. W. Swain (1915), is attributed to Eliot by Louis Menand and Sanford Schwartz in "T. S. Eliot on Durkheim: A New Attribution" (*MP* 79:309–15). At the other end of Eliot's career his nine meetings with John Malcolm Brinnin between 1950 and 1957 are recalled in Brinnin's *Sextet: T. S. Eliot and Truman Capote and Others* (Delacorte, 1981). Brinnin publishes for the first time a statement written by Eliot during the winter of 1954–55 in opposition to "the Soviet persecution of dissident Jewish intellectuals."

Two bibliographies make welcome appearances this year. *An Annotated Critical Bibliography of Modernism* by Alistair Davies (Barnes and Noble) contains a 50-page chapter on Eliot criticism from the beginning to 1981. Davies lists 128 books, chapters of books, and articles, dividing them into 17 categories and annotating each item more informatively than either Mildred Martin in *A Half-Century of Eliot Criticism* (1972) or Beatrice Ricks in *T. S. Eliot: A Bibliography of Secondary Works* (1980). Elsewhere, Armin Paul Frank presents "T. S. Eliot in Germany, 1965 to the Present: An Estimate and a Bibliography" (*YER* 7:123–37). Frank lists books and dissertations on Eliot published in Germany or by German scholars between 1965 and 1978 and chapters of books and articles published between 1965 and 1976. Both of these useful studies will save other scholars many hours of work.

*b.* **General Studies.** If 1982 is a lean year for textual and biographical studies, it is a fat one for general studies. Two of the best emphasize the importance of Eliot's philosophical and religious ideas to the understanding of his poetry. In *T. S. Eliot's Intellectual and Poetic Development, 1909–1922* (Humanities) Piers Gray charts Eliot's responses to Jules Laforgue, Henri Bergson, Josiah Royce, F. H. Bradley, Émile Durkheim, and Lucien Lévy-Bruhl, among others. Gray makes especially good use of the unpublished essay on "The Interpretation of Primitive Ritual," written by Eliot for Royce's seminar at Harvard. Through close readings marred at times by a schoolmasterly tone and repetitive style, Gray shows how Eliot's ideas are incarnated in the language of his poetry and critical prose. In *T. S. Eliot's Negative Way* (Harvard) Eloise Knapp Hay concentrates upon the ideas of "void and path" as "developing patterns that reveal a striking design in Eliot's entire poetic corpus." Hay argues that Eliot's "embracing of the austere regimens of the Christian *via negativa* was possible only because he began by taking a way of even more appalling rejections"—namely, the negative way of Bradleian epistemological skepticism and Buddhist philosophical resignation. Hay shows, among other things, that Irving Babbitt's thinking about Buddhism influenced Eliot no less profoundly than did his thinking about European romanticism.

Such influence is the central concern of Leonard Unger's *T. S. Eliot's Compound Ghost: Influence and Confluence* (Penn. State). Unger posits "a dynamics of correspondence by which a variety of sources becomes both a confluence and an influence" upon a poet's work. He demonstrates such a confluence in Eliot's echoings of Edward FitzGerald's translation of *The Rubáiyát of Omar Khayyám*, of A. C. Benson's 1905 life of FitzGerald, of Joseph Conrad's short story "The Return," and of Milton's *Paradise Lost*. This brief but elegant study is itself influenced more by John Livingston Lowes than by Harold Bloom.

Two other books on Eliot published this year exemplify the difference between a good primer and a bad one. Before his death in February Philip R. Headings completed *T. S. Eliot: Revised Edition* (Twayne). Headings expands his 1964 handbook from 9 to 14 chapters, incorporating much new material. His special sympathy with the Dantesque dimensions of Eliot's poetry and with his plays remains strong. In contrast, Burton Raffel in *T. S. Eliot* (Ungar) dislikes most of the poetry Eliot wrote after 1927. "The poetic failure of *Ash-Wednesday* and the comparative failure of *Four Quartets* is thus paralleled, if not precisely mirrored, in Eliot's plays." Raffel's grammar is frequently shaky, his use of critical terms is often imprecise, his footnotes are gratuitously contentious, and his tone of voice is excessively self-regarding. Beginning students should head for Headings.

Like John J. Soldo in his study of *Fireside*, Charles Sanders emphasizes the playful, childlike quality of Eliot's literary voice. In " 'But Where's the Man': The 'Double Part' of T. S. Eliot" (*YER* 7: 3–9) Sanders argues that "like the child . . . with his imaginary 'play'-mate for whom he speaks two parts in two voices through one instrument, Eliot communicates with Eliot as much as with and through" the writers of the past. Similarly, Sally M. Gall stresses Eliot's "many-tongued and multiple language" as an exemplary contrast to the monotones of recent "Domestic Monologues: The Problem of 'Voice' in Contemporary American Poetry" (*MR* 23:489–503). In "Landscape and Voice in T. S. Eliot's Poetry" (*CentR* 26:33–50) John N. Serio relates the emergence of "a more personal voice" in Eliot's later poetry to his increasing use of "natural and particularized" landscapes. Having noted this connection, however, Serio is unable to account for it in an illuminating manner.

The tension between Eliot's revolutionary poetics and his reactionary politics concerns both Wolfgang Wicht in "The Ideological Background of T. S. Eliot" (*ZAA* 30:101–18) and Cairns Craig in *Yeats, Eliot, Pound and the Politics of Poetry: Richest to Richest* (Pittsburgh). Wicht takes a straightforward Marxist line, arguing that although Eliot's poems anatomize "the state of bourgeois man and manners" in a "monopolist society," they also "serve an antirevolutionary function in intentionally disregarding any forces that have the potential to really alter social conditions." For his part Craig links Eliot's social views to an elitist theory of audience demanded by his aesthetic dependence upon the associational memories of his readers. "Yeats, Eliot and Pound were driven to politics in order to maintain the institutions and the patterns of society which preserved and promulgated the kinds of memory on which their poetry relied. . . . The open poem demanded as its counterbalance the closed society." Craig's interesting argument is incompletely documented and not entirely persuasive.

c. **Relation to Other Writers.** The most ambitious treatment of Eliot's relation to other writers this year is Fred D. Crawford's *Mixing Memory and Desire: "The Waste Land" and British Novels* (Penn. State). Crawford examines the works of 17 modern British novelists from Richard Aldington to Anthony Burgess, identifying allusions, echoes, images, and themes indebted to Eliot's poem. Lacking an adequate theory of literary influence, Crawford overstates some of his claims (Ford "structured his plot so that *Last Post* functions as a gloss on some lines from *The Waste Land*") and states others so broadly and banally as to render them tenuous ("The characters in *Antic Hay*, like those in *The Waste Land*, feel that the burdens of modern life are too great for religious belief to mitigate").

But Crawford's strength as a researcher appears in his sensitive record, documented by quotations from unpublished letters, of the troubled personal and literary relationship between Eliot and Aldington.

Another troubled relationship is the subject of "Bertrand Russell and T. S. Eliot: Their Dialogue" by Gladys Garner Leithauser and Nadine Cowan (*Russell* 2:7–28). The authors map the personal and intellectual rifts that divided Russell and Eliot after 1920 but do not focus the philosophical differences between the two men sharply enough. In "The Irritant and the Pearl: 'Jones's Karma' and the Poetry and Drama of T. S. Eliot" (*CRCL* 9:188–99) P. S. Padmanabhan argues that a short story by May Sinclair published in *The Criterion* in 1923 influenced the treatment of Hindu themes in Eliot's subsequent writings. Noting a coincidence of imagery in "Burnt Norton" and D. H. Lawrence's "Preface to New Poems," Donald Gutierrez proceeds to contrast Eliot's consciousness of history and desire for transcendence with Lawrence's "poetics of instantaneity" in " 'Quick, Now, Here, Now, Always': The Flaming Rose of Lawrence and Eliot" (*Univ. of Portland Rev.* 34:3–7).

This year's studies of Eliot's relation to other American writers are noticeably weaker than the studies of his British affinities. In "T. S. Eliot as an American Poet" (*CentR* 26:147–71) Sam S. Baskett surveys Eliot's responses to American landscape and writers, drawing no new conclusions and ignoring much previous work on the subject. In "Black Cottages: Frost, Eliot, and the Fate of Individualism" (*Cithara* 22:37–52) Stephen J. Adams forces an artificial comparison between "Gerontion" and Robert Frost's "The Black Cottage" in order to illustrate the poets' disparate reactions to "the tradition of New England individualism stemming chiefly from Emerson." In "Melville and Eliot's Missourians" (*AN&Q* 19[1981]:78–81) Terry Britton suggests that certain lines in "The Love-Song of J. Alfred Prufrock" have a plausible source in Herman Melville's *The Confidence-Man*.

Four essays this year treat Eliot's relation to writers in classical and Romance languages. John J. Soldo's "T. S. Eliot and the Classics: The Influence of Petronius" (*MarkhamR* 11:36–40) provides a useful summary of Eliot's courses and grades in the classics, both in preparatory school and in college. Soldo also unearths a previously unpublished note from Eliot to John Hayward about Petronius.

However, these new materials do not lead their finder to any new conclusions. The same is true of Soldo's "Eliot's Dantean Vision, and His Markings in His Copy of the *Divina Commedia*" (*YER* 7:11–18). This essay lists the passages maked by Eliot in his bilingual edition of Dante (London: J. M. Dent, 1909–10), but generates no significant interpretive argument from the evidence. In "The Tradition of Italian *Poesia Ermetica* and T. S. Eliot" (*RLMC* 35:55–66) Joseph Pivato quaintly seeks to establish the existence of an "international tradition of hermetic poetry" consisting of the medieval Italian *stilnovisti*, the Renaissance English metaphysicals, the 19th-century French Symbolists, and the 20th-century Modernists. In "T. S. Eliot and the *Leçon de Valery*" (*CritQ* 24:69–77) Tony Pickney argues that in *Four Quartets* Eliot is guilty of precisely the same "rigid dualisms" for which he had earlier criticized Valery.

Eliot's relation to German and Scandanavian artists is the subject of two studies this year. His debt to Wagner receives fresh attention in Stoddard Martin's *Wagner to "The Waste Land": A Study of the Relationship of Wagner to English Literature* (Barnes and Noble). Martin fully acknowledges the findings of Herbert Knust in *Wagner, the King, and "The Waste Land"* (1967) but goes beyond Knust in emphasizing the central importance to Eliot's poetry of Wagner's *Parsifal*. Elsewhere, H. Neville Davies explores Eliot's connections with Kierkegaard and Strindberg in "Repetition and Renewal in T. S. Eliot's 'Marina': A Scandinavian Perspective" (*Scan* 21: 67–78). Davies argues that "Marina" traverses "Kierkegaard's three stages or spheres of existence—the aesthetic, the ethical, and the spiritual," and also that the poem is "directly indebted" to "the recognition scene from Strindberg's *Till Damaskus*, Part 2, Act IV." Davies cannot show, however, that Eliot knew either Kierkegaard's writings or Strindberg's play by 1930, when "Marina" was first published.

*d.* **The Poems and Plays.** *T. S. Eliot: The Critical Heritage*, ed. Michael Grant (Routledge), is a two-volume collection of contemporary ("immediate") reviews of Eliot's poems and plays. It contains 181 reviews first published in England and America between 1916 and 1963. The editor's introduction surveys the history of Eliot's poetic and dramatic publications, their reception, and the growth of his literary reputation. Although it is convenient to have a modern reprint of these scattered pieces, the usefulness of the collection is limited by an editorial decision to include no reviews of Eliot's prose writings. Comparable volumes on Dryden, Johnson, Coleridge, Arnold, Pound, and Woolf in the same series include reviews of their critical as well as their creative works.

Eliot's early poems attract only three significant essays this year, while *The Waste Land* and *Four Quartets* receive the lion's share of attention. In "Time and Irony in T. S. Eliot's Early Poetry" (*MSE* 8:39–52) Isaiah Smithson applies Kierkegaard's distinction between mastered and unmastered irony to the personae of "Prufrock," "Portrait of a Lady," and "Gerontion," who speak ironically but fail to achieve "mastered irony as a means of gaining insight into time and the human condition in general." In "Mysteries of the Broad Backed Church: T. S. Eliot's 'The Hippopotamus'" (*CP* 15:11–18) Bruce Ross invokes the biblical contexts of the poem's epigraphs to argue that the hippo becomes "a symbol of Church mysteries," specifically "of the actuality of the flesh and blood Christ." In "The House of Mirrors: Language in Eliot's 'Gerontion'" (*CollL* 9:44–53) Diane Stockman Bonds offers a perceptive close reading of the poem informed by deconstructionist principles. Bonds finds in the speaker's language a self-referential mirroring of signifiers which gesture toward meaning but ultimately reflect only its absence.

Bonds applies deconstructionist theory more appropriately and subtly than does Ruth Nevo in "*The Waste Land*: Ur-Text of Deconstruction" (*NLH* 13:453–61). Nevo labels *The Waste Land* "as a deconstructionist Ur-text, even as a Deconstructionist Manifesto . . . totally, radically nonintegrative and antidiscursive . . . an apogee of fragmentation and discontinuity." But she does not justify these hyperboles with a persuasive critical analysis. A better-supported reading of the poem in structuralist terms occurs in Mutlu Konuk Blasing's "*The Waste Land*: Gloss and Glossary" (*ELWIU* 9:97–105). Blasing stresses the "structural dissonance" between the fragmented, irrational text of the poem and the continuous, rational "metatext" implied by Eliot's notes. The notes, he concludes, only "fragment further the sensibility of the poem." The other end of the poem receives the attention of Richard A. Sullivan in "The Sibyl and the Voice: Eliot's Epigraphs to *The Waste Land*" (*YER* 7:19–27). Both the epigraph from Petronius' *Satyricon* and the cancelled epigraph from Conrad's *Heart of Darkness* function differ-

ently, according to Sullivan, from "traditional" epigraphs such as
that of Tennyson's "Mariana." This difference, however, is not convincingly illustrated in the essay.

Another essay and several notes are devoted to specific passages
of *The Waste Land* and to "Journey of the Magi." In "The Tarot
Fortune in *The Waste Land*" (*ELH* 49:908–28) Betsey B. Creekmore offers an ingenious new interpretation of the Madame Sosostris
episode and its structural and symbolic relevance to the poem as a
whole. Creekmore argues that Madame Sosostris uses the Waite/
Smith Tarot to tell a coherent fortune in answer to the question
"May I die?" Elsewhere, in "T. S. Eliot and William Cowper: A New
*Waste Land* Source" (*N&Q* 29:347) A. V. C. Schmidt links lines 98
and 104 of "A Game of Chess" to a poem by Cowper. In "*The Waste
Land* in St. Louis" (*YER* 7:50) Charles T. Dougherty notes the existence in St. Louis of a Metropole hotel, built in 1912 and famous until
1920 for catering to prostitutes. Finally, Neil Taylor locates "A Possible Source for T. S. Eliot's 'Journey of the Magi' " (*N&Q* 29:347–
48) in R. B. Cunninghame Graham's story "The Fourth Magus"
(1910). Delayed in his journey for 33 years, Graham's magus arrives
in time to witness Christ's crucifixion, and concludes that "birth and
death are not so very different after all."

*Four Quartets* remains fertile ground for scholarly tillage, to
judge from the recent crop of studies. For A. E. Dyson in *Yeats, Eliot,
and R. S. Thomas: Riding the Echo* (Macmillan, 1981), the poem is
"neither more or less Christian than *The Waste Land* . . . I see the
*Quartets* now not as a 'great Christian poem,' but as the last, and
perhaps most teasing, enigma that the poet left." Dyson devotes 100
pages to a discursive, highly personal reading of the poem, ripened
during many years of university lectures and tutorials. For Sister
Corona Sharp in " 'The Unheard Music': T. S. Eliot's *Four Quartets*
and John of the Cross" (*UTQ* 51:264–78), on the other hand, the
tone, structure, imagery, and symbolism of the poem are all profoundly indebted to the Christian writings of St. John of the Cross,
which Eliot knew in the translation of E. Allison Peers. Sister Corona's essay has much in common with Hay's *T. S. Eliot's Negative Way*.

The linguistic, metrical, and musical aspects of the *Quartets* are
treated in several recent essays and books. In "*Ing* Forms in *Four
Quartets*" (*ES* 63:23–31) Frances O. Austen concentrates upon
Eliot's present participles and gerunds, showing how their represen-

tation of "unfinished or recurrent actions" embodies the poet's sense of the "endless succession" of historical time. In "Covert Rhyme in the Scheme of Eliot's 'East Coker'" (*PLL* 18:421–27) Frank Burch Brown identifies an elaborate and symmetrical, though unobtrusive rhyme scheme in the first 17 lines of section 2. The "covert" quality of Eliot's rhymes and meters is also emphasized by Charles D. Hartman in *Free Verse: An Essay on Prosody* (Princeton, 1980). By using only "recognizable *parts* of familiar 'alternate patterns,'" according to Hartman, Eliot "creates the awareness of movement—of rhythm in the broadest sense—without giving awareness anything stable to focus or depend on." Elsewhere, six previously published essays on musical forms in Eliot's poetry are conveniently gathered and reprinted in *Literature and Music: Essays on Form*, ed. Nancy Anne Cluck (Brigham Young, 1981). Written by Paul Chancellor, Helen Gardner, D. Bosley Brotman, Herbert Howarth, Harvey Gross, and Thomas R. Rees, most of these studies center upon *Four Quartets*. Finally, the closing lines of "Little Gidding" are the subject of Rob Jackaman's "Patterned to Perfection: The Conclusion of *Four Quartets*" (*SHR* 16:201–09). Jackaman brings new enthusiasm to some rather old ideas about the poem.

For comic relief from serious explication one may turn to Robert F. Fleissner's "About the Mews: Catching Up with Eliot's Cats" (*Thalia* 4:35–39). Fleissner offers a clever, tongue-in-jowl, allegorical reading of *Old Possum's Book of Practical Cats*, stressing its Christian symbolism and "cat-holic" qualities.

Eliot's plays attract no separate studies this year, although they are treated in the general studies of Hay, Headings, and Raffel. If this neglect suggests that the plays no longer have much to say to readers in the English-speaking world, the reverse appears to be true in Poland, where a production of *Murder in the Cathedral* at St. John's Cathedral in Warsaw and at Wawel Cathedral in Cracow is the major theatrical event of the year, with significant political overtones. In "New Productions: 'Murder in the Cathedral' by T. S. Eliot" (*The Theatre in Poland* 24:8–11) Marta Fik calls it "the first play of such wide scope to be produced since martial law was declared in Poland." In the circumstances the theme of the play which stood out most clearly for the audience was "antitotalitarianism"; "a moment of great tension" occurred when the knights pounded upon the doors of the cathedral and "the public became a populace under siege." To judge from Fik's report, at least one of Eliot's plays may have a timeless relevance to recurring human conditions.

**e. The Criticism.** Both the earlier and the later criticism of Eliot is examined in several essays this year. The "pervasive Aristotelianism" of Eliot's early critical principles is stressed by B. L. Reid in "T. S. Eliot and *The Sacred Wood*" (*SR* 90:227–39). Reid suggests that the 13 occasional essays which make up *The Sacred Wood* are organized into three distinct groups, giving the book a coherent and symmetrical structure. Two essays on Eliot's criticism by Richard Shusterman vary considerably in quality. In "Eliot and Logical Atomism" (*ELH* 49:164–78) Shusterman argues that Eliot's early criticism is indebted for four of its basic linguistic and epistemological assumptions to the philosophy of Bertrand Russell. But all four assumptions are so general that they might have come from many other sources. The same critic is more persuasive in his discussion of "Objectivity and Subjectivity in Eliot's Critical Theory" (*OL* 37:217–26). Here Shusterman argues that the "extreme objectivism" of Eliot's early critical theory gives way in his later writings to "an outlook which not only accepted but encouraged critical subjectivity."

An analogous movement "from aesthetics to broader cultural concerns" in Eliot's later criticism is noted by William Bedford Clark in "Cleanth Brooks: Mr. Eliot's Christian Critic" (*SoR* 18:73–83). Having first documented Eliot's belief during the 1930s "that the critic's role is fraught with significant social responsibility," Clark proceeds to nominate Cleanth Brooks as the critic who best fulfills Eliot's conception of that role. Finally, Eliot's 1953 address on "American Literature and the American Language" is viewed by Anne Paolucci and Henry Paolucci, in "Poet-Critics on the Frontiers of Literature: A. D. Hope, T. S. Eliot, and William Carlos Williams" (*RNL* 11:146–91) as a "masterpiece in the genre" of comparative studies which show "how new national literatures emerge out of inherited and shared languages." The Paoluccis also discuss the ambivalent responses to Eliot of Williams and Australian poet and critic A. D. Hope.

In connection with the question of literary nationality raised by the Paoluccis and Sam S. Baskett we might note, in closing, that 1982 marks only the tenth anniversary of Eliot's inclusion in *ALS*. Before 1973 he was counted more a British than an American author. Even now he is described as one of the "major British Modernists" on the dustjacket of Alistair Davies' *Annotated Critical Bibliography of Modernism*. It is a tribute to Eliot's extraordinary sensitivity to local idiom that he is reckoned a native by the scholars of two different English-speaking nations.

*University of New Mexico*

# 9. Faulkner

*Karl F. Zender*

Of the five years for which I have written this chapter 1982 was the least interesting. With the exception of John T. Matthews' *The Play of Faulkner's Language*, Louis Daniel Brodsky's and Robert W. Hamblin's *Faulkner: A Comprehensive Guide to the Brodsky Collection*, and Bruce F. Kawin's *Faulkner's MGM Screenplays*, little work that was new or complex or challenging appeared during the year. Even deconstruction, that great woolly bear, seems to have been tamed and made predictable. As a confirmed Faulknerian, I am obliged to wonder how much of this sense of staleness and satiety is in the eye of the beholder. Perhaps the next couple of years will give me an answer, because I intend to step away from *ALS* for a time to pursue some projects of my own.

## i. Bibliography, Editions, and Manuscripts

The major bibliographical event of the year was the appearance of Louis Daniel Brodsky's and Robert W. Hamblin's *Faulkner: A Comprehensive Guide to the Brodsky Collection*, vol. 1: The Biobibliography (Miss.). As its title indicates, this handsomely produced and scrupulously edited volume is a descriptive catalog of the Brodsky collection of Faulkneriana. The collection it describes is an impressive one, ranging in content from manuscripts of early poems to first editions to over 300 letters by Phil Stone, Estelle Faulkner, and Faulkner himself. The catalog's very full descriptive comments and occasional facsimile reproductions of letters tantalize, for they suggest that the collection contains important biographical information, particularly about the later years of Faulkner's life. One awaits with expectation the promised publication of the contents of the collection itself; in the meantime, this preliminary volume should prove

Professor Linda Wagner (Michigan State University) will do the Faulkner chapter for the next two years.—Ed.

148 Faulkner

indispensable not only to bibliographers but to critics and biographers as well.

Several other useful bibliographical aids appeared during the year. Essentially a compilation of dissertation abstracts from the last 30 years, Tetsumaro Hayashi's *William Faulkner: Research Opportunities and Dissertation Abstracts* (McFarland) should be of value to any graduate students temerarious enough to wish to write on Faulkner. In addition to the abstracts themselves the volume contains a brief essay on research opportunities by Richard F. Peterson and indexes listing the dissertations by author, director, title, university, and subject. Unfortunately the essay is not very illuminating and the indexes contain several errors. In "The Books of William Faulkner: A Revised Guide for Students and Scholars" (*MissQ* 35: 265–81) James B. Meriwether undertakes to supplement and revise his 1977 guide to the relative reliability of the various editions of Faulkner's work. The new guide issues a timely warning about errors that have crept into recent press runs of at least two of the Vintage editions of Faulkner's novels. The year also saw the publication of Petra M. Gallert's "German-Language Translations of Faulkner" (*MissQ* 35:283–300) and Fumiyo Hayashi's and Shizue Uchida's "William Faulkner: An Annotated Checklist of Research and Criticism in Japan: VII" (*WiF* 4,ii:95–105). The first of these items updates the list of German-language translations of Faulkner's fiction contained in James B. Meriwether's *The Literary Career of William Faulkner*; the second supplements earlier checklists of work on Faulkner appearing in Japanese journals. Finally, it should be noted that the annual Faulkner issue of *Mississippi Quarterly* continues to publish a survey of scholarship similar to this one and that the *Faulkner Newsletter & Yoknapatawpha Review* continues to offer information for book collectors, chatty reviews, and brief notes.

The publication of previously unpublished work by Faulkner slowed almost to a standstill in 1982. Of the three brief items that did appear during the year the most important is "Pierrot, Sitting Beside the Body of Colombine, Suddenly Sees Himself in a Mirror," ed. J. B. M. [James B. Meriwether] (*MissQ* 35:305–08). This early poem, written in Faulkner's Swinburnian mode, anticipates a number of his later themes and displays a surprisingly mature command of narrative method. (For a different account of the poem's provenance from the one given by Meriwether see the Brodsky and Hamblin

*Comprehensive Guide*, p. 17). The annual Faulkner issue of *Mississippi Quarterly* also contains "Faulkner's Speech at Nagano, August 5, 1955," ed. Joseph Blotner (*MissQ* 35:309–11). As Blotner suggests in his headnote, this speech was an attempt by Faulkner to make up for the intemperateness of some earlier off-the-cuff remarks about American culture. Finally, in "William Faulkner: Poet at Large" (*SoR* 18:767–75) Louis Daniel Brodsky reprints and discusses an early draft of Faulkner's poem "Pregnacy" [*sic*] and a letter pertinent to the poem, written in 1924. The letter is also reprinted (in facsimile) in Brodsky's and Hamblin's *Comprehensive Guide*. The last item to be considered in this category is a disappointing one. Taken together, Leland H. Cox's *William Faulkner: Biographical and Reference Guide* and *William Faulkner: Critical Collection*, Gale Author Handbooks 1 and 2 (Gale) purport to be a self-contained guide to the study of Faulkner, but they are too restricted in outlook to perform this function well. In his sampling of criticism entitled "Critical Assessments," for example, Cox reprints no work whatsoever by deconstructionists, by structuralists, or by psychobiographers. In a list of recommended readings of over 200 items he does not mention John Irwin's *Doubling and Incest*, André Bleikasten's *Most Splendid Failure*, David Minter's *William Faulkner: His Life and Work*, Donald Kartiganer's *The Fragile Thread*, or even Irving Howe's *William Faulkner: A Critical Study*, to mention only the more glaring omissions. A similar restriction in focus characterizes the brief biography and the set of critical introductions to Faulkner's works that together make up the first volume of this two-volume set. In both the biography and the introductions Cox deemphasizes the darker and more complex aspects of Faulkner's life and vision in favor of a morally upbeat view of him as an advocate of the eternal verities.

## ii. Biography

Only two significant pieces of work on Faulkner's biography appeared in 1982: Panthea Broughton's long interview with Meta Carpenter Wilde (*SoR* 18:776–801) and Jay Martin's "'The Whole Burden of Man's History of His Impossible Heart's Desire': The Early Life of William Faulkner" (*AL* 53:607–29). One comes away from Broughton's interview with a renewed sense of Meta Wilde's intelligence and warmth of personality, but with little new information about Faulkner. Despite the best efforts of interviewer and interviewee alike, the connections between Faulkner's relationship with Wilde and his art remain shadowy. Martin's essay is a stimulating attempt to understand Faulkner's early career in psychoanalytic terms. Martin identifies several of the central questions that must concern students of Faulkner's career and makes some insightful observations about the repressive character of Faulkner's early art, but he finally is defeated by the slenderness of our knowledge of Faulkner's childhood. Curiously, he misreads one of the documents most central to his case, attributing to one of Faulkner's aunts qualities Faulkner ascribes to another. Finally, mention should be made here of the *Dictionary of Literary Biography* (Gale). Faulkner is the subject of a 30-page essay by Linda W. Wagner in volume 9 (*American Novelists, 1910–45*) and of a 12-page essay by M. Thomas Inge in volume 11 (*American Humorists 1800–1950*).

### *iii.* Criticism: General

*a.* **Books.** The year saw the publication of three books of general criticism, one collection of essays by several hands, and a book in which Faulkner receives two chapters of attention. The most important item in this array of material is John T. Matthews' *The Play of Faulkner's Language* (Cornell). As I have already reviewed this book at length (*Criticism* 25[1983]:80–83), I will only summarize my remarks here. *The Play of Faulkner's Language* is a perceptive and stimulating, though not entirely successful, attempt to read Faulkner's fiction in the light afforded by Jacques Derrida's critique of the metaphysics of presence. Matthews focuses on four novels: *The Sound and the Fury, Absalom, Absalom!, The Hamlet,* and *Go Down, Moses.* The book's strengths are most evident in the chapters on the first two of these novels, where Matthews presents state-of-the-art readings of the ways Faulkner multiplies and disorients the meanings he purports to convey. Especially admirable is Matthews' exploration of the various languages of loss—Benjy's, Quentin's, Jason's, and Faulkner's own—in *The Sound and the Fury.* Less successful are the chapters on *The Hamlet* and *Go Down, Moses,* where Matthews fails to give sufficient emphasis to the representational and developmental aspects of the novels. By concentrating almost exclusively on the play of repetition and variation, Matthews abstracts Faulkner's characters (most notably Ike McCaslin) from their careers in time and thereby diminishes our sense of their tragic complexity. Despite this limitation Matthews' book is a significant event in the history of Faulkner studies. The first full-scale attempt to apply deconstructionist theories and methods to the canon, it merits the attention of all serious students of Faulkner's fiction.

The other book-length studies to appear during the year can be more briefly treated. According to its dust jacket, John Pikoulis' *The Art of William Faulkner* (Macmillan) is only the second book on Faulkner published in the United Kingdom (excluding, of course, books first published in America). This survey of the fiction from *Sartoris* to *Go Down, Moses* exhibits both the strengths and the weaknesses of a distant view of its subject. The strengths are moral sanity, critical balance, and elegance of phrasing; the weaknesses are occasional eccentricities of judgment (as when Pikoulis excludes *As I Lay Dying* and *Light in August* from the list of Faulkner's major novels) and a sense of disengagement from the ongoing critical dialogue. All in all, one could do worse than to advise a beginning student of Faulkner to start with this book. The other book-length study, Yasuhiro Yoshizaki's *Faulkner's Theme of Nature* (Kyoto: Yamaguchi Shoten), is awkwardly written, loosely organized, and critically naive. It does not merit comparison with the considerable body of good work now being created by Japanese critics.

Doreen Fowler's and Ann J. Abadie's *Faulkner and the Southern Renaissance* (Miss.) reprints the proceedings of the eighth annual Faulkner and Yoknapatawpha conference. In both presentation and content this volume exhibits a decline from the high standard of quality established in this series in the last few years. To a large extent the problems with the content of the volume arise from the shopworn character of the conference theme: what, after all, is one to do with Faulkner and the Agrarians at this late date? The better essays in the volume, of which there are several, respond to this problem by taking a flexible approach to the definition of their subject. Among these, David Minter's "'Truths More Intense than Knowledge': Notes on Faulkner and Creativity" (pp. 245–65) is especially noteworthy. Minter focuses on the dialectic between conservative and radical elements in Faulkner's creativity, defining the one as an emphasis on repetition, remembering, and copying, and the other as a playful decentering of meaning and value. The strength of Minter's essay lies in his insistence (absent in Matthews' *The Play of Faulkner's Language*) on the historical character of Faulkner's deconstructive impulse. Though Faulkner's novels "withhold certitude and forego closure," Minter says, they resist postmodernism by their continuing insistence on "the possibility of evaluation and meaning." Similarly far-ranging and insightful is Richard H. King's "Memory and Tradition" (pp. 138–57). Using Nietzsche on history and Freud on memory as points of departure, King provides a succinct overview of the crisis character of modernism and of Faulkner's changing relationship to modernist beliefs. Also of value, though less far-ranging, are two other essays by Minter and King. In "Family, Region, and Myth in Faulkner's Fiction" (pp. 182–203) Minter explores the connection between Faulkner's fiction and the modern history of the family. In "Framework of a Renaissance" (pp. 3–21) King places the Southern Renaissance in a variety of contexts, most notably that of the postwar scholarly and critical validation of the phenomenon itself.

Of the eight remaining essays five seek to locate Faulkner in the context of the Southern Renaissance. The most rewarding of the five, Louis D. Rubin, Jr.'s "The Dixie Special: William Faulkner and the Southern Literary Renascence" (pp. 63–92) is a graceful and temperate statement of the mixed character of Faulkner's relation to his southern heritage. Less temperate are two essays by Floyd C. Watkins, "What Stand Did Faulkner Take?" (pp. 40–62), and "The Hound Under the Wagon: Faulkner and the Southern Literati" (pp. 93–119). In the second of these essays Watkins notes that Faulkner had no significant ties to the other southern writers of his time, then uses this fact as the basis for an assertion that Faulkner's true allegiance was to the folk oral tradition. In the first essay Watkins seeks to assimilate Faulkner to a southern chauvinism of an unsophisticated sort. At one point Watkins says that "those who have read Faulkner correctly are usually Southern or rural or extraordinarily empathetic." Perhaps the first place to pause in this statement is at the word "correctly." In the fourth of the five essays, "Faulkner and the Fugitive-Agrarians" (pp. 22–39), Cleanth Brooks asserts that Faulkner and the Agrarians differed very little in their attitudes toward southern life. He arrives at this assertion by way of an attempted disproof of Daniel Aaron's claim that the Agrarians only tardily acknowledged Faulkner's greatness. Finally, in "Faulkner and Continuance of the Southern Renaissance [*sic*]" (pp. 158–81), Alexander Blackburn approaches the subject of the conference from the modern end, by seeking to determine where the Southern Renaissance went after Faulkner. Though sometimes quirky, this essay makes occasional insightful comments about Faulkner's parodic presence in later southern fiction.

The remaining three essays in the Fowler and Abadie volume can be briefly treated. In "Faulkner's Ultimate Values" (pp. 266–81) Cleanth Brooks enumerates the virtues Faulkner especially cherishes and concludes, not surprisingly, that "Faulkner's conception of the human being is . . . right in the mainstream of the great classical-Judaic-Christian tradition." Elizabeth Spencer's "Emerging as a Writer in Faulkner's Mississippi" (pp. 120–37) is a largely anecdotal account of her encounters with Faulkner's fiction while growing up in Mississippi in the 1930s and 1940s. She concludes with a welcome plea that we not "get folksy and cosy about our great writer." The last of the three remaining essays, Patrick Samway's "Faulkner's Poetic Vision" (pp. 204–44) is only tangentially related to the theme of the conference. It will be discussed in section *v.* below.

The final item in this category, Bruce F. Kawin's *The Mind of the Novel*, devotes parts of two chapters to *The Sound and the Fury*, *As I Lay Dying*, and *Absalom, Absalom!* In his preface Kawin asks that "the reader agree for the duration of this book to consider the possibility that the self exists apart from any self-image, projection, or symbolic category constructed by words and by the conscious mind." This is fair enough; but unfortunately Kawin rides Faulkner's texts rather hard in an effort to prove that they affirm a similar conception of the self. In the instance of *Absalom, Absalom!*, for example, he bases nearly his whole argument for the existence of a transcendental meaning—what he calls "the mind of the story"—on the biblical allusion contained in the novel's title. Kawin brings considerable knowledge and intellectual ability to bear on his investigations, but I wish he had approached them in a more disinterested way.

*b.* **Articles.** Only three articles on general themes appeared during 1982. The first, Judith Bryant Wittenberg's "William Faulkner: A Feminist Consideration" (*American Novelists Revisited*, pp. 325–38), provides an intelligent and balanced overview of the place of women in Faulkner's fiction. Wittenberg emphasizes the limitations of seeing Faulkner "as either a misogynist or a gyneolatrist"; she uses psychoanalytic concepts to good effect, particularly in discussing the androgynous elements of Faulkner's characters. The second article, Michael Oriard's "The Ludic Vision of William Faulkner" (*MFS* 28: 169–87), is an informed but somewhat tendentious analysis of the theme of game-playing in Faulkner's fiction. Oriard has some good things to say about the ways in which games serve as metaphors for freedom for Faulkner, but he lessens the force of his argument by broadening the category of "game" to include other forms of human conflict. In "Southern Fiction and the Pattern of Failure: The Example of Faulkner" (*GaR* 36:755–70) Elmo Howell says that Faulkner was not comfortable with introspection, was impulsive as an artist, was deficient in imagination, and was not gifted with either a long attention span or stability of mind. He says that Faulkner was a freak genius. He says that Faulkner is not as good a writer as Trollope and that *Light in August* is his last wholly original work. After this, what remains?

### iv. Criticism: Special Studies

*a.* **Ideas, Influences, Intellectual Background.** The short list of works in this category is headed by Daniel Joseph Singal's *The War Within*, an ambitious but flawed attempt to write the history of the transition from Victorianism to modernism in the South. Singal presents a familiar view of Faulkner as a man divided between the past and the present. His readings of the fiction are marred by biographical reductionism and by too-easy recourse to sweeping symbolic interpretations. His view of modernism may strike literary critics as a curious one, for it owes less to Nietzsche, Freud, and the literary avant-garde of the 1920s than it does to contemporary historians and social theorists. A second historical study, Lawrence Schwartz's "Malcolm Cowley's Path to William Faulkner" (*JAmS* 16:229–42), provides some interesting information about Cowley's personal and political reasons for turning to work on the *Portable Faulkner* when he did, but many readers will wish to reject Schwartz's conclusions about the relationship between Faulkner's "greatness" (Schwartz's quotation marks) and "the prevailing reactionary aesthetics of the post-war era."

The remaining items in this category are all influence studies. An attempt to trace James Joyce's influence on Modernist and post-Modernist American fiction, Craig Hansen Werner's *Paradoxical Resolutions* (Illinois) suffers from the narrowness of its conceptual base. Werner sees Joyce as having healed the breach between Richard Chase's realistic and romantic modes of the American novel. What this means for Faulkner, strangely enough, is that *Go Down, Moses* is more Joycean than either *The Sound and the Fury* or *As I Lay Dying*. In "Faulkner and the Comic Perspective of Frederick Burr Opper" (*JPC* 16:139–50) Richard A. Milum uses Faulkner's sole reference to Alphonse and Gaston as the occasion for a discussion of the presumed influence of the comic strips on Faulkner's comic vision. The essay begins unpromisingly, with a misidentification of the circumstances of the debate in which the reference occurs; it does not cite any specific, substantial evidence for the influence of the comics on Faulkner. Finally, Carmen Chaves McClendon's "A Rose for Rosalinda: From Yoknapatawpha to *Ópera dos Mortos*" (*CLS* 19:450–58) presents an impressive list of parallels between Faulkner's "A Rose for Emily" and the work by Autran Dourado named in the title of the essay. Dourado is a contemporary Brazilian writer who has acknowledged Faulkner's influence on his fiction.

*b.* **Style and Structure.** No studies devoted specifically to the style or structure of Faulkner's fiction appeared during 1982.

*c.* **Race.** After the spate of interest in Faulkner's racial themes in 1981, matters settled back to normal in 1982. The only item to appear during the year, a chapter in John R. Cooley's *Savages and Naturals* (Delaware), rehashes Faulkner's depictions of blacks in *Sartoris, The Sound and the Fury*, and "The Bear," and arrives at predictable conclusions about Faulkner's failure to depict "a black character rebellious and verbal enough to anticipate the growing independence and demand for social justice among southern blacks."

#### *v.* Individual Works to 1929

As is usually the case, studies of *The Sound and the Fury* dominate the work on the first decade of Faulkner's career, but there are also a few items on the early poetry, *Soldiers' Pay*, and *Mosquitoes* to be considered. Patrick Samway's "Faulkner's Poetic Vision" (*Faulkner and the Southern Renaissance*, pp. 204–44) is a long but inconclusive survey of Faulkner's poetry. Samway clearly values the poetry highly, but his ability to persuade us to share his opinion is impeded by his failure to establish a clear and consistent aesthetic frame of reference. Of interest in this essay are the restrictions on *Vision in Spring*, one of Faulkner's early unpublished collections of poems. Each time Samway quotes from this work, he cites Judith Sensibar, a 1982 University of Chicago Ph.D., as its "exclusive copyright licensee." The only other item on Faulkner's poetry to appear during the year, Emily Dalgarno's "Faulkner's Pierrot" (*NMW* 14:73–76), notes another instance—in addition to those identified by Martin Kreiswirth (see *ALS 1980*, pp. 156–57)—of Faulkner's borrowings from Robert Nichols' *Ardours and Endurances*.

Francis J. Bosha's *Faulkner's "Soldiers' Pay": A Bibliographic Study* (Whitston) consists in the main of a careful collation of the first edition of the novel, the bound typescript in the Alderman Library at the University of Virginia, and an earlier typescript in the Berg Collection of the New York Public Library. The collation is supported by a long introduction and by appendixes containing, among other things, transcriptions of Faulkner's notes for the novel and of rejected manuscript and typescript pages from the Berg Collection. The introduction is sometimes infelicitously phrased, and some of the key editorial decisions merit fuller explanation, but all in all the book looks like a good job of work. The only item on *Mosquitoes* to appear during the year, Ilse Dusoir Lind's "Faulkner's *Mosquitoes*: A New Reading" (*WiF* 4,ii:1–18), unfortunately does not fulfill the promise made in its title. Lind arrives at the familiar conclusion that the central concern of the novel is "the problem of the artist, in particular the modern American artist who is writing fiction."

The long list of items on *The Sound and the Fury* is headed by two collections of criticism, André Bleikasten's *William Faulkner's "The Sound and the Fury": A Critical Casebook* (Garland Faulkner Casebooks, vol. 1 [Garland]) and Arthur F. Kinney's *Critical Essays on William Faulkner: The Compson Family* (Critical Essays on American Literature [G. K. Hall]). Because of substantial differences in focus and emphasis, these two volumes are more complementary than competitive. Bleikasten's *Critical Casebook* is tightly focused on the novel itself. In addition to a number of previously published essays the volume contains a selection of Faulkner's own comments on the novel, a newly written genetic study by Gail M. Morrison, an intelligent introduction by Bleikasten, and a full and well-annotated bibliography. In selecting materials Bleikasten has chosen to pass over the widely known studies by Brooks, Millgate, Vickery, et al. in favor of less accessible items. He also has chosen to deviate in his introduction from the general editor's promised "overview of scholarly study," providing instead an original critical essay on the themes of presence and absence and on the nature of our engagement in "the hazardous, reiterative, never completed business of [the story's] tellings." The effect of these decisions is mixed. On the one hand, they display a welcome openness to recent directions in the study of *The Sound and the Fury*; on the other, they lead to an emphasis on the individual sections of the novel at the expense of the whole and to a neglect of the relation of the novel to Faulkner's other works.

Kinney's volume, by contrast, is both more broadly focused and more traditional in its critical orientation. As its subtitle suggests, its subject is not *The Sound and the Fury* alone (though most of its contents focus on the novel) but all appearances of the Compson family in the Faulkner canon. It contains 23 critical essays (compared to eight in the Bleikasten volume), a section of early reviews, a variety of materials by Faulkner that anticipate or discuss *The Sound and the Fury*, a long introduction by Kinney, and a short story by Alan Cheuse that purports to trace Caddy Compson's fortunes after she leaves Jefferson. Of the 23 critical studies three—Donald M. Kartiganer's "Quentin Compson and Faulkner's Drama of the Generations," John W. Hunt's "The Disappearance of Quentin Compson," and Joan Williams' "In Defense of Caroline Compson"—are published here for the first time. Kartiganer presents an intriguing alternative model for the study of generational conflict to the one used by John Irwin in *Doubling and Incest* and applies it to several novels; he also draws a valuable distinction between Faulkner's characterizations of Quentin Compson in *The Sound and the Fury* and *Absalom, Absalom!* Hunt's essay has the intriguing topic of when and why Quentin Compson disappears from the Faulkner canon, but his discussion would have been strengthened had he paid attention to Quentin's role as an artist manqué. As its title suggests,

Joan Williams' essay is a plea for a sympathetic reassessment of Caroline Compson. Kinney's introduction to the volume is a revised and expanded version of a talk given at LeMoyne College. It contains a fresh new discussion of the theme of blood, but it sometimes overwhelms by force issues that one would prefer to see discussed in a more detached and provisional way.

*The Sound and the Fury* is the subject of seven other studies that appeared during 1982. Three of these—André Bleikasten's "Bloom and Quentin," François L. Pitavy's "Joyce's and Faulkner's 'Twining Stresses': A Textual Comparison," and Nancy Walker's "Stephen and Quentin"—appear in *The Seventh of Joyce*. Evidently the three critics were asked to choose a passage from Faulkner and then were provided with a passage from Joyce with which to compare it. Perhaps inevitably, this exercise led to a fair amount of repetition, but it also produced moments of real insight, especially in Pitavy's essay. Both he and Bleikasten demonstrate convincingly how much more radical and inward is Faulkner's use of stream of consciousness than is Joyce's.

The remaining four items on *The Sound and the Fury* can be briefly treated. Leon Howard's "The Composition of *The Sound and the Fury*" (*MissouriR* 5:111–38) is an impressionistic study of the topic identified in its title. Howard asserts, without much evidential support, that Faulkner began the novel by writing a "core story" about the Compson children on the day of their grandmother's death. He attempts to reconstruct this story, largely by rearranging several parts of the Benjy section into chronological order. Linda W. Wagner's "Language and Act: Caddy Compson" (*SLJ* 14,ii:49–61) is a character study of Caddy, distinguished from its predecessors by its emphasis on Caddy's "role as language-creator and giver." Also concerned with language is Seiji Sasamoto's "The First Section of *The Sound and the Fury*: Benjy and His Expressions" (*WiF* 4,ii:19–36). Sasamoto's close analysis of Faulkner's choice of verbs, conjunctions, and adjectives leads to several worthwhile observations, as when he says that Faulkner omits conjunctions that involve "reason, cause, assumption, condition, and concession." Finally Austin M. Wright's *The Formal Principle in the Novel* (Cornell) contains a balanced and well-written but somewhat old-fashioned analysis of the plot of *The Sound and the Fury*. Wright says that Benjy, Quentin, and

Jason form a compound protagonist and that the plot of the novel
consists of the deflation of the Compson's pretensions.

### vi. Individual Works, 1930–39

The dominance of *Absalom, Absalom!* over the attention of Faulkner critics slackened considerably in 1982. Of the 21 studies devoted
to the fiction of the 1930s five are on this novel, three on *As I Lay
Dying*, and five on *Light in August*—surely a healthier state of affairs
than last year's, when 12 out of 21 essays were on *Absalom, Absalom!*
The three studies of *As I Lay Dying* are headed by François L.
Pitavy's "Through Darl's Eyes Darkly: The Vision of the Poet in
*As I Lay Dying*" (*WiF* 4,ii:37–62). This complex and stimulating
analysis of Darl as a figure of the poet extends Stephen Ross's comments on the place of voice in the novel (see *ALS 1979*, p. 148) in
important ways. One wishes that Pitavy had pressed his insights
further by placing Darl's monologues more firmly in the context of
the other monologues in the novel and by asking why this sort of
study in artistic self-erasure should have interested Faulkner at this
point in his career. The second and third items on *As I Lay Dying*
are both of limited value. William Rodney Allen's "The Imagist and
Symbolist Views of the Function of Language: Addie and Darl Bundren in *As I Lay Dying*" (*SAF* 10:185–96) is a schematic analysis
of Addie and Darl as representatives of imagism and symbolism respectively. Deborah E. Whitely's close reading of Whitfield's monologue in her "Phenomenological Psychology and the Interior Monologue: Interpreting Whitfield's Passage" (*CEA* 44:33–36) does little
more than recapitulate the process by which Whitfield decides to
remain silent about his affair with Addie. Finally, I wish to mention
an overlooked item from 1981, Robert J. Kloss's "Addie Bundren's
Eyes and the Difference They Make" (*SCR* 13[1981]:85–95). Kloss
makes some good observations about Darl Bundren in the course of
this psychoanalytic study of eye imagery, but he never addresses the
central question posed by Pitavy in his essay: how *can* we psycho-
analyze characters in a novel in which voice and personality are so
deliberately discontinuous?

Only two items appeared on *Sanctuary* during the year, neither
of much significance. Lance Lyday's "*Sanctuary*: Faulkner's *Inferno*"

(*MissQ* 35:243–53) is a forced attempt to educe parallels between Faulkner's novel and Dante's poem. One would think that the compositional history of the novel would work against Lyday's claim that structural parallels exist between the openings of the two works, but he asserts that this is not so. The second item on *Sanctuary*, Kiyoyuki Ono's "Sanctuary of the Heart: An Interpretation of *Sanctuary*" (*WiF* 4,ii:63–78) discusses the novel in traditional terms, as the story of Horace Benbow's discovery of evil. The phrase "sanctuary of the heart" in the essay's title refers to one's ability to hide ignoble feelings behind a mask of respectability.

Heading the list of materials on *Light in August* is the second in the series of Garland Faulkner Casebooks, François L. Pitavy's *William Faulkner's "Light in August": A Critical Casebook* (Garland). Like André Bleikasten's volume in this series (see section *v.*), Pitavy's book contains a selection of criticism, a thoughtful introduction, and a well-annotated bibliography. Like Bleikasten too, Pitavy chooses to pass over commonly available materials in favor of less known and more recent items and to deviate from the stated purpose for the introduction in favor of an original contribution of his own. Though I have reservations about some of Pitavy's editorial decisions—the amount of space he devotes to an excerpt from R. G. Collins' "*Light in August*: Faulkner's Stained Glass Triptych," for example—my overall impression is that his book provides a good, sound introduction to the current state of knowledge of the novel. I come away from this volume, too, with the sense that the standard readings of *Light in August* may be ripe for substantial reworking.

The remaining four items on *Light in August* are of varying quality. The most impressive of the four, John Tucker's "William Faulkner's *Light in August*: Toward a Structuralist Reading" (*MLQ* 43:138–55) investigates "the problem of the novel's unity" and seeks to determine "the binary distinctions according to which the communal world of Jefferson organizes itself." The first of these efforts produces some good insights into the novel's structure, but the second never moves much beyond familiar oppositions between black and white and male and female. Marianna Torgovnick's *Closure in the Novel* (Princeton) contains a chapter entitled "Story-Telling as Affirmation at the End of *Light in August*" (pp. 157–75) in which Torgovnick attempts to prove that "the basic function of the furniture dealer's narration is . . . to prevent the ending of *Light in August* from seeming too grandly or artificially affirmative." Presumably the too grandly affirmative ending in question is some alternative version of the story of Byron and Lena, not the somber penultimate chapter of the novel. In "The Death of Joe Christmas and the Power of Words" (*TCL* 28:252–68) James Leo Spenko attempts, though with little success, to explain why Joe Christmas allows himself to be killed. The reason, Spenko says, is that Percy Grimm's use of the epithet "Jesus Christ" brings out the passive, victimized side of Christmas' personality. Finally, Judith Halden's "Sexual Ambiguities in *Light in August*" (*SAF* 10:209–16) is a rather contentiously argued attempt to trace Joe Christmas' and Joanna Burden's interpersonal difficulties to a sexual source. Halden uses phrases like "natural sexual identity" and "fundamental, natural sexuality" with enviable assurance.

Before turning to *Absalom, Absalom!* mention should be made of the one item to appear on *Pylon*. Hugh M. Ruppersburg's "Image as Structure in Faulkner's *Pylon*" (*SAB* 47:74–87) makes a convincing case for the importance of imagery in the novel; the essay is particularly strong in its discussion of images of language. The five items on *Absalom, Absalom!* are headed by Peter Brooks's "Incredulous Narration: *Absalom, Absalom!*" (*CL* 34:247–68). Brooks uses Roland Barthes and Gérard Genette as points of departure for an examination of the ways in which *Absalom, Absalom!* sums up "the entire nineteenth-century tradition of the novel—particularly its concern with genealogy, authority, and patterns of transmission—while subverting it." Brooks's observations are not startlingly new, but he expresses them with balance and lucidity. Also of value is William J. Schultz's discussion of the creative elements of Mr. Compson's narration in "Just Like Father: Mr. Compson as Cavalier Romancer in *Absalom, Absalom!*" (*KanQ* 14:115–23). The way in which Mr. Compson's storytelling serves his own needs has been studied before, but not so exhaustively. I disagree, though, with Schultz's claim that Mr. Compson emphasizes the love relationship between Charles Bon and Judith Sutpen; such an emphasis would be inconsistent with Mr. Compson's self-indulgent view of Bon as a sophisticate lost among Mississippi yokels.

Two brief studies of *Absalom, Absalom!* appeared in the annual Faulkner number of *Mississippi Quarterly*. The first, Loren F. Schmidtberger's "*Absalom, Absalom!*: What Clytie Knew" (*MissQ* 35:255–63), is another in the long series of attempts to pin down the events of the novel according to the canons of realistic fiction. Unfortunately Schmidtberger's conclusion—that Clytemnestra knew Bon was Judith's half-brother—is no less speculative than Quentin's and Shreve's version of the Sutpen story. The second *Mississippi Quarterly* study, Geraldine E. LaRocque's "*A Tale of Two Cities* and *Absalom, Absalom!*" (*MissQ* 35:301–04), is a modest but convincing study of parallels between the two novels. Finally, in "Faulkner, Naipaul, and Zola: Violence and the Novel" (*The Artist and Political Vision*, pp. 291–315) Peter C. Sederberg uses *Absalom, Absalom!* as a test case for a theory about the social and psychological functions of art. The theory derives largely from Morse Peckham's concept of a rage for disorder; the conclusion reached about *Absalom, Absalom!* is that its formal difficulties provide a salutary preparation for our encounters with the ambiguities of the real world.

The *Unvanquished* is the subject of two brief studies and "Old Man" of one. Beth Burch's "Rosa Millard and the Railroad: A Note on William Faulkner's *The Unvanquished*" (*MSE* 8,ii:1–3) argues that the railroad in the novel symbolizes Rosa Millard's moral state: the rails come to be twisted, and so do Rosa's values. In "William Faulkner's Black Exodus: Multiple Narratives in *The Unvanquished*" (*SCB* 42:144–48) George W. Van Devender retraces a familiar argument in claiming that Faulkner alludes to the imagery and events of the Exodus story in "Raid." Doreen A. Fowler's "Measuring Faulkner's Tall Convict" (*SNNTS* 14:280–84) attempts to recruit the tall convict into the ranks of the supporters of order, responsibility, freedom, and civilization. The level of abstraction at which the argument is pitched makes it difficult either to accept or to oppose.

The last item to be discussed in this section, Bruce F. Kawin's *Faulkner's MGM Screenplays* (Tenn.), is a work of substance and worth. This lengthy book reprints four treatments and three screenplays written by Faulkner during his first tour of duty in Hollywood. (The screenplays are *Today We Live*, *War Birds*, and *Mythical Latin-American Kingdom Story*, a fascinating, though incoherent script that Faulkner evidently wrote on speculation; another screenplay, *Louisiana Lou*, was not released for publication by its owner.) The book also includes a general introduction recounting Faulkner's stay at MGM in considerable detail, analytic introductions to each script, explanatory footnotes, and a bibliography. Though Kawin

acknowledges that the scripts are not great art, he sometimes succumbs to the temptation to interpret them as if they were. This one
caveat to the side, I have only praise for this book. Even those readers
of Faulkner who are reluctant to give much attention to his movie
work—and I count myself among their number—will profit greatly
from Kawin's book.

### vii. Individual Works, 1940–49

The only item on *The Hamlet* to appear in 1982, Dwight Eddins'
"Metahumour in Faulkner's 'Spotted Horses'" (*ArielE* 13,ii:23–31)
begins promisingly with a claim that the "Spotted Horses" section of
*The Hamlet* "represents not only a vintage specimen of humour, but
a profound analysis of the role humour plays in our existence."
Rather than pursue this idea, though, Eddins contents himself with
retelling the story and with analyzing dubious instances of "anti-
humour." The remaining items in this section are all studies of *Go
Down, Moses*. In "Providence and the Structure of *Go Down, Moses*"
(*SoR* 18:495–505) Warren Akin, IV, does a good job of disentangling
the personal, social, and racial strands of Ike McCaslin's view of
history and of showing the limitations of each. Akin bases his argument almost entirely on the discursive content of the fourth section
of "The Bear"; he could have made an even stronger case had he
been more attentive to imagery and symbol. In "Faulkner's Storied
Novel: *Go Down, Moses* and the Translation of Time" (*MFS* 28:
109–27) Ronald Schleifer uses Jacques Lacan, Jacques Derrida, and
their epigones as points of departure for an interpretation of *Go
Down, Moses*. This is a thoughtful study, but it uses the language of
deconstruction while disregarding its metaphysical implications: for
example, Schleifer views Lucas Beauchamp's relation to the past as
an authentic act of recovery, not as an elaboration of desire. Another
attempt to apply contemporary critical methods to *Go Down, Moses*
occurs in John Duvall's "Using Greimas' Narrative Semiotics: Signification in Faulkner's 'The Old People'" (*CollL* 9:192–206). Unfortunately Duvall never really substantiates his claim that using
Greimas' method can provide insights unavailable to an intuitive
reader. The final item in this section, K. J. Phillips' "Waste Land in
Faulkner's *Go Down, Moses*" (*IFR* 9:114–19), is an awkwardly or-

ganized attempt to find evidence of Faulkner's use of the grail legend in *Go Down, Moses*. The parallels Phillips cites are predictable ones: Hubert Beauchamp's silver cup is the grail, and so forth.

### *viii.* Individual Works, 1950–62

Though no truly outstanding work was done on the fiction of this period, two essays appeared that give promise of future achievement. The first, Dinnah Pladott's "Faulkner's *A Fable*: A Heresy or a Declaration of Faith?" (*JNT* 12:73–94), examines the theme of sacrifice in the novel. Pladott distinguishes between "affirmative" and "destructive" instances of sacrifice. Not surprisingly she finds that Faulkner affirms affirmation; where she deviates from expectation, though, is in her willingness to acknowledge the divergences of the novel from its biblical analogues and to question what those divergences mean. Even more promising is Charlotte Renner's "Talking and Writing in Faulkner's Snopes Trilogy" (*SLJ* 15,i:61–73). This sprawling essay has a central idea of real merit, though the reader must work to break it free of a distracting concern with evaluative issues. Renner argues that the Snopes trilogy depicts the shift from an oral to a print culture and that this depiction is linked in intricate ways to the narrative strategy of the three novels. At one point she observes that Faulkner's postwar "concern for the survival of his entire fictional community" fosters "more collaboration than competition among [his] narrators." I wish she had pressed this observation further, for I think she is on the verge of a real insight into the changing character of Faulkner's style.

The remaining items in this section are of less significance. William T. Stafford's "Contractive Expansiveness at the End of *The Mansion*" (*NMAL* 6:Item 16) is an appreciative tribute to Faulkner's mastery of style and technique. In *The Businessman in American Literature* Emily Stipes Watts views Linda Kohl in the context of other postwar depictions of the children of capitalists and concludes that for Faulkner "the children of the rich are not necessarily doomed to corruption or communism." Finally, in "Faulkner's Nobel Prize Address: A Reading" (*SAQ* 81:94–104), Jerry A. Herndon subjects Faulkner's speech to close analysis. Herndon is so predisposed in favor of the humanistic message of the speech as not to have much of interest to say.

### ix. The Stories

Most of the work on the short stories consists of brief explications of individual stories. Two exceptions to this observation are Walter Allen's *The Short Story in English* (Oxford) and Joseph M. Flora's "The Device of Conspicuous Silence in the Modern Short Story" (*The Teller and the Tale*, pp. 27–45). Allen allots eight pages of his magisterial survey to Faulkner. He discusses "The Bear," "Dry September," "A Rose for Emily," and "That Evening Sun" and is duly appreciative of Faulkner's genius, both as a short story writer and as a novelist. Flora's essay is a competent if unspectacular analysis of the device of deliberate silence in a number of modern short stories, including "Dry September" and "That Evening Sun." Flora's suggestion that Faulkner crosses a naturalistic subject matter with a Chekhovian interest in silence deserves further exploration. Also broadly based, but not very illuminating, is Jeffrey J. Folks's "Honor in Faulkner's Short Fiction" (*SoR* 18:506–16). This portentous analysis of "Shingles for the Lord" and "Honor" loads these interesting but minor stories with the whole weight of the conflict between tradition and modernity in Faulkner's fiction.

Five studies of individual stories remain to be discussed. Paula Sunderman's "Speech Act Theory and Faulkner's 'That Evening Sun'" (*Lang&S* 14[1981]:304–14) uses speech act theory in an attempt to determine what conversational exchanges reveal about Faulkner's characters' perceptions of themselves and of each other. So far as I can see, Sunderman's method uncovers little that should not be apparent on a first reading of "That Evening Sun." Frank A. Littler's "The Tangled Thread of Time: Faulkner's 'A Rose for Emily'" (*NMW* 14:80–86) is a study of the attitude of the townspeople of Jefferson toward Emily Grierson. Littler observes that the townspeople envy Emily's resistance to change. The ironic allusions mentioned in the title of John T. Jacobs' "Ironic Allusions in 'A Rose for Emily'" (*NMW* 14:77–79) are to Homer the poet and to "baron." In the course of the six paragraphs of this brief note we are given "climatic" for "climactic," "Illiad" for "Iliad," and "poinsoning" for "poisoning." Finally, both Robert Crosman's "How Readers Make Meaning" (*CollL* 9:207–15) and George L. Dillon's "Styles of Reading" (*PoT* 3:77–88) use reader-response methods in analyzing "A Rose for Emily." Crosman argues for the equal validity of two opposed readings of the story, while Dillon examines several readings in an effort to determine whether they reveal underlying "regularities in performance." Dillon uses phrases like "specialists in story comprehension" and "top-down guidance," and he cites a work entitled *New Directions in Discourse Processing.* New directions indeed!

*University of California, Davis*

# 10. Fitzgerald and Hemingway

### Scott Donaldson

Two significant developments marked the year's work on Fitzgerald and Hemingway. First, most of the important criticism, including Joseph M. Flora's book on the Nick Adams stories and Jackson R. Bryer's collection of articles on Fitzgerald's stories, concentrated on the short fiction rather than the novels. Second, the overall standard of published scholarship was unusually high.

### i. Bibliography, Letters, and Biography

*Hemingway: The Critical Heritage*, ed. Jeffrey Meyers (London: Routledge & Kegan Paul) supplements and expands on Robert O. Stephens' *Ernest Hemingway: The Critical Reception* (1977). Both print reviews of all of Hemingway's books, but where Stephens supplies portions of 12 reviews of *Green Hills of Africa*, for example, Meyers includes four reviews in their entirety, each preceded by a word about the author and followed by annotations. In making his selections Meyers leans toward English (and, at times, Continental) reviewers and toward Hemingway's fellow novelists; his lengthy and thoughtful introduction is enlivened by little-known quotations from James Joyce, Saul Bellow, Norman Mailer, and Ralph Ellison. Meyers also takes reviewers to task on occasion, as in his persuasive defense of *Across the River and Into the Trees*.

Two separate volumes addressed themselves to the question of books Hemingway owned and read. Michael S. Reynolds' *Hemingway's Reading, 1910–1940: An Inventory* (Princeton, 1981) limits its focus to the pre-Cuban period. His fine introduction, dealing with his own unsuccessful quest for a Cuban visa and his discovery of the Oak Park high school reading lists in an attic, makes literary research read like adventure. There are minor differences between Reynolds' approach and that of James D. Brasch and Joseph Sigman in their

thorough and scholarly *Hemingway's Library: A Composite Record*
(Garland, 1981)—Reynolds attempts to ascertain what Hemingway
read, Brasch and Sigman what books he owned—but both consist
basically of a catalogue and a subject index that documents Hemingway's interest in biography and autobiography, military history,
hunting and fishing, and art and poetry. However, Brasch and Sigman draw on the 1966 inventory of the Finca Vigia library by Cuban
authorities to itemize more than three times as many books as does
Reynolds: more than 7,000 in all. In their introduction they make
interesting observations on Hemingway's reading habits, outline their
sources and methods of procedure, and inveigh against biographical
criticism as, presumably, incompatible with textual study.

Yet another major bibliographical resource is the two-volume
*Catalog of the Ernest Hemingway Collection at the John F. Kennedy
Library* (Hall). On more than 1,400 oversized pages, ten items to a
page, are reproduced the cards from the Hemingway collection at
the Kennedy library in Boston. Fewer than half of the manuscripts
noted here were included in Young's and Mann's inventory (1968);
moreover, this catalog lists both outgoing and incoming correspondence and some 3,000 newspaper clippings. Even without an index
these volumes represent a valuable guide to a collection whose use
is virtually obligatory for serious Hemingway scholars.

Hemingway's letters to his sister Sunny, recently made available,
throw light on his six months as a reporter for the *Kansas City Star*
during 1917–18, as Michael Culver's "'The Short-Stop Run': Hemingway in Kansas City" (*HemR* 2,i:77–80) reveals. In addition to
identifying two unsigned articles Hemingway wrote—one on a suicide, one on a fire—the letters disclose that he joined the Missouri
National Guard and straighten out some confusion about where and
with whom he lived. An important Hemingway document written
more than 20 years later appeared in the *Washington Post* for 28 Nov.
1982 (F1,F15). Discovered by William B. Watson, "Humanity Will
Not Forgive This!"—which was published in *Pravda* on 1 August
1938—represents as intensely partisan a statement about the Spanish
Civil War as Hemingway ever made. *Sara & Gerald: Villa America
and After* (New York: Times Books), by Honoria Murphy Donnelly
with Richard N. Billings, depicts Hemingway sympathetically as kind
and tutorial with Honoria; Sara Murphy would not say a word against
him. The material on Fitzgerald is more familiar, less surprising.

## ii. Criticism

*a.* **Full-Length Studies.** *The Short Stories of F. Scott Fitzgerald: New Approaches in Criticism* (Wis.), ed. Jackson R. Bryer, constitutes a significant addition to Fitzgerald studies. Consisting of 22 new articles, a fine introduction by Bryer, and an extremely useful 75-page checklist of criticism on the stories, this book gives the stories the type of attention they deserve. In his introduction Bryer cites the "deplorable absence of worthwhile commentary" and concludes that there have been only about 20 "serious critical essays" on Fitzgerald's stories, fewer on all of Fitzgerald than on Hemingway's "Macomber" and "Snows." The articles in his collection go far toward remedying this neglect. Joseph M. Flora's *Hemingway's Nick Adams* (LSU) considers the Nick stories as a whole. Admirable in its attention to echoes and interconnections and usually keen in interpretation, the book would have been better had the author consulted drafts of the stories.

*b.* **General Essays.** Politics, sport, and sex figure in the essays on Fitzgerald. Ronald J. Gervais' generally authoritative "The Socialist and the Silk Stockings: Fitzgerald's Double Allegiance" (*Mosaic* 15, ii:79–92) elaborates on the divided political loyalties reflected in Fitzgerald's fiction: though Marxism provided an outlet for his idealism, Fitzgerald owed allegiance to the class he came from and tended to "depict lovingly the charm and grace" of the upper class he regarded as doomed. Gervais is particularly insightful in his treatment of "May Day" and *The Last Tycoon*. Dealing at some length with Fitzgerald's well-established interest in Princeton football, Robert J. Higgs in *Laurel and Thorn: The Athlete in American Literature* (Kentucky, 1981) traces the disappearance of the athletic hero in his fiction as Tom Buchanan, the moral antithesis of strength and beauty, replaces the rest of his "clean-living, all-round, upper-class heroes and would-be heroes." In this connection Leverett T. Smith, Jr.'s "Why Tom Buchanan Played End at New Haven" (*AN&Q* 20: 77–79) interestingly demonstrates the particular appropriateness of Tom's position, for it was the ends, swift and powerful, who covered the punts and slammed down the small and graceful Hobey Bakers whom Fitzgerald admired and once hoped to emulate. With curiously convoluted reasoning Lindel Ryan's "F. Scott Fitzgerald and the Battle of the Sexes" (*LiNQ* 8,iii[1980]:84–94) indicts Fitzgerald for insensitivity to the plight of women in a society which values them almost solely for their attractiveness to men, yet draws the evidence to support this argument from statements made by his characters and situations depicted in his fiction.

In her opening survey for the British number of the *Hemingway Review*, "A Change in Emphasis: Hemingway Criticism in Britain over the Last Twenty-Five Years" (*HemR* 1,ii:2–19), Moira Monteith discusses the comments of Richard Hoggart, D. S. R. Welland, Tony Tanner, Malcolm Bradbury, and David Lodge. She detects an ameliorative tone in the reviews of Hemingway's *Selected Letters* which may signal a hiatus to "dumb ox" interpretations and disparagements of the author as maker of his own myth. Graham Clarke's "Hemingway in England: Bibliography" (*HemR* 1,ii:76–84) is a checklist designed to provide a "map" of British response to Hemingway's writing. Andrew Gibson considers the opposite side of the question in his comprehensive and well-reasoned "Hemingway on the British" (*HemR* 1,ii:62–75) and decides that his attitudes toward the British were basically ambiguous. He admired the British for their coolness of behavior and reticence of language, yet at the same time suspected that their decorum concealed superciliousness and an unwillingness to confront reality.

With the assistance of documents not previously consulted, like Fitzgerald's critique of "Fifty Grand" and Perkins' attempts to get the aborted beginning of *The Sun Also Rises* restored, Scott Donaldson's "The Wooing of Ernest Hemingway" (*AL* 53:691–710) details the process by which Hemingway was enticed into the Scribner camp. According to Ann Edwards Boutelle's interesting psychological interpretation in "Hemingway and 'Papa': Killing of the Father in the Nick Adams Fiction" (*JML* 9:133–46), the "combination of lucidity and elusiveness" in the Nick stories suggests something unnamed and unapproachable at the center. That something, she believes, is the ritual killing of the father. In "Fathers and Sons" Nick sits in the woodshed contemplating patricide. Moreover, Hemingway consistently associates Doctor Adams with Indians, and in "Indian Camp" and "Ten Indians" a dead Indian stands in for the undisposed-of father. Boutelle miscounts by a decade in stating that Hemingway was 39 when his father committed suicide. Jeffrey Walsh takes up more overt warfare in "Emblematical War: Representation of Combat in Hemingway's Fiction" (*HemR* 1,ii:45–57). Walsh's overlong article concludes sensibly that Hemingway aimed to de-glamorize war in his writing; less convincing are additional assertions such as that *For Whom the Bell Tolls* "is founded upon the notion of litera-ture as the signification of working class struggle."

Two first-rate essays deal with technique. Mark Wilson's percep-tive "Ernest Hemingway as Funnyman" (*Thalia* 3,i[1980]:29–34) isolates a "consistent strain of humor" in Hemingway and concen-trates on the use of two devices—the deadpan narrator and the con-trast of rhetorics—characteristic of his humor and that of the Old Southwest (and Mark Twain) from which he undoubtedly learned. Stephen R. Portch's "The Hemingway Touch" (*HemR* 2,i:43–47) breaks important ground in exploring Hemingway's "superb use of the non-verbal," and particularly of awkward extended silence, in "Hills Like White Elephants" and "The Killers."

*c.* **Essays on Specific Works: Fitzgerald.** The best of the scholar-ship concerned the stories and, in one notable case, an essay. Bryer's collection alone includes ten general studies or "overviews" as well as a dozen articles concerned with individual stories. Among the overviews Richard Lehan's sweeping "The Romantic Self and the Uses of Place in the Stories of F. Scott Fitzgerald" (*Stories*, pp. 3–21) illuminates the connections between the stories and novels; Lehan regards "The Swimmers," for example, as a transition piece between the still romantic *Gatsby* and the disillusioned *Tender*. That story, according to Melvin J. Friedman's " 'The Swimmers': Paris and Vir-ginia Reconciled" (*Stories*, pp. 251–60), belongs to a transatlantic literary sequence, contrasting Paris and Virginia, that "starts with Edgar Allan Poe and carries to Yves Berger and William Styron."

Scott Donaldson's "Money and Marriage in Fitzgerald's Stories" (*Stories*, pp. 75–88) traces the theme of love and money (whose symbiotic relationship has often been considered in the novels) through a number of stories, including such usually overlooked ones as "Presumption" and "A Snobbish Story." C. Hugh Holman's "Fitz-gerald's Changes on the Southern Belle: The Tarleton Trilogy" (*Stories*, pp. 53–64) is an illuminating cultural study of the southern belle and of Fitzgerald's three belles from Tarleton (Montgomery) who simultaneously embodied the tradition and sought indepen-dence from it. John Kuehl's well-written "Psychic Geography in 'The

Ice Palace' " (*Stories*, pp. 169–79) asserts what is tacit in Holman: that the most crucial geographical distinction in Fitzgerald is that between North and South. In "The Ice Palace" reincarnation and a romantic past seem far preferable to "preservation through refrigeration" in a frozen labyrinth.

A thoughtful essay which treats a previously neglected subject, Lawrence Buell's "The Significance of Fantasy in Fitzgerald's Short Fiction" (*Stories*, pp. 23–38) classifies five "main forms" of fantasy in his work—among them the combination of the fantastic and the ironic in "The Diamond as Big as the Ritz." Joseph Mancini, Jr., addresses another important subject in "To Be Both Light and Dark: the Jungian Process of Individuation in Fitzgerald's Basil Duke Lee Stories" (*Stories*, pp. 89–110). Mancini argues—sometimes at excessive length—that in depicting Basil's coming of age Fitzgerald rendered a "psychology of youth" similar to Jung's, but disconcertingly takes evidence where he finds it in the Basil stories without identifying its context or the particular story involved.

Two excellent articles consider Fitzgerald's short fiction of the 1930s. Sprinkled with sharp evaluative commentary, Ruth Prigozy's "Fitzgerald's Short Stories and the Depression: An Artistic Crisis" (*Stories*, pp. 111–26) outlines a number of themes in his work during 1929–35, including the deterioration of marriage, the loss of character, the erosion of old values, and the effects of social class on individuals. Kenneth E. Eble's "Touches of Disaster: Alcoholism and Mental Illness in Fitzgerald's Short Stories" (*Stories*, pp. 39–52) goes beyond "Babylon Revisited" to the considerable number of stories that center on alcoholism and mental illness. Both diseases have a similar effect on Fitzgerald's characters, Eble observes: they "rob their victims of purposeful vitality, let loose the chaotic violence that flows beneath, and nullify the rational processes by which the sober and sane maintain control."

Alan Margolies' " 'Kissing, Shooting, and Sacrificing': F. Scott Fitzgerald and the Hollywood Market" (*Stories*, pp. 65–73) and Robert A. Martin's "Hollywood in Fitzgerald: After Paradise" (*Stories*, pp. 127–48) take up the writer's relationship with the movies. Margolies provides an exceedingly knowledgeable review of Fitzgerald's sometimes successful attempts, in the first half-decade of his professional life, to sell his stories to Hollywood. "Dice, Brass Knuckles & Guitar," for example, "blatantly reflected the hoped-for Holly-

wood sale." Martin conclusively demonstrates how financially dependent Fitzgerald was on Hollywood throughout his career, and
not only during the last three and a half years. According to Martin,
"Jacob's Ladder" and "Magnetism" "form the nucleus of Fitzgerald's
entire Hollywood theme." Three times he quotes the author's hunch,
in *The Crack-Up*, that "the talkies would make even the best selling
novelist as archaic as silent pictures." Benefiting from correspondence
with Arnold Gingrich, James L. W. West, III's first-rate "Fitzgerald
and *Esquire*" (*Stories*, pp. 149–66) contends that his association with
the magazine, where his work appeared 45 times between 1934 and
1941, gave him a necessary outlet for essays and short fiction as his
long connection with the *Saturday Evening Post* was coming to an
end. West also insightfully analyzes "Three Acts of Music" and "The
Lost Decade," two short, elliptical pieces Fitzgerald wrote for *Esquire*.

A good general essay on the stories not included in Bryer's collection, William J. Brondell's closely reasoned "Structural Metaphors in
Fitzgerald's Short Fiction" (*KanQ* 14,ii:95–112) examines three of
Fitzgerald's "five-act" stories which successfully blend form and substance: "Absolution," "The Freshest Boy," and "Babylon Revisited."
In each, Brondell finds, a superstructure carries the central action of
the plot, while a deep structure reflects the protagonist's psychological condition as he responds to the action.

One of the major virtues of James W. Tuttleton's admirable "Seeing Slightly Red: Fitzgerald's 'May Day'" (*Stories*, pp. 181–97) is its
insistence that the author's politics are to be taken seriously in studying his fiction. Another is its meticulous reading of this early story,
which "combines with uncommon adroitness the social and the psychological, the public and private tensions of Fitzgerald the man
and the historical moment." Tuttleton provides useful background
on the historical moment with an account of what actually happened
in Manhattan on May Day, 1919. In an unusually important essay,
"'No Americans Have Any Imagination': 'Rags Martin-Jones and
the Pr-nce of W-les'" (*Stories*, pp. 217–25) Victor Doyno brilliantly
shows how this slight story rewards a variety of critical approaches:
"Stylistic, folkloristic, thematic, structural, genetic, and contextual."
Perhaps most valuable is the genetic method wherein Doyno illustrates how Fitzgerald improved the story in revision.

Carlos Baker's graceful "When the Story Ends: 'Babylon Revisited'" (*Stories*, pp. 269–77) brings fresh insight to bear on this story by revealing its "double theme of freedom and imprisonment." Despite an occasionally donnish tone, Sheldon Grebstein contributes a very skillful explication in "The Sane Method of 'Crazy Sunday'" (*Stories*, pp. 279–89). Peter Wolfe's "Faces in a Dream: Innocence Perpetuated in 'The Rich Boy'" (*Stories*, pp. 241–49) characterizes Anson Hunter as an emotional infant who resists change and growth while the world around him develops. Rather controversially, Wolfe contends that Fitzgerald's narrator stays neutral and does not insist on a "concluding judgment" against Hunter's immaturity. Irving Malin's "'Absolution': Absolving Lies" (*Stories*, pp. 209–16) usefully points out that all three principals—Rudolph, his father, and Father Schwartz—are suffering from severe mental unbalance. This story, Malin believes, "demonstrates clearly that [Fitzgerald] is a religious writer." Neil D. Isaacs' "'Winter Dreams' and Summer Sports" (*Stories*, pp. 199–207) declares unpersuasively that the continuing appeal of this story derives in good part from its sport-mindedness.

Although she detects some confusion in Doctor Moon's double role as symbol and moralist, Christiane Johnson concludes in "Freedom, Contingency, and Ethics in 'The Adjuster'" (*Stories*, pp. 227–40) that this story occupies an important place in the Fitzgerald canon, since it bodied forth for the first time the ideal of the mature, responsible woman. James J. Martine's interesting "Rich Boys and Rich Men: 'The Bridal Party'" (*Stories*, pp. 261–68) contrasts the way male figures respond to blackmail in "The Bridal Party," "Magnetism," and "May Day." In Fitzgerald's fiction, he determines, it is not money but character, and not a romantic but a pragmatic world view, that makes the man. George Monteiro unearths a biographical subtext in "Two Sets of Books, One Balance Sheet: 'Financing Finnegan'" (*Stories*, pp. 291–99). According to Monteiro's argument Fitzgerald was "setting Hemingway up as his own scapegoat" in this story, partially in response to the crack about "poor Scott" in "The Snows of Kilimanjaro." Finally, Stephen L. Tanner's insightful "Fitzgerald's Lost City" (*BRMMLA* 35[1981]:55–62) discloses how Fitzgerald used the techniques of fiction in one of his finest essays. "My Lost City" expresses the essence of his dual artistic vision: the contrast between what Tanner calls the "Romantic Promise" and a "Diminished Thing."

Of the seven articles on Fitzgerald's novels the two most important are on *Gatsby.* In "Fitzgerald, Perkins, and *The Great Gatsby*" (*JNT* 12:210–20) Carla Mulford makes a convincing case that the "biography" of Gatsby—the Dan Cody story which Fitzgerald moved forward from the eighth to the sixth chapter of the novel at Perkins' behest—might better have been left where it stood in the uncorrected galleys. Use of this material later in the novel allows additional time to establish Gatsby's legendary stature, underscores his innocence, and strengthens the implications of Nick's final peroration. Richard Godden's challenging "*The Great Gatsby*: Glamour on the Turn" (*JAmS* 16:343–71) reads the novel in the light of Lukács, Veblen, Brecht, Raymond Williams, and Karl Marx, as a socioeconomic parable. Sometimes Godden oversimplifies, as in observing that "Gatsby loves Daisy because she is his point of access to a dominant class." Solely? But his article is often illuminating, and it offers fresh interpretations of the two principal figures. For example, Godden attributes the more telling gaffes of Gatsby (or Jay Gatz, as he persistently misnames him) to two causes. The first is Brechtian: they prevent the reader/spectator from fully identifying with the character; second, Gatsby presents himself as a commodity (the shirts) since he recognizes that, in the world he inhabits, desire is often "commodified." Nick romanticizes Gatsby despite these lapses largely as a way of avoiding self-knowledge of his "distaste for the human and for himself." This essay is not the first to offer a Marxist interpretation of the novel, but it is the most sophisticated so far. Another article with a revisionary approach, Duane Edwards' "Who Killed Myrtle Wilson? A Study of *The Great Gatsby*" (*BSUF* 23,i:35–41) advances the improbable thesis that Gatsby was lying when he acknowledged that Daisy was driving the "death car." As Edwards points out, certain details support this radical reading. But for Gatsby (who lied shamefully about his origins) to lie *in order to accuse Daisy falsely* involves him in a cynicism that violates the logic of the novel.

Joan Kirkby's "Spengler and Apocalyptic Typology in F. Scott Fitzgerald's *Tender Is the Night*" (*SoRA* 12[1979]:246–61) significantly observes that each of Fitzgerald's novels is "characterized by an end of time feeling" and that, in each, personal crises mirror larger historical crises. In *Tender* the apocalyptic hints of the other novels are fully developed: the last days are underway. This novel (like *Tycoon,* though Kirkby doesn't say so) was undoubtedly influenced by the dark vision of Oswald Spengler, Fitzgerald's philosopher-guide. John M. Howell's "Dr. Tom Rennie and *Tender Is the Night*" (*ICarbS* 4[1981]:111–15) suggests that the young, handsome, and charming Dr. Rennie, one of the psychiatrists who treated Zelda in Baltimore, may both have served as a partial model for Dr. Diver and have taught Fitzgerald something about psychiatry. This suggestion may well warrant further research.

The most telling conclusion of Lloyd Michaels' "Auteurism, Creativity, Entropy in *The Last Tycoon*" (*LFQ* 10:110–18), a study of the Hollywood version of *Tycoon*, is that the film-makers tried and failed to solve one problem Fitzgerald had yet to work out in his draft of the novel: "How to link Stahr's infatuation with Kathleen Moore . . . to the political intrigues within the studio that eventually were to bring about his demise." Following a reprise of familiar material Edward J. Piacentino's note on "The Illusory Effects of Cynthian Light: Monroe Stahr and the Moon in *The Last Tycoon*" (*AN&Q* 20[1981]:12–16) discusses the use of moon imagery to "emphasize the magic, the fantasy, and above all the mystique that invades Stahr's dreams." No mention is made of the moon-person in Fitzgerald's 1925 novel.

Several notes and articles are devoted to influence studies, in both directions. After a useful review of what Geismar, Miller, and Piper have had to say about connections between the two writers, Tom Quirk in "Fitzgerald and Cather: *The Great Gatsby*" (*AL* 54:576–91) asserts on circumstantial grounds that *Alexander's Bridge* and "Paul's Case," instead of *My Ántonia* and *A Lost Lady*, exerted "the most suggestive influence" on Fitzgerald. An article longer than its content requires, Olatubosun Ogunsanwo's "George Meredith and F. Scott Fitzgerald: Literary Affinities: Narrative Indirectness and Realism" (*Neohelicon* 8,ii[1981]:191–216) finds that *Gatsby* and Meredith's *One of Our Conquerors* both employ introspective narrators who achieve sympathetic understanding without becoming sentimental. Elsa Nettels' "Howells's 'A Circle in the Water' and Fitzgerald's 'Babylon Revisited'" (*SSF* 19:261–67) is a first-rate comparative study that notes a "striking resemblance" in plot, situation, and character between the two stories. Instead of insisting on immediate influence, Nettels stresses a crucial difference in attitude between the two writers. In Howells "pain and failure are balanced by the promise of happiness," while "nothing compensates" Fitzgerald's characters "for the loss of youth and fortune."

Two articles see Fitzgerald as influencing Pynchon and Brautigan, respectively. Charles Baxter's persuasive "De-Faced America: *The Great Gatsby* and *The Crying of Lot 49*" (*PNotes* 7[1981]:22–37) regards *Gatsby* as a forerunner of Pynchon's novel, for in the first the "disparity between past ideals and present actuality" leads to a situation, in *Lot 49*, where "history has literally become unreadable." Lonnie L. Willis' "Brautigan's *The Hawkline Monster*: As Big as the Ritz" (*Crit* 23,ii:37–47) maintains that Brautigan's 1974 novel shares with "Diamond" "not only a sense of futility but also more than a few similarities in organization and theme"; moreover, both works resemble Twain's *The Gilded Age* and its mountain full of coal.

Three separate pieces, two by Linda Wagner, concern Zelda Fitzgerald. Wagner's "*Save Me the Waltz*: An Assessment in Craft" (*JNT* 12:201–9) makes a powerful case for the artistry of this novel, Fitzgerald's literary declaration of independence. The "ornamental" and "rococo" rhetoric at the beginning of *Save Me the Waltz*, Wagner observes, appropriately reflects the adolescent flightiness of the protagonist, while the language turns somber and spare as her father dies and she becomes ill. The result is "an ironic fiction which paints the dispirited modern woman as vividly as Eliot's *The Waste Land* did the modern temper." In "A Note on Zelda Fitzgerald's *Scandalabra*" (*NConL* 12:4–5) Wagner comments that in her apparently lighthearted play (written after *Waltz*) Fitzgerald was once again exploring the kind of marital infidelity that embittered the heroine of her novel. William H. Epstein's "Milford's *Zelda* and the Poetics of New Feminist Biography" (*GaR* 36:335–50) characterizes the book as a tragedy of isolation, suppression, and madness. *Zelda* constitutes one of the first examples of a "new subgenre" of biography that involves rewriting the lives of women according to feminist perspectives.

*d.* **Essays on Specific Works: Hemingway.**   As with Fitzgerald most of the principal contributions concentrated on the stories rather than the novels. Michael Stubbs's overly methodological "Stir Until the Plot Thickens" in *Literary Text and Language Study* (London: Arnold, pp. 56–81), ed. Ronald Carter and Deirdre Burton, builds upon David Lodge's approach to "Cat in the Rain" (1981) by analyzing capsule plot summaries of the story. These summaries underline Hemingway's use of apparent ambiguity, mixed with strong implication, at the end of his stories. Keith Carabine's original and important " 'Big Two-Hearted River': A Re-interpretation" (*HemR* 1,ii:39–44) disputes the Cowley-Young-Benson view of the story as a "nightmare at noonday," instead emphasizing "the existential pleasure" Nick earns from control of his sensations. The story represents "one of the best accounts of euphoria in the language," Carabine states. Robert P. Weeks's critically sensitive "Wise-Guy Narrator and Trickster Out-Tricked in Hemingway's 'Fifty Grand' " (*SAF* 10:83–91) stresses the comic elements in the story, which depend upon use of a reliable if limited first-person narrator other than the protagonist, exactly the situation in "A Matter of Colour" (which Hemingway wrote in high school) and in Twain's jumping-frog story.

Working in close touch with the author's revisions in manuscript, Kenneth G. Johnston's " 'Hills Like White Elephants': Lean, Vintage Hemingway" (*SAF* 10:233–38) does the best job yet of illustrating the accomplishment of this beautifully articulated story. Johnston's " 'The Three-Day Blow': Tragicomic Aftermath of a Summer Romance" (*HemR* 2,i:21–25) sniffs down every clue—to *The Ordeal of Richard Feverel* and *The Forest Lovers* and the Black Sox scandal, for example—in assessing this bittersweet tale of Nick Adams' education. Unsurprisingly, two articles belabor the waiters' dialogue in "A Clean, Well-Lighted Place." David Kerner's well-researched "The Manuscripts Establishing Hemingway's Anti-Metronomic Dialogue" (*AL* 54:385–96) elaborates on his earlier argument (1979) that Hemingway knew what he was doing when he wrote the dialogue by citing a number of other examples, in manuscript, of his assigning two consecutive indented speeches to the same character. C. Harold Hurley's "The Manuscript and the Dialogue of 'A Clean, Well-Lighted Place': A Response to Warren Bennett" (*HemR* 2,i:17–20) disputes Bennett's assertion (1979) that the callous "What does it matter if [the soldier who's picked up a girl] gets what he's after?" should be attributed to the older waiter. For further developments watch this space.

Using "Macomber" as a text, Robert J. Bresnahan's enlightening "Ernest Hemingway: A Reader's Perspective" (*MidAmerica* 8[1981]: 22–35) demonstrates how the iceberg technique fits into Wolfgang Iser's reader aesthetics. Confronted with gaps in the text and with multiple perspectives, the reader adopts expectations that must continually be altered as further information is supplied. In "Margot

Macomber's Gimlet" (*CollL* 8,i[1981]:12–20) Bert Bender acknowledges that sexist values are "embedded in the story from beginning to end" but contends, convincingly, that this does not justify interpreting the story to exonerate Mrs. Macomber. Three notes suggest two different models for the character of Francis Macomber. Bruce Morton's "Hemingway's 'The Short Happy Life of Francis Macomber'" (*Expl* 41,i:48–49) regards the story's publication in the wake of *The Crack-Up* articles as evidence that Macomber was modeled on Fitzgerald. Expanding on this view in "Macomber and Fitzgerald: Hemingway Gets Even in 'The Short Happy Life of Francis Macomber'" (*ZAA* 30:157–60), Morton finds "a compelling accumulation of textual and circumstantial evidence" that Hemingway "was drawing a bead on Fitzgerald." The argument is provocative if not entirely convincing. Arthur Coleman's unusual "Francis Macomber and Sir Gawain" (*AN&Q* 19[1981]:70) casts its eye further back for an avatar. Hemingway's story, Coleman maintains, is "a twentieth-century rendition of a theme and situation" dramatized in *Sir Gawain and the Green Knight*. The common archetypal theme is "the ceremonial conquest of fear" by way of the knightly (or Hemingwayesque) code.

In *Expl*, in two adjoining notes bearing the same title, "Hemingway's 'Soldier's Home,'" both George Monteiro (40,i:50–51) and John D. Boyd (40,i:51–53) catch the irony invalidating Horace P. Jones's view (1979) that Hemingway erred in saying that Krebs returned home "years" (instead of merely months) after the war was over. A second "error" Jones mentioned—calling Krebs a "soldier" though he served in the Marines—Boyd also attributes, rather less successfully, to the author's irony. The question of possible errata is also at issue in Kenneth G. Johnston's "Nick/Mike Adams? The Hero's Name in 'Cross-Country Snow'" (*AN&Q* 20:16–18). On the basis of his study of the manuscripts Johnston concludes with good reason that *Nick* Adams was originally to be called *Mike*; then, despite this evidence, he insists that Hemingway intended the confusion of the two names in "Cross-Country Snow."

Three other notes complete the scholarship on the stories. Charles Stetler and Gerald Locklin's brief "Beneath the Tip of the Iceberg in Hemingway's 'The Mother of a Queen'" (*HemR* 2,ii:68–69) asserts that the rather bitchy narrator of the story plays the role of surrogate mother to the homosexual bullfighter. According to Gary D.

Elliott's "Hemingway's 'The Light of the World' " (*Expl* 40,i[1981]: 48–50), the title refers to Nick's difficulty in casting light on the dark world he encounters. Alice Hall Petry in "Hemingway's 'The Light of the World' " (*Expl* 40,iii:46) refers to the *Dictionary of American Slang* as authority that "C. and M." stand for "Cocaine and Morphine."

Among articles on Hemingway's novels James Hinkle's engaging "Some Unexpected Sources for *The Sun Also Rises*" (*HemR* 2,i:26–42) locates some 60 passages from largely unexpected sources that are echoed in the novel and so confirms the author's wide and eclectic reading. Hemingway sounds most of these echoes (to George Ade, Ernest Boyd, Eleanor Clarage, Homer Croy, and Robert L. Duffus, to name a few) in "the tone of a pleasantly mocking salute." Besides demolishing various myths about Hemingway's service during World War I, Robert W. Lewis' knowledgeable "Hemingway in Italy: Making It Up" (*JML* 9:209–36) establishes G. M. Trevelyan's *Scenes from Italy's Wars* as a vade mecum for *A Farewell to Arms*. But the basic point of Lewis' article is that Hemingway blends and transforms all his sources, including those derived from personal experience, talk, and reading, into an end-product that reaches beyond journalism to art. Paul Smith's "Almost All is Vanity: A Note on Nine Rejected Titles for *A Farewell to Arms*" (*HemR* 2,i:74–76) usefully adds to the list of tentative titles Hemingway considered for his novel nine from *Ecclesiastes*, whence came *The Sun Also Rises*.

Four articles, all of high quality, consider Hemingway works rarely examined. Daniel R. Barnes's "Traditional Narrative Sources for Hemingway's *The Torrents of Spring*" (*SSF* 19:141–50) documents use of two folk legends—the dead woman who disappears overnight and the man who unwittingly performs in a sexual exhibition—in *Torrents* and suggests that the author was satirizing more than Anderson's *Dark Laughter* in that book. Allen Josephs' authoritative "*Death in the Afternoon*: A Reconsideration" (*HemR* 2,i:2–16) regards *Death* as "One of the most original books in American literature" and essential to understanding the rest of Hemingway's writing. Hemingway's exaltation of *toreo*, Josephs believes, amounted to "embracing an ancient mystery" and "rejecting much of what passed for modern Western values." Josephs' contention gains support from Arthur Coleman's "Hemingway's *The Spanish Earth*" (*HemR* 2,i:64–67), the first careful reading of Hemingway's narration for the 1938 documentary film. Hemingway does not condemn political tyranny therein, Coleman points out, but instead laments the war's threat to the traditional Spanish way of life. Finally, Gerry Brenner's extremely important "Are We Going to Hemingway's *Feast?*" (*AL* 54:528–44) establishes that Mary Hemingway and/or L. H. Brague of Scribner's substantially altered the text of *A Moveable Feast* prior to its publication in 1964. According to Brenner, Hemingway's public image has suffered from these additions, subtractions, and rearrangements. Particularly affected is the ending, where he emerges as both more sentimental and more cruelly judgmental than in typescript. Hemingway apparently intended, for instance, to "exclude from his book all the material about the 'pilot fish' and the rich," to assume himself the full burden of guilt for leaving Hadley, and to absolve her of any complicity in the breakup.

Adopting a comparative approach in "The Champion and the Challenger: Hemingway and O'Hara" (*JOHJ* 3,i–ii[1980]:22–30), Carlos Baker demonstrates the competitive nature of the correspondence between the two writers, comments on O'Hara's unsuccessful attempt to strike an appropriate note of camaraderie, and concludes that, alike though they may have been in family background and education, the two were vastly different as writers. Baker illustrates the point by contrasting the quietly moving "Fathers and Sons" with O'Hara's sociologically oriented "The Doctor's Son." Five other pieces reported on similarities rather than distinctions. Robert E. Gadjusek's extensive "Dubliners in Michigan: Joyce's Presence in *In Our Time*" (*HemR* 2,i:48–61) claims "close and deliberate parallelisms" between *Dubliners* and *In Our Time*; these probably stem, he suggests, from shared attitudes about the condition of the world and a common awareness of psychic dualisms. Charles Harmon Cagle's " 'Cezanne Nearly Did': Stein, Cézanne, and Hemingway" (*MQ* 23:268–78) presents a readable though hardly original review of what others have said on this subject.

One study points to Hemingway's influence on Salinger, another to Salinger's influence on Hemingway. Cynthia M. Barron's "The Catcher and the Soldier: Hemingway's 'Soldier's Home' and Salinger's *The Catcher in the Rye*" (*HemR* 2,i:70–73) asserts that Hemingway's story exerted substantial influence on Salinger's novel. In both works male protagonists seek "a return to the realm of childhood"; in both childhood is exemplified by an innocent younger sister and children's games. Sandra W. Spanier's "Hemingway's 'The Last Good Country' and *The Catcher in the Rye*: More Than a Family Resemblance" (*SSF* 19:35–44) mentions these and other parallels to propose that Hemingway's story/novel-in-progress, written after 1952, was influenced by *Catcher*. Spanier then extravagantly proposes that Hemingway dropped "The Last Good Country" when he sensed that "it was not new or real or even truly his own." The best of the influence studies, William Rodney Allen's "All the Names of Death: Walker Percy and Hemingway" (*MissQ* 36:3–19), designates Hemingway as the "American writer who seems to haunt Percy." Hemingway or his characters appear in disguise in each of Percy's five novels, Allen shows. Moreover, both writers are preoccupied with suicide as a theme; but where Hemingway seems to advocate stoicism as a reaction to a troubled existence, in Percy's fiction a stoical stance leads only to despair.

**e. Dissertations.** There were three dissertations, all with promising titles and abstracts, on Fitzgerald. For the first time in many years, no single dissertation dealt exclusively with Hemingway, though his work is considered jointly with others' in two cases.

As a valediction I propose that those of us who write and teach about Hemingway and Fitzgerald clasp hands and vow never to utter "macho" or "Jazz Age."

*College of William and Mary*

*Part II*

# 11. Literature to 1800

*William J. Scheick*

In 1906 Arthur Symons wrote, "Criticism is properly the rod of divination: a hazel switch for the discovery of buried treasure, not a birch rod for the castigation of offenders." Symons' observation emphasizes the value of the critic; it also implies the critic's responsibility to unearth *treasures*. This year many obscure and forgettable early American writings were disinterred, and one can only wonder in what sense they are treasures except to their editors, who kept busy at something to swell their list of publications. Occasionally critics disclosed some hidden riches in writings by Edward Taylor, Charles Brockden Brown, and some Early National authors; but on the whole critical divination was absent not only in the printing of early American writings of little or no merit but also in the uninspired proliferation of surveys, plot summaries, biographical reviews, self-evident thematic readings, and rehearsals of well-worn arguments. The scholarship for this year calls to mind James McNeill Whistler's angry remark: "Two and two continue to make four, in spite of the whine of the amateur for three, or the cry of the critic for five."

## i. Puritan Poetry

In "Anne Bradstreet and Her Children" (*Regulated Children*, pp. 10–23) Ross W. Beales concludes that Bradstreet responded to her children ambivalently, though she appreciated their complexity, tolerated their moods, and respected their individual personalities. Concerning Bradstreet's verse, Eileen Margerum argues in "Anne Bradstreet's Public Poetry and the Tradition of Humility" (*EAL* 17:152–60) that the poet was not in the least ambivalent; her self-deprecating apologies are merely conventional poetic formulae disguising her self-assurance as an author. A. Owen Aldridge (*Early American Literature*, pp. 25–52) pursues a similar line of thought by comparing the verse of Bradstreet and that of a Mexican poet to reveal their mutual Renaissance interest in structural complexity and in the theme of the grandeur of the universe. An inaccurate and "modernized" edition of Bradstreet's writings is accompanied by a banal introduction in Adelaide P. Amore's *A Woman's Inner World: Selected Poetry and Prose of Anne Bradstreet* (Univ. Press), a book which ought not to have been published.

Edward Taylor, who owned an edition of Bradstreet's poems, worked within conventions too. In fact, in "Reading Taylor Exegetically: The *Preparatory Meditations* and the Commentary Tradition" (*TSLL* 24:347–71) Jeffrey A. Hammond convincingly contends that Taylor is often less original in his poetic associations than we have suspected; the apparent random shifts from image to image in his verse (e.g., "Meditation 2.25" and "Meditation 2.149") tend to evince an underlying unity derived from the exegetical traditions of his time. The tradition of the baroque manner concerns A. Owen Aldridge (*Early American Literature*, pp. 53–87), who too simply compares Taylor's work to that of Spanish and Italian contemporaries to demonstrate not only a mutual fascination with the evocation of wonder through language but also (unconvincingly) the absence in Taylor's verse of any special connection between words and metaphysics. The tradition of number symbolism interests Ursula Brumm, who in " 'Tuning' the Song of Praise: Observations on the Use of Numbers in Edward Taylor's *Preparatory Meditations*" (*EAL* 17: 103–18) reaches for the uncertain conclusion that Taylor used stanzas of six ten-syllabic lines and controlled word frequency in stanzas and total word count in poems to express his meaning. Like Hammond and Brumm, Anthony Damico perceives order rather than randomness in Taylor's technique; in "The Conceit of Dyeing in Edward Taylor's *Preparatory Meditations*, Second Series, Number One" (*EAL* 17:227–38) Damico discusses well Taylor's use of the image of a scarlet dye as a metaphor conveying how a type (the shellfish source of the dye) is superseded by its antitype (Christ's saving blood), so that by substitutional atonement the Savior's dying dyes souls.

Christ's and his own death were on Taylor's mind in a special way during his last 12 years of life, when in his verse he focused on Canticles. Taylor's fascination with the Canticles allegory during his last years, Jeffrey A. Hammond argues in "A Puritan *Ars Moriendi*: Edward Taylor's Late Meditations on the Song of Songs" (*EAL*

17:191–214), provided the poet with comfort against the approach of death and became, in a sense, a rehearsal for singing the song of the Bride. The strengths of this reasonable reading notwithstanding, Hammond perhaps goes too far by claiming that Taylor unequivocally (and presumptuously?) considered himself one of those to whom Canticles applied. Taylor's Canticle poems also interest David H. Watters, whose *"With Bodilie Eyes": Eschatological Themes in Puritan Literature and Gravestone Art* (Ann Arbor, Mich.: UMI Research Press, 1981) discusses how in the poet's later poems the traditional symbols of death (e.g., the hourglass and the skull) are transformed into symbols of life and how the poet's eschatological vision of personal perfection yielded metaphors forced to the very edge of the distinction between the literal and the figurative.

Watters also gives a superb reading of Samuel Torrey's epitaph for William Thompson. And Leo M. Kaiser has published "A Census of American Latin Verse, 1625–1825" (*PAAS* 91:197–299), a chronological list with indexes of first lines and authors.

### ii. Puritan Prose

Watter's study also discusses Taylor's friend Increase Mather, who reconciled a premillennial theology emphasizing a disjunction of heaven and earth with an eschatological system emphasizing the spiritual union of the saints on earth and in heaven. Watters argues well that, like Taylor, Mather transformed images of death into images of personal triumph.

Increase's father is the subject of B. R. Burg's *Richard Mather* (TUSAS 429), a book which not only utterly fails in its expressed goal to discuss the literary features of Mather's writings but which is dishonest in pretending to be anything other than an embarrassing duplication of Burg's earlier study (see *ALS 1976*, pp. 175–76). Increase's father-in-law receives careful attention in Edward H. Davidson's "John Cotton's Biblical Exegesis: Method and Purpose" (*EAL* 17:119–38), which discloses that in biblical exegesis Cotton and other first-generation divines were not limited to the Ramist system; ministers often used the syllogism with an implacable consistency signifying the complete subservience of personal and social matters to the divine ways literally set forth in the Bible. A letter by Cotton, explains Slayden Yarbrough in "The Influence of Plymouth

Colony Separatism on Salem: An Interpretation of John Cotton's
Letter of 1630 to Samuel Skelton" (*Church History* 51:291–303),
reveals that (contrary to Perry Miller's opinion) separatist Plymouth
colony was the source and model of the New England practice of
congregational polity.

John Cotton's grandson wrote extensively about familial polity.
Although not punitive in discipline or insensitive to the special needs
of his children, Cotton Mather experienced difficulty in respecting
their autonomy and in achieving emotional distance from them (N.
Ray Hiner, "Cotton Mather and His Children: The Evolution of a
Parent Educator, 1686–1728," (*Regulated Children*, pp. 24–43).
Mather's perception of the autonomy of a religiously nonconforming
people of pure belief figures in Ursula Brumm's "'What Went You
Out Into the Wilderness to See?': Nonconformity and Wilderness in
Cotton Mather's *Magnalia Christi Americana*" (*Prospects* 6[1981]:
1–15). Brumm notes that although the literal wilderness was de-
stroyed in the making of history, the idea of it remained as a meta-
phor for later Puritans. A brief Latin poem (c. 1704) sent to Mather
by an unidentified eminent person is translated and annotated by
Leo M. Kaiser in "An Addendum to Jantz from Cotton Mather's
*Paterna*" (*NEQ* 55:110–12).

An outspoken opponent of the Mathers is the subject of "Solomon
Stoddard and the Process of Conversion" (*EAL* 17:215–26), in which
Michael Schuldiner suggests that behind Stoddard's later doctrine of
open admission to the Lord's Supper is the belief that individuals
who give a profession of faith and manifest proper behavior already
evidence their conversion. Schuldiner defines three stages in the
Stoddardian view of the conversion process (being of faith, increase
of faith, growth in faith), but his distinction between the last two
remains too fuzzy and opens many questions (unentertained by
Schuldiner) about Stoddard's understanding of the distinction between the enlightenment of reason and the turning of the heart in
the Puritan morphology of conversion. The difference between Stoddard and first generation Puritan divines can be measured by a reading of *Thomas Shepard's Confessions*, ed. George Selement and Bruce
C. Woolley (Boston: Colonial Soc. of Mass., 1981), a record of statements made by 51 applicants for membership in the Cambridge
church that reveals (contrary to Selement's opinion) that Shepard
had high standards for admission. Shepard's blighted relationship

with Nathaniel Eaton, Harvard's first administrator, is documented in Susan Drinker Moran's "Thomas Shepard and the Professor: Two Documents from the Early History of Harvard" (*EAL* 17:24–42).

Not conversion but worldly things are the subject of "The Other Diary of Samuel Sewall" (*NEQ* 55:354–67), in which Mary Adam Hilmer claims that Sewall's private writings inadvertently express a litany of the sufferings of the body that matter more as distinct bodily manifestations than as emblematic spiritual indicators.

### iii. The South

In "The Revolutionary War Poems of St. George Tucker" (*TSL* 26[1981]:48–65) Carl Dolmetsch edits several primarily public poems reflecting the spirit of their time. A more pessimistic view of human nature is recorded in a poem edited by J. A. Leo Lemay in "Southern Colonial Grotesque: Robert Bolling's 'Neanthe'" (*MissQ* 35:97–126), which suggests that the exaggerated conclusion of this poem mirrors Bolling's idea of reality.

The exaggeration of nature's extremes, its horrors and its beauties, is reconciled not philosophically but by the juxtaposition of civilization and wilderness in William Bartram's accounts: so contends Hugh Moore in "The Southern Landscape of William Bartram: A Terrible Beauty" (*EAS* 10[1981]:41–50). Exaggeration of another sort characterizes "'A Certain Amount of Excellent English': The Secret Diaries of William Byrd" (*SLJ* 15:101–19), in which Ross Pudaloff asserts that Byrd's writings either control (through ironic perspective) or erase (through banal language) his feelings; through the ordinary power of his language Byrd achieves personal, political, and historical identity.

### iv. Edwards and the Great Awakening

There was a lull this year in scholarship on Edwards, but an interesting article by M. E. Grenander appeared on the psychiatric relevance of Edwards' concept of each person as a moral agent responsible for his ethical choices: "The Fourfold Way: Determinism, Moral Responsibility, and Aristotelean Causation" (*Metamedicine* 3:375–96). An Edwardsian disciple receives attention, particularly concerning his religious thought, in Joseph A. Conforti's *Samuel Hopkins and the New Divinity Movement* (Grand Rapids, Mich.: Christian Univ. Press, 1981). The New Divinity ministers appalled Isaac Backus, who claimed to be "much better acquainted with Edwards's writing than they are." Now *The Diary of Isaac Backus*, ed. William G. McLoughlin (Brown, 1980) is available in three volumes.

Sometimes in political and religious affairs Backus collaborated with Quakers. According to Donald Brooks Kelley in "'A Tender Regard to the Whole Creation': Anthony Benezet and the Emergence of an Eighteenth-Century Quaker Ecology" (*PMHB* 106:69–88), the Quakers urged individual self-restraint as a solution to ecological abuse; because they valued all life as a manifestation of the divine mystery in creation, they condemned any disrespect for flora, fauna, or humanity. As critical of the Quakers as he was of Baptists like Backus—and no advocate of Edwards' writings—Ezra Stiles read his grandfather Edward Taylor's poem on the natural wonder of some bones and, reports Cora E. Lutz in "Ezra Stiles and the Bones of the Giant of Claverack" (*YULG* 57:18–25), he thought them to be the remains of some gigantic humanoid creature. That Stiles might have been influenced by George Berkeley is suggested in William H. McGowan's "The Dream of Ezra Stiles: Bishop Berkeley's Haunting of New England" (*SECC* 11:181–98).

"Ministers vs. Laymen: The Singing Controversy in Puritan New England, 1720–1740" (*NEQ* 55:79–96), an informative essay by Laura L. Becker, reviews the debate over how the Psalms should be sung and explains that singing by note replaced the improvised manner (in spite of laity opposition) in part because its ministerial supporters emphasized how the New Way bolstered family cohesion, encouraged personal discipline, aided uniformity within churches, and stemmed the declension of religion.

### v. Franklin, Jefferson, and the Revolutionary Period

In "Religious Liberalism and the Founding Fathers" (*Two Centuries of Philosophy in America*, ed. Peter Caws [Totowa, N. J.: Rowman and Littlefield, 1980], pp. 22–45) Nicholas Gier remarks that, properly speaking, the religious beliefs of the leaders of the Revolutionary period were not Deistic, but liberal; viewed collectively these beliefs are eclectic and inconsistent, albeit a fine expression of religious tolerance, love of reason, and adherence to principle. Such beliefs inform the "Speech of Polly Baker," which A. Owen Aldridge (*Early American Literature*, pp. 97–130) claims was probably influenced by Boccaccio's *Decameron* and in turn influenced various French writers. Franklin not only held these beliefs but his *Autobiography* is said in Jean A. Perkins' "Contexts of Autobiography in the Eighteenth Century: France and America" (*Enlightenment Studies in Honour of Lester G. Crocker*, ed. Alfred J. Bingham and Virgil W. Topazio [Oxford: Voltaire Foundation, 1979], pp. 231–41) to reflect a faith in pragmatic solutions, rationality, and compromise in both personal endeavors and political life. In "Benjamin Franklin's *Autobiography*: The Self and Society in a New World" (*MQ* 22[1981]: 93–104) Tom Bailey claims that in his book Franklin displaces mindless self-reliance with a more generous concern with public welfare. In contrast, Jesse Bier asserts in "Benjamin Franklin: Guilt and Transformation" (*PMHB* 106:89–97) that in his book Franklin justifies and vindicates the self by converting his fugitive psychological vengeance against authority figures (father, elder brother, king) into historical respectability. Possibly pertinent to this debate is Ruth A. Banes's "The Exemplary Self: Autobiography in Eighteenth Century America" (*Biography* 5:226–39), which I have not seen. Hardly exemplary is Peter Allaire, who in Claude-Anne Lopez' "The Man Who Frightened Franklin" (*PMHB* 106:515–26) is unmasked as a spy.

To the Federalists Jefferson was equivalent to a spy, "a man of curds" who surrendered his principles for mere words. The Federalist indictment of Jefferson as an atheist and Jefferson's subsequent self-defense are documented in Constance B. Schulz's " 'Of Bigotry in Politics and Religion': Jefferson's Religion, The Federalist Press, and the Syllabus" (*VMHB* 91:73–91). The vicissitude of Jefferson's image as a cultural hero is usefully surveyed in Eugene L. Huddleston's *Thomas Jefferson: A Reference Guide* (G. K. Hall), an annotated bibliography reviewing all major scholarship on Jefferson since his death. Huddleston's introduction is flawed, owing to his evident seduction by Fawn Brodie's speculations concerning Jefferson's personal life.

Possible influences on Jefferson are discussed in Kathleen Hardesty's "Thomas Jefferson and the Thought of the *Encyclopédie*" (*Laurels* 52 [1981], 19–31), which remarks the correspondence between the ideas of the French Encylopedists and Jefferson's political, ethical, and religious thought. In "Thomas Jefferson's Notes on Divorce" (*WMQ* 39:212–23) Frank L. Dewey detects Miltonic echoes which appear to be derived from Jefferson's reading of Samuel Pufendorf. Not Milton but the Greek and Roman classics, as well as the Judeo-Christian notion of a teleological universe and the scientific value of empirical method, inform Winfield E. Nagley's "The Materialism of Jefferson" (*Two Centuries of Philosophy in America*, pp. 52–60).

Jefferson's adherence to an agrarian conservatism implicit in classical republicanism is revised in "What Is Still American in the Political Philosophy of Thomas Jefferson?" (*WMQ* 39:287–309), Joyce Appleby's well-documented analysis of Jefferson's use of Antoine Louis Claude Destutt de Tracy's economic theory to refute Charles Secondat, Baron de Montesquieu's ideas about small republics. Similarly revisionist is "The Transatlantic Background of Thomas Jefferson's Ideas of Executive Power" (*SECC* 11:163–80), in which Ralph Ketcham studies Jefferson's attempt to maintain his faith in people (self-government) at the same time as he recognizes the importance of the quality of individual leadership (virtue).

If Jefferson entertained dialectical ideas, so did Michel-Guillaume Jean de Crèvecoeur, who according to James L. Machor ("The Garden City in America: Crèvecoeur's *Letters* and the Urban-Pastoral Context" (*AmerS* 23:69–83) believed that pastoral America could exist only in combination with urbanization; this belief is also mirrored in the *Letters* in a balanced design of multiple levels of personal and national experience. The writings of a Loyalist contemporary of Crèvecoeur are presented in "The Hudibrastic Poetry of Jacob Bailey" (*EAL* 17:54–64) by Bruce Granger. And a work by one of Bailey's contemporaries, who, like Crèvecoeur, scrutinized the relationship between private and public virtue, is presented in " 'Philosophic Solitude' and the Pastoral Politics of William Livingston" (*EAL* 17:43–53) by Frank Shuffelton.

Raymond Hedin briefly observes in "The American Slave Narrative: The Justification of the Picaro" (*AL* 53:630–45) that 18th-century slave narratives reveal an unself-conscious assimilation of the slave-owner's ethics. Assimilation is also the subject of "Slavery in the African Imagination: A Critical Perspective" (*WLT* 55[1981]: 21–25), in which S. E. Ogude suggests that Phillis Wheatley's poems are deficient in feeling and resort to Scripture instead of the poet's own imagination because slavery had ideologically conditioned her thought. A disappointing round of articles on Wheatley appears in *Critical Essays on Phillis Wheatley* (Hall), ed. William H. Robinson. This volume includes (besides 16 blank pages resulting from a printing error) an uninspired poem, an excerpt from a forthcoming book, Albertha Sistrunk's simplistic "The Influence of Alexander Pope on the Writing Style of Phillis Wheatley," John C. Shields' largely derivative but readable "Phillis Wheatley and the Sublime," and Mukhtar Ali Isani's reductive "Phillis Wheatley in the Elegiac Mode."

### vi. The Early National Period

Emory Elliott's *Revolutionary Writers: Literature and Authority in the New Republic, 1725–1810* (Oxford) provides a valuable survey mapping how past religious forms were adapted to new circumstances and audiences, how Early National fear of chaos and materialism redefined the vocations of clerics and poets, and how the emergence of new literary strategies, particularly the disguise of authorial voice, might reveal the genetic code for the role of the American artist. Especially good is Elliott's identification of such literary masks as "the philosopher in the forest" and the "hermit-pilgrim" who is neither a romantic idealist nor a misanthrope; both of these personae suggest artists who are apart from, rather than above their audience and who pursue their own pilgrimage to truth.

This quest for truth was vexed by the Early National writer's sense of a gap between cause and effect, good intentions (what rulers professed) and events (what rulers did). This realization, according to Gordon S. Wood's important "Conspiracy and the Paranoid Style: Causality and Deceit in the Eighteenth Century" (*WMQ* 39:401–41), resulted in a prevailing fear of conspiracy evident even as late as Charles Brockden Brown's romances; this fear, a rational attempt to come to terms with the gap perceived between promise and practice, served as an ordering principle of thought and assisted in the decoding of the concealed pattern of human wills. That conspiracy and confidence games are kin is implied in William E. Lenz's "Confidence Games in the New Country: Hugh Henry Brackenridge's *Modern Chivalry*" (*CLQ* 17:105–12), which notes that older literary conventions were inadequate to express conditions in the New World and discusses Brackenridge's sense of the confidence game as paradigmatic of an American society encouraging corruption and undermined by chaos.

In contrast Joel Barlow, the "Wicked Wit" from Connecticut, had a firmer faith in culture. Like Johann Gottfried von Herder, explains J. A. Leo Lemay in "The Contexts and Themes of 'The Hasty-Pudding'" (*EAL* 17:3–23), Barlow believed that culture originated from folkways, that the dominant social institutions derived from familial patterns and natural cycles, and that the resultant customs were artful, ritualistic expressions of humanity's religious nature. The poetry of Barlow, Philip Freneau, and Timothy Dwight imitates the style and aesthetic theory of classical models but repudiates many of the intellectual traditions associated with them; moreover, explains A. Owen Aldridge (*Early American Literature*, pp. 158–85), Federalist verse and critical writings parallel the European quarrel with classical authors. A quarrel of a different kind informs the paintings of John Trumbull. In a good essay ("John Trumbull and the Representation of the American Revolution" [*SIR* 21:341–56]) Ronald Paulson focusses on Trumbull's images of sundering and joining to emphasize the painter's sense of the essence of the Revolution: that kingly or fatherly authority is based on covenantal agreement (a belief attacked by Thomas Paine). The writings of Trumbull's, Dwight's, and Barlow's fellow Connecticut Wit are reviewed in Edward M. Cifelli's *David Humphreys* (TUSAS 428), which includes several new attributions of works to Humphreys.

Similarly, a poem by Belknap is identified and printed in "Poetry as Payment: Jeremy Belknap" (*EAL* 17:161–64) by Lewis Leary. A review of Belknap's career and occasional psychological notes on his writings comprise George B. Kirsch's *Jeremy Belknap: A Biography* (Arno Press). Another Federalist Bostonian is the subject of "John Lathrop, Jr.: The Quiet Poet of Federalist Boston" (*PAAS* 91[1981]: 39–89), in which Lewis Leary offers snippets of Lathrop's mediocre verse within an overview of his career. Federalist writers are also the concern of "Federalist Mock Pastorals: The Ideology of Early New England Humor" (*EAL* 17:139–51), Cameron C. Nickels' argument that members of the Joseph Dennie circle feared mob politics—which they associated with Jeffersonian agrarianism—and consequently employed countrified language to attack the rustic Yankee, whom they stereotypically portrayed as the foolish lover and bumpkin engaged in misadventures. An extended witty item by Dennie appears in "'A

Kind of Burr': Colonial New England's Heritage of Wit" (*New England Heritage*, pp. 11–28), in which Harrison T. Meserole reminds us of early American humor.

Satire certainly characterizes Early National drama. A survey of these plays, with special attention to the plots of Royall Tyler's *The Contrast* and William Dunlap's *André*, makes up the first quarter of Jack A. Vaughn's *Early American Dramatists: From the Beginnings to 1900* (Ungar, 1981). A review of the career of another playwright appears in "Mercy Otis Warren: Playwright, Poet, and Historian of the American Revolution" (*Female Scholars: A Tradition of Learned Women Before 1800*, ed. J. R. Brink [Montréal: Eden Press Women's Publications, 1980], 161–82), in which Joan Hoff Wilson and Sharon L. Bollinger also urge that Warren's "formidable and independent mind" be judged in the context of times which limited women. And Benjamin Franklin, V, in "A Note on Mercy Otis Warren's 'The Defeat'" (*EAL* 17:165) prints a section of a play that was previously illegible.

While Warren was formulating views concerning a revision of the direction of the rising American republic, another woman was revising the captivity narrative in 1787. In this revision, the subject of Annette Kolodny's "Turning the Lens on 'The Panther Captivity': A Feminist Exercise in Practical Criticism" (*CritI* 8[1981]:329–45), white women's vulnerability in the wilderness is deemphasized, the conflict between civilization and wilderness is replaced by different ways of relating to the American landscape, and a new fantasy emerges, reflecting the hopes and anxieties of American women about the frontier. The frontier of publishing a new magazine concerns Thomas H. Brown, whose "Friends and Foes: Noah Webster's Involvement in Personal Politics in Eighteenth-Century American Periodical Publishing" (*LC* 45[1981]:104–14) traces the brief life of Webster's *American Magazine* with an eye to the determinative role of personalities, loyalties, and animosities in the success or failure of Early National periodicals.

Finally, in "The Early National Period and the New England Literary Tradition" (*New England Heritage*, pp. 29–49) Lawrence Buell argues that an appreciation of the Romantic movement in America requires a better understanding of its literary predecessors. And in "Republicanism and Early American Historiography" (*WMQ* 39:334–56) Robert E. Shalope presents a reasonable irenicon urging scholars who engage in the current conflict between ideological (the causal power of ideas) and sociological (the subservience of ideas to economic and social pressures) historiography of republicanism to unite; if both sides treated republican language as a clue, they would find common ground in their mutual recognition of the dynamic interaction of social reality (life) and ideas (language).

### vii. Brown and Contemporaries

Novels by Hannah Webster Foster, Elizabeth Helme, Harriet Lee, Susanna Rowson, and Anna Seward are considered in Sally Allen McNall's *Who Is in the House? A Psychological Study of Two Centuries of Women's Fiction in America, 1795 to the Present* (Elsevier, 1981, pp. 12–32). In these works McNall discovers three themes: the young woman unprotected by an absent (dead or bad) mother, the duplicity of males, and the dependency of heroines as they experience the emotional extremes of self-hate and communal bliss. In the writings of many of these same authors, including Charles Brockden Brown, there exists a disjunction between the social demand for public morality announced in prefaces and the covert meanings implied in the actions of the characters. This is the defendable thesis of "Flirting With Destiny: Ambivalence and Form in the Early American Sentimental Novel" (*SAF* 10:17–39) by Cathy N. Davidson, who suggests that the humanization of villains, the portrayal of wives who suffer from bad marriages for nothing they have done, and the depiction of marriage as no haven from the cruel world subvert the explicit authorial claims that these novels advocate simple virtue.

Such disjunctions necessarily coerce the reader to create his or her own meaning in these books. In fact, argues Walter Hesford in "'Do You Know the Author': The Question of Authorship in *Wieland*" (*EAL* 17:239–48), Brown's fictional world is so decentered that all of its models of authority (God, Carwin, ideologies) are "deconstructed"; this fact makes the involved reader share in Clara's plight, for in the absence of any clear origin of events in the book the reader becomes the author of their meaning. Absence at the center of the text is similarly the concern of "Construing Brown's *Wieland*: Ambiguity and Derridean 'Freeplay'" (*SNNTS* 14:43–54), in which Michael Kreyling concludes that Brown's romance concerns the play of verbal signals, the problematic nature of human perception, and the decentralization of an alienated reader's consciousness at stake in the game of the text. Norman S. Grabo is also fascinated by the manifest ambiguities in Brown's works. In *The Coincidental Art of Charles Brockden Brown* (N.C., 1981) Grabo makes a good case for seeing the alleged defects of coincidence, repetition, doubling, and digressions as deliberate fictional techniques whereby Brown conveys psychological reality in an allegorical mode rather than viewing them as attempts to copy phenomenological events in a realistic mode. Grabo is especially instructive on the Maxwell-Stuart-Conway digression in *Wieland* and on the bizarre adventures of Sarsefield and Weymouth in *Edgar Huntly*; he also gives such interesting readings as the observation that Sophia's role in *Ormond* might be a testing of Clara's solution in *Wieland*. Brown might have sought to balance authorial generative energy and the need for restraint, with the result, Grabo suggests, that his characters possibly project psychological features of himself and that his use of coincidence and doubling imparts an architectural form to his works. Repetition also interests Beverly Lyon Clark, whose "Charles Brockden Brown's Contagious Unreliability" (*IFR* 8[1981]:91–97) argues that the unreliability of the senses in any one scene in a Brown romance infects the reader's response to parallel scenes.

Not cohesion through parallelism or repetition, but the lack of an integration of artistic imagination and social conventions interests Maurice J. Bennett, whose "A Portrait of the Artist in Eighteenth-Century America: Charles Brockden Brown's *Memoirs of Stephen Calvert*" (*WMQ* 39:492–507) studies an incomplete work to show Brown's artistic conflicts and his alienation from America. Brown's sensitivity to the matter of integration is also implied in Robert D. Newman's "Brown's *Edgar Huntly*" (*Expl* 40:25–26), which notes that trees mark the intersection of terrible wilderness and secure settlement. Brown's introduction of the Dark Lady to American fiction is the subject of "Born Decadent: The American Novel and Charles Brockden Brown" (*SoR* 17[1981]:501–19), in which Philip Young claims that the portrait of Achsa in *Arthur Mervyn* is influenced by Rousseau.

Incest in *Wieland* and in William Hill Brown's *The Power of Sympathy* contributes to the theme that the sins of the father haunt and destroy his children; so explains James D. Wilson in *The Ro-*

*mantic Heroic Ideal* (pp. 139–53), which also suggests that Charles Brockden Brown believed in the possibility of allying art and reason, self and society. Reviewing the critical reaction to William Hill Brown's book in "Boston's Reception of the First American Novel" (*EAL* 17:65–74), Richard Walser concludes that, despite some controversy over it, the work barely registered its existence.

Replying to an article by Mukhtar Ali Isani (see *ALS 1981*, p. 193), Edward W. Pitcher in "The 'Fragment' in Early American Literature: A Response" (*SSF* 19:169–71) explains that narrative fragments are not indigenous to America but have their source in British models. Pitcher has also identified the non-American origins of stories appearing in three early American periodicals: "An Unacknowledged Source for Essays in the *Town and Country Magazine* in 1787–1788" (*PBSA* 75[1981]:192–94); "The Fiction in the *Columbian Magazine*: An Annotated Checklist" (*AEB* 5[1981]:16–24); "The Fiction in *The American Museum* (1787–1792): A Checklist with Notes on Sources" (*AEB* 5[1981],100–106).

### viii. Miscellaneous Studies

Of tangential interest to literary studies of early American writings are 11 essays on the colonial American family (*WMQ* 39:1–242) and Ann Kibbey's "Mutations of the Supernatural: Witchcraft, Remarkable Providences, and the Power of Puritan Men" (*AQ* 34:125–48). Kibbey advances the dubious argument that the crime of the victims at Salem was not merely that they were witches but that they were women engaging in activities which Puritan culture associated with adult male sexual identity.

Anyone interested in Perry Miller's effect on the study of Puritan American literature will want to consult *Sources for "The New England Mind: The Seventeenth Century,"* ed. James Hoopes (Williamsburg, Va.: Institute of Early Amer. Hist. and Culture, 1981); a symposium of essays reevaluating Miller's contribution (*AQ* 34:3–94); and Bruce Tucker's "Early American Intellectual History After Perry Miller" (*CRevAS* 13:145–57), which remarks the artistic coherence of Miller's vision. Also, anyone interested in Richard Beale Davis' effect on the study of American Southern Colonial literature will want to read "A Colloquium of the Present State of the Study of Early American Literature and the Contributions of Richard Beale

Davis to This Study," ed. Michael A. Lofaro (*TSL* 26[1981]:1–47).

Concluding thus, critiquing critics on critics (Borges-like mirror-work, as it were) might have tickled Charles Brockden Brown's fancy. Much of the other types of "duplication" in this year's account of early American literary scholarship would, I fear, have defied even his genius for appreciating doubleness, parallelism, and repetition.

*University of Texas at Austin*

# 12. 19th-Century Literature

## George Hendrick

My worktable is beginning to crack from the weight of books and articles to be noted in this section. In the midst of financial crises on virtually every campus, scholars have gone on exploring topics in the 19th century. These studies can hardly be seen as "escapist," however, since that century was fully as troubled as our own. Much of the work this year is useful, and it is obvious that the spirits of my coworkers have not been broken by financial problems in higher education or by difficulties in our discipline.

### i. General Studies

Joy S. Kasson in *Artistic Voyagers: Europe and the American Imagination in the Works of Irving, Allston, Cole, Cooper, and Hawthorne* (Greenwood) has a simple—even old-fashioned—thesis: "During the half-century that preceded the Civil War, American art and literature flowered in an extraordinary renaissance of self-conscious national expression. Yet most of the major figures of that period, both writers and painters, were drawn to visit, learn from, and come to artistic terms with the Old World. Even while pursuing the goal of artistic nationalism, these artists found something stimulating and sustaining in their exposure to Europe." Kasson intelligently discusses that "pull toward Europe" in this carefully researched study.

Cheryl Walker's *The Nightingale's Burden: Women Poets and American Culture before 1900* (Indiana) does not throw much new light on this important subject. Emily Stipes Watts's *The Poetry of American Women from 1632 to 1945* (1977) is still the standard study. Walker writes well, however, and has useful observations about women poets.

Donald A. Ringe's *American Gothic: Imagination and Reason in Nineteenth-Century Fiction* (Kentucky) is a wide-ranging, perceptive study with impressive chapters devoted to Charles Brockden Brown, Washington Irving, Edgar Allan Poe, and Nathaniel Hawthorne. The Irving chapter gracefully draws on previous scholarship, and Ringe clearly shows the rationalistic and psychological Gothic influences. He concludes that Irving maintained a balance—"firmly committed to an objectively real and knowable external world, but admitting at the same time the power of the imagination to create a world of appearances that has a psychological reality for the mind that perceives it." Ringe sees that Irving pointed out human foibles and that he also imbued his stories with "good-natured humor that, in the last analysis, is his unmistakable trademark." All the chapters have useful insights into American Gothic.

Perry D. Westbrook in *The New England Town in Fact and Fiction* (Fairleigh Dickinson) deals with the New England town from the time of Timothy Dwight's *Greenfield Hill* to the present. Much of the text is devoted to the 19th century, and Westbrook says some standard things about town life in works by Catharine Sedgwick, Longfellow, Dr. Holmes, Harriet Beecher Stowe, Mary E. Wilkins Freeman, Edward Bellamy, Sarah Orne Jewett, and others. The literary judgments are standard, and the chapters on town government are pertinent and useful in understanding the literary works. Westbrook does, as he promised in his preface, indicate how New England towns "have contributed to the formation of an American mystique of democracy, or, less frequently, in their negative aspects have generated misgivings concerning our national political and social norms."

Helen Winter Stauffer and Susan J. Rosowski, editors, in *Women and Western American Literature* (Whitston) have included over 20 original essays under these general headings: "Shaping the Western Frontier: Women in History," "From Fact to Fiction: Myth As Filter," "Images in Transition and Conflict," and "Shaping Imaginative Frontiers." Though the quality of the essays varies, the topics written about are consistently interesting and important. The essays on "Women's Organizations and Western American Literature," "Women in Western American Fiction: Images, or Real Women?," "Sacajawea of Myth and History," and "Hamlin Garland's Feminism" are particularly perceptive. One might wish that the "Preface" had contained more theoretical material, but that is a minor matter, for the collection is indeed useful to cultural and literary historians.

Nicolaus Mills in "The Crowd in the Classic American Novel"

(*CentR* 26:61–85) poses a problem of concern to many writers of the last century: "Could American democracy be anything more than the coercive mass democracy of the crowd?" Mills's essay treats Cooper, Hawthorne, Melville, and Mark Twain. The beginning section on Cooper's fear of a tyrannical majority is particularly well illustrated by some close analysis of the last of the Littlepage novels, *The Redskins*. Mills is convincing and writes with clarity.

Harold Woodell in "The Preacher as Villain and Fool in Nineteenth-Century Fiction" ( *CLAJ* 25:182–96), gives an excellent analysis of this subject from the works of John Pendleton Kennedy, John Esten Cooke, Thomas Nelson Page, Mary Ann Cruse, William Falconer, Frances Hood, Caroline Lee Hentz, Mrs. G. M. Flanders, George Washington Cable, and others. Woodell examines the preacher in romances, in propaganda novels, and in local color stories and suggests how the literary character of the preacher was developed in southern literature.

Joan Zlotnick in *Portrait of An American City: The Novelists' New York* (Kennikat) has a good subject, but the treatment, from chapter 1 ("The Colony and the Early Republic") through chapter 10 ("The Contemporary Scene") is perfunctory. There is too much plot summary and too little analysis. The bibliography of novels, stories, and sketches concerning New York may prove useful to some readers.

Robert C. Bray in *Rediscoveries: Literature and Place in Illinois* (Illinois) concentrates on Illinois writers of the 19th century (Francis Grierson, Joseph Kirkland, Henry Blake Fuller, Edward Eggleston, and others) and on diarists and travel narratives of that period, but he does include discussions of later figures and is particularly perceptive on Sandburg. This well-written study helps us rediscover some writers from Illinois.

Perhaps the most impressive general study of the year is Emily Stipes Watts's *The Businessman in American Literature* (Georgia). Watts finds that antibusiness sentiment was present in American literature and culture long before Howells' *The Rise of Silas Lapham*. In one of her best chapters, "The Yankee Peddler and the Con Man," she depicts the economic and sexual image of this folk character. Watts explores a variety of themes—radical and utopian anticapitalist sentiment, capitalist optimism, easy money and tainted money— in Thoreau, Emerson, Hawthorne, Melville, Whitman, Mark Twain, and other writers of the 19th century, but she does not confine herself to that century. She is also convincing when she deals with 20th-century literary presentations of the businessman. One of the best scholarly books of the year.

Carl Sandburg said of one of his English professors at Lombard College: "Some of us had our suspicions that his learning weighted him down, there was so much of it." James D. Wilson's *The Romantic Heroic Ideal* (LSU) is certainly weighted down—with references and with tortured writing, and with learning. It is hard to find the individualist heroes among the rhetoric. I offer as evidence the first sentence in chapter 1: "A survey of the many manifestations of the chameleon-like romantic hero, coupled with a critical evaluation of the various scholarly attempts to locate a common denominator sufficiently broad to include the multiple types of romantic heroes, might well bring one to A. O. Lovejoy's assessment that, because of the sheer number and bewildering diversity of academic approaches, the term 'Romantic' has come to mean so many things that, by itself, it means nothing."

William F. Wu's *The Yellow Peril: Chinese Americans in American Fiction* (Archon) deals with racism in this country, but the literature discussed is generally not of high quality. Wu finds that some American writers did believe in the "Yellow Peril" and its cultural and sociological dangers.

Janet Holmgren McKay in *Narration and Discourse in American Realistic Fiction* (Penn.) was afraid that readers would be troubled by the "reductive géometrie of linguistics." She had reasons to be fearful. After a dense introductory chapter on "Accounting for Voices," the author has dense chapters on *The Bostonians*, *The Rise of Silas Lapham*, and *Huckleberry Finn*.

Glen A. Love in *New Americans: The Westerner and the Modern Experience in the American Novel* (Bucknell) has mistitled his book, for several of his major figures—Hamlin Garland, Willa Cather, Sherwood Anderson, and Sinclair Lewis—can more properly be considered midwesterners. The frontier traditions and assumptions of the Middle West and the Far West were not always the same, though, and Love's simplifications vitiate his study. Still, what Love has to say about individual writers confronting the conflict of frontier values and those of an industrial age are useful and often perceptive. It is

too bad Love did not publish the individual chapters without linking
them together with a thesis that doesn't quite work.

Eric J. Sundquist in *American Realism: New Essays* (Hopkins)
has brought together some excellent essays on American Realism.
Praise should go, in particular, to Richard H. Brodhead for his "Hawthorne among the Realists: The Case of Howells," William E. Cain
for "Presence and Power in *McTeague*," and Julia Bader for "The
Dissolving Vision: Realism in Jewett, Freeman, and Gilman." All
of the essays in the collection (some had previously been published)
are of high quality. The editor's introduction is worthy of this fine
collection.

Karl-Heinz Schönfelder in "From Benjamin Franklin to Frank
Algernon Cowperwood: Changes in the Image of the American Businessman" (*ZAA* 30:213–18) briefly surveys the presentation of the
businessman and finds that writers at the end of the 19th century put
forward forerunners of Dreiser's tycoon.

Karen Call in "A Bibliography of Nineteenth-Century Women
Writers in Rhode Island" (*ATQ* 47–48:199–224), presents bibliographies of approximately 90 authors. Primary works of these writers
(most of whom are obscure) are listed.

### *ii.* Irving, Cooper, and Their Contemporaries

The most important publication on Irving this year was volumes 3
and 4 of Irving's *Letters* (Twayne). The editors—Ralph M. Ader-
man, Herbert L. Kleinfield, and Jenifer S. Banks—of these concluding
volumes of meticulously edited letters cover the years 1839–59. The
copious annotations are thorough and consistently helpful. The four
volumes contain 2,656 letters written by Irving, plus a few newly
located letters. In addition, the editors include a list of unlocated
letters sent by Irving, listings of located and unlocated letters received by Irving, and a fascinating section on spurious Irving letters.
The index is unusually thorough, and these volumes are of great value
to literary scholars of the 19th century.

Irving's *The Alhambra*, with an introduction by Andrew B. Myers
and with the F. O. C. Darley illustrations, has been reprinted in a
facsimile edition by Sleepy Hollow Press. The 1851 illustrated text
published by George P. Putnam (Irving's revised edition) has been

reprinted. This is a handsome volume, with a gracefully written, useful introduction on American publishing history at midcentury and on Irving's interest in Spanish subjects. The Darley illustrations are worth the price of the book.

Richard J. Zlogar's " 'Accessories That Covertly Explain': Irving's use of Dutch Genre Painting in 'Rip Van Winkle' " (*AL* 54:44–62) is certain to influence future readings of one of Irving's best-known stories. Zlogar treats a complex subject clearly and convincingly. It is too bad that *AL* couldn't have included color plates of some of the Dutch paintings.

*Washington Irving's Tales of the Supernatural*, selected and with an introduction by Edward Wagenknecht (Owings Mills, Md.: Stemmer House) contains a brief introduction and some fine illustrations by R. W. Alley. John A. Gunnison-Wiseman in "Addendum to *BAL*: The Second American Edition of Part 1 of Irving's Tales of a Traveller" (*PBSA* 76:81–82) describes a previously unnoticed second American edition of *Tales of a Traveller* containing the introduction, four additional stories, and final corrections contained in the English edition but missing from the first American edition.

Cooper scholarship, I am glad to report, has had a good year. Cooper's *Wyandotté, or the Hutted Knoll*, edited, with a historical introduction by Thomas and Marianne Philbrick, has appeared as part of The Writings of James Fenimore Cooper (SUNY). This 1843 novel has not been easily available, but one suspects there will be little popular demand for it, though scholars will certainly find this edition useful.

*Gleanings in Europe: England* (SUNY) is another triumph for The Writings of James Fenimore Cooper project. Donald A. Ringe and Kenneth W. Staggs have included an excellent "Historical Introduction" and "Explanatory Notes." This is a model edition of an important work.

In an attractive paperbound volume Wayne Franklin in *The New World of James Fenimore Cooper* (Chicago) deals with Cooper and the shaping of the American literary imagination. Better than any other Cooper scholar I have read, Franklin shows that Cooper's economic anxieties allied him with the economic instabilities and anxieties of his age. The study is a delight to read.

Several better than ordinary Cooper articles appeared this year. Allen M. Axelrad in "The Order of the Leatherstocking Tales: D. H.

Lawrence, David Noble, and the Iron Trap of History" (*AL* 54:189–211) argues that readers should not follow Lawrence and read the Leatherstocking Tales in the chronological order of publication. Instead, they should follow David Noble's ordering and read the novels in "the chronological order of Leatherstocking's life." While the article could have been reduced in length, Axelrad does argue persuasively for Noble's ordering.

Wilson Carey McWilliams in "Fenimore Cooper: Natty Bumppo and the Godfather," in *The Artist and Political Vision*, begins with a compelling thesis: "From the start defending or defining America has required coming to terms with barbarism." McWilliams is a political scientist, and it is refreshing to see the perspective he brings from that discipline on the subject of Cooper and barbarism: "Natty Bumppo, the man 'without a cross of blood,' is compelled by his devotion to the virtues and morals in which he was reared to become the ally of the civilization he disdains." McWilliams has cogent views on the Corleones also. This is a well-written, thought-provoking article.

David G. Pugh in "The Jacksonian Mystique: Images of an Emerging American Character Type" (*MarkhamR* 11:72–80) begins with a Freudian reading of the mythic character of Rip Van Winkle reminiscent of Leslie Fiedler. Pugh also has some tried-and-true things to say on Jacksonianism and on Cooper's use of the Jacksonian myths in his own fictional creations.

Christine Bold in "How the Western Ends: Fenimore Cooper to Frederic Remington" (*WAL* 17:117–35) has produced an important theoretical study. Bold is convincing in her discussion of Cooper, Remington, and Wister. Finally, Leland Krauth in "Laughter in *The Pioneers*" (*SAmH* NS 1:79–88) works hard to find humor in Cooper's "frontier novel of manners." Unfortunately, there wasn't much to find, and Krauth's article is too long for the small subject.

Cathy N. Davidson in "Isaac Mitchell's *The Asylum*; or, Gothic Castles in the New Republic" (*Prospects* 7:281–99) gives a useful overview of the Gothic novel before turning to an extended discussion of *The Asylum* (1811). Davidson rightly points out that in its denouement the novel "warns that the actions of humans can be as frightening and unpredictable as any incursions of the supernatural. Later American authors from Poe to Hawthorne . . . Bierce and James . . . Faulkner and Flannery O'Connor will make much the same points in something of the same fashion."

### iii. Popular Writers of Midcentury

Little has been written on Longfellow during the last decade, and *Papers Presented at the Longfellow Memorial Conference, April 1–3, 1982* (Washington, D.C.: Government Printing Office) is a welcome addition to Longfellow scholarship. The papers are as follows: the late Andrew Hilen, "Longfellow and Scandinavia Revisited"; Rita Gollin, " 'Standing on the Green Sward': The Veiled Correspondence of Nathaniel Hawthorne and Henry Wadsworth Longfellow"; Edward Wagenknecht, "Longfellow in His Family Relations"; J. Chesley Mathews, "H. W. Longfellow's Interest in Dante"; Edward Tucker, "Longfellow's Play *John Endicott*"; Rena Coen, "Longfellow, Hiawatha, and American Nineteenth Century Painters"; Frederick Wagner, "Longfellow, Emerson, and Emerson's 'Gossips': Alcott, Channing, and Thoreau"; and Steven Allaback, "Longfellow Now." Rena Coen's article is perceptive and contains many good illustrations, and Rita Gollin gives us some fascinating glimpses of the Hawthorne-Longfellow correspondence. The entire collection is highly recommended.

The Whittier item this year is William J. Kimball's "Whittier's *Leaves from Margaret Smith's Journal*" (*NEQ* 60,ii:276–84), a rather too long discussion of this didactic work. Kimball comes to a standard conclusion, namely that the purpose behind this and almost all of Whittier's writings was "a plea for love and understanding that would conquer strife."

Turning to an earlier and more obscure writer than Whittier, Kathryn Zabelle Derounian in "Lost in the Crowd: Rebecca Rush's *Kelroy* (1812)" (*ATQ* 47–48:117–26) argues that this early work is a novel of manners. The article suffers (understandably, given the obscurity of the novel) from too much plot summary. *Kelroy* deserves some more attention, however, and readers may wish to consult Harrison T. Meserole's "Some Notes on Early American Fiction: Kelroy Was There" (*SAF* 5:1–12) and Henri Petter's *Early American Novel* (see *ALS 1971*, pp. 164–65). Cathy N. Davidson also works this early period in "Flirting with Destiny: Ambivalence and Form in the Early Sentimental Novel" (*SAF* 10:17–39), arguing convincingly that the roots of fiction in the United States are to be found in sentimental novels. Davidson believes—and her examples from *The Coquette* are especially well chosen—that these sentimental novels are "subtle, ironic, complex, almost—in a modern sense—unsentimental." Kathe-rine Hanley's "Death as Option: The Heroine in Nineteenth-Century Fiction" (*CLAJ* 25:197–202) is too sketchy to be of much value.

David S. Reynolds in *George Lippard* (TUSAS 417) has written about a reformer-writer too little known by our cultural and literary historians. Reynolds correctly points out that "from several tested literary modes Lippard forged new best-selling formulae that pointed toward such later genres as the city novel, muckraking fiction, the gangster story, biblical and Social Gospel fiction, and modern fiction of the grotesque and surreal."

Was there really a need for another book on Horace Greeley? Certainly one may be inclined to answer negatively after reading Eric S. Lunde's *Horace Greeley* (TUSAS 413). Concentrating on Greeley's ideas and his writing style, Lunde does not really tell us anything new.

There is a need for a good study of Elizabeth Stuart Phelps, but Carol Farley Kessler's *Elizabeth Stuart Phelps* (TUSAS 434) is a disappointment. The book is narrowly conceived: Phelps's feminist beliefs are emphasized, but her interest in homeopathy, equally im-portant to Phelps, is not. Many of the readings of individual stories and novels are perfunctory.

Two articles on popular writers of the time are noteworthy. Evelyn Shakir's "Ednah Dow Cheney: 'Jack of all trades'" (*ATQ* 47–48:95–115) gives us a carefully argued study of a writer most often remembered now as the author of *Louisa May Alcott, Her Life, Letters, and Journals*. Shakir shows that Cheney (1824–1904) de-voted much of her adult life "to improving the educational, occupa-tional, and political opportunities available to women," and draws convincing examples from Cheney's fiction and nonfiction. Mary E. Quinlivan in "Race Relations in the Antebellum Children's Litera-ture of Jacob Abbott" (*JPC* 16:27–36) finds that this once popular writer was opposed to slavery but did not become involved in the antislavery movement. Abbott presented Negro children in his sto-ries, however, and he suggested that racial prejudice could be over-come. Though the scope of the article is small, it contains useful information.

Melody Graulich in "'Wimmin is my theme, and also Josiah': The Forgotten Humor of Marietta Holley" (*ATQ* 47–48:187–98) writes well about a humorist worth reading and about Holley's fine comic character, Samantha Allen. Holley, through Samantha, "attacks conventional and narrow thinking." Graulich has a light touch when discussing Holley's humor, and she is effective in demonstrating Holley's commitment to the women's rights movement.

Three minor writers must share this paragraph. Maurice Kramer in "Alone at Home with Elizabeth Stoddard" (*ATQ* 47–48:159–69) admits that Stoddard's novels are not masterpieces, but he believes they are of interest "because of her awareness of the contrast between transcendental aspiration and psychological limitation." Sheila A. Tully in "Heroic Failures and the Literary Career of Louise Imogen Guiney" (*ATQ* 47–48:171–86) argues that Guiney's inability to lead a heroic life—as her father, a Civil War hero, had done—shaped her literary career. Allen Shepherd in "Sweet Little Ways: Elsie Dinsmore" (*MarkhamR* 11:57–59) does not have much of importance to say about Martha Finley (1828–1909) and her once-famous character.

This was not the best possible year for scholarship on Harriet Beecher Stowe. The Harriet Beecher Stowe volume published by the Library of America contains *Uncle Tom's Cabin*, *The Minister's Wooing*, and *Oldtown Folks*. The notes and chronology are by Kathryn Kish Sklar. The lack of a critical introduction and significant biographical sketch is a serious flaw in this volume. Josephine Donovan in "Harriet Beecher Stowe's Feminism" (*ATQ* 47–48:141–57) rightly points to Stowe's feminist concerns, but the arguments are not always convincing, especially in the discussion of *The Pearl of Orr's Island*. Donovan believes that Stowe moved away from some of her feminist concerns because of Victoria Woodhull's "proclamations on free love" and "her scandalous allegations that Henry Ward Beecher, Stowe's favorite brother, had been involved in an adulterous affair with a parishioner, Elizabeth Tilton." Certainly the radicalism of Woodhull and Elizabeth Cady Stanton offended Stowe, but Donovan's explanations seem simplistic.

#### iv. Local Color and Literary Regionalism

Though there is continued interest in the New England local colorists, the work this year is not of a high order. The five articles on Jewett are certainly uneven in quality. Marjorie Pryse in "Women 'At Sea': Feminist Realism in Sarah Orne Jewett's 'The Foreigner'" (*ALR* 15:244–52) gives a limited reading of that story, ignoring Mrs.

Tolland's early life, certainly needed for an understanding of the story. Pryse is more interested in issuing a manifesto: "Let us provision the house of American criticism, like Captain Tolland, as if our women were going to put to sea the same as our men. Only then will the inner lives of women cease to be foreign, and women themselves cease to be foreigners."

Michael Atkinson in "The Necessary Extravagance of Sarah Orne Jewett: Voices of Authority in 'A White Heron'" (*SSF* 19:71–74) emphasizes voices of authority in this story of innocence preserved. George Held pecks away at the same story in "Heart to Heart with Nature: Ways of Looking at 'A White Heron'" (*CLQ* 18:55–65). Held gives a close reading of this sensitive story and shows that "the heron's life has become the equivalent of the girl's life, at least of her existence heart to heart with nature." Held's reading is more substantial than Atkinson's.

Marco A. Portales in "History of a Text: Jewett's *The Country of the Pointed Firs*" (*NEQ* 60:586–92) points out that three sketches —"A Dunnet Shepherdess," "William's Wedding," and "The Backward View"—were added by Mary Jewett to *The Country of the Pointed Firs* after Jewett's death. It is not known on whose authority these sketches were added. Curiously enough, Portales used *American Literary Manuscripts* (1960) instead of the much augmented *ALM* (1977) in his search of libraries to see "if Jewett left any written or oral directive or if Mary R. Jewett's transactions with the Houghton Mifflin Company regarding the 1910 and 1919 editions of *Pointed Firs* exist and are available." Marcia McClintock Folsom works with the same collection in "'Tact Is a Kind of Mind-Reading': Empathic Style in Sarah Orne Jewett's *The Country of the Pointed Firs*" (*CLQ* 18:66–78). Folsom finds that the style of the stories keeps them from being sentimental or merely quaint. She chose her illustrations from Jewett's work well, and her conclusions are sound.

Only one other New England local colorist was written about this year; Katherine Kleitz in "Essence of New England: The Portraits of Rose Terry Cooke" (*ATQ* 47–48:127–39) argues that Cooke's best works are *Somebody's Neighbors* and *The Sphinx's Children and Other People's*: "In a leisurely, almost gossipy style, these portraits relate their subjects' entire lives, concentrating on births, deaths, and marriages in a reportial fashion. For depth of character study and realistic portrayal of a distinctive American way of life, these stories are unequalled." Kleitz includes too much plot summary, and this weakens the article, but is convincing in making the case that Cooke's stories do evoke New England.

Turning to the South, I find five articles of note. Charles S. Watson in "Simms and the Beginning of Local Color" (*MissQ* 35:25–39) argues that Simms's *Voltmeier* and *The Cub of the Panther* are "precursors of local-color fiction." John McCluskey in "Americanisms in the Writings of Thomas Nelson Page" (*AS* 57:44–47) lists and defines 42 Americanisms not previously recorded in Page's work. Raymond Hedin in "Uncle Remus: Puttin' On Ole Massa's Son" (*SLJ* 15,i:83–90) argues that Uncle Remus, though showing affection for the young white boy hearing the tales and seemingly showing loyalty to the boy's parents, is actually moving the boy toward the world of manipulation and cunning found in the stories. Hedin makes his points well. Robert O. Stephens in "Cable's Bras-Coupé and Merimee's Tamango: The Case of the Missing Arm" (*MissQ* 35:387–405) meticulously researches the history of the original Bras-Coupé in fact and legend and shows that Cable originally used that story in his "Bibi." Later the story became an integral part of *The Grandissimes.* Stephens is consistently perceptive as he shows the influence of "Tamango" on Cable. He is also convincing when he argues that the missing arm was "more metaphorical than literal" and that Cable had "found the way to open the story of a local rebel to large meanings about the conflict of cultural values within the Creole world." Bill Christophersen in " 'Jean-Ah-Poquelin': Cable's Place in Southern Gothic" (*SDR* 20:55–66) argues that Edward Stone in "Usher, Poquelin, Miss Emily: The Progress of Southern Gothic" (*GaR* 14 [1960]:433–43) underrated Cable's story. After sifting through the evidence, Christophersen concludes that Cable used a conventional resolution of plot in his story and that Faulkner concentrated on the workings of a morbid mind, thereby moving beyond Cable. Christophersen concludes that "Cable's story adumbrates Faulkner's at the deepest levels of theme as well as at the more superficial levels of plot and characterization."

Rayburn S. Moore's *A Man of Letters in the Nineteenth-Century South: Selected Letters of Paul Hamilton Hayne* (LSU) is impeccably edited. Hayne (1830–86) is now almost forgotten, but during his last years he was called the "poet laureate of the South" and was much read and admired. He corresponded with many prominent writers, including Dr. Holmes, Whittier, Longfellow, Sidney Lanier, and Wilkie Collins. From the more than 1,500 surviving letters, Moore prints 128. Hayne often expressed himself with great vigor; consider this 1876 comment on Whitman: "the big, shameless *Beast* in his 'Leaves of Grass,' actually *'apotheosizes,'* (if I may use that term), his own *genital organs*; falls down, & *worships* them(!), as if some visible deity glowed in the spherical beauty of his (doubtless) enormous testicles, and equally enormous *Penis*!! (Pardon such vulgar expressions; but *apropos* of *Whitman*, one becomes necessarily, & involuntarily vulgar!)." As Louis D. Rubin, Jr., observes in his foreword, these letters by Hayne "have much to tell us about the region, its writers, its social and cultural life, the literary values of the Genteel Tradition, and the pursuit of literature as a profession in late nineteenth-century America." Moore has given us a first-rate piece of scholarship.

Several works on humorists need to be reported. James B. Meriwether in "Augustus Baldwin Longstreet: Realist and Artist" (*MissQ* 35:351–64) argues that Longstreet should be considered a southern, not a southwestern, humorist. Even this designation is not quite proper, Meriwether decides, for Longstreet was a realistic social historian. Meriwether persuasively sketches some of Longstreet's literary strengths and asserts that the writer has not yet received due recognition. Robert Micklus in "Sut's Travels with Dad" (*SAmH* NS1:89–102) emphasizes that Harris' humor "derives not only from Sut's manner of telling the tales, but also from the plain fact that the plots of the tales are . . . so repetitive. . . ." Micklus tussles with his thesis considerably and finds many examples to prove it to a scholarly audience.

William Bedford Clark in a carefully researched "Col. Crockett's Exploits and Adventures in Texas: Death and Transfiguration" (*SAmH* NS1:66–76) shows Richard Penn Smith at work fabricating the Crockett at the Alamo myth for "pecuniary profit and political gain." Carey & Hart, the publishers, had a large number of unsold copies of Crockett's *Tour Down East*, and Carey suggested that a book on Crockett in Texas would sell and would help clear out the backlog of the other books. Smith wrote his literary hoax quickly; it did sell, and it did sell copies of *Tour Down East*. Smith's book also ridiculed Jackson and Van Buren, using the techniques of the southwestern humorists. Clark rightly sees the importance of the work as a "prototype of today's westerns" and as "an exercise in national hagiography." Another impressive study is Milton Rickels' "Elements of Folk Humor in the Literature of the Old Southwest" (*Thalia* 4: 5–9). Citing all the right humorists, including the unjustly ignored Taliaferro, Rickels concludes: "We can glimpse in the work of the Southwestern humorists one of the ancient and extensive elements of the folk culture—that is, the culture of humor. This culture, by its forms, creates a little world within the larger 'real' world. It provides a second set of values, of aesthetic perspectives which seem essentially subversive of the standard culture. It keeps alive an image of a Golden Age of abundance and freedom."

Willene and George Hendrick in *On the Illinois Frontier: Dr. Hiram Rutherford, 1840–1848* (So. Ill.) present surviving accounts of the professional life of the physician-writer Hiram Rutherford, who wrote the sketch on John Richman used by Mark Van Doren in his long narrative poem *The Mayfield Deer*. Several previously unpublished stories by Dr. Rutherford are reprinted, including a fine comic piece in the best tradition of the frontier humorists—"Jonas Bragg—A Personal Sketch."

Although many articles, on humorous and nonhumorous topics alike, seem padded, David B. Kesterson in "The Literary Comedians and the Language of Humor" (*SAmH* NS1:44–51) rushed through a book-length topic in seven pages. The examples are splendid.

### v. Henry Adams

Is a new biography of Henry Adams needed? My first reaction was that Ernest Samuels' magisterial study will last this century. After reading Edward Chalfant's *Both Sides of the Ocean: A Biography of Henry Adams: His First Life, 1838–1862* (Archon) I am convinced there should be room on our shelves for this new Adams biography. Samuels has not been superseded, but Chalfant includes fascinating material not found in Samuels. Chalfant appears to be more of a partisan of Adams than Samuels was, but no complete evaluation of Chalfant's study can be made until he publishes the concluding two volumes.

Wayne Lesser in "Criticism, Literary History, and the Paradigm: *The Education of Henry Adams*" (*PMLA* 97:378–91) argues that the "paradigm achievement" of the work was "an inquiry into 'historical being.'" Systems offering such broad answers to Adams's great work are ultimately unsatisfactory.

### vi. Realism and the Age of Howells

I will begin this long section with two general studies. Teresa Kieniewicz in *Men, Women, and the Novelist: Fact and Fiction in the American Novel of the 1870s and 1880s* (Univ. Press) is heavily indebted to Jerzy Topolski in her account of "social consciousness inscribed into late nineteenth century novels." This study is highly derivative. Of more significance is Alfred Habegger's *Gender, Fantasy, and Realism in American Literature* (Columbia). Habegger has a strong thesis and unfocused evidence. He has also written a quarrelsome book. In his attempt to show that the realistic novel is "a principal type of American fiction," he adopts a graduate student stance and attacks Richard Chase, Lionel Trilling, and several other major critics. He sets out "to discover the books that were in the air at the time," and "the sort of people who read and liked these books." In part 2 Habegger takes a look at male and female humor. He does well in his presentation of female humor but is not convincing in his account of the frontier humorists. This provocative, rambling book ends on a curious note: an attack on the New Critics and Partisan Reviewers who "canonized" James. Jamesians will laugh and cry their way through this section.

This was a year in which Howells scholars were active, even hyperactive. I begin with two books. The Library of America published another of its useful volumes: *William Dean Howells: Novels 1875–1886*. The following novels are included: *A Foregone Conclusion, A Modern Instance, Indian Summer*, and *The Rise of Silas Lapham*. The texts used are those established for A Selected Edition of W. D. Howells. Three of the titles have been published by Indiana University Press, and copy supplied by the Howells Center was used for *A Foregone Conclusion*. The notes and chronology were prepared by Edwin H. Cady. One wishes for a gracefully written introduction instead of a stark chronology, but it is good to have these novels together in one volume. Kenneth E. Eble's *William Dean Howells* (TUSAS 16) replaces the earlier (1962) Twayne book on Howells

by Clara and Rudolf Kirk. This is one of the best Twayne books. Eble
has used the Howells papers, which had been restricted until 1972.
His literary judgments are based on mature reflection. He writes a
plain prose, clear and to the point. His purpose is admirable: "to
furnish an acquaintance with Howells which may lead readers to
read his works." He has succeeded.

Ginette de B. Merrill and George Arms in "Howells at Belmont:
the Case of the 'Wicked Interviewer' " (*HLB* 30:153–78) play detective and are successful, finding the author of a sensational, unsigned
review to be George Parsons Lathrop—a possible prototype for
Bartley Hubbard in *A Modern Instance*. In "Two Howells Collections" (*RALS* 11:81–90) Merrill describes the Howells collections
at Alfred University and at the Massachusetts Historical Society.
Brenda Murphy in "Laughing Society to Scorn: The Domestic Farces
of William Dean Howells" (*SAmH* NS1:119–29) finds that Howells'
"domestic farces were a means of releasing . . . ambivalent feelings,
a way of presenting the ridiculousness of the situation, and hinting
at the essential evil involved in it, without taking responsibility for
it, to purge guilt and anxiety through laughter."

*The Old Northwest* has devoted its spring and summer issues to
Howells. There is space to note only a few of the essays. Walter
Havighurst gives nostalgic accounts of Howells' early life ("Howells
of Hamilton [Ohio]," 8:7–11). With the help of unpublished letters
and diaries, Ginette de B. Merrill throws new light on "The Meeting
of Elinor Gertrude Mead and Will Howells and Their Courtship"
(8:23–47). James Woodress makes use of Howells' unpublished
Venetian journal, now at Harvard, in "*Venetian Life*: Background,
Composition, Publication, and Reception" (8:49–67). In "Realism
and the Dangers of Parody in W. D. Howells's Fiction" (8:69–80)
Don L. Cook sees two sides to his parody: "straight-faced seriousness" akin to frontier humor, and a mocking of the style and rhetoric
of other writers.

Of the six essays in the summer issue of *The Old Northwest* that
are noteworthy here, we should mention these four: Joel M. Jones's
"A Shaker Village Revisited: The Fading of the Familial Ideal in the
World of William Dean Howells" (8:85–100); William E. Lenz's
"*The Leatherwood God*: William Dean Howells' Confidence Man"
(8:119–30); George Arms on "Howells' Last Travel Book" (8:131–

55); and David J. Nordloh's description of "The Howells Collection at Miami [University of Ohio]" (8:189–95).

Robert Weimann's "Realism, Ideology and the Novel in America (1886–1896): Changing Perspectives in the Work of Mark Twain, W. D. Howells, and Henry James" (*ZAA* 30:197–212) finds unmistakable "signs of crisis and transition" in the three writers. Weimann believes Mark Twain "anticipates some of the profoundly ironic parabolic forms of twentieth-century realism" and that in Howells' *A Hazard of New Fortunes* realism helps to "come to terms with life as . . . it is lived in the present," and that James used his narration as a "form of vengeance upon his audience."

### vii. Fin-de-Siècle America: Stephen Crane and the 1890s

With a few exceptions, much of the work on Crane this year concentrates on minor problems. An exception is Joseph Katz, "The Estate of Stephen Crane" (*SAF* 10:135–50). Katz tries to set the record straight; he believes the melodramatic accounts of the settlement of Crane's estate in Gilkes' *Cora Crane*, which were adopted by other writers on Crane, are largely based on misinformation. William Howe Crane, an older brother of the writer, was not a villain as he has been portrayed, and Cora, who was "wilfull, misinformed, paranoid," kept the estate matters in a muddle. Katz clarifies many puzzles in this sprightly written, informative article.

Erminio G. Neglia's "Fictional Death in Stephen Crane's 'The Blue Hotel' and Jorge Luis Borges' 'El Sur'" (*Chasqui* 10,ii–iii:20–25), while naive in the use of Crane sources, does point out Borges's admiration for Crane and similarities between two well-known stories by Crane and Borges. I wish Neglia had cast his net wider, had not restricted himself to two stories, for a larger-scale study would have been more useful. Frederick Newberry in "*The Red Badge of Courage* and *The Scarlet Letter*" (*ArQ* 38:101–15) believes that Henry "can be identified" with various aspects of Calvinism, especially "in the psychological and symbolic ways Hawthorne represents them." Newberry's evidence on Crane's indebtedness to Hawthorne is not altogether convincing.

More substantial is Nicholas Delbanco's *Group Portrait*. In 1890 Conrad, Crane, F. M. Ford, Henry James, and H. G. Wells were neighbors, and Delbanco works out their relationships. Delbanco is a good storyteller and writes gracefully about Crane at Brede Place. An extract from this book appeared as "Figures in a Landscape" (*Antæus* 44:100–115).

Harvey Binder's edition of *The Red Badge of Courage* (Norton) is based "as fully as possible" on "Crane's handwritten manuscript." The history of the texts of that novel is complicated: after Crane's initial failures to find a publisher, it was brought out as a newspaper serial and reduced in length from 55,000 to 18,000 words. In 1895 D. Appleton & Co. accepted the novel, but deletions were made before publication. Crane made some of the deletions and changes but others were made in the Appleton office. Binder asserts that "Crane *finished* the story as he wanted it before *any* of the cuts was made." That is easier to assert than to prove. Binder does his best with this point, but the evidence about Crane's views on the extensive changes in the manuscript is scanty. Binder provides useful information about the deletions, the ways the original manuscript was reshaped, about the differences in the presentation of Henry in the original draft and in the Appleton edition. Although the Appleton edition poses problems for readers, some of the deletions and changes seem called for, especially some of Henry's jejune philosophical speculations. Will Binder's text now become the standard edition?

Ambrose Bierce has not been forgotten this year. Cathy N. Davidson has edited *Critical Essays on Ambrose Bierce* (Hall) and has brought together a useful selection of Bierce criticism. One might quarrel about inclusions and omissions, but the collection will be used by undergraduate and graduate students in American literature who have an interest, or are forced to have an interest, in Bierce. Davidson's introduction is informative. Davidson also published "Re-Structuring the Ineffable and Ambrose Bierce's 'The Secret of Macarger's Gulch'" (*MarkhamR* 12:14–19). Her point is that Bierce uses the conventions of the popular gothic tale "to serve his own artistic purposes." Davidson's prose rather overwhelms the Bierce story.

Louis Filler in "Hoosier David Graham Phillips: 'Radical'?—'Conservative'?" (*ON* 7:325–37) comes to the conclusion that Phillips was both. Filler handles his materials with ease, and the article is a pleasure to read.

Patrick K. Dooley in "Fakes and Good Frauds: Pragmatic Religion in *The Damnation of Theron Ware*" (*ALR* 15:74–85) attempts, not entirely successfully, to ally the pragmatism in Frederic's novel with William James's pragmatism. Since Dooley does not show that Frederic knew James's philosophy, the article seems to exist in a vacuum.

Timothy Frazer in "Joseph Kirkland's *Zury* as Linguistic Evidence" (*AS* 57:190–97) convincingly argues that *Zury: The Meanest Man in Spring County* is a valuable linguistic document. Kirkland, a New Yorker, moved to Vermilion County, Illinois, in 1858 and lived there for ten years. He used that county and its speech patterns in *Zury*. Kirkland lived in Vermilion County long enough "to develop a good ear for the local idiom, but not long enough to become deaf to it."

Jon Christopher Hughes in "*Ye Giglampz* and the Apprenticeship of Lafcadio Hearn" (*ALR* 15:182–94) contributes a useful study of a relatively unknown period in Hearn's life—his Cincinnati journalist years. Hearn edited the humorous journal *Ye Giglampz* for nine weeks. Hughes deftly shows Hearn at work.

Leland Krauth in "*Boy Life on the Prairie*: Portrait of the Artist as a Young Man" (*MarkhamR* 11:25–29) argues that Hamlin Garland is now too little known and read. Krauth makes the case for the importance of *Boy Life on the Prairie*. Marcia Jacobson in "The Flood of Remembrance and the Stream of Time: Hamlin Garland's *Boy Life on the Prairie*" (*WAL* 17:227–41) makes much the same case, but she is wordier than Krauth. More useful than these two articles is *Critical Essays on Hamlin Garland*, ed. James Nagel (Hall). Sixty-six articles and reviews are included, one of which is new. Nagel's long introduction is judicious; he does not claim too much for Garland: "He was among the finest of the regional realists." It is unlikely that there will be a Garland revival soon, but anyone interested in the retrospective record will find these well-chosen articles and reviews invaluable.

There are four small-scale studies of Frank Norris this year. Martha Dimes Toher in " 'The Music of the Spheres': The Diapason in Frank Norris's Works" (*ALR* 15:166–81) stretches a small subject into a long article. Toher goes on at length to show that Norris "repeated the diapason images for . . . subtle thematic purposes. . . ." John Jolly in "The Genesis of the Rapist in *The Octopus*: Frank Norris' Revision of *Vandover and the Brute*" (*WAL* 17:201–11) argues

that Norris drew on *Vandover* (not published in Norris' lifetime) in
*The Octopus* and that the rapist in *The Octopus* is Vanamee. Jolly
believes (but the proof he offers would probably not be considered
valid by most) that Vanamee's "paroxysms of grief are but the outward manifestation of the struggle between the fleshly and spiritual
elements of his being." Robert F. Sommer in "Norris' *McTeague*"
(*Expl* 41,i:39–40) works hard to explain Norris' calling Polk Street
an "accommodation street." Since the meaning is self-evident in the
context, and since the Darwinian applications of the term are also
self-evident, the explication seems overly long.

Robert C. Leitz, III, in "The *Moran* Controversy: Norris' Defense of His 'Nautical Absurdities'" (*ALR* 15:119–24), reprints, with
an informative introduction, Norris' rather heavy-handed response
to a review of his first novel.

James Kinney in "The Rhetoric of Racism: Thomas Dixon and the
'Damned Black Beast'" (*ALR* 15:145–54) does not throw much new
light on Dixon and his fear of miscegenation, for there is too much
plot summary in the article and too little analysis.

It isn't that interest in Kate Chopin is dying; rather, I suspect,
there is a gathering of the forces. This year I noted only four articles
on Chopin, but I wouldn't be surprised if that number is not doubled
next year. Robert S. Levine in "Circadian Rhythms and Rebellion in
Kate Chopin's *The Awakening*" (*SAF* 10:71–81) writes about the
"sleepiest" novel in American literature. Levine does his best to
enliven a somnolent subject, but others—most notably George Arms
—have already said what needed to be said. Madonne M. Miner in
"Veiled Hints: An Affective Stylist's Reading of Kate Chopin's 'Story
of an Hour'" (*MarkhamR* 11:29–32), using an idea proposed by
Stanley Fish in *Self-Consuming Artifacts*, gives a predictable reading, reminding one of a classroom exercise. Winfried Fluck in "Tentative Transgressions: Kate Chopin's Fiction As a Mode of Symbolic
Action" (*SAF* 10:151–69) elaborates on Anne Scott's notion in "The
Ever Widening Circle" (*Hist. of Education Quar.* 19 [1979]). Fluck
argues that "in its freedom to arrange, construct, and interpret reality
according to its own rules and interests, fiction can be seen as a
mode of symbolic action." Fluck's examples drawn from Chopin's
works all fit the thesis. Elaine Gardiner's "'Ripe Figs': Kate Chopin
in Miniature" (*MFS* 28:379–82) is a sensitive reading of that brief
Chopin sketch. Gardiner identified a cyclical pattern in many Chopin

stories—including "Ripe Figs"—noting that they often end "where they began, albeit not without significant change in the characters or their situations."

Laura Hapke in "Girls Who Went Wrong: Fallen Women in Turn-of-the-Century Fiction" (*MarkhamR* 11:61–64) gives an overview of the conventional presentation of "the fallen woman" and points out that *Can She Atone?* and *Little Lost Sister* are not entirely formulaic. Hapke demonstrates the shift from writers concerned with "sin" and the fate of the sinning woman to progressives who used the fallen woman "to arouse reform impulses."

Christopher P. Wilson in "American Naturalism and the Problem of Sincerity" (*AL* 54:511–27), using examples from Jack London, Upton Sinclair, David Graham Phillips, and Frank Norris, attempts to show that the naturalism of these writers "reflected positive thinking, a triumph of the will." Wilson argues that these naturalists gave the reading public credibility instead of truth, and that this was done "not for sincerity, but only what looked like it." Wilson brings together many good examples, but I suspect his conclusions will be greeted by some with skepticism. Another general article is Don Graham's "Naturalism in American Fiction: A Status Report" (*SAF* 10:1–16). Graham points out that several critics have ignored "the continued presence of naturalism in American fiction," and puts Norman Mailer, Donald Barthelme, Edward Dahlberg, and others in the naturalistic tradition. Graham concludes that the "commitment to facticity and actuality . . . may be the most abiding contribution of naturalism to American fiction."

*University of Illinois at Urbana-Champaign*

# 13. Fiction: 1900 to the 1930s

*John J. Murphy*

It was an unusually fruitful year for criticism on the writers of this period. Two book-length Jack London studies appeared, as did two on Ellen Glasgow. Dreiser's *American Diaries* and a Mencken letter collection were published for the first time, and there were two special issues of journals devoted to Willa Cather. Several general studies offer significant essays on these writers. Fleischmann's *American Novelists Revisited* is important for probing essays on Cather, Wharton, Stein, and Dreiser. Glen A. Love's *New Americans* suggests new approaches to Cather, Lewis, and Anderson. Although more specialized, Helen W. Stauffer and Susan J. Rosowski's *Women and Western American Literature*, Faulkner and Luebke's *Vision and Refuge*, and Ikonné's *From DuBois to Van Vechten* explore lesser-known as well as major figures. Two articles on Dreiser appeared in Sundquist's *American Realism: New Essays*, and Pizer's *Twentieth-Century American Literary Naturalism* contains an important consideration of Dos Passos' *U.S.A.* On the most general level Erisman and Etulain's *Fifty Western Writers* offers as many essays by specialists on novelists as diverse as Mary Austin and Max Brand, O. E. Rølvaag, and Owen Wister. While gathering the many items from 1982 and several overlooked from 1981, Katherine Anne Porter's comment on this period came to mind: "[I]t was as rich and fruitfully disturbing a period as literature has to show for several centuries."

### i. Willa Cather

As in most recent years Cather's fiction generated more critical response than any two or three of the other major writers covered in this chapter. Besides broad cultural approaches to the fiction, activity in Cather's case divides according to two interests: studies primarily devoted to the woman herself—her sexual preferences, childhood, etc.—and studies attempting to analyze the techniques of the fiction or explore it within world and American literary contexts.

In "The Cowboy in the Laboratory: Willa Cather's Hesitant Moderns" (*New Americans*, pp. 107–69) Glen A. Love includes Cather in the group of early modern novelists (with Norris, Garland, Anderson, and Lewis) attempting a new, machine-age version of the American Adam by fusing (in Leo Marx's terms) the machine and the garden, applying the frontier heritage to the mechanized present. Love reminds us that many Cather heroes are of their own times as much as of the past times they idealize, are the bridge builders, railroaders, scientists of 20th-century America. Analyses, longer and murkier than they should be, of *Alexander's Bridge* and *The Professor's House* highlight this essay, for both these novels frame active heroes with their reflective mentors, and both depict "Cather's characteristic conflict [usually involving sex] between the obligations to the self and to society." Tom Outland, who inspires the title of Love's essay, becomes the culmination of the modern Catherian hero. "Outland is the vanguard of the very forces his creator deplores, and [his] 'princely gifts' . . . include the darker consequences of his heroic new pioneering." What is probably the late Bernice Slote's last completed essay, "Willa Cather and the Plains Culture," appears in the last volume edited by her friend, the late Virginia Faulkner, *Vision and Refuge* (pp. 93–105), a volume hampered by a restrictive topic. The Slote essay is a case in point, reiterating commonplaces about Cather's uprooting from Virginia, about Cather's thesis that "human history is a record of an emigration, an exodus from barbarism to civilization," and how this is paralleled in *My Ántonia*; about Cather's use of varied nationalities to enrich her imaginative world; and about her "late" discovery of Indian culture. One detail reminds us of the significance of Slote's best work: Jim Burden's childhood experience in his grandmother's bowlike garden in *My Ántonia* is paired with his scene in Ántonia's cuplike orchard. "These two moments of the epiphany of sun and earth . . . mirror each other like a grown person and the child he was."

The best of the criticism devoted to Cather herself is Sharon O'Brien's contribution to *American Novelists Revisited*: "Mothers, Daughters, and the 'Art Necessity': Willa Cather and the Creative

Process" (pp. 265–98). Focusing her examination on Cather's struggle to combine identities of woman and artist while analyzing her relationship to her mother "and the other women whom she loved," O'Brien reviews major works supporting her thesis. That thesis explains Cather's "masculine" period as a love/hate reaction to her mother as well as an association with a male literary tradition. While there is too much purposeful selectivity in the use of early stories to fit her thesis, O'Brien offers sensible and helpful readings of *O Pioneers!* and *The Song of the Lark* as Cather's successful development of a unique autonomous female hero. The male perspectives used in *My Ántonia* and *A Lost Lady*, which are related to Cather's possible lesbianism, are "necessitated by cultural and perhaps personal pressures that camouflage her own 'unnatural' attachments." The late fiction is seen as reflecting Cather's increased understanding of her deceased mother. This is an important essay, fine criticism of its kind; O'Brien is cautious enough to suggest possibilities rather than make claims about Cather's private self.

Much less responsible is Deborah Lambert's "The Defeat of a Hero: Autonomy and Sexuality in *My Ántonia*" (*AL* 53:676–90). Lambert begins by concluding that "Cather was a lesbian who could not, or did not, acknowledge her homosexuality and who, in her fiction, transformed her emotional life and experiences into acceptable, heterosexual forms and guises." She includes Annie Sadilek Pavelka (prototype for Ántonia) among Cather's loves and blames Cather for making Ántonia a domestic heroine, for submitting to convention and acquiescing to a paternalistic world. How, one wonders, could such an unsubstantiated argument be so well placed? One might ask the same question of Jennifer Bailey's "The Dangers of Femininity in Willa Cather's Fiction" (*JAmS* 16:391–406), another entry in the growing tradition of Cather criticism as feminist polemic. Bailey begins with worthy insights into Cather's untraditional approach to the frontier, equating it with Glasgow's and E. M. Roberts' as an alternative to Henry Nash Smith's view of settlement as a feminizing consequence of cultivating virgin land. The logic then leaps: conventional relationships between women and men are those "felt to be undesirable or abnormal. . . . In Cather's major novels, this conviction is to be found in the virtual absence of such conventional relationships." Bailey's reading of *O Pioneers!*, *My Ántonia*, *A Lost Lady*, and *The Professor's House* support this unconventional

Cather; however, other novels supportive of a traditional Cather
and conventional aspects of these novels are ignored. "Discoveries"
here about the harmful effects of Cather's "fastidiously conservative
men" have been a major topic in Cather criticism for more than a
decade. John Randall's *The Landscape and the Looking Glass* (1960)
is the most recent Cather criticism cited, although gender-critical
theories into the 80s are represented. Like a voice in the wilderness
is Helen C. Southwick's "Willa Cather's Early Career: Origins of
a Legend" (*West. Penn. Hist. Mag.* 65:85–98). As Cather's niece
Southwick encourages restraint in conclusions about Cather's lesbianism, noting that most of the evidence cited is from a 1950 memoir
*These Too Were Here: Louise Homer and Willa Cather* by Elizabeth
Moorhead Vermorcken, who recalled the facts when she was in her
eighties. Cather's living arrangement at the McClung home, the reception afforded her there, and the decade of the visit were misrep-
resented by Moorhead. This plus the fact that Cather's friendship
with Isabelle McClung lasted through the latter's marriage and until
her death and that it was Cather's penchant to destroy all correspondence, not just letters to Isabelle, should at least suggest restraint among responsible critics in "proving" the lesbianism charge.
In discussing the "corruscating view of the institution of marriage"
in *A Lost Lady* and *My Mortal Enemy*, novelist Doris Grumbach has
the good sense, in "Heroes and Victims: Willa Cather's Marriage
Theme" (*QJLC* 39:242–49), to ask questions rather than make conclusions. Grumbach seems to favor the husbands' parts in these
novels, seeing both Captain Forrester and Oswald Henshawe as
wronged by their beautiful and charming wives. In the process of
writing a Cather biography, Grumbach concludes with questions:
"Is it safe to reason from the fates of Myra Henshawe and Marian
Forrester that Cather's moral is misogamist? Is this her fictional answer to the marriage of Isabelle McClung, the beautiful young
woman we know to have been the one true romantic attachment of
Cather's life?" Loretta Wasserman also has the wisdom of restraint
in using Cather's life to interpret her works in "The Lovely Storm:
Sexual Initiation in Two Early Willa Cather Novels" (*SNNTS* 14:
348–58). "[A]ny argument from life . . . has to be made very tentatively," she claims, while suggesting the importance of the "Julio
episode" during Cather's first visit to the Southwest. Her argument
is that Cather is not, as some traditional critics have maintained, an

asexual novelist. Fred and Thea's Arizona affair in *The Song of the Lark* and Jim's Lincoln affair with Lena in *My Ántonia* are sexual episodes awakening the artist to the natural rhythms of life. Within the context of her times Cather was brave in "running some risk in describing the two illicit affairs as fully as she did."

A special Cather issue of *Great Plains Quarterly* (2:193–248) presenting the papers from the first national Cather seminar (1981) contains biographical as well as source and technical studies. In "The Uses of Biography: The Case of Willa Cather" (pp. 195–203) James Woodress describes the difficulties encountered in writing Cather's biography, especially in the light of Cather's attempt to destroy her correspondence. Woodress explores the autobiographical aspects of several novels, including *The Professor's House*, key to the profound crisis of Cather's middle years. Mildred R. Bennett reviews the Red Cloud and Virginia scenes of Cather's childhood in "The Childhood Worlds of Willa Cather" (pp. 204–9), while in "An Exploration of Cather's Early Writing" Bernice Slote explores Cather's early non-fictional writing and the ideas about art, music, and literature reflected in the mature work (pp. 210–17). This is a much more fitting final essay than the one in *Vision and Refuge*; in it Slote offers valuable departing wisdom: "We must admit . . . that we have handicapped ourselves by fashionable judgments: by critical assumptions made, held, and never reexamined, by our own ignorance of the nineteenth-century milieu in which Cather developed . . . and by the neglect of clues and allusions within the work that in T. S. Eliot's *The Waste Land* . . . would have drawn forth tomes of analysis." In "Marriage and Friendship in *My Ántonia*" (pp. 224–31) David Stouck approaches the classic from a biographical perspective, considering it "less a novel about the growth and conditions of the country than of the recalling of one's youth, a taking stock of life" that Cather found necessary after Isabelle McClung's marriage in 1916. Three essays in this volume approach individual novels from more literary perspectives. Bruce P. Baker, II, analyzes Cather's epigraph poem "Prairie Spring" as a key to the relationship between the two parts of Cather's first Nebraska novel in "*O Pioneers!*: The Problem of Structure" (pp. 218–23). In "*One of Ours* as American Naturalism" (pp. 232–38) John J. Murphy examines this Pulitzer Prize novel, Cather's only attempt to deal directly with large contemporary issues, within the tradition of turn-of-the-century American realism and naturalism

rather than as a typical Catherian novel démeublé. Susan J. Rosowski
examines the manipulation of historical and symbolical narrative
modes in "Willa Cather's *A Lost Lady*: Art versus the Closing Frontier" (pp. 239–48), noting the tension developed "between the en-
croaching real world of change and experiences of unity—of symbolic
meaning—that become increasingly difficult to reach in that world."
This novel is also the subject of Paul Comeau's "The Importance of
*Hamlet* to Cather's *A Lost Lady*" (*MarkhamR* 11[1981]:1–5), a superior example of analysis through literary association. Comeau
makes the point that association with world literature was an instinc-
tive aspect of Cather's creative process, that the Shakespeare play is
not a model to which she is indebted but that both play and novel
reflect worlds in transition. Using Cather's epigraph from Ophelia's
mad speech as a starting point, he explores similarities between Niel
Herbert and Hamlet; Marian and Ophelia and Gertrude; Captain
Forrester and Polonius, etc. A less successful attempt at the same type
of analysis is Jeanny Ross Pontrelli's "The Archetypal Hero in *Death
Comes for the Archbishop*" (*HK* 15,ii:31–39), which compares Father
Latour to Aeneas and the two priests to knights in quest of the Grail
while somewhat forcing the thesis that the intellectual Latour's success in New Mexico (discovery of the Grail) depends on his absorbing
"heart" from his vicar. *Archbishop* is also the subject of two essays
in a special Cather issue of *Western American Literature* (17:3–60).
In "Cather's *Archbishop* and Travel Writing" (pp. 3–12) David
Stouck places this novel in the tradition of *A Week on the Concord
and Merrimack Rivers, Typee, Their Wedding Journey*, etc. Not only
do the novel's structure and the occasion of its composition resemble
the "oldest form of narrative indigenous to North America," so do
its other worldly aspects as a journey to the next world and the
contemplative loneliness of its hero: "In the *Archbishop* this contemplative mode which coexists with the action of travelling directs
us to a vision of the next world and the spiritual dimension of human
existence." The spiritual aspect of this novel and *Shadows on the
Rock* is also the subject of John J. Murphy's "Willa Cather and Catholic Themes" (pp. 53–60), which touches on Cather's seeking refuge
in Catholic subjects. The spiritual mystery residing in otherwise
mundane events romanticized the world for Cather and her characters, enabling them to believe "in the mystery and importance of
their own little lives." This issue includes two essays on *The Pro-

*fessor's House* containing material valuable enough to be recast more successfully. In "St. Peter and the World All Before Him," Missy Dehn Kubitschek reads both Professor St. Peter's and Tom Outland's stories as Edenic myths in which the protagonists cannot accept a fallen world of imperfect people. Her paralleling of Henry Atkins and seamstress Augusta as antidotes to self-righteousness is of interest, as are her insights into other details; however, the essay belabors literary associations and implications. L. Brent Bohlke's "Godfrey St. Peter and Eugene Delacroix: A Portrait of the Artist in *The Professor's House?*" (pp. 21–38) employs Delacroix's *Journal* in a top-heavy, almost interminable if intriguing list of parallels between Cather's protagonist and the French artist in attitudes, habits, and physical resemblances. *Perhaps*, runs the conclusion, Delacroix is the prototype for the Professor, who *might* be the St. Peter that Delacroix never painted. Rounding out the special issue is Mildred Bennett's equally interminable citing of parallels, mostly characters, from work to work in "Willa Cather's Bodies for Ghosts" (pp. 39–52), somewhat based on the premise that Cather kept experimenting with certain characters from work to work until she got them just right. Examples range from the perceptive to the obvious or forced.

The Cather essays in *Women and Western American Literature* treat *My Ántonia* and *A Lost Lady*. Patricia Lee Yongue in "Marian Forrester and Moll Flanders" (pp. 194–211) makes the point that the heroine of *A Lost Lady* resembles Defoe's as "a prisoner of the male imagination and of the socio-economic, psychological, and moral conditions which issue from that initial imprisonment." Although much of this argument is generally confined to possibilities of Cather's intention, Yongue's interpretation of details like the flowers put on Captain Forrester's grave and the graceless gossips that invade the Forrester place are contributive. John J. Murphy discusses Cather's and Wister's manipulations of first-person points of view to portray representative western heroes in "The Virginian and Ántonia Shimerda: Different Sides of the Western Coin" (pp. 162–78). After detailing the careers of Ántonia and Jeff and the roles of Jim Burden and the Eastern Tenderfoot, Murphy compares the Wests of Cather and Wister according to what their heroes variously represent: Wister's is the establishment West of old stock Americans, Ántonia "represents a counter culture in the West, a backward life rather than progress." Edward J. Piacentino offers a thorough analysis of suggestive imagery in "Another Angle of Willa Cather's Artistic Prism: Impressionistic Character Portraiture in *My Ántonia*" (*MidAmerica* 9:53–64). Although most of the article concerns Ántonia and Lena in terms of earth vs. light color tones, use of detail in minor portraits is also treated. Merrill Maguire Skaggs considers Cather's last and first novels in two essays in *Mississippi Quarterly*. In "Willa Cather's Experimental Southern Novel" (35:3–14) Skaggs examines *Sapphira and the Slave Girl* for its unexpected handling of clichés of southern fiction, especially the contrast between the aristocratic southern woman Sapphira is supposed to be and the one she actually is. Skaggs also suggests innovations in structure and point of view. "[T]he contrary directions in which the story seems to run" and its pace are symbolized in the "beautiful double-'S' in the road to Timber Ridge." In "Poe's Shadow on *Alexander's Bridge*" (35:365–74) Skaggs argues that Cather rejected her first novel because Poe influenced her writing of it, making it rationally rather than imaginatively creative. The parallels drawn between "The Fall of the House of Usher" and the novel are valid, especially regarding the protagonists' crises and the roles of Lucius Wilson and Poe's narrator. Literary association functions in the opposite direction in Tom Quirk's "Fitzgerald and Cather: *The Great Gatsby*" (*AL* 54:574–91), which explores Fitzgerald's debt to Cather's *A Lost Lady* and *My Ántonia* in matters of style and form and to "Paul's Case" and *Alexander's Bridge* in matters of theme. Cather's first novel, like *Gatsby*, is the story of the divided self, the mid-life pursuit of lost vitality. In a brief second section, Quirk speculates on "a certain divided quality" in "nearly every line" of *Gatsby* and in Fitzgerald himself, who identified with both Gatsby and Carraway. Although this divided self aspect is not applied to Cather, I think Quirk approaches the key to a new understanding of her fiction and life.

    In order to establish a long-needed canon of authority and accuracy, Joan Crane has published *Willa Cather: A Bibliography* (Nebraska). This volume lists all editions and printings of Cather's books and periodical pieces to date, every original collection of her writings, works she edited, anthologies, editions for the blind, translations, etc. The bibliography is descriptive of illustrations, bindings, paper, dust jackets, etc. L. Brent Bohlke offers an addition to the Cather canon in his note, "Willa Cather and *The Life of Mary Baker G. Eddy*" (*AL* 54:288–94), having discovered in a letter from Cather to a librarian friend a detailed description of her extensive involvement during her *McClure's* years in the writing of Georgine Milmine's *The Life of Mary Baker G. Eddy and the History of Christian Science*. Bohlke feels this work needs study for possible influences on Cather's subsequent fiction.

Finally, Susan J. Rosowski suggests in "Discovering Symbolic Meaning: Teaching with Willa Cather" (*EJ* 71,viii:14–17) a valuable place for Cather's fiction in the high-school curriculum. Cather is able to take students from the emptiness of their own reading experiences through remembered scenes of youth to combinations of these into a whole, "guid[ing] the reader in transforming objects into symbols of universal significance."

## *ii.* Ellen Glasgow, Edith Wharton, and Gertrude Stein

Either coincidence or something unique in Willa Cather's work distinguishes scholarship on her from that on these other major women writers. All but a few of the studies on them are by women and about women. The best of this criticism approaches questions of gender universally, but much other work concerns little more than the particular experiences of these particular women.

The year's two book-length studies on Ellen Glasgow illustrate these two different approaches. Marcelle Thiébaux's *Ellen Glasgow* (Ungar's Modern Literature Series) introduces in Glasgow a spirit divided between romanticism and realism, orthodox Christianity and intellectual rejection of it, traditional restraint and modern freedom, and then arranges the novels according to subject: that of a woman artist torn between love and whole-hearted commitment to her work, appraisals of the South's attempts to recover from the Civil War, the spawning of new Virginia leaders from the poor white and upper classes, the industrialization of Virginia, the plight of the southern heroine dealing with inferior men, satiric estimates of changing sexual mores, and reaffirmations of old values against the materialism between the world wars. Thiébaux considers six novels of enduring value: *The Deliverance*, an achievement anticipating Faulkner; *The Miller of Old Church*, "the most confidently written, the most unified of her early works in terms of character and society"; *Virginia*, "an American naturalistic novel of major importance"; *Barren Ground*, a rich evocation of the region if flawed by shrill femi-

nism, and *The Romantic Comedians* and *The Sheltered Life*, spark-
ling and dark social satires respectively. Glasgow's scope and vision
were significant in that she explored women's viewpoints and relations as well as the sweeping social and political changes that occurred from the Civil War to 1939, touching upon Darwinism and
Calvinism along the way.

The other study, Linda W. Wagner's *Ellen Glasgow: Beyond
Convention* (Texas), although proceeding from the reasonable thesis
that Glasgow developed from writing novels dominated by males to
those concentrating on female situations and problems, does little to
extend the reputation of this novelist beyond certain areas of women's
studies. If Glasgow went beyond convention, she never got beyond
herself, the study seems to argue, and Wagner explores the novels as
barometer readings of the passions, disappointments, and frustrations
of the novelist herself. Midway through the study there is a distorting application of Glasgow's statement that "realities of experience"
should inform the contemporary novel and "intense consciousness"
be its objective, Wagner concluding that this "implies" that "her
fiction may have been a means of analyzing her emotions." An example of the contradictory effects of biographical paralleling from so
restricting a perspective is the curious conclusion that Glasgow's
"favorite character," John Fincastle (*Vein of Iron*) is the medium
of "the sometimes contradictory feelings she had known in her own
eventful life as woman—and as that most complex of persons, woman
writer"!

A better side of female criticism, although occasionally forced
and unnecessarily complicated, is Anne Goodwyn Jones's "Ellen
Glasgow: The Perfect Mold" in *Tomorrow Is Another Day: The
Woman Writer in the South, 1859–1936* (LSU, 1981; pp. 225–70),
which explains Glasgow's ambivalence toward the South's feminine
ideal and its victims, her "obsession" with as well as "protest against
the female practice of stacking life on the single emotion of love. . . ."
Glasgow was more realist as a novelist than as a critic, according to
Jones; what she commented on as the "pure selflessness" of the
heroine of her novel *Virginia*, she "shows clearly in her fiction . . .
[as] not absolutely pure and that the 'perfect' mould [of the feminine
ideal] breaks not by anyone's choice but because of its own imperfections." In *Life and Gabriella* Glasgow "shows a southern lady rebelling . . . against her role"; this novel "forms a perfect companion

for *Virginia*, paralleling, reversing, developing, and reinforcing the patterns in *Virginia.*" Ambivalence on a more universal scale is the subject of "Ellen Glasgow and the Tide Water Renaissance" in Daniel Joseph Singal's *The War Within* (pp. 83–110). Singal sees Glasgow as the post-Victorian whose Darwinism enabled her in *Virginia* to acknowledge openly the animal component in human nature while lamenting and identifying with the vanishing, inhibiting life of the past. After World War I she sought in *Barren Ground* a mechanism to repress the very biological instincts she had acknowledged. Singal concludes that "in her case, the Calvinist conscience, detached from its religious base, had been permitted to float freely, through her thought. . . ."

*Barren Ground* was the topic of three other articles. Debra D. Munn's "A Probable Source for Glasgow's *Barren Ground*" (*MarkhamR* 11:21–25) sees the extension of woman to land as similar to that in Cather's *O Pioneers!* Through careful paralleling of plot and character and descriptive passages, Munn makes her point that "resemblance . . . seems too striking to be coincidental." This comparison with the Cather novel could easily be extended meaningfully into the psychological dimensions of female autonomy explored in Mary Castiglie Anderson's "Cultural Archetype and the Female Hero: Nature and Will in Ellen Glasgow's *Barren Ground*" (*MFS* 28:283–93), which interestingly if repetitiously attempts to establish Dorinda Oakley as Everywoman, who has broken the "psychological, social, and moral inertia" of her community by "turn[ing] 'feminine' transforming power outward." Dorinda Oakley's accomplishment also concerns Jan Zlotnik Schmidt in "Ellen Glasgow's Heroic Legends: A Study of *Life and Gabriella, Barren Ground,* and *Vein of Iron*" (*TSE* 26[1981]:117–41), which views the heroines of all three novels as Glasgow's elect, variously tested by people, nature, and urban life. Their heroic visions achieved in struggle "affirm . . . that man's and woman's development of character is fundamental to the continued existence of modern civilization itself." Finally Tonette L. Bond makes available the seven letters of Ellen Glasgow to Marjorie Kinnan Rawlings and a fascinating letter from Rawlings to Glasgow in which Rawlings describes a dream about Glasgow (*EGN* 16:3–6).

*The Age of Innocence* and *Summer* were emphasized by Edith Wharton's critics. The Wharton entry in *American Novelists Revisited,* Elizabeth Ammons' "Cool Diana and the Blood-Red Muse:

Edith Wharton on Innocence and Art" (pp. 208–24), argues that in
*The Age of Innocence* old New York preferred the athletic achievements, innocence, and dependence of May Welland to the artistry,
experience, and freedom of Ellen Olenska, that Wharton identified
with Ellen and thus recorded her rejection of and by old New York.
One wonders if May is as "empty" as Ammons claims and if there is
not more ambivalence in Wharton's feelings toward the society of
her girlhood, the demise of which in *A Backward Glance* she associated with the country's present moral impoverishment. Judith P.
Saunders' "Becoming the Mask: Edith Wharton's Ingenues" (*MSE*
7,iv:33–39) provides a more informed portrait of May Welland by
noting that socially demanded innocence in young girls is at least
as much the design of young women as it is of men—"the entrapment
[is] from within as well as from without." May's knowledge of
Archer's feelings for Ellen, her offer to release him from their engagement, and her lie about her pregnancy are "dramatic evidence that
the innocence required in young women is a mask more than a reality." The article is flawed, however, in that Newland Archer's
opinions and the critic's preferences for nature over culture are construed as Wharton's. Cushing Strout approaches the same novel with
less predisposition in a comparative study: "James's Lady and Wharton's Age" (*HudR* 35:405–15), which stresses Wharton's sharing
with James a respect for the value and price of renunciation. Ellen
Olenska in this reading "accepts the code of decency observed in
[Newland Archer's] society rather than backing her own personal
claims." Strout takes issue with recent Wharton critics who attempt
to dissociate Wharton from James, for "the fear of linking her to
James reduces the idea of influence to discipleship." James's observations on what might be construed failures in his novel "gave her an
opening for her own talent to take up [what he left out] by putting
the psychological in a social context, telling the male side of the story
more fully, and seeing the heroine and the hero through to the end
of their situation."

In "The Unmastered Streak: Feminist Themes in Wharton's
*Summer*" (*ALR* 15:86–96) John W. Crowley through careful textual
analysis supports the pessimistic conclusion that Charity Royall's
marriage amounts to final entrapment in dependent childhood rather
than autonomous adult identity. As an examination of paternalistic
assumptions about women conditioned to think of themselves as tro-

phies to be captured, while in actuality sex objects upon which men may gratify sexual needs while denying women the right to such gratification, *Summer* is "radically a feminist novel." The distinguishing thing about Linda Morante's "The Desolation of Charity Royall: Imagery in Edith Wharton's *Summer*" (*CLQ* 18:241–48) is its taking the plight of the heroine beyond woman's dilemma. Through "a tapestry of wasteland imagery," Wharton represents in Charity Royall's situation the poverty of Americans trapped within a mausoleum of mediocrity and separated from their cultural heritage. Wharton's unfinished novel is the subject of Carol Wershoven's "Edith Wharton's Final Vision: *The Buccaneers*" (*ALR* 15:209–20). Seen as a companion piece to her first novel, *The Valley of Decision*, in that both depict "the impact of change on a repressive, reactionary old order," this last novel transforms Wharton's fears into a new hope, because the accomplishment of its dual heroines would be "a reconciliation of opposing elements: of American classlessness and British hierarchy, of tradition and innovation, in a merger which bodes well for the future." Finally, in "Two Novels of 'The Relatively Poor': *New Grub Street* and *The House of Mirth*" (*NMAL* 6:Item 12) Adeline R. Tintner convincingly attributes the repetition of the phrase "the relatively poor" and Lawrence Selden's "republic of the spirit" speech in Wharton's novel to George Gessing's novel.

Cynthia Secor's "The Question of Gertrude Stein" (*American Novelists Revisited*, pp. 299–310) was the year's most general consideration of Stein and her work, grouping *The Making of Americans*, *Mrs. Reynolds*, and *Ida, a Novel* with *Middlemarch* and *The Portrait of a Lady* as "works that have earned a secure place in the canon of Anglo-American fiction. These three Stein novels are complex statements about the relation of individual to society, culture, geography, and history. They are about the ecology of human life." Concentrating on the fiction before World War I and before World War II, Secor clarifies aspects to be considered in evaluating Stein's contribution: interest in the composing human mind taking her beyond the confines of the patriarchal literary tradition, a distinctly marginal angle of vision (Jewish, lesbian, female, expatriate), and fundamental values essentially feminine (sensual, domestic, nurturing, healing). "Gertrude Stein's Landscape Writing" (*WS* 9:221–39) by Marianne DeKoven is a fascinating study of Stein's development of unified vision in her "landscape writing," in which body, spirit, and nature are integrated. The achievement of this female vision indicates Stein's acceptance of her femaleness, her association of femaleness with genius. DeKoven sees the novel *Lucy Church Amiably* as successful landscape writing but devotes much of her essay to analysis of *Four Saints in Three Acts* because Stein's plays are even more successful examples. Using the plays to illustrate and explore the various contortions and deformities of experimental language, Elizabeth Fifer in "Rescued Readings: Characteristic Deformations in the Language of Gertrude Stein's Plays" (*TSLL* 24:394–428) concludes that Stein forced knowledgeable readers into a special relationship of rescuing her meaning and distracted those who would disapprove of the sexual self-identity she consistently explored. This search for identity through friendship is the subject of Carolyn Burke's "Gertrude Stein, the Cone Sisters and the Puzzle of Female Friendship" (*CritI* 8:543–64), which traces Stein's use of her incipient intimacy with Etta Cone, eventually replaced by Alice B. Toklas, and Etta's relationship with her sister Claribel in her "self-discovery" through female relationships. Stein's use of Mabel Dodge in her attempts to define herself and Americans of her turn-of-the-century generation is the subject of Lois P. Rudnick's "Radical Visions of Art and Self in the 20th Century: Mabel Dodge and Gertrude Stein" (*MLS* 12,iv:51–63). Dodge, who had flashes of insight into Stein's linguistic revolution, suffered identity confusion similar to Stein's in her relationship with her brother; both women were guilty of a "detached view of human beings, as though they existed for the sole purpose of providing interesting specimens for their psycho-aesthetic laboratories."

A first rate, well-reasoned article is Lisa Ruddick's " 'Melanctha' and the Psychology of William James" (*MFS* 28:545–56), which applies *Psychology: The Briefer Course* to Stein's portrait. The relationship of Jeff Campbell and the heroine becomes a struggle for mental dominance between interdependent progressive and conservative mental tendencies, an opposition between "preconception" and "mind wandering." While "Melanctha" is recognized as a serious exercise in mental stability in Ikonné's *From DuBois to Van Vechten* (pp. 19–22), it is said to be marred by prejudice: "Not being absolutely confident of her knowledge of Negroes, Stein, in her attempt to convert her white characters and white situations into black characters and black situations, could not resist the temptation of using existing Negro stereotypes as a frame of reference." Finally, in "The Chicago Renaissance Discovers Gertrude Stein" (*AN&Q* 20:111–13) Ray Lewis White describes as guarded ridicule the reception of *Tender Buttons* by the popular press in Chicago.

## *iii.* Theodore Dreiser, Jack London and John Dos Passos

"[I]f not a feminist, at least a fellow traveler, allied with feminists in a struggle against patriarchy," concludes Susan Wolstenholme about Dreiser in "Brother Theodore, Hell on Women" in *American Novelists Revisited* (pp. 243–64). Although a bit emotional toward the end, this is a fine study of the conflict in Dreiser's major novels, especially *An American Tragedy*, between a mechanistic, amoral system and a humanistic, moralistic one. The author follows Robert Penn Warren's division of the novels into those written "under the aegis of the mother" and the Cowperwood trilogy "under the aegis of the father." A result of our social-sexual arrangement is that males feel compelled to escape the dark fearful mermaid world from which life springs and thus victimize women as Clyde Griffiths does Roberta Alden. Also feminist in its approach is Walter Benn Michaels' "Dreiser's *Financier*: The Man of Business as a Man of Letters" in *American Realism* (pp. 278–95). Michaels' thesis is that Cowperwood's experiences with his wife and his mistress "provide paradigms for the major competing accounts of value" in the novel. Dreiser comes down on the side of nature and speculation, "not only think[ing] of capitalist production as natural" but "of nature in all her manifestations [love] as capitalistic."

The womanizing that Dreiser equated with business ventures is evident throughout all seven hitherto unpublished *American Diaries, 1902–1926* (Penn.), carefully edited with an excellent introduction by Thomas P. Riggio and textual apparatus by James L. W. West, III, and Neda M. Westlake. The first or Philadelphia diary, kept at the suggestion of Dreiser's doctor when Dreiser was suffering from exhaustion while trying to write *Jennie Gerhardt*, betrays a "strangely Chaplinesque figure" inadequate to either the self-imposed task of being an antigenteel literary force or the sexual conquests he associated with it. Less concerned with bowel movements and sleep is the Savannah diary of 1916, which, though rich in details of setting, reveals Dreiser as still worried about his potency. The Greenwich

Village diary of the following year continues the amorous adventures, while the subsequent Indiana diary records a return to source that seems to prepare Dreiser for his masterpiece, *An American Tragedy*. The Hollywood diary, 1919–24, details Dreiser's life with his young cousin, actress Helen Richardson, who made him painfully aware of his age and meager finances. Confessed fears about satisfying Helen indicate "his experience was pushing him to imagine scenarios that held the germ of [*Tragedy*]." Valuable as these contributions are to our concept of the American scene and the novels, the primary contribution is undoubtedly biographical, revealing, according to Riggio, a man absorbed by women yet resisting engaging his feminine side in his relationships with them. "The diaries are virtually written around [the women he knew] . . . perhaps no male writer of the period—with the exception of Henry James—was as interested in the lives of women. . . . The diaries present Dreiser interacting with the originals of his *Gallery* [*of Women*] characters." In a related article, "Dreiser's Debt to His Contemporaries" (*DrN* 13,i:1–9) Richard W. Dowell examines the Philadelphia diary to call attention to Dreiser's unacknowledged dependence on other writers during his struggle to complete *Jennie Gerhardt*. Besides reading works of Frederic, Garland, and Howells, he discovered Blake Fuller's *With the Procession* and Brand Whitlock's *The 13th District*, works he later included in his list of admired American novels. Ida Tarbell's *Life of Lincoln* moved him deeply, and he identified with Lincoln's suffering. In *Dreiser in New York: A Diary Source* (*DrN* 13,ii:1–7), Hilbert H. Campbell includes impressions of Dreiser's crudities and grandeur as well as his dealings with Sherwood Anderson from Eleanor Copenhaver Anderson's sporadically kept 1933–34 diary.

The more interesting of two articles on *Sister Carrie*, Philip Fisher's "Acting, Reading, Fortune's Wheel: *Sister Carrie* and the Life History of Objects" (*American Realism*, pp. 259–77) relates the rising and falling action of the Ferris wheel to Carrie Meeber's rocking chair as emphasizing the Darwinian and economic order of Dreiser's world. Fisher makes distinctions between the Chicago or Bildungsroman half of the novel and the New York or rise-measured-by-decline half. Robert A. Morace's "Dreiser's Contract for *Sister Carrie*: More Fact and Fiction" (*JML* 9:305–11) is yet another rendition of "L'affaire Doubleday"; this one absolves Frank Norris of blame while detailing Arthur Henry's impractical intransigence contributing to the novel's stillbirth.

Three articles are devoted to various aspects of technique in Dreiser. The point of Paul A. Orlov's "Plot as Parody: Dreiser's Attack on the Alger Theme in *An American Tragedy*" (*ALR* 15:239–43) is Dreiser's ironic use of plot devices from the rags to riches stories: the "lucky" discoveries of a patron and long-lost relative are combined and lead to tragedy because the benefactor proves more practical than charitable and the protagonist lacks the "pluck" of his Alger counterparts. Joseph Griffin's "Dreiser Experiments with Form: Five Stories from *Chains*" (*ESC* 8:174–86) carefully reviews the short stories as Dreiser's attempts "to pin down this elusive *genre*." "Chains" and "Fulfillment" alternate paragraphs of interior monologue and objective framework; "The Shadow" juxtaposes a wife's and a husband's monologues; "The Hand" presents a deteriorating mind in calendared segments of interior monologue and remarks of observers, and "The Victor" views a man from different perspectives before he is thwarted by forces beyond his control. Philip L. Gerber's "Cowperwood Treads the Broads" (*DrN* 13,ii:8–17) presents an interesting record of Rella Abell Armstrong's persistent if unsatisfactory (to Dreiser and mistress Kay Sayre) attempts to telescope the first two novels of Dreiser's trilogy into a topical 1920s stage play.

The two book-length studies of Jack London have the dubious distinction of trying to prove the inadequacies of the man and artist. What emerges from John Perry's *Jack London: An American Myth* (Nelson-Hall [1981]) is a tragic and unpleasant figure incapable of rising above race prejudice and materialism or of understanding what he happened to read in Marx and Jung. Using memoirs by contemporaries and later biographers and criticism, Perry credits London's erratic temperament and physical constitution to his astrologer father. London's rejection by his father generated notions of survival of the fittest, efforts to establish a family line at his baronial estate, a compulsion for material success, and somewhat contradictory class-revolution attitudes. London's money-making mania becomes the basis of the deterioration of his art and health, for he turned to booze when failing to repeat the success of *The Call of the Wild*. Joan D. Hedrick's *Solitary Comrade: Jack London and His Work* (N.C.) should have focused on London as representative of the contradictions and denials of his society and time (which it does in places) rather than repeatedly blame him for what he failed to do. As it is, London becomes a literary whore: "Accommodation to his society created in him the psychic satisfactions of a prostitute." *The Sea Wolf* records his selling out, moving as it does from Wolf Larsen's terrible version of a "'piggish' world of social Darwinism and laissez-faire capitalism" to the sentimental consciousness (which "heralded the death of London's art") of Hump Van Weyden, whose mothering by Maud Brewster dramatizes the refuge London sought in domestic life with Charmian Kittredge. Except for *The Call of the Wild, Martin Eden,* and a few short stories in the cause of socialism, London's output was an attempt to veil the naked truths he glimpsed, a substitution of the individual for the cosmic consciousness.

The authors of the year's several articles seem to like London better. In "Resentment and Revolution in Jack London's Sociofantasy" (*CRevAS* 13:179–92) Gorman Beauchamp explores the generating nature of London's resentment of the bourgeois order and desire for a better one in *The Iron Heel, The Scarlet Plague,* "Goliath," and other works: "Images of violent apocalypse provide him with the fictive scenario that satisfies both impulses, imaginatively elevating his personal rancor to the level of world-historical class conflict." Katherine M. Littell, in "The 'Nietzschean' and the Individualist in Jack London's Socialist Writings" (*JLN* 15:76–91), summarizes London's final humane vision as distinct from yet nourished by socialist and Nietzschean philosophies as well as capitalism and Christianity: "Progress must come from 'individuals' capable of inspiring and leading the less gifted members of the human race toward maximum self fulfillment rather than into exploitation." Helpful to the teacher of London, Michael Qualtiere's "Nietzschean Psychology in London's *The Sea-Wolf*" (*WAL* 16:261–78) carefully examines the philosopher's Revaluation of Values, Long Sickness, and psychic paralytic disturbance, and applies each to the character of Wolf Larsen, concluding that similarities are hardly accidental. Finally, in a fascinating source study, "Adam Strang in Cho-Sen: The Korean Episode in *The Star Rover*" (*JLN* 15:1–36), Victor R. S. Tambling cites Korean history and records of famous Pacific voyages to establish that London used actual persons and the names of persons in

*The Star Rover* and also suggests that he provided clues to guide his readers to this factual content.

Dos Passos studies were confined to technique in *U.S.A.* and *Manhattan Transfer.* Donald Pizer's "John Dos Passos: *U.S.A.*" in his *Twentieth-Century American Literary Naturalism* (pp. 39–64) is an excellent analysis of the trilogy as a naturalistic tragedy of America's failed potential. Through consideration of character "interlacing," narrative "cross-stitching," indirect discourse, narrative clusters, ironic biographies, news reels, and the Camera-Eye, Pizer argues for the work's powerful and complex unity. In "The Structure of John Dos Passos's *U.S.A.* Trilogy" (*ArQ* 38:229–34) Michael Clark takes pains to prove the structural unity of the trilogy through (what Pizer terms character interlacing) a system of reciprocal characters balanced between Rovers and Muckers, exploiters given to abstractions and creators who work with their hands. Finally, Phillip Arrington, in "The Sense of an Ending in *Manhattan Transfer*" (*AL* 54:438–43), a somewhat densely packed note insightful on fire references and the consummation of individuals, sees the novel as the "brazen trumpet" of an "American anti-Jeremiad" warning endless fall rather than destruction, for "the values . . . destroying America . . . continually recreate America."

#### iv. Sherwood Anderson, Sinclair Lewis and Ole Rølvaag

The major essays on these midwestern writers appeared in *New Americans* and *Vision and Refuge.* Glen A. Love's study on Anderson in the former volume, "Sherwood Anderson: Stilling the Machine" (pp. 170–218), is primarily a consideration of *Marching Men* and *Poor White,* and secondarily of *Windy McPherson's Son, Kit Brandon,* and *Winesburg, Ohio.* Anderson's approach to the urban-pastoral conflict in America is seen as a "struggle toward resolution between the hero and a threatening society," the acquisitive culture fostered by the new technology. From novel to novel this struggle moves back and forth from village to city, the new American variously a wanderer in search of purpose, an organizer of the silent masses, a spokesman for the failed souls of forgotten pastoral America, a socially concerned and exploited technocrat, a disillusioned new woman. Out of this jumble of the good and bad effects of industrial

America emerges "the Andersonian artist himself . . . who, in his unyielding determination to encompass the diverse forces of his times, in his refusal to deny the age he cannot accept, emerges as the only assuredly heroic figure from among all [Anderson's] new Americans." The in-between American is also the subject of David D. Anderson's "Sherwood Anderson's Technologically Displaced Persons" (*SSMLN* 12,iii:9–20), which theorizes that Anderson's failure to understand his father is evident in his failure to connect the craftsman displaced by time and circumstance in *Poor White* to the fumbling father unable to comprehend a factual world in *Windy McPherson's Son.*

In the biographical area William Baker's "Sherwood Anderson in Springfield" (*ALR* 15:47–61) provides details of Anderson's year (1899–1900) at Wittenberg Academy, how he learned more from the helpful people he met at "The Oaks" boarding house (many, doubtless, prototypes for *Winesburg* characters) than in school, and how the discarded manuscript "Talbot, the Actor" (on the reverse sides of the *Winesburg* manuscript) is clearly a record of that year and of Anderson's sublimating "the freak" in himself and finding the path to adventure. Details of this Springfield year are included in Anderson's summary of his life in a newly discovered 1926 letter to a *Herald Tribune* writer (*WE* 7,ii:3–4). Escaping "the freak" is also the subject of "Sherwood Anderson and *Dark Laughter*: Discovery and Rebellion" (*SSMLN* 11,ii[1981]:23–31) by David M. Lockwood, who sees the escape of Bruce Dudley and Aline Grey as toward the direction of "those impulses which may lead to greater personal fulfillment. They will in turn allow us to see a closer relationship with the great river of humanity [Mother Ohio, Mother Mississippi] that is everywhere around us."

The reverse side of the *Winesburg* manuscript occupies Ray Lewis White in two *Winesburg Eagle* notes. In "'Death in the Woods': Anderson's Earliest Version" (7,ii:1–3) he summarizes "A Death in the Forest," an almost complete narrative typed by Anderson on the manuscript in the Newberry Library. White edits and reprints a version of "Nobody Knows" from the same manuscript in "*Winesburg, Ohio*: the Unique Alternate Draft of 'Nobody Knows'" (8,i:3–5). Also valuable in assessing Anderson's craft is Raymond Wilson's carefully organized and detailed "Rhythm in *Winesburg, Ohio*" (*GrLR* 8:31–43), in which he applies E. M. Forster's notion of rhythm to the three functions of Anderson's use of hands: as providing objective correlatives to inner needs, as motivation factors, as elements in characterization. Distinguishing between rhythm and conventional indications of unity in narratives, Wilson notes that while " 'Departure' does not resolve the maturity theme . . . the story does carefully conclude the 'hands' rhythm." Finally, in "Sherwood Anderson and Ben Hecht: Fancy and Fact" (*WE* 8,i:1–2) Walter Göbel offers an anecdote revealing Anderson's use of fancy to beautify and idealize reality.

Glen Love's offering on Lewis, "Sinclair Lewis: New Pioneering on the Prairies" (pp. 219–54), concentrates on *Main Street, Babbitt, Arrowsmith,* and *Dodsworth* in considering Lewis's juggling the careers of Westerners seeking quality life through balance between the new technology and nature. In their various ways his characters are ennobled by this effort yet fail: Carol Kennicott is too visionary, George Babbitt not enough so; Martin Arrowsmith withdraws from conventional society, while Sam Dodsworth decides to improve it. Love believes that the affirmative aspects of Lewis' work have been neglected, at least as a possible controlling set of ideas in the fiction. Like Cather and Anderson, Lewis believed "that the old stalemate between machine and garden might be transformed into a progressive synthesis." In "Sinclair Lewis vs. Zane Grey: *Mantrap* as Satirical Western" (*MidAmerica* 9:124–38) Robert E. Fleming, also using a Western approach, sees this Lewis novel as intentionally reversing American mythic versions of the Indian, mountain man, effects of the wilderness on hero and heroine, and the circumstances of the adventurous canoe chase. "Read as parody," concludes Fleming about this critically maligned novel, "*Mantrap* makes perfect sense and provides one more example of Sinclair Lewis's versatility as a humorist and a novelist."

The increased interest in Rølvaag's work is evident in Nebraska's making available in Bison editions the sequels of *Giants in the Earth, Peder Victorious* and *Their Father's God.* Three essays in *Vision and Refuge* concern the Rølvaag trilogy, particularly *Giants in the Earth.* Dorothy Burton Skårdal provides a helpful context in "Life on the Great Plains in Scandinavian American Literature" (pp. 71–92) as she examines this ethnic literature between the 1870s and World War II. Rølvaag's novels provide constant evidence in concluding that "the Scandinavian heritage can be summed up [in the literature] as love of land, strong loyalty to the extended family, thrift and honesty, respect and work, obedience to both civil and religious law, and Protestant piety. The qualities in the American culture that [these novelists] value most highly are individual freedom, lack of class distinctions, and economic opportunity." In "Agrarian versus Frontiersman in Midwestern Fiction" (pp. 44–63) Barbara Howard Meldrum sees the conflict between farmer virtues and the lawless, grasping qualities of frontiering as inevitably joined in agriculture on the plains and as central both to Per Hansa's character and his difficulties with his wife. Beret's Cassandralike warning is against the sin of materialism: "Here where 'Earth takes us' man has no time to think of God, only of self and pressing material needs." Paul Reigstad in "Myth Aspects of *Giants in the Earth*" (pp. 64–70) explores the novel's Faustian and *askeladd* overtones and applies the "giants" of the title to the "monstrous" within the settlers themselves, "their potential for evil." The dangers of the settling are also the subject of Emilio DeGrazia's "The Great Plain: Rølvaag's New World Sea" (*SDR* 20,iii:35–49), which argues that life away from the watery sea and on the prairie sea sends the existential self into hiding and urges individuals away from creative living. The essay has some value for attempting to place Rølvaag squarely within the American literary tradition encompassing Melville, Lewis, Fitzgerald.

Finally, Catherine D. Farmer in "Beret as the Norse Mythological Goddess Freya/Gerthr" (*Women and Western American Literature*, pp. 179–93) argues that Per Hansa's neglect of his wife causes her to surrender to the land her role as seductive fertility goddess and results in Per Hansa's lapse from his role as vegetation, sunshine god Frey/Freyr and become in death the figure of winter.

### v. H. L. Mencken, Humorists, and Others

The year's Mencken book, *Letters from Baltimore: The Mencken-Cleator Correspondence*, ed. P. E. Cleator (Fairleigh Dickinson), seems at first and actually is self-indulgence on the part of the editor, especially the six-page "Personal Preamble," in which we learn more about the editor than about Mencken. Yet the collection of letters dating from 1936–48, with notes from Mencken's secretary from 1948–56, becomes fascinating as a record of Mencken's responses to the war, hospitals, organized religion, bureaucracy, and his estimates of Churchill, Roosevelt, Truman, Dewey, etc., as well as to Cleator, his English friend, an amateur scientist and professional writer. The letter exchange between Cleator and Rosalind C. Lohrfinck after Mencken's death tells the story of Cleator's unsuccessful attempt to persuade her to record her 27 years' secretarial experiences with Mencken. Mencken letters also concern Walter C. West in "H. L. Mencken Letters in the University of North Carolina Collection" (*Menckeniana* 81:1–3), a description of the 500-item collection recently opened for research of Mencken's letters to Duke professor Fred Hanes, his wife Betty, and sister De Witt. Most of the letters reveal attitudes of Mencken evident in those to Cleator, although a few after the death of Sara Haardt Mencken in 1935 directly express Mencken's distress and personal vulnerability. In "Missives from Henry: the Mencken-Hanes Correspondence" in the same issue (pp. 4–5) the nephew of Fred Hanes, Frank Borden Hanes, reminisces about his uncle and aunts and the earthy, fun-loving Mencken ("an annual guest at their cottage. The vulnerable side of Mencken ("sentimental, generous, and unwavering," according to Alfred A. Knopf) surfaces in Robert F. Nardini's fine essay, "Mencken and the Cult of Smartness" (*Menckeniana* 84:1–12), on Mencken's popular following in the 1920s. The important point is made that, as in the case of most popular heroes, the reasons for the fame of this castigator of both backwoods barbarism and Boston propriety were essentially frivolous: "Not ideas, but a jaunty style drew the majority of Mencken's following; they slipped it on like a fashion in clothes." When the Depression came fame went, never to return.

The influence of Mencken, especially of "The Sahara of the Bozart," on the successful attempts of H. L. Davis and James Stevens to still the Emmeline Grangerford school of Northwest writing in their 1927 *Status Rerum* pamphlet is the subject of Glen A. Love's "Stemming the Avalanche of Tripe: or, How H. L. Mencken and Friends Reformed Northwest Literature" (*Thalia* 4[1981]:46–53). Mencken is noted in Lawrence E. Mintz's "American Humor in the 1920s" (*Thalia* 4:26–32), a valuable if sometimes plodding examination of the likes of Ring Lardner and Dorothy Parker, Charlie Chaplin and Mae West, concluding that the era's culturally inept "little man" represents a lapse from the optimism of the commonsense hero of an earlier America. Lardner is one of several writers reviewed in *Laurel and Thorn: The Athlete in American Literature* (Kentucky

[1981], pp. 22–31) by Robert J. Higgs, who stresses the serious side
of this writer's surprise attack on America's spurious athlete-heroes,
whose blood lines can be traced through southwestern humor to
Greek, Arab, and Indian mythology. The achievement of Lardner's
best work is exposure, in the ironic manner, of both the absurdity of
and corruption in hero worship based on conceit and games. Gordon
Bordewyk in "Comic Alienation: Ring Lardner's Style" (*MarkhamR*
11:51–57) recognizes uncommon skill in his subject's use of the vernacular voice, and applies various stories ("My Roomy," *You Know
Me Al,* "Zone of Quiet," "Haircut," etc.) to the four types of communication breakdown contributing to their alienation theme: in-
articulateness, literalness, chattering, and deception. The humor of
William Sydney Porter is the subject of Kent Bales's contribution,
"O. Henry, 1862–1910," to *American Writers: A Collection of Literary
Biographies,* 2,i[1981]:385–412. Bales attempts to rescue Porter's
dead literary reputation by emphasizing his gift of parody capable
of corroding the literary and social conventions it discloses. To most
readers Porter's art remains merely a delightful play of surfaces,
and he hid "suggested meanings" well in order to maintain a popular
audience. His position in American letters is transitional, deconstructing through parody the formulae of a dying literary tradition
and paving the way for reform.

Ida H. Washington has prepared an informative critical biography in *Dorothy Canfield Fisher: A Biography* (New England).
Canfield, the child of a crusader and an artist, "carried the two conflicting natures of her parents within her own personality and wres-
tled with them to create meaning out of their differences." She led a
remarkably full life, enjoyed a successful marriage and literary fame,
raised two children, and worked in war relief and adult education.
Vermont was as important to her novels as Virginia was to Glasgow's,
but, like Glasgow, her concerns were universal, primarily the potential of human beings. In *The Deepening Stream* she traced the
process of her own maturity—including the tragic relationship between her parents, her experiences in France, her marriage, the birth
of her children, and the war—in the story of her heroine Penelope
Gilbert. Canfield's view of life was that of a tough Yankee. If her
fiction lacks greatness, it is perhaps the result of self-control, of
insufficient mystery, of her insistence on being an active crusader in
one's time. This biography suffers as a result of the rationalism of

the subject, so evident in generous quotations from her letters; yet Washington performs a worthy service, encouraging us to look again at a novelist who considered untraditional roles for men and women in her treatment of human growth. The major work of an early contemporary of Dorothy Canfield Fisher, New Mexico novelist Mary Hunter Austin, is the subject of James C. Work's "The Moral in Austin's *The Land of Little Rain*" (*Women and Western American Literature*, pp. 297–310). Work notes that the pattern of this impressionistic nature book revolves around three questions: "What are the essential qualities of the land? What is the relation of life forms to the land and to each other? And what is the proper role of a human animal in relation to the land and the life of it?"

*Merrimack College*

# 14. Fiction: The 1930s to the 1950s

## Louis Owens

### i. "Art for Humanity's Sake"—Proletarians and Others

Two major looks at the literature of the proletarian '30s appeared this year in *Literature at the Barricades: The American Writer in the 1930s* (Alabama), ed. Ralph F. Bogardus and Fred Hobson, and the special *Book Forum* issue on the '30s (6,ii). *Literature at the Barricades* provides an exceptional overview of this difficult decade with reprints of such classics as James T. Farrell's "The End of a Literary Decade" (pp. 204–10) and essays by such authorities as Irving Howe, Hugh Kenner, Louis D. Rubin, Jr., and Daniel Aaron. In "The Thirties in Retrospect" (pp. 13–28) Howe sketches what he calls the "whole sad story of the leftward-moving writers in the thirties" and comes close to a dismissal in spite of himself when he concludes: "But concern for the truth must force us also to admit that it was a time in which talent betrayed itself to the wardens of authoritarianism." Louis D. Rubin, Jr.'s "Trouble on the Land: Southern Literature and the Great Depression" (pp. 96–113) focuses on such writers as Erskine Caldwell and James Agee as he argues that most southern literature of the '30s does not concern itself with the problem of social consciousness characteristic of "proletarian" literature. The *Partisan Review* and such associated figures as Philip Rahv, William Phillips, and Dwight McDonald are the subjects of Alan Wald's excellent "Revolutionary Intellectuals: *Partisan Review* in the 1930s" (pp. 187–203), which might be effectively summed up in Wald's own words as a study of "the literary and political peregrination of *Partisan Review*" during the decade. Wald's essay, which originally appeared in *Occident* (1974), is worth a second look. In addition to his representation in "The End of a Literary Decade" James T. Farrell is himself the subject of Donald Pizer's fine chapter, "James T. Farrell and the 1930s" (pp. 69–81), which begins by pointing out the dangers inherent in period criticism and goes on to

conclude that we can understand the permanence of such a work as
*Studs Lonigan* if we "view it as a work whose strength derives from
the distinctive strengths of the two impulses . . . called the 1920s and
the 1930s." Less impressive is chapter 7 of this volume, Victor A.
Kramer's "The Consciousness of Technique: The Prose Method of
James Agee's *Let Us Now Praise Famous Men*" (pp. 114–25), an
essay concluding that "because his impressions and imaginative
wanderings are central, the text must ultimately be approached as
poetry." Daniel Aaron's "Edmund Wilson's Political Decade" (pp.
175–86) offers more valuable insight into Wilson's complexities,
pointing out Wilson's diffidence in *The American Jitters* toward the
"Jewish, ethnic, or black associates" of the left.

In his "Friendship Won't Stand That: John Howard Lawson
and John Dos Passos's Struggle for an Ideological Ground to Stand
On" (pp. 44–66), another of the more useful essays in this volume,
Townsend Ludington documents the widening gap between the
political positions of these two writers throughout the '30s as Lawson moved toward a rigidly Marxist position while Dos Passos grew
increasingly conservative. Jack B. Moore shows us another side of
'30s fiction in his "The View from the Broom Closet of the Regency
Hyatt: Richard Wright as a Southern Writer" (pp. 126–43). Moore
laments the "typical invisibility of black writers" in studies of southern fiction and then goes on to study the stories in *Uncle Tom's
Children* and *Eight Men*, pointing out that in contrast to the view
of southern farming held by the Agrarians, "land is no foundation
for Wright's characters as it is in other southern writing. . . ." Still
another writer outside the proletarian mainstream in the '30s is the
subject of Glenda Hobbs's "Starting Out in the Thirties: Harriette
Arnow's Literary Genesis" (pp. 144–61). Hobbs depicts Arnow's
difficulties getting started while writing fiction during this period
and, in a well-written essay, argues that "an aesthetic reassessment
is overdue."

*Book Forum's* special issue on the '30s does not carry the impact of *Literature at the Barricades*, consisting of much anecdotal
and biographical memory searching in addition to several essays
deserving mention here. One of the more readable of these is Douglas
Wixson's "Jack Conroy, The Sage of Moberly" (*BForum* 6:201–06),
a brief sketch of Conroy serving to distinguish him from the New

York circle of radical authors led by Mike Gold. Wixson's essay serves as a worthwhile reminder of this author whose *The Disinherited* has been reissued this year (Westport, Conn.: Lawrence Hill). A similar but more lengthy essay in this issue is Erika Duncan's "Coming of Age in the Thirties: A Portrait of Tillie Olsen" (pp. 207–22), a combination of biography, uncritical admiration, and critical glances at Olsen's *Yonnondio*. More concise, but offering little more than introductory biographical sketches, is Diane Levenberg's "Three Jewish Writers and the Spirit of the Thirties: Michael Gold, Anzia Yezierska, and Henry Roth" (pp. 233–44). However, any reminder of these three writers is valuable. The same might be said of Bill Whelan's "The Hardest-Shelled Protestant Episcopalian" (pp. 245–47), a very brief and rather unfocused account of James Gould Cozzens' *Men and Brethren*.

Perhaps the most substantial essay in this issue of *Book Forum* is Oliver Conant's "The Hunger and the Journey: Communism in the Thirties" (pp. 248–56), which contrasts and compares Richard Wright's *American Hunger* and Lionel Trilling's *The Middle of the Journey*, labeling both "the most deeply felt and memorable critical accounts of the Communist mentality and the appeal of communism in the thirties that exist in our literature." Finally, in "The Arguments of the Thirties: Of Politics, Journalism and Art" (pp. 257–62) Phyllis Zagano offers an educational view into the world of leftist journals during the '30s, with closest attention to *The Nation, The New Republic*, and *Partisan Review*, along with the chief figures associated with those journals.

Undoubtedly the most ambitious book-length study of this period this year is Daniel Joseph Singal's *The War Within: From Victorian to Modernist Thought in the South, 1919–1945* (N.C.). In this interdisciplinary study Singal traces the passage of Southern thought from the Victorianism and Cavalier myth inherited by Faulkner and the Agrarians to Modernism and, with an excellent focus on Robert Penn Warren, Existentialism. In the process Singal illuminates this period in the South with remarkable clarity. Posing for himself the question of where the "desire to rebel against the inherited culture" in the South came from, he answers the question convincingly while providing meaningful discussions of such figures as Ulrich Phillips, Ellen Glasgow, Faulkner, and Warren. In the somewhat unpliable thesis approach, there is a residue of its dissertation origins, but the result is a valuable addition to our understanding of the South and its literature.

*a.* **James Agee, Delmore Schwartz, and Others.** James R. Fultz adds to Agee criticism "A Classic Case of Collaboration . . . *The African Queen*" (*LFQ* 10:13–24), in which Fultz traces the evolution of the film from Forster's 1935 novel through Agee's and Huston's scripts. Fultz notes that in Agee's rough draft for the script, "Agee presents moral ambiguities that are not in the film." The problem of Jewish identity is the subject of Irving S. Saposnik's "Delmore Schwartz's America" (*SSF* 19:151–55), in which Saposnik focuses on Schwartz's "America! America!" as the story most "indicative of Schwartz's maturing attitude toward his Jewish-American identity." Erika Duncan reminds us of another little-noted figure in American letters with "Writing and Surviving: A Portrait of Meridel Le Sueur" (*BForum* 6:37–43), an essay containing fulsome praise for the beauty and strength of this author but very little else. Linda Ray Pratt offers a more valuable study in her view of William Carlos Williams as critic of American culture in "Williams's Stetcher Trilogy: 'The Pure Products of America'" (*SAF* 10:41–54). Pratt's thesis is that in the novels *White Mule, In the Money,* and *The Build-Up* "Williams implicitly questions the myth that America was made great by immigrants who represented the best and most vital of the European peoples."

*b.* **John Steinbeck.** The number of essays appearing this year on Steinbeck suggests at least a sustained interest in Steinbeck's work. As usual, *Steinbeck Quarterly* led the field in the number of works, and as usual the quality and significance of these studies vary considerably. *StQ* 15,i–ii begins with Tetsumaro Hayashi's tribute to Steinbeck's agent, Elizabeth Otis, in "Elizabeth Otis as I Remember Her" (pp. 6–8) and contains a brief autobiography written by Otis (pp. 9–10). Of greater interest to Steinbeck students will be Sylvia Cook's "Steinbeck, the People, and the Party" (pp. 11–23), which originally appeared in *Literature at the Barricades,* ed. Ralph F. Bogardus and Fred Hobson (Alabama). In an attempt to define Steinbeck's place in the proletarian '30s, Cook points out Steinbeck's isolation from the political and publishing center in New York and, in tracing Steinbeck's development from the early fiction to *The Grapes of Wrath*, argues that "Steinbeck's evolving concern for the migrants has led him to a new and less dispassionate metaphor for his scientific interests" in *The Grapes of Wrath*. In this same number of *StQ*, John Ditsky's "Between Acrobats and Seals: Steinbeck in the U.S.S.R." (pp. 23–29) compares Steinbeck's *A Russian Journal* with Arthur Miller's *In Russia* and declares that "while Miller's text is thoughtful and literary in its emphases, Steinbeck's clearly intends to entertain. . . ." Ditsky concludes, not very convincingly, that "John Steinbeck's *Russian Journal* would seem to be a sort of trial run for the notion that the public artist in an absurd time can do little more or better than to don a mask and bedevil the powers that be." In "Jim Casy: Politico of the New Jerusalem" (*StQ* 15,i–ii:30–37) Helen Lojek provides little new insight regarding Jim Casy while attempting to place this character from *The Grapes of Wrath* in the context of the Social Gospelers. Lojek concludes that "Jim Casy comes to believe that America can achieve an earthly millenium through redemptive labor organizing." A more insightful essay in this number of *StQ* is Michael W. Shurgot's "A Game of Cards in Steinbeck's *Of Mice and Men*" (pp. 38–43). Shurgot focuses on the significance of George's solitaire games throughout the novel, declaring that "the game of cards is the central symbol of the entire novel." The card games, he suggests, provide "an exact symbol of the unpredictable, often merciless world" of the novel. The final essay, Douglas L. Verdier's "Ethan Allen Hawley and the Hanged Man: Free Will and Fate in *The Winter of Our Discontent*" (pp. 44–50), points out Steinbeck's accurate use of the tarot deck and states (overstates, perhaps) that "the plot of the novel turns" on the incident of Ethan's tarot session with Margie Young-Hunt. *StQ* 15,iii–iv offers two additional essays on Steinbeck's fiction before devoting itself to Tetsumaro Hayashi's "Interviews with Outstanding Steinbeck Scholars." In "Charles G. Norris and John Steinbeck: Two More Tributes to *The Grapes of Wrath*" (pp. 90–96), Richard Allan Davison attempts to demonstrate the influence of *The Grapes of Wrath* on Charles Norris' *Flint*, quoting at length from both works to support his thesis. Bradd Burningham's "Relation, Vision, and Tracking the Welsh Rats in *East of Eden* and *The Winter of Our Discontent*" (pp. 77–90) argues that *The Winter of Our Discontent* is the sequel to *East of Eden*, claiming that "in *Eden* is the genesis of much that was to culminate in

Winter." Burningham spends much of his time explicating the familiar Cain-Abel theme of *East of Eden* and tracing parallels in theme and characterization between the two novels. Hayashi's "Interviews with Outstanding Steinbeck Scholars" are conducted with tact and superb knowledge of Steinbeck studies, but the result is uneven. Outstanding among the interviews is that with Jackson J. Benson, Steinbeck's biographer. In his interview (pp. 97–103) Benson observes that Steinbeck's style "seems to have a far greater range" than Hemingway's and that "Steinbeck, of all his novelist contemporaries, was probably the brightest as well as the best read and most scholarly." Martha Heasley Cox and John Ditsky, other interview subjects here, offer little beyond Ditsky's claim that "Steinbeck's works and mind . . . have been vastly underrated all along," while interviews with Maurice Dunbar and Lee Richard Hayman provide tips for anyone teaching a Steinbeck course.

Among essays on Steinbeck appearing outside *StQ* this year, the most valuable may be Warren Motley's "From Patriarch to Matriarchy: Ma Joad's Role in *The Grapes of Wrath*" (*AL* 54:397–412), which effectively demonstrates Steinbeck's debt to Robert Briffault's *The Mothers* in his characterization of Ma Joad. *The Grapes of Wrath* came in for additional attention in Mark Hamilton Lytle's "Hollywood Realism and the Depression Era" (*BForum* 6:117–84), which points out persuasively John Ford's elimination of "social class tension" from the movie version of that novel, and in *Twentieth Century Interpretations of* The Grapes of Wrath, edited by Robert Con Davis (Prentice-Hall). In addition to the familiar mainstays of Steinbeck criticism—essays by Warren French, Peter Lisca, and R. W. B. Lewis—this collection is noteworthy for its excellent introduction by Davis and its inclusion of an interesting and previously unpublished essay on Ma Joad, Joan Hedrick's "Mother Earth and Earth Mother: The Recasting of Myth in Steinbeck's *The Grapes of Wrath*" (pp. 134–43). Hedrick finds Ma Joad to be "emphatically not a realistic portrait of a woman," and concludes that "in Steinbeck's telling, she had no inner self." In "Camelot East of Eden: John Steinbeck's *Tortilla Flat*" (*ArQ* 38:203–16) Louis Owens focuses on Steinbeck's use of Arthurian materials in *Tortilla Flat* and argues, contrary to most previous criticism, that *Tortilla Flat* is "a remarkably unified and artistically successful novel. . . ." Also attempting to set the critical record straight is James C. Work, whose "Coordinate

Forces in 'The Leader of the People' " (*WAL* 16:278–89) begins with the declaration that the "principle interpretations of Steinbeck's 'The Leader of the People' seem shallow," and goes on to apply the frontier thesis of 19th-century writer John Mason Peck to an explication of the story. Perhaps of more immediate use to Steinbeck critics is Robert S. Hughes, Jr.'s "Steinbeck Stories at the Houghton Library: A Case for Authenticity of Four Unpublished Texts" (*HLB* 30,i:87–95). Hughes provides a distinct service to Steinbeck scholarship as he traces the peregrination of four Steinbeck stories and looks at internal evidence to support his claim that "The Days of Long Marsh," "East Third Street," "The Nail," and "The Nymph and Isobel" are "indeed genuine Steinbeck." Of less significance but very accurate is John Tibbett's review of Metro-Goldwyn-Mayer's film based on *Cannery Row* and *Sweet Thursday*, "It Happened in Monterey: John Steinbeck's *Cannery Row*" (*LFQ* 10:82–84). Tibbetts finds the movie a disappointment, declaring that "Doc and Suzy move in a subterranean world, oddly empty, oddly quiet, and . . . rather boring."

### ii. Social Iconoclasts—Salinger and West

The most significant study of Nathanael West to appear this year is Kingsley Widmer's *Nathanael West* (TUSAS 423). Widmer warns us in his preface that his emphasis will be "broader than the usual summary and explication," and he is true to his word as he blends much excellent critical insight with a surfeit of homespun wisdom concerning politics, morality, Southern California architecture, and the petit bourgeois. Widmer's thesis centers upon West's obsession with masquerading in his personal life and fiction and upon what Widmer refers to incessantly as the "masturbatory" element in West's fiction. A much less significant because less ambitious addition to West criticism is Joy Walsh's note, "*Miss Lonelyhearts*: The Problem of Touching and the Primary Need for Fictions" (*NMAL* 6:Item 1). Walsh notes that "Miss Lonelyhearts desperately desires to touch his readers through the letters," but finally "the collapse of his hope in the sexual as well as linguistic dimensions of communication leave him . . . stranded in the novel's final pages with nothing to touch." Correcting errors is the intent of David R. Mesher's "A Note on Nathanael West Bibliographies" (*AN&Q* 20,v–vi:79–80), in which Mesher points to errors in William White's *Nathanael West: A Com-*

*prehensive Bibliography* (1975) and the duplication of these errors in Helen Taylor's "An Annotated Bibliography" in *Nathanael West: The Cheaters and the Cheated*. Mesher laments what he calls the "shoddy bibliography" exemplified in such errors.

Two essays worthy of mention this year consider J. D. Salinger's *The Catcher in the Rye*. In "In Memoriam: Allie Caulfield in *The Catcher in the Rye*" (*Mosaic* 15:129–40) Edwin Haviland Miller wonders whether this novel "has been praised for the right reasons" and argues that "most critics have tended to accept Holden's evaluation of the world as phony, when in fact his attitudes are symptomatic of a serious psychological problem." Miller proposes that we read this novel as "the chronicle of a four-year period in the life of an adolescent whose rebelliousness is his only means of dealing with his inability to come to terms with the death of his brother." Similarities between *The Catcher in the Rye* and Hemingway's posthumous "The Last Good Country" are the subject of Sandra Whipple Spanier's "Hemingway's 'The Last Good Country' and *The Catcher in the Rye*: More Than a Family Resemblance" (*SSF* 19:35–43). Labeling both works "contemporary American romances with some surprising similarities," Spanier speculates that Hemingway did not finish this work because he may have "realized he was coming awfully close to a story that had already been written [*Catcher*]."

### *iii.* Expatriates and Emigrés

*a.* **Henry Miller, Anaïs Nin.**   Richard R. Centing kept both Miller and Nin in view this year with *Seahorse: The Anaïs Nin/Henry Miller Journal* (1:ii), published and edited by Centing to take the place of *Under the Sign of Pisces*. The first number of *Seahorse* contains Centing's "Writings About Henry Miller: A First Supplement" (pp. 10–16) and "Writings About Anaïs Nin: An Eighth Supplement" (pp. 5–9). This issue also features an interview by Kenneth Merrill with Samson de Brier (pp. 1–4) attesting to de Brier's adulation of Anaïs Nin. A 1970 interview with Anaïs Nin conducted by Maxine Molyneux is the subject of "Looking Again at Anaïs Nin" (*MinnR* 18:86–101) by Maxine Molyneux and Julia Casterton. Focusing upon the third volume of the journals discussed in the interview, Casterton notes in her commentary "how uneasily [Nin's] work sits in the history of women's writing in this century" and the difficulties raised by the problematic quality of Nin's writing for feminist critics. Observing that Nin fails to mention the erotica in the interview, Casterton states, "The erotica stand, I believe, as a salutary warning against the unified self that looms at the reader in the interview."

*b.* **Vladimir Nabokov.** This year continues to add to Nabokov studies with the appearance of *Nabokov: The Critical Heritage,* ed. Norman Paige (Routledge). A valuable addition to Nabokov scholarship, this volume provides a concise overview of the belated, contradictory, and complex critical reaction to Nabokov's novels, from the emigré journal period to English and American reviews of the later works. A less useful volume to appear this year is David Packman's *Vladimir Nabokov: The Structure of Literary Desire* (Missouri), a brief volume heavily laden with structuralist paraphernalia. Referring frequently to Borges, Barthes, and intertextuality, the author argues that *Lolita, Pale Fire,* and *Ada* are "reflexive" in presenting effects not resolved in the texts. Packman quotes at length and offers somewhat thin explication burdened by a tendency toward opacity of language. Another sometimes turgid but admirably structured essay is D. Barton Johnson's "Spatial Modeling and Deixis: Nabokov's *Invitation to a Beheading* (*PoT* 3,i:81–98). Johnson examines the thematic oppositions and "pure spatial dimension" of this minor work and suggests that "the linguistic category of deixis be posited and utilized as the appropriate intermediate level between 'reality' which is directly describable in spatial terms and verbal art which is only indirectly accessible to spatial modeling." D. Barton Johnson shifts his focus to *Ada* in "The Scrabble Game in *Ada* or Taking Nabokov Clitorally" (*JML* 8:291–303), declaring that "of all of Nabokov's writings, the one most riddled with word play is *Ada.*" Johnson cleverly deciphers the anagrammatic sexuality of the Van/Ada/Lucette relationship and finds in the scrabble game "an anagrammatic motif echoing the theme of Lucette's passionate obsession with her halfbrother." An equally clever piece of detective work is found in Paul R. Jackson's "*Pale Fire* and Sherlock Holmes" (*SAF* 10:101–05), in which Jackson follows the tracks of the "second bird" in *Pale Fire* to "The Final Problem," the story in which Doyle prematurely killed off Holmes only to resurrect him later. In "Necrophilia in *Lolita*" (*CentR* 26:361–74) Lucy B. Maddox notes Nabokov's allusions to Poe's "Annabel Lee" and "Ligeia" and argues that

"Nabokov exploits the psychological implications of necrophilia" in the novel and that Humbert's madness is "the psychological distortion resulting from love for a female who is immune to change and who therefore cannot be lost." Less conspicuously clever but insightful nonetheless is David Cowart's "Art and Exile: Nabokov's *Pnin*" (*SAF* 10:197–207). Cowart complains that critics have heretofore not recognized that *Pnin* "ranks among the author's best works," and he concludes that Pnin is "a symbol of the human condition as it is perceived in the modern age." A larger view of Nabokov is the aim of Robert J. Nelson's "The Gnoseologist and the Nosologist: Vladimir Nabokov and Edmund Wilson on Literature and Politics" (*GaR* 36,i:133–47). In a perceptive study of Wilson-Nabokov letters Nelson attempts to define "the roots of the socio-genetic incompatability that makes the Nabokov-Wilson friendship a fascinating encounter of owl and pussycat."

### iv. Southerners

*a.* **Robert Penn Warren, Allen Tate, and the Agrarians.** Of greatest interest to Warren scholars this year will most likely be James A. Grimshaw, Jr.'s *Robert Penn Warren: A Descriptive Bibliography, 1922–1979* (Virginia), a comprehensive and intelligently organized bibliography of primary and secondary material, including manuscripts, unpublished works, and translations. Three rather slight essays focusing on Warren also bear mentioning here. In "Robert Penn Warren's *Brother to Dragons*: Irony and the Image of Man" (*MissQ* 35,i:15–24) Mark Royden compares the Jefferson of this Warren work to Ike McCaslin of Faulkner's "The Bear," stating that both "have attempted to preserve an idyllic view of life. . . ." R. P. W. of *Brother to Dragons* Royden compares to Cass Edmonds in "The Bear" and argues that "the resolution achieved by the two principal speakers of *Brother to Dragons* would seem to strike the precarious moral balance demanded by a modern Party of Irony." Diane S. Bonds compares Warren and Hardy in "Fleshly Temptation in Robert Penn Warren's *A Place to Come To* and Hardy's *Jude The Obscure*" (*AN&Q* 19,ix–x:144–46). Bonds adds little to Warren scholarship in pointing out "distinct resemblances" in characters' names in the novels and in noting the similarities in the roles of Rozelle and

Arabella as "embodiments of fleshly temptation." Also lightweight is Kenneth Tucker's "The Pied Piper—A Key to Understanding Robert Penn Warren's 'Blackberry Winter'" (*SSF* 19:339–42). Tucker claims that "the story's parallel to the medieval German legend of the Pied Piper . . . guides the reader's perceptions of the fictional events. . . ."

Allen Tate is the subject of Robert Buffington's encomium in "Allen Tate: Society, Vocation, Communion" (*SoR* 18,i:62–72). Declaring Tate to be "one of the heroes of the modern republic of letters," Buffington provides a biographical illustration of Tate's commitment to "high seriousness." A more stimulating study this year is Louis Fuller's "Prophets in the Promised Land" (*BForum* 6:263–69), an impressive attempt to comprehend the place of the Agrarians of *I'll Take My Stand* in the '30s and the seeming incongruity of their lasting influence on American letters. One of the Agrarians, Andrew Lytle, receives special attention in John Yew's "Alchemical Captains: Andrew Lytle's Tales of the Conquistadors" (*SLJ* 14,ii:39–48), a discussion of *Alchemy* and *At the Moon's End*, concluding that "Lytle demonstrates that from its outset the Spanish incursion is marked by a perversion of motive . . . a perilous confusion . . . of means and ends."

*b.* **Conrad Aiken.** Aiken receives the attention this year of a special issue of the *Southern Quarterly* (21,i:1–159), an issue which begins with Irving Malin's introduction raising the question of whether Aiken can reasonably be considered a southern writer (*SoQ* 21,i: 3–6). Malin concludes that Aiken "takes the South as a given, but he cannot dissociate himself from it. He must *transform* it—through art." In one of the more effective essays in this issue, "*Great Circle*: Conrad Aiken's Autoplastic Journey into Childhood" (pp. 39–63), Steven E. Olsen compares this novel to "Young Goodman Brown" and "The Bear" as a "classic tale of initiation. . . ." Olsen reads the Duxbury section of the novel as a reshaping—"autoplastic 'self-shaping'"—of childhood for the author. In "Conrad Aiken's Fiction: 'An Inordinate and Copious Lyric'" (pp. 9–27) in this number of *SoQ* Mary Martin Rountree assesses the reasons for Aiken's failure to achieve popular or critical success with his fiction and concludes: "He was at no point attuned to the spirit of his time." Aiken's critical theory is the subject of Nancy Ciucevich Story's "Conrad Aiken: A Functional Basis for Poetry and Criticism" (*SoQ* 21,i:132–47). Focusing on the "relativism" of Aiken's criticism, Story states broadly: "His criticism . . . elevates Aiken to the status of the superior critic who teaches us how, not what, to think." Aiken and criticism are also the subjects of Ted R. Spivey's "Conrad Aiken and the Life of Reason" (*SoQ* 21,i:148–57). Depending heavily upon an elucidation of the philosophy of Santayana, Aiken's teacher at Harvard, Spivey argues that in Santayana's concept of the life of reason can be found the key to "Aiken's own pursuit of the life of reason" and the way to read Aiken's heavily autobiographical works. A less substantial study is "Conrad Aiken and the Supernatural" (*SoQ* 21,i:119–31), by Douglas Robillard, who notes that "the importance of Poe should not be overlooked in Aiken's development" and is almost as shallow in his scrutiny of *The Jig of Forslin* and "Mr. Arclaris."

A more valuable perspective on the fiction is Joseph C. Voelker's " 'A Collideorscape!': Sigmund Freud, Malcolm Lowry, and the Aesthetics of Conrad Aiken's *A Heart for the Gods of Mexico*" (*SoQ* 21,i:64–81). Voelker finds the "two sides of Aiken, the Freudian modernist and the Unitarian minister" at war with one another, and, while detailing Aiken's complex relationship with Lowry, declares this novel to be "an exposition of *Beyond the Pleasure Principle* and an explicit acceptance of Freud's pessimisim concerning the possibilities of individual perfectability. . . ." In "The Artist and the Art Novel: A Reappraisal of Conrad Aiken's *Blue Voyage*" (*SoQ* 21,i:28–37) Sanford Pinsker declares *Blue Voyage* "an especially good place to see . . . the assets and liabilities of Aiken's aesthetic." Pinsker concludes that this novel is "an extended meditation—in the form of a prose poem—about consciousness, Art, and how the two are ineluctably related." Edward Butscher shifts the focus to Aiken's short works in "Conrad Aiken's Short Fiction: The Poet's Story" (*SoQ* 21,i:99–118) to examine "Silent Snow, Secret Snow," "Mr. Arcularis," and "Strange Moonlight," noting Aiken's debt to Katherine Mansfield, Chekhov, Poe, and Freud. In an essay not marked by clarity of style, "The Ushant Dream of Conrad Aiken" (*SoQ* 21,i:82–98), James L. Wheeler delves into the difficulties of *Ushant* and Aiken's verse in an attempt to solve the secret of the Ushant dream, finding that the dream "set the dominant structure and atmosphere of Conrad Aiken's stream of consciousness autobiography. . . ."

**c. Eudora Welty.** Welty continues to receive a great deal of attention from critics. Jennifer Lynn Randisi's *A Tissue of Lies: Eudora Welty and the Southern Romance* (Univ. Press) places Welty in the context of the tradition of southern romance writers and provides a particularly cogent discussion of the significance of place in Welty's work. Welty is also the subject of a special issue of the *Southern Quarterly* (20:iv) this year as well as a number of additional essays. Ruth M. Vande Kieft begins her "Eudora Welty: The Question of Meaning" in the *SoQ* special issue (pp. 24–39) with a facile dismissal of "semiotics or of a French disease called post-Saussurean linguistics," and argues at length in favor of her own rather personal brand of humanistic search for meaning in Welty's fiction. *The Optimist's Daughter* this critic declares to be "an elegy without an apotheosis. . . ." In "Images of Memory in Eudora Welty's *The Optimist's Daughter*" (*SLJ* 14,ii:28–48) Marilyn Arnold documents the imagery of this novel, noting "an ingenious blend of time and bird imagery," and argues that "through the use of imagery, symbol, ritual, and parable" Welty weaves her several themes "into one thematic whole." A more significant essay is Michael Kreyling's "Modernism in Welty's *A Curtain of Green and Other Stories*" (*SoQ* 20,iv:40–53). Citing the Modernist dilemma as defined by Krutch, Barzun, and others, Kreyling suggests that Welty's "artistic voice addresses her age's moral and philosophical dilemmas as directly as anyone else's."

The remaining items in *SoQ*'s Welty issue are somewhat less profitable. In "Eudora Welty: The Metaphor of Music" (pp. 92–100) Elizabeth Evans examines musical metaphors, images, and allusions. Albert J. Devlin treats "Jackson's Welty" (*SoQ* 20,iv:54–91) or should it be "Welty's Jackson"? That is, the reflection of Jackson, Mississippi, topography in her fiction. W. U. McDonald, Jr., offers guidelines to more needed textual study ("An Unworn Path: Bibliographical and Textual Scholarship on Eudora Welty," *SoQ* 20,iv: 101–7). In addition to being an interview, Martha Van Noppen's "A Conversation with Eudora Welty" (*SoQ* 20,iv:7–23) demonstrates difficulties in interviewing Welty—contending with Welty's coyness, for example. A similar difficulty confronts interviewer John Griffin Jones in *Mississippi Writers Talking*, vol. 1 (Miss.). Jones approaches Welty with a "yes'm" style and worshipful desire to avoid any question that might startle. However, this interview should interest Welty readers because of a scattering of candid Welty remarks.

*The Golden Apples* is the subject of two of the more effective Welty essays to appear this year. In "Dreaming of the Other in *The Golden Apples*" (*MFS* 28:415–33) Lowry Pei examines the technical devices of this work in light of what this critic sees as the central thematic issues of the collection: "how we perceive or constitute reality, how we turn it into language, and how we achieve communication . . . between the accustomed subjectivity that is over here and the bewildering one that is over there." *The Golden Apples*, Pei concludes, "can be seen as a book about how people use many things which are not equal to the world—language, dreams, memory —to make the world available and bearable. . . ." Occasionally more strained than Pei's essay is Elaine Upton Pugh's "The Duality of Morgana: The Making of Virgie's Vision, the Vision of *The Golden Apples*" (*MFS* 28:435–51). In dismissing prior attempts to "decode" specific mythical references in this volume Pugh argues that "Welty is working inside a mythical frame that absorbs and supersedes disparate mythic events. It seems that *The Golden Apples* grows out of a cyclical conception of history and myth, and from this cyclical history a fundamental or archetypal duality emerges." Two noteworthy studies of *Delta Wedding* also appeared this year. In "*Delta Wedding* as Pastoral" (*Interpretations* 13:59–72), Allison Goeller argues that the novel "deserves to stand beside *Moby-Dick*, *The Great Gatsby*, and other important pastorals . . . where the American garden of Eden is found to be seriously flawed." Also noting the darker side of *Delta Wedding* and *Losing Battles*, Sara McAlpin suggests in "Family in Eudora Welty's Fiction" (*SoR* 18:480–94) that the family functions not only as a nurturing element in these works but "also as a decidedly restrictive and diminishing force." Patricia S. Yaeger takes yet another approach to Welty's fiction in "The Case of the Dangling Signifier: Phallic Imagery in Eudora Welty's 'Moon Lake'" (*TCL* 28:431–52). Phallic imagery, Yaeger claims, "provides the dominant set of metaphors" in this story and "presides over the plot . . . in unexpected ways." Though a bit top-heavy with Lacanian baggage, Yaeger's essay provides a thoughtful perspective on this story and Welty's fiction as a whole. Somewhat less stimulating is John L. Idol, Jr.'s "Edna Earle Ponder's Good Country People" (*SoQ* 20,iii:66–75), which suggests that Edna Earle bridges the worlds of town and country in *The Ponder Heart*: "This optimistic daughter of the Ponders sees . . . a continuing need for good country people as well as the urgency of upholding the best features of life in a small town as she has come to know them in Clay." The broadest approach to Welty's fiction in this year's essays, Richard C. Moreland's "Community and Vision in Eudora Welty" (*SoR* 18:84–99) claims that Welty's "dramatic resolutions . . . have tended increasingly in the direction noted by [Robert Penn] Warren, away from history and toward idea. . . ." Moreland reviews *The Golden Apples, The Ponder Heart, Losing Battles,* and *The Optimist's Daughter* to support this thesis. A final note here must take into consideration the *Eudora Welty Newsletter,* which continues to furnish a miscellany of valuable material on Welty, including a textual study of the English edition of *Delta Wedding* by W. U. McDonald, Jr. (*EWN* 6,i:6–12; ii:4–8). Also notable are McDonald's "Works by Welty: A Continuing Checklist" (*EWN* 6:i) and O. B. Emerson's "A Checklist of Welty Scholarship" (*EWN* 6:ii).

*d.* **Carson McCullers and Katherine Anne Porter.**   McCullers is the subject of several essays this year, with perhaps the least ambitious being Barbara C. Gannon's note, "McCullers' *Ballad of the Sad Cafe*" (*Expl* 41,i:59–60), which suggests that the song of the chain gang in this novel serves as an envoy and "encapsulates *The Ballad of the Sad Cafe.*" Only slightly more significant is Clifton Snider's "On Death and Dying: Carson McCullers's *Clock Without Hands*" (*MarkhamR* 11:43–46), which traces the five stages of dying outlined in Kubler-Ross's *On Death and Dying* in this McCullers work. Louise Westling turns her attention to *The Ballad of the Sad Cafe* in "Carson McCullers' Amazon Nightmare" (*MFS* 28:465–73) and begins with the declaration that "Miss Amelia's freakishness has not been seriously examined" heretofore. Westling concludes: "The form of *The Ballad of the Sad Cafe* . . . allows McCullers to indulge the impulse to appropriate male power and thus escape the culturally inferior role of woman." In "Autistic Gestures in *The Heart Is a Lonely Hunter*" (*MFS* 28:453–63) Frances Freeman Paden suggests that in this work "McCullers endows her characters with a kind of psychology that is profoundly autistic" and that the novel's conclusion is positive in that Brannon experiences an "epiphanic moment" of self-recognition as he gazes into the mirror and gathers the courage "to turn away . . . from his own reflection."

In " 'The Other Side of Silence': Katherine Anne Porter's 'He'

As Tragedy" (*MFS* 28:395–404) Bruce W. Jorgensen offers a corrective to what he sees as the errors of recent criticism of this story and
argues that "Miss Porter's subject in 'He' . . . is simply the tragic
nature of ordinary familial love." Like Jorgensen, Debra A. Moddelmog in "Narrative Irony and Hidden Motivations in Katherine Anne
Porter's 'He'" (*MFS* 28:405–13) cites the varied critical history of
this story, but unlike Jorgensen Moddelmog argues that the story is
heavily ironic and that Mrs. Whipple is "a moral monster."

Richard S. Kennedy provides additional insight this year into the
editorial industry surrounding Thomas Wolfe in "Thomas Wolfe and
Elizabeth Nowell: A Unique Relationship" (*SAQ* 81:202–13). Primarily a tribute to the indefatigable Nowell, this essay gives large
credit to Wolfe's agent and editor for sharpening Wolfe's style.
James Boyer also focuses on Wolfe in a note, "The Metaphysical
Level in Wolfe's 'The Sun and the Rain'" (*SSF* 19:384–87). Claiming that this story "is convincing on the literal and the symbolic
level," Boyer concludes that "the simplicity of character, of plot and
of language all reinforce the theme: that one must find wisdom not
in learning, not even in experience, but in the strength that comes
from the earth."

A 1981 publication meriting attention this year is Richard S.
Kennedy's "The 'Wolfgate' Affair" (*Harvard Mag.* 84,i:48–62). Replying with refreshing vehemence to John Halberstadt's argument
that Wolfe's last novels, *The Web and the Rock* and *You Can't Go
Home Again*, are the creations not of Wolfe but of Edward C. Aswell,
Wolfe's editor, Kennedy sets out "to stop this defamation of a dead
author and his work" by once again detailing the editorial process
which produced these posthumous works. Although Kennedy weakens his defense of Aswell somewhat by admitting certain editorial
trespasses, Kennedy's defense of the integrity of the novels is persuasive and should convince us to consider again before dismissing
them as "fraud."

### *v.* Popular Writers—Erskine Caldwell, Margaret Mitchell, James Thurber, and Others

Erskine Caldwell is the subject of an entertaining but insubstantial
interview conducted by Elizabeth Pell Broadwell and Ronald Wesley
Hoag and published as "'A Writer First': An Interview with Erskine

Caldwell" (*GaR* 36:83–101). Of greater interest to Caldwell readers and critics will be William White's "About Erskine Caldwell: A Checklist, 1933–1980" (*BB* 39,i:9–16), while more entertaining but less profitable is Howard Baker's "From the Top of the Tree" (*SoR* 18:427–41), a personal reaction to, rather than a critical study of, Caroline Gordon.

William Boozer offers insight into the character of Jesse Stuart in "Jesse Stuart to William Boozer: A Decade of Selected Letters" (*Register of the Ky. Hist. Soc.* 80,i:1–64). Unfortunately, however, the insight offered is not very positive. These hundred or so letters register primarily Stuart's concern for the durability of his reputation as he denounces and denigrates such competitors as Sinclair Lewis, John Steinbeck, and Hemingway and measures success exclusively in numbers of volumes sold and monetary reward reaped. A rather sad display.

One of the more thoughtful essays this year deals with Margaret Mitchell. In "*Nick of the Woods* and *Gone With the Wind*: Racism, Literature and the American Chivalric Myth" (*MarkhamR* 12:1–5) Margaret E. Stewart depends heavily upon Richard Slotkin's thesis of "regeneration through violence" as she examines what she terms a "fundamental American myth"—the "romanticized character of the vigilante"—in both *Nick of the Woods* and *Gone With the Wind*. Pointing to the contradiction between the vigilante mystique's dependence upon the image of the helpless female and Scarlett O'Hara's competence, Stewart declares that "the tension between feminine mystique and female reality is all too easily resolved within the romantic terms of *Gone With the Wind*." Margaret Mitchell's feminism also figures in Darden Asbury Pyron's "Margaret Mitchell: First or Nothing" (*SoQ* 20:19–34), a somewhat anecdotal account of Mitchell's life, stressing the tensions which provided "the sources of her creative energy and the larger dilemmas she confronted as a Southerner and a woman." A less prominent and less popular writer than Mitchell is the subject of Mary Jane Lupton's "Zora Neale Hurston and the Survival of the Female" (*SLJ* 15,i:45–54), in which Lupton looks at Hurston's *Their Eyes Were Watching God* and, in a sometimes less-than-cogent discussion, argues that in Janie of that novel "Hurston is giving us a 'New Woman,' a woman whose actions are larger, even, than heroic." Still another neglected female voice is the subject of Mitzi Berger Hamovitch's "My Life I Will Not Let

Thee Go Except Thou Bless Me: An Interview with Janet Lewis"
(*SoR* 18:299–313), which may stimulate new interest in Lewis'
writing while providing a few interesting glimpses into Lewis' life
with Yvor Winters and her pre-Winters years in Paris. Finally, James
Thurber receives attention in Ann Ferguson Mann's well-written
"Taking Care of Walter Mitty" (*SSF* 19:351–57), which briefly defends the oft-scorned Mrs. Mitty and argues that "Mrs. Mitty's behavior can just as easily be understood as a response to, and not a
cause of, Mitty's fantasy life. In fact, Mrs. Mitty can be considered
the ideal wife for Walter Mitty."

### vi. Detectives and Westerners

Raymond Chandler is the subject of another volume this year, William Luhr's well-researched *Raymond Chandler and Film* (Ungar).
Though damaged by repetition and an at times less-than-sparkling
style, Luhr's study provides both an excellent background synopsis
of Chandler's life in Hollywood and revulsion for the trade of screen-
writer, and a close examination of the movies made from Chandler
material. Chandler and Dashiell Hammett together are the subjects
of Paul Skenazy's monograph *The New Wild West: The Urban Mysteries of Dashiell Hammett and Raymond Chandler* (*WWS* 54), an
intelligent study contrasting Hammett's "morally ambiguous" detec-
tives with Chandler's detective hero "in search of a hidden truth."
Though perceptive, the monograph is flawed by Skenazy's attempt
to deal with more material than a monograph allows for, a problem
highlighted by the abrupt dismissal of Chandler and an addendum
discussing the detective fiction of Ross Macdonald (Kenneth Millar)
in three pages. Even less focused is Joseph Agassi's "The Detective
Novel and Scientific Method" (*PoT* 3,i:99–108), a brief essay inves-
tigating the nature of scientific investigation with much reference
to Bacon and notice of Poe. Agassi makes distinctions between the
"romantic detective, spy, and suspense novel" and its "realistic counterpart," and, in a few paragraphs on Chandler finds Chandler's
detective not to be romantic in the way Chandler claimed he was
but "rather immoral in small ways. . . ." Chandler's apprenticeship to the pulps, most notably *Black Mask*, is the focus of Roy
Meador's "Chandler in the Thirties: Apprenticeship of an Angry
Man" (*BForum* 6:143–53), an essay which helps explain the appear-

ance of *The Big Sleep* at the end of the decade. Horace McCoy, another practitioner of "hard-boiled" fiction, is the subject of a quick overview in Mark Royden Winchell's monograph, *Horace McCoy* (*WWS* 51), a discussion of several McCoy novels in an attempt to view McCoy as a regionalist and Hollywood as his region.

Mari Sandoz continues to generate critical attention this year, particularly from Fritz Oehlschlaeger. In "Passion and Denial in Mari Sandoz's 'Peachstone Basket' " (*Great Plains Quar.* 2:106–13) Oehlschlaeger dutifully notes that Sandoz's reputation "will undoubtedly rest primarily on her nonfiction" and then goes on to a careful and insightful reading of "Peachstone Basket" as a "mythic interpretation of American character, an interpretation that has affinities with those suggested by Ralph Waldo Emerson." Surely the most significant work on Sandoz this year is Helen Winter Stauffer's *Mari Sandoz: Story Catcher of the Plains* (Nebraska), the first full-length biography of this major western writer. Stauffer chronologically and methodically traces Sandoz's life and literary career from the sandhills of Nebraska to success and New York, discussing the genesis of each work along with Sandoz's tortured wranglings with editors and critics. Stauffer's research is exhaustive, and she admirably avoids the small talk of biography to give us a clear and convincing portrait with a useful bibliography attached. Of less critical import is Claire Mattern's "Mari Sandoz and *Capital City*: The Writer and Her Book" (*BForum* 6:222–32), which consists primarily of biographical sketching with brief commentary upon resemblances between the fictional Capital City and the real Lincoln, Nebraska. Biography is also the chief aim of Jane Nelson's monograph on another little-read author, *Mabel Dodge Luhan* (*WWS* 55), a light-handed introduction to Luhan's life and work which takes a quick look at the six Luhan volumes published in the '30s.

*California State University, Northridge*

# 15. Fiction: The 1950s to the Present

## Jerome Klinkowitz

In 1967, when at the start of his doctoral studies this reviewer purchased his first book-length study of postwar American fiction, there
were less than half a dozen to choose from. At last count the shelf for
such contemporary studies now holds over 60 books, with a half
dozen or more being added each year. Glancing through this field,
which was born and has flourished before our eyes much like time-
lapse photography of a beautiful and intricate plant coming into
bloom, one is amazed how little repetition there has been from volume to volume. Perhaps it is the unsettled, anticanonical nature of
contemporary literature which encourages such idiosyncratic approaches; but the highly personal nature of responses to recent fiction especially characterizes the several major studies offered this
year. From polemic to worry and wonder, each scholar seems anxious to orient his or her approach according to one's most intimate
responses. In some cases the result is virtually confessional; but for
all it is apparent that contemporary fiction has not lost its ability to
enthuse and even enchant.

### i. General Studies

In *The Metafictional Muse* (Pittsburgh) Larry McCaffery has presented not only the year's best study, but one of the most valuable
books yet written on the structural innovations which have characterized American fiction since the late 1960s. Robert Coover, Donald Barthelme, and William H. Gass are McCaffery's personal favorites, but his selection is a strategic one as well since these three
writers cover the range of innovations from parody and satire through
myth to a self-conscious examination of language and the fiction-

The author wishes to acknowledge the substantial contribution of his research assistant, Gary Arms.

making process. McCaffery reaches beyond their individual works to
notice an even deeper complementary trend in both the history of
science and popular culture: a metasensibility which redirects attention from the product of a system to its process. As a result the reader
may be surprised to find McCaffery discussing Werner Heisenberg
in one paragraph and comedian Steve Martin or the Blues Brothers
in the next, yet his argument is that "this 'meta-sensibility' is evolving
into the characteristic sensibility of our age, the inevitable product
of our heightened awareness of the subjectivity and artifice inherent
in our systems, our growing familiarity with prior forms, our increased
access to information of all sorts." Within these parameters Robert
Coover distinguishes himself by his convincing demonstrations that
"mythic impulses lie behind the creation of *all fictions*" while Donald
Barthelme concentrates on building a new artifice out of these otherwise discredited materials (and in the process making thematic concerns out of his technical problems). For McCaffery, however, William H. Gass is the master, whose masterpiece of aesthetic theory,
*Fiction and the Figures of Life*, qualifies him as the Pound of our
era. Gass is most of all sensitive to words: how their meaning differs
in literature from that in life, and how they (and not what they
signify) are fiction's true component material. Gass "thickens" his
medium in order to reduce our tendency to "see through" his medium
to its referents; only the text itself is capable of generating meaning.

Part of McCaffery's success with previous studies of innovative
fiction is that he believes there is much more to these novels than
authorial or textual self-reflexiveness. Such reflexion is by itself a
dead end, he admits, but he quotes Raymond Federman to the point
that in the decades since these disruptive fictions were first presented
there has been less emphasis on *self*-consciousness and more on self-
*consciousness*. Federman's formulation anticipates both the title and
the method of this year's other truly excellent study, Bruce Kawin's
*The Mind of the Novel*. For Kawin fiction has not been "exhausted"
or even radically turned around by revolutionary "postmodern" con-
victions; instead he believes that "most genres evolve out of a self-
consciousness achieved within the context of their parent forms."
With this sense of evolution in mind, Kawin can answer such nagging
questions as whether or not innovative fiction is genuinely "new," or
whether all its techniques were employed two centuries before by

Laurence Sterne. To answer this latter objection, Kawin takes the example of Steve Katz's *The Exaggerations of Peter Prince* to show how, unlike Sterne, Katz is "both the author of the system and inside it," a tactic which only self-consciousness of both form and of tradition can provide. "Sterne's reader could draw the analogy between narrator and author," Kawin advises, "but here Katz (like Ron Sukenick in his first novel, *Up*) joins the two directly." Some of the arguments in *The Mind of the Novel* are familiar (such as technical complexity being a way of foregrounding process) while others are a genuine surprise (such as Kawin's desire to link the self-conscious novel's mind with the extremes of Hindu philosophy and feminist utopias), but these idiosyncracies are more than balanced by the author's breadth of analysis, which runs with great detail from as far back as Richardson and Sterne to as recent a group of authors as Carlos Castaneda, Sukenick, Federman, and Katz. The parallel with mysticism is justified, Kawin believes, because "Reflexive fiction strives to imitate the structure of the human mind and its territory —to become a limited whole"; this constitutes "a confrontation with the ineffable, since it presents the operations of consciousness to itself." Whereas earlier fictions used a series of filters to make this process apparent (such as the multiple narrative sections in *As I Lay Dying*), writers from Beckett on have sought to face the unnamable directly.

The three other book-length additions to our shelf of general contemporary studies are far less satisfactory, though each has its individually helpful analyses. Their syntheses fail, however, because the authors have failed to test their personal beliefs against the greater evidence of three decades' innovation—in short, their views are monolithic rather than productively idiosyncratic. Craig Hansen Werner uses the ready-made structure of the master's thesis for his disappointing *Paradoxical Resolutions*. From inception to execution his method is annoyingly reductive: Joyce's general influence on the course of post-*Wake* fiction is turned into a hobby-horse on which everyone from William Faulkner to Ronald Sukenick is given a ride; yet by keeping the discussion within Joyce's terms we are never allowed to see what the newer writer can do on his or her own. Even more regrettable is Werner's pedantic graduate-student manner of arguing with previous critics instead of addressing the novels themselves. A potentially valuable discussion of Ronald Sukenick in terms of performance theory is counterbalanced by an unfortunate and uncontrolled rapture over the works of Thomas Pynchon.

A less reductive style of enthusiasm is found in Annie Dillard's *Living by Fiction* (Harper), though the author's sense of wonder for contemporary fiction suffers for its lack of testing against firmer standards. For Werner's Joyce she substitutes Nabokov and Borges as her points of measure, but does not define their achievements more sharply than a general sense of self-referentiality and gamesmanship. Dillard is astute in pointing out how innovative fiction actually "requires *more* coherence than traditional fiction does" because of the daring with which it "bares its own structure." Its sphere of activity is not society but the novel itself, with the result that writing has taken the same course as painting, "from depth to surface, from rondure to planes, from world to scheme, from observation to imagination, from story to theory, from society to individual, from emotion to mind." From contemplating cosmology literature has turned "to abstracting pattern itself" which Dillard sees Robert Coover, Donald Barthelme, Ronald Sukenick, and Italo Calvino doing, in the tradition of Nabokov's *Pale Fire*. These writers "flaunt the speculative nature of their fiction." The weaker half of Dillard's book is just the part she claims to be most important: that despite this emphasis on artifice innovative fictionists still draw their materials from the world and address its human concerns. Her commonsense refutation of deconstructionist theory is amateurish, detracting from the fine analyses which precede it.

Even less satisfactory as a commonsense approach is Alvin B. Kernan's *The Imaginary Library: An Essay on Literature and Society* (Princeton). From his routine readings of four contemporary novels, all of which express unease with the current state of affairs in both letters and society, Kernan concludes that the great tradition is in danger of eclipse. Certainly Bellow's *Humboldt's Gift*, Malamud's *The Tenants*, Nabokov's *Pale Fire*, and Mailer's *Of A Fire on the Moon* boast little affection for the currency of social and literary deconstruction; but Kernan limits his discussion to each author's thematics, shying away from the structural inventions of Nabokov and of Mailer in particular. His basically negative approach is revealed in such disclaimers as "Any attack on the texts—from literal book-pulping to deconstructive criticism—contains potentially the most dangerous consequences for literature as a whole." To equate mass-marketing policies on book returns to the aesthetic discoveries in Paris and New Haven is hardly the sign of a discriminating mind. Indeed, much of *The Imaginary Library* reads as if it were written 20 years ago: seeing the major division as between science and poetry "for the control of reality" ignores completely Michel Foucault's thesis that science and poetry each draw their authority from the same set of governing cultural constraints and definitions. Kernan fixes the outcome by choosing not genuinely disruptive fictionists such as Ronald Sukenick and Steve Katz on which to test his arguments, but rather self-confessed "old-fashioned, very standard romantic" figures such as Malamud and especially Mailer, who by the very terms of their approach are fated to lose.

A much more reliable index to the forces of literary and social change may be found in the "Postface 1982: Toward a Concept of Postmodernism" (pp. 259–71), which concludes the second edition of Ihab Hassan's seminal *The Dismemberment of Orpheus* (Wis.). The brilliance of Hassan's approach is in his sharp discrimination between two contrasting sets of values for literature produced within the cultural conditions of either modernism or postmodernism. By examining Hassan's criteria of hierarchy versus anarchy, distance versus participation, totalization versus deconstruction, through his succeeding oppositions of synthesis/antithesis, paradigm/syntagm, metaphor/metonymy, selection/combination, depth/surface, signified/signifier, determinacy/indeterminacy, and finally transcendence/immanence, one can get a sense of the true confrontation which eludes Kernan and Dillard. How these oppositions which are most clearly expressed in American fiction extend to British writing as well is outlined by Jerome Klinkowitz in his preface (pp. xi–xiv) to the third edition of *Contemporary Novelists*, ed. James Vinson (St. Martin's).

### ii. Saul Bellow and Other Jewish-Americans

The anticipated surge in Bellow scholarship has come this year with three fine books and several helpful articles. Most notable is fellow novelist Malcolm Bradbury's *Saul Bellow*, which inaugurates Methuen's "Contemporary Writers" series. Bradbury's posture is triply unique, for in addition to being a fiction writer himself he writes from the perspective of the British and as a member of the informally organized "Trilateral Group" of European Americanists (so named because of their respective affiliations with the Universities of East Anglia, Paris-III, and Würzburg). The Trilaterals (who are the major contributors to Methuen's series) combine an analytically sharp judgment of American culture with a textual approach unobtrusively based in the latest European theories, and much new light is cast upon Saul Bellow's fiction by this fresh methodology.

Bradbury finds Bellow to be a uniquely important writer because his work stands at the intersection of naturalism and psychological modernism, reflecting Bellow's interest in both the world and the individual. It is the tension between these two realms which helps create the intellectual substance he is famous for, what Bradbury calls "the sense of existence and the sense of self come into conflict." The struggle between "outward history and inner freedom" qualifies Bellow as an extender of the great American tradition of romantic selfhood versus the world, and it is this author's special sense of history which lends stature to his "step beyond absurdism toward a recovered moralism." There is a progress in Bellow's work which Bradbury organizes into decades: the philosophic density of the 1940s novels, the exuberance of adventure finally characterized in Henderson's wide-ranging language at the end of the 1950s, Herzog's posture of silence beyond all language in the 1960s, and the self-conscious probe of our contemporary cultural history evident in Bellow's work of the past ten years. Bellow's genius, Bradbury believes, can be traced to his ability to so finely articulate Philip Rahv's "much-discussed tension between the imaginative myths of fiction and the commanding powerhouse of historical process." The more Bellow's protagonists are lulled by the dreams of their creative imaginations, the more rudely they are discomforted by the nightmares of history. Bradbury's own work as a comic mannerist is evident in his decision to devote most space to *Henderson the Rain King*; but Henderson is pivotal to Bradbury's thesis only because he is such a richly energetic character, and it is this broadly social sense of Bellow's comedy which this study most perfectly expresses.

Robert R. Dutton's *Saul Bellow* (TUSAS 181) is less thesis-oriented and more of a series book than Bradbury's, though it is distinguished by its attention to Bellow's productive tension between individual and society. Dutton in fact goes much farther than Bradbury in viewing Saul Bellow as an intellectual novelist: "He uses character," Dutton believes, "in the old allegorical tradition: to dramatize a preconceived idea." This may be an overstatement which Dutton himself soon qualifies, citing the "multilevel roles" of Bellow's protagonists, "one of which projects his thematic implications back into history." Dutton agrees with Bradbury that in the wake of *Mr. Sammler's Planet, Humboldt's Gift,* and especially *The Dean's December* "we will see less of the comic spirit that marked the trails" of Henderson and Herzog; "Rather, we will have the heirs of Mr. Sammler and Charlie Citrine, pilgrims who confront the world on a quest not only for self-justification or for self-realization, but offering themselves as point-men for our passage through the debilitating thicket of today's moral and spiritual malaise."

In *Quest for the Human: An Exploration of Saul Bellow's Fiction* (Bucknell) Eusebio L. Rodrigues provides a workmanlike account of the humanistic themes evident in each of Bellow's novels from *Dangling Man* through *Humboldt's Gift.* Like Bradbury, Rodrigues privileges *Henderson the Rain King* because of its major emphasis on "awakening and hope." *Humboldt's Gift,* however, is seen as the prime achievement, largely due to what Rodrigues feels is its Transcendental call for American rededication and rediscovery. Here one feels more comfortable with Malcolm Bradbury's analysis of Bellow as a more critical examiner of the American imagination, a position Rodrigues might well share had his study included treatment of *The Dean's December.*

In an essay originally written for Richard Kostelanetz's massive and authoritative *American Writing Today* (Washington, D.C.: Forum Books/Voice of America Editions, 1982, vol. 1, pp. 115–26) and reprinted for stateside audiences in *AR* (40:266–73) under the title "Saul Bellow," Ihab Hassan traces Bellow's development as a densely serious writer who has found his true *métier* in comedy, a style which in his hands is "more energetic, wiser, and manlier." Like Bradbury and Rodrigues, Hassan singles out *Henderson the Rain King* as having "the largest, the freest sense of life," but adds that *Herzog* and *Mr. Sammler's Planet* are somewhat uneven responses to the "distractions" of the 1960s. In *Humboldt's Gift* Bellow recovers his characteristic "amplitude of vision." In " 'The Hollywood Thread' and the First Draft of Saul Bellow's *Seize the Day*" (*SNNTS* 14:82–94) Alan Chavkin studies the growth through manuscript revisions

of Bellow's belief that his hedonistic characters can only affirm life
once they accept the regeneration which comes with suffering.
Another view of Bellow's thematics of acceptance is demonstrated,
rather reductively, by Barbara L. Estrin in "Recomposing Time:
*Humboldt's Gift* and *Ragtime*" (*DQ* 17,i:16–31); both novels use
such common devices as the destruction of an automobile and the
antics of Harry Houdini to initiate discussions of catastrophe and
death. Everything and everyone is repeatable, these novels teach,
and therefore nothing fundamental can ever be destroyed. The most
delightful of the year's essays is "Bellow's Moving Day," written by
the novelist's close friend Richard Stern and included as a chapter
in his *The Invention of the Real* (Georgia; pp. 13–26). In addition
to many personal insights into Bellow's commerce with the quotidian,
the reader can share Stern's appreciation of his friend: "Comedian
to the depths, Bellow is a visionary who feels through the farcical
spin of things the Unmoved Mover."

Bernard Malamud and Isaac Bashevis Singer drew little attention
this year, just Rita K. Gollin's "Malamud's Dubin and the Morality
of Desire" (*PLL* 18:198–207) and Judith Rinde Sheridan's similarly
thematic "Isaac Bashevis Singer: Sex as Cosmic Metaphor" (*MQ* 23:
365–79) which explains the uniqueness of these sexual themes within
the more reserved Yiddish tradition (sexual aberration is in fact a
characteristic of hellish mortal life). Cynthia Ozick receives some
long overdue attention in Ruth Rosenberg's fine "Covenanted to the
Law: Cynthia Ozick" (*MELUS* 9,iii:29–38); Ozick tests her readers'
perceptions of her ironies, asking them to think like Jews.

Philip Roth continues to attract strong and insightful scholarship.
Especially notable is Thomas Blues's "Is There Life After Baseball?
Philip Roth's *The Great American Novel*" (*AS* 22,i[1981]:71–80),
which ties the novel's theme to baseball's own history and to the
mythic elements of the game as characterized by Jacques Barzun.
The Jamesian influence in Roth's later work is traced by Adeline R.
Tintner in "Hiding Behind James: Roth's *Zuckerman Unbound*"
(*Midstream* 28,iv:49–53), which reveals the inside joke about masturbation central to Roth's theme. The year's major contribution,
however, comes from Hermoine Lee's volume in the Contemporary
Writers series, *Philip Roth* (Methuen). Lee's thematic study isolates
the tensions in Roth's work: moral authority versus social restraint,
the roles of being a writer versus being a son, and above all the

inner voice which provides Roth such strong vehicles for the expression of these polarities. Roth's difficulties as a writer are paralleled by his character's problems; theme provides technique, giving each novel a strong sense of integrity.

### iii. Norman Mailer

As always, Mailer's own historical figure dominates the scholarship on his fiction, a disposition which this year's additions strongly reinforce. *Pieces and Pontifications*, ed. Michael Lennon (Little, Brown) collects Mailer's essays and interviews. The overwhelming bulkiness of Mailer's social record (and his life is far from over!) is documented with admirable dispassion by Hilary Mills in her *Mailer: A Biography* (Empire Books), capitalizing on the illogic of Mailer's career and his self-sustaining unrealistic expectations for charting his epic life. At times Mailer seems a creature of the public life he fancies, but this same fascination has led to the triumphs of experimentation in such works as *Armies of the Night* and *Of a Fire on the Moon*. Mailer's tampering with his own text is the subject of Hershel Parker's finely researched "Norman Mailer's Revision of the *Esquire* Version of *An American Dream* and the Aesthetic Problem of 'Built-in Intentionality'" (*BRH* 84[1981]:405–30). Parker believes Mailer's intention for the psychological equality of the novel's male characters changed between his initial composition and final revision, with the result that many narrative passages have been weakened. One of these characters, Shago Martin, interests John Cooley in his chapter on Mailer's work in *Savages and Naturals: Black Portraits by White Writers* (Delaware, pp. 137–60); the image of the hipster is here personified as an educator of the white man, showing Mailer's "cultural primitivism." Yet there is a complexity to Mailer's vision that some critics (here feminist) misread, as Jessica Gerson argues in "Norman Mailer: Sex, Creativity and God" (*Mosiac* 15,ii:1–16); his true affinity, Gerson says, is not to sexual macho but rather to the cabalistic notion of male/female duality. But above all Mailer is interested in creating *himself* in the world, mirroring his public self in the social arena (as opposed to the more private and mysterious behavior of other writers), argues Albert E. Stone, who takes *Armies of the Night* as a representative text for his "Factual Fictions" chapter (pp. 265–324) in *Autobiographical Occasions*.

## iv. Flannery O'Connor, William Styron, and Other Southerners

A new book on O'Connor plus a new edition of an earlier study provide a welcome balance to the customary sheaf of predictable essays on this most explicatible of authors. In *Flannery O'Connor: The Imagination of Extremity* (Georgia) Frederick Asals notes O'Connor's "attraction to polarities" and claims these tensions were fed by her religious beliefs. "The middle is always *mediocris* in O'Connor," Asals explains, "a condition ultimately of illusion, for in the world she dramatizes only extremes have genuine existence." Among her works *Wise Blood* stands alone, because its "disorienting realism" and sense of "waking nightmare" are not based in the author's customary sense of the "sacramental." As in Poe and West, these wasteland themes reflect "our broken condition" which force O'Connor to be an antimaterialist; only later will she come to terms with the materiality of life. Above all, she is a theological writer: ascetic, visionary, and apocalyptic, characteristically given to the either/or. For an exactly opposite interpretation one may turn to Kathleen Feeley's newly reprinted *Flannery O'Connor: Voice of the Peacock* (Fordham); here we learn that "the theological basis of O'Connor's fiction adds a dimension, and subtracts nothing," a lesson Feeley learned when testing her book's thesis on non-Christian audiences in Japan.

The year's essays on O'Connor are as usual plentiful and, with few exceptions, unexciting. Worth noting is Russ McDonald's "Comedy and Flannery O'Connor" (*SAQ* 81:188–201), which locates the author firmly within the comic tradition and its fundamental methods. Her comic view is complementary to her Christianity, both of which see man as dreadful but salvageable. Among her typical character types are the too proud hypocrite, the innocent, and the viceful. What is unique in O'Connor is her tendency to use Vice as her spokesman; providential assistance always arrives in some surprising and terrifying shape, with the result that "O'Connor's main characters get the fool knocked out of them." A complementary view is provided by Lucinda H. MacKethan in "Hogpens and Hallelujahs: The Function of the Image in Flannery O'Connor's Grotesque Comedies" (*BuR* 26,ii:31–44). Laughter and the comic sense are more important than O'Connor's often-noted moralism, MacKethan insists; her grotesque images are intended to connect and combine the commonplace with the sacred, a theme often referred to in her letters. This intentionality, again as shown in O'Connor's letters, is studied by Clara Clairborne Park in "Crippled Laughter: Toward Understanding Flannery O'Connor" (*ASch* 51:249–57).

Among the workmanlike explications of O'Connor's stories are several demonstrations of how "Gothic" her approach is. More originality can be found in André Bleikasten's "Writing on the Flesh: Tattoos and Taboos in 'Parker's Back,'" (*SLJ* 14,ii:8–18). There is much more to this story than religious allegory, Bleikasten argues; the signifiers of tattoos and taboos interplay on many levels, with the conclusion that identity comes not from the individual but from God. Two studies by James J. Napier also combine originality with genuine helpfulness. "Flannery O'Connor's Last Three: 'The Sense of an Ending'" (*SLJ* 14,ii:19–27) claims that O'Connor's concluding work reveals new techniques and varieties of emphasis within her tragicomic mode. Her use of time, for example, here becomes more complex and flexible, and her opposing sides of tragedy and comedy find resolution in the central experience of humiliation. From humiliation the enlightenment to effect change may or may not follow, but it is the chastening that makes change possible. Victor Lasseter's "The Children's Names in Flannery O'Connor's 'A Good Man Is Hard To Find'" (*NMAL* 6:Item 6) traces the influencing sense of how the outlaw names John Wesley Hardin and Belle Starr enhance the story's religious meaning.

William Styron is the subject of two newly translated essays and one original article in *Critical Essays on William Styron*, ed. Arthur D. Casciato and James L. W. West, III (Hall). Valarie M. Arms's "William Styron in France" (pp. 306–15) is an outdated existentialist account. Holding up better are Roger Asselineau's 1967 essay "Following *The Long March*" (pp. 53–59) and Michel Butor's "Oedipus Americanus" (pp. 135–45), which introduced the French edition of *Set This House on Fire* in 1962. Asselineau's thesis is that Styron capitalizes not on style per se but rather "subordinates his stylistic effects to his intention of preserving a past experience in transparent amber. Therefore, inversely to what happens in his [longer] novels, where time waves criss-cross and blur the outlines, he has in this case courageously simplified and stylized," choosing the manner of

Flaubert over Joyce and Faulkner. Butor's point is that "Cass Kin-solving's behavior . . . expresses an admonition to stand firmly on one's origins and to reformulate the whole of history."

Essential for any Styron file is William Styron's own *This Quiet Dust and Other Writings* (Random House). The author is, of course, a pleasing stylist, but in addition to the predictable essays on the grace and terror of the American South are a frank introduction (pp. 3–8) to this section of essays which answers the historical and racial arguments against *The Confessions of Nat Turner*. Later on, in a fine essay on F. Scott Fitzgerald (pp. 77–86) Styron evokes a strong sense of sympathy for a brother writer maligned by his own public image.

In *Shelby Foote* (TUSAS 431) Helen White and Redding S. Sugg, Jr. provide an able survey of this writer's talents. Foote's historical and universalizing capability within the "Jordan County" materials is emphasized. There is a deteriorating factor among Foote's delta planters, from a sense of noblesse oblige to a smug "I've got mine," yet in the author's sociology of the region his delta characters rank superior to the hill folk. As a third generation delta writer Foote can declare his "pure vocation as an artist" apart from the social distrac-tions, which then become free for use as genuine artistic themes. An interview with Shelby Foote can be found in *Mississippi Writers Talking*.

Much of the special issue, "Women Writers of the American South" (*MFS* 28,iii), is devoted to conventional analyses of O'Con-nor and Welty. Are there no younger women writers in this region?

### v. Older Realists and New Mannerists: Jackson, Vidal, Cheever, and Updike

The least amount of work in several years has been devoted to this group of writers, but what we have is a sound addition to scholarship. In "The Escape Theme in Shirley Jackson's 'The Tooth' " (*SSF* 19: 133–39) Richard Pascal shows the Faustian nature behind the urge to escape. Another short story of an equally commanding writer is Robert Phillips' subject in "Gore Vidal's Greek Revival: 'The Ladies in the Library' " (*NMAL* 6:Item 3). Variations on the Aeneas myth provide the structure for "an allegorical tale of one man's unwilling quest and his victimization by the fates."

With surprisingly little writing on John Updike, the late John

Cheever is our main mannerist studied this year. John Gerlach applies Poe's theories of composition to two of Cheever's masterpieces in "Closure in Modern Short Fiction: Cheever's 'The Enormous Radio' and 'Artemis, the Honest Well Digger' " (*MFS* 28:145–52), yielding singleness of effect, surprise, and logical inevitability in the former while relying upon theme in the latter—all to show that the modern "open" short story is merely an adaptation of Poe's principles of expectation and satisfaction. Cheever's novels are surveyed by Robert G. Collins in "From Subject to Object and Back Again: Individual Identity in John Cheever's Fiction" (*TCL* 28,i:1–13). Increasing alienation is the central theme, making man but a peripheral spectator to a social process which has little need of individuals. Only in *Falconer* is this problem resolved by shedding "social identities" and accepting the individuality of someone else, part of Melville and Thoreau's "New England tradition." Collins has also done an admirable job in commissioning ten new articles for his *Critical Essays on John Cheever* (Hall). Chief among these are Samuel Coale's "Cheever and Hawthorne: The American Romancer's Art" (pp. 193–209), which finds the same Manichean distinction between narrator and story in each writer; Richard R. Rupp's "Of That Time, Of Those Places: The Short Stories of John Cheever" (pp. 231–51), in which we see the progress of Cheever's heroes through various stages of individualism and community; and Burton Kendle's "The Passion of Nostalgia in the Short Stories of John Cheever" (pp. 219–30), which shows how a shared history provides the basis for the author's strongest themes.

Most of the new work on John Updike this year is contained in William R. Macnaughton's finely edited *Critical Essays on John Updike* (Hall). The most significant contribution to the volume is Macnaughton's own introduction (pp. 1–36), which, in the process of surveying nearly three decades of scholarship on Updike, manages to synthesize the essentials of his writing career. The early appraisals of Updike as a sensuous stylist have given way to more profound understandings of his theologically ponderous thematics. The five essays Macnaughton has commissioned reflect both this deepening within Updike's career itself and within scholarship, especially in George J. Searles's reappraisal, "*The Poorhouse Fair*: Updike's Thesis Statement" (pp. 231–36). This early novel is characteristic of the mature Updike, Searles argues, because of its strongly voiced concern

with a lapse of high moralism in American life. Looking to the middle
of Updike's canon, Gordon J. Slethaug suggests in "*Rabbit Redux*:
'Freedom is Made of Brambles'" (pp. 237–53) that freedom is a relative notion, and that the independence a younger Harry Angstrom
sought in *Rabbit, Run* is in this later and more mature novel shown
to be a most insidious trap in itself. "Americans, implies Updike" in
the book's references to 1969's cultural reality, "need to learn that
unrestricted freedom can not exist, and that when one is most free,
one may paradoxically become the most enslaved and enslaving."
Kathleen Verduin's "Fatherly Presences: John Updike's Place in a
Protestant Tradition" (pp. 254–68) shows how family order, particularly childhood's familial world, is Updike's characteristic index
of rightness. Concluding essays by Gary Waller and Joyce Markle on
*A Month of Sundays* (pp. 269–80) and *The Coup* (pp. 281–301) show
respectively how Updike balances dialogue against narrative comment and how his only apparently atypical African leader sounds a
familiar call for man's spiritual elegance.

A freshly sympathetic look at John Updike's fiction is provided
by Elizabeth Tallent in *Married Men and Magic Tricks: John Updike's Erotic Heroes* (Berkeley: Creative Arts Book Co.). Rather
than repeat the notion that Updike's prose is stylistically sensuous,
Tallent looks deeper to find how its thematics demand a constant
sense of movement and a sense of the male hero creating his female
counterpart; almost always Updike's women soon become wives if
they are not so already. In *The Poorhouse Fair* Hook courts death,
just as in *Rabbit, Run* Harry Angstrom feels threatened by death and
decay and must therefore animate the world he inhabits. The best
of Updike's lovers have the sense of being "drawn," as one of them
praises the drawing in Vermeer; because of his vital sense of risk,
Henry Bech stands as the perfect antitype to Updike's more familiar
erotic protagonists who create reality with their visions.

### vi. New Realists: Gardner, Doctorow, Oates, and Others

Robert A. Morace and Kathryn VanSpanckeren are the editors of
*John Gardner* (So. Ill.), a comprehensive collection of original essays
covering all aspects of Gardner's fiction. There is a "dark Manichean" strand to the early work, Samuel Coale argues in "'Into the
Farther Darkness': The Manichean Pastoralism of John Gardner"

(pp. 15–27), complementing David Cowart's "*Et in Arcadia Ego*: Gardner's Early Pastoral Novels" (pp. 1–14). Helen B. Ellis and Warren U. Ober study the debts to Blake which are evident in *Grendel* (pp. 46–61), while Jerome Klinkowitz regrets this novel's unproductive trickery (pp. 62–67). The volume's strongest essay is Donald J. Greiner's "Sailing Through *The King's Indian* with John Gardner and His Friends" (pp. 76–88), a collection which Greiner praises for its methodical survey of various styles of textual artifice. From his studies of mediaeval literature Gardner has taken the folk technique of embedding and perfected it as a structural element in his own work, as Kathryn VanSpanckeren shows (pp. 114–29), while her co-editor Robert A. Morace explores the moral fiction issue Gardner has raised as a critic (pp. 130–45).

That Gardner's arguments can be turned back upon themselves is shown quite handily by R. Barton Palmer in "The Problem with Gardner's *On Moral Fiction*" (*Renascence* 34:161–72). Gardner's power as a fictionist, however, is ably demonstrated by Kay K. Rout in "The Ghoul-Haunted Woodland of Southern Illinois: John Gardner's 'The Ravages of Spring'" (*SSF* 19:27–33). Rout traces the psychological uncertainty which comes to control this story; indeed, Gardner here proves himself master of the schizophrenic removal from reality which has characterized such classic works as "Young Goodman Brown" and *The Turn of the Screw*.

The staying power of E. L. Doctorow's *Ragtime* is the subject of Charles Berryman in "*Ragtime* in Retrospect" (*SAQ* 81:30–42). Its enigmatic narrator, its mixture of fiction and history, and the novel's double theme of disintegration and renewal provide the basis for Doctorow's transformations of the central characters. Life is in flux, the narrative shows: nothing can be firmly fixed, and men who try to do so find that life drifts out from beneath them. The one satisfied figure in the novel is the immigrant father, who can rise to power and fortune in Hollywood because he knows that history is a fabric of illusion. A substantial interview is conducted by Richard Trenner in "Politics and the Mode of Fiction" (*OntarioR* 16:5–16).

The one substantial piece of work on Joyce Carol Oates this year is Leif Sjöberg's "An Interview with Joyce Carol Oates" (*ConL* 23: 267–84). The uncanny beauty of the familiar world when seen "emptied of ourselves" is shown to be one of Oates's fascinations; we believe we exist in terms of the world, and when we are taken out of it that world seems all the more wondrous. Higher mathematics and physics share this sense of beauty, she insists; what the poetic rejects is simply "bad science": "The novel, like all forms of art, is an expression of a subjectivity which might then be translated into the *universal,* while science deals only with the universal or the representative." Beauty itself is fully relative, a cultural prejudice which does not lend itself to such scientific measure. Oates's own standards of judgment for literature are breadth of vision and a sense of the interlocking determinations of "politics, religion, economics, and the mores of society." Her novel *Bellefleur* is described as a "complex parable of American aspirations and tragic shortcomings" which is written in both the symbolic and historical modes.

Year by year Stanley Elkin approaches the status of major novelist, and a good survey of his career is provided by John Ditsky in " 'Death Grotesque as Life': The Fiction of Stanley Elkin" (*HC* 19,iii: 1–11). Singled out for highest praise is the author's "splendid ear," his ability to capture American and especially Jewish-American speech, all nicely couched in humor. "Elkin is the funniest writer alive," Ditsky claims, noting Elkin's mastery of "the small catalogue of pertinent details" on which this humor is based. His prose style is luxuriant, even though his usual character is the humble salesman (for Elkin "the characteristic American type").

Among the many authors not treated to scholarly examination in the usual course of events are James Salter and William Maxwell. In "Glimpses of a Secular Holy Land: The Novels of James Salter" (*HC* 19,i:1–13) Margaret Winchell Miller praises Salter's ear for lyrically poetic language and his obsession with the power of desire. His male characters seek the perfect woman, even though the author rarely develops these female characters well. The heroes worship Woman, not any specific woman, and are irritated by any imperfections which crop up in between. The single Ideal Woman in all of Salter's works, Miller believes, is Nedra of *Light Years.* In "Memory and Imagination in William Maxwell's *So Long, See You Tomorrow*" (*Crit* 24,i: 21–37) James F. Maxwell finds the death of a boy's mother a "recurrent, autobiographical incident in William Maxwell's novels." There is an inextricable relationship between art and life, making invention the better part of remembering; writing about such events is just the opposite of purging them, since fiction memorializes them in a uniquely lasting way. "When one feels, one *is*; and by remembering feeling, one can almost *be* again."

### vii. Early Innovators: Jack Kerouac, James Purdy, Paul Bowles, and Others

Although during his lifetime Jack Kerouac was celebrated as an undisciplined writer of "spontaneous prose"—the classic illustration was of his rolls of Western Union paper run nonstop through the typewriter—recent studies of his manuscript archives reveal that he wrote and revised carefully according to a lifetime "grand design for literature." Such is Ann Charters' conclusion to her carefully researched "Kerouac's Literary Method and Experiments: The Evidence of the Manuscript Notebooks in the Berg Collection" (*BRH* 84:431–50). Kerouac's French-Canadian heritage as a shaping influence on his work is the subject of Richard S. Sorrell's "Novelists and Ethnicity: Jack Kerouac and Grace Metalious" (*MELUS* 9,i: 37–52). A valuable resource has been made available by Jay Landesman in his reprinting of the full run (1948–51) of the Beat magazine *Neurotica* (Humanities). With its contributions by writers as diverse as Marshall McLuhan and Lawrence Durrell and as historically important as Carl Solomon and Chandler Brossard, *Neurotica* impresses one even today with its fresh sense of cultural innovation.

John O'Brien's massive *Review of Contemporary Fiction*, now (1983) in its third volume, has distinguished itself as the scholarly and critical voice for the style and generation of writers who stand between the Beats of the early 1950s and the more popularly accessible innovative fictionists of the 1960s and 70s. Early issues focused on Gilbert Sorrentino, Paul Metcalf, and Hubert Selby (the titans of this academically overlooked period), plus substantial numbers on Douglas Woolf and Wallace Markfield (2,i) and on Paul Bowles and the younger Coleman Dowell (2,ii). The most helpful survey of Markfield's career is provided by Melvin J. Friedman in "The Enigma of Unpopularity and Critical Neglect: The Case for Wallace Markfield" (pp. 36–44); John O'Brien's interview (pp. 5–29) collects the author's own feelings on this legacy of anonymity. Especially noteworthy in the issue's second half is Eric Mottram's "Douglas Woolf's Escapes from Enclosure" (pp. 66–81), which shows how the writer defines his fictions by the social and technical limits they struggle to eclipse, and John O'Brien's " 'All Things Considered' in Douglas Woolf" (pp. 113–19), which argues for his place in the modernist mainstream.

One of the most substantial studies yet made is Eric Mottram's "Paul Bowles: Staticity and Terror" (pp. 6–30), in which this author's work is placed within the 20th-century background (from Werner Heisenberg through Timothy Leary) and described as the forerunner of contemporary experiments by Thomas Pynchon and Richard Fariña. Though Bowles is suspicious of constraining systems, it is the mythology of man's individualism which he finds creating the most sinister traps. Paul Metcalf's notes on each of Bowles's books are also helpful (pp. 32–41), though the best insights into the author's techniques are provided by Lawrence D. Stewart ("Paul Bowles and 'The Frozen Fields' of Vision," pp. 64–71) and Robert Hauptman ("Paul Bowles and the Perception of Evil," pp. 71–73); Bowles is especially adept at using the subconscious without imposing judgments on it, even when its materials are confirmed by memory. Coleman Dowell's *Island People* gets the majority of attention in the second half of this *RCF* issue; most astute are Gilbert Sorrentino's brief remarks (pp. 122–23), perceiving a deft use of antiform (an author who is not an author, chapters which are not chapters, etc.).

A reminder of how John Rechy's nightmare world provides a stimulus to fresh narrative technique is offered by Ben Satterfield in "John Rechy's Tormented World" (*SWR* 67,i:78–85). Lest James Purdy's pioneering work in narrative voice be forgotten, Donald Pease has prepared a careful analysis of his "transitive beginnings" in "False Starts and Wounded Allegories in the Abandoned House of Fiction of James Purdy" (*TCL* 28:335–49); the author's "protected paradises" are often horticultural gardens, replacing James's "house of fiction" as a metaphor for point of view. A new magazine which features this latter generation of pioneer innovationists is Bradford Morrow's *Conjunctions*. Its third number features an important interview with James Purdy (pp. 97–111), covering topics such as early influences (including Sherwood Anderson's use of the American vernacular), Purdy's disinfatuation with Henry James, his early work as a little magazine editor, and the reader's role in creating his texts. The author's sentence-by-sentence method of composition is also explained.

### *viii.* Ken Kesey and Joseph Heller

An important reading of Ken Kesey's major work may be found in William C. Baurecht's "Separation, Initiation, and Return: Schizophrenic Episode in *One Flew Over the Cuckoo's Nest*" (*MQ* 23:279–93). This psychological/mythic examination stresses the importance of male bonding, citing Leslie Fiedler's classic theory. McMurphy is seen as a particularly American hero: a working class individualist with outlaw tendencies who must learn that love and not the masculine imperial will is the key to our national male mythology. The novel's high-spirited quality is due to Kesey's belief that the character Chief Broom embodies an Indian spirit who spoke to the author directly; Broom parallels the steps of a schizophrenic "episode" with a mythic hero's journey, emerging as a healed potential leader of men.

The first extended study to take full measure of Ken Kesey's career—which now includes not just the two novels but two decades of what some have seen as artistic procrastination in his fragmentary works known as "The Demon Box"—has been published this year by M. Gilbert Porter. His *The Art of Grit: Ken Kesey's Fiction* (Missouri) combines excellent readings of *One Flew Over the Cuckoo's Nest* (where Kesey parallels the hero's reintegration of society with a textual movement from fragmentation to wholeness) and *Sometimes a Great Notion* (where the hero is seen in a quest for essential selfhood) with a detailed analysis of Kesey's later work. This fragmentary material of the past two decades has disturbed and confused critics, who have failed to see how it contributes to Kesey's purpose: the writer must stand as a protector between the evils of the world and the innocence of his readers.

A similarly strong study of Joseph Heller has been produced by Stephen W. Potts for "The Milford Series: Popular Writers Today" published by R. Reginald/Borgo Press. *From Here to Absurdity: The Moral Battlefields of Joseph Heller* is one of the first studies to find a useful scheme for viewing all of this author's work: not just the often-studied *Catch-22*, but the author's plays and his troublesome novel *Good as Gold* as well. Each work features the lingering presence of death, often presented as an unexpected surprise; the sign of an absurd universe, it is a constant test of accommodation for Heller's antiabsurdist heroes. In "Insanity is Contagious: The Mad World of *Catch-22*" (*CentR* 26:86–113) Beverly Gross extends previous studies of the way the theme of insanity provides a structuring principle for the novel.

### ix. Kurt Vonnegut and Jerzy Kosinski

Kurt Vonnegut continues to maintain his position as the most-talked about contemporary novelist. In his Contemporary Writers series study *Kurt Vonnegut* (Methuen), Jerome Klinkowitz shows how Vonnegut's successes both as a popular and as an avant-garde writer are based on his own self-characterization of the American experience as it made its way through the 1920s, the Depression, World War II, and after. The present complex form of his writing is the result of a carefully plotted incorporation of biographical elements into his novels, climaxing in his personal fictions of the 1970s, each of which begins with an autobiographical preface locating the novel's theme and technique within the experience of his own life. Vonnegut's care in avoiding conventional racial stereotypes in *Cat's Cradle* is the subject of John Cooley's Vonnegut chapter in *Savages and Naturals* (pp. 161–73). Bokonon has created a radically different society thanks to his own vision of the world's troublesome complexity which only simplistic ritualism can ameliorate. At the root of this success is Vonnegut's sympathy: he "manages so successfully with black character here because he cares about all his characters in a very individual and whimsical way." A more comprehensive view of this same novel is provided by Lucien L. Agosta in "Ah-Whoom! Egotism and Apocalypse in Kurt Vonnegut's *Cat's Cradle*" (*KanQ* 14: 127–34). Here we find Vonnegut presenting "ego on its own"—ego that no longer mediates between the demands of id and superego, but which rushes to its own annihilation because of its lack of both passion and conscience. Unable to give or to receive love, Felix Hoenikker fathers not just the atom bomb but also three children who are versions of the Freudian psyche fragmented: Frank as ego, Angela as superego, and Newt as id. The character Mona represents the unified psyche.

Vonnegut's vision (and there are many versions of it!) continues to inspire the best criticism. That his work of the 1970s ran against the more popular grain of pessimism is expressed in Kermit Vanderbilt's "Kurt Vonnegut's American Utopias" (pp. 137–73 in *The Utopian Vision: Seven Essays on the Quincentennial of Sir Thomas*

*More*, ed. E. D. S. Sullivan [San Diego]). According to Vanderbilt, contrary to common belief, there is nothing easy or simplistic about Vonnegut's work. The new communal sense of man and the positive role of the writer in his society is a theme that can be traced back to *Player Piano*. The false ideals of material progress and unlimited growth is countered by Vonnegut's more forceful vision of pure human worth, just as the themes of human depravity are a counter-test throughout *Mother Night*. Kilgore Trout is Vonnegut's prime projector of utopias, and as he emerges as a character in *God Bless You, Mr. Rosewater* and afterwards he is uniquely positioned to both express a utopian ideal and also to suffer the author's critique of these same notions. Vonnegut's own optimism has been tested by his vulnerability as a highly visible public writer, able to dare the suggestion (as he does at the end of *Jailbird*) that the Sermon on the Mount expresses the most practical ideal utopia possible. In two complementary articles Kathryn Hume distinguishes herself as one of the brightest new Vonnegut critics. Her "The Heraclitean Cosmos of Kurt Vonnegut" (*PLL* 18:208–24) argues that the flux and transformation favored by Vonnegut reveal the key to his literary philosophy: that knowledge is relative, that polarizations tend to dissolve into identities, but that amid all this, human consciousness and decency will prevail as valid stabilities. "Vonnegut's Self-Projections: Symbolic Characters and Symbolic Fiction" (*JNT* 12:177–90) argues that Kilgore Trout and other of Vonnegut's self-proclaimed autobiographical projections are alter-egos which express "courage in the face of chaotic unreason" and the writer's "ability to respond with words, with creative effort, to events and situations that the rest of us tend to filter out and forget," an insight which helps explain the appeal of Vonnegut's most recent "personal" novels.

In one of the best essays yet published on Jerzy Kosinski, Paul R. Lilly, Jr., explains how the violence in this author's novels is less worthy of close attention than "the shifting identity of victim and oppressor." Power and not violence is what fascinates Kosinski, and power is the only antidote to victimization. Each person is "intensely alone," Kosinski's novels teach, and everyone else is a potential enemy. Norman Lavers' *Jerzy Kosinski* (TUSAS 419) makes this same point, but is weakened by the critic's willingness to let Kosinski write his book for him. Interviews are cited almost as often as the text, and unverifiable biographical stories are accepted without question (such as Kosinski's self-proclaimed status as an "Associate Professor" at the highly esteemed Polish Academy of Sciences when he was barely 24 years old and holding only a Master's degree in History and Political Science). Lavers sees *The Painted Bird* as Kosinski's strongest work, another sign that biography has outweighed literary analysis; a better survey of Kosinski's work would take more trouble to explain the increasing self-affectation in such later works as *Blind Date* and *Pinball*.

### x. John Barth and Thomas Pynchon

John Barth's preeminence as an innovationist is debated by Jerome Klinkowitz in "John Barth Reconsidered" (*PR* 49:407–11). Because his novels are not things in themselves but are instead "imitations of imitations," Barth is more properly a "closet Aristotelian."

According to Tony Tanner in his *Thomas Pynchon* (Methuen), this elusive author is more than an innovationist: his three novels virtually recapitulate the history and experience of fiction, with *V.* functioning much like *Don Quixote* (Stencil as Quixote, Benny Profane as Sancho), *The Crying of Lot 49* as an archetypal mystery story, and *Gravity's Rainbow* as a rehearsal of the reading process itself. "Does nature have its own language of signs, or do we 'alphabetize nature in looking at it?' " Because this question is central to Pynchon's work, his fiction is ultimately self-conscious of the epistemological processes of life.

The best Pynchon scholarship continues to appear in *PNotes*. In "Godolphin—Goodolphin—Goodol'phin—Goodol-Pyn—Good ol'-Pym: A Question of Integration" (no. 10, pp. 3–17) Hanjo Berressem outlines Pynchon's use of Poe's theories of composition as expressed in *The Narrative of Arthur Gordon Pym*. Marion Brugiére presents a strong case that Oedipa's search is a never-ending perpetual motion machine in "Quest Avatars in Thomas Pynchon's *The Crying of Lot 49*" (no. 9, pp. 5–16), while Pynchon's talent for constantly changing the distance between his text and his readers by mixing tones and styles is demonstrated by Brooke Horvath in "Linguistic Distancing in *Gravity's Rainbow*" (no. 8, pp. 5–22). Among other journals, the most helpful piece would be Carolyn S. Pyuen's "The Transmarginal Leap: Meaning and Process in *Gravity's Rainbow*"

(*Mosiac* 15,ii:33–46). The overall vision of this novel is rooted in a non-Newtonian text, and is therefore hard to locate; its open network is "a continuation of reality which extends from the natural world, through the author and his text, and includes the reader as an element in its interconnected tissues of meaning." What is needed, Pyuen claims, is a new critical approach which considers this mutual interpenetrability of text and reader.

### xi. Donald Barthelme and William H. Gass

Two short books on Donald Barthelme eclipse the limits of their form and become, especially when read together, substantial additions to scholarship on this author who has been acclaimed as the "most imitated" and most influential of our current age. Charles Molesworth's contribution to the "Literary Frontiers" series, *Donald Barthelme's Fiction: The Ironist Saved From Drowning* (Missouri), favors this author's penchant for satire and parody. Barthelme's mechanics of collage are an alternative to the "wild visions" of other innovationists; it is an ideal method to accompany the leveling of values otherwise expressed as Pop Art. Barthelme's special success is that in his work "the parodic center is itself parodied." Molesworth stops short of appreciating Barthelme the experimental stylist and expresses dislike for the stories which consist of only dialogue. These newer fictions which characterize *Great Days* are the meat and potatoes of Maurice Couturier and Régis Durand's "Contemporary Writers" study, *Donald Barthelme* (Methuen), for they are the perfect example of how Barthelme anchors his fictions in nothing other than themselves. For these French critics Barthelme is less an ironist than a comedian, paralleling the shift in postmodernism away from irony and toward humor. Indeed, Barthelme can be read either way, as these two studies show, depending on whether one's sympathies are with the modern or postmodern. Couturier's and Durand's best advice is that Barthelme is not a metafictionist. No sterile theoretician, he is instead concerned with the presence of performance; replacing the stable center of reference with an indeterminate play of surface, Barthelme indicates the brilliant effects possible when one's signifiers are left to function as themselves. As the author's adult protagonist nightmarishly returned to sixth grade remarks from his superior

position of experience, "Signs are signs, and some of them are lies."
One of Barthelme's single-page *New Yorker* stories is given profitable analysis by William N. Warde, Jr., in "Barthelme's 'The School':
Pedagogical Monologue and Social Commentary" (*NOR* 8:149–53).
His earliest collection of stories is treated by Jochen Achilles in "Donald Barthelme's Aesthetic of Inversion: Caligari's Come-Back as
Caligari's Leave-Taking" (*JNT* 12:105–20). A substantial overview
may be found in Thomas L. Leitch's "Donald Barthelme and the End
of the End" (*MFS* 28:129–44). In his fiction apparent subjects such
as love and death are always ideas or objects, never concrete experiences which engage the emotions or invite commitment. As parodies
of the genres they imply, these pieces are innocent of true narrative development. Barthelme's special flavor comes from his mixture of flat tone with fantastic situations. Two interviews prove that
Barthelme is an astute commentator on his own works: Jo Brans'
"Embracing the World: An Interview with Donald Barthelme" (*SWR*
67:121–37) and Larry McCaffery's excellent "An Interview with
Donald Barthelme" (*PR* 49:184–93). McCaffery is especially sharp
in his ability to draw Barthelme out on the subjects of improvising
from spontaneous sentences, the physicality of language, the French
new novelists, and his dialogue method in *Great Days* and *The Dead
Father*.

William H. Gass, who has not published a novel or story collection for a decade and a half, helps redirect critics' attention to his
literary theory in his essay, "Representation and the War for Reality" (*Salmagundi* 55:61–102). His argument that "words get their
power from other words" and not from the things they describe is
answered by Alvin H. Rosenfeld (pp. 103–09) and Ihab Hassan (pp.
110–18), the former cautioning that Gass's aesthetic will not work
when its subject is the holocaust (his work in progress) and the latter
complaining that Gass's language does not sufficiently contest itself,
creating "a poverty of life on the page." A full chapter on Gass the fictionist and the theorist occupies pp. 139–202 of Elizabeth W. Bruss's
*Beautiful Theories* (Hopkins), where the point is made that Gass
makes his fiction more literary at the same time that stylistic over-attention distracts from his aesthetic arguments. His ontology of literature shares much with the New Criticism, though his postmodern
affinity for consciousness through language marks him as more of a
rebel.

### *xii.* John Hawkes and Robert Coover

An excellent synthesis of John Hawkes's complex career as a novelist has been made by Patrick O'Donnell in *John Hawkes* (TUSAS 418). Drawing on the close stylistic analyses of Pierre Gault (who is the most sensitive of Hawkes's readers), O'Donnell praises Hawkes's ability to stretch language to accommodate his extreme psychic visions, noting that metaphors become virtually new linguistic tools in his hands. The author's bleak vision is more than balanced by his comic spirit, "and this integration of comedy and disaster allows Hawkes to fictionalize the unbearable, to perform the artistic act." The author's most recent works are discussed in companion essays by Paul Rosenzweig. In "Aesthetics and the Psychology of Control in John Hawkes's Triad" (*Novel* 15:146–62) *The Blood Oranges, Death, Sleep and the Traveler,* and *Travesty* are seen as the vehicles by which "artistic" narrators attempt to impose order on reality and in the process disorder themselves. Each has a facade of objectivity which masks a self-serving psychology aimed at excusing the narrator from responsibility. Death, however, proves the ultimate reality which they cannot change or escape. "John Hawkes's Novels of the Seventies: A Retrospective" (*ArQ* 38:69–77) adds *The Passion Artist* to this trilogy with an emphasis on the author's increase of self-conscious control (as the sex and violence mount). The structure of these novels mimic and mock the narrators' attempts to impose order, making them "highly stylized structures containing chaos."

The year's most written about writer is Robert Coover. Whether in individual analyses, surveys of contemporary fiction, or in syntheses of literary style, Coover's work inspires excellent scholarship. Foremost among this year's contributions is Lois Gordon's *Robert Coover: The Universal Fictionmaking Process* (So. Ill.). Coover's mixture of fact and fiction help to understand how he considers reality a relative notion, less central to human endeavor than the myth-making structures through which we view it. By tracking the "human need for significance" as Gordon does in the several novels and many short stories, one can find coherence among the author's various styles and themes (indeed, Gordon's comprehensive study of virtually everything Coover has written and said mark this as the definitive study against which future efforts will be measured).

Coover's *The Public Burning* is the topic of a gathering of essays in *Critique* 23,i. One of the best of Coover's critics is Thomas LeClair, and his "Robert Coover, *The Public Burning*, and the Art of Excess" (pp. 5–28) applies his theory of deliberate overkill; the "artist of excess" purposefully attracts and repels his audience in order to give his ideas power. At first the reader drives the artist over the edge and condemns him for it, but later, understanding this need to eclipse limits, he begins to desire such spectacle in the novel. In "Meta-fiction, the Historical Novel, and Coover's *The Public Burning*" (pp. 29–42) Raymond R. Mazurek explains how Coover has written a new style of work which treats history as a form of discourse. History is neither text nor narrative, but those forms are the only access we have to it. Media warp events to the extent that the words become their objects; by using words we may alter history, as Coover does in this novel. A more particularized study is Louis Gallo's "Nixon and the 'House of Wax': An Emblematic Scene in Coover's *The Public Burning*" (pp. 43–51). The mishaps and confusions of the man who thinks he is watching a 3-D movie parallel Nixon's own experiences, providing a surreal emblem of the novel as a whole. John Ramage covers much ground in "Myth and Monomyth in Coover's *The Public Burning*" (pp. 52–68), arguing that when the romantic hero is cut off from history there is no chance of rebirth (because there has been no preliminary dissolution), and that here may be found the roots for the corruption of the American dream.

Coover's ability to serve as a key type of novelist in a wide-ranging synthesis of fiction's full history is obvious from Zahava Karl McKeon's *Novels and Arguments: Inventing Rhetorical Criticism* (Chicago). McKeon chooses the first novel, *The Origin of the Brunists* (pp. 130–76) to show how the thematic contrasts between Marcella's and Happy's judgments sum up the novel's intentionality as "qualitative rhetoric," one of McKeon's types in the novel's progress. One of the most attractive interviews yet conducted with Coover has been published by Thomas Alden Bass. His "An Encounter with Robert Coover" (*AR* 40:287–302) describes a visit with the author when he lived in England (Coover spent most of the 1970s in the United Kingdom). In addition to providing an intimate portrait of his personal and professional life Bass manages to draw Coover out on such subjects as his student years at Chicago, his studies with Richard McKeon, and the genesis of his first stories. Much detail is accorded the composition of *The Public Burning*.

### *xiii.* John Irving and Tom Robbins

Still riding the crest of fame provided by *The World According to Garp* and *The Hotel New Hampshire*, John Irving is now more frequently interviewed than he is studied. Even the first book-length treatment, Gabriel Miller's *John Irving* (Ungar), concludes with an interview covering the usual topics from family life as a metaphor to the use of Vienna as a symbol of Old World decadence. Miller's study is distinguished by its appreciation of the essential optimism which distinguishes John Irving as a writer from his character Garp as shown through Irving's complex use of autobiography: only by combining traumatic memories of the past with a reshaping imaginative vision can the world be properly approached. Larry McCaffery's "An Interview with John Irving" (*ConL* 23:1–18) shows a strong understanding of the author's fiction; once a black-sheep style of scholarship, interviews have lately become the virtual equal of well-researched essays when the questions are as pertinent as McCaffery's. Irving is particularly lucid on the superiority of imaginative material to biographical, even though the latter may be an important impetus to the former. He also reveals that *Garp* was his breakthrough book because by writing it he discovered that he did best when he truly admired the characters he created, preferring breadth and complexity to "easily psychoanalyzed" entities. Joyce Rewick's "John Irving: An Interview" (*FInt* 14:5–18) reveals that the subject may have been interviewed to death. But among new items of discussion are his practice of beginning with each novel's ending, his affinities with and divergences from his teacher Kurt Vonnegut, the genesis of Jenny Garp as a character, and the role of sex and violence in his novels.

"Misfits: Tom Robbins' *Even Cowgirls Get the Blues*" (*NDQ* 50,iii:36–51) by Beverly Gross singles out Robbins' characteristic "unbridgeabilities" as the key to both his humor and his vision: paradox, contradiction, and opposition are shown to be part of a larger synthesis which Robbins champions over sterile conformity.

### *xiv.* Ronald Sukenick and William Gaddis

Charlotte M. Meyer provides an illuminating treatment of innovative fiction in "An Interview with Ronald Sukenick" (*ConL* 23:129–44). The major focus is how Sukenick "ascribes to the imagination the power of reality-making," and its expression on "the peripheries of language where language gets created: the edge of language, where there's a fresh contact between language and whatever is out there." Most instructive is Sukenick's belief that "the artist becomes the inventor of experience from mere phenomena: that is, we're confronted with phenomena and we want experience. Experience is phenomena taken in and made relevant to the individual psyche," a Romantic notion the author draws from both Wordsworth and Wallace Stevens. How these beliefs are expressed in one of the author's seminal fictions is explained by Stanley Trachtenberg in "The Way That Girl Pressed Against You on the Subway: Ronald Sukenick's Real Act of the Imagination" (*JNT* 12:57–71). In *Autobiographical Occasions* Albert E. Stone finds Sukenick (pp. 269–74) to be a handy contrast to Mailer's public self; Sukenick prefers the private mysteries of "parafiction" in which there is "no self, only linguistic structures" which are meant to disorient the reader's customary distinctions between history and imagination. As for pressures of fact, Sukenick resists them. How Sukenick's imaginative values are represented in the social changes of the 1960s is detailed by Jerome Klinkowitz in "New American Fiction and Values" (*AASt* 2:241–48).

William Gaddis is given full treatment in the *Review of Contemporary Fiction* 2,ii; best among the issue's eight contributions is Stephen Weisenburger's "Paper Currencies: Reading William Gaddis" (pp. 12–22) in which words are characterized as currencies of exchange (with a resultant shift of meaning in the narrative). Susan Strehle's "Disclosing Time: William Gaddis's *JR*" (*JNT* 12:1–14) shows that when the narrative is studied, time shifts become complex indeed, making necessary a work such as Stephen Moore's *A Reader's Guide to William Gaddis's "The Recognitions"* (Nebraska), which explains the structural metaphors that bind together the immense resource of references, each of which is then listed.

### xv. Fiction of the Vietnam War

Because the war disrupted so many military and social traditions, expressing it in fiction was no easy matter. As a result there has been more attention to the novels and stories which resulted from the experience than has been accumulated in thrice the time since World

War II. What will certainly be the definitive work for many years to come is Philip D. Beidler's *American Literature and the Experience of Vietnam* (Georgia). Beidler divides the literature into three phases, based on the military conduct of hostilities. The earliest fiction set the style for concentrating on self-generating roles—both in the war itself and in the fictions about it. Realistic conventions were of little use in dealing with a war which defied reality itself. With no point of reference writers had little choice but to construct metafictions; as for traditions, "the whole apparatus of mythic consciousness seemed to have gone on permanent short-circuit, pure overload." In *Vietnam in Prose and Film* (McFarland) James C. Wilson regrets "a new revisionism" which tries to traditionalize the war; Jeffrey Walsh's chapter (pp. 185–207) in *American Literature, 1914 to Vietnam* (St. Martin's), however, makes the case that the wealth of experimentalism makes any normative interpretation of the war and its literature impossible.

### xvi. Science Fiction

Thanks to Marshall B. Tymn's production of *The Year's Scholarship in Science Fiction, Fantasy and Horror Literature* (Kent State), *ALS* need comment on only trend-setting books and essays. One of these would be David Mogen's *Wilderness Visions: Science Fiction Westerns* (R. Reginald/Borgo Press), which shows how America's frontier heritage provides deeper roots for fantasy literature than most appraisals of "space-opera" allow. Using the same myths as Western pulp sagas, these SF Westerns use space as a frontier for comments on civilization. Of interest to all readers (and not just SF buffs) is Larry McCaffery's contribution to *Bridges to Fantasy*, ed. George Slusser, Eric S. Rabkin, and Robert Scholes (So. Ill.), "Form, Formula, and Fantasy: Generative Structures in Contemporary Fiction" (pp. 21–37). If literature is a game, as authors such as Roger Zelazny and Robert Coover suggest, "it becomes quite natural for writers to wish to explore literary games which can be played with fresher, more vital rules." Hence Samuel R. Delany's wish to deconstruction SF in *Einstein's Intersection* and Steve Katz's rewriting of pop mythologies in *Creamy and Delicious*; Robert Coover is the most complex with his shuffling of possible narrative sequences.

*xvii.* Women Writers and Women in Fiction

In *Lilith's Daughters: Women and Religion in Contemporary Fiction* (Wis.) Barbara Hill Rigney finds that the protest literature of Mary Gordon, Marge Piercy, and Annie Dillard argues with established ideals of a male God and other philosophies of pertinence to female sexual identity. In this respect their literature is a "challenge of the sacred" in order to create "a kind of garden wrested from the wilderness of patriarchal language and ideology." Female Christ-figures and erotic Mary-images are part of this reconstruction of the Garden along lines that are not male-dominant.

"On Feminist Utopias" (*WS* 9:241–62) is Anne K. Mellor's study of how genre-free societies have been posited as an ideal in works by Ursula Le Guin and Marge Piercy. Their "challenging imaginative vision of a historically possible gender-free society toward which feminists might aspire and pragmatically work" is seen as a stimulus to feminist theory. A more abstract style of novel is described by Jennifer L. Randisi in "The Journey Nowhere: Didion's *Run River*" (*MarkhamR* 11:41–43); Joan Didion changes the river myth from one of voyage and escape (Dante and Twain) to one of going nowhere. Kay Mussell provides an interesting preface to *Twentieth-Century Romance and Gothic Writers*, ed. James Vinson (Gale; pp. v–vii), commenting that the American 1970s trend of sex as a positive experience has changed the publishing history of this subgenre in favor of more explicit "details of women's personal lives." In Patricia Altner's entry on Rosemary Rogers (pp. 593–94) we see this same shift from the author's early "bodice busters" (which treated such sexual characteristics negatively) to her more contemporary settings in recent novels, where the same "sweet/savage" clichés nevertheless remain.

*xviii.* The American West, Native American and Chicano Writers, and Oriental-American Literature

In his preface to *Twentieth Century Western Writers*, ed. James Vinson (Gale; pp. vii–xiv) C. L. Sonnichsen makes a concise summary of this subgenre and finds its informing mythology as equal to that of the Bible, the Arthurian legends, and the Norse sagas. Setting is less important than this mythic background, which during the 1940–

80 period experiences a complete reversal of values as a "West that never was" (such as in Larry McMurtry's *Horseman, Pass By*) replacing the West that really was. Helen Winter Stauffer and Susan J. Rosowski have collected a good set of essays in *Woman and Western American Literature* (Whitston). Most helpful is Barbara Howard Meldrum's "Women in Western American Fiction: Images, or Real Women?" (pp. 55–69), which cites Vardis Fisher's *Mountain Man*, Wallace Stegner's *Angle of Repose*, and Frederick Manfred's *The Manly-Hearted Woman* to show that "very few central actions can be imagined as being performed by female protagonists" unless they adopt male characteristics in doing so. Women characters are Lynn Waldeland's subject in "Plains Song: Women's Voices in the Fiction of Wright Morris" (*Crit* 24,i:7–20). Many of these are overbearing creatures who make life miserable for men, but they are forced to be this way because the men refuse to be co-responsible partners. *Plains Song*, however, is "the best feminist novel of the past fifteen years" because women carry the novel without using men as foils.

Jessamyn West and Henry Wilson Allen (who uses the two pen names "Will Henry" and "Clay Fisher") are given full treatment in the Western Writers Series by Ann Dahlstrom Farmer and Robert L. Gale respectively, but the Western writer accorded most attention this year is Wallace Stegner. In "Wallace Stegner's Family Saga: From *The Big Rock Candy Mountain* to *Recapitulation*" (*WAL* 17: 101–16) Forrest G. Robinson shows how Stegner's notion of "being born to write one story" becomes a fictional process motivating the return to childhood whereby Bruce Mason reports his mission in life. Three new essays grace Anthony Hiller's collection, *Critical Essays on Wallace Stegner* (Hall). William C. Baurecht's "Within a Continuous Frame: Stegner's Family Album in *The Big Rock Candy Mountain*" (pp. 98–108) praises the accurate social context of American folkways and dreams. In "*Angle of Repose* and the Writings of Mary Hallock Foote: A Source Study" (pp. 184–209) Mary Ellen Williams Walsh shows how the effect is one of re-creation and not chronicle. Merill Lewis's "Wallace Stegner's *Recapitulations*: Memory as Art Form" (pp. 210–21) treats the novel as a homecoming, much as Robinson does in his essay.

What are destined to become the standard interpretations of N. Scott Momaday, James Welch, Leslie Marmon Silko, and Gerald Vizenor is the substance of Alan R. Velie's *Four American Indian*

*Literary Masters* (Oklahoma). Puerto Rican literature of New York is described by Eugene V. Mohr in *The Nuyorican Experience: Literature of the Puerto Rican Minority* (Greenwood); fiction first striking a high profile as immigrant literature soon found its home in New York's Puerto Rican community, and after going through an autobiographical phase has now produced challenges to tradition and calls for a new multicultural identity (represented respectively by Piri Thomas and Nicholasa Mohr). A similar state of affairs is described by Elaine H. Kim in *Asian American Literature* (Temple), where cultural myths and stereotypes generated from outside the Asian-American community challenge its writers to create beyond caricatures. *Three American Literatures* (MLA) edited by Houston A. Baker, Jr., collects valuable essays geared toward the teaching of Chicano, Native American, and Asian-American literatures. The most written-about minority work continues to be the subject of William C. Clements' "The Way to Individuation in Anaya's *Bless Me, Ultima*" (*MQ* 23:131–43), which classifies the book as an "individuation novel" according to Jung. A more complete reading of Anaya may be found in Antonio Márquez's "The Achievement of Rudolfo A. Ananya," the central piece (pp. 33–52) in *The Magic of Words: Rudolfo A. Ananya and his Writings*, ed. Paul Vassallo (N. Mex.).

*University of Northern Iowa*

# 16. Poetry: 1900 to the 1940s

## Richard Crowder

The year 1982 brought publication of three bibliographies (Ransom, Aiken, and Harry Kemp) and a descriptive catalogue of the paintings of Cummings. Of essay collections there were four: on the Agrarians, on Frost, and two on Crane. Books of criticism treated Williams (two), Frost (two), Crane and Williams in a study of visionary poetry, Moore, and Millay in a revised edition of TUSAS 116. A 1981 work on Stevens came to my attention. There were biographical studies of Masters, H.D. (two, of which one was autobiographical), and Williams' mother (a reissue of a 1959 memoir of the poet). Brief notes appeared in *Expl* 40,ii,iii, and 41,i; *NMAL* 5, *NConL* 12, and *MP* 80—one each on Moore and Stevens, two on Williams, and 12 on old standby Frost. Twenty-nine dissertations considered 14 of the poets (exclusively or in part) of the 60 (some very minor, granted) I have touched on in this chapter since *ALS 1969*—Robinson, Winters, Fletcher, Stein, H.D., Aiken, Bogan, and Hulda Saenger Walter (1867–1929), one each; Frost and Cummings, two each; Crane and Moore, three; Stevens, four; and Williams, seven. That's quite a dwindling from the 36 dissertations reported last year.

### i. Group Studies

One article and four books gave consideration to groups of our poets. Maxine Kumin contributed " 'Stamping a Tiny Foot against God': Some American Women Poets Writing between the Two Wars" (*QJLC* 39:48–61). Taking off from Theodore Roethke's 1961 attack on poetry by women, the author gives brief sympathetic summary statements on the work of Amy Lowell, Moore, H.D., Teasdale, Millay, Bogan, and, from the next generation, Muriel Rukeyser, arguing that with grace, clarity, and strength they accomplished in large part what they set out to do.

In 1980 Thomas Daniel Young delivered the Lamar Memorial Lectures at Mercer University and has used his material in writing *Waking Their Neighbors Up: The Nashville Agrarians Rediscovered* (Georgia). The book explains what Tate, Ransom, and their colleagues wanted to achieve and shows that time has proved them prophetic. Just as Thoreau's antimaterialism advocated a reexamination of assumptions about what is necessary for a good life, so the Agrarians warned their readers against almost total commitment to the applied sciences. The "Postlude" recounts the activities of the group from the publication of *I'll Take My Stand* (1930) through *Understanding Fiction* (1943).

We are not likely to be allowed soon to forget this generation of southerners. A symposium celebrating the 50th anniversary of the publication of *I'll Take My Stand* was held at Vanderbilt on 30 and 31 October and 1 November 1980. Taking part were experts on the period, including among others Lewis P. Simpson, Robert B. Heilman, and Louis D. Rubin, Jr. There was also a discussion by Andrew Lytle, Lyle Lanier, and Robert Penn Warren, moderated by Cleanth Brooks. A collection of this material, edited by William C. Havard and Walter Sullivan, who have written an introduction, is called *A Band of Prophets: The Vanderbilt Agrarians after Fifty Years* (LSU). The book provides a review of the famous "movement" and an estimate of its place in the American literary tradition. Though there is no emphasis on the poetry, there is ample picturing of the sources of the works of imagination by the original coterie. The essays treat such subjects as sectionalism, the southern concept of a Republic of Letters, the relation of the movement to the European intellectual community, and its reputation in the universities of the country. Brooks's panel was concerned with "Culture, Economics, and Society in a Technological Age."

Selected from the *Hound & Horn* Archive (Beinecke Library, Yale) are *The "Hound & Horn" Letters*, ed. Mitzi Berger Hamovitch (Georgia). Lincoln Kirsten, co-founder of the magazine as a Harvard undergraduate, has written a foreword. These letters faithfully and with spirit and insight reflect the period of 1927–34. Among the writers were Tate, MacLeish, Cummings, Moore, Williams, and Winters —their very names a sure promise of high energy, important issues, and unabating creativity. The letters testify to a profound interest in ideologies, literature, and culture in general and trace the development of high critical responsibility in the United States. This is an important anthology, of interest to students of the period and to the general reader alike.

The first chapter of Hyatt Waggoner's *American Visionary Poetry* (LSU) developed from a colloquium at Brown, became first an essay in *SR* 79, and now with some changes introduces the chapters that follow in this book on specific poets. Waggoner defines a visionary as "one who sees better or farther, deeper and more truly than we," that is, is attached to the "perceivable world," but can make "positive implications." After a chapter on Whitman ("I and the Round Earth") the author presents his ideas on Hart Crane ("Only in Darkness Is Thy Shadow Clear"), a "good late Symbolist" who had to seek ways of shaking up the senses in order to envision the epiphanies he felt he could not experience in the quotidian world. Waggoner links Crane to Whitman and Blake as visionaries, but more importantly to Arthur Rimbaud, whom the poet discovered through Eliot.

In a chapter headed "Naturalizing the Unearthly" the author fits Williams into his scheme because after the initial Imagist-Objectivist phase he indicated that he had an eye which saw "with the aid of memory and thought" beyond the grimness and waste of the everyday scene toward an interpretive vision. Waggoner says, however, that *Paterson* fails because Book IV ends in nostalgia. In Book V (seven years later) the poet insists that an artist must create his own world (as Jackson Pollock did with his "blobs"). "Asphodel, That Greeny Flower," says Waggoner, goes beyond the kind of visionary poem Williams was writing in mid-career (cf. "Desert Music"). It is a poem of "light remembered." In an appendix ("Seeing and Believing") Waggoner gives brief attention to Frost and Stevens, among others.

### *ii.* The East

Tributes to Archibald MacLeish offered at his funeral in 1982 have been collected in *MR* 23:657–704. (The pages of the section are actually unnumbered.) Henry Steele Commager ("Beauty & Wisdom") calls the man a "Roman in his sense of virtue" and "an Athenian in his sense of beauty." Joseph Langland ("In Our Time for a Long Time") proclaims MacLeish's truly human quality, his profound feeling for the aesthetic, a wide-ranging sympathy, a command of language, and an intuitive perception of what constitutes an authentic "cultural heritage." Langland quotes from the correspondence as evidence of his generosity and modesty, for he knew that —in the company of Pound, Blackmur, Tate, Hemingway, and the others—he was not the best writer of his generation. Langland lists 31 titles of poems familiar to American readers, however, to prove that he was nevertheless significantly present "in the scene."

John William Ward ("Archibald MacLeish & Education") pictures his subject as gentlemanly, morally stern, and capable of "controlled anger against individual and social wrong." He saw that colleges have the responsibility (often neglected) of teaching "people who want to know, what there is to know and what things are conditions precedent to what other things and in what order." For him the purpose of the humane man is "to strive to be fully human and to sustain a critical engagement with life." Donald Junkins' contribution is a poem, "Reaching Out: After Reading MacLeish Succumbs at Eighty-nine," in which he paints the poet as a keen observer and a creative recorder. "Arch, take care, take/true: aim for the heart/ again."

Added to this cluster of encomiums is a television interview conducted with MacLeish by William Heyen and Anthony Piccione on 2 October 1974 at SUNY College, Brockport, N.Y. "The Shine of the World: A Conversation with Archibald MacLeish" touches on numerous subjects beginning with "Ars Poetica" and its roots in the poet's life. MacLeish speaks of many contemporaries from Louis Untermeyer ("an anthologist") to Pound, who had berated MacLeish in his infamous Rome broadcasts. Other topics include Jews, fascism, his own *Frescoes for Mr. Rockefeller's City*, Chaucer, Sandburg, Learned Hand, F.D.R., Rimbaud, Crane, and more. They reveal the man's broad sympathies, his sensitivities, and his deep-seated virtues.

Helen Hagenbüchle's "Antennae of the Race: Conrad Aiken's Poetry and the Evolution of Consciousness" (*HLQ* 45:215–26) contends that Aiken always was preoccupied with shaping and refining his "I-World" relationship. He saw poetry as the point at which "the unconscious turns conscious." For him the act of writing itself was "the prototype of this process of transformation." "Linear time" in his early poetry becomes "spiral time" in his later work. For him "the eternal principle underlying time" is "a consciousness-becoming life

principle." What is for the individual a transitory moment is preserved in the cosmic consciousness, "where permanence and progress
are coeval." Aiken deserves more serious attention like this.

F. W. and F. C. Bonnell have compiled *Conrad Aiken: A Bibliography (1902–1978)* (Huntington), in which the works are divided
into five categories: books and pamphlets, contributions to books,
contributions to periodicals (including juvenilia from the Middlesex
School and pieces in the *Harvard Advocate*), translations, and such
miscellanea as foreign editions, recordings, films, and "Books Announced but Not Published." The listings are devoted entirely to the
work of Aiken himself (nothing *about* him). The index appears
complete and usable. This bibliography of "primary works" will be
important for both serious collecting and critical research.

Cummings has been neglected this year. The sole work on him is
a catalogue of an exhibition of his paintings, which critics are relating
more and more to his poetry. Milton A. Cohen is author of the catalogue *E. E. Cummings' Paintings: The Hidden Career* for the two
showings at the University of Texas at Dallas and the Dallas Public
Library. The exhibition affirms, as nothing else can do, that Cummings was a serious artist. It is a strong addition to the work of
Rushworth Kidder (*ALS 1975*, p. 372, and *ALS 1976*, p. 330).

Two books of essays on Crane show the wide interest in the poet
in the past years, though this year produced only two articles in
journals (by women, it so happens). David R. Clark's *Critical Essays
on Hart Crane* (Hall) charts the uneven course of Crane's critical
reception. Clark's introduction thoroughly surveys all relevant scholarship. Of the 20 essays three are original: Mary Jean Butts concentrates on "Atlantis," Allen Grossman studies the "intense poetics" of
"The Return," and Donald Pease considers Crane in the role of epic
prophet. Some other essays are by Tate, R. W. B. Lewis, Malcolm
Cowley, and Yvor Winters.

The other anthology is *Hart Crane: A Collection of Critical Essays*, ed. Alan Trachtenberg (Prentice-Hall). The editor's 12-page
introduction points out particularly the critically slighted quality of
"intensity of reflection" in the poetry. Trachtenberg claims that it is
necessary to come to an "awareness of cunning compressions" to get
at the poet's form (and subsequently the "meaning"). Following the
introduction the editor presents Crane's own "General Aims and
Theories" and then a set of 15 critical commentaries by a dazzling

array of literary thinkers including Tate, Winters, Blackmur, and Harold Bloom. All the essays are reprints, a few being condensed. They range in time from 1926 to 1982, the last essay being a chapter from Bloom's *Agon: Towards a Theory of Revisionism* (Oxford), where Crane is characterized as "a prophet of American Orphism." Crane's canon, says Bloom, may be "truncated," but it is undeniably "overwhelming."

Miriam Fuchs reviews the well-known details of the Crane-Kahn connection in "Poet and Patron: Hart Crane and Otto Kahn" (*BForum* 6:45–51). Fuchs fleshes out the skeletal story with quotations from unpublished letters of Crane at Columbia and Kahn at Princeton. A couple of times she uses the phrase "cordial but cool" in describing Kahn's attitude. His $2,000 loan in the mid-twenties "triggered an extremely productive period of writing" for Crane. "Whatever Crane considered him to be and whatever Crane's parents considered him to be, Kahn apparently did not view himself as anyone's surrogate father. He remained, from start to finish, a gracious and humane patron of the arts."

The other article, by Suzanne Clark Doeren, is called "Theory of Culture, Brooklyn Bridge, and Hart Crane's Rhetoric of Memory" (*BMMLA* 15:18–28). The author advocates the use of the techniques of comparative literature and American studies in getting at Crane, who challenges "the closed history of America's ideology of progress." *The Bridge*, if read adequately, must stimulate "the play of differentiation, rupture, and recovery engendered by passionate history." This is a thoughtful, quickening article.

William Brevda's dissertation at Connecticut in 1980 was entitled *Harry Kemp: The Last Bohemian*. From that work he has culled two publications—an essay and a bibliography. "Harry Kemp: A Bibliography of Primary Sources" (*BB* 39:191–94) lists published books, foreign editions, his periodical *Provincetown Tideways*, contributions to periodicals, and manuscripts. Brevda's article, "At the Crossroads of Vagabondia, Hobohemia, and Bohemia: Harry Kemp's *Tramping on Life*" (*MarkhamR* 11:46–50), describes how Kemp took to the open road always with the idea of returning to the East. In his army blankets he wrapped "a second-hand Shakespeare, in one volume, of wretched print, with a much-abused school copy of Caesar" in Latin ("of whose idiomatic Latin I have never tired"), as well as a volume of Keats subsequently stolen from him by other tramps. A muscular Bohemian, Kemp undertook to prove that it was not "shameful and unmanly" to be sensitive to beauty. This essay supplements the work of Marshall Brooks (see *ALS 1980*, p. 365).

### *iii.* The Midwest, South, and West

Lindsay's writing is "overtly moral, declaratory, expansive," hence "American Bardic," near to oblivion in the present-day "hierarchy of genres." So says Donald Wesling in "What the Canon Excludes: Vachel Lindsay and American Bardic" (*MQR* 21:479–85). Wesling opines that Harold Bloom would classify Lindsay as weak, unaware of what the entire problem of writing amounts to. A strict "hierarchical canon" must establish certain standards and genres and "give a common body of reference," as well as set up its own criteria for greatness. Wesling thinks it would be almost impossible to carve out "an explicit, authoritative American poetic canon," for a canon has to exclude what it cannot fit within its standards. Nowadays American Bardic is hardly countenanced and thus cannot be included as indispensable.

Another Midwest-born poet is the subject of his son's memoirs. Hilary Masters, son of Edgar Lee Masters by his second marriage, has written *Last Stands: Notes from Memory* (Godine), which focuses on two old people, his mother's mother and his own father. This recollection of boyhood fortunes, estranged parents, the father's physical breakdown, and other family crises is in a novelistic style with more metaphoric suggestiveness than the usual autobiographical account.

*A Gallery of Southerners*, ed. Louis D. Rubin (LSU), is a collection of essays originally printed elsewhere. Chiefly concerned with writers of fiction, it does preserve the editor's "Allen Tate, 1899–1979" (pp. 107–14) first published in *SR* 87 (*ALS 1979*, p. 323). It expresses Rubin's feeling of deep indebtedness to the influence of Tate, who had served as his model. "He was worthy of one's esteem." Martha E. Cook's "A Literary Friendship: Allen Tate and Donald Davidson" (*SoR* 18:739–54) reviews and expands on the Tate-Davidson letters (*ALS 1981*, pp. 313–14), tracing the diminishing warmth in their personal relationship, though they continued to write to each other about literary matters, sometimes after considerable silence. Tate helped Davidson in his ongoing struggle for recognition. "Their friendship was of a higher kind which transcended personal misunderstandings." Their literary connection lasted nearly 50 years. Robert Buffington continues his examination of the Vanderbilt group with "Allen Tate: Society, Vocation, Communion" (*SoR* 18: 62–72). This is a chronological account of the ups and downs of Tate's economic situation as he pursued his writing, supporting himself now by teaching, now by free-lancing. He was constantly distinguishing between company (propinquity) and society ("presence fully human"), between career (what one chooses to do) and vocation (that to which one is called), between communication (which we use) and communion (in which we participate).

The original leader of the Fugitives-Agrarians is the subject of the indefatigable Thomas Daniel Young's *John Crowe Ransom: An Annotated Bibliography* (Garland), including a 26-page introduction. A volume in the Modern Critics and Critical Schools Series, it will be highly serviceable to scholars in the literature of the South.

Robert Ian Scott seeks to correct the views of Joseph Wood Krutch especially with respect to Robinson Jeffers. Scott thinks Krutch ignored the possibility of change through understanding of the cause by systematically examining "the widest possible range of relevant facts." In "Berkeley to Barclay's Delusion: Robinson Jeffers vs. Modern Narcissism" (*Mosaic* 15,iii:55–61) he describes how Jeffers set out to show that such delusions as Krutch's could be avoided "if we would see the universe and not some narcissistic reflection of ourselves in God." In *The Woman at Point Sur* (1927) the Reverend Dr. Barclay renounces World War I and the Christian faith, which did not prevent the death of his only son in battle. Scott sees Barclay as a parody of Bishop Berkeley (d. 1753) and his belief that only through God's perception does the world exist. Barclay on the other hand believes that "the world exists to satisfy us" and dies under that self-deception (a kind of narcissism). One of Jeffers' frequently recurring opinions is that egocentricity causes much otherwise avoidable misery. Responsible adults, in the poet's view, will discover what they "can and cannot and should not do in relation to the universe." It is vain to "hope that our words and emotions can rule the world." *RJN* 60 (pp. 5–16) and 61 (pp. 18–38) have provided two installments of a collection of letters from Una Jeffers to the poet's friend

Albert Bender. A third installment is contemplated. An interesting map of Jeffers country with a relevant reading list appears in *RJN* 61:41.

### iv. The Women

A quite different sort of book from Bonnie Costello's *Marianne Moore: Imaginary Possessions* (*ALS 1981*, p. 318) is Elizabeth Phillips' *Marianne Moore* (Ungar). In five chapters Phillips covers the facts of Moore's life and presents through explications her view of the poet's work. In the first chapter (biographical) she uses 68 footnotes, testimony to her reliance on "secondary sources" as the basis of her account, though many of the references are to Moore's own words in interviews and to the poet's essays recounting her past. The next two chapters explicate many poems roughly in the order of their publication to show Moore's growth from haughtiness and bluntness through frank confession and honesty to an old age characterized by a humility born of sorrow and helplessness but always with a conscious mindfulness of the world of large issues. One chapter dwells on Moore's reliance for strength on the Christian faith. (She remained a staunch Presbyterian.) The last chapter, "In the Public Garden," shows Moore to have been very much aware of political and social problems. She became a public poet because she passionately wanted good to survive.

In an article devoted to women Susan R. Van Dyne writes of Moore as very reticent but determined to achieve a view without illusions. "Double Monologues: Voices in American Women's Poetry" (*MR* 23:461–85) demonstrates how Moore uses her wit and "deflections" both to protect herself and to attack what she does not like. In pointing to faults of others which she fears are her own weaknesses, she "tests the limits of her own comprehension," reaching "full consciousness" through precise use of voice and eye. Van Dyne gives as an example "The Grave," a poem colored by the reserve of negation.

In "History in the Text" (*TSLL* 24:329–46) Jonathan Morse argues that the search for symbols can lead only to "the mirage of the source of the sources of the sources." If we are aware of a poem's history, we will put any textual resistance to work in getting to "know the originating language of our reading selves." Moore's poem "Peter"

in the 1979 *Norton Anthology of American Literature* is burdened
with critical views mingling with factual material. To equate the cat
Peter with Christ's disciple is misleading. The cat in Morse's opinion
is an animal in a poem which shapes "his naturalness into syllabic
lines of perfect idiosyncracy."

"Meeting Marianne" (*IowaR* 13:96–100) is based on Mary Barnard's letters home while she was visiting New York for the first time
in 1936. The article is excerpted from *Assault on Mount Helicon*,
scheduled for publication in 1983. A typical comment: "She also
chided me gently for not writing better prose." Barnard considers
"What Are Years" to be "one of the great modern lyrics."

Though Moore and her particulars and Stevens and his abstractions appear to have little in common, they viewed each other as
kindred spirits, says Bonnie Costello in "Marianne Moore's Debt
and Tribute to Wallace Stevens" (*CP* 15,i:22–33). His influence on
her is in fact quite evident, especially his exotic imagery, which
fertilized her own "riot of gorgeousness." They were comparable to
each other and different from their contemporaries in "their musi-
cality, their use of figuration, their way of writing about the imagination, their definitions of heroism, their images of combat, their sense
of America." In 1950 Moore's "Pretiolae" made explicit reference to
Stevens' Hartford and Reading, and in 1951 Stevens was a judge of
the National Book Awards, in which Moore's *Collected Poems* won
the poetry prize. As last year's book proves, Costello is an astute
Moore scholar.

Janice S. Robinson's *H.D.: The Life and Work of an American
Poet* (Houghton Mifflin) is a breakthrough study disclosing the biographical provenance of H.D.'s work. It examines carefully her poetry
and her prose (published and unpublished) and links them closely
with her Moravian girlhood and her relationships later with Pound,
her unfaithful husband Richard Aldington, D. H. Lawrence, Freud,
and Bryher (Winifred Ellerman). Under the influence of this book,
12 years in preparation and based on thousands of manuscript pages,
letters, and books in the Beinecke Library and elsewhere, no one's
reading of H.D. can ever be the same. Even if not altogether objective, it is nevertheless unromanticized and honest and goes far beyond any preceding H.D. study, including Susan Stanford Friedman's feminist *Psyche Reborn* (see *ALS 1981*, p. 317). In no way
should it be passed over.

H.D.'s autobiographical novel *Hermione*, released in 1981 by New Directions, was written in 1927. According to Carol Camper in her article "The Autobiography of a Future Poet from Pennsylvania" (*ConL* 23:377–80) it has many irritating flaws but serves to introduce the reader "to the mythologizing impulse behind H.D.'s poetry" and her search for "symbolic analogues for personal values." It gives voice to "a woman whose alienation profiles patriarchy's most blighting effects."

Perdita Schaffner writes an introduction to her mother H.D.'s *The Gift* (New Directions), an autobiographical account of the poet's childhood. The book fills out even farther the story as told by Janice Robinson. It is colored by the kindliness of H.D.'s family and relatives. "The gift," inherited from her maternal grandmother, was the ability to enter the very memories of her 18th-century Moravian ancestors. It actually blossomed in London one day during the Blitz when the poet suddenly "saw" a jar of "prewar apple jelly which she was saving for Edith Sitwell." (The words are daughter Perdita's. Does this not parallel Proust's "petite madeleine"?)

That *Helen in Egypt* (1961) is a lyrical epic marked by a sustained intensity is the judgment of Albert Gelpi ("Hilda in Egypt," *SoR* 18:233–50), who contrasts the work with Emily Dickinson's ambivalent, contradictory brief love poems. It develops extensively a "woman's myth" and presents the mother-figure as supreme. Hilda is "self-born in Helen." This sympathetic reading would find parallels in the work of Friedman.

Norman A. Britten has revised his *Edna St. Vincent Millay* (TUSAS 116). Except for a grudging acknowledgment of the author's 17 pages of comment on the plays (p. 254), *ALS 1967* makes no mention of the first edition. This new version differs from the first in several ways. Reduced biographical detail is in general used only as background for the poetry. In addition, Britten finds room for more emphasis on Millay's prose, her relation to the feminist movement, and her place in what is called "High Modernism." The arrangement of the subject matter follows the usual TUSAS order —mostly year by year with a conclusion about the poet's achievement. For many readers Millay's life was that of "a full-bodied participant" in her half of the 20th century, and as poet she "enunciates a credo for private lives and public issues."

Marjorie Perloff's *The Poetics of Indeterminacy: Rimbaud to Cage*

(Princeton, 1981) contains a chapter entitled "Poetry as Word System: The Art of Gertrude Stein" (pp. 67–108), in which the author considers Stein's Cubist syntax, her mode of repetition, and the Dada attitude and style. Perloff sees Dada as the informing trait of *Tender Buttons*, the text of which "has remained peculiarly resistant to interpretation." Objects here have Cubist qualities of fragmentation and decomposition and "serve as false leads, forcing the reader to consider the very nature of naming."

Helped by the critical study of Virginia M. Kouidis (*ALS 1980*, pp. 354–55), revival of interest in Mina Loy now has its golden opportunity. The Jargon Society of Highlands, N.C., has published Loy's *The Last Lunar Baedeker*, including not only her previously published poems but 50 pages of new material ("Didactic, Polemical, and Prescriptive Writings," "Profiles and Interviews," and "Ready Mades") and photographs of Loy herself and of her paintings, sculptures, "constructions," and one of her calla lily lamps. Roger L. Conover's long, knowledgeable introduction is both freshly biographical and unsentimentally appreciative. It is followed by a generously annotated "Time Table" (chronology). Question: Is Loy intrinsically major, or will this book be collected as a fascinating relic of the Pound Era?

Helen P. Trimpi has written a laudatory commentary on the poems of Yvor Winters' widow, Janet Lewis, born in 1899. Trimpi explains that Lewis' collected poems begin with the work of 1918, "The Freighters," which gained her membership in the Poetry Club at the University of Chicago. On the other hand, "Words for a Song" was composed after she had celebrated her 80th birthday. It considers with strength and concentration the "complexities of human love." Trimpi's article is punctuated with such statements as "The rhetorical movement is masterly" and "The structure within this small area is tightly organized by alliteration and by repetition."

### v. Stevens

Following his 1978 dissertation on *Wallace Stevens: The Pursuit of Mastery* Milton J. Bates has been plowing the Stevens field with persistence and assiduity. Now again he is pursuing the biographical approach in "Selecting One's Parents: Wallace Stevens and Some

Early Influences" (*JML* 9:183–208). This is a thorough study—with photographs—of the effect on Stevens of his immediate ancestry as well as his experiences at Harvard (fellow students, faculty, the *Advocate*, the clubs) and his ambivalent attitude toward his hometown of Reading.

Joseph Kronick looks at "the poet's genealogy" in the wide sense in "Of Parents, Children, and Rabbis: Wallace Stevens and the Question of the Book" (*Boundary* 10,iii:125–54). He considers the poet's connection with Emerson, Thoreau, his father, and fellow poets. He shows how important it was to Stevens to collect and order the leaves of his world in books and concludes by interpreting Stevens' several references to a rabbi as "the secular reader and his texts." He identifies what Stevens is after as bringing balance to "the fluctuations and shades of difference in human love." The ideal secular reader must be able to lighten dark places with "a moment's interpretation" and must be "free from the bondage of genealogy," standing outside any "linear descent" whether father-son, teacher-student, or priest-congregation.

Marjorie Perloff discusses "Pound/Stevens: Whose Era?" (*NLH* 13:485–514), saying that the two poets had no time to read each other's work and that Pound's experimentation and invention were at loggerheads with the "discipline" of Stevens. Top-notch critics such as Hugh Kenner (Pound) and Harold Bloom (Stevens) have supported their chosen poets with vigor. William Carlos Williams, on the other hand, defended both at once while he vilified Eliot. Naming the leader of an era—whether he be Pound or Stevens—is in the long run a toss-up. *Chacun à son gout.* In "Wordsworth, Frost, Stevens, and the Poetic Vocation" (*SIR* 21:87–100) David Bromwich, though emphasizing Wordsworth, proposes that a chief concern for Stevens is "the continuity of poetry for the poet" and for Frost "the justification of poetry to the world"—both of which problems troubled Wordsworth.

"Stevens and Lawrence: The Poetry of Nature and the Spirit of the Age" (*SoR* 18:44–61) by Jerome Bump points out how the nature poetry of these two men "asks us to determine the signifiance of the shift in the humanities from the traditional values of 'humane letters' to the imitation of science's apparent objectivity, abstraction, and rationality." Both poets are interested in "the origins of our new environmental ethic and the increasing infatuation . . . with solipsism, decreation, nihilism, and death." At the end of his life, particularly, Stevens tried to get in touch with "the thing as it exists separate and apart from ourselves." Lawrence's "Tortoise Shout" contrasts with Stevens' "The Course of a Particular" in that Lawrence's "cry" is uttered by an actual woman, baby, coal miner, whereas in the Stevens poem the exertion of being "part of everything" eventually diminishes to nothingness.

The one book on Stevens to come to my attention was published in 1981: Michael Sexson's *The Quest of Self in the Collected Poems of Wallace Stevens* (vol. 1 of Studies in Art and Religious Interpretation; Lewiston, N.Y.: Edwin Mellen Press). In the introduction the author proposes a thesis that Stevens is determined, even heroic in "trying to achieve an unbreakable unity." Though the poet fails, he does decide that existence is inextricable from the imagination. There follow four chapters examining the major works in Jungian depth and disclosing what may be called "psychopoesis" rather than psychology at work. The conclusion, "The Deeper Feminine," obviously Jungian in its affirmation, presents the belief that, as Frost puts it, "The Secret sits in the middle and knows."

A related theme is developed by Alfred Corn in "Wallace Stevens: Pilgrim in Metaphor" (*YR* 71:225–35), one of a series of talks given at George Mason University, where Corn was poet-in-residence in October 1981. The author says that in his early years Stevens was inhibited by a sense of nothingness, but his total scepticism brought him to the view that the imagination could be valued "as absolute, no less comprehensive than a belief in the divine." He could also claim, however, that "the ultimate value is reality," whose marriage to the imagination he was always seeking (the vocation of a poet). The way to the "central imagination" is through language and its sound. Poetic style is all-important. Stevens' later poems, though, looked to metaphor as the means of turning an empty "thing" into something at the same time fulfilling and "unreal." The vacancy of his early poems was "replaced by a sense and a rhetoric of fullness."

Three of Stevens' poems received individual attention: "The Comedian as the Letter C" (early), "The Idea of Order at Key West" (middle), and "The Sail of Ulysses" (late). The first of these is a record of Stevens at the crossroads in current American literature.

Which way should (would?) he go? As early as 1900 (while a senior at Harvard) he expressed dissatisfaction with local color. Martha Strom, in "Wallace Stevens' Revisions of Crispin's Journal: A Reaction against the 'Local'" (*AL* 54:258–76), explains that the poet could not assume the tone of Paul Rosenfeld, James Oppenheimer, and other advocates of direct response to the American environment. "From the Journal of Crispin" was finished at about the time of the appearance in the *Dial* of Santayana's "The Comic Mask" and "Carnival," which influenced him to make long excisions from his original poem testifying to his "divergence from the localists." In the final version Crispin is pictured as separate from Stevens, whose emphasis on the "intelligence" is far removed from Crispin's soil.

Allan Chavkin suggests that "The Idea of Order at Key West" is Stevens' expression of the theme of "Tintern Abbey" and "The Solitary Reaper": the placing of hope in "the passionate imagination." Through the words thus created one can "transform an alien (ghostly) modern world into some kind of home for man." Chavkin's article is called "Wallace Stevens' Transformation of the Romantic Landscape Meditation" (*CEA* 44,iii:2–4).

Michael Ryan considers the same poem in "Disclosures of Poetry: On Wallace Stevens and 'The Idea of Order at Key West'" (*APR* 11,iv:29–34), in which he reaches the conclusion that what is important is not subject matter but "the magnificent fury of his belief in poetry" (Chavkin's "passionate imagination"). Ryan looks at the poem in terms of sound, syntax, and structure and sees that it grows from Stevens' complete commitment to poetry. The reader is obligated to listen for the sentence variety and the relationship of the sentences against the blank verse and the few end rhymes. The music is difficult to get at because the sounds "are potentially meaningful in a discursive way."

One of Stevens' last compositions is the subject of Nancy W. Prothro's "The Wealth of Poverty, the Jewel of Need: Wallace Stevens' 'The Sail of Ulysses'" (*CP* 15,ii:1–10). The poem in question balances "a knowledge of unresurrectable death with a life vitally redeemed by a new sense of self." The "voice" of the poem is profound, the result of "long years of struggle, of hope and faith." The poet's last works portray him as remarkably humble, but vital, strong, whole, and mentally healthy.

## *vi.* Williams

*Yes, Mrs. Williams: A Personal Record of My Mother* (2d ed.) (New
Directions) is William Carlos Williams' 1959 record of memories of
his Puerto Rican mother, augmented now with an introductory
memoir by William Eric Williams about his grandmother—a warm,
loving, well-detailed series of anecdotes and remembered scenes.
Hugh Kenner, in "Poets at the Blackboard" (*YR* 71:173–84), reconstructs the remarks he made in observation of the 75th anniversary of
the graduation in 1906 from the University of Pennsylvania of Ezra
Pound (M.A.) and Williams (M.D.). He thinks "*With Bill and Ez
at College* would be a marvelous silent film," following the various
hilarious escapades of the two young geniuses. Williams' experience
in what we call "the humanities" at Horace Mann High School had
sufficed: he never took a college course in language or literature,
yet many a Williams poem uses the themes of ancient mythology
couched in the diction of New Jersey. (In 1903 at the University he
carefully absented himself from a reading by Yeats.) His learning
(as well as Pound's) was acquired in a manner analogous to that of
successive professors erasing just enough of what's on a blackboard
to make room for their own expositions, resulting in a palimpsest of
the day's variety of instruction. ("Creative writing" courses would
not have helped either man.)

We welcome an essay from a scholar up to now occupied with
earlier American literature. In "William Carlos Williams and the
Efficient Moment" (*Prospects* 7:267–79) Cecelia Tichi tells how the
middle-class movement of Scientific Management, founded by Frederick W. Taylor, a mechanical engineer, was absorbed by Williams
probably about the time of his graduation and helped bring along
his own turning away from Keatsianism toward a personal efficiency
that produced a full literary experience in the interstices of his busy
life as a physician. His poems themselves are "vivifying instants of
perception that define life, in which he gives body to the advan-
tageous jumps, swiftnesses, colors, movements of the day." In both
his life and his writing he seized the moment constantly and ef-
ficiently.

Williams, as we know, wrote in other genres than poetry. David
A. Fedo's "The Meaning of Love in William Carlos Williams' *A
Dream of Love*" (*ConL* 23:169–90) analyzes what several keen critics

have considered the poet's best play, all things considered. The leading man (a doctor-poet) and woman each has a "special dream of love at once agonizing and consoling." Fede explores the Greek tragic parallels. Because the plot is obviously autobiographical, Williams found it difficult to objectify his feelings. In the end, after the man's death, the wife comes to forgive her husband's infidelity: she has learned from tragedy how to live—how to survive.

Linda Ray Pratt gives consideration to three interrelated novels in "Williams' Stetcher Trilogy: 'The Pure Products of America'" (*SAF* 10:41–54). *White Mule* (1937), *In the Money* (1940), and *The Build-Up* (1952) avoid the clichés often encountered in stories of immigrants and the American experience. They maintain balance and objectivity in drawing "compelling portraits from historical and sociological" points of view. An effort on the part of Williams to tell "the truth about us," they open up further implications and delights which readers can find in the poetry.

William Wasserstrom uses as springboards two exhibitions, "*The Dial* and the *Dial* Collections, 1920–1929" (Worcester Art Museum, 1959) and "William Carlos Williams and the American Scene, 1920–1940" (Whitney Museum of American Art, 1979). He develops the thesis that "custodians of high culture" these days are displaying in museums the "spent spirit of progress," "the remains of utopia." Williams' work, Wasserstrom maintains, advocated the idea that "the dynamism of American culture" generated the energy of American art. In "William Carlos Williams: The Healing Image" (*BR* 10[1981]: 40–53) Wasserstrom sees Williams as trying to bring about the re-energizing of his country through the power of line and sentence, creation being basically "a moving process" with emphasis on the verb "to make." This is a widely allusive essay drawing deeply on the author's various areas of research in the past couple of decades: William James, Henry Adams, Stephen Spender, John Dewey, James Oppenheim, Van Wyck Brooks, Robert Lowell, and many others.

In *The Poetics of Indeterminacy* (see Stein discussion above) Marjorie Perloff writes on Williams in "'Lines Converging and Crossing': The 'French' Decade of William Carlos Williams" (pp. 109–54). She looks on *Spring and All* (1922) as the Williams composition most influenced by the French poets and painters of the '20s—such as Apollinaire, Rimbaud (translated in *The Dial* in 1920), Duchamp, Braque, and Gris. Her argument places *Spring and All* as the model for the serial poems that followed—"a discontinuous structure in which meaning is created by the resonance of contiguous images." Perloff opines that Williams' influence on the poets of our time is found in the earlier work rather than *Paterson*: "He is the poet as passionate defender of the faith that 'to engage roses/becomes a geometry.'" Though neither poststructuralist nor deconstructionist, Perloff draws considerably on critics like Barthes, Todorov, and Derrida, seeing Williams as the opposite of the Romantic, the symbolist, the referential.

The influence on Williams of the visual arts, particularly painting, is drawing a good deal of critical attention. William Marling's *William Carlos Williams and the Painters, 1909–1923* (Ohio) is a top-drawer account of Williams' relationship with the avant-garde artists. The book opens with the poet's statement that he "almost became a painter." He certainly "sought out and made friends with painters all his life." Evidence is piling up that he read very little of the authors supposed to have influenced him (see "Poets at the Blackboard" above), but rather relied on his brother, his mother, his college acquaintances, and the friends he made later to keep him *au courant*. Marling maintains that the work and friendship of important painters of the day made his poetry what it was. For example, just as Juan Gris thought in terms of the paint itself, Williams was primarily devoted to words (more than content). All his life Williams explored and reported the conflict between the inner man and his century. In the poems he transferred to the "color and form and nuance of speech" his sense of "the primordial relations of things" to "the human consciousness." This book from now on will be indispensable in reaching the heart of Williams' works.

Joan Burbick focuses on another artist in "Grimaces of a New Age: The Postwar Poetry and Painting of William Carlos Williams and Jackson Pollock" (*Boundary* 10,iii:109–23). To the weight of the painters of the 1920s analyzed by Perloff can be added the similarities in composition between Williams and Pollock, whom the poet admired: they both shifted to the epic in imaging the sublime, using collage and "found objects." After World War II they both built their realities out of "speed and high contrast." In *Paterson* Williams, like Pollock, produced "a stream of fractured energy relentlessly in motion." The world of the two artists explodes "into a million separate threads, still contained within the same field of force." The new "grimace" was "a poetics of 'seeing' that went beyond *The Waste Land* into paradoxically disturbing fascination with the chaos."

Towards the end of his book *The Space Between: Literature and Politics* (Hopkins, 1981) novelist and cultural essayist Jay Cantor uses Williams quotations (e.g., from "The Burning of the Greens" and *Paterson*) to underscore his attitude toward Vietnam and the early 1970s. He makes continued use of the poet's motto "No ideas but in things" to support his explanation of the revolution in art from Duchamp (the 1913 Armory Show) to Andy Warhol. Cantor's writing is interesting and imaginative.

Charles Doyle dubs his *William Carlos Williams and the American Poem* (St. Martin's) "an introductory study," but it is more than just a primer. Articles drawn from the manuscript appeared in *Modern Poetry Studies, West Coast Review*, and elsewhere. Doyle looks at the poems, many of them in detail, in the order of their publication. He devotes a chapter to each of the five *Paterson* books. In the chapter entitled "The Odorless Flower" he looks into the poet's obsession with measure during his last 15 years. Williams, he says, worked hard at presenting "the quality of American experience direct and without interference." In thorough coverage Doyle relates the prose works to the poetry. Despite his modesty he has given us an important book.

James Laughlin, editor of New Directions Press, published Williams' *White Mule* in 1937 much to the author's pleasure, and their relationship was warm and close ever after. In "William Carlos Williams and the Making of *Paterson*: A Memoir" (*YR* 71:185–98) Laughlin traces the composition of Williams' epic, which New Directions also published. The author tackles the problem of structure, which he analyzes as "an extended intellectual mosaic," all parts interacting, all cemented with frequently reappearing themes. As others have noted, Williams ignored totally everything he ever learned at school and college. He disregarded "conventional narrative," normal syntax, grammar rules, and unity of subject matter. Laughlin was in a particularly fortunate position to observe the poet's fellow feeling with Dadaists and Cubists. He reveals that his friend wrote something every night even if he had to resort to automatic writing à la Gertrude Stein. He was a very satisfactory collaborator. Confesses Laughlin, "Working with Williams was one of the high points of my life."

David Hurry sees the influence of *King Lear* in many of Williams' poems, of which tragic heroes are part and parcel. He admits in "Shakespeare, Heroes, and Fools in William Carlos Williams' *Paterson*" (*LitR* 25:317–30) that *Paterson* could not be directly in the tragic mode because of the presence of "ironic disguises and qualifications," partly because of our loss of faith in language (particularly rhetoric). The heroes are "betrayed by bureaucracy, religious dogma, and political machinations," to which betrayal Williams felt himself peculiarly vulnerable, a trait he felt compelled to protect. In *Paterson* he avoids the melodramatic, bombastic, and sentimental by "dispersed identification," shifts in subject matter, and a certain comic element, borrowing, Hurry insists, from *King Lear*. Williams also makes use of fools: he plays both King and Fool in *Paterson*," always with "an eye for the pompous, the bigoted, and the bombastic—or for the accurate and beautiful." As Fool Williams is able to "express and control the tragic and heroic element of *Paterson*."

### vii. Frost

Donald Hall bemoans Edward Connery Latham's 1969 edition of Frost's poems. In "Robert Frost Corrupted" (*AtM* Mar.: 60–64) he reports 1,364 emendations of which Latham offers no justification for 1,117, chiefly of punctuation. Hall hears changes in inflection and actual meaning because of the editor's alterations. He recommends a conscientiously edited variorum, restoring the poet's intended punctuation (from the first editions) and at the same time recording variations. He insists above all that "the poet's sentence-sounds must return to the poet's page."

Kerry McSweeney can find no consensus yet among critics on Frost's ranking as a poet—great? major? or even modern? His "Frost's Commentators: The Weak and the Strong" (*CritQ* 24,ii:19–25) cites five recent critics showing the variation in judgment—William H. Pritchard, W. J. Keith, David Perkins, John C. Kemp, and Richard Poirier. Frost, he says, needs a critic whose discourse is as lucid as his argument is sophisticated, recognizing the Romantic-naturalist context and letting "claims for the size of Frost's achievement remain largely implicit." He feels that we had such a critic in Reuben A. Brower (see *ALS 1963*, pp. 165, 168).

Unpublished letters of 45 years ago and an essay on "An Afternoon with Robert Frost" (a "charming episode") constitute J. Albert Robbins' little book *Interlude with Robert Frost: A Brief Correspondence with the Poet and Recollections* (Bloomington, Ind.: Private Press of Fredric Brewer). There are two letters from college student Robbins to Frost and two in reply from Frost dated April and May 1937 and a note from Frost in Amherst dated 23 November 1937. Frost shatters any notion that New England is decadent and offers helpful comments on "The Black Cottage," "The Census-Taker," "A Servant to Servants," "West-Running Brook," and several other poems. Robbins' essay quotes random remarks by Frost on E. A. Robinson ("He was the thoughtful one of the lot") and candid comments on putting a poem together.

Charles H. Miller's *Auden: An American Friendship* (Scribner's, 1983) is the source of Miller's "American Friendship: Auden at Middlebury: Frost at Dartmouth" (*MR* 23:741–49). The author recalls his various encounters with Frost and Dartmouth professor Sidney Cox in Hanover. A native of Michigan, Miller had attended the University of Michigan, where he knew Auden. In fact he bought Auden's green Pontiac but did not tell feisty Frost (in New Hampshire later) whose car he was riding in (for there could conceivably have been Frostian trouble). Miller, Frost, and Cox talked of Auden but also of many other matters recorded in this excerpt, the conclusion of which tells of Auden's visit to Middlebury. For our chapter the chief interest is in Frost's comments in various directions.

Frost's granddaughter, Lesley Lee Francis, a specialist in Spanish literature and language, says the poet was fascinated by "pre-Columbian artifacts and the search for man's origins." Her "Robert Frost and the Majesty of Stones upon Stones" (*JML* 9:3–26) expresses Frost's feeling for archeological problems and discoveries, especially in Central and South America, which he visited late in life —as well as Israel and Greece. At his subsequent readings around the United States he recollected with profound pleasure the "tangible signs of early civilization and man's shadowy origins."

Philip L. Gerber is responsible for two books on Frost. The first is his revised edition of *Robert Frost* (TUSAS 107, ALS *1966*, p. 190). Virtually reversing opinions stated in the first edition, Gerber introduces recent critics' recognition of Frost's relationship with Emerson. He has added a chapter on "Testing Greatness: Frost's Critical Reception," a year-by-year summary of what serious readers wrote through the years from 1917 to 1979. The "Secondary Sources" division of the bibliography is necessarily highly selective but reflects the enormous industry of scholars since the 1966 edition.

As his second book Gerber has edited *Critical Essays on Robert Frost* (Hall), in large part reprints of articles which the editor considers of permanent importance. They range from Pound's early commendations (1913–14) to a 1978 essay by Roberts W. French. The editor has drawn from scholarly journals as well as from the *Detroit News*, the *Boston Post Magazine*, and the *New York Times Book Review*. Gerber's substantial introduction reviews the entire enterprise of Frost criticism. He admits that the production of Frost studies is ever flowing: there will be more. The book concludes with an original essay by Donald J. Greiner on "The Indispensable Robert Frost" in which Greiner nominates "After Apple-Picking" as the most important of the poems, "another of Frost's explorations of what he considered to be man's greatest terror: that our best may not be good enough in Heaven's sight." Greiner's judgment is that Frost's "best work will be forever necessary to the cultural health of the nation."

T. R. S. Sharma's *Robert Frost's Poetic Style* (Humanities Press, 1981), based on a Ph.D dissertation, is clearly stated and an intelligent commentary. Sharma has good things to say about the poet's origins, his values, and his approaches to the writing of poetry. The style is disarming and informal to the point of being conversational. Another 1981 study that failed to come to my attention is John T. Gage's "Humour en Garde: Comic Sayings in Robert Frost's Poetic" (*Thalia* 4,i:54–61). Gage indicates how central humor is to Frost's practice of the art. Both his direct and his indirect humorous assaults are masterly, and his reasoning is often humorous in a positive way. Sudden juxtaposition, aphorism, repetition, black humor, charm, pun, playful rhyme, "rigamarole," metaphor (which will never quite shape the complete truth from the given evidence), irony—all these techniques are at Frost's command as he seeks to have fun in his verse. Though humor is redemptive for Frost, it is also rhetorical in that it induces the reader, like the poet, "to compose and endure." The games Frost plays serve as therapy and also as arguments toward "an available attitude." Gage quotes from many poems to support his points, not the least of which is a warning against adopting any belief that is too easy.

Scholars this year couple Frost with a disparate crowd of other writers, ranging from D. W. Winnicott and Kenneth Burke to Emerson, Hardy, Thoreau, and Eliot. Richard Poirier returns to Frostian studies (see *ALS 1977*, p. 358) with "Frost, Winnicott, Burke" (*Raritan* 2:114–27). Poirier invokes the British psychoanalyst D. W. Winnicott to show how wrong it is to consider Frost as "an old seventeen" all his life, "lost in play" like a child, his task occupying "his whole nature." He cites Kenneth Burke as echoing Emerson in understanding "things" to be "the signs of words." For Emerson, Burke, Winnicott—as for Frost—"things" are magical and full of meaning. For Frost the richness of metaphor is indispensable, and through metaphor and the emphasis on voice the poet hides himself, "is essentially unknowable and undefinable." This essay opens up new ways to think about Frost.

Robert Langbaum sees both Hardy and Frost as enemies of modernism. Both wrote of nature, which many modern poets have rejected as subject matter. He says, however, in "Hardy, Frost, and the Question of Modernist Poetry" (*VQR* 58:69–80) that their nature resists the pathetic fallacy, except in instances as in "Hyla Brook," where it purposely shows itself to be inadequate or irrelevant. Frost's really great poems are never controlled by an idea. They end, rather, not in a Hardy-like "irony or pat remark," but "with an enigma," for which reason Hardy may be minor whereas Frost is probably major. They both nevertheless "show how to be modern without being modernist." Frost, for example, finds music in "the modern flatness of voice" and is without doubt, in Langbaum's opinion, "our best nature poet since Wordsworth" without "transforming and transcending quotidian reality."

Stephen J. Adams points out similarities between Frost's "The Black Cottage" and Eliot's "Gerontion" in "Black Cottages: Frost, Eliot, and the Fate of Individualism" (*Cithara* 22:39–52). Both poems are dramatic monologues; deal with time, change, and history; center on the house as symbol (Frost's less complex than Eliot's); and are related to British poems in which the house is the image of ordered society. Adams uses "An Old Man's Winter Night" for its metaphysical desolation, but he believes "The Black Cottage" is one of the very few American poems equal in power and significance to "Gerontion." Both poems have their roots in Emersonian individualism.

Margery Sabin in "The Fate of the Frost Speaker" (*Raritan* 2:

128–39) finds flaws in Reuben Brower's proposal to train the ear to
follow Frost's efforts at "talk" crossed almost at once with sounds
beyond mere conversation. (Kerry McSweeney would no doubt disagree with her. See "Frost's Commentators" above.) According to
Sabin, Brower tends to falsify ever so slightly the "sounds" of the
poet. Likewise, Frank Lentricchia (*ALS 1975*, p. 364) in Sabin's
view mistakenly tries to combine "close reading" with the French
"criticism of consciousness." Sabin points to the "double action" in
the poetry: "It shielded private experience behind the communal
front of language," but at the same time "it reached out to a more
general human life through human gestures." Poststructuralists have
claimed that such "communal characteristics of speech" are just "ob-
stacles to desire." Sentence sounds in Frost are meant "to control the
desire for full presence that may be a less ambivalent motive for
readers than for the poets they want to meet."

Herbert Marks, a graduate student at Yale, has been writing a
dissertation on biblical "naming" and poetic etymology. His essay
on "The Counter-Intelligence of Robert Frost" (*YR* 71: 554–78) is
in three parts. First he examines the phenomenon of concealment in
Frost's work, such as in "layers of connotation." A large concern is
the tension between freedom and restraint. Then he looks at Frost's
poems about women. For the poet "the fata morgana was Eve." It
is necessary for fallen man to conceal, no matter how reluctantly,
but confusion is the result. Marks concludes that one must try, nevertheless, to bring the fragments of life into a whole, no matter how
enigmatic. In fact all history "is a choice of figments." This is the
way he reads Frost.

In "The Faces of Robert Frost" (*CRevAS* 13:223–29) Wayne
Tefs reminds us that Frost's books are fraught with "apprehension,
regret, hostility, and fear," qualities many readers refuse to acknowledge but rather accept at face value the farmer-sage image the poet
sought to project. Actually his poems are stimulated by "a pervasive
tension." His achievement is based on "his poetic triumph over such
fears" as come from confronting "desert places." The "nightmares
of being human" are "redeemed by the mind's own transformative
powers."

John Oliver Perry says that the good-hearted old New England
farmer-sage image too often seems to dominate Frost's "romantic,
potentially extremist, poetic, visionary" self. In "The Dialogue of

Voices in Robert Frost's Poems" (*SAQ* 81:214–29) Perry expands on such dialogue in Frost as (1) the obvious exchange between two characters in conversation, (2) the communication in the dramatic monologues between the overt speaker and the implied poet, and finally (3) the ironic interplay of two meanings. It is in "conversations of spirit and flesh that our double needs are most satisfied."

Fritz Oehlschlaeger calls attention to a pun on the name of Thoreau in the last lines of "A Drumlin Woodchuck": "so instinctively thorough/About my crevice and burrow." His essay "Two Woodchucks, or Frost and Thoreau on the Art of the Burrow" (*CLQ* 18: 214–19) expresses the opinion that Frost intended the entire poem to be read in the perspective of Thoreau. The woodchuck, Frost, and Thoreau all insist that work and play be indistinguishable. As Frost says in "Two Tramps in Mud Time," work is "play for mortal stakes."

Pursuing that same theme, David Kann in "Deadly Serious Play: Robert Frost's 'Design'" (*HSL* 14:23–32) sees in "Design" the poet challenging the tradition established by Whitman by playing with the material "in an old-fashioned way." Kahn studies the finished poem (1936) as well as its earlier version ("In White," 1912). "Design" portrays the narrator as being in charge (the poem begins with "I") whereas "In White" works over "the threatening material through abstraction and depersonalization." The Petrarchan sonnet form and the rhyme scheme give the narrator "the mastery of the fantasy material." (Actually, Kann observes, the rhyme scheme is even tighter than the Petrarchan formula calls for.) "Design" gives the lie to the argument that the old forms are not adequate to deal with modern thought. It is the play in the lines of the sonnet that stays the confusion of today's terror.

*Purdue University*

# 17. Poetry: The 1940s to the Present

## Lee Bartlett

In introducing his recent collection of essays, *The World, the Text, and the Critic* (Harvard), Edward W. Said sees the contemporary literary critic as operating in one or more of four primary forms: (1) the "practical" work of the review, (2) the traditional literary history, (3) explication and "appreciation" (what we do most usually in the classroom), and (4) literary theory. Donald Hall rather charmingly subsumes the first three forms under one rubric, seeing the critic's task as either doing the parish work of textual scholarship or attempting to define or utilize the theology of literary theory. Obviously, as we work to establish the contemporary canon—and whether or not we admit any interest in that Arnoldian activity, it is what we are up to at every turn—most of our efforts must be of the parish variety because there are so many rudimentary things we simply do not know. Yet just as most postmodern American poets themselves have found the formulation of a poetics a necessary adjunct to their primary vocation, contemporary verse remains an open field for the kinds of questions currently obsessing theorists: audience response, textuality, erasure, and so forth. Laszlo K. Géfin's study of the ideogram, solid biographies of Robert Lowell and John Berryman, Marjorie Perloff's and Charles Altieri's explorations of primary modes, Susan R. Dyne's provocative piece on the particular problem of the "self-deception of unexamined language" encountered by women poets, Brian Swann's collection of essays on Native American oral literature, Henry M. Sayre's assessment of performance poetry, and a good batch of essays by and interviews with poets themselves make this a lively year in our field. While as usual I've encountered a few superficial and/or redundant studies written most probably with an eye too close to the rail of tenure and promotion, generally both parish priests and high-church theologians have through their labors taken our collective soul perhaps a half-step closer to that perfect "knowledge of the shadow line," that heaven of "a distant resolution" of which we all, like John Ashbery, dream.

### i. Groundwork

In 1919 the *Little Review* published Ezra Pound's edited version of Ernest Fenellosa's essay "On the Chinese Written Character as a Medium for Poetry," an article drawn from the 16 manuscript notebooks the poet had received from the scholar's widow six years before, and it proved to be an event which helped transform the landscape of American poetry. Through the years much has been written about the ideogram and Pound's relation to it, but Laszlo K. Géfin's *Ideogram: History of a Poetic Method* (Texas) is the first full-length study of Fenellosa's ideas and their impact on both modern and postmodern American verse, and it is generally very good. The first three chapters of the book (which deal with Fenellosa, Pound, and Williams) are intriguing. Géfin worked with the Fenellosa manuscripts in the Pound collection at Yale, and he presents a fascinating summary of the ways in which Pound tampered with the original essay to stress his belief that Fenellosa's breakthrough had been "the juxtaposition of seemingly unrelated particulars capable of suggesting ideas and concepts through their relations," i.e., the ideogrammic method. One example of Géfin's approach is his very thorough analysis of the significant (and silent) contractions, excisions, and revisions Pound made on Fenellosa's draft before attempting publication. This book will be reviewed in chapter 8, but of particular interest to readers of this essay are the later treatments of the objectivist poets, as well as of Charles Olson, Robert Duncan, Robert Creeley, Allen Ginsberg, and Gary Snyder. Géfin demonstrates how while each of the objectivists came to his poetic from a different source (Zukofsky, the Bach fugue; Reznikoff, the law report; Oppen, mathematics), all worked within and amplified the "ideogrammatic method" in their collective sense of the poem as an open field of particulars working through relation. In his clear discussion of Olson's poetics, Géfin argues that "Projective Verse" is the "only document which utilizes" Fenellosa's ideas with the fervor and consistency of Pound. In reading Duncan's difficult "Passages," Géfin demonstrates how the poet's sense of "rime" as a "force within a field of force" and his notion of the "grand collage" are

sourced in Fenellosa; further, he sees Creeley's "active transformations," Ginsberg's insistence on "the synthesizing act in language,"
and Snyder's interest in elliptic juxtaposition as landmarks along a
continuous tradition of the paratactic method of composition as outlined in Fenellosa's essay. While at times Géfin's study simply summarizes fairly well-known material, and his later chapters especially
often do little more than hint directions for further research, *Ideogram* can be highly recommended. Extremely well researched, judicious, and highly readable, this book is a solid study of perhaps the
major modernist contribution.

This year's special issue of *Contemporary Literature* (23,iv:407–
559) devoted to "American Poetry of the Seventies" offers a second
general study of interest. Following a brief preface by Thomas
Gardner (pp. 407–10), the journal is divided into two parts: the first
includes three thematic essays; the second, four essays on individual
poets (William Bronk, John Ashbery, Robert Lowell, and Charles
Simic), the latter reviewed in appropriate sections of this chapter.
In "From Image to Action: The Return of Story in Postmodern
Poetry" (pp. 411–27) Marjorie Perloff once again divides poets into
two camps: (1) "a late variant of the paradigmatic modernist lyric"
which offers a "solitary 'I' in the timeless moment" and relies on "the
consort of images to create meaning" (James Wright, Robert Lowell,
Robert Bly) and (2) "fragmented, dislocated, and often quite literally non-sensical narrative" (Frank O'Hara, Ed Dorn, Norman
Howard). Giving a penetrating reading of Dorn's *Slinger*, Perloff
finds this second mode—narrative—more useful than the first in the
contemporary self's adjusting "to the phenomenology of the present."
Henry M. Sayre's lucid "David Antin and the Oral Poetics Movement" (pp. 428–50) argues that the lack of critical work being done
on the "performance" poets—Antin, Jerome Rothenberg, Jackson
Mac Low, and John Cage—is in the main due to "oral performance
poetry's self-willed outlaw status." Sayre usefully outlines some of
the tenets of these poets, referring to important essays like Rothenberg's "New Models, New Visions" and Mac Low's "Statement" on
chance and indeterminacy. He discusses the political implications
of a "non-categorical" poetics (anti-imperialist and anti-expansionist),
contending that these poets attempt to create, like both the beat and
Black Mountain poets before them, a "situation" over against an
artifact. I find much of value in the program of the performance

poets, though I continue to have difficulty responding to poetry which seems to be created out of theory rather than impulse. Still the profound influence of the performance poets cannot be denied, and these writers seem truly committed to their project. Finally, in "Sensibility, Rhetoric, and Will: Some Tensions in Contemporary Poetry" (pp. 451–77), Charles Altieri discusses what he terms the poetics of "highly crafted moments of scenic empathy" (Perloff's first category) which currently, he feels, dominates our verse. In a wide-ranging essay (touching on Stanley Plumly, Louise Glück, Carl Dennis, Robert Hass, and Robert Pinsky), Altieri concludes that John Ashbery and Adrienne Rich have "strong claims to being the major poets of our minor age."

A second symposium of note this year is *OhR's* issue on free verse (vol. 28), in which the editors ask nine poets and a critic to analyze the state and status of free verse ("What it expresses, what it bodies forth, and what it *speaks* in American poetry"). Though interesting, the poets' articles (by Reg Saner, Bin Ramke, Donald Hall, Wayne Dodd, Marvin Bell, Louis Simpson, Lucien Stryk, William Matthews, and Michael Heller) are often too brief to do more than hint their author's concerns. Charles Hartman's "At the Border" (pp. 81–92), however, provides a rather good discussion of the precarious "border" between "the nonmetrical and the metrical" with reference to W. H. Auden and Marvin Bell.

Both of these special issues are commendable, though they raise a question: the title of each symposium promises if not inclusiveness at least range, yet all *ConL's* four concluding pieces are on male poets of primarily the same eastern geography, while all ten of the essays in *OhR* are written by men. In the first instance are we to assume that somehow these four poets are representative of the '70s, and in the second that women (or blacks or Native Americans) have no concern with the uses and abuses of free verse?

Finally, two other symposia are worth mentioning this year. In *Poetry East*, no. 7, "The Inward Society: Surrealism and Recent American Poetry," editors Richard Jones and Kate Daniels collect "statements" by "a number of leading American poets on what has been called the neo-surrealist movement in recent American poetry." As with the *OhR* pieces on free verse, one often wishes for more extended treatments (the longest essay is Jones's brief "The Question of Surrealism," (pp. 7–12), though the notes by Carol Muske, David

Ignatow, Ira Sadoff, Gregory Orr, James Tate ("schools of poetry are not worth whale spit when you are face to moose with a poem"), Charles Simic, Mekeel McBride, Louis Simpson, Roger Shattuck, and Walter Korte, as well as the closing surrealist chronology are of interest. A number of writers (Aaron Kramer, Donald Hall, Louis Simpson, Diane Wakoski, Theodore Weiss, David Perkins, and Robert Bly) responded to Frederick Turner's "Mighty Poets in Their Misery Dead: A Polemic on the Contemporary Poetry Scene" in an issue of the *MissR* (5:171–97). Turner is editor of the new *Kenyon Review* (our literary equivalent to the *National Review*), and his article (which appeared in *MissR* in 1980) argued that "no truly great poetry has been written in English since the Second World War" due to a poetic taste which is one "of the most rigid and mandarin in history." As one might expect, the responses, while both entertaining and informative, betray a certain lack of patience.

Other important theoretical issues are addressed this year in two essays by Richard Jackson and Paul Kameen. Jackson's "The Deconstructed Moment in Modern Poetry" (*ConL* 23:306–22) interestingly attempts to examine some of the ways "modern and postmodern poets have deconstructed traditional moments of timelessness," with reference to Derrida and Lacan. He looks briefly at poems by Mark Strand (wherein the "deconstructed moment of presence" becomes "non-presence"), Charles Simic (a "poetic world" located in a "fading trace of Being"), Philip Levine (for whom "the moment is emptied when a relation to the past seems lost"), James Wright (who has an interest in "the refusal of language to name"), and others. Like Charles Altieri, Paul Kameen sees recent American poetry involved in a "competition" between the symbolist and immanentist modes. His "Madness and Magic: Postmodernist Poetics and the Dream" (*Criticism* 24:36–47) argues that the first mode ("essentially negative . . . grounded on the assumption that the irrational" is "an aberrant and unpredictable state of mind") reaches its apex in the confessional poets; the second ("grounded on the assumption that the irrational" dis-closes "itself as prophetic insight") moves through Olson to the deep image poets. Keenen follows with a short discussion of John Berryman and James Wright as examples of each mode.

Last year I noted a number of substantial items focusing on questions of translation and ethnopoetics, and this year two more important texts appeared. Seeing the possibility of translation as perhaps "the central issue of our time," KR devotes vol. 4, no. 2 to the subject, with essays by Wolfgang Bauer, George Steiner, Emery George, and Robert Bly. All of these pieces are substantial, though Bly's "The Right Stages of Translation" (pp. 68–89) is of particular interest, as the poet takes us step by step through the "eight stages" of translating a poem, here number XXI from Rilke's Sonnets to Orpheus. Even more signal is Brian Swann's Smoothing the Ground: Essays on Native American Oral Literature (Calif.), a collection of 20 solid essays by folklorists, linguists, literary critics, and ethnopoets. In their discussions of the problems of translation, the role of the critic, and the interpretation of Native American oral literature these pieces are rich and varied, and taken as a group represent amply the first-rate work currently being done in this area. Of particular interest are the five essays by Dennis Tedlock, John Berhorst, Jeffrey F. Huntsman, Karl Kroeber, and Willard Gingerich on general questions of translation and criticism, as well as Kroeber's "Poem, Dream, and the Consuming of Culture" (pp. 323–33). Oddly, the editor himself provides only a brief introduction and no bibliography or other apparatus, though the quality of the other essays make this volume signal in Native American poetry studies. Further, this year saw the publication of what I think is the first "scholarly" volume on the work of a folk singer/rock & roller, Betsy Bowden's Performed Literature: Words and Music by Bob Dylan (Indiana). Although Bowden is often a bit too hip in the casualness of her style (making the book seem, at times, an extended Rolling Stone piece) and sometimes a little glib in her overgeneralizations about the music and politics of the counterculture sixties, her book closely analyzes the Dylan corpus. Arguing cogently that Dylan's lyrics are not, strictly speaking, poems but rather songs, "words and music combined for oral performance" (an obvious fact that some earlier academic aficionados have chosen to overlook), Bowden takes into account in her explication not only lyrics but instrumentation, vocal inflection, tempo, pauses, and so forth. This volume would have been helped immeasurably had the author demonstrated an acquaintance with current theories of oral poetries and ethnopoetics (or at least of the influence of the Beat Generation poets—McClure, Ginsberg, and Kerouac especially—on Dylan), but even so this is an unusual and interesting study.

Bruce-Novoa's *Chicano Poetry: A Response to Chaos* (Texas) is, amazingly, the first book-length study of Chicano poetry. Arguing that the primary thread woven through all Chicano verse is a reaction to "the threat of loss," Bruce-Novoa presents chapter-long explications of work by Rodolfo Gonzales, Alurista (Alberto Urista), Sergio Elizondo, Ricardo Sanchez, and Gary Soto, among others. In the future much of this poetry (most of which appeared in the '70s) will probably be forgotten. Always engaged, it often suffers from cliche; still, work by writers like Gonzales and Soto has already achieved a place in the more general tradition of American verse, one which Bruce-Novoa's seminal study can only reinforce.

The discussions in the first half of Harold Bloom's substantial *Agon: Towards a Theory of Revisionism* (Oxford) range from Gnosticism and the Kabbalah to Freud and the sublime, and typically for Bloom are eclectic, bizarre, brilliant, and preoccupied with paradigm; the second half of the book focuses on a number of "strong American poets," including both Ashbery and Ammons. In "Measuring the Canon" (pp. 270–88) Bloom reads Ashbery's "Tapestry" "on the High Romantic crises-poem model of six revolutionary ratios" and "Wet Casements" as "a beautifully forlorn poem, a hymn to lost Eros"; further, Ashbery himself is "the culmination of this very American solitude" which is the legacy of Frost, Stevens, and Crane. In "The Menorah as the White Light of Trope" (pp. 289–317) Bloom reads John Hollander's *Spectral Emanations: New and Selected Poems*; the title work, he argues, is "manifestly a sequence of seven poems, each one named by one of the seven spectral colors," each depending for its "form and scale on the seven-branched quality of the menorah itself," which for Bloom is the "central visual trope of the Jewish tradition."

Two books this year concern what is certainly the most sustained American poetic tradition, the visionary, as Hyatt Waggoner's *American Visionary Poetry* (LSU) attempts to define the impulse through a series of essays examining a number of writers in the Whitman tradition (including Roethke, Ammons, and Waggoner), while the editors of *Walt Whitman: The Measure of His Song* (Holy Cow!) examine the tremendous influence of Whitman on contemporary verse. In his definition of the visionary Waggoner does not really break any new ground (he explains, for example, that the visionary poem differs from the Imagist poem in that it "does not assume a dichotomy between the perceiver and the perceived," and thus "runs counter to the poetry of alienation"), but as in his earlier books (*American Poetry* especially) Waggoner is on all counts convincing and articulate in his summary of those things we know; his comments on individual poets are mentioned in the appropriate subsections of this chapter. For their massive tribute to Whitman, editors Jim Perlman, Ed Folsom, and Dan Campion have gathered a number of essays and poems on the poet by many postmodern writers, including Ginsberg, Eberhart, Jonathan Williams, Berryman, Levertov, James Wright, Nemerov, Ferlinghetti, Kinnell, Simpson, Dave Smith, Bly, and June Jordan, among others. Rich and various (in a blurb, Gay Wilson Allen calls the volume "a major contribution . . . colossal," and I'll second that), this labor of love is the kind of book you'll want to read straight through, then use as a reference again and again. Small press publishing at its best.

The question of "voice" has been a recurrent concern in our area at least since the modernists, and this year two critics contend again with the question. In "Domestic Monologues: The Problem of 'Voice' in Contemporary American Poetry" (*MR* 23:489–503) Sally M. Gall argues that a misconception of the nature of voice by younger poets has led to a lot of bad poetry. Here she wishes to offer a rather obvious "reminder both to critics and poets" that a speaker's voice is "a possibility, not a necessity," and that a poem works or fails not according to "what someone is saying," but to what language "is creating." More substantial is Susan R. Van Dyne's fine "Double Monologues: Voices in American Women's Poetry" (*MR* 23:461–85). Sandra Gilbert has suggested that the female poet has an exaggerated sense of a "double self"—the public and social over against the private and subversive—which she attempts through her art to reconcile. Van Dyne expands upon this notion, arguing that this "doubleness" is not only endemic to American women poets, but "is as often treasured and coolly exploited by the poet as it is transcended." Thus, she asserts, for a woman poet, choosing her "voices" becomes the most crucial activity, one centered on a full understanding of the nature and uses of language. For Van Dyne, Adrienne Rich and Elizabeth Bishop are related to Emily Dickinson and Marianne Moore in their rigorous avoidance of "the self-deception of unexamined language"; further, Anne Sexton, while on the surface "exhibitionistic," shares "some of the same rhetorical strategies for confronting her situation."

Two more items rather wide ranging are William Everson's *Birth of a Poet: The Santa Cruz Meditations*, ed. Lee Bartlett (Black Sparrow), and Michael McClure's *Scratching the Beat Surface* (North Point). The first book comprises a year's worth of Everson's "meditations" given at the University of California at Santa Cruz during the 1975–76 academic year: the first six meditations center on the vocation of the poet, the second six on the role of the poet in America, the third six on the particular situation of the American poet living in the West. According to the *American Book Review*, *Birth of a Poet* "provides a thorough analysis of the consequences of dis-placed art," giving us "an extraordinarily odd opportunity to overhear an old poet teaching himself, his craft, his tradition." While Michael McClure does not seem to have the same interest in the nature of language as the structuralists or, more recently, the deconstructionists, he does base his exploration of revolt in an exploration of *sound*. A few years ago Robert Peters likened McClure's poetry to action painting, wherein "the energy screaming (at times) streaming (at others) is as important as any direct poetic statement." As a "mammalian communicator" (Peters' term) McClure's task has been to register the raw, animal, sexual possibilities of the howl, the grunt, the spontaneous cry. The first half of *Scratching the Beat Surface* is a retrospective poetry anthology with commentary. Composed of McClure's Gray Lectures given at SUNY, Buffalo, the volume takes us on a fascinating tour through some of the verse and personalities of the San Francisco/Black Mountain poetry scenes. While some of what he gives us is old hat, much—his discussion of the influence of Francis Crick on "biophysical thinking," his meditations on the interest of his contemporaries in nature, his memories of the Six Gallery reading, his interest in systems theory in relation to Olson's—is compelling. Further, the four meditations which make up "Wolf Net," the second part of the volume, continue McClure's graceful sorties into man's animal nature.

Both because of their daily attention to language and their commitment (sometimes misguided and often, as in the two volumes just mentioned, delightfully eccentric), poets generally make lively essayists and reviewers. Last year I noted a number of first-rate collections (by Thomas Merton, Jerome Rothenberg, Diane Wakoski, and others), and this year I can do the same as Robert Peters, Hayden Carruth, Jonathan Williams, Marge Piercy, and Donald Hall have all published solid collections, and Richard Kostelanetz and Hall have edited two others. Peters' *The Great American Poetry Bake-Off, Second Series* (Scarecrow) is as perceptive, entertaining, and sometimes bitchy as his "first series" of reviews and notes published in 1979. These 72 pieces have all been written since 1979, and they cover a number of well-known (James Dickey, Robert Duncan, Robinson Jeffers, David Wagoner) and lesser-known (Rochelle Ratner, Jerry Ratch, Rosemarie Waldrop) poets, as well as more general topics like "opening lines" and poetry and baseball. Peters considers himself an iconoclast in the tradition of Carlyle, Rexroth, and Bly, charmingly viewing "the critical act as a sexual congress between the critic and his subject" raising "a few hairs of affection or lust." Rather more extended and traditional are Hayden Carruth's selected essays and reviews collected in *Working Papers*, ed., intro. Judith Weissman (Georgia). Drawn from Carruth's prose of three decades, this volume offers reviews of Pound, Williams, Auden, Stevens, and Eliot, as well as a number of Carruth's contemporaries, including Lowell, Berryman, Schwartz, and Jarrell. A few of Carruth's longer meditations on poetry and politics, poetic form, and the writer's situation are also included.

"As a man, a poet, and a joyous laborer in the literary world," James Dickey has written of Jonathan Williams, "my generation has not the equal of Jonathan Williams, or anything like it." *The Magpie's Bagpipe* (North Point) is probably one of the most typographically satisfying books to be published in our area this year, pulling together 39 vigorous short essays on literature, photography, and travel by the founder of the Jargon Society. Additionally, two new volumes in Michigan's "Poets on Poetry" series appeared this year, *Parti-Colored Blocks for a Quilt* by Marge Piercy, and Donald Hall's *The Weather for Poetry*. As we might expect, Piercy's essays and interviews are always both engaging and engaged, as she discusses her life and work, questions about the relationship between feminism and art, and politics; of particular interest are her ten reviews, eight of which focus on writing by contemporary women poets and novelists. Donald Hall's second collection in the Michigan series (of which Hall is general editor) collects 45 of his essays, reviews, and notes on poetry published between 1977 and 1981. While Hall alerts us in his introductory note that he now makes his living through free-lance writing rather than teaching and thus many of these pieces were written to "boil the pot," in general the prose is seldom trivial. Hall has through the years been one of our strongest apologists for the value of verse in the 20th century, and this book continues his tireless celebration.

As Pound's "A Few Don'ts," Olson's "Projective Verse," Snyder's "Poetry and the Primitive" show, the history of both modern and postmodern poetics has been written primarily in the essay, not the book. Therefore collections like Donald Allen's and Warren Tallman's *Poetics of the New American Poetry* usefully draw together essays which may otherwise be difficult to track and give our students a handy overview of what poets have been saying about their craft. This year two good volumes can be added to our shelves: *The Avant-Garde Tradition in Literature*, ed. Richard Kostelanetz (Prometheus) and *Claims for Poetry*, ed. Donald Hall (Michigan). To talk about an avant-garde "tradition" (or like Harold Rosenberg a "tradition" of the "new") seems an oxymoron; still, most experimental writers in English seem to take earlier experimental writers as masters (with Stein as a kind of vortex), and as the avant-garde has a "history," a body of art and theory existing in time, it can be said, I suppose, to establish a certain course. Kostelanetz' book collects 27 extended and important pieces which either attempt to survey some aspect of the avant-garde (Judy Ramson's "Italian Futurism," Bob Cobbing's "Concrete Sound Poetry 1950–1970," and Hugh Kenner's "Art in a Closed Field") or function as manifestos (Olson's "Projective Verse" and Rosemarie Waldrop's "A Basis of Concrete Poetry"). Of particular interest is David Antin's seminal "Modernism and Post-Modernism: Approaching the Present in American Poetry," which, like many other pieces in this volume, has never been collected previously. Hall's *Claims* brings together "ideas of contemporary American poets on the subject of their art" by 43 writers. Hall attempts to be up to date (all but two of the poets—O'Hara and Hugo—are living), drawing together pieces ranging from Bly's comments on the image, Duncan's, Carruth's, and Hass' ideas on form, and Levertov's comments on the line to Mac Low's notes on chance and Silliman's essay on language poetry. There are important limitations here (there is nothing by Olson or Rexroth, for example; one of

Rothenberg's pieces on ethnopoetics or Everson's on the vocation of
the poet would have added to the volume), but *Claims* is fairly
representative.

Two other anthologies of interest should be noted. *Literature and
the Urban Experience*, ed. Michael C. Jaye and Ann Chalmers Watts
(Rutgers, 1981), collects essays by a number of writers (including
Lawrence Ferlinghetti, Amiri Baraka, David Ignatow, and Marge
Piercy) first presented at the Conference on Literature and Urban
Experience held at Rutgers in 1980. Elly Bulkin's and Joan Larkin's
*Lesbian Poetry* (Persephone) offers work by 64 poets, tracing "the
flowering of lesbian poetry that began slowly in the late '6os and had
reached full bloom by the mid-'7os." While some of this work is far
too "message-oriented" to be of more than passing interest regardless of our political sympathies, the volume generally is an extended
collection of intensely felt and well-crafted verse. Additionally,
Charles Bernstein provides a selection of work by writers involved
in "one of the most frequently mentioned and least understood developments in American poetry in recent years," "Language Poetry"
—"a writing that takes as its medium, or domain of intention, every
articulable aspect of language"—in "Language Sampler" (*ParisR*
86:75–125).

Questions of form seemed to occupy little attention this year. In
"The Contemporary Villanelle" (*MPS* 11:113–27) Ronald McFarland interestingly examines a variety of poems by Theodore Roethke,
Marilyn Hacker, James Merrill, Rachel Hadas, Gilbert Sorrentino,
Richard Hugo, and others. McFarland sees Roethke's "The Waking"
as the first important "breakthrough" villanelle in its use of slant-
and eye-rhyme, and gives Merrill credit for developing the contemporary villanelle's "flexibility." Albert Cook's rather odd "The Syllabic Module" (*MPS* 11:1–19) argues that contemporary poets
"should be producing metrical modes, analogous to the structure of
serial music"; instances of Cook's own verses are cited as examples.

Finally, a number of eclectic articles appeared this year. In "Literature in Contemporary American Prison Writings" (*SJS* 8,i:26–37)
Emanuel Diel discusses post-1960 prison poetry, which has appeared
primarily in small-press books and small magazines. Diel sees much
of this work as undistinguished, though he finds the poetry of five
writers—Michael Hogan, Gene Fowler, Etheridge Knight, Ed (Foots)

Lipman, and Pancho Aguila—to be "good to excellent literature."
Tom Hansen's "On Writing Poetry: Four Contemporary Poets" (*CE*
44:265–73) briefly examines essays and interviews by Donald Hall,
William Stafford, Robert Bly, and Richard Hugo as "testaments of
similar faiths in the vocation of the poet." Caroline Slocock discusses
the difficult publication history and impact of the 1972 volume of war
poems by Vietnam veterans in "*Winning Hearts and Minds*: The 1st
Casualty Press" (*AmerS* 16:107–18). Richard Howard's "The Resonance of Henry James in Recent American Poetry" (*ConP* 5,i:1–11)
looks very briefly (and thus not fully convincingly) at Elizabeth
Bishop, Anthony Hecht, James Merrill, Howard Moss, and John Hollander, declaring that "for the American poet since 1950, any descriptive account of ANYTHING will be Jamesian, insofar as the Jamesian
tone, the muster of language under the ravaging wing of memory
and credence, will afford an access to the physical world which
prosody has funked." Michael Davidson, curator of the Archive for
New Poetry at the University of California at San Diego, discusses
"the new 'oralism' in recent poetry" and the importance of the archive's collection of Paul Blackburn's extensive library of poetry
tapes in " 'By ear, he sd'/: Audio-Tapes and Contemporary Criticism"
(*Credences* [Buffalo, N. Y.] 1,i:105–17). "By listening over and over
again to a reading, the listener begins to hear what a page can never
render: the emphasis and character of the line," Davidson comments.
And last, in "Turning Back on the Road to the Absolute" (*MPS* 11:
164–88) Hank Lazer argues that the "function of the image, especially in recent poetry, is to make the other world palpable." After
an interesting discussion of Rilke's sense of the "angel" in the *Dueno
Elegies*, Lazer briefly looks at the figure in poems by Merrill, Olson,
Levine, Levertov, and others.

### ii. The Middle Generation

*a.* **John Berryman, Robert Lowell.** Biographies of writers are the
literati's *Dallas* and *General Hospital*; we read them for their won-
derful gossip as much as anything else, and in John Haffenden's *The
Life of John Berryman* (Routledge), Eileen Simpson's *Poets in Their
Youth: A Memoir* (Random House), and Ian Hamilton's *Robert
Lowell: A Biography* (Random House) we are not disappointed. All

three of these books have received much press, and, for "literary" books, all three must be best-sellers. In fact, I'm sure that everyone reading this chapter has at least dipped into each of these volumes, and many have immersed themselves in the three books' combined 1,250 pages. Thus, as space has become a premium in *ALS*, I'll simply offer a few observations. Biographers Haffenden and Hamilton had fairly full access to Berryman's and Lowell's papers, and interviewed, seemingly, scores of the poets' friends, ex-wives, relatives, publishers, colleagues, students, and enemies. The Berryman biography in particular is extensively researched and, most probably because Lowell led a more "public" life, seems the more revelatory of the two (Haffenden's good critical companion to Berryman was reviewed in this chapter in 1980); interestingly, however, only Hamilton documents all his sources fully. Both books set the records straight on the poets' writing and publication histories, their relationships (crucial in both cases) to their families, and their singular madnesses. Haffenden goes perhaps into a bit too much detail, too frequently discussing Berryman's interminable sexual adventures, though most often he does demonstrate the effect these affairs had on the poet's work. Eileen Simpson unravels her fascinating narrative from a privileged vantage point; not only is she a psychotherapist, but she was married to Berryman from 1942 to 1956. Thus we get the "inside scoop" not only on Berryman, but also on R. P. Blackmur, Randall Jarrell, Delmore Schwartz, and Lowell (and their various ladies), and Jean Stafford. Aside from the numerous anecdotes which run the gamut from charming to rather pathetic (and are always telling), one of the most interesting facets of the book is Simpson's discussions of her ex-husband's peccadillos wherein the analyst's objective tone is sometimes broken, almost imperceptively, by the voice of the hurt wife ("For the obsessive love, which turned into excessive hate—Lise's self-assurance now appeared to him as arrogance, her insoucience coldness, her vitality destructive—to run its course took exactly the time Cal had allowed"). There will be, of course, later biographies and memoirs of these two poets, but these books by Haffenden, Simpson, and Hamilton will stand as benchmarks.

Written prior to the availability of either of the Berryman studies above, Robert Hahn's "Berryman's *Dream Songs*: Missing Poet Beyond the Poet" (*MR* 23:117–28) looks for biographical clues in

*Recovery* and Eileen Simpson's novel *The Maze*. Hahn equates the characters Dr. Alan Severance (*Recovery*) and Benjamin Bold (*Maze*) with Berryman/Henry, and argues that all fail because of their inability to persuade "us of the existence of the poet beyond the poet, so that the troubled speaker becomes an actor in his own drama." J. P. Ward's intriguing *Poetry and the Sociological Idea* (Humanities), in outlining the "five main trends in sociological thought"—phenomenology, interactionism, functionalism, social anthropology, and Marxism—discusses Thomas Hardy and Berryman as poets "in the Sociological World"; Berryman in particular, Ward argues, is tied to an attributive language because for him "there is no nub reality being expressed."

In their preface to *Robert Lowell: A Reference Guide* (Hall) Steven Axelrod and Helen Deese explain that Lowell "became an academic industry" with the publication of *Life Studies*; from 1959 on, they reckon, criticism on the poet appeared at the rate of 2.5 books and 67 shorter pieces a year. This totals, from 1943 through 1980, 1,736 items (!), which Axelrod and Deese list year by year and usefully annotate. A later edition of the book will have to include Robert B. Shaw's "Lowell in the Seventies" (*ConL* 23:415–27), which focuses on *History*, *The Dolphin*, and *Day by Day*; Shaw finds the first volume, in its "audacity of design" and "solid and subtle craftsmanship" a success, the second "an adventurous experiment gone wrong," and the last book the recovery of Lowell's "authentic voice."

**b. Elizabeth Bishop, Randall Jarrell.** In "Elizabeth Bishop's Surrealist Inheritance" (*AL* 54:63–80) Richard Mullen argues that while Bishop is quite obviously not a surrealist in technique, she "explores the workings of the unconscious and the interplay between conscious perception and the dream." Further, Mullen contends, like André Breton, Bishop is concerned with the "otherness of objects," though she does not attempt a "dissociative" poetics. Mullen reads closely three poems ("The Monument," "Rainy Season; Sub-Tropics," and "The Weed") in terms of their "surrealist sources" in his effort to demonstrate Bishop's fusion of the subjective with a poetics of presence. This is a curious essay. Certainly, to be interested in the unconscious and the dream life is an inheritance almost all postmoderns share; Bishop can hardly be located in the surrealist camp because of it. As if realizing this, each time Mullen draws an interesting connection between Bishop and the surrealist project, he finds it necessary to undercut his own argument, as if to remind us of the obvious, that the poet wasn't truly a surrealist at all. Still, this essay has value both for its readings of the poems and for serving as a brief case study of the general influence of the surrealist program on a mid-century American poet. Bonnie Costello in "Vision and Mastery in Elizabeth Bishop" (*TCL* 28:351–70) is interested in the "rhythm of vision—receding and yielding" in Bishop's work. Costello reads a number of poems, commenting on their "recurrent compositional elements in Bishop's descriptions," "a predominance of horizontal and dynamic form, strewn with the detritus of previous life."

The suicides of poets seem to draw investigators almost as surely as the assassinations of presidents, and in "The Death of Randall Jarrell" (*VQR* 58:450–67) Jeffrey Meyers turns his investigative talents to the circumstances surrounding Jarrell's death when hit by an automobile in 1965; was it an accident or a suicide? Meyers gives us a brief biography of Jarrell, noting his bouts with depression and their probable causes, then examines the events surrounding the death. Looking at newspaper reports, Jarrell's Certificate of Death, the coroner's report, and the 18-page report of the autopsy, Meyers concludes that "it was will, not fate, that determined" the poet's death. Peter Steele's "A Dialogue with the Father: Jarrell's Mutations" (*Meanjin* 41:410–19) is a short discussion of "Jerome," as well as passages from a few other poems, in terms of Jarrell's sense of Freud as a "sponsoring presence." In "Randall Jarrell: Poet-Critic" (*ASch* 52:67–77) William H. Pritchard first convincingly argues the case for Jarrell as perhaps rivaled only by R. P. Blackmur as critic of earlier 20th-century American poetry, then turns to Jarrell's own verse, "making an attempt at Jarrellian characterization and appreciation." Finally, Meyers offers a second Jarrell item in his "Randall Jarrell: A Bibliography of Criticism, 1941–81" (*BB* 39:227–34), listing 325 entries.

**c. Theodore Roethke.** Of all the "middle generation" poets, Theodore Roethke has been, for the past few years at least, the most influential, and of these poets he appropriately gathered the most critical attention this year, with two books, a chapter each in two others, plus three additional articles. In *Theodore Roethke: The Journey From I to Otherwise* (Missouri) Neal Bowers contends that "Roethke's manic-depressiveness, which troubled him most of his life, produced in him a propensity for mystical insight." Making use of both the poet's published work and his 277 notebooks, Bowers examines Roethke's three stages in his "search for identity": "the outward journey, inward growth, and the consummation of a love relationship." The book's early chapters on Roethke's place in the mystical tradition and the foreshadowing of his later concerns in his early work are particularly illuminating, and while Bowers at times stays a bit too close to his thesis (which would have irritated the poet himself), on the whole this is a solid and sensitive study. Norman Chaney's *Theodore Roethke: The Poetics of Wonder* (Univ. Press) is rather undistinguished, its 89 pages of text reading much like an unrevised dissertation. While there will not be much here for even those relatively new to the poet's work, Chaney is, in fact, interesting when he hints at Roethke's relation to thinkers like Paul Tillich and Conrad Bonifazi, but in general these pages are too few.

In "Blake and Roethke: When Everything Comes to One" (*William Blake and the Moderns*, ed. Robert J. Bertholf and Annette S. Levitt, SUNY, pp. 73–91) the poet's best commentator continues his exploration of Roethke, this time developing his sense that Blake was "the single most important poet for Roethke, not so much on the level of style . . . but at the deeper level of mythopoetic action." Like the writers above, Hyatt Waggoner is also concerned with Roethke's visionary stance in his "Learning to See in the Dark" (*American Visionary Poetry*), though, unlike Parini, he argues that it is Whitman, not Blake, who emerges finally as the primary master. Two articles look rather closely at the poet's craft: in " 'Intuition' and 'Craftsmanship': Theodore Roethke at Work" (*PLL* 16:58–76) Don Bogan interestingly examines the various stages of composition of "Where Knock Is Open Wide" (making use of Roethke's drafts) to demonstrate the poet's delicate balance between the importance of the unconscious and the revision process; and Allen Hoey's "Some Metrical and Rhythmical Strategies in the Early Poems of Roethke" (*CP* 15,i:49–58) attempts to trace briefly the poet's evolving metrical craft, from the "awkwardly handled title poem" of *Open House* to the greenhouse poems, finding the later poems not truly "free verse,"

but rather metrically formal "in slightly modified dress." Last, in
"Theodore Roethke: The Manic Vision" (*MPS* 11:152–64) Neal
Bowers presents a piece of his longer study.

### *iii.* A Kind of Field

Last year I had the pleasure of mentioning the publication of the
first issues of Clayton Eshleman's *Sulfur*; this year saw the appearance of the first three issues of a second important new journal, one
sure to take its place among the three or four most important in our
field. *Sagetrieb*, edited by Carroll F. Terrell, Burton Hatlen, and
Constance Hunting (with Basil Hunting and George Oppen listed
as "senior editors") is a tri-quarterly devoted to poets in the Pound–
H.D.–Williams tradition, that is, poets including Zukofsky, Niedecker, Reznikoff, Olson, Creeley, and, more tentatively, Duncan and
Snyder. Modeled on Terrell's decade-old *Paideuma*, the journal will
print general essays, explication, biography, documents, and reviews,
as well as special issues devoted to a single poet.

*a.* **Charles Olson.** The year saw the Olson-Creeley *Complete Correspondence* (Black Sparrow) almost half finished, as editor George
F. Butterick gave us another 150 pages covering, as for the earlier
volumes, just a few months—in this case 8 November 1950 to 11
February 1951. Again, as with the earlier collections, more of Creeley's letters than Olson's are available, and once again there is not
only much information on developing lives and poetics but also
previously unpublished poems and parts of poems. Although both
sides of the correspondence remain elliptic to the point of hermeti-
cism in their syntax and typography, and thus often frustrate the
reader for whom these poets are not a life's work, certainly this series
has emerged as a signal event in the publication of postmodern literary documents. With issue 3 of *Sulfur*, Paul Christensen's edition
of "The Letters of Edward Dahlberg and Charles Olson" (pp. 122–
23) is now complete. This installment covers the years 1950–55, the
years of the two poets' "final feud," which Christensen perceptively
attributes to the fact that by the mid-'50s "Dahlberg was devoured
by despair, and Olson was not." Once again we are forced to make
our way through the Scylla and Charybdis of both men's epistles sans
notes, and this is too bad, though certainly for Christensen's tran-

scriptions and Clayton Eshleman's publication of them both men deserve at least an acre each in Dogtown, free and clear.

Last year I noted the selected passages of Merton M. Sealts, Jr.'s correspondence with Olson concerning Melville which appeared in *CL*. This year, the relationship between the two men, with many sections from Olson's letters, is related by Sealts in part 2 of his *Pursuing Melville, 1940–1980* (Wisconsin). The correspondence ran from 1940 to 1964, initiated by then graduate student Sealts in an attempt to get Olson to read an essay he had written on one of Melville's stories at the request of Eleanor Melville Metcalf, Melville's granddaughter. Most of Olson's comments in the subsequent 80-item correspondence centered on the subject of Melville's library (Sealts's *Melville's Reading*, much influenced by Olson's ideas, appeared in 1966), though questions of the general state of Melville scholarship, poetry, and the universities were often broached. Anyone with an interest in Olson's scholarship and his passion for Melville will not want to overlook this study by one of Melville's most serious and perceptive critics.

Fielding Dawson's memoir of Olson appears this year in "On Olson, with References to Guy Davenport" (*Sagetrieb* 1:125–32), while in "Modern Literary Manuscripts and Archives: A Field Report" (*Credences* 1,i:81–103) George Butterick describes in fascinating detail the organizing, care, and feeding of the Olson Archives at the University of Connecticut. Philip Eggers' "Old Mother Smith: The Offshore Hero of Charles Olson's Counter-Epic" (*ConP* 5,i:30–44), reading *Maximus* as a "counterepic" (that is, not a celebration of Gloucester's history, but "history as it might and should have been"), interestingly examines the poem's "Aeneas"—Captain John Smith—as the product of Olson's reconciliation with the mother figure. Finally, in "The Pleistocene in the Projective: Some of Olson's Origins" (*AL* 54:81–97) George Hutchinson outlines the chronology and shape of Olson's interest in Pleistocene culture, an interest which greatly influenced both the poet's "Projective Verse" essay and *Maximus*. Of special note is Hutchinson's speculation concerning the probable influence of Max Raphael's work on cave paintings on Olson's sense of "the motive of reality" as "process rather than goal."

*b.* **Robert Creeley.** From the start, Robert Creeley's purpose has been, as he says in *Pieces*, to "Hear, goddamnit, hear," and of the poets of the "Olson group" he has certainly emerged with the most continually interesting ear. This year *Sagetrieb*'s first special issue (1,iii) is devoted to Creeley, drawing together appreciations, general essays, explications, bibliography, and photographs. "The Vortex" opens with Creeley's moving elegy "Oh Max," followed by poems and short prose by Anne Waldman, Michael McClure, Cid Corman, Anselm Hollo, and Burton Hatlen. The essays include Mosch's "Robert Creeley's Epistemopathic Path" (describing Creeley's attempts at "overcoming metaphysics," pp. 57–85), Charles Bernstein's "Hearing 'Here': Robert Creeley's Poetics of Duration" ("writing comes to desire to make actual its own conditions in/as writing by making audible the process of writing," pp. 86–95), Jerry McGuire's "No Boundaries: Robert Creeley as Post-modern Man" ("the tension that has attracted so many readers to Creeley's work is that of a language act attempting to eradicate its other/ness even as that otherness is felt and desired as a presence and an absence," pp. 97–118), George Butterick's "Robert Creeley and the Tradition" (Creeley continues to return "to the larger literary tradition for periodical reactivation and refreshment," pp. 119–54), and Albert Cook's brief "The Construct of Image: Olson and Creeley" (Creeley "can be thought of as re-aligning the practice of Williams through complications—and simplifications—induced by Olson," pp. 135–39). "The Explicator" gives us four pieces by Cynthia Dubin Edelberg (on the "sequences," pp. 143–62), Jed Rasula (on *Pieces*, pp. 163–70), Michael Heller (on *Words*, pp. 171–74), and Linda W. Wagner (on Creeley's sense of place, pp. 175–81). Finally, following a series of photographs, Timothy Murray (Curator of Manuscripts for the Washington University Libraries in St. Louis) outlines the holdings of "what is probably the largest collection of material relating to Robert Creeley's work in the world" (pp. 191–94) at Washington University. Informative and highly readable, this issue rests solidly alongside *Boundary*'s earlier Creeley symposium.

Of Creeley's poetry Olson wrote, "It is a study, how Creeley lands syntax down the alley, and his vocabulary—pure English—to hit meter and rhymes all of which are spares and strikes." This year, in their *Collected Poetry of Robert Creeley* (Calif.) the editors have given us the whole bowling alley. The massive (670-page) volume collects eight books published between 1945 and 1975, as well as "In London" from *Daybook*, 11 previously uncollected poems, a short preface, and an index of titles and first lines. At $28.50 the book is certainly priced beyond the reach of many of Creeley's readers (though perhaps a later paper edition will be more reasonable); still, the publisher has produced a lovely work of typography, choosing to give each poem its own page, thus reinforcing Creeley's syntactic intent. A major piece of publishing, with Olson's complete *Maximus* and Blackburn's translations to follow, this volume demonstrates the myriad opportunities for other university presses.

*c.* **Louis Zukofsky, George Oppen, Lorine Niedecker, Charles Reznikoff.** Interest in the Objectivist poets, while not outstripping their most well-known inheritors Olson and Creeley, seems to intensify each year, perhaps simply because of the rather recent republication of much of their long out-of-print work. A number of good pieces appeared on Zukofsky this year, the best of which was Burton Hatlen's "Zukofsky, Wittgenstein, and the Poetics of Absence" (*Sagetrieb* 1:63–93), an essential bit of reading. In a long and complex discussion Hatlen analyzes Zukofsky's movement from an image-centered poetics of presence in "An Objective" to a later Wittgensteinian sense of absence—"what language might become / in a 'state of perfect rest' "—in *Bottom: On Shakespeare.* Tom Sharp's "Sincerity and Objectification" (*Sagetrieb* 1:255–66) takes as its text Zukofsky's manuscript of his essay "Charles Reznikoff: Sincerity and Objectification" (only about half of which was published in the 1931 issue of *Poetry* devoted to the Objectivists), describing for us the poet's debt to Pound in his emerging aesthetic. In "Louis Zukofsky: Songs of Degrees" (*Credences* 1,ii–iii:122–49) John Taggart usefully offers "something of an introduction to the poetics and poetry," reading the seven-poem series as "a range of real and imagined song." Finally, in *Sagetrieb* both Reno Odlin (1:100–02) and Ted Pearson (1:307–08) publish notes on *A*, while David Gordon adds a few memories to the poet's biography (with references to Zukofsky's *Catullus*) in "Zuk On His Toes" (1:133–41), and Cid Corman's "Ryokan's Scroll" (1:285–89) briefly traces Zukofsky's use of a poem of Ryokan's on a scroll Corman purchased in Kyoto in the late '50s.

As if to catch their breath after last year's massive collections on George Oppen, the poet's interested readers published no new work this year on his verse. *Sagetrieb*, however, did run four pieces on Lorine Niedecker and Charles Reznikoff. The longest and best of these is Kathryn Shevelow's "History and Objectification in Charles Reznikoff's Documentary Poems, *Testimony* and *Holocaust*" (1:290–306), which convincingly argues that Reznikoff's primary contribution resides in his "work with the historical poem, in which he seeks through the methodology of objectivist poetics" the translation of the historical into the poetic. In her discussion Shevelow interestingly sets passages from actual court transcripts alongside Reznikoff's later verse reworkings of them. August Kleinzahler gives us perhaps the year's most eccentric and elliptic note on a poet in his exceedingly odd two-page piece on Zukofsky's "The Walker" (1:103–04). In "Lyric Minimum & Epic Scope: Lorine Niedecker" (1:268–76) Donald Davie "annotates" "Lake Superior" with reference to Janet Lewis' *The Invasion*, while in "The Evolution of Matter" (1:278–84) Jane Augustine investigates Niedecker's early Imagist-Objectivist poetics and her later extension "beyond."

#### iv. The Autochthonic Spirit

Of all the "groups" of poets treated in this chapter, the San Francisco Renaissance/Beat poets continue to be the most slighted, and this is unfortunate. A number of book-length works (including studies of Duncan and Ferlinghetti, two volumes of essays on Rexroth, and an edition of Everson's forewords and afterwords) are scheduled for publication in 1983, and perhaps these will spur further critical interest. In 1982, however, these poets, save for Duncan, were shamefully neglected. There was one article only on Snyder and one on Ginsberg, and a Ferlinghetti bibliography and interview; no work appeared on Jack Spicer, Philip Whalen, Gregory Corso, William Everson, Diane DiPrima, or Ron Lowensohn—the list goes on and on—and one of the most vital poets, essayists, and translators of our age, Kenneth Rexroth, has attracted just a three-page note.

An issue of *Credences* (3,ii–iii) devoted to Robert Duncan offered four new essays on the poet by James Broughton, William Everson, Dennis Cooley, and George Quasha. Broughton's "Homage to the Great Bear" (pp. 140–45) and Everson's "Of Robert Duncan" (pp. 147–51) are memoirs of these poets' important relationships in the Bay Area of the late '40s and '50s; Everson's is especially good in his account of the San Francisco/Berkeley split caused by *Ark*, as well as its sense of Duncan's homosexuality as an embodiment of the

Apollonian. In "Robert Duncan's Green Wor[l]ds" (pp. 152–60) Dennis Cooley closely reads "The Fire" and "Earth's Winter Song," arguing that Duncan's "green world"—"a dream of grass blowing / east against the source of the sun"—is his sustaining myth. The issue concludes with George Quasha's extended piece on "Duncan Reading" (pp. 162–75), which finds both our reading of Duncan's text and the poet's own reading done "in and around the making of his work" to be "directed by his heretically multiple poetics," for "reading is a root principle of consciousness." Following is a penetrating discussion of a number of poems (especially "Passages") as examples of the "non-developmental and non-teleological" process the poet endorses. Another solid piece this year is Michael Andre Bernstein's "Bringing It All Back Home: Derivations and Quotations in Robert Duncan and the Poundian Tradition" (*Sagetrieb* 1:176–89); here Bernstein sees sources of Duncan's fusion of the poet, critic, and translator in Pound's work, traces out the poet's sense of "permission," and discusses Duncan's interest in "the relationship between imagination and desire."

While readers will want to look at the whole of *William Blake and the Moderns*, ed. Robert J. Berthoff and Annette S. Levitt (SUNY), two essays collected there are of particular interest. In "Robert Duncan: Blake's Contemporary Voice" (pp. 92–110) Berthoff argues that Duncan, like Blake, "has searched out in conscious maneuvers the texts which immersed him in the continuous contention of universal contraries." He then continues with a discussion of the correspondence between the two poets, including each's sense of the "visionary" (for Blake, Christ is the emblem of the imagination, for Duncan it is Eros), their attempts to overcome the subject/object dualism, and the importance for both poets of the creation of a "prophecy of mythological reality." Following, Alicia Ostriker's "Blake, Ginsberg, Madness, and the Prophet as Shaman" (pp. 111–31) looks to Blake as source for "*Howl*'s tenor of 'madness,'" and the poem's argument that "to accept is to redeem."

Donald Gutierrez takes Kenneth Rexroth's "Time Spirals" (a section from *The Dragon and the Unicorn*) as the subject of his brief but interesting note in "Going Upstream" (*NMAL* 6:Item 9), seeing the poem's message as a kind of stoicism amid "the living vividness and latent doom of the present." Finally, Lee Bartlett's "Gary Snyder's *Myth and Texts* and the Monomyth" (*WAL* 17:137–48) argues that the long poem's three parts mirror the archetypal monomyth (separation/initiation/return), offering a reading of the poem's movement as an affirmation of the Dionysian over the Apollonian and a call for a transformation of values.

Bill Morgan's well-researched (with the cooperation of the poet) *Lawrence Ferlinghetti: A Comprehensive Bibliography* (Garland) more than lives up to its subtitle. The 400-page volume gives full descriptions of 58 separate books, pamphlets, and broadsides through 1981, as well as the poet's hundreds of translations, contributions to periodicals, interviews, films, etc. Unfortunately, the book's checklist of criticism, though exhaustive—598 items are listed—is unannotated. Finally, Jean Jacque Lebel's 1980 interview with the poet for an essay in *Le Monde* is translated in Ferlinghetti's *The Populist Manifestos* (Grey Fox, 1981).

### v. Dream of a Common Language

Following hard upon the publication of Plath's *Collected Poems*, *The Journals of Sylvia Plath*, ed. Frances McCullough and Ted Hughes (Dial) appeared this year. The book is divided into three parts, the first covering entries from 1950 to 1955 (Smith College); the second, from 1955 to 1958 (Cambridge and Smith); and the third, from 1958 to 1962 (Boston and England). The topics include the poet's difficulties and successes with her writing, her college experiences, her marriage to Hughes, the birth of her children, discussions about her parents, and comments on other writers. Unfortunately, passages from these journals have been deleted; though the editors claim that the excisions have no real effect on the thrust of the volume, a scholar who has seen the originals tells me that in fact they change the tone (especially in the area of Plath's relationship to Hughes) in a fashion that is unnerving. Having never seen the originals myself, I cannot attest to the accuracy of this criticism, though I suspect there is some truth to it. Still, in places this is a powerful book and often Plath's style approaches the lyrical as she describes struggles with various real and imagined demons.

Three articles on Plath this year signal a return of interest to the poet's earlier work. With " 'Burned-up intensity': The Suicidal Poetry of Sylvia Plath" (*Mosaic* 15,i:141–51) Fred Moramarco contributes to a general "Death and Dying" symposium with a discussion of Plath's grappling with Camus' only "truly serious philosophical question." Moramarco finds in the early *Colossus* poems "suicidal fixations" which intensified as the poet's technical skill matured, and argues (against last year's study by Mary Lynn Brose) that Plath's work from the start "becomes a long funeral dirge." Christopher Morris' "Order and Chaos in Plath's 'The Colossus'" (*CP* 15,ii:33–42) argues that his rather extended reading of the title poem is the first to explain its two levels: "the speaker's effort to understand existence by recollecting her father" and the "inability to find, through poetry, a clear understanding of her position." Morris traces a series of allusions in the poem which, he believes, advance the theme from the "private past" to a general "death of authority," ending with an analysis of the poem's structure and language. In his "Further Reflections on Plath's 'Mirror'" (*HSL* 14:11–22) Robert J. Kloss explains (though, mysteriously, without reference to Jacques Lacan's seminal essay on the "mirror image") that "it is an intrinsic part of Plath's design to faithfully reflect the individuation process," with particular reference to the mother.

"A Poetry of Survival: The Unnaming and Renaming in the Poetry of Audre Lorde, Pat Parker, Sylvia Plath, and Adrienne Rich" (*CLQ* 18:9–25) by Pamela Annas attempts to examine "the relation of a woman poet to language." Annas begins by establishing the "five stages in the process of renaming" that "other-defined groups need to work through" (acceptance, dual consciousness, unnaming, renaming the self, and renaming the world), then perhaps a bit too briefly she discusses the four poets above in terms of these stages, concluding that "the woman artist is more aware both of potentialities and of limitations." In "Poets in Bedlam: Sexton's Use of Bishop's 'Visit to St. Elizabeth's' in 'Ringing the Bells'" (*CP* 15,i:37–47) Joyce M. Wegs reads Sexton's poem not as a fairly "straight-forward personal narrative" of her hospitalization, but rather as a "highly personal reaction" to Elizabeth Bishop's earlier poem on the same topic.

### vi. A Complex of Occasions

The notion of the literary group or school is, finally, a fiction, though for surveys like this it is a useful one. Still, at this point each year I run into a problem: while earlier subsections have some obvious rationale—either diachronic or synchronic—I end with any number of items on writers who are not so easily categorized.

*a.* James Wright, Robert Bly. The poet Dave Smith's edition of *The Pure Clear Word: Essays on the Poetry of James Wright* (Illinois) seeks, Smith writes in his introduction, to attract to Wright "more genuine intelligent readers of good will." By his death in 1980 Wright had become, in fact, one of the major influences of the next generation as he grew into his later style, and this book is a solid tribute to his achievement. Following an introduction wherein he outlines some of the poet's central concerns, Smith reprints his long 1979 interview with Wright (pp. 3–42). Of the following 13 essays, 11—by W. H. Auden (foreword to Wright's *The Green Wall*), Robert Bly (two essays on "Crunk"), William Matthews, James Seay, Edward Butscher, Stephen Yenser, Leonard Nathan, Robert Haas, Bonnie Costello, and Smith—are reprinted, while Henry Taylor, Peter Stitt, and Miller Williams contribute original pieces. In "In the Mode of Robinson and Frost: James Wright's Early Poetry" (pp. 49–64) Taylor discusses the poet's first two books as hardly "false starts," but rather displaying "the self-reliance that characterizes most of Wright's work'; for Taylor, the later shift in style was "a survival tactic." Stitt's "James Wright: The Quest Motif in *The Branch Shall Not Break*" (pp. 65–77) argues, as its title implies, that the basic strategy Wright employs in *Branch* is that of a quest, one tracing "in his own intimate kinship with the animals a release from self-consciousness and death-consciousness." Last, Williams offers "James Wright, His Poems: A Kind of Overview, in Appreciation" (pp. 234–46), making the wonderful observation that when a writer dies all his work becomes "simultaneous," while Smith closes the volume with an extended bibliography of Wright's work (pp. 247–57).

Two other good essays on Wright appeared this year. Of particular interest is Nicholas Gattuccio's fascinating "Now My Amenities of Stone Are Done: Some Notes on the Style of James Wright" (*CP* 15,i:61–76). Gattuccio takes his title from the title of Wright's suppressed 1961 collection *Amenities of Stone* (discovered among the poet's papers in 1980), which is the "missing" transitional volume between *Saint Judas* and *Branch*. Not the least intriguing is the discovery that about two-thirds of *Branch* (including "Lying in a Hammock" and "A Blessing") was written earlier than we might assume, between later 1959 and early 1961. Edward Lense regards Wright as a visionary poet (he certainly could have been included in Waggoner's study). His "This Is What I Wanted: James Wright and the Other World" (*MPS* 11:19–32) looks at both *Branch* and *We Gather at the River* as books which embody "a traditional myth of the other world . . . that gives force to his otherwise conventional poetry."

In *ALS 1981* I discussed at length *Poetry East's* special number devoted to Robert Bly; in 1982 the massive issue was reprinted as *Of Solitude and Silence*, ed. Richard Jones and Kate Daniels (Beacon Press). In "Camphor and Gopherwood: Robert Bly's Recent Poems in Prose" (*MPS* 11,i–ii:88–102) William V. Davis, feeling that the prose poem for Bly was "inevitable," reads *This Body Is Made of Camphor and Gopherwood* as a return to "his beginnings," the Boehme-influenced voice of *Silence in the Snowy Fields*. Bly is interviewed this year by Joseph Shakarchi in *MR* 23:226–43.

*b.* **James Merrill, W. S. Merwin, John Ashbery, Frank O'Hara, A. R. Ammons, James Dickey.** James Merrill, a much-awarded poet whose Ouija trilogy *The Changing Light at Sandover* finally appeared in one volume this year, had two books devoted to his work. Ross Labrie's *James Merrill* (TUSAS 427) is a useful introduction to "one of the most hermetic writers America has produced," containing discussions of the poet's life, his plays and fiction, the shorter poems, and his long poem. Labrie is measured in his comments—he is obviously taken with the poet, but he is not overwhelmed by him—and this first full-length study of the Merrill corpus, concise and non-thesis-ridden, does the poet's readers a service. In 1980 David Lehman edited a series of essays on John Ashbery called *Beyond Amazement*; this year, with Charles Berger, he has published a similar volume, *James Merrill: Essays in Criticism* (Cornell). Following Lehman's introduction, which clearly sets the context but accepts perhaps too much as a given Merrills "greatness," there are 11 new essays on a number of aspects of the poet's work. Lehman writes on Merrill's "unity"; J. D. McClatchy and Samuel E. Schulman on books of shorter poems; David Kalstone, Peter Sacks, Willard Spiegelman, Richard Saez, and Stephen Yenser on Merrill's epic; Rachel Jacoff on Merrill and Dante; Charles Berger on Merrill and Pynchon; and David Jackson (the poet's companion for 30 years) charmingly on "lending a hand" with Merrill's Ouija board. Both of these books include selected bibliographies. James Merrill is also the subject this year of *Paris Review's* "The Art of Poetry XXXI" interview (84:184–219), conducted by J. D. McClatchy.

Two good articles appeared on W. S. Merwin this year. In "For a Coming Extinction: A Reading of W. S. Merwin's *The Lice*" (*ELH* 49:262–85) Hank Lazer examines Merwin's sixth collection as a "planetary elegy," "an extended myth of uncreation." Lazer argues that while a few of the poems in the volume have specific political occasions (the war in Vietnam most obviously), generally Merwin's work "is more likely to fashion a political poetry which is a mythology of forces." Still, he feels, the book must be read as an extension of Merwin's "search for continuity and personal identity" in the midst of "the insubstantial, the empty, and the silent." The silent is also a concern of Anthony Libby in "Merwin's Planet: Alien Voices" (*Criticism* 24,i:48–63), as he senses Merwin's "curious landscape" as that of a "terminal pessimist," a place of "silence and exclusion." Libby traces a number of the poet's concerns with the "non-human," arguing that "Merwin's growing preference for the visionary aphorism and the language of incantation over the aphorism of logic and the language of analysis are consistent not only with Merwin's distrust of humanity but with his developing interest in dumb beasts."

Only three articles appeared on Ashbery this year, though all are of note. Bonnie Costello's "John Ashbery and the Idea of the Reader" (*ConL* 23:491–514) comments that reading is a primary subject for Ashbery, allowing his "self-reflexiveness" an escape from "banal solipsism." Arguing that "convexity is Ashbery's paradigm of the psychic and ontological distance between writer and reader," that the mirror "reminds us that a text, whether we are its writer or its reader, calls for both active and passive responses," Costello traces this strategy from *Rivers and Mountains* through the most recent work. That Wallace Stevens served as one of Ashbery's masters is no secret, and in " 'Thinking Without Final Thoughts': John Ashbery's Evolving Debt to Wallace Stevens" (*ELH* 49:235–61) Lynn Keller outlines the relationship. Keller argues that Ashbery's first important volume, *Some Trees*, rather "unabashedly adopts" both the theories and practice of the early Stevens, while from the "transitional" *Rivers and Mountains* on, Ashbery has approached more fully Stevens' later discursive and meditative mode. In addition, Keller finds that the two writers share a passion for paradox, "a sense of man's isolation in the cosmos," an insistence on the value of the imagination, and a common vocabulary. With reference to both Jacques Lacan and Jacques Derrida, Mutlu Konuk Blasing examines Frank O'Hara's last major poem as an example of a "tongue that is playing with language" in an attempt to combat "the alienation of language," in "Frank O'Hara's Poetics of Speech: The Example of 'Biotherm' " (*ConL* 23:52–64). The overarching metaphor in the poem, Blasing points out, is food, "a metaphor for everything one takes in and processes." Further, Blasing finds an affinity between O'Hara and Artaud in that for both poets words are "wholly body."

Thomas A. Fink in "The Problem of Freedom and Restriction in the Poetry of A. R. Ammons" (*MPS* 11:138–48) reads through a few of Ammons' poems to trace the poet's "long-time obsession' as "the desire to maintain a sense of unity and diversity" in poetry and perception which has "fundamental ramifications." Finally, Lee Bartlett and Hugh Witemeyer trace one of the myriad debts of contemporary poets to Ezra Pound in their "Ezra Pound and James Dickey: A Correspondence and a Kinship" (*Paideuma* 11:290–312). Dickey met Pound at St. Elizabeth's in August of 1955, and an exchange of letters followed; this article prints the 15 surviving pieces of correspondence with a running commentary.

*c.* **Richard Wilbur, J. V. Cunningham, Robert Pack, William Meredith, Ann Stanford.** Each of these poets has produced a substantial body of work, and the articles concerning them this year are all more or less general reassessments. In "Wilbur's Words: The Poetry of Richard Wilbur" (*MR* 23:97–111) Bruce Michelson feels that Wilbur is "misvalued," that his poetry is "neither charming ornament nor gimmick," but rather "as daring an experiment in poetry as we have seen in the past three decades." Reading closely Wilbur's early "Regatta" and the later "Year's End," "In a Churchyard," and a few other poems, Michelson argues that Wilbur's incessant "word play" is meant to be regenerative, "catching not just diversity, but the unity beyond diversity." Interesting reading for anyone who has a concern for either Wilbur or the pun. A second article, Joe Reibetanz's "What Love Sees: Poetry and Vision in Richard Wilbur" (*MPS* 11:160–85), attempts to counter Randall Jarrell ("his poems are all scenes") and James Dickey ("Wilbur has an unwillingness or inability to think or feel deeply") on the poet. Beginning with Wilbur's 1976 collection *The Mind-Reader*, Reibetanz examines the development from the early to the later, more imaginative and "natural" work.

In " 'The Vacancies of Need': Particularity in J. V. Cunningham's *To What Strangers, What Welcome*" (*SoR* 18:286–98), R. L. Booth looks at Cunningham's sequence of 15 poems as a reversal of the poet's earlier sense of "haeceity." Robert Pack's selected poems occasion Paul Mariani's "Fresh Flowers for the Urn: Reassessing Robert Pack" (*MR* 23:715–32). Mariani argues that Pack has "tried to establish a poetics based on creating a Wordsworthian tranquility," though his "real father" is the late Keats struggling with transience and mortality. Wordsworth is also invoked in Neva Herrington's "The Language of the Tribe: William Meredith's Poetry" (*SWR* 67:1–17), an essay which discusses the range of Meredith's poetry in terms of the "meditative tradition." Last, a poet not often written about, Ann Stanford, is the subject of Joan Johnstone's brief "On Ann Stanford" (*SoR* 18:280–85), an appreciation of "a poet of the seasoned lyric composed in a plain style"; Karla Hammond provides us with a long interview with the poet in the same issue (314–37).

*d.* **Muriel Rukeyser, William Bronk, Diane Wakoski, Wendell Berry, Richard Hugo, Galway Kinnell, Stanley Kunitz.** Two poets who are certainly underattended to are Muriel Rukeyser and William Bronk, though each drew a good essay this year. In "Finding Her Voice: Muriel Rukeyser's Poetic Development" (*MPS* 11:127–38) David S. Barber, who feels that the lack of much critical interest in Rukeyser is the fault of the poet's early attempts at a "transcendental language" in the manner of Whitman which emerged as "merely vague," traces the strong "development of a more personal, individualized, reflective speaking voice" in the later work. Norman M. Finkelstein in "William Bronk: The World as Desire" (*ConL* 23:480–92) says Bronk is "one of the most significant poets writing in English today." Bronk's "single great constant" is "desire for the world"; his individual poems "unfold as a phenomenology of desire" reflecting back upon one another producing what is really a single work of skeptical "self-negating rhetoric."

Desire also plays a role in Taffy Wynne Martin's good "Diane Wakoski's Personal Mythology: Dionysian Music, Created Presence" (*Boundary* 10,iii:155–72). Martin argues that while the poet's verse "strays about as far as possible from the detached irony of a well-made modernist poem," through an acknowledgment of loss her work emerges with an Eliotic coherence "in which desire functions as an enabling drive." Although much of Wakoski's work is highly personal, Martin finds that the struggle between flesh and spirit provides the central conflict of every Wakoski poem. In "A More Mingled Music: Wendell Berry's Ambivalent View of Language" (*MPS* 11:35–56) Robert Collins explains that for Berry "the abuse of language is largely responsible for the cultural, physical, and spiritual wasteland in which Americans are living today." The poet admires Williams especially, both for his concern for place and his insistence on the value in human terms of verse, yet Collins feels Berry shows a progressive "paradoxical development in his poetry which increasingly emphasizes the importance of silence."

Michael S. Allen's *We Are Called Human: The Poetry of Richard Hugo* (Arkansas) is a solid and concise introduction to Hugo's work. Opening with a good discussion of the influence of Roethke, Allen proceeds with an orderly discussion of each of Hugo's eight books, from the 1961 *A Run of Jacks* to *The Right Madness on Skye* (1980). He discusses Hugo's major themes—the landscape of the west, the nature of defeat, the "triggering town"—concluding that "at a time in our literature when poets are praised for closing their doors in self-absorbtion and evasion, Hugo's poetry calls us to be human in our songs and in our common need."

No substantial work on either Galway Kinnell or Stanley Kunitz appeared this year, though both men were interviewed: Thomas Hilgars and Michael Molloy chat briefly with Kinnel (*MPS* 11:107–12), while *Paris Review*'s "Art of Poetry, XXXIX" (conducted in 1977 by Chris Busa) focuses on Kunitz (83:202–46).

*e.* **Carolyn Forché, Louise Glück, Charles Simic, Madeline DeFrees.** The current attacks on the Sandinistas in Nicaragua and the struggle of the left in El Salvador, Chile, and Guatemala have in America rekindled interest in the political or social resonsibility of the poet. While in this chapter I generally do not have space to mention either new books of poetry or reviews (no matter how extended), here I must note the publication of Carolyn Forché's second volume of poetry *The Country Between Us* (Harper), as it served as a focus for an intense debate on the whole question of politics and poetry. In her essay on El Salvador in *APR* (July–August 1981) Forché argues that "there is no such thing as non-political poetry," that to use language is to take a position. In "Poetry and Commitment" (*OhR* 29: 15–30) Jonathan Holden takes issue with this position, claiming that Forché is wrong, that "it is precisely when the distinction between what is political and what is not breaks down or is denied that the quality of art declines." Holden examines "political" poems by Forché, Rich, and Ginsberg (finding them not good art) beside similar poems by Stevens and Simpson, which he argues are "first-rate political poetry . . . neither smug nor hysterical." He closes by setting two poems about prisoners (Charles Simic's "The Prisoners" and Forché's "The Visitor") side by side, finding Simic's a "brilliant reversal of perspective," Forché's "strong" but not as "fully realized" due to the poet's "making an ideology of emotion." A second, even more scathing indictment of Forché (serving as a corrective to the scores of laudatory reviews her book has gathered) is Eliot Weinberger's piece in *Sulfur* (6:158–64), wherein he accuses Forché of mere "formula" writing, of being a "student-profound" whose work belongs "to the genre of revolutionary tourism."

Robert Miklitsch provides an overview in "Assembling a Landscape: The Poetry of Louise Glück" (*HC* 19,iv:1–13), tracing influences (Lowell and Plath), developing themes, and analyzing language through the poet's three major books. In "*White*: Charles Simic's Thumbnail Epic" (*ConL* 23:528–49) Peter Schmidt discusses Simic's poem-sequence as "ur-lyric," a "private collection of beginnings, of summonings" of chapters, situations, and themes which are developed in other work. Finally, Carol Ann Russell interviews Madeline DeFrees in *MR* 23:265–69.

*University of New Mexico*

# 18. Drama

## Walter J. Meserve

In all probability the confusion between drama and theater will persist because people are careless with words and, despite St. Augustine's admonition, they will presume. There is, however, a difference between the two terms—between the written work of art and the place where that work is to be created as an event for an audience by whatever number of "mechanics" may be required. Theater people in particular find any distinction meaningless while further clouding the terminology by using the word "script" indiscriminately to refer to the written work, thus reducing the art of the dramatist to something merely "written," that is, in progress and ready for their final touch. There is, of course, a certain amount of truth in their reaction, but perhaps because the distinction between the two terms can be made so readily, numerous people continue to explain it with the expected and natural result.

The focus of this essay is the drama, the American drama as it has been written, commented on, and evaluated by scholars, critics, and practitioners of theater. Nevertheless, the necessary and complementary fusion of the art of the dramatist and the arts practiced by people of the theater make the consideration of both drama and theater not only an obligation but a distinct advantage for American literary scholars. One may be studied without the other, but, as Emerson and others have observed, the whole can be more than the sum of its parts.

The number of books and essays on American drama and theater published this year was clearly remarkable. Even with some careful pruning there will be more than 100 references in this essay. All, of course, are not equally valuable or even worth reading, but that knowledge, too, can be helpful. An obvious conclusion points to the vitality of the area of scholarship, surely desirable as a sign of healthy curiosity from which excellence may develop.

### i. Histories and Books of General Interest

Few scholars have attempted a full chronological study of American drama and theater. Garff Wilson is one, and the second edition of *Three Hundred Years of American Drama and Theatre* (Prentice-Hall) adds material from the decade of the '70s but is, unfortunately, much shortened from the original 1973 publication. Reducing the number of pages from 536 to 350, Wilson cuts the early history unmercifully, especially the material on playwrights, arriving at the mid-19th century on page 80 rather than page 129. The bibliography is updated, but original errors remain uncorrected. The emphasis is now upon the modern and contemporary periods, and although the evaluations are astute, the volume loses some of its value as a history. Edward Wagenknecht comments occasionally on theater and drama in *American People, 1900–1909* (Mass.), an enthusiastic memoir, delightful and perceptive. It is surely not an overstatement to say that Wagenknecht, with more than 80 books to his credit, has written more about American writers than any other living scholar. In this book about the people he admires and who impressed him during this decade of his early growth he mentions the theater many times and also devotes a chapter to "The Many-Faceted Theater." "It was," he wrote, "a theater geared to entertainment, neither a clinic, an agency of social reform, nor a brothel."

C. W. E. Bigsby is a more traditional historian of American drama. In *A Critical Introduction to Twentieth-Century American Drama, 1900–1940* (Cambridge) Bigsby begins with the Provincetown Theater, allows O'Neill nearly a third of his pages, and comments with his customary insight and clarity on the various theaters of the period and on the dramatists who created for them. The opening section on Susan Glaspell is particularly good as is the chapter on black drama. With the contributions of Wilder and Hellman, however, he brings his observations to a rather abrupt close. From a more limited perspective, Thomas A. Greenfield in *Work and the Work Ethic in American Drama, 1920–1970* (Missouri) provides a fresh view but is clearly too enthusiastic in his claims that work forms the thematic or intellectual center of all American drama. "War as a job" may be an interesting metaphor, but Greenfield does not create a compelling argument. The persistent attempt to interpret American drama continues with Ruby Cohn's *New American Dramatists: 1960–1980*

(Grove), part of a new series that is "written for people interested in modern theatre who prefer concise, intelligent studies of drama and dramatists, without an excess of footnotes." Cohn provides no footnotes at all, but the volume is a well-written and intelligent introduction to contemporary plays as scripts for production and as dramatic literature. Commenting on the various approaches to theater—actor-activated, radical, black, gay, visual—she climaxes her evaluation with worshipful praise for Shepard. "The Word is my Shepard," she writes, in an impulse she should have squelched.

Each year a number of books on various aspects of American literature include references or commentary on American dramatists. Surely the handsomest volume this year is *The Oxford Illustrated Literary Guide to the United States* (Oxford) by Eugene Ehrlich and Gorton Carruth. State by state and region by region the traveler may find his favorite writers here. With a fine sense of importance the authors-compilers start with Maine, listing information about the following writers who also created for the theater: Owen Davis, Mary Ellen Chase, Thomas Wolfe, Kate Douglas Wiggin, Edna St. Vincent Millay, Booth Tarkington, W. D. Howells, Nathaniel Parker Willis, H. W. Longfellow, and John Neal. Emily Stipes Watts in *The Businessman in American Literature* (Georgia) refers to a few modern plays to support her claim that American writers mounted attacks on businessmen and capitalism: *The Hairy Ape, Death of a Salesman*, Barry's *Holiday*, Rice's *Adding Machine, Beggar on Horseback* by Kaufman and Connelly, and Charles Gordone's *No Place to Be Somebody*. Watts does not, however, mention the plays of Bronson Howard or take proper advantage of the Yankee plays, and many would object to her assertion that Silas Lapham is "an American Cousin of Ebenezer Scrooge." Elaine H. Kim has a perceptive and substantive section (pp. 180–89) on the plays of Frank Chin in *Asian American Literature: An Introduction to the Writings and Their Social Context* (Temple).

## ii. Reference Works

Few people seem to write bibliographical essays or to describe distinctive collections. The need is there, however, and aids to scholarship of this character would be most welcome. D. J. Woodard's description of the "Mackaye Collection: A Wealth of Americana" (*ThS*

23:108–10) at Dartmouth is a good if brief example, and the collection begs for scholarly attention. J. P. Wearing's "Nineteenth-Century Theatre Research: A Bibliography for 1981" (*NCTR* 10:93–109) is also valuable.

Compilers of "information sources" (if that is an appropriately clear literary category) created a number of useful volumes—some more useful than others—for drama and theater scholars. Brenda Coven's *American Women Dramatists of the Twentieth Century: A Bibliography* (Scarecrow) has two sections: a general bibliography of about 75 items, mostly since 1970, and individual bibliographies of 133 playwrights who have had at least one successful play in New York. Most of the playwrights listed, however, are too minor to have stimulated criticism, and the items noted are carelessly compiled, very selective, and lack dates and page references. The *Dictionary of Literary Biography, Documentary Series*, vol. 2, ed. Margaret A. Van Antwerp (Gale) includes photographs, MS facsimiles, letters, notebooks, interviews, and contemporary assessments. Richard H. Harris' *Modern Drama in America and England, 1950–70* (Gale), vol. 34 in the Guide to Information Sources, includes some 255 dramatists, listing plays written prior to 1975 and criticism before 1970. The criticism, however, is skimpy and poorly annotated. Donald Koster in *American Literature and Language* (Gale), vol. 13 in the same series, admits to being "highly selective" and lists only books. Among the individual authors in his volume are 14 dramatists representing two centuries of literature. Essentially, however, Koster simply repeats information more effectively presented in other Gale Research volumes.

*The Lively Arts Information Directory*, ed. Steven R. Wasserman (Gale) is another resource volume which provides a tremendous amount of helpful information under such headings as "National and International Organizations," "State and Regional Arts Agencies," "Government Grant Programs," "Foundations" (too general to be helpful), "Colleges and Universities" (very selective), "Schools That Do Not Award Degrees," "Journals" (very poor, with only 29 listed for theater), "Arts Consultants," "Special Libraries," "Research Information Centers," "Festivals" (944 listed), and "Awards"—all related to the "lively arts." Stan A. Vrana attempted an ambitious and valuable research tool in *Interviews and Conversations with 20th-Century Authors Writing in English: An Index* (Scarecrow). With a listing of more than 3,500 interviews involving 1,600 writers during the period from 1900 to 1980, the book appears more complete than it is. In fact, the listing is very scattered and particularly poor for dramatists because major sources are omitted. For most of the writers included, only a single interview is listed. Clearly, the idea behind the volume is excellent, but it is not well executed. *Theatre Profiles 5* (New York: Theatre Communications Group) is an illustrated reference guide to America's nonprofit professional theaters, providing information on facilities, finances, and productions for 159 theaters.

### iii. Anthologies

Teachers of American drama and theater have never had much choice among play anthologies, particularly collections that included plays written before 1920. This year that situation was improved, although there is still no collection of 19th-century American drama in print. *The Longman Anthology of American Drama*, ed. Lee A. Jacobus (Longman), includes 22 plays, 6 before O'Neill and 10 after World War II. It certainly fills a need and the plays are well chosen, but the introductions to individual plays are brief, not always well written, and suggest insufficient knowledge of sources and subject matter. Otis L. Guernsey, Jr.'s *Best Plays of 1980–81* (Dodd, Mead) includes five American plays with *Lunch Hour* by Jean Kerr listed as the "best American play." Dorothy Mackin's *Melodrama Classics, Six Plays and How to Stage Them* (Sterling) includes three American melodramas but is essentially a "how-to" book by the director of the Imperial Players at Cripple Creek, Colorado, where these plays were successfully produced. *Modern Drama in America* (Wash. Square) is the first volume of a new series. Volume 1, *Realism from Provincetown to Broadway, 1915–1929*, ed. Alvin S. Kaufman and Franklin D. Case, will be useful to teachers of American drama, for it shows an excellent choice of plays and provides valuable background and commentary for each play. One hopes that bibliographies will be included in future volumes.

*New Plays USA 1*, ed. James Leverett (New York: Theatre Communications Group) is another first volume in a new series of yearly "manifestos" designed to introduce new American plays to a reading public. The six plays, each with playwright's notes, production history, and brief playwright's biography, are introduced by Michael

Feingold's essay on "American Playwriting: The State of the Art, the State of the Union" (pp. xi–xvi) which in spite of an inadequate understanding of theater history—*The Octoroon* (1859), for example, is not really a Civil War melodrama—shows an interesting rebellion from the trashiness of Broadway and a concern for an alternative theater. *Three Plays by Louisiana Playwrights* (Baton Rouge, La.: Oracle) has a very poorly devised introduction by Clinton Bradford and is mainly of interest for G. Stevens' adaptation of "Royal Tyller's" (*sic*) *The Isle of Barrataria. The Random Review, 1982*, ed. Gary Fisketjon and Jonathan Galassi (Random House), is the first in a series of annual anthologies that reprints the best stories, poems, and essays from some 600 periodicals. It would be appropriate to focus upon drama and theater in some future issue.

### iv. 19th-Century Plays, Playwrights, and Theaters

As the number of articles and books on various aspects of American drama and theater have increased markedly this year, a greater interest in Pre-O'Neill drama has developed. *Nineteenth-Century Literature Criticism*, vol. 2, ed. Laurie L. Harris (Gale), does not show an overwhelming concern for dramatists, but the sections on William Dunlap (pp. 207–18) and William Wells Brown (pp. 45–56) are substantial, and references are made to the plays of Longfellow and James Kirk Paulding. *The Writing Women of New England, 1630–1900*, ed. Arlen and Perry Westbrook (Scarecrow), an anthology, simply ignores the fact that women wrote an incredible number of plays during these years. In *Plotting the Golden West* (Cambridge, 1981) Stephen Fender refers to the plays of John Brougham but otherwise ignores the many dramatists whose work would have helped illustrate his thesis in an exciting fashion.

Among the spectacles on the 19th-century stage *Mazeppa* enjoys a rather notorious reputation. Wolf Mankowitz's *Mazeppa: The Lives, Loves and Legends of Adah Isaacs Menken* (Stein and Day) should have been an exciting book. As a "biographical quest," however, it is not a serious study, and the author relies heavily on pictures for his effect. Totally lacking in documentation, presumptuous and self-conscious in style, the volume shows a careless writer whose approach to his material is stilted and trite. Five other 19th-century plays, however, were the subjects of revealing essays. Bruce A. Mc-

Conachie has discovered a fascinating letter concerning a version of *Uncle Tom's Cabin* which he elucidates in terms of the politics of the period: "H. J. Conway's Dramatization of *Uncle Tom's Cabin*: A Previously Unpublished Letter" (*TJ* 34:149–54). Gary A. Richardson provides a different view of "Boucicault's *The Octoroon* and American Law" (*TJ* 34:155–64) by exploring slavery as a theme and basic metaphor in the play. With comment, pictures, and reprinted pages from the stage manager's book Stephen Johnson gives an act-by-act re-creation of "Joseph Jefferson's *Rip Van Winkle* (1865)" (*TDR* 26:i,3–20). Unfortunately, his comment is little more than a retelling of the plot. Leigh George Odom uses more imagination and material to recreate the 1866 production of "*The Black Crook* at Niblo's Garden" (*TDR* 26:i,21–40). In "*Margaret Fleming* in Chickering Hall: the First Little Theater in America?" (*TJ* 34:165–71) Barnard Hewitt presents a history of the production and a carefully considered positive response in this well-written essay. Hamlin Garland was, of course, involved in Herne's production, and *Critical Essays on Hamlin Garland*, ed. James Nagel (Hall) reprints some 66 articles and reviews, some of which refer to his theater experiences. Nagel's introduction to the volume is excellent.

Three additional essays relate to American drama and theater at the turn of the century. Susan Carlson Galenbeck attempts to inspire more interest in Henry James's abortive ventures into the theater in "British Comedy of Manners Distilled: Henry James's Edwardian Plays" (*HJR* 4:61–74). G. W. Schuttler brings rather little insight or information to his subject, "William Gillette and Sherlock Holmes" (*JPC* 15:31–41). Although "Bronson Howard, Dean of American Drama 1842–1908" (*ALR* 15:112–18) offers considerable opportunity for a bibliographical study, Barbara Gannon's selected entries are hardly satisfying.

Clearly, published research on the American theater during 1982 shows the fascinating diversity waiting for the young scholar. For example, David Ritchey's *A Guide to the Baltimore Stage in the Eighteenth Century: A History and Day Book Calendar* (Greenwood) appends a scanty history to a complete calendar and includes two contemporary items relevant to performers of that early period. It is one kind of labor of love performed by theater historians. *Theatrical Touring and Founding in North America*, ed. L. W. Conolly (Greenwood), a collection of essays, is another kind—with a completely different objective. It includes 13 essays by various contemporary scholars on individuals (Ernesto Rossi, Henry Irving, Thomas W. Keene, and Ambrose Small) and theaters (Woodland, California; Group Theatre; Margo Jones Theatre). Richard Moody's essay on "The Formative Decade" (pp. 113–34) is particularly provocative and provides a factual and anecdotal commentary on an important period in American theater history. C. D. Johnson's *19th Century Theatrical Memoirs* (Greenwood) is still another kind of source for American theater historians.

### v. Eugene O'Neill and His Dramas

The contributions of Eugene O'Neill still provide a major focal point for scholarly study of American drama. This year there were five books and more than a score of essays that dealt with his work: his thought, his plays, his women characters, his techniques in comparison with his contemporaries. One of the most revealing books for students of O'Neill is *"The Theatre We Worked For": The Letters of Eugene O'Neill to Kenneth Macgowan* (Yale), edited by Jackson R. Bryer and introduced in a substantial and provocative essay by Travis Bogard. Divided into four sections represented by 164 letters, the volume includes all surviving correspondence. James A. Robinson's *Eugene O'Neill and Oriental Thought* (So. Ill.) is an extremely illuminating study of O'Neill's fascination with Eastern mysticism and the tension it created within him as it warred with his Western heritage. Developing his thesis from *The Fountain, Marco Millions, The Great God Brown,* and *Lazarus Laughed,* as well as *Strange Interlude, Dynamo, Day's Without End,* through *The Iceman Cometh* and *Long Day's Journey into Night,* Robinson very astutely concludes that O'Neill probably always had a "divided vision." Michael Manheim's *Eugene O'Neill's New Language of Kinship* (Syracuse) is a very personal reaction to O'Neill's plays in terms of motifs. Essentially there is no "new language" but rather a new interpretation of O'Neill's work by one who is fascinated with the personal struggles that evoked such expressions of creativity. *O'Neill on Film* (Fairleigh Dickinson) by John Orlandello traces the 50-year history of some 13 adaptations of O'Neill's plays. On the whole the author provides a clear-headed evaluation along with the interesting anecdotes that come with good research. Normand Berlin's *Eugene*

*O'Neill* (Grove) begins with a thoughtful discussion of *Long Day's Journey*, degenerates into a pedantic discussion, and concludes on a defensive tone. Chronological and mainly perfunctory, such books hold too strongly personal observations to provide good introductions to a subject. Two essays consider O'Neill from a relatively general point of view. Joseph J. Moleski discusses "Eugene O'Neill and the Cruelty of Theater" (*CompD* 15:327–42) and Romulus Linney provides a personal view of O'Neill's fall from favor in "About O'Neill" (*EON* 6,iii:3–5).

With O'Neill's advent into the realm of world theater, comparativists joined theater historians from theater departments and drama critics from departments of English to evaluate a new phenomenon: an American dramatist whose plays found audiences throughout the world. Michael Hinden argues that Peter Shaffer is the major living heir to the O'Neill legacy. Comparing *Equus* with *The Great God Brown* and *Amadeus* with *The Iceman Cometh*, Hinden develops a theory that both create ritualistic elements and metaphysical themes in a personal search for a god: "When Playwrights talk to God: Peter Shaffer and the Legacy of O'Neill" (*CompD* 16:49–63). Michael Manheim concludes from a discussion of the "Dialogues Between Son and Mother in Chekhov's *The Sea Gull* and O'Neill's *Long Day's Journey into Night*" (*EON* 6:i,24–29) that the two saw life in similar ways. In a two-part essay, "O'Neill and Frank Wedekind" (*EON* 6:i,29–35;ii,17–21), Susan Tuck attempts to show the influence of Wedekind's *Frühlings Erwachen* and *Erdgeist* upon *Ah, Wilderness!* and *Strange Interlude* respectively.

The women in Eugene O'Neill's plays have been the subject of more than one Ph.D. dissertation over the past 20 years and several articles and book chapters, but the subject seems always open to reinterpretation, more particularly as the women in modern society adjust their views and sharpen their opinions. Accommodating to new perspectives, vol. 6, issue no. 2 of the *Eugene O'Neill Newsletter* focuses upon "O'Neill's Women." The general view is presented to rather little effect by Doris Nelson, "O'Neill's Women" (pp. 3–6). Trudy Drucker categorizes certain recurring female types in "Sexuality as Destiny: The Shadow Lives of O'Neill's Women" (pp. 7–10). A curiously cryptic discussion by Bette Mandl argues for "Absence as Presence: The Second Sex in *The Iceman Cometh*" (pp. 10–15). "Mother and Daughter in *Mourning Becomes Electra*" (pp. 15–17) are compared by William Young. The most valuable of the essays in this issue is Linda Ben-Zui's "Susan Glaspell and Eugene O'Neill" (pp. 21–29) in which O'Neill's personal life and professional writing are shown to have received substantial support from Glaspell.

Most of the essays that appear in the *Eugene O'Neill Newsletter* are brief comments, short notes that draw attention to an idea, suggest a comparison or source, or describe a production. There are few fully developed theses and substantially documented theories. Issue no. 3 of vol. 6 focuses upon O'Neill's short plays. Robert Sarlós comments on the original production of *The Rope*: "Nina Moise Directs Eugene O'Neill's *The Rope*" (pp. 9–12). "O'Neill's Use of Language in *Where the Cross is Made*" (pp. 12–13) is the subject of Robert Perrin's very brief observations. Stephen King sees a relationship between " 'The Formless Fear' of O'Neill's Emperor and Tennyson's King" (pp. 14–15). In "*Fog*: An O'Neill Theological Miscellany" (pp. 15–20) Gerald Lee Ratliff tries to gather the strands of O'Neill's eclectic theology. Esther Timar lists "Possible Sources for Two O'Neill One-Acts" (pp. 20–23); the plays are *Recklessness* and *In the Zone*. Gordon Bordewyk and Michael McGowan suggest "Another Source of Eugene O'Neill's *The Emperor Jones*" (pp. 30–31).

One interesting point concerning O'Neill scholarship is its inclusive character and the variety of approach. Scholars are obviously interested in O'Neill the man and writer and a broad spectrum of his plays. In "The Longing for Death in O'Neill's *Strange Interlude* and *Mourning Becomes Electra*" (*L&P* 31[1981]:37–48) Robert Feldman acknowledges the past analysis that has focused on the Oedipus complex in Freudian psychology and argues that the Freudian notion of a death instinct expressed in *Beyond the Pleasure Principle* is even more meaningful in understanding the two plays. Through his reading of modern and contemporary plays Albert Wertheim has concluded that in *Days Without End* O'Neill created a new technique for which more recent playwrights should be grateful: "Eugene O'Neill's *Days Without End* and the Tradition of the Split Character in Modern American and British Drama" (*EON* 6:i, 5–9). *To Hold a Mirror to Nature: Dramatic Images and Reflections*, vol. 1, ed. Karelisa V. Hartigan (Univ. Press) includes an interesting essay concerned with the concept of time and the control of the tempo of a play through its structure. The author of the essay, Betsy Greenleaf Yarrison, uses *The Emperor Jones* to illustrate her argument of "The Future in the Instant" (pp. 137–60). In "O'Neill's Transcendence of Melodrama in *A Touch of the Poet* and *A Moon for the Misbegotten*" (*CompD* 16:238–50) Michael Manheim argues, largely through assertion rather than analysis and firm supporting evidence, that O'Neill was capable of writing only melodrama prior to these two plays, which show him using "the free and open pathos of traditional tragedy." To say the least, it is not a well-designed or compelling piece of scholarship. Among the more thoughtful commentaries on O'Neill's work is Peter Egri's monograph, which was originally published in Budapest in 1980. The *Eugene O'Neill Newsletter* printed the second part, "*The Iceman Cometh*, European Origins and American Originality" (6:i,16–24).

#### vi. Drama and Theater Between the World Wars

Among American dramatists no one has achieved a position of importance and influence in playwriting circles with fewer plays to his credit than Edward Sheldon. Now there is a carefully researched and generally well-documented book on this man, *Edward Sheldon* (TUSAS 401), by Loren K. Ruff. Although limited by the format of this series, Ruff has been fortunate to have excellent sources for his discussion, and all of Sheldon's work is presented in the framework of the society that make the plays possible. Ruff's major contribution is his explanation of Sheldon's influence on other American dramatists and the American theater in general. One of Sheldon's forgotten contemporaries, Jessie Lynch Williams, won the first Pulitzer Prize for drama with *Why Marry?* in 1918. Considering the recent changes in society, it was probably inevitable that someone would rediscover this play, and Judith L. Stephens presents a limited analysis in "*Why Marry?*: The 'New Woman' of 1918" (*TJ* 34:183–96). Stephens' approach is one of skepticism, as she discusses the heroine of the play in terms of four characteristics often assigned to female characters and concludes that she was more of a "transitional character" than a complete "New Woman." Another dramatist who wrote very few plays and survived his last work by more than two score years was Marc Connelly. In "*Green Pastures*, American Religiosity in the Theatre" (*American Culture* 5:51–58) Walter C. Daniel is determined to praise the play as a religious experience.

One of the best written and most important articles on dramatists

of this period is Douglas Wixson's "Thornton Wilder and Max Rein-
hardt: Artists in Collaboration" (*StHum* 9:ii,3–14), which explores
the friendship that existed between the two men, explains some of
their similar approaches to theater and comments perceptively on
their collaboration in the first production of *The Merchant of Yon-
kers.* Another fine article showing the careful scholarship that should
accompany a good idea is Richard J. Altenbaugh's "Proletarian Drama: An Educational Tool of the American Labor College Movement"
(*TJ* 34:197–210). After a detailed study of the social and educational
purposes and programs of three labor colleges, Altenbaugh concludes
that their drama "resembled agit prop and served as a vital pedagogical tool." Townsend Ludington uses some unpublished letters along
with the plays of John Howard Lawson and John Dos Passos to create
a substantial and well-ordered study of the political stance of these
writers and their work together in the New Playwrights group. His
essay is entitled "Friendship won't stand that: John Howard Lawson
and John Dos Passos' Struggle for an Ideological Ground to Stand
On" (pp. 46–66) in *Literature at the Barricades: The Writer in the
1930's* (Alabama), ed. Ralph F. Bogardus and Fred Holson. Another
writer who has seemed always at the barricades is Lillian Hellman,
the subject of Bernard F. Dick's *Hellman in Hollywood* (Fairleigh
Dickinson). The best parts of the book are the detailed analyses of
the scripts Hellman wrote for the movies and the movie adaptations
others created from her plays. The writing, however, is uneven, and
Dick ostentatiously uses *Julia* to try to explain Lillian Hellman to
posterity.

    During the 1930s Edna Ferber was undoubtedly America's most
popular female writer. An essay on "The Americanization of Edna:
A Study of Ms. Ferber's Jewish American Identity" by Steven P.
Horowitz and Miriam J. Landsman (*SAJL* 2:69–80) refers to her ten
plays to establish that identity. Another essay in the same volume,
Harold Cantor's "Odets' Yinglish: The Psychology of Dialect as Dialogue" (pp. 61–68) provides an excellent analysis of Odets' conscious
attempt to create an "art language from Yiddish roots."

    Theater between the two world wars usually attracts historians
interested in the Group Theatre, Playwrights Theatre, Federal Theatre, or Theatre Guild movements. Those researching the Provincetown generally concentrate on O'Neill or another of the big three—
O'Neill, Jones, Macgowan—but Robert Sarlós has now written about

that theater from the perspective of Jig Cook in *Jig Cook and the Provincetown Players, Theatre in Ferment* (Mass.). There are nine sections in the book. Some of them have appeared in print previously, yet the volume is extremely valuable—well documented and effectively illustrated, with each production described in clear detail. Jig Cook left the Provincetown and America in 1922, and the book ends that year, but Sarlos also provides a very thoughtful annotated dramatis personae of some 90 people involved in activities of the Provincetown. *Uncle Sam Presents: A Memoir of the Federal Theatre, 1935–1939* by Tony Buttetta and Barry Witham (Penn.) is a personal account of this theater project by Buttetta, who worked with the New York unit of the Federal Theatre Project and reported for the *Federal Theatre Magazine*. In 40 scenes Buttetta tells his story; it is a personal response, not a history, and completely lacking the mechanics of scholarship. It is an interesting story although occasionally tedious, and one misses the names of other workers and the obligatory sentence that gives Dirksen his villainous due.

In a detailed discussion of Robert Edmond Jones's designs and Hopkins' direction, Jennifer Parent recreates "Arthur Hopkins' Production of Sophie Treadwell's *Machinal* (1928)" (*TDR* 26:87–100). Parent's objective is to focus upon the expressionistic technique that distinguished an otherwise common story. In a comparable effort to recreate a production David Harris describes "The Original *Four Saints in Three Acts* (1934)" (*TDR* 26:102–30), the opera by Gertrude Stein and Virgil Thompson, as a "seminal work of the American avant-garde." Rather little has been written about Stein's plays; "Rescued Readings: Characteristic Deformations in the Language of Gertrude Stein's Plays" by Elizabeth Fifer (*TSLL* 24:394–428) focuses upon the one area in which Stein's plays can stand analysis. The final item relevant to this period is valuable only as a personal reflection by Erskine Caldwell, who discusses his attendance at a recent production of *Tobacco Road* at the Beverly Hills Playhouse and the memories it evoked: "Night in November/Beverly Hills, California" (*GaR* 36:102–11).

### vii. Arthur Miller, Tennessee Williams, and Edward Albee

The major contribution to Miller scholarship this year was a collection of essays in the Twentieth Century Views series edited by Robert

A. Martin, *Arthur Miller* (Prentice-Hall). The volume consists of
general views and specific commentary and includes the thoughts of
some of the best-known critics of modern American drama. Of the
14 essays six were written especially for this collection, and to these
are added Charles A. Carpenter's "Studies of Arthur Miller's Drama:
A Selective International Bibliography, 1966–1979" (pp. 205–19)
and an illuminating "Introduction" (pp. 1–12) by Martin, who builds
his thesis around Miller's "obsessive subject—and his best one—" the
American Dream and its effect upon the family.

In "The Mills of the Gods: Economics in the Plays of Arthur Miller" (pp. 75–96) Thomas E. Porter finds Miller to be "a quintessential
American playwright" for centering his dramatic conflicts always in
the struggle between the ideal and the actualities of society. Enoch
Brater in "Miller's Realism and *Death of a Salesman*" (pp. 115–26)
considers Miller's realism as "emblematic," a realism that "holds the
naturalistic and the symbolic in perfect equilibrium." In "*The Crucible*: 'This Fool and I' " (pp. 127–38) Walter J. Meserve argues that
Proctor "is that common man who frequently lacks good judgement
and acts the fool that all men who contend honestly with life suffer
and understand, becoming finally a wiser man than he realizes, one
who can be mistaken for a heroic figure." J. L. Styan writes a delightfully phrased and compelling essay explaining "Why *A View from
the Bridge* Went Down Well in London: The Story of a Revision"
(pp. 139–48). As he says, "When Miller displays dramatic insight
beyond mere literacy, he is irresistible." "Pessimism in *After the Fall*"
(pp. 159–72) exposes for Stephen S. Stanton the new philosophy of
life Miller presumably accepted in 1964. The other eight essays in
the collection are reprinted from the writings of such Miller scholars
as Ruby Cohn, Gerald Weales, Leonard Moss, and Benjamin Nelson.

At a conference held at the University of Michigan, 9–11 April
1981, entitled "The Writer's Craft: The 50th Anniversary Hopwood
Festival" Miller gave the keynote address. Published as "American
Writer: The American Theatre" (*MQR* 21:4–20) the speech includes
the personal observations of this winner of two Hopwood Awards
and some interesting, sometimes humorous, comments about changes
in the theater from the 1930s through the present where Miller finds
the theater caught between "greed and irresponsibility"—as if this
conclusion suggested a change! In an essay published in *English
Studies* (63:32–36), "Society vs. the Individual in Arthur Miller's

*The Crucible*," Jean-Marie Bonnet appears surprised to discover that the play is difficult to classify because Miller fuses the individual to society. Such a structure, she complains, does not allow her to draw a neat conclusion. The reissuing of Richard L. Evans' *Psychology and Arthur Miller* (Praeger, 1981) adds only a new introduction of a single paragraph in which Evans praises Miller as a writer well equipped to exchange ideas with a psychologist. Neil Carson's *Arthur Miller*, a new study published as part of the Grove Press Modern Dramatist series, does little for Miller scholarship. An uncertain appraisal of either vague or conventional commentary, the work finally underscores Miller as a religious writer. With the exception of Martin's collection and Miller's speech, the year provided nothing lasting for Miller scholarship.

Tennessee Williams added to his published autobiographical observations in "The Man in the Overstuffed Chair" (*Antæus* 45–46: 281–91) but attracted very little critical comment this year. One essay well worth reading, however, is Brian Parker's "The Composition of *The Glass Menagerie*: An Argument for Complexity" (*MD* 25:409–22). A number of scholars have dealt with the composition of *The Glass Menagerie*, but Parker points out that new materials at the Humanities Research Center of the University of Texas will affect these previous discussions as well as the final interpretation of the play. Parker also comments on the use of projections in the play and their impact on later drama. From a comparativist's point of view Gilbert Debusscher discusses "French Stowaways on an American Milk Train: Williams, Cocteau and Peyrefitte" (*MD* 25:399–408). Debusscher sees a definite pattern which Williams could have borrowed from Cocteau's *L'Aigle à deux têtes*, but he's less certain of the influence of Roger Peyrefitte's novel, *L'Erilé de Capri*. Both essays show a serious and spreading interest in the works of Williams, who will clearly be the subject of many more articles in 1983.

It is a revealing point that the three major American dramatists of the mid-20th century found time either to write or to speak about themselves. Edward Albee was interviewed at Berkeley on 23 September 1980, fielding a variety of topics about himself and his work: Matthew C. Roudané, "An Interview with Edward Albee" (*SHR* 16:29–44). Otherwise, most of the publications on Albee were reprints. Harold P. Blum's "A Psychoanalytic View of *Who's Afraid of Virginia Woolf?*" (1969) appeared in *Lives, Events and Other Play-*

*ers, Directions in Psychobiography*, ed. Joseph T. Coltreca (Jason Aronson, 1981, pp. 272–83). The same collection included Jules Glenn's "The Adoption Theme in Edward Albee's *Tiny Alice* and *The American Dream*" (pp. 255–69, original pub. 1974). Richard E. Amacher published a revised edition of *Edward Albee* (TUSAS 141) with comments on eight plays since his first edition (1969)—a chapter on six of them and references to *Adaptation* and *Lolita* (unpublished). The format of the book remains the same, and Amacher has provided short sections on "Albee Today" and "Albee Tomorrow" in which he hedges all statements. The only new essay on Albee is interesting mainly as a sociological observation that Albee, in the late 1950s, wrote three plays concerned with abandonment when he was temporarily estranged from his parents: *Zoo Story, Bessie Smith,* and *Sandbox.* The observer is Lucinda P. Gabbard, "Edward Albee's Triptych on Abandonment" (*TCL* 28:14–33).

### viii. Some Contemporary Dramatists

Although the names of successful dramatists of the 1930s appear occasionally in books or articles dealing with themes related to their work, there is relatively little attention paid to such dramatists as Maxwell Anderson, Robert Sherwood, Elmer Rice, Paul Green, Lillian Hellman, Rachel Crothers, S. N. Behrman, William Saroyan, and others whose plays caught headlines in *Variety* for years. The dramatists since 1950—other than the three just treated—have generally lacked the sustaining power of these comparative giants from the near past. William Inge had it, but his unwarranted neglect by critics will eventually be discovered.

There is also relatively little current concentration of criticism on contemporary dramatists as scholars scan the theatre front for interesting subject matter. In "The McCarthy Era and the American Theatre" (*TJ* 34:210–22), for example, Albert Wertheim studies the impact of HUAC and Senator McCarthy on American drama. Barry Witham looks at a number of plays and assesses three—*5th of July, Loose Ends,* and *Alfred Dies*—as reactions to the social and political situation in America around the mid-1970s. Ellen Schiff's *From Stereotype to Metaphor, The Jew in Contemporary Drama* (SUNY) surveys the presentation of the Jew on stage. She shows a sense of history by identifying George Jessop's *Sam'l of Posen* (1881) as a modest beginning and then jumps to more modern periods. Plays by Odets, Chayefsky, Miller, and Inge are plumbed for Jewish types while Hansberry's *The Sign in Sidney Brustein's Window* reveals the "new Jew." Judith Olareson's presentation of *The American Woman Playwright: A View of Criticism and Characterization* (Whitson, 1981) appears defensive and resentful as she emphasizes the work of 17 playwrights. Her thesis is simple if forced: 40 years ago women in plays were simple, passive, and socially subjugated; today they are complex, active, autonomous beings. Waving this thesis like a banner throughout her discussions, Olareson condemns all who do not believe as she does. One is reminded of the views of Amanda Cross, a writer of mystery stories, who says that a woman is not liberated until she stops caring what other women think. What a vastly different approach is reflected in John Jones's "Interview with Beth Henley" in *Mississippi Writers Talking* (vol. 2; Miss.; pp. 169–90), who, in spite of the inexperienced oral historian conducting the interview, comes across as an intelligent, perceptive, and charmingly youthful person.

From the scattered essays on contemporary drama and dramatists a few old and respected names appear among the new. Houghton Mifflin will soon publish the letters of Archibald MacLeish, and in the *Paris Review* (24:104–44) readers get a preview from the 1926–69 letters: R. H. Winnick and Archibald MacLeish, "Archibald Mac-Leish: Selected Letters." Within these letters, however, there is nothing on MacLeish's plays. Another poet and dramatist, William Carlos Williams, is the subject of a fine study by David A. Fedo: "The Meaning of Love in William Carlos Williams' *Dream of Love*" (*CL* 23:169–90). Concentrating on the two major characters in the play and the different ideas of love presented, Fedo provides a thorough and well-written discussion of the development of the play and some of the reasons why it is generally cited as Williams' best play. Not poetry but language and structure, a "non-traditional collage-like form," interests Michael O'Neill as he discusses "History as Dramatic Present: Arthur L. Kopit's *Indians*" (*TJ* 34:493–504). Kopit, the writer argues, employs diverse techniques to create a mosaic of scenes and images superimposed on a myth from history and counterpointed by contemporary events.

The single exception to the theory of scattered scholarship pertaining to contemporary drama is Sam Shepard, a popular subject for comment and assessment. Critics like Ruby Cohn vie with themselves to create titles appropriate to the praise in their essays, or perhaps titles to match the titles of Shepard's plays. At any rate, writers find something different in his plays, something close to America—in fact, in fiction, in spirit, and in manner. Shepard fascinates because he appears to present Americans with a new view of themselves and in a startling fashion. He seems to have an answer; he is "Sam Shepard: Escape Artist" (*PR* 49:253–61), according to R. Wetzstean. A new myth of America appears on stage, Mark Siegel explains, in "Holy-Ghosts, the Mythic Cowboy in the Plays of Sam Shepard" (*BRMMLA* 36:235–48). Critics also see Shepard as a dominant force in the development of contemporary American drama. After summarizing the activities of playwrights who were successful in the 1960s, Richard L. Homan suggests that only Lanford Wilson and Shepard have continued to produce significant work during the '70s. Although his essay, "American Playwrights in the 1970's: Rabe and Shepard: (*CritQ* 24:73–82), has a dual focus which is never reconciled and attempts too much to provide well-considered conclusions, Homan's selection of Shepard is logical and appropriate. As if to provide a stamp of critical approval for this relatively recent appearance into American theatre history, Twayne Publishers have a new volume by Doris Auerback, *Sam Shepard, Arthur Kopit and the Off-Broadway Theater* (TUSAS 432). This very slight book follows the usual pattern of the series with brief chapters—seven for Shepard, five for Kopit, and one on the history of the Off-Broadway Theater. But it says something about the considered importance of number 5 on the scholarly list: O'Neill, Miller, Williams, Albee, Shepard.

### *ix.* Contemporary Theater and Theaters

The concept of theater is constantly changing. Perhaps that is the single essential unchanging aspect of theater. And surely theater must always be contemporary; it must always be now. It was to the Greeks and Romans, to the people in the pit at Shakespeare's Globe, to the Kabuki audiences of 17th-century Japan, to the Bowery b'hoys of Brooklyn in mid-19th-century America. For the most part, historians and compilers of information have kept track of theater in New York. Californians are now beginning to assert themselves along this line. *California Theater Annual: 1982* (Performing Arts Network), ed.

Barbara Isenberg, is designed to record the state's professional theater activities for 1981–82. Fully documented and very well illustrated with information according to regions, the annual indicates that there are a surprising number of plays produced each year, both traditional and contemporary.

To suggest some of the oddities on stage now accepted as theater, Theodore Shank has written *American Alternative Theater*, part of a new series from Grove Press, "written for people interested in modern theatre," etc. but "without jargon and an excess of footnotes." Fortunately, this volume has notes and a bibliography, although no one could write about contemporary theater without using jargon. At any rate, the book purports to describe the alternative theater being offered to the complacent middle-class society of America. Shank deals mainly with works existing "only in the audible, visual, and social circumstances of performance" appearing in the 1960s and 1970s. Providing a running explication of theater actions and situations such as a section on "Self as Content," Shank shuns a conclusion, while the reader is probably relieved to know that there is an alternative to "alternative theater."

*New Broadways, Theatre Across America, 1950–1980* (Rowan and Littlefield) attempts to fill out the picture of theater in America. Gerald M. Berkowitz, the author, has no startling observations or a clear thesis; he simply provides a 30-year survey of Off-Broadway, Regional, and Alternative theater with a glimpse of Broadway and some exceptionally well-chosen illustrations.

Among the ethnic theaters that have gained prominence during the last quarter of a century, black theater has been most active and warrants special attention. *Black Theater in America* (Crowell) is the title of James Haskins' survey of black theater from the beginning to the present. Mainly concerned with black actors and black theaters, Haskins has a reasonably balanced approach: the post-Civil War, the Depression years and on to the '60s and '70s. The book is a serious study of an important part of American theater, and it is well written. It is unfortunate, however, that Haskins did not envision a serious audience. He eliminated notes, sources, and all but a sketchy bibliography; otherwise, the book could have been a valuable addition to existing scholarship. *Black American Literature Forum* (16: iv) also provides another kind of historical review of black acting and black theater. It must suffice here, however, to provide only a list of the essays, all quite brief and introduced by James V. Hatch and Andrzej Ceynowa: John Dewbury, "The African Grove Theatre and Company" (pp. 128–31), Errol Hill, "S. Morgan Smith: Successor to Ira Aldridge" (pp. 132–35), Edward A. Robinson, "The Pekin: The Genesis of American Black Theater" (pp. 136–38), John G. Monroe, "Charles Gilpin and the Drama League Controversy" (pp. 139–41), Andrea J. Nouryeh, "When the Lord Was a Black Man: A Fresh Look at the Life of Richard Berry Harrison" (pp. 142–46), VeVe A. Clark, "Katherine Dunham's *Tropical Revue*" (pp. 147–52), Stephen M. Vallillo, "The Battle of the Black Mikados" (pp. 153–57), Rosetta Reitz, "Hot Snow: Valaida Snow (Queen of the Trumpet Sings and Swings)" (pp. 158–60), Kathy Anne Perkins, "Black Backstage Workers, 1900–1969" (pp. 160–63), Thomas D. Pawley, "Three Views of the Returning Black Veteran" (pp. 163–67), and James V. Hatch, "Sittin' at the Banquet, Talkin' with Ourselves (An Open Letter to Theatre Scholars and Historians on the Status of Black Theatre Research and Publication" (pp. 168–70). Neither of these volumes, however, treats the black playwright fairly, and the reason is not clear. Certainly, there are distinguished black contemporary playwrights worthy of scholarly analysis. One essay this year on Amiri Baraka, however, reveals an interesting confrontation between two moving forces in the modern theater, Sandra L. Richards, "Negative Forces and Positive Non-Entities: Images of Women in the Dramas of Amiri Baraka" (*TJ* 34:233–40). Richards condemns Baraka's portrayal of women as "instructive of what writers must not continue to do."

### x. Conclusion

Any attempt to evaluate or comment on scholarship relating to American drama during a given year is certain to be frustrating. As scholars from different disciplines become involved, the definition of terms—drama and theater—presents a problem. When playwrights, for example, produce plays that are essentially created by actors through trial and error movements and speeches, discussions of the theories of performance from essays and books dealing with history and criticism seem necessary. The editor of *Modern Drama*, for example, included an essay by Marie Claire Pasquier on "Richard Foreman: Comedy Inside Out" (25:534–44) because she saw some value in Ontological-Hysteric Theatre where one of Foreman's frequent concerns is an "impatience with our bodily limitations," according to Pasquier. This essay was followed in *Modern Drama* by Herbert Blau's "Comedy Since the Absurd" (pp. 548–68) in which Blau's syntax presents as much challenge as his ideas. "When we think on the subject of comedy," he writes, "then, any time since the Absurd, we may be thinking of a very painful subject, or subject and object appallingly confused, which is the congenital tragic substance of the most incisive comedy since Oedipus breached the confusion with his mother's brooch." If critical commentary is meant to be esoteric, why are not clear comments by playwrights more meaningful to scholars?

Presumably, any well-researched commentary on theaters has value for those who will assess American drama. "Portraits in Words" (*PerfAJ* 6:27–8) and "Photo History of La Mama" (*PerfAJ* 6:18–26), therefore, should be noted for historians of the plays performed at Ellen Stewart's La Mama. People interested in "intercultural performances" and an "ethnography of performance" should read "Performance in 'America's Little Switzerland': New Glarus, Wisconsin" (*TDR* 26:111–24) by Phillip Zarrilli and Deborah Neff. On the international front Bonnie Marranca presents the reactions of foreign critics to avant-garde theater in America: "American Theatre Abroad —The European View, Interviews with Phillippa Wehle, Ritsnert Ten Cate and Attansio De Felice" (*PerfAJ* 6:iii). But if one wants to know something about the most impressive productions across the country of American plays during the 1981–82 season, read Gerald Weales' "American Theater Watch, 1981–82" (*GaR* 36:517–29). In this article Weales comments with his customary wit and wisdom on some 15 plays that may or may not remain on the American stage or appear in histories of American drama but have some merit as literature and theatre art. All of these views or approaches to the study of American drama have potential scholarly value, and a certain amount of attention should be paid to them—if only by the writer of this essay.

*Indiana University*

# 19. Black Literature

## *John M. Reilly*

Though it underlies all approaches to black literature, a didactic motive is most clear in thematic studies and prescriptive theories of criticism. The former focus on the special experiences related by black writing, while the latter propose to strengthen the black community. There is also in criticism nearly as strong a devotion to the task of securing appreciation for black writers as skilled artists. Theoretically there may be contradiction. The assumed moral dimension of art would be more evident in tracts than in the sophisticated structures created by literary imagination. Yet black culture is replete with marvelous aesthetic effects in music and oral utterance. How can the critic fail to stress the counterpart effects in literature? More to the point, how can the peculiarly literary qualities of imaginative writing be synthesized in critical practice with the moral dimension of black literature?

Reintegration of art and social purpose occurs most completely in studies of genre and period formation. As the often-quoted words of W. E. B. Du Bois on double consciousness assert, the black writer works within two traditions. One is received from the shared possession of European-American culture, the other derives from the modifications of an African-American heritage. The available genres of the novel, verse, and drama are reconstructed in some degree or another when undertaken by an Afro-American artist. Similarly the evolution of black writing proceeds in large measure through the phases familiar in the dominant American literary histories. There are as many romantic and naturalistic black writings as there are white writings in those modes, but the chronology is not synchronized exactly with the progress of Euro-American belles lettres. To the extent that there are historical causes for the manner and modes of writing, or political and social events providing rubrics for the sense of association among writers in time, those causes and rubrics are specialized and differentiated by Afro-American experiences. So the literary history of black writing must be constructed in and for itself, with reference to but not duplication of "white" literary history.

The reader will see that many critics of the work of 1982 speak directly to these issues. There are too many to name as examples here, but even when studies are not explicitly directed to genre or literary period, they are increasingly informed by awareness of a necesssary reconstruction. More and more of the basic materials for constructing literary history are being recovered; the Afro-American canon expands; and the interpretation of texts increasingly finds content through form.

### *i.* Bibliography

*Early Black Bibliographies, 1863–1918* (Garland), compiled with an introduction for each of 19 rare, out-of-print references by Betty Kaplan Gubert, recovers such interesting documents as *A Select Bibliography of the Negro American,* prepared under direction of W. E. B. Du Bois for the Tenth Atlanta Conference in 1905. Periodical citations make this bibliography particularly valuable. Other items in Gubert's book will be of varying use to the literary scholar, but certainly ready availability will encourage consultation of the 113 years of publications listed in the *Catalogue of Anti-Slavery Publications in America* published by Samuel May, Jr., in 1863 and the Library of Congress publications prepared by A. P. C. Griffin on the Negro Question (1903) and the 14th and 15th Constitutional Amendments (1906). Other Library of Congress listings of references on the Ku Klux Klan (1913), Ethnography (1916), and the history of slavery (1917) provide useful representations of contemporary study. A *Catalogue of Rare Books and Pamphlets* prepared by Robert M. Adger in 1894 presents 320 items in a dealer's sale list; Daniel A. P. Murray's *Preliminary List . . .* for the Paris Exposition in 1900 features works by black authors; the holdings of William Carl Bolivar, a founding member of the American Negro Historical Society, are shown in the catalogue of his library (1914), while the preeminent collector Arthur A. Schomburg appears in the volume through the collectors' guide he prepared for the first annual exhibition of the Negro Library Association. For the modern investigator Gubert ties the 19 bibliographies together with an author index.

Another work providing guidance to important older publications is Walter C. Daniel's *Black Journals of the United States*, the first in the Greenwood Press series, Historical Guides to the World's Periodicals and Newspapers. Daniel details 107 publications, including two from the West Indies, in essays on the historical origins, an index of source locations, and publication history. Covering publications issued from 1827 to 1980, the profiles are arranged alphabetically beginning with *Abbot's Monthly* and continuing to *The Western Journal of Black Studies*. Drawing upon the *Annual Magazine Subject Index* published by F. W. Faxon Co. from 1907 to 1949, Richard Newman has edited *Black Index: Afro-Americans in Selected Periodicals, 1907–1949* (Garland, 1981). Approximately 350 periodicals were consulted, and 1,000 articles are indexed in this work, with Newman's particular contribution being provision of author access in addition to the topical references in the alphabetical listing. Because it is separately indexed, the *Journal of Negro History* is omitted from the listings.

Since 1975 the publications catalogued by the research departments of the New York Public Library and the Library of Congress have been noted in annual guides, the latest of which is *Bibliographic Guide to Black Studies in 1981* (Hall). Main entries, titles, and subject listings are integrated in a single alphabetical arrangement providing LC catalog and ISBN information. Entries from volumes 11–15 of *American History and Life* pertaining to Afro-America have been selected by Dwight L. Smith and compiled in *Afro-American History: A Bibliography*, vol. 2 (Santa Barbara, Calif.: ABC-Clio, 1981). The present volume provides 4,113 abstracts from periodical literature published between 1974 and 1978. Literary topics may be located within the categorical arrangement of the volume and by aid of subject and author indexes.

Concentrating specifically on literature, Margaret Perry has prepared *The Harlem Renaissance: An Annotated Bibliography and Commentary* (Garland). Attempting to be comprehensive, though admittedly not exhaustive, Perry lists secondary works up to 1980 in eight categories: bibliographical and reference material, literary histories, general studies, studies of 18 representative major authors, miscellaneous materials such as newspaper columns, anthologies, holdings in libraries and special collections, and dissertations.

One of the poets treated by Perry receives more ample coverage in Robert G. O'Meally's "An Annotated Bibliography of the Works of Sterling A. Brown" (*Callaloo* 5,i–ii:90–105). This revised and expanded version of a listing originally prepared for *CLAJ* (1975) presents the works chronologically within eight categories that cover poems, short stories, and critical writings, as well as reviews and recordings. Andrea B. Rushing's "An Annotated Bibliography of Images of Black Women in Black Literature" (*CLAJ* 25[1981]:234–62) is another updated listing, this one originally issued in 1978 in *CLAJ*. The 66 items include books, articles, and dissertations published from 1955 to 1979.

The exemplary model for establishing an author's canon is found in *Richard Wright: A Primary Bibliography* by Charles T. Davis and Michel Fabre (Hall). Drawing upon the resources of the Wright archive in the James Weldon Johnson Collection at Yale University, the book presents published works chronologically, in generic subdivisions, indicating and describing extant typescripts and carbons; distinguishing versions of the same work in draft; and cross-referencing to reprints. A second section presents a similar though more limited description of typescripts for 178 unpublished works arranged alphabetically by Wright's working title or by a title assigned for identification in the archive. Unpublished correspondence, still controlled by Mrs. Wright, is omitted from the listing and prevents the volume from being definitive, but what is described and indexed offers scholars the chance to study the evolution of texts and, thus, Wright's application to technical problems of composition. Margaret A. Van Antwerp's entry on Richard Wright (pp. 397–460) in the *Dictionary of Literary Biography, Documentary Series*, vol. 2 (Gale) is selective, though it provides lists of works, biographies, and bibliographical sources.

The possibility of definitive work necessarily eludes bibliographers of contemporary authors, so *Ishmael Reed, A Primary and Secondary Bibliography* by Elizabeth A. Settle and Thomas A. Settle (Hall) provides the most help in listing works about Reed. These secondary works are entered alphabetically within an annual chronology through 1980. They are annotated and indexed. Primary works are presented according to the Hall format by genre within annual listings. Those, too, are annotated. In a review of the book Joe Weixlmann (*BALF* 16:81–83) sharply criticizes the loose use of bibliographical terms and the failure to differentiate paperback editions.

Scholars wishing to initiate studies in contemporary black fiction will find help in "A Chronological Checklist of Afro-American Novels, 1945–1980" prepared by Peter Bruck and Wolfgang Karrer, with the help of Kurt Westermann, in their edited volume, *The Afro-American Novel Since 1960* (pp. 207–25). The list aims to be definitive through inclusion of paperback original, small-press, and "vanity" editions, all provided with place and date of publication.

James V. Hatch addresses scholars in "Sittin' at the Banquet, Talkin' with Ourselves (An Open Letter to Theatre Scholars and Historians on the Status of Black Theatre Research and Publication)" (*BALF* 16:168–69). Hatch comments on the growth of the body of research in the last 20 years, argues that black theater history must enter "mainstream" books, and provides "A Bibliography of Some Black Theatre Arts Publications, 1970–1982," listing 22 bibliographical and reference works, 23 historical-critical studies, 24 biographical works, 51 available acting editions of plays, and special issues of periodicals and anthologies in print.

### *ii.* Fiction

*a.* **Douglass, Chesnutt, Steward.** Among the contents of the volume *Autographs for Freedom* (1853), published to raise funds for *Frederick Douglass's Paper*, was an adaptation of the story of Madison Washington, leader of a revolt on *The Creole*, written by Douglass himself. In "Storytelling in Early Afro-American Fiction: Frederick Douglass' 'The Heroic Slave'" (*GaR* 36:355–68) Robert B. Stepto shows the artful parallel Douglass produces between the slave hero and the white heroes of Virginia and the subtle techniques that originated in Douglass' immediate rhetorical need to establish the authenticity of slave testimony.

Two of the year's essays on Charles W. Chesnutt attribute new significance to his first novel. In "Rena Walden: Chesnutt's Failed 'Future American'" (*CLAJ* 15:74–82) Sally Ann H. Ferguson relates the narrative of Rena and John Walden to the articles Chesnutt published in the *Boston Evening Transcript* during 1900, developing his theory that if the United States were left free to follow natural patterns, an octoroon population would secure the acceptance of blacks in the dominant culture. In Ferguson's reading John Walden is the prototype of the new American, Rena with her naiveté and ignorance an antitype programmed to fail. P. Jay Delmar treats the novel in "Coincidence in Charles W. Chesnutt's *The House Behind the Cedars*" (*ALR* 15:97–103). Delmar examines five occasions of plot coincidence and judges four of them functional means of emphasizing the role played by forces external to character in creating a nearly tragic action. In his article "Romanticism in the Fiction of Charles W. Chesnutt: The Influence of Dickens, Scott, Tourgée, and Douglass" (*CLAJ* 26:145–71) Richard O. Lewis attempts to account for the persistence of romanticism in Afro-American writing during an age of realism. The inquiry is apt, and the examples of congeniality between Chesnutt's outlook and the legacy of romanticism are critically acceptable as parallels, but the opportunity for a pointed thesis is lost in an overly general argument about universal themes said to have pulled Chesnutt onto the firmer ground of realism.

William L. Andrews memorializes the obscure T. G. Steward in "Liberal Religion and Free Love: An Undiscovered Afro-American Novel of the 1890s" (*MELUS* 9,i:23–36), a study of *A Charleston Love Story: or, Hortense Vanross* (1899). Pastor, educator, and historian, Steward devoted his only work of fiction to a presentation of Christian fundamentalism suggesting comparison to Harold Fredric's *The Damnation of Theron Ware*. Equally important is the fact that Steward, as a black historian, refused the practices of such reactionary fiction as the novels of Thomas Dixon to narrate a tale of the South in transition.

*b.* **Toomer, Fisher, Hurston.** Like Richard O. Lewis, Barbara E. Bowen also takes up the presence of romanticism in Afro-American writing. Bowen's "Untroubled Voice: Call-and-Response in *Cane*" (*BALF* 16:12–18) is, however, considerably more successful in focusing her conclusions and interpreting Jean Toomer's declaration that his book was a swan song. She sees *Cane* as investing the Afro-American call-and-response form with the problem of the romantic lyric: unity with nature. Narrators listen for a voice that will embody Toomer's new cultural myth, but the untroubled assumption that it will be heard is no longer possible; thus, *Cane* serves as an elegy for spiritual life. "Healing Songs: Secular Music in the Short Fiction of Rudolph Fisher" (*CLAJ* 26:191–203) by John McCluskey, Jr., describes Fisher's experimental use of music to suggest a spiritual collectivity, a seriousness of purpose that transforms such stock items as the cabaret dance scenes of the Harlem Renaissance.

Each of the year's articles on Zora Neale Hurston examines her most familiar work and offers an interpretation intended to be corrective. Wendy J. McCredie's "Authority and Authorization in *Their Eyes Were Watching God*" (*BALF* 16:25–28) distinguishes three phases in Hurston's development of a female voice of authority, that is to say, an autonomous assertion of self by the character Janie. "Listening and Living: Reading and Experience in *Their Eyes Were Watching God*" (*BALF* 16:29–33) by Maria Tai Wolff can be read as amplification of McCredie, for Wolff applies Ralph Freedman's conception of the lyrical novel to discern successive scenes of self-recognition that mark the transition to Janie's full womanhood. Mary Jane Lupton in "Zora Neale Hurston and the Survival of the Female" (*SLJ* 15:45–54) is struck by critical oversight of the disturbingly violent resolution of Janie's life with Tea Cake. The act by which Janie severs the relationship with her lover—shooting him to death —shows in its ambiguity the dominance of male-female conflict on the symbolic level of the text. Making the latent feminism specific in interpretation, Lupton produces a cogent relationship between the novel and theories of female evolution in feminist writing because of the depth of detail she summons. The final essay on Hurston, entitled "Nanny and Janie: Will the Twain Ever Meet?" (*JBlS* 12:403–14) is written by Lillie P. Howard, author of the TUSAS volume on Hurston (see *ALS 1980*, p. 442). Reconsidering a minor character usually treated by critics as simply an example of means to repress Janie, Howard justifies Nanny's concern for security and argues that in the conclusion of the novel Janie has no more complete an outlook than her grandmother, and in fact shares her way of thought.

**c. Wright, Himes, Ellison, Baldwin.** Yoshinobu Hakutani's compilation of *Critical Essays on Richard Wright* (Hall) joins with the bibliography by Davis and Fabre to make 1982 a banner year for Wright studies. Hakutani's introduction describing trends and citing outstanding or representative interpretations serves as an excellent setting for the 12 reprinted essays, most of them classic pieces published since the time of Wright's death, and 6 new pieces written for this volume. Donald B. Gibson's contribution, "Richard Wright: Aspects of His Afro-American Literary Relations" (pp. 82–90) contrasts Wright's major fiction with works by Chesnutt and Dunbar to show that black people need not be victims, that they have power. Fred L. Standley in " '. . . Farther and Farther Apart': Richard Wright and James Baldwin" (pp. 91–103) gives us a chronology of activities and events, a summary of interpretations, and the fundamental points of disagreement. In "Richard Wright, French Existentialism, and *The Outsider*" (pp. 182–98) Michel Fabre concentrates on the period from 1946 to 1953 to emphasize possible congruences of Wright's outlook and works by Sartre, de Beauvoir, and Camus. Similarly Nina Kressner Cobb in "Richard Wright and the Third World" (pp. 228–39) refers to modernization theory and the sociology of religion not so much to demonstrate a source for Wright's *Black Power* or *Pagan Spain* as to explicate his pro-Western attitude and sympathetic identification with Westernized elites. John M. Reilly takes as his subject the persona of autobiographical writings in "The Self-Creation of the Intellectual: *American Hunger* and *Black Power*" (pp. 213–27), arguing that autobiography is more guise than genre, as Wright creates a record not of fact but of the emergence of an autonomous imagination. In the sixth original essay for the Hakutani volume Robert Tener conducts an intense examination of Wright's 23 published haiku. "The Where, the When, the What: A Study of Richard Wright's Haiku" (pp. 273–98) attributes the production of a mass of verse in the disciplined haiku form during Wright's last year of life to his desire for an orderly universe and a unity with nature adumbrated in earlier works.

   More than once Wright spoke of the effect Gertrude Stein had on his work; yet the technical influence is apparently limited to some experimental passages in *Lawd Today* and in the unpublished "Tarbaby's Dawn." In "Richard Wright and Gertrude Stein" (*BALF* 16: 107–12) Eugene E. Miller explores the literary relationship with the aid of a manuscript in the archive entitled "Memories of My Grandmother." Miller concludes that Stein's *Melanctha* defamiliarized and then legitimized the familiar language of Wright's youth, and the shock of recognition he felt through Stein stimulated imaginative insights deeper than style. Günter H. Lenz looks squarely at the folk dimension of Wright's imagination in "Southern Exposures: The Urban Experience and the Re-Construction of Black Folk Culture and Community in the Works of Richard Wright and Zora Neale Hurston" (*NYFQ* 7[1981]:3–39). Lenz argues that while writers of the '20s sought to reclaim a folk culture that had been discredited by white stereotypes, the writers of the '30s had to revise the aesthetic tenets of the Renaissance to produce a more realistic literature. Through careful analysis of point of view in works from *Lawd Today* through *12 Million Black Voices* Lenz traces the emergence of a voice speaking from within felt history. As a contrast Hurston is represented as learning to speak naturally in a folk manner but ahistorically. John M. Reilly's "Richard Wright Preaches the Nation: *12 Million Black Voices*" (*BALF* 16:116–19) agrees with Miller and Lenz that Wright had to learn his cultural perspective and, with Lenz, asserts that a major source of knowledge was the theory of the Chicago school of sociology. The burden of Reilly's article is to characterize the simulated oral utterance in which Wright expressed the national consciousness he had earlier demanded in *Blueprint for Negro Writing*.

Claudia C. Tate's "Christian Existentialism in Richard Wright's *The Outsider*" (*CLAJ* 25:371–95) renews study of the philosophical underpinning of Wright's second novel. Where earlier criticism dealt with concepts of guilt and saw a major problem in the negative characterization of Cross Damon, Tate seeks resolution of the problem through a full reading of the novel's adaptation of Kierkegaard's psychological system. On a more limited scale Earle V. Bryant's "The Sexualization of Racism in Richard Wright's 'The Man Who Killed a Shadow'" (*BALF* 16:119–21) also offers a reading with reference to psychological concept. In this case the concept of sexual ambivalence resulting from racist conditioning finds its label in the writing of Calvin C. Hernton, its expression in the concentrated violence of the short story. Yet another article constituting a reworking of previous critical work is "Style and Meaning in Richard Wright's *Native Son*" by Joyce Ann Joyce ( *BALF* 16:112–15). Though the idea that Wright worked his craft meticulously is not new, it continues to require careful demonstration. It receives that in Joyce's attentive analysis of syntactic structures and patterns of sound in key passages.

Each of two essays on Chester Himes is devoted to his work in exile. "Chester Himes in France and the Legacy of the *Roman Policier*" (*CLAJ* 25[1981]:18–27) by Robert P. Smith, Jr., recounts

Himes's career with Marcel Duhamel's "Série noir," showing that his style makes for effective detective fiction, and then reporting the history of the French translation of *Cast the First Stone*, published in 1978. Jay R. Berry, Jr., in "Chester Himes and the Hard-Boiled Tradition" (*ArmD* 15:38–43) outlines Himes's innovations in hard-boiled writing as characters related to the "bad nigger" of folklore, a point of view that permits him to feature a wealth of minor characters, and an application of history to evoke Harlem. The appearance of these articles reminds us of a problem of scholarly audience. Much of what they say, particularly in Berry's case, has been available before, but not to the readers of the specialized journals in which they have published: readers of *CLAJ* would have found Berry's analysis previously in several articles in quarterlies, while readers of *ArmD* are likely to be acquainted with the *roman policier*.

Robert N. List's *Dedalus in Harlem, The Joyce-Ellison Connection* (Univ. Press) traces at length parallels of image and treatments of language in *Invisible Man, Ulysses,* and *Finnegan's Wake*. In addition to the formal basis for similarity, and the obvious influence Joyce has had upon his successors, List further justifies his study through assertion that Ellison, as well as Richard Wright, would naturally be attracted to Joyce's treatment of race. Simulating the way the black authors may have read Joyce, he gathers textual references linking the oppression of the Irish and blacks. But some readers may balk at the claim that eye imagery in *Invisible Man* is an index of castration anxiety.

In "Ellison and Ellison: The Solipsism of *Invisible Man*" (*CLAJ* 25[1981]:162–81) Timothy Brennan argues that the novel documents a pilgrimage by Ellison from Wrightian protest to affinity with symbolic methods that sublimate racial conflict in consciousness of the self. In particular the discussion of the Golden Day episode illustrates Brennan's first-rate ability to show a conflict of premises emerging in the art and style of the novel. In "*Invisible Man* and the Indictment of Innocence" (*CLAJ* 25:288–302) Mike W. Martin presents the narrator as a willing dupe. For this characterization the Trueblood passage becomes central as rendition of the moral responsibility one assumes in submitting to harmful illusions. Despite Martin's representation of gullibility he finds that the novel concludes with an assumption of authentic commitment. In "The Ending of Ralph Ellison's *Invisible Man*" (*CLAJ* 25:267–87) Per Winther notes that the narrator's role is that of an artist who gives form to chaos and finds in the advice of his grandfather, "Yes them to death," preconditions for the political work of using democracy to destroy racism. Eugenia Collier's "Dimensions of Alienation in Two Black American and Caribbean Novels" (*Phylon* 43:46–56) attends to the didactic function of the representation of alienation on several levels of *Invisible Man* and George Lamming's *In the Castle of My Skin*. The final article on Ellison, "The Old Order Shall Pass: The Examples of 'Flying Home' and "Barbados' " (*CLAJ* 25:303–14) by Chikwenye Okonjo Ogunyemi reads the structure and symbols of the works by Ellison and Paule Marshall to argue, in dispute with other critics, that the stories are similarly optimistic as they relate initiation into blackness, in the case of Ellison's protagonist, and in Marshall's story the old order replaced with a new generation of self-determining blacks.

The year's two essays on James Baldwin give us suggestive new treatments of the blues in his work. Keith E. Byerman in "Words and Music: Narrative Ambiguity in 'Sonny's Blues' " (*SSF* 19:367–72) finds that the story's narrator persistently misreads messages and distances himself from Sonny because of his reliance on language that is at once rationalistic and metaphoric. Even in the concluding scene, so often praised by critics, he cannot escape his prison-house. The second essay, Marlene Mosher's "James Baldwin's Blues" (*CLAJ* 26:112–24) considers the blues to manifest the theme of surviving victimization through honest creativity and traces Baldwin's use of specific blues compositions, allusions, and blues style of characterization in drama and fiction.

**d. Williams, Marshall, Demby, C. Wright, Murray.** In a brilliant study Wolfgang Karrer charts the adaptation of a Jamesian narrative technique by a black writer. His essay, "Multiperspective and the Hazards of Integration: John Williams' *Night Song*" (*The Afro-American Novel*, pp. 75–101), examines the novel of new bohemia as a product of the Cold War climate that deflected protest into conventional literary modes. On this historicist foundation he examines the functional value of the quadrangular point of view for treating racism, analyzing in the process the intrusion of a covert narrator

and revealing the evidence of racism in the privileged point of view
of the white character in the novel. The inadequacy of the well-made
novel then leads Karrer to comparative references to other Williams
novels and speculation about the author's uneasy compromises with
publishers' requirements.

Karrer's "The Novel as Blues: Albert Murray's *Train Whistle
Guitar*" (*The Afro-American Novel*, pp. 237–63) matches his work
on Williams in a strongly argued and similarly constructed statement
of the problem addressed by the novel and detailed translation of
the answer. In this case the problem is how to use the blues as more
than allusion. The answer appears in dialogue informed by blues
language or patterns, and a narrative voice that employs the AAB
stanzaic structure. The study leads to a complex description of the
novel's voice as nostalgically rooted in oral culture but selectively
reproducing folklore so it is assimilable by readers in the dominant
American culture.

Deborah Schneider's "A Search for Selfhood: Paule Marshall's
*Brown Girl, Brownstones*" (*The Afro-American Novel*, pp. 53–73)
implies distinction between the narrative and the discourse by which
the author directs readers' evaluation, for her reading relates the
Electra attachment of Selina Boyce to her father with the consequent
rejection of her mother while permitting one to see that the evaluations Selina makes are projections of her consciousness alone. Others
are possible.

In "William Demby's *The Catacombs*: A Latecomer to Modernism" (*The Afro-American Novel*, pp. 123–44) Klaus P. Hansen re-
assesses a novel that critical opinion, in marked contrast with popular response, has accorded the status of a minor classic. Hansen denies
the presence of existentialism in Demby's writing by arguing that the
early novel *Beetlecreek* is linked to naturalism through the influence
of Sherwood Anderson and asserting that the intricacy of *Catacombs*
owes as much to *Tristram Shandy* as it does to postmodernism. Hansen's purpose in clarifying Demby's lineage, which includes also
Joyce and writings of *Lebensphilosophie*, is to establish the *oeuvre*
as symptomatic of the eclectic adoption of models carrying ideological patterns not applicable to black experience.

Eberhard Kreutzer's "Dark Ghetto Fantasy and the Great Society:
Charles Wright's *The Wig*" (*The Afro-American Novel*, pp. 145–66)
adds to an explanation of the accommodationist fantasies in Wright's

tragicomic novel the judgment that the work is decidedly limited by redundancy and unfilled possibility.

***e*. Kelley, Gaines, Morrison, Jones, Reed, Young, Walker, McPherson.** Marienne Sy's "Dream and Language in *Dunfords Travels Everywheres*" (*CLAJ* 25:458–67) remarks yet another of the Joycean experiments in modern black writing, the novel by William Melvin Kelley in which the author supplements a surface realism with dream passages that remodel conventional English in the same fashion as black English does. Sy describes Kelley's misunderstood purpose as creation of a narrative of collective unconsciousness through application of Joycean tools to writing language with an African flavor. In "Romance as Epistemological Design: William Melvin Kelley's *A Different Drummer*" (*The Afro-American Novel*, pp. 103–22) Peter Bruck also reveals complexity where critics have rested content with a single, in this case political, interpretation. Kelley's text made discontinuous by introduction of varying points of view employs the genre of romance to reflect the multiple layers of meaning for Tucker Caliban's spontaneous withdrawal. Bruck claims that the Thoreauvian echo in the book's title reminds us to read that act as a fictional version of noninstitutional civil disobedience, while through the geneological references he takes us to other Kelley texts so that we recognize an attempt at a full saga of black life.

According to Albert Wertheim in "Journey to Freedom: Ernest Gaines's *The Autobiography of Miss Jane Pittman*" (*The Afro-American Novel*, pp. 219–35), Gaines's famous novel is written as folk autobiography complete with epic travels and a series of leaders and martyrs of almost biblical stature. These components combined in the narration by the title character produce a double pulse: radical events and characters played off against Miss Jane's abiding conservatism. The swings from defiance to perseverance gain momentum through the story until Miss Jane's own significant act at its conclusion. The striking achievement of Wertheim's study is to uncover through analysis of imagery and literary echoes the process by which Gaines reconstructs and amalgamates the genres of fiction and autobiography.

Susan Willis' "Eruptions of Funk: Historicizing Toni Morrison" (*BALF* 16:34–42) is methodologically outstanding among the year's studies of Morrison. Willis notes that her critical interest is not in the confirmation of social fact, the didactic motive, but is instead in how texts subvert the limitations in which they are written. Still, she achieves synthesis of moral and formal study by representing Morrison as writing against reification, the ultimate horror of bourgeois society. The same issue concerns Elizabeth J. Ordnóñez in "Narrative Texts by Ethnic Women: Researching the Past, Reshaping the Future" (*MELUS* 9,iii:19–28) where Morrison's *Sula* is one of the exhibits illustrating female writers' reshaping history by disrupting genres, displacing patriarchal texts, and inventing matrilineal traditions.

Dorothy H. Lee adopts a more conventional approach to Morrison in "*Song of Solomon*: To Ride the Air" (*BALF* 16:64–70) but is not to be faulted for that, because, while her study of Milkman's progressive divestiture of old ego may be familiar, Lee's observation of metaphors exhaustively but not ploddingly establishes Morrison's right to be termed a magical realist. Peter Bruck writes freshly about Morrison's use of folklore and theme in "Returning to One's Roots: The Motif of Searching and Flying in Toni Morrison's *Song of Solomon*" (*The Afro-American Novel*, pp. 289–304) by a sophisticated presentation of motifs actualized through reading, by showing Morrison's strategy of selective omniscience, and by showing awareness of previous published criticism. In contrast Wilfrid D. Samuels' "Liminality and the Search for Self in Toni Morrison's *Song of Solomon*" (*MV* 5,i–ii[1981]:59–68) takes up Houston Baker's recommendation to contextualize literature in an "anthropology of art" (see *ALS 1980*, p. 466) and sets out to parallel Milkman's career with the traditional hero described by Lord Raglan and the rites of passage described in other "literary" anthropological works. The results are a predictable presentation of laid-on background and need not be repeated here or in future criticism. Charles Scruggs in "The Nature of Desire in Toni Morrison's *Song of Solomon*" (*ArQ* 38:311–35) suggests how the novel is centered on a tension between desire, which is close to the Eros of Plato, and wisdom, and how the tapestry of the novel derives in part from the contrasts among the biblical books of Proverbs, Ecclesiastes, and Solomon. Keith E. Byerman's "Intense Behaviors: The Use of the Grotesque in *The Bluest Eye* and *Eva's Man*" (*CLAJ* 25:447–57) explains that Morrison's character Pecola and Gayl Jones's Eva are grotesques that show not only their own insane behavior but also show that their grotesque world is ultimately our world.

Gayl Jones receives special treatment in a section devoted to her in the October issue of *Callaloo*. This includes an interview conducted by Charles Rowell, five pieces of short fiction, and two poems, as well as two critical essays. The essay on fiction written by Jerry W. Ward, Jr., is entitled "Escape from Trublem: The Fiction of Gayl Jones" (*Callaloo* 5,iii:95–104). Ward opens his impressive article with a discussion of the reader's imitation of the creative process by which Modernist writers manipulate fictions in an associative process. Application of the theory to Jones's writing demonstrates that thinking through fictions, by readers and by a writer sharing the character's cognition, reveals how women and men conceptualize a slavery of limits. Short as it is, this essay is unquestionably one of the year's most provocative.

Michel Fabre's excellent "Postmodernist Rhetoric in Ishmael Reed's *Yellow Back Radio Broke Down*" (*The Afro-American Novel*, pp. 167–88) unites an explanation of Reed's large-scale project of deconstructing American myths and dismantling genres with a distillation of his fictional aesthetic from the inverted techniques, absences, and discontinuities of Reed's satiric Western novel. Fabre's literary sensitivity and scholarship are responsible for an essay that becomes the necessary and best starting place for future studies.

Elizabeth Schultz's "Search for 'Soul Space': A Study of Al Young's *Who Is Angelina?* and the Dimensions of Freedom" (*The Afro-American Novel*, pp. 263–87) gives intensely serious attention to a writer justly compared to Mark Twain for his creation of memorable character. Schultz defines that character by notation of Young's provisions of unique traits and by intriguing comparisons between Angelina and that other classic heroine, Henry James's Isabel Archer.

"Collective Experience and Individual Responsibility: Alice Walker's *The Third Life of Grange Copeland*" (*The Afro-American Novel*, pp. 189–218) by Klaus Ensslen measures the title character against the ideal of unself-conscious oneness Walker finds in black music and the writing of Zora Neale Hurston. Ensslen concludes that although Grange dramatizes essential parts of collective experience, his positive enhancement results from Walker's reduction of fictional motivation to individual traits.

Mary A. Gervin's "Developing a Sense of Self: The Androgynous Ideal in McPherson's 'Elbow Room'" (*CLAJ* 26:251–55) explicates the title piece of James Alan McPherson's 1978 Pulitzer Prize volume of short stories to show the characters' relationship in a paradigm of androgyny that makes race secondary to personality.

*f.* **General Criticism of Fiction.** Trudier Harris in *From Mammies to Militants: Domestics in American Literature* (Temple) chooses 11 examples of the female domestic in black literature and classifies them as either fully accepting their Mammy role, as moderates who wear a mask like John the slave in folklore, or as subversive militants. A chapter on the sociology of domestic labor grounds the study in historical reality, as do references to interviews the author conducted with maids. While Harris has a tendency to overexplain, her book represents not only retrieval of fictional characters usually deemed minor but provides explanatory background for the striking plots of such works as Alice Childress' *Like One of the Family*, Barbara Woods's "The Final Supper," and new black drama, including Douglas Turner Ward's *Happy Ending* and Ted Shine's *Contribution*.

Future studies of the reconstruction of genres by Afro-American authors will draw heavily upon Craig Hansen Werner's *Paradoxical Resolutions: American Fiction Since James Joyce* (Illinois), an investigation of the use of Joycean concepts and techniques to mediate between the modes of romance and realism. Werner treats six black authors in this broad study: Wright, Gaines, Baldwin, Morrison, Kelley, and Ellison. In some cases, as in the reading of Gaines's *Bloodline*, observation of possible Joycean influence results in altered readings, while in the case of Baldwin there is a Joycean manner used to repudiate a Joycean concept. Discussion of Kelley's use of dream language, confirming points made by Sy in the article noted earlier, and Ellison's acknowledged Joycean efforts in the encyclopedic novel are probably the most successful of Werner's treatments of black writing, but the entire project is provocative because Werner conceives his work as a study of Joyce's relevance to general problems of American fiction rather than proposing interpretations that depend upon acceptance of point-by-point argument for validation.

Four articles on fiction from 1982 may be classified as contributing to a differential black literary history. Sondra O'Neale in "Race,

Sex and Self: Aspects of *Bildung* in Select Novels by Black American Women Novelists" (*MELUS* 9,iv:25–37) observes that black female authors are not preoccupied with adolescent recognitions, physical awakening, or conflict and reconciliation with family. More often than not they invert the *Bildung* conventions to depict an internal struggle to achieve self-realization rather than simple adulthood. Codifying the pattern, O'Neale indicates that art is possibly the freest choice available to female protagonists. Carolyn A. Naylor confirms O'Neale's argument with her own in "Cross-Gender Significance of the Journey Motif in Selected Afro-American Fiction" (*CLQ* 18:26–38). Taking up the idea that the *Bildungsroman* is the most salient form for neofeminism, Naylor contrasts Hurston's *Their Eyes Were Watching God* and Morrison's *Song of Solomon* with Wright's "The Man Who Lived Underground" and Ellison's *Invisible Man* to argue that Janie and Pilate relinquish false views of themselves and achieve an androgyny that honors the male as well as female principle, while the protagonists of the male authors fail to understand their own human complexity. In "The Structuring of Emotion in Black American Fiction" (*Novel* 16:35–54) Raymond Hedin seeks to account for the tendency he finds in black fiction to mute depiction of anger and the strategic emphasis writers have placed on literary structure. Hedin finds explanation in the writers' awareness that part of their audience doubts the full humanity of blacks; thus, conventional forms clearly displayed and modified anger are rhetorical choices to convey rationality. That the forms of culture shape the forms of fiction is also the burden of Kathryn Hunter's study of Afro-American dissent from materialism in "Possessions and Dispossessions: Objects in Afro-American Novels' (*CEA* 44,iii: 32–40). From William Wells Brown's *Clotel* to Ishmael Reed's *Free-Lance Pallbearers*, material possessions in black fiction represent cultural imposition rather than a means to define character, so characters learn to despise or destroy the objects that confirm their subjugation.

### iii. Poetry

*a.* **Wheatley, Heard.** Supplementing his publication of *Phillis Wheatley: A Bio-Bibliography* (see *ALS 1981*, p. 391) William H.

Robinson fills out the representation of Wheatley's literary reputation with *Critical Essays on Phillis Wheatley*, also published by G. K. Hall. An introduction allusively titled "On Being Young, Gifted, and Black" (pp. 1–12) comments on the disposition of critics to focus on the issue of Wheatley's race, whether they are racists, abolitionists, or modern militants. The body of the collection reflects the history of Wheatley criticism with 37 brief comments, most of them from the 18th century; 17 reprinted essays, including several occasioned by the 1834 reissue of *Poems on Various Subjects*; and seven essays published during the 1970s. Four additional essays were written especially for this volume. In the first of these, "The Influence of Alexander Pope on the Writing Style of Phillis Wheatley" (pp. 175–88), Albertha Sistrunk deems it a fact that, of course, Wheatley internalized the model of Pope along with other influences of her American environment. What remains is to determine the extent of that influence, and Sistrunk finds it considerable in aesthetic values as well as in the poetic practice she categorizes so carefully. The conclusion that Wheatley must be judged historically in relation to 18th-century poetics is unobjectionable, though demanding reiteration in view of the record of critical judgments Robinson's work has prepared for us. John C. Shields takes up a favored theory of the poet's time in "Phillis Wheatley and the Sublime" (pp. 189–205), recounts the theory from summary of primary sources which he matches with citations of Wheatley's verse, and thus argues effectively for her participation in a tradition that foreshadows romanticism. Mukhtar Ali Isani, who has shown dedication and astuteness in many previous essays on Wheatley, also presents her as a poet well within tradition in "Phillis Wheatley and the Elegaic Mode" (pp. 208–14). Approximately one-third of the poems we know Wheatley composed are elegies displaying the evident influence of New England models, but, as Isani shows through examination of Wheatley's revisions and variant versions, the poet achieved an individualized voice, earning her a place among the poets who were "widening the range of eighteenth century sensibility while working within the basic tradition of the age." The contribution by Henry Louis Gates, Jr., to the Robinson collection is taken from his forthcoming study *The Idea of Blackness in Western Discourse*, titled for the present volume "Phillis Wheatley and the Nature of the Negro" (pp. 215–33). The excerpt from an intellectual history of the philosophical conflict over human enslavement concerns references to Wheatley in the debate over the mental capacity of Africans and confirms her relevance to obsessive American bad faith.

Asking "Whoever Heard of Josephine Heard?" (*CLAJ* 26:256–61), Renate Maria Simson explains that the author of *Morning Glories* (1890) was esteemed in her day for conventional love and religious poems, one of which, "Black Samson," might be read as metaphoric of the rising race.

*b.* **McKay, Brown, Tolson.** Despite an apparent new interest in Claude McKay, only one essay on his work, "Theme and Technique in Claude McKay's Poetry" by Isaac I. Eliminian (*CLAJ* 29[1981]: 203–11), has appeared since my last report, and its topical surveys of the verse with notation of imagery must be termed an introductory rather than investigative piece.

Meanwhile the celebration of the accomplishments of Sterling Brown that began some years ago has borne rich fruit both in publications and presentations to scholarly meetings. Latest is a special section on Brown in *Callaloo* (5,i–ii:11–105) that includes photographs by Roy Lewis; the annotated bibliography by Robert G. O'Meally noted earlier; reprints of Brown's poems "Strange Legacies," "Strong Men," and "When De Saints Go Ma'ching Home," along with his critical essay "Negro Characters as Seen by White Authors" (1933); a poem dedicated to Brown by Sherley Anne Williams; and two interpretive essays originally prepared for delivery at an MLA session. In the first of the essays, "Sterling Brown's After-Song: 'When De Saints Go Ma'ching Home' and the Performances of Afro-American Voice" (pp. 33–42), Kimberly W. Benston analyzes the reenactment of call-and-response by which Brown, in such a poem as "Saints," makes the past available as a version of existence established between memory and realization, a possible present. Benston's sensitive reading and skilled explication of the essential quality of Brown's poetry locates a tension between autonomous and collective enactment that broke the constraints of literary dialect to release the complexity of Afro-American "saying" into modern verse. Robert G. O'Meally's "'Game to the Heart': Sterling Brown and the Badman" (pp. 43–54) studies a number of poems adapting the white stereotypes and black creations of badmen and "nachul" men. Each character violates social conventions, and Brown's treatment of that violation results in songs of an unsinkable human spirit. A third essay, by Vera M. Kutzinski, called "The Distant Closeness of Dancing Doubles: Sterling Brown and William Carlos Williams" (*BALF* 16:19–25) provides a comparative study that associates Brown's symbolically charged landscapes, geographical interconnections, and multicultural representations with *Paterson*.

Worth noting as additions to recent publication on Melvin B. Tolson are the poet's own memoir "The Odyssey of a Manuscript" (*NewL* 48[1981]:5–17) and Robert M. Farnsworth's edition *Caviar and Cabbage: Selected Columns by Melvin B. Tolson from the "Washington Tribune," 1937–1944* (Missouri). The memoir speaks of the composition of *A Gallery of Harlem Portraits* and the struggle to get it read by publishers. The newspaper columns initiated when Tolson was 39 and beginning to gain a literary reputation are provided substantial introduction by Farnsworth, who situates their composition in Tolson's literary milieu.

*c.* **Brooks, Baraka, Rodgers, Jones.** "Gwendolyn Brooks's Way with the Sonnet" by Gladys Margaret Williams (*CLAJ* 26:215–40) is a set piece in approach. There is analysis of theme, prosody, and embodied vision; but they are appropriate means to demonstrate the plasticity of the prescribed form in the hands of the artist who adapts the sonnet for her fictions in *A Street in Bronzeville* and *Annie Allen*. This is solid work in the best sense of the term.

"'All is Permitted': The Poetry of LeRoi Jones/Amiri Baraka" by W. D. E. Andrews (*SWR* 62:197–221) is also first-rate, though it would appear to be covering familiar ground by tracing the development of Baraka's aesthetic from participation in the Beat Generation to the later hortatory style. The virtue of Andrews' work lies in his detection of a logic of development due in part to psychological imperatives and partly the result of historical change. By positing an ultimately synthetic and intensely subjective core to Baraka's aesthetic, Andrews is able to show the coherence in the selection of influences and changes of tack. In short, the varied output of Baraka is seen as an intelligible canon.

Estella M. Sales's "Contradictions in Black Life: Recognized and

Reconciled in *How I Got Ovah*" (*CLAJ* 25[1981]:74–81) finds Carolyn Rodgers reconsidering the dichotomies of revolutionary tactics
and Christian ethics along with the slave past and the black present
in a selection of verse thematically shaped by the metaphoric crossing
of symbolic bridges. The result is Rodgers' provision of unique connotation to the popular expression that gives her volume title.

"A Spiritual Journey: Gayl Jones's Song for Anninko" is Trudier
Harris' contribution to the special treatment of Jones in *Callaloo*
(5,iii:105–11). Describing Almeyda's exploration of memory and
history in the poem, Harris intends not only to show the emergence
of a character who becomes representative of Luzo-Africans of the
17th century, but also to offer an appealing description of an in-
sufficiently known poem.

*d.* General Criticism of Poetry. Several of the year's best general
essays confront the persistent demand by critics for a "universal"
literature. Poets like Baraka have attacked the concept steadily, and
now scholars are beginning to detail how it has damaged past practice. Arnold Rampersad's "The Universal and the Particular in Afro-
American Poetry" (*CLAJ* 25:1–17) describes the function of "universalism" in a colonial situation as a way to defuse political analysis.
Rampersad is concerned to show that the traditional evaluation of
white middle-class history as the sum of universal human nature has
distorted the texture of black poetic art.

By creating a theory of black poetics in *Understanding the New
Black Poetry* (1973), Stephen E. Henderson did much to raise awareness of the spectrum of possibility in verse untrammeled by extrinsic
demands for conformity to universal values. His 1977 speech at Southern University reprinted as "The Blues as Black Poetry" (*Callaloo*
5,iii:22–30) repeats the message through contradiction of the idea
that literary genres derive from subliterary forms. Henderson argues
for the view that folk sources are the most distinctly black aspect of
writers' tradition.

The editors of *Callaloo* have coupled Clyde Taylor's " 'Salt Pea-
nuts': Sound and Sense in African/American Oral/Musical Creativity" (5,iii:1–11) with Henderson's piece since Taylor also directs
critical attention to substrata of poetry, particularly a matrix of communication patterns that include symbolizations in music and lan-

guage of entire cultural outlooks. He terms their content mytho-
phones; their provenance, African values. Evidence of distinctively
oral qualities in poetry, along with a psychological withdrawal from
Western ways supply the burden of "Oral Tradition and Recent
Black American Poetry" by Chikwenye Okonjo Ogunyemi (ZAA 4:
325–33). The exhibits include elegies by Sonia Sanchez and Etheridge Knight, Keorapetse Kgositsile's "When Brown Is Black (For
Rap Brown)," and Lebert Betune's "To Strike for Night."

### iv. Drama

*a.* **Baraka, Shange.**   The year's major project in drama is a historical issue of *BALF* that will be noted among literary historical studies.
Otherwise there are some provocative articles to report. W. D. E.
Andrews carries his analysis of Baraka's work into dramatic genres
with "The Black Revolutionary Drama of LeRoi Jones" (*BRMMLA*
36:259–78). Andrews indicates that early plays such as *Dutchman*
and *The Slave* preserve the qualities of familiar social drama while
beginning a progression toward revolutionary theater. The later, more
schematized plays, however, subordinate dramatic dialectic to polemical purposes. Despite its utility, Andrews' essay shares the culpa-
bility described by Sandra L. Richards in "Negative Forces and
Positive Non-Entities: Images of Women in the Dramas of Amiri
Baraka" (*TJ* 34:233–40). Andrews' evaluations, like others, overlook the fact that Baraka's dramaturgy has been until recently overwhelmingly male-dominated and woman-hating. Because Baraka
summons powerful eloquence to denounce black women who traffic
with racism in *Black Mass*, establishes evil in the person of aggres-
sively independent white women, discounts the intelligence of female characters used as mouthpieces for political positions, and so
ignores the double oppression of black women, Richards can argue
that he has disregarded much of historical reality in conceiving his
dramas.

Andrea Benton Rushing's "For Colored Girls, Suicide or Struggle?" (*MR* 22[1981]:539–50) reports personal responses to Ntozake
Shange's choreopoem to instigate inquiry into its strange effect.
Without doubt the drama appeals to audiences deeply; yet it ignores
racism and capitalism, glorifies individualism, and offers simplistic
explanations. Rushing is disturbed by the results of her inquiry, but

stops short of prescriptive criticism, though she implies a version of Richards' charge that the playwright obscures historical reality.

*b.* **General Criticism of Drama.** Rhett S. Jones advances an ingeniously suggestive theory in "Politics and the Afro-American Performing Arts in Environmental Perspective" (*Callaloo* 5, i–ii:175–95). Contrasting the experience of Africans and Afro-Americans in control of the land and economy, Jones argues that performing arts in American segregated space became largely improvisational, while African ability to control living space fostered a formal art just as it did popular politics. Distinct American experience thus channeled energy into folk performing arts that required only brief control of space and demanded a subtle, depoliticized manner of performance.

### *v.* Slave Narratives and Autobiography

The primacy of Frederick Douglass among fugitive slave authors continues to be affirmed in 1982, first by the appearance of the second volume of *The Frederick Douglass Papers*, ed. John W. Blassingame (Yale). This carries Series 1, "Speeches, Debates, and Interviews," through the years 1847–54, a period when Douglass shifted from the position of a strict Garrisonian. Of the approximately 650 speeches delivered during the period, 59 are reprinted here, with the texts for 37 taken either from *The North Star* or *Frederick Douglass's Paper*. The apparatus continues to be of high quality: notes are provided as needed, the volume is fully indexed, and in addition the editor provides an itinerary of Douglass' travels. The record is also enhanced by William L. Andrews' report of research in "Frederick Douglass, Preacher" (*AL* 54:592–97), indicating that biographers have erred in not pursuing the evidence that Douglass was a licensed preacher. In "Biblical Allusion and Imagery in Frederick Douglass' *Narrative*" (*CLAJ* 25:56–64) Lisa Margaret Zeitz explicates a preacherly black homiletic identification with the Israelites and adds some detail to a familiar reading.

In "The American Slave Narrative: The Justification of the Picaro" (*AL* 53:630–45) Raymond Hedin concentrates on the shifting rhetorical demands made on slaves' life writings and demonstrates that the picaro character who originally appeared in 18th-century narratives because the experiences of writers such as Briton Ham-

mon and John Marrant were picaresque, metamorphosed as resistance to slavery and the duty to escape its bonds became plausible
expression of increasing political awareness. In part the picaro was
purified by authorial deflection of responsibility for actions such as
thievery back on slavery itself, but above all the narrators' assumption
of the "put on" as a tactic to invert slavery's false assumptions shows
a developed power to transcend the limitations of historical circumstances.

A similar presentation of the slave narrative as a source of black
literature is made by the late Charles T. Davis in "The Slave Narrative: First Major Art Form in an Emerging Black Tradition." Written
as the introduction to an edited volume, the essay appears in the collected writings of Davis published as *Black is the Color of the Cosmos*
(83–119; see closing paragraph for complete citation). Davis also
studies the form against the background of shifting abolitionist goals,
noting in general the artful use of testimonial detail, voice, and sentiment; and examining specifically the organizing principles in works
by Frederick Douglass, William Wells Brown, and Henry Bibb.

Jesse Craig Holte's comparative study "The Representative Voice:
Autobiography and the Ethnic Experience" (*MELUS* 9,ii:25–46) includes *The Autobiography of Malcolm X* as an illustration of the
conversion of the genre originating as self-examination into the statement of a spokesman for a community. R. Baxter Miller defends Alex
Haley's *Roots* against charges of faulty history and derivativeness in
"Kneeling at the Fireplace: Black Vulcan—*Roots* and the Double
Artificer" (*MELUS* 9,i:73–84). Extracting the myth of Vulcan from
the text, Miller uses it as armature for a consideration of the tension
between myth and history, a story that begins as an African epic but
concludes as a new-world narrative.

Surely the most important publication of the year on black autobiography is the chapter of Albert E. Stone's book *Autobiographical
Occasions and Original Acts: Versions of American Identity from
Henry Adams to Nate Shaw* (Penn.) entitled "Two Recreate One:
The Act of Collaboration in Recent Black Autobiography" and separately published in *YREAL* (pp. 227–66). Conceived on the principle that autobiography is content, not any particular form, Stone's
book explores the linkages between public and private history
through comparative studies; thus, W. E. B. Du Bois and Henry
Adams are paired for examination of old men recreating their his-

torical identity, while the self-constructions of Richard Wright and Louis Sullivan represent the preoccupation of artists with childhood sources of genius. The astute readings uncovering the ascending circle of Du Bois' *Autobiography* and the psychosocial cluster of emotions and motives in *Black Boy* define as extremes the scope of recreation and expression in black autobiography. Remarking the developing conventions of collaborative autobiography evident in the stories of Dick Gregory, Mahalia Jackson, and Ossie Guffy, Stone proceeds to thoughtful analysis of *All God's Danger: The Life of Nate Shaw*, written with Theodore Rosengarten; *The Autobiography of Malcolm X*, written in collaboration with Alex Haley; and a conclusion generalizing the procedure for a multifaceted analysis of texts as tandem performances. Stone's book impresses because of its careful study of such matters as the tension between the motive that led Rosengarten to provide the real Ned Cobb with the alias "Nate Shaw" and the authenticity of Cobb's narrative power, and because in pursuing tropes and metaphors in Malcolm X's narrative he fills out the most thorough interpretation to date of that multilayered story.

To discuss another form of the art of life-writing, Bernard W. Bell presents "Black Literary Biography: Theory and Practice" (*CLAJ* 25[1981]:141–61), which characterizes William E. Farrison's biography of William Wells Brown as a materialist documentary, J. Lee Green's life of Anne Spenser as a rescue mission, Arnold Rampersad's book on Du Bois as a critical rather than biographical study, Fabre's biography of Wright as psychologically astute but constrained by the author's acceptance of the writer's self-image, and Robert Hemenway's biography of Zora Neale Hurston as a compelling rendition that is nevertheless torn between loyalty to subject and loyalty to truth.

### *vi.* Literary History, Criticism

Under the direction of James V. Hatch, the noted bibliographer and editor of black drama, and Andrzej Ceynowa of the University of Gdansk, *Black American Literature Forum* has begun a three-part series on drama with a special issue (16,iv) on historical figures and productions. The five articles on performers are Errol Hill's "S. Morgan Smith: Successor to Ira Aldridge" (pp. 132–35), a presentation

derived from theatrical newspapers of the career of the Philadelphia
black man who played Othello within a month of his arrival in London in 1866 and performed for years in provincial engagements; John
G. Monroe's account in "Charles Gilpin and the Drama League Controversy" (pp. 139–41) of the racism evoked by Gilpin's candidacy
for the Drama League Award of 1920 in recognition of his performance in *The Emperor Jones*; Andrea J. Nouryeh's "When the Lord
was a Black Man: A Fresh Look at the Life of Richard Berry Harrison" (pp. 142–46), which summarizes the career and personality
of the actor who lived his life as humbly as he performed the star
role in *Green Pastures*; Vèvè A. Clark's detailed analysis of the bal-
letic performance of African and Caribbean themes in "Katherine
Dunham's *Tropical Revue*" (pp. 147–52); and Rosetta Reitz's recovery of the significance of a feature performer in Sissle and Blake's
*Chocolate Dandies* and the English cast of *Blackbirds*, "Hot Snow:
Valaida Snow (Queen of the Trumpet Sings & Swings)" (pp. 158–
60). The four articles on dramatic production are "The African Grove
Theatre and Company" (pp. 128–31) in which Jonathan Dewberry
summons contemporary reports to outline a history of the early 19th-
century company; Edward A. Robinson's discussion of the first black
stock theater in "The Pekin: The Genesis of American Black Theater"
(pp. 136–38); Stephen M. Vallillo's description in "The Battle of the
Black *Mikados*" (pp. 153–57) of the struggle in 1939 between the
Federal Theatre and Michael Todd over the right to tap the popularity of black performances in the adaptation of Gilbert and Sullivan; and Kathy Anne Perkins' quick look at the problems of theater
workers seeking admission to the stage employees' union in "Black
Backstage Workers, 1900–1969" (pp. 160–63).

The research of Mary Frances Berry and John W. Blassingame on
the transformative effect of slavery on culture (*ALS 1979*, p. 423)
has now been incorporated in a full-length study, *Long Memory,
The Black Experience in America* (Oxford). A narrative history
arranged thematically according to institutions, the work makes frequent use of literature, along with a storehouse of secondary sources
that are appropriately summarized, to stress a capacity for survival
as observed from within black culture.

Berndt Ostendorf's *Black Literature in White America* (Barnes &
Noble) draws upon Du Bois' conception of double consciousness,

Ellison's emphatic assertion of the key role of folklore, and Robert B. Stepto's thesis in *From Behind the Veil* (see *ALS 1979*, pp. 423–24) to develop a sociological approach to the function and content of culture. Ostendorf's high regard for folklore leads him to make a point of rejecting the largely discredited pathological models of black adaptation to American life, and to employ examples of linguistic usage, improvisational performances, and the arts of minstrelsy and jazz to describe popular arts as a method of dealing with ambivalence and cathartically resolving conflict. Considerations of literature follow from these premises in a study of black writers from Wheatley, whom Ostendorf dismisses as a cultural mimic, to Ellison, in whose "Flying Home" he sees the capacity of folk culture to counteract routinized behavior and lift the consciousness.

The acknowledged models for Wilson Jeremiah Moses in his study *Black Messiahs and Uncle Toms: Social and Literary Manipulation of a Religious Myth* (Penn. State) are Henry Nash Smith's *Virgin Land* and John William Ward's *Andrew Jackson*; thus, he seeks to delineate the process by which a concept is fused with collective emotion. Moreover, in keeping with American Studies methodology he frankly asserts the belief that novelists are at the center of a culture, their works defining its deepest impulses. Possibly the highpoint of the study is the analysis of Du Bois' fiction, particularly since *Dark Princess* emerges, despite its operatic manner, as a precursor of Wright's *The Outsider*, Ellison's *Invisible Man*, and John Williams' *The Man Who Cried I Am*. This book is an important addition to self-aware criticism.

Several of the notable recent efforts in literary history are devoted to the Harlem Renaissance. *When Harlem Was in Vogue* (Knopf, 1981) by David Levering Lewis was omitted from last year's report but deserves notice because of its aggregation of excellent cameo biographies and reconstructions of key events, such as the party held in 1924 by Dr. Charles S. Johnson at which the idea was conceived for a special issue of *Survey Graphic* on the New Negro. I remarked on the quality of that reconstruction upon its first publication (see *ALS 1979*, p. 425) and have no reason to revise my estimate of Lewis' ability to adapt primary sources for narrative history. Though the book is not intended as an interpretive study, it postulates its subject as the story of a small elite whose distance from the experience of the masses of Harlem accounts for its limited influence, lack of power to represent Afro-America more than metaphorically, and inevitable failure.

The editors of *The Afro-American Novel Since 1960* have provided useful essays in critical theory. Peter Bruck's introductory essay, "Protest, Universality, Blackness: Patterns of Argumentation in the Criticism of the Contemporary Afro-American Novel" (pp. 1–27) locates tokenism and an ahistorical content-bound opposition of protest and art in notable studies by whites, but makes clear that black critics too have allowed universalism and tokenism to prevail. Bruck proposes a break from preoccupation with a canon composed of Wright, Baldwin, and Ellison. Wolfgang Karrer's "Integration or Separatism: The Social History of the Afro-American Dilemma after World War II" (pp. 29–52) insists that black novels of the last 35 years have reflected social history faithfully. The history experienced by blacks has a unique particularity.

In "'I Yam What I Am: Naming and Unnaming in Afro-American Literature" (*BALF* 16:3–11) Kimberly W. Benston founds a study of Jay Wright upon the comprehensive significance of the geneological impulse in Afro-American culture. Newly freed persons authenticate the self by the dual process of unnaming the immediate past designations of slavery and deliberately adopting new names that signify both independence and continuity with a past preceding enslavement. For Benston, Jay Wright thoroughly integrates the naming process into his poetic vision, centering poems upon a core of desire to align the self with a universal order.

To close this report on the critical enterprise in black literature, it is appropriate to signal the appearance of *Black is the Color of the Cosmos: Essays on Afro-American Literature and Culture, 1942–1981* (Garland), the collection of essays by Charles T. Davis edited by Henry Louis Gates, Jr. Gates characterizes these largely reprinted works as meditations on the tropes of blackness, which indeed they are. Let us add that their publication is testimonial also to a scholar whose contributions to Afro-American studies away from his desk were probably more notable than the writings. The example he set and the environment he created had incalculable influence on many of the critics whose work is annually recorded in these *ALS* reports.

*State University of New York at Albany*

# 20. Themes, Topics, Criticism

## Michael J. Hoffman

It is now three years since I last wrote this chapter for *ALS* after having done it for the previous six volumes. Getting back after a break to reading so many works of criticism and theory has given me a chance to assess changes that have taken place in literary scholarship and theory during the intervening years. What changes have in fact occurred?

The main one I can discern is that the "new" criticism—by which I refer to theory developed principally in Europe, and particularly in France—has taken much stronger hold in American letters, not only in literary theory but also in writings about American literature. The interest in various "post-Structuralist" movements, including semiotics and deconstruction, seems to be not just a passing fad but a part of the mainstream of literary study. A revisionary impulse is riding high, an impulse that—in American literary studies, for instance—has set about revising our assessments of the classic works, reinterpreting them in the light of new approaches, rather than simply adding other works of traditional scholarship to library shelves. What the lasting value will be of this revisionary fervor we should leave to history to decide, but the excitement of being part of such an age of transition is quite tangible.

In writing this chapter again, I have continued the tradition established in *ALS 1973*—and maintained so ably in the last three years by Jonathan Morse—of writing exclusively about full-length works, under the assumption that critical ideas of genuine importance will soon find their way into the pages of a book. Even limiting myself that way, however, I still had to read more than 100 books; and so, I feel secure in suggesting that I have taken a comprehensive look at both general literary theory and at the overviews of American literature that were published during 1982.

Given space limitations, I have had to be somewhat selective, and so I could not write about all the books I read. I have therefore adopted certain principles. Because *ALS* is intended primarily for specialists in American literature, I have written about *all* the works on appropriate American topics that came my way. In the second section—which is concerned with works of general theoretical and critical interest—I have written on only half the books I examined. I chose to write about what I thought were the most stimulating books, even if that meant that some categories were slighted that during other years may be more fully populated. Those books that did not fall easily into conventional groupings I have gathered into a category called "Special Topics."

### *i.* American Literature

*a.* **Works by Major Figures.**  The works in this miscellaneous group are all by prominent figures in American literary studies. Three volumes are collections of periodical essays, one is an intellectual autobiography, and the other a poetics of popular culture full of autobiographical reference. All are interesting and well written.

Leslie Fiedler's latest book, *What Was Literature? Class Culture and Mass Society* (Simon and Schuster), is a summa of his long, prolific career. Its tone is highly personal and full of references to Fiedler's academic combats as the heroic Jew in the WASP university. In Fiedler's mind his own rise and that of what he stands for corresponds to the decline of "elitist" literature. The book is polemical and essayistic, and, as one might expect, it is often weak on facts and long on opinion. Still the writing is so provocative and full of ideas that even when we are most infuriated by Fiedler's cavalier manner, we find the book impossible to dismiss.

It is Fiedler's thesis that most "elitist" writing is readable only by literature students and professors, whereas what we call popular literature and culture reflects the deepest needs and desires of a society. The yearning of America—its set of unconscious mythic priorities—is much better reflected in *Hill Street Blues* and *Mork and Mindy* than in the latest novel of Saul Bellow or in a formally perfect older one by Henry James. Although he opposes categories like "high," "middle," and "low" culture, Fiedler does engage in a reverse snobbism that sets him proudly before television soap opera, popular movies, and best-selling novels. But since he has also been trained in traditional canonical literary studies, the combination gives him a range of cultural experience that is unusual among English professors.

The book is divided into two sections, the first of which ("Part One: Subverting the Standards") contains most of the theoretical and polemical prose, including such chapters as "Who Was Leslie A. Fiedler?," "What Was the Novel?," "What Was the Death of the Novel?," and "From Ethics and Aesthetics to Ecstatics." Part Two is called "Opening Up the Canon" and contains a number of provocative readings of such popular novels and other unclassifiable works as *Uncle Tom's Cabin, Gone With the Wind, The Clansman,* and *Roots.* Fiedler refers to these as "inadvertant epics" (this book was originally announced as *The Inadvertant Epic*), by which he means that they reflect the mythic yearnings of the culture (substitute tribe, race, or people) better than other cultural forms. The search for lost ancestry, relations between the races, the sentimentalization of the past, all find expression in works so powerful that millions continue to buy them as books, and watch them as films, plays, or television mini-series. Fiedler knows how to write interestingly about such works, and he does not fall into the trap of doing close readings as if they were by Conrad, James, or Dostoyevsky. Often ill-tempered and over-stated, *What Was Literature?* states a position that all of us in American literature need to confront.

Paul Fussell, author of the fine book *The Great War and Modern Memory,* has produced a volume of essays and book reviews entitled *The Boy Scout Handbook and Other Observations* (Oxford), all of which appeared in such journals as *New Republic, Encounter, Harpers, New York Times Book Review,* and *Spectator.* Written on a variety of literary, cultural, and historical topics, these essays have as subjects not only the boy-scout handbook but such matters as Poe and Whitman, "Can Graham Greene Write English?," travel, things British, and the Second World War.

The title essay alone is worth the price of the book. Fussell's rapier prose might make a serious boy scout think the essay a sober paean to the bible of their movement. Still, with all of Fussell's ironic wit, the essay views the boy-scout handbook with gentle affection, as something left over from a simpler world where the Protestant work ethic was mixed with a draught of American optimism. "In the current world of Making It and Getting Away with It, there are not many books devoted to associating happiness with virtue" (p. 7), he says.

The essays on the Second War are all informative, factually and emotionally. The book's final autobiographical essay, "My War," helps us understand why Fussell writes so well about war, even that other, First one that he has made his own without having had to live through it himself.

I wrote a glowing review of Irving Howe's magisterial *World of Our Fathers* in *ALS 1976*, and all of us have made use of his many essays and books. Howe has now produced a magisterial intellectual autobiography entitled *A Margin of Hope* (Harcourt). This book succeeds in being both sensitive and moving in spite of the author's resolute unwillingness to use the intimate details of his own life unless they have something directly to do with the development of his mind. The only exceptions are a number of references to his father and, in particular, to his father's death. He barely mentions, for instance, his marriages.

*A Margin of Hope* is the intellectual odyssey of a 1930s Jewish socialist man of letters. Howe divides the life of his mind into its major episodes: the '30s, the Stalinist/Trotskyite conflict, the Second War (which he spent mostly in Alaska with lots of time for reading), the postwar period (*Dissent* and *Partisan Review*), the period of Jewish identity (Yiddish anthologies with Eliezer Greenberg) and the conflict over Hannah Arendt's *Eichmann in Jerusalem*, the McCarthy period (during which Howe did his first college teaching), the '60s (and battles with the New Left), and the '70s (which are written up as a series of fragments, as if that period was not yet clearly in focus). The final two sections are by far the weakest, but the book until about 1960 is an excellent history of urban social and political ideas since the Great Depression. The following quotation will give the reader a taste of the book's analytical flavor: "The New York intellectuals formed the first group of Jewish writers coming out of this immigrant milieu who did not define themselves through either a nostalgic or a hostile memory of Jewishness. By the late thirties Jewishness as sentiment and cultural source played only a modest part in their conscious experience. What excited them was the idea of breaking away, of willing a new life. They meant to declare themselves citizens of the world and, if that succeeded, might then become writers of this country" (p. 137). This beautifully written book is the equal, in its way, of the retrospective works of Alfred Kazin that cover the same period.

Diane Johnson, the distinguished novelist, has collected her essays and book reviews in *Terrorists & Novelists* (Knopf), most of which appeared in the *New York Times Book Review* and the *New York Review of Books*. The book's first section, "Self-Deceptions," is concerned with those forms of fictional and nonfictional writing "where strategies of self-dramatization require the truth-teller to hold some traffic with fiction" (p. x). In this section are pieces on such topics as Flaubert's letters, Brooke Hayward's memoirs, and Alice and Henry James. In part 2, "Fictions Stranger Than Fiction," the pieces are "concerned with the connection of history to fiction" (p. x). This section has pieces on Norman Mailer's novel, *The Executioner's Song*, Saul Bellow's *The Dean's December*, and E. L. Doctorow's *Loon Lake*. The third section, "The Real World," contains Johnson's well-known pieces on rape, Jonestown, and Patty Hearst.

The author's sensibility is sane and skeptical, and free of ideology, qualities that make her an excellent social commentator as well as a perceptive reviewer. Her tone is graceful, urbane, and unpretentious, her novelist's insights enabling her to understand the bizarre complexities of the Hearst case or the mass suicide at Jonestown better than anyone I have read. And her scholarly background lends an authority to the three pieces on John Ruskin that one does not expect from a literary journalist.

Louis D. Rubin, Jr., has produced a new collection of essays called *A Gallery of Southerners* (LSU) on a number of southern topics including William Faulkner, Thomas Wolfe, Allen Tate, Flannery O'Connor, and *Gone With the Wind*. While all the essays seem to be occasional pieces, they do express a coherent point of view which Rubin describes in his introduction as a position of outsidership growing out of his combined status as both southerner and Jew, a point of view that has enabled him to see his culture and its literature clearly. The pieces on Faulkner and Wolfe are very good, based as they are on a lifetime of scholarship. There is also an excellent essay relating *Gone With the Wind* to Faulkner's novels of the 1930s, such as *Absalom, Absalom!*, as well as a very good essay on Shelby Foote's lengthy history of the Civil War. This is a book for dipping into rather than reading through.

*b.* **Studies of American Fiction.**   Brief mention goes to the first work in this section, a study of the use of myth in science fiction, written by Casey Fredericks and entitled *The Future of Eternity: Mythologies of Science Fiction and Fantasy* (Indiana). Concerned largely with American writers such as Ursula K. Le Guin, Samuel R. Delany, Philip José Farmer, and Roger Zelazny, and written for a general audience, the book should also be useful to students of science fiction. A few chapter titles will give the reader some sense of Fredericks' approach: "Old and New Myths in Science Fiction," " 'Estrangement' in Myth and Science Fiction," "The Return to the Primitive." A good selected bibliography will help those readers interested in exploring the subject further.

A stimulating application of reader-response theory to works of American fiction is *Interpretive Conventions: The Reader in the Study of American Fiction* (Cornell), by Steven Mailloux. The book begins with an excellent summary of five major theorists: Stanley Fish, Wolfgang Iser, Jonathan Culler, Norman Holland, and David Bleich, of whom the first three are more socially oriented, the latter two more psychologically. But Mailloux finds neither orientation to be satisfactory. Holland's and Bleich's psychological models will not work "because they lack the intersubjective base assumed by the discipline and necessary for the kind of practical criticism that dominates American literary study" (p. 64). The other three writers do attempt to establish ways by which shared reading conventions operate, but even their theories lack a sufficient intersubjective base. Mailloux proposes to take the best from Fish, Iser, and Culler and supply "what is missing: *a social model of reading that supports a reader-response approach to literary criticism*" (p. 65; Mailloux's italics). The rest of the book tries to supply that kind of approach through both theoretical and practical criticism.

Mailloux's discussions of "Rappaccini's Daughter," *Moby-Dick*, and *The Red Badge of Courage* are convincing readings that establish how the shape of the text depends on the ways readers respond to it. Especially ingenious is the way Mailloux establishes how even so "scientific" a literary method as textual criticism depends on interpretive conventions. The proof lies in his discussion of how readers' responses to *The Red Badge of Courage* not only established the original ending of the published version but have resisted all attempts to re-instill it in new editions. When used this well, reader-response criticism may have much to say about how the new history of American literature will be written.

Some mention ought to be made here of John Carlos Rowe's *Through the Custom-House: Nineteenth-Century American Fiction and Modern Theory* (Hopkins), which applies different types of revisionist theory to six 19th-century American texts. Rowe applies Heidegger's late essays to *A Week on the Concord and Merrimack Rivers*, Sartre on the imagination to *The Blithedale Romance*, Freud to *The Narrative of Arthur Gordon Pym*, Derrida's revision of Freud to "Bartleby the Scrivener," Nietzsche to *Pudd'nhead Wilson*, and the structural linguistics of Saussure and Benveniste to *The Sacred Fount*. I shall not deal with any of these readings here, because they will be discussed in other chapters of *ALS*. Instead I shall point readers to the difficult but stimulating introduction that justifies the applications by contending that the forms of 19th-century American literature are so unusual that conventional readings cannot account for them. Rowe suggests that this fact arises from the perpetual sense of belatedness felt by all serious American writers at that time. He quotes from Harold Bloom to make his point: "Our poets' characteristic anxiety is not so much an expectation of being flooded by poetic ancestors, as already *having been* flooded before one could even begin": (*A Map of Misreading*, p. 52). This anxiety explains the generic confusion that exists in the period. "What major work of nineteenth-century American literature," asks Rowe, "belongs to any recognizable genre?" (p. 25). It's a good question, which by implication suggests that the belatedness felt by 19th-century American authors was translated into works that in fact prefigured modernism—thereby justifying the use of modernist interpretive theory to anlyze the works themselves. Perhaps so, but in the final analysis Rowe's interpretations can be justified only by their own valid relation to the texts themselves.

Two other works complete this section. The first, by Emily Stipes Watts, is *The Businessman in American Literature* (Georgia). This historical study, which focuses chiefly on the novel, is organized chronologically around thematic clusters. In the early chapters, which explore the Puritan attitude toward money, Watts challenges as "wrongheaded" Max Weber's theory of the Puritan ethic and the rise of capitalism. She claims that the Puritans had much more suspicion of accumulative gain than we have been led to believe. Their views of piety gave rise in American literature to a predominantly negative view of the businessman which was sustained throughout the 19th century by writers such as Melville, Howells, Twain, and James. Although Sinclair Lewis parodied the businessman in *Babbitt*, that novel was written out of a basic understanding and acceptance of business values foreign until then to most other American writers. Even Dreiser, who stood in awe of the animal graspingness of Cowperwood, did not fundamentally embrace his values. By the 1930s, however, the general view of business had changed, and since that time the businessman has become something of a hero in works by Kesey, Vonnegut, and even Bellow. How long that will last remains to be seen, since the burgeoning scale of American business threatens to destroy the very concept of the businessman.

Joan Zlotnick's *Portrait of an American City: The Novelists' New York* (Kennikat) studies the use of New York City as a setting in American writings since colonial times. The chapter titles are a clear guide to the book's historical organization: e.g., "The Emerging Metropolis," "The Gay Nineties," "From Shtetl to Sweatshop," "The Roaring Twenties," "The Great Depression," "The Contemporary Scene." While the material is fascinating, the plodding quality of the chapter titles gives a clue to the imaginative level of the book. As an overview this is a useful compendium, with lots of quotations from the novels; but there is a good bit of carelessness here, and one is not always inclined to trust the author. For example, the hero of Dreiser's *The "Genius"* is consistently misspelled as Wilta, and the main character of Bellow's novel is referred to as *Morris* Herzog (p. 195). A good editor would have protected the author from such embarrassments.

*c.* **Ethnic Literatures.**   Brief mention goes to *Three American Literatures: Essays in Chicano, Native American, and Asian American Literature for Teachers of American Literature,* ed. Houston Baker, Jr., intro. Walter J. Ong (MLA). While these essays are not original contributions, they are well-informed pieces of work, written by individuals who are leaders in their fields. The essays on Chicano and Native American literatures are probably the best, particularly Raymund A. Paredes on "The Evolution of Chicano Literature" and Kenneth Lincoln's "Native American Literatures: 'old like hills, like stars.'" The pieces on the Asian American literatures (Chinese American and Japanese American) are not as good, although a lengthy piece written by four authors contains a number of useful references.

It reads, unfortunately, as if it had been written by four authors. A more comprehensive overview appears in Elaine H. Kim, *Asian American Literature: An Introduction to the Writings and Their Social Context* (Temple), which covers Chinese, Japanese, Korean, and Filipino literatures, primarily writings in English. Kim begins with a discussion of the stereotypes of Asians that have long appeared in American literature, embodied in such characters as Mr. Moto, Fu Manchu, and Charlie Chan. She then turns to the slim 19th-century beginnings of a literature written by Asian Americans, and to the increasing body of work done in this century. In the early chapters she mentions writers as familiar as Lin Yutang and devotes a long section to the Filipino author Carlos Bulosan.

Chapters follow entitled "Second-Generation Self-Portrait," which includes discussions of Pardee Lowe and Jade Snow Wong, and one called "Portraits of Chinatown," which contains a discussion of *Flower Drum Song*, the source of a well-known Rodgers and Hammerstein musical. A chapter called "Chinatown Cowboys and Warrior Women" contains discussions of contemporary writers Frank Chin, Jeffrey Paul Chan, and Maxine Hong Kingston. "New Directions" covers Asian American responses to the Vietnam War, experimental poetry, racism and annihilation, ethnic self-definition, and writing by women. Kim is careful to present a balanced discussion of each ethnic group, claiming that while these literatures deal in multicultural perspectives, they are not assimilationist.

Charles M. Tatum's *Chicano Literature* (Twayne) attempts a full historical, generic account of Chicano writings. (Although Tatum is an Anglo-Saxon name, we are informed that his mother was a native of Mexico.) The first chapter presents historical backgrounds and the second traces the history of Chicano literature from the 16th century through the 1950s. Four chapters follow on the theater, short story, novel, and poetry. Most of this literature is recent and is understandably involved with establishing a sense of cultural pride. Tatum stresses the fact that many oral forms still survive in these writings, particularly in drama and poetry. The only name at all widely known is that of John Rechy, author of *City of Night*. All in all, *Chicano Literature* is a solid, though unimaginative introduction to the field.

Murray Baumgarten's *City Scriptures: Modern Jewish Writing* (Harvard) studies 20th-century Jewish writers from the point of

view of their urban nature and their concern with human identity.
Baumgarten claims that when Jews began to leave the ghettoes, they
were faced with the choice of what identity they might assume now
that they were no longer rigidly defined as "Jews": " 'Who am I?
Who will I become? What will my children become?' There was a
dizzying array of answers: 'I am Reform; I am a Zionist; I am Marxist; I remain Orthodox.' It is this question of identity—underscored
by the dynamics of an immigrant experience—that has informed so
much of modern Jewish writing" (p. 162). Baumgarten believes that
this peculiar situation of Jewish writers—he is primarily, though not
exclusively concerned with those who come from a Yiddishist background—makes them important critical thinkers for the modern sensibility. "Leaving behind old habits," Baumgarten says, "the critical
thinker takes along old values. Self-definition depends on the honor-
ing of two commitments: his independence can be maintained only
insofar as he recognizes his traditional values. . . . His dual allegiance
leads the modern Jewish writer to an intensive exploration of the
conditions for character and individuality" (p. 31).

The book is not driven by a thesis so much as by certain themes
that the author follows through a number of writers from diverse
backgrounds, including some Americans—e.g., Sholem Aleichem,
I. B. Singer, Isaac Babel, Philip and Henry Roth, Saul Bellow, Bernard Malamud, Jorge Luis Borges, and Samuel Agnon. The chapter
titles indicate some of the major themes: "Dual Allegiances," "Cloth-
ing and Character," "Community and Modernity," "Folk Speech and
Holy Tongue," "City Premises." Baumgarten also makes some convincing connections between the modern Jewish writers and the classic writers of the American Renaissance: "The writers of the American Renaissance, like the modern Jewish writers, emerged from a
religious culture centered on the notion of election, on the idea of
their chosenness; and both work with a language of tradition while
seeking to articulate an idiolect expressive of a critical view of their
communal religious past and their modern individualist present in
response to the crisis of modernity" (p. 33). This is a well-written,
stimulating book whose insights transcend its subject.

*d.* **The Media and Technology.** This section contains four books
that focus on the various media and technologies that affect Ameri-

can literature and culture. The first, Daniel J. Czitrom's *Media and the American Mind: From Morse to McLuhan* (N.C.) is concerned with three media: the telegraph, motion pictures, and radio. In part 1 of this intellectual and social history of American communication the author shows the ways the media grew in the United States and how they changed the conduct of American life. For instance, "Before the telegraph there existed no separation between transportation and communication. Information traveled only as fast as the messenger who carried it" (p. 3); or, "Whereas the telegraph had inspired mystery and wonder by transforming the nature of communication, the motion picture confronted the accepted standards of culture itself. Movies introduced more than a new communication technology; they quickly became the principal new (and most popular) art form of the 20th century" (p. 30). There are also fine insights about the impact of radio on modern culture.

Part 2 studies various contemporary theorists. One chapter focuses on early sociologists of communication, such as Charles Horton Cooley, John Dewey, and Robert E. Park. There is another chapter about the development between 1930 and 1960 of the study of communications as an intellectual discipline. A final chapter on Harold Innis and his disciple, Marshall McLuhan, explains how those thinkers went beyond data collection to focus on *how*, or *on the way* media affect people.

John A. Kouwenhoven has long been an important name in American cultural studies, and one of his books, *Made in America*, is a classic. His latest book, *Half a Truth Is Better Than None: Some Unsystematic Conjectures about Art, Disorder, and American Experience* (Chicago), is a collection of essays that add up to a statement of Kouwenhoven's theory of American culture, artifact, and media. All the essays are informed by the author's intimate knowledge of technology and cultural artifact, and they reflect a definition of "American" civilization as "that often untidy vernacular ferment produced when the technology of manufactured power and the democratic spirit work together" (p. 5). There are a number of delightful essays in this book, all of them characterized by skeptical sanity, light wit, and excellent prose. Among my favorites are "American Culture: Words or Things?," "Democracy, Machines, and Vernacular Design," and "Design and Chaos: The American Distrust of Art"; two wonderful essays on photography, "Living in a Snapshot World" and "Photographs as Historical Documents"; and a masterpiece of cultural-technological generalization, "The Eiffel Tower and the Ferris Wheel." This book represents not old-fashioned American studies, but rather the middle generation of such studies that emphasized cultural theory and the cultural lessons to be learned from technology.

The remaining two works in this section are concerned with the book industry. The first, by Lewis A. Coser, Charles Kadushin, and Walter W. Powell, *Books: The Culture & Commerce of Publishing* (Basic Books), is a sociological study of the publishing industry that uses all the apparatus of field research, including interviews, questionnaires, and statistical analyses of found and solicited data. The authors study marketing techniques, career patterns, hidden and covert decision-making, the roles of authors, middlemen, and distributors, and the situation of women in the industry. The sociological detachment of tone adds to the unsettling nature of the findings, which suggest that the industry on which we depend as teachers and writers is in serious trouble. The coolness of tone is, however, broken by many vivid anecdotes and quotations from interviews, all of which add up to a probing look at the publishing industry.

Leonard Shatzkin's *In Cold Type: Overcoming the Book Crisis* (Houghton Mifflin) is a prescription by a long-time publishing executive and consultant for dealing with what he considers a sick industry. While Shatzkin's conclusions are similar to those in the previous book, they come from a management rather than sociological perspective, and he is polemical in presenting solutions. He sees waste in the sales, distribution, and overall economic policies of publishing, and he sees no hope that the industry will turn itself around unless it makes a series of basic reforms. The problem, as Shatzkin sees it, is not that there are too many books being published; rather, it is an inadequate sales force and an antiquated policy of returns that cause a multitude of abuses. In addition, the companies do a poor job of preparing the sales force concerning new publications, and they have a marginal understanding of the differences among local markets. The book is not well written, and it does tend to be repetitious, but if *ALS* readers look it over along with the one by Coser et al., they will receive good insights into the current dismal situation in publishing.

*e.* **Special Topics.** In this section I shall treat a series of works not as easily categorized. Not surprisingly, many of this year's more interesting works fall into this group.

*Grammar and Good Taste: Reforming the English Language* (Yale), by Dennis E. Baron, is a historical study of attempts to reform the American language from colonial times up to Edwin Newman and William Safire, with primary emphasis, however, on the 18th and 19th centuries. While almost all such attempts have been futile, the focus of the controversy has been widespread, concerned by various authors with spelling, pronunciation, grammar, and usage, or with grammar as prescription or description, or with English versus American usage. Some of the theorists of prescriptive reform were Noah Webster, Benjamin Franklin, Richard Grant White, Goold Brown, Lindley Murray, and Henry James. Baron's own approach is detached and nonprescriptive, and he writes with sly, skeptical humor. For example: "The cyclical popularity of school grammar in our education system may partly be a result of the misconception of grammar as a body of etiquette rules to be learned and applied rather than as a body of knowledge to be studied for its own sake. We do not teach biology in the schools so that students can be better able to use their bodies. We teach it so they can understand how bodies work. But we do not feel the same way about English language instruction" (pp. 166–67). While many of us tend to think of grammar in the way Baron makes fun of, this lively book should give all prescriptivists a better sense of what we are up against.

Philip D. Beidler's *American Literature and the Experience of Vietnam* (Georgia) is a very personal book, at least partly because Beidler himself, as a veteran of the war, contributes much of his own vivid memory of how it felt to be there. Beidler characterizes the literature of Vietnam as "a mixup of American mythic consciousness and realized experiential fact so dense and entangled that from the very beginning there would never be any real hope of sorting it out" (p. 31). The book's opening chapter tries to capture the experience of the war through evocative quotation from a series of writings, while the second chapter places the material in the context of American literature. Three long chapters then survey the writings by historical periods: 1958–70; 1970–75; 1975 to the present. Beidler tries to suggest that the literature of the war is characterized by both shifting emphases and a continuous development, but in this I did not find him successful. Still, the book is an excellent introduction to the literature of that unfortunate war. Because the author assumes the reader has read little of the writing, he summarizes most of the works he discusses and performs few lengthy analyses.

The next book is a reference work that will seduce any student of American literature. It is *The Oxford Illustrated Guide to the United States* by Eugene Ehrlich and Gorton Carruth (Oxford), written, the authors claim, so that travelers can "find places associated with the lives and works of writers" (p. vii). The book is organized encyclopedically, first by regions, then by cities ("1,586 hamlets, villages, towns, and cities"). Places where writers have lived and written are listed, and the texts connected with each city, town, hamlet, and village relate the places to the lives and works of the various writers. There are also many photographs, at least one on each page, of both writers and settings. In the front of the book, names of states and cities are listed alphabetically, so that if you wish to explore the book geographically, you can do so. If you wish to find references to a specific author, you consult the alphabetical index at the end. To give you some sense of the scale of things, the section on Salem, Massachusetts, has barely 2 pages; that of New York City, organized by boroughs and sections, has 43. I challenge any reader not to spend a lot of time browsing through this fascinating book.

The recent interest in John Reed, Louise Bryant, and that generation of writers that was reflected in the celebrated movie *Reds* is also reflected in a book published around the same time, Leslie Fishbein's *Rebels in Bohemia: The Radicals of The Masses, 1911–1917* (N.C.). This book studies the radical culture of the period, using as its focus *The Masses* and the people and social movements related to that journal. The place is New York City; the neighborhood, Greenwich Village; the time, the six years before the entry of this country into the First World War. The book is a good historical study of a transitional period in American culture, one that saw an ascension of public interest in Marx, Freud, feminism, sex, and the arts of modernism. There was a cult of youth, and contemporary thinkers confused youthful rebellion with the interests of a class, choosing "to root [rebellion] in the fleeting modernity of adolescence, thereby imperiling the very survival of that rebellion into maturity" (p. 57). The writers here are numerous—including John Reed, Floyd

Dell, Max Eastman, Louise Bryant, George Cram Cook, Mary Heaton
Vorse, Emma Goldman, Mabel Dodge, Hutchins Hapgood, and many
others—and though there are no major figures among them, they
are all of historical literary interest. Fishbein is successful in showing
how the radical pose of most of these figures was contradicted by
their basically middle-class lives and values.

One of the better books of 1982 is Gary Lindberg's *The Confidence
Man in American Literature* (Oxford). Primarily concerned with
works of fiction, Lindberg makes *excursi* into the works of Franklin,
Emerson, and Thoreau. This excellent, often wise book is brash and
sometimes polemical, but the author comes to his work with a definite
vision of American culture. As a result, this is not just a history of the
use of the confidence man in American literature; it is a study of how
the concept developed as a trope, the study of which can help us
"understand some important things about our history and our values"
(p. 4).

Lindberg begins with Melville's novel to establish the basic model
of the con man and the kinds of belief he both establishes and exploits. He then turns to Franklin and traces the historical background
giving rise to the American need for individualistic exploitation and
"confidence." Chapters follow on the development of the various
types of con man in Melville, Poe, and Twain. The ingenious chapter
on Thoreau is preceded by one on Emerson in which Lindberg characterizes the Oversoul as a Jack-of-All-Trades. Along the way Lindberg has interesting things to say about P. T. Barnum, Jack Kerouac,
Ken Kesey, Joseph Heller, Saul Bellow, John Barth, and Watergate.
This is the best work I know on the confidence man in American
literature.

Two large, valuable works about the South will get only brief
mention here, because I didn't have the time to read them all the
way through. The first is by Bertram Wyatt-Brown, *Southern Honor:
Ethics & Behavior in the Old South* (Oxford), which traces the evolution of the code of honor in the antebellum South. Wyatt-Brown's
approach to history is sociological, and the insights he derives about
the nature of the southern character remind me of Cash's *The Mind
of the South*. The author defines the notion of honor that developed
in the South, tracing it to the sense of family and kinship structures
as well as the elaborate sense of gentility that evolved as the region
did. He talks about the roles of mothers, fathers, women, and men,

and defines the South's characteristic quality of male dominance. Wyatt-Brown's prose is elegant, and the book reads much like a narrative.

Daniel Joseph Singal is also a historian, whose book, *The War Within: From Victorian to Modernist Thought in the South, 1919–1945* (N.C.) is a first-rate study of the development of modern thought in the South. It focuses on writers in a variety of fields, including history, fiction, publishing, sociology, and poetry, showing in the process how important it was for writers to break free of the Cavalier myth, so elegantly described by Bertram Wyatt-Brown, in order to become modern thinkers. While the book is not a literary analysis, it is informed by a literary sensibility. Its excellent chapters on Ellen Glasgow, William Faulkner, the Agrarians (as a group), Allen Tate, and Robert Penn Warren make it essential reading for students of Southern literature.

In *Autobiographical Occasions and Original Acts: Versions of American Identity from Henry Adams to Nate Shaw* (Penn.), Albert E. Stone studies autobiography as a manifestation of culture. Autobiographies, he claims, "are indeed centrifugal cultural works. They resist closure and the nonreferentiality of art, while remaining art. In choosing this mode or convention of communication, the writer deliberately eschews the aesthetic freedom and integrity his discourse might have possessed had it taken other narrative forms" (p. 4). By extension, the form of the autobiography determines the way reality is remembered. While the theory of autobiography expressed here is not terribly innovative, the specific readings are convincing, and the range of the writers discussed is wide, including Henry Adams, Black Elk, Louis Sullivan, Richard Wright, Margaret Mead, Anaïs Nin, Malcolm X, Norman Mailer, and Lillian Hellman. Beyond the opening chapter that states Stones's view of autobiography in America, the rest of the book will reward dipping into more than reading straight through.

While on the face of it, Bryan Jay Wolf's fascinating book, *Romantic Re-Vision: Culture and Consciousness in Nineteenth-Century American Painting and Literature* (Chicago), is more a study of paintings than writing, what he has to say is of great relevance to students of literature. Wolf reads paintings as if they were texts, influenced here by an immersion in contemporary theory, most apparently in Harold Bloom and revisionary readings of Freud. For

Wolf Romantic paintings were engaged in the same "dialectic of consciousness with itself" as were the writings. Perhaps most interesting is that he treats paintings as intertextual documents, or as artifacts created within traditions and quoting from predecessors and precursors.

The book focuses on three American Romantic painters—Washington Allston, John Quidor, and Thomas Cole—and it includes ingenious readings of a number of their works, perhaps most memorably Quidor's *The Return of Rip Van Winkle* and Cole's *Snow Squall, Winter Landscape in the Catskills.* Wolf asserts that Allston defines himself by his references to other painters and traditions, and he generalizes from his readings of Allston as follows: "Parody liberated 19th-century Romanticism from the assumptions and biases of more referential modes of discourse, providing it instead with a thrust toward modernism that emphasized syntactic enclosure over referential intent. . . . By shifting the burden of meaning in a work of art from the ostensible subject to its organizing principles, it wed literary or visual formalism with linguistic self-awareness" (pp. 17–18). Coming as it does out of analyses of Allston's paintings, this generalization strikes me as quite fresh and useful to students of American Romanticism.

Wolf's reading of Cole is more in the deconstructive mode, as in this summation of the artist's masterpiece, the *Expulsion from the Garden of Eden*: "Cole's achievement in the *Expulsion from the Garden of Eden* is to have created a myth of Romantic selfhood that validates the individual's act of assertion by a process of reversal: Cole's *repudiation* of the constraints of Eden is transformed into a tale of expulsion and defeat, masking through its imagery of loss the force of its own refusal" (pp. 102–03). This is one deconstructive reading that does more than merely present a sophisticated poetics. It illuminates a text.

Space hinders me here, but let me mention how effective is Wolf's reading of Quidor's marvelous painting, *The Return of Rip Van Winkle*, as a drama of belatedness similar to Harold Bloom's reading of American Romantic literature. So too are Wolf's discussions of other paintings that Quidor based on the writings of Washington Irving, such as *The Money Diggers* and *Antony Van Corlear Brought into the Presence of Peter Stuyvesant.* "Quidor's art," Wolf writes, "is a deconstructive mode of art, premised not on the possibility of

authentic vision but on its absence" (p. 130), a reading that fits the
paintings very well. This book's value lies not so much in what it
has to tell us about the paintings or their period as in its providing
us with examples of how contemporary theory can fruitfully explain
our major texts.

## ii. General Works of Theory and Criticism

*a.* **Writings about Theorists.**  It is quite clear that acts of criticism
and theory are increasingly being equated with poetry, fiction, and
drama. In fact, some writers suggest they represent a higher order of
creative thought. As that attitude has become widespread, and as
theory has come closer to philosophy, it is not surprising that the
theorist has become something of a literary culture hero, about whom
serious books are being written with analytical readings that have
heretofore been reserved for "belletristic" writers. In this section I
shall write about seven works that analyze the writings of leading
theorists.

Elizabeth W. Bruss had finished the draft of *Beautiful Theories:
The Spectacle of Discourse in Contemporary Criticism* (Hopkins)
before her untimely death at the age of 36. It is a wise, erudite book,
and reading it gives one a sense of great loss, although had Bruss
lived to see it through publication with a good editor she might well
have cut it down to a more manageable size. The book attempts to
explain the present Age of Criticism, and some of her general propositions are as good as I have read. "But theory," she writes, "was also
attractive for its capacity—as an extraordinary and invented language—to go beyond the range of the familiar and the usual that are
the province of ordinary language and that never even appear problematic as long as terms derived from ordinary language seem inevitable. The unconscious and the ideological are precisely what are
hidden to habitual perception" (p. 21). Such theoretical speculations were more fertilely spawned in continental European countries
of more idealistic philosophical traditions than those of the more
empirical Anglo-American tradition.

In her first chapter Bruss explains *why* an age of criticism has
occurred, and in the second chapter she explores the process of *how*
theory became of an interest equal or superior to that of "literature."
The book's third chapter discusses various strategies for entering the

different kinds of theoretical texts currently being written. All this is preparation for a series of lengthy chapters on William Gass, Susan Sontag, Harold Bloom, and Roland Barthes. An afterword tries to tie together these four theorists with the common thread that they are *re*readers. (Doesn't all criticism involve *re*reading?) It seems to me that other critics might have worked just as well, but the analyses Bruss offers of each one are helpful, if wordy.

Eugene Lunn's *Marxism & Modernism: An Historical Study of Lukács, Brecht, Benjamin, and Adorno* (Calif.) studies four major Marxist thinkers with divergent assessments and theories of aesthetic modernism. According to Lunn, none of these theorists were truly orthodox Marxists, although Lukács probably came the closest to being one. Lunn places them historically through presentation of historical context as well as reference to the work of other writers. "Benjamin and Adorno each developed rich and penetrating dialectical readings of the modernist experience since Baudelaire which showed a wider grasp and sympathy than either Brecht or Lukács. But these interpretations, in turn, were contrasting ones: Benjamin . . . was particularly drawn to the spatializing, metaphorical, and depersonalized literature of modern Paris. . . . Adorno's analyses, on the other hand, were indebted to Austro-German musical and philosophical traditions and to the crisis of subjectivity registered in the Viennese modernism of Freud and Schoenberg" (pp. 149–50).

The astute individual analyses arise from Lunn's informed understanding of Marxism. In stressing the many intellectual connections and interactions among his four critics, Lunn creates a sense of a vital German Marxist intellectual community. This book is both erudite and densely textured.

In *Literary Criticism and the Structures of History: Erich Auerbach and Leo Spitzer* (Nebraska) Geoffrey Green studies Auerbach and Spitzer as if they were poets, showing how their critical points of view grew out of their lives as German-Jewish expatriates during the rise of the Third Reich. Each critic was trained in classic German philology, but their experiences forced them to develop a vision of the world that went beyond the philological. "We need," Green says, "the sensibilities of both scholars—the historicistic humanism of Auerbach devoted to the study of man and his literature across a historical evolution of present times; the stylistic spiritualism of Spitzer devoted to the analysis of what is human in art and life across a historical continuum of human visions of the eternal—in order to attain a balanced and working understanding of our own complex and exceptional era" (p. 165).

Annette Lavers, who has translated a number of books by Roland Barthes, has written a full-scale interpretation of his work, *Roland Barthes: Structuralism and After* (Harvard), which contains a clear, relatively concise account of the development of Barthes's thought. This is an intellectual biography rather than a story of Barthes's life, and Lavers seems to share with her subject a reticence about personal detail. There is a helpful exposition of structuralism (good discussions of Piaget and Lévi-Strauss) and of what Lavers claims are four stages in Barthes's career as a theorist. After some opening general chapters, Lavers goes through all of Barthes's works in order, discussing his diachronic and synchronic theories as well as his rhetoric. She not only knows Barthes, she understands the critical and philosophical issues behind the works.

An old culture hero, Kenneth Burke, was the subject of discussions at the 1977 English Institute, which were ultimately the core of *Representing Kenneth Burke*, ed. Hayden White and Margaret Brose (Hopkins). The volume, which contains a number of essays by well-known American theorists, is an excellent introduction to Burke. Although not a systematic survey of his writing, the volume has a coherence and intellectual quality that is rare for such a collection. I particularly recommend the pieces by Fredric Jameson, William Wasserstrom, Frank Lentricchia, and Angus Fletcher.

Two books that explain the writings of Michel Foucault are worth a serious look by either admirers or skeptics. The first and more straightforward one is by Hubert L. Dreyfus and Paul Rabinow, *Michel Foucault: Beyond Structuralism and Hermeneutics* (Chicago). This overview of Foucault's work, written by a philosopher and an anthropologist, is chronological in approach, treating one work at a time, in both summary and critique. The book is designed to show how Foucault's work dramatizes one of the bold tensions in modern thought: between the attempts in hermeneutics and structuralism to solve the dilemma posed by phenomenology of a transcendental subject that provides meaning. The structuralists avoid the problem by positing structures in "reality" that are there regardless of a perceiving subject. Hermeneutics does not seek meaning in the perceiving subject but rather in literary texts and social structures.

Foucault moves between the two poles and then beyond. This is a good introduction to Foucault's work because it is orderly and clear, but one should be familiar with the primary texts before trying to read it.

Another co-authored book, this one by a philosopher and a sociologist, takes a different tack on Foucault. (Does he really need two authors from different fields to explain him?) Charles C. Lemert and Garth Gillan, in *Michel Foucault: Social Theory and Transgression* (Columbia), study Foucault's theories with an emphasis on his development of a special vocabulary. This more synchronic study, often as difficult as one of Foucault's books, is helpful in explaining such special Foucault concepts as episteme, power-knowledge, discourse, and transgression. Crucial to the argument is Foucault's theory of power, which suggests in fact that power lies in theory. "Critical social theory," the authors assert, "is not transcendence of the social, but transgression. . . . Truth is in power. Theory is politics" (p. 28). Quite useful to the reader is a chronological listing of Foucault's publications and a glossary of "Concepts Used by Foucault."

*b.* **Theory of Fiction.** Four works make up this section, all of them interesting, but none embodying a major contribution to the theory of fiction. Three are products of the Chicago school of criticism, which is still at the center of any discussion of literary genres.

David Carroll's *The Subject in Question: The Languages of Theory and the Strategies of Fiction* (Chicago) attempts to relate the most advanced forms of contemporary critical theory to the novel, eventually applying them for the most part to the novels of the French "new" novelist, Claude Simon. Carroll discusses a number of theorists and theories, including Freud, Lacan, Lukács, structuralism, and deconstruction before making his applications. It is an interesting attempt but of limited usefulness to *ALS* readers. For one thing, others have done a better job explaining some of the theories; for another, most readers will not be familiar enough with Claude Simon to be able to see how well Carroll applies the various theories.

*Novels and Arguments: Inventing Rhetorical Criticism,* by Zahava Karl McKeon (Chicago) applies the principles of formal rhetoric to novels in order to use them as analytical tools. McKeon invokes the names of Aristotle and Cicero on many occasions as she establishes four modes of organization: dialectical, grammatical, poetic, and rhetorical. We can choose to analyze a text from any of these points of view, but it is rhetoric itself that provides the overall unifying principle. McKeon applies her theory to specific novels and tales by Günter Grass, John Fowles, Robert Coover, and Flannery O'Connor. Unfortunately, the book is written in such a turgid, multisyllabic prose that it was all I could do to finish it. *Novels and Arguments* is advertised on the book jacket as "the first comprehensive exploration of the rhetoric of the novel"; but whether that claim is true, one might well prefer a less "comprehensive" but far more useful study of the rhetoric of the novel, Wayne Booth's *Rhetoric of Fiction* (out in a new edition in 1983).

Austin M. Wright, a novelist and formally a student at the University of Chicago, is the author of *The Formal Principle in the Novel* (Cornell). He has written a book about the primary structuring principle of the novel, a unity he identifies with the discredited notion of plot. In the first part, called "The Hierarchy of Form," Wright discusses various theoretical matters, including conventions, formal principles, imitation, plot and mimesis—all characteristic of the Aristotelian approach long associated with Chicago. Wright's discussions, while not dogmatic, do seem a bit prescriptive, but the book is too sophisticated to be simply a handbook for writing a novel. The second part of the book contains good readings of *Portrait of a Lady*, *The Sound and the Fury*, *Invisible Man*, and *Pale Fire*. The final chapter explains the usefulness of a theory of fiction to a novelist.

The most interesting work in this section is by Bruce F. Kawin, *The Mind of the Novel: Reflexive Fiction and the Ineffable* (Princeton), which treats the discovery of the self as both theme and technique in the "reflexive" novel. For Kawin the reflexive novel is primarily concerned with what cannot be expressed, with what he frequently refers to as the "ineffable." "The self," he says in his preface, "is not named in these works largely because it is extralinguistic. What is named is the problem of naming" (p. xiii). Kawin focuses primarily on different varieties of the first-person narrator who are the most frequent self-seekers of reflexive fiction. He also distinguishes well between reflexiveness and self-consciousness in fiction, defining the latter as being "a slightly higher order of apprehension" (p. 16). There are analyses of a number of novels, including *Moby-Dick*, *Absalom, Absalom!*, *Pale Fire*, and *Gravity's Rainbow*, and the text is studded throughout with quotable, witty passages. But the prose also gets a little sentimental and lyrical at times, and I must confess that I, for one, get nervous with a book that tells me that "one of the biases of the book you are reading is that the ultimate vision is of a wholeness that can be called Love and that in talking about it we feel our joy expand" (p. 10). Such sentiments betray a softness that often robs Kawin's arguments of a rigor that would ultimately have made *The Mind of the Novel* better than it finally is.

**c. Deconstruction.** This section must begin with mention of a fine new translation by Alan Bass of Jacques Derrida's *Margins of Philosophy* (Chicago). This collection, first published in France in 1972, contains ten essays and a preface, all of which have some interrelationships and most of which are fairly accessible. Many of Derrida's difficult concepts are best confronted in essays rather than in full-length works like *Of Grammatology*. One might well approach his work by reading the first essay in *Margins of Philosophy*, "Différance," which explains how the neologism *différance* arises from the combination of differing and deferring in order to express the inability of language to make the spatial and temporal distinctions on which discourse relies. Language is always temporally and spatially at a distance from fully self-aware utterance. At best, we can but recall, retain, or represent a trace of the original thought giving rise to utterance. The fact that the "a" of Derrida's neologism is not pronounced emphasizes the fact that the concept is inexpressible in speech and expressible only in writing. The concepts of the trace and the primacy of writing loom large in all these essays. Committed Derrideans will want to read the whole book. Others might wish especially to try "The Ends of Man," "The Linguistic Circle of Geneva," and "The Supplement of Copula: Philosophy before Linguistics."

An easier way to get started on a study of deconstruction would be to read an excellent introduction, Christopher Norris' *Deconstruction: Theory & Practice* (Methuen), a handbook written clearly and on a high level. Rather than give a strict definition (what would such a definition be?), Norris conveys the process of working with deconstructive ideas, so that if you read the book carefully you will understand the concept well enough to read the primary works. Norris also traces deconstruction historically, from the diacritical notions of Saussure through structuralism to poststructuralist writings. The sections on Derrida not only discuss the major texts but expound on the key ideas, such as the trace and *différance*. Norris then harks back to Nietzsche and Marx as deconstructionist precursors of Derrida. In a long chapter discussing American deconstructionists, he contrasts Geoffrey Hartman and Hillis Miller (deconstruction 'on the wild side') with Paul de Man (who has the kind of logical rigor Norris associates with Derrida). There is a useful selected bibliography for those who wish to read further.

Jonathan Culler's *On Deconstruction: Theory and Construction After Structuralism* (Cornell) is another book by this author on the emergence of the "new" criticism and theory, this one being in my judgment one of the better works in English on the theory and implications of deconstruction. Written in a tone of calm and rational exposition, the book distinguishes quite clearly between the deconstructive and structuralist projects. Culler shows how deconstruction begins with a recognition that works are structured on binary oppositions—such as, in Freud's case, normal/abnormal. It often continues by showing how the term conventionally considered primary may in fact be the secondary term; that, for instance, we may understand normality only by having abnormality against which to measure it. Deconstruction then works to reveal the contradictions inherent in a text that either the text itself or conventional readings of it have sought to conceal. Texts are their own best guides as to how we are to read them: "Deconstruction emphasizes the self-referential moments of a text in order to reveal the surprising effects of employing a portion of a text to analyze the whole or the uncanny relationships between one textual level and another or one discourse and another" (p. 205).

The book covers a great deal of ground, since it is mostly a summary exposition of the field. Culler is a synthesizer, not an original critic like Derrida, de Man, or Hartman, but what he substitutes for his own original relationship to literary texts is a genuine ability to demonstrate the relationship among the various new schools of criticism. He is well versed in 20th-century philosophy, and he reads theoretical texts closely and persuasively.

The final section focuses on specific critical applications of the method of deconstruction. Emerging as the closest thing to Culler's model critic and theorist is Paul de Man, whose subtle readings embody the fullest understanding and application of the work of Derrida. Others whom Culler admires are Barbara Johnson, Neil Hertz, and Shoshanna Felman. The book concludes with an excellent bibliography of most of the essential writings in the field.

Another distinguished book on deconstruction is by Susan A. Handelman, *The Slayers of Moses: The Emergence of Rabbinic Interpretation in Modern Literary Theory* (SUNY), which is part of the SUNY Series on Modern Jewish Literature and Culture. The four specific "slayers of Moses" are Sigmund Freud, Jacques Lacan, Jacques Derrida, and Harold Bloom, who embody for Handelman an essential struggle in contemporary intellectual history between Hebrew and Hellene, Jew and Greek.

Handelman's theory is that the "new" criticism is a return to Hebraic ways of thought and interpretation, and as such it constitutes a revolt against the remnants in Western thought of our Greek intellectual heritage. "What Greek thought split asunder—word and thing—Derrida seeks to rejoin," Handelman says, in order to restore or reconstitute " 'what was originally represented,' the 'primary meaning' " (p. 18). This is similar to "one of the most interesting aspects of Rabbinic thought," which "is its development of a highly sophisticated system of interpretation based on uncovering and expanding the primary concrete meaning, and yet drawing a variety of logical inferences from these meanings without the abstracting, idealizing movement of Western thought" (p. 19).

By trying to reunite language with its primary referent, the slayers of Moses are elevating the status of the text much as the Rabbinic tradition elevated the Torah. But if the text is paramount, then interpretations of it become equivalent to the text itself. If Torah, Midrash, Talmud, and later commentary all have comparable status within Rabbinic tradition—and are therefore, of necessity, treated intertextually—so there is also at least a rough equivalence between Derrida and Hegel when the former interprets the latter. All interpretation of Hegel from now on will have to contend with Derrida as much as with the texts of Hegel. The ultimate in intertextuality is shown by Handelman's reproduction (p. 48) of a page from the Vilna edition of the Talmud, which, except for its Hebrew, looks suspiciously like a page from *Glas*, Derrida's gloss on Hegel, or *Saving the Text*, Hartman's gloss on Derrida's gloss on Hegel.

Space prevents my going on, but it should be clear that I think this a very stimulating book. Not as coherent an overview as Culler's, it nonetheless contains more original ideas. The theory is quite convincing, and the writing is clear even when it deals with difficult concepts. The metaphor in the title combines references to both Freud and Bloom.

Brief mention goes to *Yale French Studies*, no. 63, ed. Barbara Johnson, entitled *The Pedagogical Imperative: Teaching as a Literary Genre*. Starting from the deconstructive theory that texts teach us how to read them by exposing their own internal oppositions and differences, this collection of essays "asks not: how should *we* teach literature? but rather: what does literature have to teach *us* about the act of teaching?" (p. iii). The essays are written by a number of figures associated with contemporary theory, including Paul de Man ("The Resistance to Theory"), Shoshana Felman ("Psychoanalysis and Education: Teaching Terminable and Interminable"), Michael Ryan ("Deconstruction and Radical Teaching"), Neil Hertz ("Two Extravagant Teachings"), and Jacques Derrida himself ("All Ears: Nietzsche's Octobiography"). The essays contain an interesting mixture of theory and practical advice, and they represent one of the first attempts to translate deconstructionism into practical pedagogy.

A promising but utimately disappointing book is *Marxism and Deconstruction: A Critical Articulation* by Michael Ryan (Hopkins), which ostensibly sets out to demonstrate the similarities between Marx and Derrida. Ryan claims that "how we read or analyze and how we organize political and social institutions are related forms of practice" (p. iv). Ryan's early thesis is convincing insofar as he can demonstrate that both Marxism and deconstruction are involved in similar reductive (not reductionistic) analyses. His opening expositions of Derrida are helpful, although the use of language and special vocabulary are absolutely uncompromising in relation to the reader.

Even so, one could tolerate a certain inelegance of style if there were no other serious problems. But the book gets bogged down in its need to maintain a radical, action-oriented pose. Both Marxism and deconstruction are instruments designed to expose ideologies, but this book becomes ideological (in its very unquestioned assumptions) in ways its ostensible deconstructionist program proposes to expose. Jargon also abounds. Everything has a label, and -isms proliferate. Let me quote a short passage out of context (perhaps unfairly so): "The categories by which one knows the world are merely a subset of the transsubjective institutional conceptual system that underwrites the construction of the social world according to logocentric or metaphysical principles" (p. 123). You could dislocate your jaw reading that bit of dogmatism aloud. A good book remains to be written on this subject.

*d.* **Hermeneutics.** I have placed in this category works of classical hermeneutics and reader-response theory, and I shall begin with two works by one of the leaders of the German school of reader-response theory.

The University of Minnesota Press has begun a series, "Theory and History of Literature," of which two books by Hans Robert Jauss constitute the second and third volumes. *Toward an Aesthetic of Reception* (vol. 2), trans. Timothy Bahti, intro. Paul de Man, brings to American readers a collection of influential writings by a colleague of Wolfgang Iser at the University of Konstanz. Influenced by Hans-Georg Gadamer, and himself an expert on French literature, Jauss attempts to unite hermeneutics and poetics. (He is a founder and co-editor of *Poetik und Hermeneutic.*) De Man's explanation is useful here: "Hermeneutics is, by definition, a process directed toward the determination of meaning; it postulates a transcendental function of understanding . . . and will . . . have to raise questions about the extralinguistic truth value of literary texts. Poetics . . . is a metalinguistic, descriptive or prescriptive discipline that lays claim to scientific consistency. It pertains to the formal analysis of linguistic entities as such, independent of signification; as a branch of linguistics, it deals with theoretical models prior to their historical realization" (p. ix). I particularly recommend the essays, "Literary History as a Challenge to Literary Theory" (an already well-known work, given by Jauss as his inaugural lecture at Konstanz) and "History of Art and Pragmatic History." Both are influential documents in the current attempt to redefine literary history.

The second book by Jauss is *Aesthetic Experience and Literary Hermeneutics* (Minn.), trans. Michael Shaw and introduced by Wlad Godzich. In contrast to the previous volume this a full-length work rather than a collection of essays. It focuses on the reader's experience of works of literature and the ways in which readers experience (primary response) and critics or hermeneutists interpret (secondary response). Jauss deals with literature from a historical perspective, but he is also fully aware of contemporary critical approaches. The first two sections, "Sketch of a Theory and History of Aesthetic Experience" and "Interaction Patterns of Identification with the Hero," are often abstract and demanding, but the remainder of the book deals more closely with literary texts. This book would be important to anyone interested in hermeneutics and reader-response criticism.

Two works by T. K. Seung arrived too late for me to read. They are *Structuralism and Hermeneutics* and its sequel *Semiotics and Thematics in Hermeneutics*, both published by Columbia. The author is a professor of philosophy at Texas who has focused directly on the major problems and authors of contemporary literary theory. Some writers he treats are Lévi-Strauss, Jakobson, Saussure, Barthes, Foucault, Derrida, Freud, Husserl, Heidegger, Gadamer, Habermas, and Louis Althusser. Seung tries to relate structuralism and hermeneutics to show how both movements and those in between are all part of an analogous effort to account for the analysis and interpretation of texts. The second volume is a more philosophical attempt to present a viable theory that will account for both structure and meaning in a text. My skimming of the two books suggests that they might well be important documents which successfully cross the boundary between criticism and philosophy, as do most important works of theory written in the past few decades.

*Autobiography: Toward a Poetics of Experience*, by Janet Varner Gunn (Penn.), studies autobiography from the point of view of hermeneutics and reader-response criticism, constituting thereby a kind of poetics of the autobiography. Autobiography, for Gunn, is a reading of life by the author which forces the reader to read him or herself while reading about the author's self. "As the reader of his or her life, the autobiographer inhabits the hermeneutic universe where all understanding takes place. The autobiographer serves, by this habitation, as the paradigmatic reader; and the autobiographical text, embodying this reading, becomes, in turn, a model of the possibilities and problems of all interpretive activity" (p. 22). Gunn chooses as her subjects *Walden*, "Tintern Abbey," *Remembrance of*

*Things Past*, St. Augustine's *Confessions*, and *Black Elk Speaks*, each of which exemplifies a different autobiographical approach or mode. A heavy use of critical jargon gets in the way more than it should in this book, but Gunn's thesis is persuasive, and she does have some fresh things to say about the genre.

I place Gerald L. Bruns's *Inventions: Writing, Textuality, and Understanding in Literary History* (Yale) in this section because it deals primarily with the interpretation of meaning, but, like most good books, this one resists being categorized. It is an excellent application of and a series of free-wheeling meditations on theories of textuality and intertextuality.

In the beginning Bruns deals with problems of secrecy and hidden meanings in both speech and in a manuscript culture. The inability of language to convey thought adequately means that secrecy is an intrinsic part of the order of communication. Allegory, for instance, is developed to exploit this ambiguity and to convert linguistic utterance into a system of signs we can understand. Modern interpretive theory has taken a number of points of view on the subject: "In Marxist and Freudian thinking secrecy possesses a short and disreputable life on the surface of what requires to be exposed. In the Nietzschean tradition the secret is somewhat more interesting: it is that across which language throws its figurative resources" (p. 17). It is in the Nietzschean tradition that Bruns situates his own theory: "The whole orientation of the interpretive task is toward the preservation of secrecy, or what amounts to the same thing, namely the preservation of the boundaries of understanding, which are not to be transgressed" (p. 40).

There are many other stimulating insights in the book, including one of the best discussions I know on how writing and printing breed differing concepts of the text; on the difference in the concepts of the text of philosophers and rhetoricians; on the meanings of *context* and *author*ity; and on the theory of intertextuality. "Writing," Bruns says, "is thus always in some sense hermeneutic, which means that it is never an original activity but is always mediated by the texts that provide access to the system. To write is to intervene in what has already been written; it is to work 'between the lines' of antecedent texts, there to gloss, to embellish, to build invention upon invention" (p. 53). This is certainly among the handful of first-rate works of theory published during 1982. Bruns is in a class with the best Yale or Johns Hopkins critics, and he writes a more lucid prose than most of them.

*e.* **Special Topics.** Alastair Fowler's *Kinds of Literature: An Introduction to the Theory of Genres and Modes* (Harvard) is one of the fullest, most sensibly argued studies I know of on the nature of literary genres and of how they are formed. Fowler's major point is that "literature should not be regarded as a class at all, but as an aggregate" (p. 3), and he argues against Northrop Frye's assertion that "'Literature is not a piled aggregate of "works," but an order of words.'" Fowler feels that this "dictum is not a very happy one. When we read literature, what we read are groups of works, or works, or parts of works: not words" (p. 4).

Although Fowler is well informed about recent theory, his writing reflects Anglo-Saxon commonsense criticism at its best. He does not argue for or discuss particular genres in detail; rather, he discusses the process of generic formation, concerning himself with such topics as "The Formation of Genres," "Transformations of Genre," "Generic Modulation," and "Hierarchies of Genres and Canons of Literature." He writes primarily about works in English, and he relates modern works to older ones to show the dangers of rigid definition and the necessity for constant flexibility in making generic distinctions.

Brief mention will go to Jane Gallop, *The Daughter's Seduction: Feminism and Psychoanalysis* (Cornell), a complex and difficult reading of Jacques Lacan in the light primarily of contemporary French feminism. "I hold the Lacanian view," Gallup says, "that any identity will necessarily be alien and constraining. I do not believe in some 'new identity' which would be adequate and authentic. But I do not seek some sort of liberation from identity. That would lead only to another form of paralysis—the oceanic passivity of undifferentiation. Identity must be continually assumed and immediately called into question" (p. xii). Gallop defines woman through a Lacanian revision of Freud, with an emphasis on puns and the complicated ramifications of sexual politics. A few chapter titles will give a flavor of the book: "Of Phallic Proportions: Lacanian Conceit," "The Father's Seduction," "Impertinent Questions," "The Phallic Mother: Fraudian Analysis." Main references to writers other than Lacan are to Juliet Mitchell, Luce Irigaray, Hélène Cixous, and Julia Kristeva. Aside from its own virtue as a feminist statement, this book is a good introduction to Lacan.

Geoffrey Galt Harpham's *On the Grotesque: Strategies of Contradiction in Art and Literature* (Princeton) is an erudite attempt to define the concept of the grotesque. "The grotesque," he says, "is embodied in an act of transition, of metonymy becoming metaphor, of the margin swapping places with the center. It is embodied in a transformation of duality into unity, of the meaningless into the meaningful. And all these discoveries were available right at the start: they were the very first things revealed about the grotesque, and they remain its primary features" (p. 47).

The first chapter seeks to define the grotesque paradoxically as both "form" and "interval," or as that which escapes the net of language. The second chapter gives a history of the concept, starting with Nero and using painting and the decorative arts as much as writing. There are many fascinating reproductions. The third chapter discusses the place of the grotesque in human culture, going back to cave art. There are, in addition, stimulating readings of *Wuthering Heights*, "The Masque of the Red Death," and a number of works by Joseph Conrad.

Another good book on the interrelationships of the arts is *The Colors of Rhetoric: Problems in the Relation between Modern Literature and Painting* (Chicago), by Wendy Steiner, author a few years ago of a first-rate book on Gertrude Stein. Steiner's desire is to explore the interrelations among writing and the various plastic arts, starting from the position that with the advent of modernism the boundaries between the various art forms were no longer clearly distinguishable and generic interrelationships along the boundaries became of necessity quite important. The first chapter "follows the history of the painting-literature analogy with specific emphasis on the modern period. Chapter 2 discusses post-Renaissance notions of artistic reference, particularly the contrast between scientific prose and nonsense" (p. xii). "Chapter 3 demonstrates the homology between Cubist painting, modern writing, and recent concepts of history and periodization" (p. xiii). There is an excellent chapter on Cubism in painting and writing, which amounts to a paradigmatic attempt at periodization. This is a well-written, thoughtful work by a younger scholar who serves notice that she will have to be taken seriously in a field dominated by such thinkers as Mario Praz and Morse Peckham.

*f.* **Works by Major Figures.** In this final section I will review works by major figures in contemporary criticism, a number of whom produced books in English in 1982. The first is by Maurice Blanchot, a prominent French critic and novelist who has been relatively unknown in the United States: *The Sirens' Song: Selected Essays, by Maurice Blanchot,* ed. and intro. Gabriel Josipovici; trans. Sacha Rabinovitch (Indiana). Blanchot is not a systematizer, but writes essays on a great variety of topics, most of them concerned with individual authors. A relative contemporary of Foucault and Barthes, he does not identify with a school. Rather he strikes me as an old-fashioned man of letters; a novelist, critic, and essayist with a strong literary sensibility. This book contains essays on Kafka and Proust, as well as an astute little piece on *The Turn of the Screw.* Of all the prominent French critics, his work may be the most worth reading as literature itself. Dipping into these essays will be a rewarding experience.

*Agon: Towards a Theory of Revisionism* (Oxford) is one of two 1982 books by the prolific Harold Bloom, the latest volumes to extend and explain his theory of influence and intertextuality. This is a collection of essays that emphasize what Bloom calls Gnosticism, by which he wishes to suggest that his theory of creative "misreading" follows from the assumption that reading is an act arising from both personal need and the will to power. "Loving poetry," Bloom says, "is a Gnostic passion not because the Abyss itself is loved, but because the lover longs to be yet another Demiurge" (p. 17).

The essays include a number on Freud and on Jewish mysticism, and quite a few on American writers like Emerson, Hart Crane, Whitman, John Ashbery, and John Hollander. As usual, both Freud and Emerson are central to Bloom's thought, the former for his formulations of defensiveness and anxiety, the latter for the example he sets of strong reading and writing. The essay on Ashbery contains a succinct statement of Bloom's theory of strong misreading: "A strong poem, which alone can become canonical for more than a single generation, can be defined as a text that must engender strong misreadings, both as other poems and as literary criticism. Texts that have single, reductive, simplistic meanings are themselves already necessarily weak misreadings of anterior texts. When a strong misreading has demonstrated its fecundity by producing other strong misreadings across several generations, then we can and must accept its canonical status" (p. 285).

Bloom's other book is *The Breaking of the Vessels* (Chicago), given originally as the Wellek Library Lectures at the University of California, Irvine. These lectures are a unified summation of the position that Bloom has evolved since *The Anxiety of Influence* (1973). In his foreword Frank Lentricchia asks whether Bloom is becoming a literary figure in his own right and not simply a critic. Perhaps so, Bloom might answer, but does it really make any difference, since personality is ultimately to be exalted above language?

Again, in this book, the major underlying figure (father) is Freud, and perhaps the best chapter in the book is entitled "Wrestling Sigmund: Three Paradigms for Poetic Originality." One statement exemplifies the exuberant wit we have come to associate with Bloom: "Karl Kraus, being Freud's contemporary, said that psychoanalysis itself was the disease of which it purported to be the cure. We come after, and we must say that psychoanalysis itself is the culture of which it purports to be the description" (p. 63). There is not much that is new to Bloom's thought here, but after many rewritings and revisions of his own basic theories, Bloom understands his own ideas well enough to write about them with control and accessibility. This might be the best beginning primer on Bloom's work.

Northrop Frye's 1982 book is *The Great Code: The Bible and Literature* (Harcourt), which "attempts a study of the Bible from the point of view of a literary critic" (p. xi). Frye applies his overall theory of literature to an interpretation of the Bible as well as to the interpreters of the Bible throughout history. He divides the book into "The Order of Words" and "The Order of Types," in each half discussing in different chapters language, myth, metaphor, and typology, using Roman numeral I after each title in the first half and II in the second. The highly theoretical first section establishes the tools Frye wishes to apply to Biblical exegesis.

The second half applies those tools to the Bible, using the traditional notion of typology which believes the New Testament is to be read by seeking the prefigurations of it that abound in the Old. The chapter on typology in part 2 is subtitled "Phases of Revelation," the various phases being creation, revolution, law, wisdom, prophecy, gospel, and apocalypse, all of them keyed to a figural interaction between the Old and New Testaments. The book is difficult, sinewy, and elusive, but it is full of brilliant insights that are the fruit of a life's thought about literature and the Bible. The method becomes clear almost by indirection, and as with much of Frye's work, one is more likely to stand in awe of it than to find an easy means to apply it.

Brief mention goes to Julia Kristeva's *Powers of Horror: An Essay on Abjection* (Columbia), trans. Leon S. Roudiez, a work by one of the most important younger French critics. For Kristeva abjection has to do with the human fascination with what repulses us; it is a mixture of disgust and almost obsessive curiosity about the object of disgust. The book explores the subject by defining it and then examining various taboos that relate to the concept of abjection. The author on whom Kristeva focuses most heavily is Ferdinand Celine. One can get a sense of the book's basic material from the following chapter titles: "Something To Be Scared Of," "From Filth to Defilement," "Suffering and Horror," "Powers of Horror." The important intellectual influences seem to be Freud and Lacan, but the range of reference is wide. Although Kristeva is known as a major French feminist, this utterly compelling book is not primarily a work of feminist criticism.

A new book by Father Walter J. Ong is *Orality and Literacy: The Technologizing of the Word* (Methuen). As part of the New Accents series, it does not represent an original contribution to knowledge. Still, the book is probably the best compendium of up-to-date thought on the subject of orality and literacy and the kinds of consciousness connected with each. Ong reviews the research of Milman Parry and Albert Lord as to how a nonliterate culture constructs the conventions of an orally transmitted epic. He shows how oral cultures need to see things contextually, and he shows how the impressive "memory" of the primitive bards is not exact (word-for-word) as in a print culture, but is compendious because there are so many general linguistic conventions on which the bard can draw.

Ong distinguishes among orality, writing, and print, claiming that deconstructionists like Derrida do not differentiate between writing and printing in their respective effects on consciousness—although we have already seen how the American critic Gerald Bruns does take these matters into account. Ong writes: "Manuscript culture is producer-oriented, since every individual copy of a work represents great expenditures of an individual copyist's time. Medieval manuscripts are turgid with abbreviations, which favor the copyist although they inconvenience the reader. Print is consumer-oriented, since the individual copies of a work represent a much smaller investment of time: a few hours spent in producing a more readable text will immediately improve thousands upon thousands of copies" (pp. 122–23).

It is interesting to observe that what seemed so revolutionary to us 20 years ago when Marshall McLuhan was expounding some of these very ideas now seems almost commonplace. We should not forget, however, that Ong's early work had a big influence on McLuhan.

Another high-level popularizer, Robert Scholes has produced a useful explanatory work in *Semiotics and Interpretation* (Yale), a book that attempts to explain semiotics and then applies the concept to specific literary texts. Scholes has always had the ability to make difficult concepts clear without either oversimplifying the ideas or patronizing the reader. Again, as in Ong's book, there is little here that is new, but Scholes, in contrast to many currently involved in semiotics, takes a humanistic approach to the material, bringing it to bear quite well on literature. He writes about the emphasis in semiotics on communicative codes, bringing in such literary critics as Roland Barthes. "Signs do not refer to things," Scholes writes, "they signify concepts, and concepts are aspects of thought, not of reality" (p. 24). He expands on this notion throughout the book, and the following paragraph makes clear the distinction between the semiotician's location of meaning and that of, say, the reader-response critic or the deconstructionist: "Under semiotic inspection neither the author nor the reader is free to make meaning. Regardless of their lives as individuals, as author and reader they are traversed by codes that enable their communicative adventures at the cost of setting limits to the messages they can exchange. A literary text, then, is not simply a set of words, but (as Roland Barthes demonstrated in S/Z, though not necessarily in just that way) a network of codes that enables the marks on the page to be read as a text of a particular sort" (p. 110).

The book contains interesting applications of this and related principles to Joyce's story "Eveline" and Hemingway's "A Very Short Story." There is a somewhat unsuccessful chapter on feminine sexuality called "Uncoding Mama: The Female Body as Text," but a useful list of definitions in a last chapter called a "Glossary of Semiotic Terminology."

The French theorist, Tzvetan Todorov, is represented by two 1982 books, both of them published by Cornell and translated by Catherine Porter: *Theories of the Symbol* and *Symbolism and Interpretation*. *Theories of the Symbol* is a history of aesthetics written from the point of view of theories of signification (semiotics). Todorov begins with Aristotle, particularly in the *Rhetoric* with its emphasis on linguistic signification. He then traces the notion of linguistic signification through Saint Augustine and the medieval thinkers to focus heavily on the 18th century in order to establish the point of view of classical linguistics about symbolism and imitation. A long section on the "Romantic Crisis" is followed by "Language and Its Doubles," a chapter concerned with theories of how language developed. Three chapters on 20th-century thinkers are concerned with Freud, Saussure, and Jakobson. This book provides an excellent historical overview of the subject and of how semiotics has expanded beyond an exclusive focus on language. It is not dominated (though it is informed) by Todorov's own theories.

Todorov's theories are the matter contained in *Symbolism and Interpretation*. The book presents a position on symbolism that tries to fuse into one theory an explanation of (1) how symbols are produced and (2) how they are received. "A text or a discourse becomes symbolic," writes Todorov, "at the point when, through an effort of interpretation, we discover in it an indirect meaning" (p. 19). Because of the influence of romantic notions of organic form, however, we are not well equipped to deal with indirect meanings that are not easily integrated. "Thus we are ill equipped to read discontinuity, incoherence, the unintegrable" (p. 38).

Todorov establishes his theory quite lucidly in the opening section, "Symbolics of Language," and in the second half of the book, "Strategies of Interpretation," he applies the theory to two major traditions: the patristic (e.g., Saint Augustine) and the philological (e.g., Spinoza). His strategy for applying theory to text is well summarized in the following paragraph: "To interpret always consists in equating two texts (the second of which need not be set forth explicitly): the author's and the interpreter's. The act of interpreting thus necessarily implies two successive choices. The first is whether or not to impose constraints on the association of the two texts. If one chooses to impose constraints, then one must choose whether to attach them to the text one is starting with (the input), to the text one ends up with (the output), or to the trajectory linking the two" (p. 166). Todorov writes extremely well. While his erudition is most impressive, it does not impede his skill in explaining complex ideas with clarity. He transcends schools in his ability to write about semiotics without being doctrinaire.

The final book is a new collection by René Wellek, *The Attack on Literature and Other Essays* (N.C.). As one might expect, in these writings Wellek is largely concerned with expressing and consolidating his already established positions; but he does so with clarity and with little defensiveness. While he is for the most part unsympathetic to the "new" criticism, he takes reasoned positions against the things he does not like, and we are all familiar with Wellek's encyclopedic knowledge. He has always been more a historian of criticism than a critic himself, and as such he has the background to weigh new critical movements in the balance of the past. The reader may wish to dip into this book rather than read it all the way through. If so, then I recommend at least the following four pieces: "The Attack on Literature," "Literature, Fiction and Literariness," "Criticism as Evaluation," and "The Fall of Literary History."

Overall, I think 1982 was a good year for criticism. There are a number of books that will remain on my permanent shelves, to which I plan to refer, in both American literature and general critical theory. It is clear how deeply the new literary theories have taken hold in this country, and it would not be inaccurate to assert that we are definitely living in an Age of Criticism.

*University of California, Davis*

# 21. Foreign Scholarship

## i. East European Contributions

### F. Lyra

In this year's survey I take notice of as many publications as are available and, when possible, will refer to works published in 1981, as well as 1982. With the help of Zoltán Abády-Nagy, I notice 1981 scholarship in Hungary; and with aid from Josef Jařab, scholarship of 1981 in Czechoslovakia. I shall comment on work of scholars in Poland—and some in Russia, though not all Russian publications have been available.

In comparison to earlier years the variety of interest in American literature expanded considerably in the Soviet Union and Poland due to the increased activity of scholars outside both countries' academic centers. As in the past, contributions on 20th-century literature dominated, but earlier periods received attention too. In the Soviet Union authors such as Ralph Waldo Emerson, Henry David Thoreau, and Henry James, whose major works are still unavailable in Russian translation, were discussed extensively. Generalizations and truisms abounded but some of the former also contained genuine insights.

*a.* **General Studies.** *Problemy stanovlenia amerikanskoi literatury* [Principal Determinants of American Literature] (Moskva [1981]: Nauka), the Soviet scholars' most weighty contribution, is a collection of ten articles by nine authors. It amounts to an exposition of a historiographical theory which in some ways resembles Robert E. Spiller's concept of the history of American literature, especially in the emphasis on regionalism. In the introduction Yasen N. Zasurskii enumerates other factors which in his view account for the uniqueness of American literature: the influence of European literature in general and English in particular, the Indians, the Afro-Americans, ethnic minorities (especially the Spanish), the frontier, the amalgamation of "book literature," journalism, and folklore. Religion is conspicuously absent in the model. Several contributors, however, have

taken it into consideration. A few of Zasurskii's generalizations may
be questioned, as, for example, his statement that southern literature became "an important component of the national literature only
thanks to Faulkner" (p. 15), or his assertion that the uniqueness of
American romanticism was determined by abolutism.

The authors' originality consists in what they choose to emphasize
and what to omit. Most of them read American literature with the
same focus as do American historiographers, albeit with differences.
In view of past distortions and omissions of important issues, the
present contributors' recognition that American literature has been
largely shaped by factors other than just social, political, and economic bespeaks a more even-handed interpretation. Maya Koreneva
stresses, for instance, the role of the Bible and the Puritans' messianic
emphasis. In her article "New England and American Literature:
Three Centuries in the Life of the Nation" (pp. 22–88) Koreneva in
several paragraphs presents a remarkably balanced view of Jonathan
Edwards. If Valentina A. Libman's *Bibliography* (ALS 1977, p. 464)
is the ultimate source of reference, then Koreneva happens to be the
first Soviet scholar to have discussed her work at some length. By
the same token in "The Middle Atlantic States and the Problem of
the National Hero in American Literature" (pp. 89–112) M. P.
Tugusheva goes on record with another Soviet "first" by crediting
John Woolman with instigating "America's sense of responsibility
for the world." In Tugusheva's opinion Woolman's ideas were distorted by later generations "to justify American imperialism." In a
brilliant display of generalizations, Tugusheva traces the American
national hero from Benjamin Franklin (Poor Richard is the first
American Adam) through the writings of John Dickinson and the
later classics down to Norman Mailer, and discovers a female variant
of the hero in the work of some woman authors of the '70s. Discussing southern literature (pp. 113–54), Nikolai A. Anastas'ev contrasts it with that of New England; he praises the Puritans for their
social conscience, which, in his opinion, the southerners lacked until
the appearance of the Fugitives, toward whom he is favorably dis-
posed. This group had good ideas, he says, and began well, but
disbanded, for the best of them—Ransom, Tate, Warren—found
southern ideals too narrow. Specialists in modernism will cheer
Aleksei M. Zverev's appreciation of the avant-gardism of *Poetry* and
*The Little Review* in his article on the Midwest (pp. 155–94). A. V.

Vashchenko skillfully combines his survey of western authors with a discussion of the function of the West in the American imagination and culture (pp. 195–216). His discussion is somewhat out of focus due to his fascination with the romantic image of the West, its realization in the Western, and his devotion to the realistic literature of the region. A. P. Saruzhanyan's piece on the frontier (pp. 217–50) contains a useful presentation of recent American scholarship on the topic, followed by a survey of authors in whose artistic works the frontier functions prominently. S. A. Chakovski's article on Afro-American literature (pp. 274–95), like Vashchenko's on the West, lacks a consistent point of view. He criticizes Booker T. Washington but praises Faulkner's imaginative treatment of the Afro-American. In his high regard for Faulkner, Chakovski comes close to an apologia for the novelist's failure to show how the black man thinks and feels. In his concluding remarks (pp. 273–77) Zasurskii reiterates the crucial importance of regionalism in the development of the national character in American literature.

The most comprehensive work on American literature of recent years published in this part of the world is *Slovník spisovalů: Spojené státy americké* [Dictionary of Writers: The United States of America] (Prague [1980]: Odeon). It covers American literature from its beginnings to the mid-'70s. The bulk of the volume was prepared by Zdeněk Vančura; after his death in 1974 Eva Masnerová assumed his editorial duties and wrote the introductory essay including a few remarks on the reception of American literature in Czechoslovakia. Besides Vančura and Masnerová the contributors include: Josef Jařab, Martin Hilský, Milan Lukeš, Radoslav Nenadál, and Zdeněk Stříbný. As Vančura was a specialist in colonial literature, his erudite entries on some earlier writers are disproportionately long compared to those on some important modern authors. Czech reviewers of the work pointed out Vančura's strong inclination toward very personal interpretation and assessment of American authors.

*b.* **Preromantic Studies.**   With his profound interest in 18th-century American writings Vančura was a rare scholar in Eastern Europe. The few contributions on early American literature are a break from the traditional neglect. I have already mentioned Koreneva's essay in the collection *Principal Determinants*. Her sensitive probing into the New England imagination leads us to expect more studies from

her in that area, especially on the early American muse, as she also
happens to be an excellent translator of English poetry, although
her brief discussion of Edward Taylor's work in her essay disappoints
as does her presentation of Anne Bradstreet and Michael Wiggles-
worth.

The only contribution devoted exclusively to Puritan literature is
Charlotte Kretzoy's "Attitude and Form: Puritan Style in 17th-Cen-
tury American Prose" (*HSE* 14[1981]:57–68), an erudite, vigorous
article on a rather banal thesis: the American Puritans' "changing
interpretations of plain style . . . were connected with changes in
attitude . . . during the first century of the settlement" (p. 57). Kretzoy
discusses the levels of style in 16th-century England and plain style
and its variety in America, which, she argues, "differed greatly from
its original English theory, therefore deserves a separate name:
*Puritan style*—a plain style with discreet compromises." American
plain style "was less plain than its English model" (p. 63). So far so
good, but none of the illustrations exemplify the Puritan style, and
she mentions the term only one more time in stressing the essential
differences "between *stylus planus*, plain style and Puritan style."
Thus the reader is left to wonder: was there or was there not a
Puritan style?

*c. The 19th Century.* Among several contributions to the study of
19th-century American literature two deserve special attention, one
from the Soviet Union, the other from Poland.

*Romanticheskie traditsii amerikanskoi literatury XIX veka i sov-
remennost'* [Romantic Traditions of Nineteenth-Century American
Literature and Contemporaneity] (Moskva: Nauka) consists of four
thematic units lucidly signaled in the anonymous introduction. The
first is made up of T. L. Morozova's essay "Nineteenth-Century
American Literature: Principal Tendencies of Development" (pp.
10–26), which accounts for the late emergence of American romanticism and its links with the enlightenment. In the second unit Yu. B.
Kovalev discusses "the chronology, topography, method of American
romanticism" (pp. 27–54), and G. V. Anikin deals with various comparative aspects between the movement in the United States and
England (pp. 55–77). The initial part of Kovalev's contribution is
particularly instructive as he criticizes earlier Soviet works on American romanticism, those by M. N. Bobrova, N. I. Samokhvalov, and

A. N. Nikolyukin. The third unit consists of five monograph essays concentrating on the literary creativity of representative romantics. The Soviet scholars' emphasis on the historical process, realism, and correlation between literary phenomena and social life is balanced by their interest in aesthetic values. If one of Anikin's conclusions concerning the "mutual penetration of the romantic and the realistic" may appear somewhat strained, his pointing to the Puritan influence, the Bible, the presence of symbolism certainly does not. O. M. Kirichenko's call for a more comprehensive look at and a reevaluation of Longfellow's poetry coincides with that of some American savants, for example, the late Howard Mumford Jones, and Morozova's reading of Emerson contrasts with the vituperations provoked by Gay Wilson Allen's recent biography of Emerson. Naturally there are arguable assertions, such as A. M. Zverev's about the South, which after Sidney Lanier's death "remained a deaf province of American literature for many decades."

The collection is complemented by a few articles on various facets of American romanticism. T. Aumin writes about "Nachalo traditsii v molodoi natsional'noi literature SSHA" [The Beginning of Tradition in the Young American Literature] ( *UZTU* 10[1981]:25–34), E. A. Nikolaeva contributes to the controversy over Washington Irving's short fiction in "O diskreditatsii fantasticheskogo elementa v rannykh novellakh V. Irvinga" [On Discrediting the Fantastic Element in Washington Irving's Early Tales] in *Vzaimodeistvie zhanra i metoda v zarubezhnoi literature XVIII–XX v.* (Voronezh, pp. 37–50). Two scholars demonstrated interest in Margaret Fuller. S. G. Shishkin's study of Fuller's participation in the editing of *The Dial* ( *Problemy zarubezhnoi literaturnoi kritike*, Tyumen' [1981]) was inaccessible; E. P. Zykova's "Literaturnaya kritika amerikanskikh romantikov. Esseistika M. Fuller" [Literary Criticism of American Romantics: M. Fuller's Essays] ( *FN* 1981, no. 5:29–36) is surveyish but competent. Zykova refrains from any critical remarks on Margaret Fuller's writings.

The other book on 19th-century American literature is Agnieszka Salska's *The Poetry of Central Consciousness: Whitman and Dickinson* (AULFL 7), the best contribution to the study of American literature in Poland during recent years and the most extensive comparison of the two poets ever undertaken. Salska is the first to admit that the idea is not original and neither are the key premises which

lead her to a stimulating exploration of both poets' imaginations
through their work, incidentally bringing together what others have
already said about their similarities and differences. The raison
d'etre for Salska's comparison is grounded in the Emersonian "view
of self as autonomous and . . . of individual consciousness as the creative center of the universe." Whitman and Dickinson explore the idea
in different directions although "their respective routes come together at important intersections" (p. 35). The contrasting identities
of the poets' selves as personae are the subject of the second chapter.
In the third Salska examines their "creative centers" in relation to
reality, which is effected through "mediation" by Whitman, through
"command" by Dickinson. In the next two chapters Salska analyzes
the poetic structure of mediation and command. The tool in the design is language, of course. She compares the poets' conception of
language as it relates to the respective types of central consciousness.
Regretfully, I must warn potential users of Salska's quotations from
the poets' as well as the critics' texts against lexical omissions and
errors in spelling and punctuation.

Among other short contributions on 19th-century literature Khalid
Husni's "Ishmael's Leviathanic Vision: A Study in Whiteness" (SAP
13[1981]:177–90) may be noted for its depth, and, less fortunately,
for its convoluted style of presentation. The gist of Husni's argument
rests in the recognition that "Ishmael's visions of the White Whale
which form the 'Doubloon' of perception in Moby-Dick are inevitably
conflicting and contradictory at various points of the circumference
of whaling . . ." (p. 179). Underlying the metaphysics of Ishmael's
narration is his emphasis on the significance of both angle and mood
of vision. His "visionary power encompasses the colourless-colourful
paradox" and "fuses the two obverse sides of whiteness." He "perceived light as well as darkness, colour as well as colourlessness, life
as well as death in the whiteness of the Whale" (p. 189). Others have
arrived at the same conclusion via different routes but few with
more sensitivity for Melville's narrative art than Husni.

In 1980 the American Studies Center at the University of Warsaw
began publication of a new annual, American Studies. In an article
in the second volume, "The Lady of the Aroostook—William Dean
Howells' International Novel" (ASW 2[1981]:77–87) Teresa Kieniewicz should be complimented for introducing Howells to Polish
students of American literature. She does it with a perceptive exegesis

of one of the author's early novels to prove that Howells offered "a possible and desirable alternative to . . . the two extremes in attitudes toward Europe embodied in Lydia Blood and Mrs. Erwin by introducing Staniford, who represents the best qualities of both extremes."

Of three Russian books dealing with American literature of both the 19th and 20th centuries, two were not available. They are collections of articles by various authors covering mostly individual authors' works. The first of these books, *Problemy realizma v zarubezhnoi literature XIX–XX vekov* [Problems of Realism in Foreign Literature of the Nineteenth and Twentieth Centuries] (Moskva [1981]) contains articles on, among others, Eudora Welty, Frank Norris, Richard Wormser, Hemingway, and Emerson. The second, *Amerikanskaya literatura XIX–XX vekov* [American Literature of the Nineteenth and Twentieth Centuries] (Krasnodar [1981]) has yet another comparison of *Moby-Dick* and *The Old Man and the Sea*, pieces on Thornton Wilder, Mary Wilkins Freeman, Hawthorne's *The House of the Seven Gables*, Whitman, and Lanier.

The third book *Ot Uitmena do Khemingueya* [From Whitman to Hemingway] (2nd ed., Moskva [1981]: Sovetskii Pisatel') is by Abel' Isaakovich Startsev. It first appeared in 1972, and since it was not reviewed in *ALS* at that time, I will now make a few comments about its second edition, as certain differences between the first and second editions illuminate one Soviet critic's modified perception of American literature during the decade. To be sure, the modifications are neither radical nor numerous. Whitman remains "a singer of idealized bourgeois democracy" and "the optimistic masses." In time the poet "came to aspire toward a classless society, a socialist order" (p. 37). Thoreau's *Walden* expresses criticism of bourgeois society and morality, although his protest is stinted by his individualistic tendencies. Melville, like most American romantics, is primarily a moralist; Ahab's pursuit of Moby Dick has no spiritual significance whatsoever; symbolically the white whale "embodies evil forces which stand in man's way to freedom and happiness." In the second edition Startsev withdrew his remark concerning Melville and Thoreau as precursors of American realism, and he also significantly changed his view of Faulkner. Startsev no longer blames Faulkner for the inability to see evil in the social and economic reality of his native land and has omitted the remark concerning Faulkner's "absorption with metaphysical evil," that his "opposition to evil has an abstract character." Startsev also has relinquished his view of Faulkner as "a victim of decadence" and relieved him from the stigma of "black pessimism." He almost excuses Faulkner for yielding to the experimental poetics of modernism prior to the publication of *The Hamlet*.

*d.* **The 20th Century.** The large quantity of work on 20th-century American literature necessitates selectivity. But this is no disaster, for much of the material adds little of note.

Aleksei Matveevich Zverev starts his *Amerikanskii roman 20-kh–30-kh godov* [The American Novel of the Twenties and Thirties] (Moskva: Khudozhestvennaya Literatura) propitiously enough by announcing in Dreiser's words that "the socialist revolution in Russia changed the direction of American literature" (p. 3). The implications of the statement are clear, but Zverev does not pursue them. After a few paragraphs on various manifestations of socialist and proletarian sympathy among American writers during the '30s he delivers nine essays on the significant novels of Dreiser, Fitzgerald, Hemingway, Wolfe, Faulkner, Dos Passos, and a few others, placing them conveniently in the framework of the "humanist art of realism" (p. 31). Zverev's historiosophical conventionality warrants no comment. His approach to particular writers, however, deserves notice although many of his judgments concern controversial problems which have been argued repeatedly; some are of little importance, while others are so general they resist argumentation. Zverev allots attention in proportion to the novelistic achievements of particular writers, devoting only one (the last) essay to the radical novel of the '30s. Briefly discussing the anthology *Proletarian Literature in the United States*—in one paragraph—he does not even mention Friedman's introductory essay, Jack Conroy's *The Disinherited*, James Farrell's Studs Lonigan trilogy, and Richard Wright's *Native Son*. Hemingway, of course, gets the greatest amount of space, but it is Faulkner he is more interested in. Faulkner's rhetoric seems to have charmed the Soviet scholar. He sees few artistic deficiencies in his fiction, and even these he manages to justify. In contrast to other Soviet critics, Zverev appreciates Faulkner's experiments. In what appears to be an attempt at neutralizing those who might accuse him of adherence to formalism, he declares: "His experimentation was never of a formal nature. Complicated reality required a correspond-

ingly intricate artistic language" (p. 118). Unfortunately, Zverev's
fine essays make up a fragmented whole. The title of the book raises
expectations of a synthesis which remains unfulfilled.

No such expectations are generated by the title of Aleksandr S.
Mulyarchik's book *Poslevoennye amerikanskie romanisty* [Postwar
American Novelists] (Moskva [1980]: Khudozhestvennaya Literatura); nevertheless his work comes closer to a synthesis than Zverev's,
although all the "chapters" are actually articles published in various
Russian periodicals or as introductions to Russian translations of
American novels. Mulyarchik aims at "throwing some light on literary phenomena and tendencies characteristic of, above all, the
movement of a critical realism in the contemporary American novel"
(p. 5). Official rhetoric notwithstanding, Mulyarchik demonstrates
perceptive readings of numerous postwar novels. He begins, however, with a discussion of Nathanael West's *The Day of the Locust*,
which epitomizes for him an earlier stage of American realism.
Mulyarchik's interpretations are grounded in the American socio-
political reality of the protagonists' lives, the novelists' perception of
that reality, and in the context of their literary biographies. The list
of authors whose work he discusses is long; those he has selected for
special consideration are R. P. Warren, James Jones, Norman Mailer,
J. D. Salinger, John Updike, Gore Vidal, John Cheever, Joseph Heller, Saul Bellow, E. L. Doctorow, and Toni Morrison. Mulyarchik's
positive evaluation of the novelists rests upon his perception of their
adherence to critical realism. His differentiation among them hangs
upon the recognition that each one of them follows it divergently;
many novelists who had begun as critical realists later embraced
artistic principles incompatible with the canons of critical realism.
In *An American Dream*, for example, Mailer mixed critical realism
with surrealism; Philip Roth compromised his talent with *Portnoy's
Complaint*; R. P. Warren in the '70s yielded to "subjectivism"; and
in *Mr. Sammler's Planet* and *Humboldt's Gift* Bellow "surrendered to
the process of spiritual stagnation and moral compromise," and with
the publication of *To Jerusalem and Back* "became a steward of Zionist ideology" (p. 344).

Mulyarchik's faithfulness to the standards of critical realism as
practiced in the Soviet Union is also reflected in his articles: "Pered
vyborom: Borba realizma i modernizma v literaturnoi zhizni SSHA"
[Facing the Choice: the Struggle of Realism and Modernism in the

Literary Life of the United States] (*LU* 1981, no., 5:169–79); "V pogranichnoi' zone: Cherty 'massovoi kul 'tury' v sovremiennoi amerikanskoi proze" [In the "Border" Zone: Features of "Mass Culture" in Contemporary American Prose] (*LO* 3:25–30); and "Na literaturnoi obochine 'Massovaya beletristika' SSHA v 70-e gody" (*VLit* 1982, no. 11:71–88). While Mulyarchik professes basically a negative attitude toward popular American writing, N. Anastas'ev inclines to grant a few popular writers some recognition as long as they deal with social problems, albeit superficially. Unless they do so their fiction amounts to *kitsch*, says Anastas'ev in "Kat stat' kumirom: Massovaya belletristika v SSHA" [How to Become an Idol: Mass Fiction in the United States] (*InL* 1982, no. 9:192–99). The "idol" is James Michener, whom Anastas'ev treats with condescending irony.

Elżbieta Grużewska deals with popular literature in a more sophisticated way, though not quite originally, concentrating on crime fiction. In "The American Detective Story—Popular Reading" (*ASW* 3:111–21) Grużewska accounts for the popularity of the genre in terms of the "aesthetics of reception," speculating that popular literature "carries out more social and psychological functions in a unified way than high literature." She then launches into an exposition of S. Lasić's poetics of the detective novel, only to finish with this statement: "Thus the problem regarding the social and psychological functions of popular literature and the reasons for its popularity in the contemporary American society require further and scrupulous examination." Her "O popularności literatury popularnej —Na przykładzie klasycznej i czarnej powieści kryminalnej w literaturze amerykańskiej" [The Popularity of Popular Literature Exemplified on the Classic and Black Detective Novel in American Literature] (*PHum* 7–9[1981]:129–40) is a useful expansion of the above article, less valuable for analysis than information.

Stephen H. Goldman in turn writes thoughtfully, though a bit pontifically, about "American Science Fiction of the Twentieth Century: Metaphors for American Attitudes Toward the Future" (*SAP* 13[1981]:163–76). He explores the reasons behind the "close association of the United States and science fiction. For these reasons can lead to an understanding of how a popular form of literature arises out of a particular society's view of itself and then changes as that view changes" (p. 163). Goldman explains the various functions of science fiction, illustrating them with close readings of J. W. Campbell's "Twilight," Isaac Asimov's *I, Robot*, and Daniel Keyes's "Flowers for Algernon."

Andrzej Kopcewicz and Marta Sienicka do not take American popular fiction as seriously as do Grużewska or Goldman, assigning no special significance to it in their *Historia literatury amerykańskiej w zarysie. Wiek XX* [A Survey of the *Literary History of the United States: XXth Century*] (Warszawa: Panstwowe Wydawnictwo Naukowe). Their impressive book typifies the strength and weakness of genre literary history, which it purports to be; yet these sections on poetry, the novel, the short story, drama, and literary theory are mixed in with chapters on literary movements, while still others deal with regions ("Poetry of the South") and periods ("The Novel of the Twenties"). There is much of value in the history but there are distressing errors of fact, and the bibliographies are in places inadequate. Nabokov's work, for example, receives a mere six lines. By sheer coincidence that deficiency is compensated by *Literatura na Swiecie*. Over half of the double 5–6 number is filled with translations of Nabokov's poetry and fragments of larger works, competently introduced, with an excellent chronology (pp. 212–25) by Leszek Engelking.

Three American 20th-century authors were subjects of book-length monographs: William Saroyan, F. Scott Fitzgerald, and Flannery O'Connor. Unfortunately, A. Zverev's *Grustnyi solnechnyi mir Saroyna* [The Sad and Sunny World of Saroyan] has not arrived for review. The publication of Andrew Turnbull's biography in Russian and Yurii Yakovlevich Lidskii's *Skott Fitsdzheral'd: Tvorchestvo* [Scott Fitzgerald: Work] (Kiev: Naukova Dumka), along with several articles in books and periodicals, make 1982 a Fitzgerald year in the Soviet Union. Though Lidskii's monograph is intended for teachers and students of philological departments, it rises above the mediocre quality American scholars have come to expect of a book intended for classroom use. Fitzgerald specialists will undoubtedly find rehashed notions in the work, but they might appreciate some of the Soviet scholar's new ideas, such as his application of M. Bachtin's concept of the "chronotope." Lidskii approaches Fitzgerald with an affirmative frame of mind that induces him to treat sympathetically even the weakest commercial stories. He is especially interested in the stylistic aspects of his subject's art and in the psychological treatment of the protagonists. In the first chapter, which deals with the short stories, he examines their relationship to the novels, though not as extensively as does John A. Higgins in his study of the short fiction. Lidskii's analyses of several stories, however, are better than those of Higgins, for they do not rely as heavily on secondary sources. Lidskii explores some stories which have drawn little attention as, for example, "The Curious Case of Benjamin Button," but devotes only two pages of general remarks to the three-story cycles. The third chapter, which deals with *The Great Gatsby* (pp. 123–249), is probably the longest discussion of the novel in any language. Lidskii makes effective use of quotations drawn from the three-volume Russian edition of the writer's works (1977). Commenting on Fitzgerald's style, he elucidates sporadically the inadequacies of translation; scholars interested in Fitzgerald's Russian reception will appreciate the relevant information.

Teresa Balazy's *Structural Patterns in Flannery O'Connor's Fiction* (Warszawa: Państwowe Wydawnictwo Naukowe) is a redundant contribution to the inflated scholarship on the writer and adds little to the debate over the primacy of religion in O'Connor's work —the main theme of the monograph. It duplicates issues discussed in past criticism such as redemption, grace, and structure anchored in Réné Girard's concept of the "triangular desire." The brief presentation of O'Connor's Polish reception (p. 72) is based on lame research and a twisted premise which—if I comprehend her halting English— implies that Polish critics, including Catholic ones, either ignore or miss the metaphysical dimension of the writer's fiction because they are unacquainted with Christian thought!

Several Polish contributions published in periodicals are thin variations on old topics; some obviously constitute fragments of dissertations rushed to press in hope of advancement in the Byzantine academic hierarchy. Outside Poland, of the numerous pieces on individual works, two items are fairly representative. M. Landor in "Tragicheskii geroi Folknera: Tyazhkoe nasledie amerikanskikh vekov v romane *Absalom, Absalom!*" [Faulkner's Tragic Hero: The Grave Legacy of American Centuries in *Absalom, Absalom!*] (*InL* 1982, no. 1:170–78) discusses Faulkner's view of southern history and the complex structure of the novel, provides a useful survey of its critical reception, and associates Faulkner with Eisenstein: both "held a tragic view of the world." In "On the Place of *Manhattan*

*Transfer* in the Development of John Dos Passos" (*HSE* 14[1981]: 37–46) Josef Grmela argues that unless "we look at *Manhattan Transfer* . . . as on a preliminary stage on the path of his development towards *U.S.A.*" rather than "as upon a prelude" to it, we shall not be able to appreciate the novel fully. It is really "almost a commonplace in the periodization of John Dos Passos [*sic*] work to 'lump together' his *Manhattan Transfer* with the trilogy *U.S.A.*"? John H. Wrenn, for one, whom Grmela quotes in the course of his article, links *Manhattan Transfer* with *Three Soldiers* and *Streets of Night*, calling them Dos Passos' first trilogy. Incidentally, Dos Passos' acknowledgment of his artistic debt to Dreiser is not in the form of a "letter" but an inscription in a gift copy of *U.S.A.* to Dreiser.

The few studies of innovative fiction or postmodernism add little to what others have already discussed with greater sophistication. But Zbigniew Lewicki's article "Entropy in Literature: What It Means and What It Does Not" (*ASW* 2[1981]:51–62) provides enlightenment on a concept that has vexed many a student of American literature. Lewicki defines entropy by analyzing Burroughs' *Naked Lunch*, Pynchon's *The Crying of Lot 49*, and Gaddis' *JR*. He demonstrates that Pynchon's novel illustrates entropy in the fullest sense of the term because it is both "an image of entropic death" and "an instrument of increasing entropy among its readers," although its setting is artificial. But Gaddis' entropic vision is more real, while Burroughs' syntactic peculiarities, says Lewicki, are not enough to render his novel entropic.

Ideas such as entropy and postmodernism are but manifestations of spiritual crisis, says A. Zverev, seemingly unaware that they mean just that to serious men of letters. Hence in "Tupik: k voprosu ob amerikanskom postmodernizme" [Blind Alley: On the Question of American Postmodernism] (*InL* 1982, no. 6:199–207) he attempts to save John Barth from himself as a reluctant follower of postmodernism. Zverev states that "Barth feels constrained by postmodernism." Not so, Susan Sontag, Zverev implies. He is particularly incensed by Sontag's elitist concept of culture, and says it may have something to do with her "antisovietism," which appears to him inconsistent with her opposition to the Vietnam war and to the U.S. government in general.

Maria [*sic*] Koreneva's "Edward Albee and the Development of Modern Drama" (*HSE* 14[1981]:47–55) and "P'esy poslednikh let i krizis amerikanskogo dukha" [Recent Plays and the Crisis of the American Spirit] (*InL* 1981, no. 7:160–68) are the only contributions on American drama in the countries surveyed. Perhaps no other critic appreciates Albee's work more than Koreneva does. She even excuses his moments of artistic weakness by turning them into "failures of a legitimate artist." One wishes Koreneva were less eulogistic and more analytical, for she demonstrates an excellent knowledge of Albee's plays. She sides, of course, with those critics who refuse to regard him as a representative of the American theatre of the absurd. Albee is not too optimistic about human nature; she argues, "he never lets himself be blind [*sic*] to all the depravity which nests in man's heart" (p. 52). Albee is a playwright who invites comparison, and Koreneva has connected him with a host of modern European dramatists. Nevertheless she keeps him firmly in the tradition of American drama with O'Neill as its epitome. In the other article Koreneva critically discusses plays by R. Patrick, Ed Bullins, Albee, Arthur Kenum, and Preston Jones. Some of the names (e.g. Kenum, Patrick) are yet to appear in the pages of *ALS*.

**e. Miscellaneous.** A variety of contributions complement, some in a substantial way, a close study of American literature. From among their number I have selected those I deem most representative. In "V poiskakh amerikanskogo mifa: Mifologicheskoe literaturovedenie SSHA" [In Search of the American Myth: Mythological Literary Theory in the United States] (*FN* 1981, no. 3:26–33) A. S. Kozlov surveys the criticism and scholarship of Gilbert Murray, Philip Young, Raymond Cook, Harry Slochower, Leslie Fiedler, and a few others, evaluating them negatively.

As a novelist Isaac Bashevis Singer has yet to have his novels translated into Polish. Maria Karpluk's "Polskie *nomina loci* w utworach I. B. Singera" (*Onomastica* 27:109–26) demonstrates that his fiction is deeply rooted in Polish soil.

High praise goes to Aleksandr Nikolaevich Nikolyukin for his *Literaturnye svyazi Rosii i SSHA: Stanovlenie literaturnykh kontaktov* [Literary Relations Between Russia and the USA: Formation of Literary Contacts] (Moskva: Nauka [1981]). In part 1, entitled "Early News from America" (pp. 15–106), Nikolyukin deals with early Russian reports about America and the Russian reception of 18th-century American writings, especially Franklin's; part 2 (pp.

107–385) is devoted to "American Romanticism and Russian Literature." Based on extensive research in archives and Russian gazettes and periodicals, the book not only provides weighty substance to Valentina Libman's *American Literature in Russian Translations and Criticism* (see *ALS 1977*, pp. 463–64) but also offers invaluable insight into the literary culture of czarist Russia, explains how the Russian critics' and writers' understanding of American literature influenced the perception of their own literature, elucidates reasons underlying the Russian censors' delay or expunction of the publication of some translated American works, provides information on the range of French and Polish mediation in the Russian translations, and sporadically fills gaps in Libman's bibliography. Nikolyukin writes extensively about Fedor Vasil'evich Karzhavin, Aleksei Grigor'evich Eustaphiev (Evstaf'ev), and Pawel Petrovich Svin'in, pioneers in Russian-American cultural relations. The greatest value of Nikolyukin's book lies in chapters 2–6 and 8 of part 2 dealing with American literature in the periodical *Moskovsky Telegraph* and the reception of Washington Irving, Cooper, and Poe. In chapter 4 Nikolyukin discusses Pushkin's attitude toward American letters, and the eighth chapter is particularly rewarding as it reveals the earliest Russian translation of *Moby-Dick* (from French) published in the gazette *Moskovskie vedomosti* in February 1853, and the first Russian translations of and articles on Hawthorne, Longfellow, and Emerson. In the Moscow State Historical Museum Nikolyukin discovered an unpublished poem by Emerson, "Marafonskaya bitva" [the Marathon Battle] (the original title is not given), dated 24 September 1824, inscribed in John Bowring's album. Nikolyukin comments on the value of the translations only occasionally, but provides essential information on the cultural, social, and political context in which they appeared, or were prevented from publication. He also writes on the influence of some American writers on Russian literature, especially Franklin and Cooper, but admittedly does not exhaust the topic. In the next-to-last chapter (7), "Russian Literature in the United States" (pp. 347–70), Nikolyukin conveniently brings together what others, including Americans, have already published on the subject.

Nikolyukin's chapter on Poe in Russia supersedes T. M. Nefedova's article "Po v russkoi literature 1840–1869 godov" [Poe in Russian Literature Between the Years 1840–1869] in *Vzaimodeistvie*

*metodov, zhanrov i literatur* [Interrelations of Methods, Genres and
Literatures] (Izhebsk: Udmurskii Gosuniversitet [1981], pp. 95–
106). Nefedova points out that the first translations of Poe resulted
from the Russians' scientific interests, particularly in psychological
phenomena. She underlines this by comparing two Russian translations (1861 and 1913) of "The Tell-Tale Heart." Whether and to
what extent V. V. Kruglevskaya's "Ob amerikano-russkikh kul'turnykh
svyazakh pervoi poloviny XIX veka" [On American-Russian Cultural
Relations of the First Half of the Nineteenth Century] in *Poetika
zhanra* [Genre Poetics] Ordzhonikidze, pp. 157–66) complements
Nikolyukin's, I was unable to ascertain.

  I owe Jack R. Cohn and Alina Nowacka an apology for having
failed to comment earlier on their *A Guide to the Study of American
Literature in Poland: Part One* (Wrocław: Wydawnictwo Uniwer-
sytetu Wrocławskiego [1979]). It was an unpardonable oversight.
The title of the 97-page publication brings to mind Lewis Leary's
*Guide* (1976). Cohn's and Nowacka's differs from Leary's both in
substance and quality. The Polish volume lacks, above all, the pedagogical value of the American scholar's book. Students of American
literature would have been better served if the compilers had written
an appropriate introduction instead of supplying such ephemeral
data as "Useful Names and Addresses" (pp. 9–12), which lists faculty
members of Polish English departments who (supposedly) teach
and write on American literature; "Library Inventory" (pp. 13–19)
containing 120 representative items on American literature available
at six English department libraries; and "Magister Essays" (pp. 21–
37). The value of the publication lies in the bibliography (pp. 39–
97), which lists Polish and foreign (translated) scholarship and
criticism. The bibliography is an indispensable tool in the study of
the Polish reception of American letters, but scholars need more
information than the entries contain. For instance, entries of books
cite neither publisher nor size (pages); collections of articles are
not itemized; entries of translated works do not provide information
about the source language and do not mention names of the translators nor the original titles. English renditions of Polish titles ensure
that the bibliography also will be useful to non-Polish students, but
the translations are not always correct. A bibliographer's cardinal sin
is to cite without sighting. Obviously Cohn and Nowacka have not
seen a great many of the items listed, otherwise they would have

corrected the misinformation contained in the secondary sources they relied on. For example, the Polish text of Alexis de Tocqueville's classic is an abbreviated version of the original; the compilers should have explained this in the annotation to the entry.

*University of Warsaw*

## ii. French Contributions

### Marc Chénetier

The year 1982 already appears as some sort of *annus mirabilis* in French Americanist production: never before has it been so abundant and of such quality. It must be known, in order to understand this double and substantial rise in quantity and quality that the French Association for American Studies (AFEA) has grown over the last ten years to reach a membership of close to 350. Research centers have blossomed in and out of the universities and American authors penetrate more and more deeply the French curricula for university degrees and *concours*. Such an *élan* finds concrete embodiment both in an increased number of specialized French publications and in the increasing studies and other enterprises (colloquia, media attention, publishing ventures, magazines, and journals) in the field of American literature. The latest European Association for American Studies (EAAS) Conference was organized in La Sorbonne, Paris, in 1982 and gathered close to 500 participants from 27 countries. "European Contributions" as a whole (the title given to a series of books published by the Amsterdam Amerika Instituut, Jodenbreestraat 9, 1011 NG-Amsterdam) are on the rise and one can clearly foresee a time when *ALS* will have to institute a separate European section.

For the first time a number of the *Revue Française d'Etudes Américaines* (*RFEA*), no. 13, was dedicated to French historiography of the United States (a field not so completely removed from literary studies as it may seem), and 1982 saw the establishment of the first Maurice-Edgar Coindreau Prize for the best American literary work in translation. This prize, jointly endowed with 10,000 FF by the Société des Amis de Maurice-Edgar Coindreau and by the

Société des Gens de Lettres, honors the name of a French translator who brought Dos Passos, Faulkner, Foote, Styron, Humphrey, O'Connor, and innumerable other American writers of the '20s, '30s, '40s, and '50s to the attention of the French public under the auspices of Gallimard and, to a certain extent, concerning Faulkner in particular, retroactively to that of the American public itself. The jury is composed of academics, professional translators, and distributors of American literature. It gave the 1982 prize to Yves di Manno for his remarkable translation of William Carlos Williams' *Paterson* (Paris: Flammarion). The 1983 prize for books published in 1982 went to J. P. Richard for his eerie rendition of Djuna Barnes's *Ryder* (Paris: Christian Bourgois).

*a.* **Bibliography and Critical Theory.** The *AFRAM Newsletter*, ed. Michel Fabre (Université de Paris III) published its 16th issue in December. It contains a large bibliographical coverage of Afro-American literature as well as of the literature of the English-speaking Third World. Fabre also edited, with Charles T. Davis, *Richard Wright: A Primary Bibliography* (Hall), complete with published and unpublished works, translations of Wright's published works, and materials by others related to Wright's published works.

Scholars now have a basic reference tool, thanks to the sponsorship of the Association Française d'Etudes Américaines and to Jacqueline Rey, general editor: *Catalogue Collectif des Périodiques intéressant les Etudes Américaines Disponibles en France (Union Catalog of Periodicals for the Study of the United States Available in French Libraries)* (Nancy: Presses Universitaires de Nancy), which lists, for each periodical, the country of origin, the ISSN number, the title, publisher, place and date of publication, and list of institutions holding issues of the periodical.

Also peripheral to our subject, but interesting as literary background, is Jean Béranger's and Robert Rougé's *Histoire des Idées aux USA du 18ème siècle à nos jours* (Paris: Presses Universitaires de France). In four parts, from puritanism to political economy via transcendentalism, Darwinism and pragmatism, it outlines as clearly as possible the history of ideas in the United States and includes a short substantial working bibliography. A somewhat longer bibliography on "The Intellectual in Great Britain and the United States" is available from the University of Orléans (45045-Orléans-Cedex), ed. Marc Chénetier and Richard Sibley.

Jean-Marie Bonnet's *La Critique Littéraire aux Etats-Unis, 1783–1837* (Lyon: Presses Universitaires de Lyon) is an abridged version of Bonnet's "Thèse d'Etat" on American criticism from revolutionary times to the publication of Emerson's "The American Scholar." It aims at facilitating an understanding of the process by which a national literature comes into existence. Bonnet uses exhaustively the American literary magazines of the period and explores the material conditions under which literary criticism emerged. Having analyzed the philosophical influences which shaped American criticism, he studies in turn critical discourse as it applies to the novel, to poetry, and to drama, defining the new profile of the critic, the form of his discourse, and the meaning of literature and literary criticism in the United States from independence to the eve of Emerson's essay. An extensive bibliography (pp. 383–413) complements this important contribution.

*b.* **18th and 19th Centuries.** Very little appeared concerning the 18th century in 1982. One notable exception is Jean Béranger's interesting study of Crévecoeur: "Transformations, paradoxes et limites des échanges dans les versions successives des *Lettres d'un Cultivateur Américain*" (*Echanges*, Actes du Congrès de Strasbourg de la Société des Anglicistes de l'Enseignement Supérieur, Etudes Anglaises no. 81, Paris: Didier Erudition, pp. 409–18) is based on a comparative study of the various editions of Crévecoeur's book in England and France.

The one noticeable publication concerning 19th-century fiction is *DeltaES*, no. 15, dedicated to Henry James, ed. Nancy Blake and Catherine Vieilledent. Of the nine articles it contains, two are dedicated to *The Turn of the Screw* (J. Carlos Rowe's "Screwball: The use and abuse of uncertainty in Henry James's *The Turn of the Screw*," pp. 1–32, and Millicent Bell's "*The Turn of the Screw* and the *recherche de l'absolu*," pp. 33–49) and three to "Louisa Pallant" (Claude Richard's "La Romance de Louisa Pallant," pp. 103–14; "Never Say: l'Art du non-dit dans 'Louisa Pallant'" by Nancy Blake, pp. 115–24, and Jacky Martin's "Les relations énonciatives dans 'Louisa Pallant,'" pp. 125–32). Catherine Vieilledent analyzes "*The*

*Wings of the Dove* and the Question of Art" (pp. 79–90), Nancy Blake's second article bears on *The Awkward Age* ("La Parole Impossible," pp. 63–78), Paul Carmignani's "La Maison Divisée" (pp. 49–62) on *The Bostonians*; Patricia Bleu addresses herself to "Fantastique et Révélation dans 'The Beast in the Jungle'" (pp. 91–102).

I announced last year the forthcoming publication of Viola Sachs's numerological study of *Moby-Dick*. It is published (Paris: Editions de la Maison des Sciences de l'Homme) under the title *The Game of Creation* and deals with "the primeval lettered language" of *Moby-Dick* as Melville's "invitation to a cosmic game." A substantial index to main signs and symbols follows seven chapters on the symbolism, based on the lore and almanacks in Melville's time. Offering an "insight into the 'mythic' in American literature," Sachs places Melville's work squarely within a time-honored American cosmological literary form and wonders *in fine* whether one can ever prove that *Moby-Dick* "constitutes a literary paradigm of mythic white Protestant American imagination."

Two articles on *Walden* came in the wake of that book's being on the syllabus of last year's "agrégation." Colette Gerbaud's "Le Sens de l'Harmonie dans *Walden*" (*Visages de l'Harmonie*, pp. 99–111) studies Thoreau's text from the triple viewpoint of a quest for "terrestrial harmonies," "human harmonies," and the "harmony of the spheres." Rather different in tone and scope is Michel Granger's "*Walden*, ou l'autographie de Henry D. Thoreau" (*RFEA* 14:199–210), which points out that Thoreau, meaning to write a sincere autobiography, in fact avoided any disclosure and created instead an ideal exemplary persona. However, the main point of this "autography" lies with Thoreau's struggle with language, aiming toward an expression "adequate to the truth of which (he has) been convinced."

More strictly thematic in his ambitions, André Poncet discusses "Anti-Racist strategies in Frank Norris's Fiction" (*Les Américains et les Autres*, pp. 55–63) in a brief article.

**c. 20th-Century Poetry and Drama.** Besides Jacqueline Ollier's "Déchiffrage et Improvisations: Clef pour *Kora in Hell*" (*AFLSHN* 43:119–24) where an entrance into Williams' volume is suggested under the guise of a sort of self-psychoanalysis dominated by a structure of opposing forces, the one important contribution to poetry studies this year is "La Poésie Américaine: Rappels et Explorations" (*RFEA* no. 15). The number opens with Jacques Darras' "Le Grand Poème Américain" (pp. 343–71), an article which outlines the main differences between French and American poets, the latter refusing obstinately to dissociate life and writing from the standpoint of life and making the poem an experiment, a voyage, a journey. Darras shows how Rothenberg, Eshleman, Antin, by keeping close to the body, the voice, and the human breath, hold a constant musical tension between language and reality. "Ce que recèlent les mots dans *The Walls Do Not Fall* de H.D." gives Jeanne Blanchenay Kerblat (pp. 373–81) an opportunity to describe this collection as a balance between destructive and constructive forces. Kerblat also has a piece on H.D., "The Rose Loved of Lover or the Heroines in the Poems of the Twenties by H.D.," in *The Twenties* (pp. 45–64). In "Anne Sexton (1928–1974) ou Comment faire taire Jocaste" (pp. 383–94), Marie-Christine Cunci attempts to delineate the contradictory aspects of Sexton's creative gesture: the poem is for her a means of self-revelation but also serves as a place of performance on which are spectacularly staged private fantasies and age-old fables. Sexton's voice, Cunci writes, is less intended to move than to seduce. Régine Lussan has contributed (pp. 395–409) "Rapports de style dans l'oeuvre de Frank O'Hara: de la poésie à la peinture," an essay essentially aiming at drawing a full parallel between abstract expressionist painters and the author of *In Memory of My Feelings*. The only article in English in this number—Kevin Power's "Michael McClure: 'Cherries Gleam Above the Blood of Geryon'" (pp. 411–37)—explores a similar vein since its main thrust consists in drawing together the neighboring arts of McClure and Jackson Pollock.

Few items on drama are worth noting this year, but I have selected the following happy exceptions. On the occasion of Richard Foreman's staging of Gertrude Stein's "Faust: Lighting the Lights" in the Théâtre de Genneviliers (the first time a Stein play was translated and performed in French), *Théâtre Public* published an issue (no. 48, Nov.–Dec.) including articles on Stein's theatre ("Stein ou le Chaos: Mode d'Emploi" by Claude Grimal, pp. 10–15, "Film, une caméra-miroir" (p. 16), and "Faust ou la Fête Electrique" (pp. 33–41) and the translation of the play, both by Marie-Claire Pasquier); a text by Richard Foreman and a variety of enlightening comments by Marie-Claire Pasquier and Claude Grimal. In the same issue are

interesting pieces by Robert Wilson and on Meredith Monk, Robert
Ashley, and Laurie Anderson, as well as interviews. Worth mentioning here in detail are Renata Molinari's "La Voix de Meredith Monk"
(pp. 65–66), Régis Durand's "Robert Ashley: Ethnovideophonie"
(pp. 69–71) and Claude Grimal's "Laurie Anderson: cantilènes de
l'ère technologique" (pp. 76–77). M. C. Pasquier has also produced
"Richard Foreman: Comedy Inside Out (*MD* 25:534–44).

Also worth mentioning briefly here is J. M. Bonnet's short piece,
"Society vs. the Individual in Arthur Miller's *The Crucible*," (*ES* 63:
32–36). But the most important event is undeniably Geneviève
Fabre's masterly book *Le Théâtre Noir aux Etats-Unis* (Paris: Editions du Centre National de la Recherche Scientifique), beautifully
illustrated. This volume of 354 large pages claims the modest ambition of posing the fundamental problems that concern the emergence
and functioning of Afro-American theatre, not of describing or
analyzing the entire black American production. Extremely well
documented (both from library and private sources), the book is
divided into three parts. The first ("L'Aventure Théâtrale," pp. 19–
84) briefly traces the historical development of black drama; the second ("Un théâtre de combat," pp. 83–173) deals with its militant
aspects; and the third ("Le Théâtre de l'Expérience," pp. 175–303)
analyzes the forms variously adopted by Gaines, Bullins, Van Pee-
bles, and P. C. Harrison. A rich critical apparatus offers a substantial
bibliography, the summaries of plays, elements of chronology, and
various tables. Sumptuously laid out and a pleasure to review, this
book is clearly a landmark in the field of American drama in France,
and there may not be better ones in the United States.

*d.* 20th-Century Fiction.   This is the area where the promises at the
end of last year's report are more than fulfilled. No less than seven
books, several collections, and many articles must be selectively
brought to the attention of *ALS* readers and, if one considers the
work now being done on 20th-century fiction, next year's harvest
seems just as promising.

This was first and foremost a Faulkner year in France. François
Pitavy edited *William Faulkner's "Light in August": A Critical Casebook* (Garland), gathering together 12 articles, a chronological appendix, and a bibliography, while André Bleikasten did the same
for *William Faulkner's "The Sound and the Fury": A Critical Case-*

*book* (Garland) with all of Faulkner's own comments on his "most splendid failure" and eight articles. But these two French Faulknerians (a rich breed in a country which rediscovered the novelist in the 1940s) have contributed more. Bleikasten has an article, "Bloom and Quentin," in *The Seventh of Joyce* (pp. 100–108). Pitavy has an essay ("Through the Poet's Eye: A View of Quentin Compson") in Bleikasten's *The Sound and the Fury* casebook, and five other pieces: two are part of his own casebook on *Light in August* ("Voice and Voices in *Light in August*" and "A Stylistic Approach to *Light in August*"); one is in *The Seventh of Joyce* ("Joyce and Faulkner's 'Twining Stresses': A Textual Comparison," pp. 90–99); *Etudes Anglaises* (35:408–19) has a fourth ("Idiotie et Idéalisme: Réflexion sur l'Idiot Faulknérien"); and finally "Through Darl's Eyes Darkly" (*WiF* 4,ii:37–62) explores the vision of the poet in *As I Lay Dying*.

The reason why I don't dwell with any particular insistence on the contents of these very remarkable texts is that, in addition, each of these two authors has published a major study of Faulkner. Pitavy's is not available yet but, I hope, will be soon. Bleikasten's *Parcours de Faulkner* (Association des Publications près les Universités de Strasbourg) is quite exemplary. Readers of Bleikasten's *The Most Splendid Failure* (see *ALS 1976*, pp. 131–32) will recognize the ambiance of that book in the second section ("La Lutte avec l'Ange"); and in the exquisitely wrought analyses of *As I Lay Dying* ("Requiem pour une Mère"), *Sanctuary* ("L'Encre de la Mélancolie"), and *Light in August* ("Versions du Soleil") that follow. Blending totally assimilated and inconspicuous modern critical theory and an uncommon eye for asperities, the stylistic delight of these chapters will not disappoint readers in the least. André Bleikasten's new task consists in editing volume 2 of the works of Faulkner in "La Pléiade." The first volume was edited by Michel Gresset, also editor of Faulkner's correspondence in French, in collaboration with Didier Coupaye (Gallimard). Gresset published part 1 of his work this year: *Faulkner ou la Fascination* (Paris: Klincksieck), the sequel to which ought to appear soon. This book revolves around the eye, the glance, oscillating between appearances and seduction. The eye is presented not as the organ of satisfaction but as that of substitution. Following an ample study of Faulkner's early work, the book fans out into a series of meticulously written, syntactically complex chapters that spell out the double movement of the eye in Faulkner's fiction: the positive force of aesthetic temptation and the shameful use of the "ominous eye." Drawing extensively on psychoanalytical notions, Gresset analyzes two effects of "le regard," designating the eye as the seat of prestige and the seat of shame.

Hardly a newcomer in the realm of Faulkner studies, Jean Rouberol authored the third major French book on the Oxford giant: *L'Esprit du Sud dans l'Oeuvre de Faulkner* (Paris: Didier Erudition). Defining the South as "that, in us, which is split, that which does not die at the hands of contradiction," Rouberol sets out to sort out "the share of the South" in Faulkner's novels. Organizing his fine thematic study around the five poles of "Roots," "The Chronicle," "Archetypes," "A Closed Society," and "The Kingdom of the Word," Rouberol meticulously visits the gallery of traits and portraits and concludes that Quentin's protest of nonhatred toward the South at the end of *Absalom, Absalom!* "expresses, in an exacerbated form, the southern consciousness of the unreconcilable which lies at the root of all Faulknerian creativity. The work," he adds," is not achieved *in spite of* but *thanks to* contradiction."

One cannot leave the South in question without mentioning still another article by André Bleikasten, one on Flannery O'Connor: "Writing on the Flesh: Tattoos and Taboos in 'Parker's Back' " (*SLJ* 14:8–18) and two pieces by Michel Bandry: "An Interview with Erskine Caldwell" (*AFLSHN* 43:125–36) and a study of the sharecropper novel in the '20s ("Le 'sharecropper novel' des années vingt," *The Twenties*, pp. 79–92). There is also an interesting essay by Jean Michelet: "Thomas Wolfe ou l'autobiographe malgré lui" (*RFEA* 14:225–36) in which it is argued that in *Look Homeward, Angel*, Thomas Wolfe does not attempt to appropriate his identity but to free himself from his past, to flee from himself; therefore, "Wolfe the autobiographer" and "Wolfe the 'raw genius' " emerge as two questionable notions.

Geneviève Hily-Mane's book *Le Style de Ernest Hemingway: La Plume et le Masque* (Paris: Presses Universitaires de France) is by a linguist and more particularly works with the theory of enunciation. In her study Hily-Mane shows to what extent the famous "simplicity" of Hemingway's style can be a fallacious notion. Behind the expert in sports and adventure is a finicky craftsman in search of techniques for a double language which may show the author-narrator at play with the lucidity of a reader felt to be at once necessary and redoubtable. The ample use of the numerous manuscripts kept by Hemingway nourishes a work with which, since it deals, after all, with style, one may feel sometimes ill at ease for reasons of . . . style. Straying away from purely referential language, this interesting and worthwhile book may give in to linguistic tics but never to jargon or lack of clarity. There is a sequel to that book in *Visages de l'Harmonie*: "L'Harmonie de la forme ou Comment Ernest Hemingway construit un paragraphe" (pp. 145–52).

A number of other articles deal with modernist authors this year, or authors strewn over the first decades of the 20th century. One thinks of Serge Ricard's "Mencken on Roosevelt: Autopsy of an autopsy" (*The Twenties*, pp. 21–34) and of another article in the same volume (pp. 121–28): Robert Silhol's "*Les Raisins de la Colère (The Grapes of Wrath)* et la Crise de 1929," but also of two essays dealing with black writers (Michel Fabre's "Richard Wright, French Existentialism and *The Outsider*, in *Critical Essays on Richard Wright*, ed. Yoshinobu Hakutani, [Hall], pp. 182–200, on the one hand, and Liliane Blary's "Claude McKay and Africa: *Banjo*," in *CE&S* 5:25–35, on the other.)

Two studies of woman writers close the pre–World War II period. One is Michel Gervaud's "Un regard autre: l'immigrant vu par Willa Cather dans ses romans de la prairie" (*Les Américains et les Autres*, Aix: Université de Provence, pp. 65–82); the other, quite impressive in length and scope, Elizabeth Béranger's *Une Epoque de Transe: l'Exemple de Djuna Barnes, Jean Rhys et Virginia Woolf* (Université de Lille III). The latter book attempts to trace woman and her images in the work of Jean Rhys to demonstrate that in Virginia Woolf's case, writing is a defensive and reconstitutive gesture (*se dé-fendre*), a sort of anti-Spaltung, and to argue that Djuna Barnes's writing is an entranced one. The third and longest part of the book is an excellent analysis of Barnes's art. Strongly informed by psychoanalysis, Béranger makes use of the latest critical equipment with great efficiency to reveal the mental structures of femininity "lived as a nightmare" and concludes that one is not born a woman but that indeed one becomes a woman, and that such a becoming is far from being simply or purely biological. This is one of the most intellectually convincing analyses of feminine writing to appear in recent years.

As to contemporary writing, I must mention Pierre Deflaux's interesting article on war novels: "Le G.I. et les autres dans le roman américain de la Deuxième Guerre Mondiale" (*Les Américains et les Autres*, pp. 83–100).

The growth of contemporary American literary studies in France over the last ten years has been impressive, and even though relatively few publications appeared this year, many are in preparation. Two of the most important items are doubtless the book Maurice Couturier and Régis Durand wrote jointly on *Donald Barthelme* (New York: Methuen; and the special issue of *DeltaES*, no. 14. *Donald Barthelme* is an astonishing book, illuminating the work of a complex author whose writing is most congenially served by the use of recent critical theories. The chapters written by the two authors blend harmoniously into a coherent whole; though their respective linguistic (Couturier) and deconstructionist (Durand) approaches could well clash, this is never the case. On the contrary Couturier's rigorous analyses are enhanced by and themselves enhance Durand's speculations, the latter mostly fed by Lyotard, Lacan, Deleuze, and Derrida.

The second issue of *DeltaES* for 1982 was entirely devoted to Grace Paley. Under the general editorship of Kathleen Hulley, it is a rich and varied collection, almost exclusively in English, contrary to the journal's ambilinguistic tradition (the one exception is Catherine Vieilledent's "Le Comique dans *Enormous Changes at the Last Minute*, pp. 129–46). An unpublished short story by Grace Paley is included: "Lavinia" (pp. 41–46), which will soon be translated into French for *Bas de Casse*. Editor Kathleen Hulley has herself contributed the introduction (pp. 3–18), an interview with the author (pp. 19–40), and a useful bibliography (pp. 147–50). Other contributors are Peter Schuman, with a series of cartoons ("The Rise of Washer Woman Grace of New York City," pp. 47–54); Carolyn Burke, with a poem entitled "New York Story, For Grace Paley" (pp. 1–2); Diane Cousineau ("The Desire of Woman, The Presence of Man," pp. 55–66); Hilda Morley ("Some Notes on Grace Paley While Reading Dante: The Voice of Others," pp. 67–72); Harry Blake ("Grace Paley, a Plea for English Writing", pp. 73–80); Jerome Klinkowitz, with a brief article on "Grace Paley: the Sociology of Metafiction," pp. 81–85); N. P. Humy ("A Different Responsibility: Form and Technique in Grace Paley's "Conversation with my Father,'" pp. 87–96), Melissa Bruce ("*Enormous Changes at the Last Minute*: A Subversive Song Book," pp. 97–114), and Joyce

Meier ("The Subversion of the Father in the Tales of Grace Paley,"
pp. 115–28).

In *RFEA*, no. 14, Claudine Thomas approaches Mailer's "autobiography" through one of Mailer's central "obsessions" in "Autobiography and the Subject of Speech: Counterplot in *Advertisements
for Myself*" (pp. 257–68): the desire to speak oneself into relevance
and, literally, self-possession; which, however, also happen to be
the very means of one's dispossession and alienation in language.
Thomas detects in this direction for research a way to account for the
latent dynamics of Mailer's autobiographical writings taken as a
whole.

John Updike is the theme of Barbara Lemeunier's "A Fable for
Modern Times: America and Africa in *The Coup*" ( *Les Américains
et les Autres*, pp. 101–16) whose thematic preoccupations are made
evident in the title. The same methodological concern structures
Elizabeth Boulot's "Rupture, Révolte et Harmonie dans *Herzog* de
Saul Bellow" (*Visages de l'Harmonie*, pp. 153–66) and Jean Marcet's
"Aspects de la Fuite dans *The Catcher in the Rye*: les Vertes Collines
d'Afrique" (*AFLSHN* 43:107–18).

Some time back, Robert Rougé contributed "Histoire, Psycha-
nalyse et Littérature chez trois romanciers américains contemporains:
Warren, Styron et Pynchon" to the Strasbourg Conference of the
Société des Anglicistes de l'Enseignement Supérieur. It is now in
print (*Echanges*, Paris: Didier Erudition, pp. 393–403) and points
to the increasing interest among French critics for the links between history and fiction. Ishmael Reed, Vladimir Nabokov, and Ken
Kesey are three other contemporary writers of fiction studied this
year. Michel Fabre deals with the "Postmodernist Rhetoric in Ishmael Reed's *Yellow Back Radio Broke Down*" (*The Afro-American
Novel since 1960*, ed. Peter Bruck and Wolfgang Karrer, Amsterdam:
B. R. Grüner, pp. 167–88); J. P. Lecourt treats "L'Enonciation et la
Quête de l'Identité: Personne, Espace, Temps dans *One Flew Over
the Cuckoo's Nest*" (*EA* 35:152–64), and Didier Machu, in "*Look
at the Harlequins!*: l'Etrange cas du Docteur Moreau" (*RFEA* 14:
245–56) examines Nabokov's work from the point of view of the
autobiography of a novelist (Vadim) who is and is not Nabokov.
Here, flesh and text keep exchanging their qualities and one may
wonder if the book tells us of a literary metamorphosis or the im-

probable passage from one state of being to another, or yet of a conversion to a different language. Machu concludes by suggesting that this might be the vanishing trick of an old conjurer who manages to spirit himself away at his farewell performance.

Last but far from least in this year's contributions in the field of contemporary American literature is a special issue of *Les Cahiers de Fontenay*, ed. Catherine Vieilledent: *Fictions Américaines: Nouvelles Voix, Nouveaux Regards* (Fontenay aux Roses: Ecole Normale Supérieure). All of the authors of this important collection are members of the Groupe René Tadlov operating at the Maison des Sciences de l'Homme, a sequel to André Le Vot's ex-Paris III Research Center. Le Vot has written the introduction to this series of essays on Robert Coover, Grace Paley, and Richard Brautigan.

In "Robert Coover's Wonder Show" (pp. 9–22) Marc Chénetier addresses the multifaceted and complex problems posed by Coover's fiction and examines the variety of Coover's lucid and controlled art. The other four essays dealing with this author are devoted to in-depth analyses of *Public Burning*, a novel outrageously underestimated in American criticism. Julian Thorsteinson studies "La Logocratie nixonienne" (pp. 23–32); Bruno Montfort, "Effets Enonciatifs dans *The Public Burning*" (pp. 33–41); Valerie Nataf, "Nixonland, USA" (pp. 42–52); Catherine Vieilledent, "Histoire et Paranoïa: la cas Nixon dans *The Public Burning*" (pp. 53–66); and Yves Abrioux, "Le jeu de la narration dans *The Public Burning*" (pp. 67–80). All methodologically acute and sophisticated, these essays on Robert Coover deliberately neglect the sheer thematic dimensions of the novel in order to concentrate on the linguistic, stylistic, and poetic effects achieved in it.

After a short introduction there are three essays on Grace Paley: one by Bruno Montfort ("Du remplacement: ironie et substitution dans une nouvelle de Grace Paley intitulée 'Faith in a Tree'," pp. 83–100), a second by Dominique Riley ("Points de vue(s) et tons révélateurs d'un Zeitgeist dans le petit monde de Grace Paley," pp. 101–12), and the third by Yves Abrioux ("Figures du Comique: récit et pouvoir dans l'oeuvre de Paley," pp. 113–28).

Two essays on Richard Brautigan complete this special issue: they are Marc Chénetier's "Drill, ye, tarriers, drill: nouvelles notes sur l'esthétique de Brautigan" (pp. 129–40) and Marie-Christine Agosto's "*Sombrero Fallout*: structure narrative" (pp. 141–53). While Chénetier plays truant with a variety of critical schools, Agosto's essay is firmly anchored in the research accomplished in the 1970s by the French "néo-rhétoriciens." A very useful series of summaries in French, English, and German (pp. 153–77) complete a volume which, emanating from a team that has based its work on enthusiasm, friendship, and antidogmaticism, reads like a veritable labor of love.

*Université d'Orléans*

### *iii.* German Contributions

### *Rolf Meyn*

The 1982 harvest of publications differs in several respects from that of the previous year. Bi- or trinational explorations of genres, motifs, and themes have increased considerably. This is not only a result of the many contributions to the *Haas Festschrift*, whose title *Die Amerikanische Literatur in der Weltliteratur: Themen und Aspekte* calls for a comparative approach, but seems to be a general trend. Also remarkable are some book-length overviews, embracing parts of American literature from colonial times to the present. These will be treated below.

*a.* **Literary Criticism and Theory: Comparative Studies.** Among the contributions to literary criticism and theory Edith Klemenz-Belgardt's *Amerikanische Leserforschung* (Tübingen: Günther Narr) stands out as the first book devoted to the field of reader-response criticism in Germany. The author notes the work of Wolfgang Iser, Siegfried J. Schmidt, Stanley Fish, David Bleich, and others, but is more interested in the empirical research of numerous American scholars. Klemenz-Belgardt's premise is that "up to now no convincing theory has been developed which integrates the various aspects of the response concept." Her intention is not to create a theory of her own, but to describe and evaluate the various attempts made in this direction. Research undertaken on the response of children, high-school students, and adults of different social and educational backgrounds is commented on. Problems arising from intelligence, the parents' influence, teaching situations, the characteristics of dif-

ferent literary texts and their effect on readers and psychic disposi-
tions are only some points considered. There is no doubt that this
work is a much-needed venture into the field of reader-response criticism which for the most part remains a *terra incognita*, especially for
those who still believe in two kinds of readers, "the immature re-
cipient on one side of the fence, and the elite of the initiated, 'cultivated' on the other." Cultural aspects, which in *Amerikanische Leserforschung* are only a segment of the complicated process unfolding
between the text and the reader, are the essense of "Landeskunde,"
the German equivalent of cultural studies. Its role in foreign-language
teaching has often been discussed in the last two decades. In contrast
to many of these debates, in which the use of literature is only of
minor importance, Karl-Heinz Tschachler in his paper "Landeskunde
und die 'Negativität' der Literatur: Ein theoretischer Versuch mit
Modellanalyse" (*ArAA* 7:23–39) has as his theme the analysis of a
literary text in regard to requirements of cultural studies. Henry
Adams' *Democracy* (1880) is singled out for a demonstration as to
how cultural issues encoded in a literary text can become part of a
"Landeskunde" model. Tschachler adopts Wolfgang Iser's concept
of the "negativity of literature," according to which a fictional text
is not in opposition to reality, but tells us something about it, and,
moreover, can be understood as an "affective reaction to it." For
Tschachler, *Democracy* can well function as a cultural studies model,
because the author's didactic intention, i.e., the unmasking of the
growing rift between American ideals and a corrupt world, is obvious. The feeling that philological studies should extend beyond
self-imposed boundaries into a wider cultural context is also at the
core of two more essays dealing with film versions of literary texts.
In Paul G. Buchloh's and Ralf J. Schröder's "Zum Problem kultureller
und medialer Umsetzung von Dramatik: Tennessee Williams *The
Glass-menagerie*" (*Haas Festschrift*, pp. 339–62) the two film versions by Irving Rapper (1950) and Anthony Harvey (1973) are
thoroughly analyzed to demonstrate the method of "close seeing,"
i.e., to compare the various signs of the original text with those realized in the films. Thus, a double effect is achieved: the text is examined with utmost scrutiny and simultaneously set in a larger
cultural context. A similar method of integrating the film into philological studies is practiced in Bernhard Reitz's " 'I've never seen

anything so unreal in my life': Unwirklichkeit als Darstellungsproblem in Coppolas 'Apocalypse Now' und Conrads 'The Heart of Darkness'" (*ZAL:A&E* 16:119–44). Both Conrad's novella and Coppola's film are taken as congenial works of art, since the latter's script is a rewriting of the former, the transposing of a journey up the river in dark colonial Africa at the turn of the century into the heart of darkness of the Vietnam War. In both works a Kurtz, who renounces his humanitarian ideals, and a narrator, who judges men by their self-control and by their moral standards, act as chief protagonists. Contrary to Conrad's *Heart of Darkness*, however, there is far less moral distance between the narrator Willard and Colonel Kurtz, although in both works the narrators succeed in transmitting the atmosphere of the unreal and absurd to their respective audiences. Yet, as Reitz holds, Coppola failed to dissolve the juxtaposition of the narrator and the narrating camera.

Problems of genre and influence are tackled in Peter Cersowsky's essay "Allegory and the Fantastic in Literature: Poe's 'The Mask of the Red Death' and Alfred Kubin's *The Other Side*" (*Sprachkunst* 13:141–50). Allegory and the fantastic are not understood as neighboring genres having a dualistic structure in common, as Louis Vax (1963) and Tzvetan Todorov (1970) insisted. Instead, Cersowsky maintains with reference to the German scholar Werner H. Sokel, there exists a mixed form, the fantastic allegory, which was of special attraction to German expressionist prose writers such as Max Brod, Franz Kafka, Alfred Kubin, and Gustav Meyrink. Cersowsky attributes much of the fantastic allegory's popularity to the influence of Poe, whose reception in Germany, partly through the intermediary of the French symbolists, was paramount around 1900. Alfred Kubin's novel *The Other Side* (1904) is presented as a striking example. Cersowsky claims a strong affinity between this novel and Poe's story "The Mask of the Red Death" because in both texts what Walter Benjamin called "objectivity as the essential cognitional characteristic of allegory" eventually gives way to the fantastic, that part of the represented world which is structured through the imagination. Also, in both texts the antagonists, personifications of decay, intrude and destroy the allegorical world, the product of their rulers. Although Cersowsky's thesis of a "counter allegory of life against the sphere of death" is debatable, since one can argue that the opposition life versus death is part of one allegorical structure, the essay ought to encourage more research on Poe's influence on German expressionist writers.

European-American interrelationships in a specific literary tradition have found their proponent in Klaus Poenicke, whose monograph *Der Amerikanische Naturalismus: Crane, Norris, Dreiser* (Darmstadt: Wissenschaftliche Buchgesellschaft) has three different aims: (1) to outline European discussions of realism/naturalism concepts from their mid-19th-century beginnings to the present, (2) to use this background for a penetrating investigation into the intellectual history of American naturalism, and (3) to evaluate the reception of Stephen Crane, Frank Norris, and Theodore Dreiser, with the help of criteria elaborated in the first two steps. This procedure makes the book more than a critical state-of-research publication. The indebtedness of American naturalism to European ideas, but also its deviance from its European counterpart, are poignantly worked out. The most important contribution is the successful attempt to arrive at definitions which are more precise than those formulated by earlier critics, whose merits and shortcomings are nevertheless depicted in all fairness. It makes Poenicke's concise summary of the Crane, Norris, and Dreiser reception the work of an authority whose comments must be kept in mind by those who want to do research in this crowded field.

*b.* **Literary History.** Of the 1982 contributions in Germany, two extensive publications covering two centuries of American literature have to be mentioned first. In his *Geschichte des Amerikanischen Dramas* (Stuttgart: Kohlhammer) Jürgen Schäfer gives German students and scholars of American theater and drama a detailed history from the first third of the 18th century to the present. In discussing the present century, Schäfer stresses the role of O'Neill in bringing American drama to new heights, examines European influences from Ibsen on, and the realistic dramatists of the '20s. Three chapters are devoted to the '30s—such forces as the Workers' Laboratory Theater, Maxwell Anderson, Robert E. Sherwood, and Lillian Hellman—and to successive decades to the present, with separate chapters on Tennessee Williams and Arthur Miller. Although Schäfer's preference for O'Neill, Williams, and Miller is obvious, this tightly structured study with its constant alternation between a focus on a decade's most important playwrights and a more general survey covers all the essentials of American theater from its beginnings to the present.

Klaus Ensslen's *Einführung in die Schwarzamerikanische Literatur* (Stuttgart: Kohlhammer) resembles in structure and scope that of Jürgen Schäfer's book. The title is an understatement; what we have here is not so much an introduction as a history of black literature. In five chapters Ensslen outlines Afro-American literature from its beginnings in the poetry of Phyllis Wheatley and Jupiter Hammon and slave narratives through the stages of abolitionism and emancipation (1820–80), of socioeconomic restrictions and the beginnings of a cultural stock-taking (1880–1930), of a deep conflict between ideology and social integration (1930–60) to the present phase which he calls "Black Literature as a political and cultural Declaration of Independence." Ensslen's conviction is clear from his introductory remarks on: black literature is the literature of an ethnic group within a "dominant culture" with all its tendencies of suppression and assimilation. Hence, argues Ensslen, modern black literature is shaped by two conflicting forces, an integrationist thrust, as can be found in Ralph Ellison's *Invisible Man*, and the cultural self-confidence of a younger generation which is proud of its ethnic roots. Although the author's preference for prose works is obvious, drama and poetry are by no means overlooked in this comprehensive study of Afro-American literature.

Brigitte Georgi's little monograph *Der Indianer in der amerikanischen Literatur: Das weiße Rassenverständnis bis 1900 und die indianische Selbstdarstellung ab 1833: Versuch einer Gegenüberstellung* (Köln: Pahl-Rugenstein) is another example of the rapidly growing interest of German scholars in the literature of ethnic groups or their portrayals in American literature. Georgi begins with a brief analysis of Puritan and 18th-century writers such as Benjamin Franklin and Philip Freneau, then focuses on such 19th-century writers as Charles Brockden Brown, James Fenimore Cooper, William Gilmore Simms, Edgar Allan Poe, Robert Montgomery Bird, John Greenleaf Whittier, Henry Wadsworth Longfellow, Herman Melville, Henry David Thoreau, and Mark Twain. For reasons unknown Nathaniel Hawthorne and Walt Whitman are not mentioned. Georgi believes three different images of the Native American emerge: the romantic, "noble" savage; the "realistic-romantic Indian" of Cooper's *Leatherstock-*

*ing Novels;* and the cruel, vicious barbarian of Robert Montgomery
Bird's *Nick of the Woods* and Mark Twain's *Roughing It.* The highest praise is reserved for Thoreau, whose Indian does not fit into any
one of these categories and who "came closer to an understanding of
the Indian's world view and his culture than most of his contemporaries."

The second part of the monograph is concerned with the autobiographies of Black Hawk, Geronimo, Plenty Coups, Two Leggins,
and others, in which Georgi discovers a growing insight into the
necessity of assimilation. In her last chapter Georgi assesses Indian
novels from Simon Pokagon's *Queen of the Woods* (1899) on. Here
she discovers a break with assimilationist tendencies beginning with
the late 1930s. D'Arcy McNickle's *The Surrounded* (1938), in structure and theme a forerunner of N. Scott Momaday's *House Made of
Dawn* (1970), marks the turn of the tide, a return to the roots. In
novels of the 1970s—e.g., George Pierce's *Autumn Bounty* (1972),
Leslie Marmon Silko's *Ceremony* (1977), and James Welch's *Winter
in the Blood* (1974)—social protest and radical confrontations are
largely absent. Instead, the emphasis is on a conflict between spiri-
tuality and transcendentalism on the one hand and a rationalistic,
materialistic world view on the other. Thus, Indian consciousness
turns into a philosophy of life. Brigitte Georgi's comparative study
leaves some questions open, simply because more than 300 years of
Indian presence in American literature cannot be squeezed into 125
pages. Yet her thesis that Thoreau is the spiritual ancestor of modern
Indian literature ought to stimulate more scrutinizing research.

Popular forms of literature have found their proponents too. In
his essay "Romance Versus Reality aus amerikanischer Sicht: Das
Problem der Western-Literatur" (*Haas Festschrift,* pp. 34–48) Karl-
Heinz Göller assumes that Timothy Flint, driven by his aversion to
what he felt as the tyranny of European culture and that of the eastern seaboard, became one of the first advocates of Western literature
containing truly national themes. Göller then turns to William Gilmore Simms, whose novel *The Yamassee* and definition of romance
he considers the first attempts to create an autonomous fiction in
theory as well as in practice. Simms, however, was not able to broach
the contradiction between romance and historical veracity. This
posed no problems for writers of dime-novel Westerns whom Göller
deems the descendants of Simms and his contemporaries. Göller

stands up for this product of popular culture, which in his opinion conveys the atmosphere and the "intentional data of an epoch," i.e., "what authors and readers thought, felt, and desired." Another genre of popular culture is embraced in Johann N. Schmidt's paper "Einwirkung und Rückwirkung: Das Melodrama in seiner europäisch-amerikanischen Wirkungsgeschichte" (*Haas Festschrift*, pp. 49–67). Schmidt points to the fact that throughout the 19th century the melodrama was one of the most popular and long-lived subgenres of the drama in France, England, and America. Its distinctive features were striking situations, uncompromising enjoyment of emotional climaxes, use of any available means of expression on stage, unscrupulous adoption of up-to-date themes and stylistic innovations, and stock characters. The melodrama's insistence on moral values, its belief in the perfectibility of man, regardless of class and social structures, predestined it for the American stage. Schmidt then views some of the most successful variants, e.g., the dipsomania play, the city melodrama, and an abolitionist melodrama, Conrad Aiken's stage version of *Uncle Tom's Cabin*. Although the melodrama lost its popularity on stage, many of its characteristics survived in films. David Wark Griffith's *The Birth of a Nation* is cited as a case in point. Correspondingly, the city and criminal melodrama provided the Hollywood gangster movie with an unmistakable iconography.

*c.* **Colonial and 19th-Century Literature.** Of particular value for scholars involved with research on American puritanism is Hans-Peter Wagner's monograph *Puritan Attitudes Towards Recreation in Early Seventeenth-Century New England: With Particular Consideration of Physical Recreation* (Frankfurt: Lang), a dissertation submitted to the university of Saarbrücken in 1979. Wagner's aim is to throw new light on a hitherto largely overlooked aspect of New England puritanism, i.e., recreation. The author uses the term as the Puritans did, denoting intellectual and physical recreation as well as recreational activities such as card and board games, convivial gatherings, and social events. Social stratification is assessed by considering three groups, i.e., the proprietors of larger estates and the affluent merchants; a middle stratum consisting of farmers, shopkeepers, merchants, and artisans; and a lower stratum made up of laborers, indentured servants, and slaves. The situation of women and children is separately analyzed. Evidence is obtained from the writings of

prominent Puritans, from town and church records, from Puritan
legislation, from letters, diaries, sermons and jeremiads, and from
the findings of other scholars such as Perry Miller, Sacvan Bercovitch,
Darrett E. Rutman, and Michael McGiffin. Wagner cogently demonstrates that all endeavors of the Puritan leaders to keep New England free from what they saw as "sin and idleness" were bound to
fail. The Puritan clergy's interpretation of recreation found no echo
among the body of laymen because in a predominantly rural New
England leisure primarily served the purpose of socialization rather
than physical recreation, especially "in such polyvalent activities as
hunting, fishing, husking, and military training." The New England
clergy, on the other hand, preferred intellectual recreation and propa-
gated a utilitarian function of physical recreation. Furthermore, even
the saints were unwilling to conform to a "new normative pattern of
behavior which ran counter to age-old customs and traditional habits." Wagner admits that evidence from the middle and lower strata
is hard to come by. All in all, however, his study is a synthetic analysis
that has to be taken into account by all future scholars of New
England puritanism.

The survey of German contributions to 19th-century literature
begins with an essay on James Fenimore Cooper, whose works, unless
in connection with larger themes, have not aroused much interest
among German scholars lately. In his " 'She springs her luff!': Coopers
Einsatz der Fachsprache im Seeroman" (Haas Festschrift, pp. 110–
27) Ernst O. Fink breaks a lance for Cooper, the underrated sea
novelist. After all, he reminds us, no lesser a writer than Joseph Conrad paid his homage to Cooper. Fink holds that Cooper was lucky
to write at a time when sea language was fully recognized as a meta-
language in fiction. Cooper had criticized Sir Walter Scott's The
Pirate for its lack of a truly nautical atmosphere, so in The Pilot and
Homeward Bound he set out to surpass his revered mentor. Cooper
succeeded because he skillfully integrated sea language in literary
language and created nautical heroes who combine an exemplary
character with highest professional efficiency and a faultless command of sea language. Cooper also plays an important role in Bruno
Schultze's paper "Die Anfänge des englischen und amerikanischen
Spionageromans" (Haas Festschrift, pp. 94–109), an abridged version of the first chapter of his monograph Die Entwicklung des Englischen Spionageromans bis 1930 (Heidelberg: Carl Winter 1977).

Schultze interprets Cooper's Harvey Birch in *The Spy* as an early example of the "patriotic spy," a traditional figure in the American 19th-century spy novel. Cooper's contemporary, Edgar Allan Poe, retained his attraction for German scholars. In Johannes Kleinstück's "Poe und Baudelaire" (*Haas Festschrift*, pp. 75–83) both poets are seen as artists who share similar esthetic views. But the concurrences are accidental. Poe's theories only confirmed Baudelaire's esthetics, which were formulated before Baudelaire became acquainted with the writings of his American counterpart: "Baudelaire did not need the 'Philosophy of Composition' to recognize the importance of the 'délibération.'" Conversely, Carla Gregorzweski, echoing Daniel G. Hoffman and F. O. Matthiessen, presents Poe as an American artist in her monograph *Edgar Allan Poe und die Anfänge einer originär amerikanischen Ästhetik* (Heidelberg: Winter).

Of the contributions on Henry James, Ludwig Borinski's paper "Die Entstehung der Moderne bei Henry James" (*Haas Festschrift*, pp. 128–43) is the most far-reaching. Starting out from the various "isms" in the early 20th century, Borinski traces modernism to Charles Dickens' *Martin Chuzzlewit*, the novels of Russian writers, and the plays of Strindberg. As for America, Borinski regards puritanism as the forerunner of modernism, because it stresses the neurotic and pathological inclinations in man. Hawthorne is the chronicler of this characteristic of puritanism; and Henry James, descended from Northern Irish Presbyterians, becomes his disciple. James's female figures are modern types of more or less emancipated women. Distorted sexual relationships abound, and the characters are complicated products of a refined, deteriorating civilization. James welds all this into his descriptions of psychological conflicts and problems resulting from a combination of egotism, lack of clarity and openness, and over-refinement. *What Maisie Knew*, with its divorce theme and its account of a child's psychological conflicts, marks the modernist breakthrough. In *The Turn of the Screw* James's modernism reaches its full maturity; the reader is thrown into the world of modern psychology, with all its subconscious complexes, neuroticism, and schizophrenia. Yet even here James does not refrain from evaluation: evil is still called evil. James remains at heart a moralist, the spiritual descendant of the Puritans. His covert moralism is also the theme of two more essays. Egon Tiedje in "Henry James in seiner Zeit: *The Spoils of Poynton* und die gesellschaftliche Wirklichkeit Englands

Mitte der neunziger Jahre" (*Haas Festschrift*, pp. 176–95) interprets *The Spoils of Poynton* as the writer's moralistic reaction to the barbarism of modern trends. Kurt Otten in his paper "Henry James im Verständnis Graham Greenes" (*Haas Festschrift*, pp. 291–303) pays tribute to Graham Greene, who not only accepted James as his master but was the first critic to point to James's preoccupation with the origin of evil, thereby making him the spiritual kin of Dostoevsky, Conrad, and Hardy. Writer and religion is also at the core of Ursula Brumm's paper "The Religious Crisis of the 19th Century in *Robert Elsmere* and *The Damnation of Theron Ware*" (*Haas Festschrift*, pp. 159–75). Brumm contrasts two writers on both sides of the Atlantic, whose novels of ideas "deal with the psychic upheaval which replaced the religious mind of Western man by a scientific mind." She convincingly pleads for a new perspctive on Harold Frederic's novel, which for the most part has been analyzed only in relation to Hawthorne and archetypical themes of innocence and initiation. For Brumm, however, there is strong evidence that Frederic's *The Damnation of Theron Ware* (1896) owes its existence to Mrs. Humphry Ward's novel *Robert Elsmere* (1888). The two works resemble each other in plot and structure, and share the theme of religious doubt and faith, centered in the figure of a clergyman. Yet where Mrs. Ward leaves the integrity of her hero intact, Frederic eight years later expresses a deterministic view of man and describes Theron Ware's damnation with a cold naturalistic precision and without any hope for atonement. Rudolf Sühnel compares Mark Twain's greatest novel and Rudyard Kipling's *Kim* from a similar point of view, although in his essay "Mark Twains *Huckleberry Finn* und Kiplings *Kim*" (*Haas Festschrift*, pp. 144–51) the problem of influence is not mentioned. Yet also for Sühnel there is no doubt that the two writers' retreat into a child's world of unmanipulated nature was caused by their reaction to a disturbing new era of technology and science. Twain, however, is more pessimistic than Kipling. Huck Finn is full of self-doubt, trying to avoid all complications, while Kim feels at home everywhere and explores life with a boyish curiosity. This explains why *Huckleberry Finn* is essentially a bitter book, and *Kim*, in contrast, "a supremely serene romance about the unchanging East."

*d.* 20th-Century Literature.    American writers affiliated with naturalism have kept their attraction for German scholars. John Martin's

"Martin Eden, a London Superman Adventurer: A Case Study of the Americanization of European Ideology" (*Haas Festschrift*, pp. 218–30) is concerned with Jack London's adoption of Nietzschean philosophy. Martin cautiously speculates that London used Nietzsche's ideology as an "aesthetic structure," and was probably aware that he took over the popular misconception of the Nietzschean superman as a blond beast who destroyed the decadent culture around him. Yet by doing this, he was able to combine the role of a typical London adventurer with that of a nihilist exposing "the decadence of American culture." Of two essays devoted to the city in American literature, Walter Göbel's "Schreckbild Stadt: Chicago im naturalistischen Roman," *Die Stadt in der Literatur*, ed. Wolfgang Haubrichs (*LiLi* 12:88–112) covers several decades, ranging from Frank Norris' *The Pit* and Upton Sinclair's *The Jungle* to Nelson Algren's *Never Come Morning* and *The Man With The Golden Arm*. In all these novels the dominant metaphors of Chicago as a battlefield for the victors, as a jungle, an octopus, a prison, or a rat cage for the defeated intensify the effect desired by the novelists: to present Chicago as a nightmare. The structures of the novels change with the city. The strong and selfish protagonists in Dreiser's novels give way to tenement and ghetto characters in Richard Wright's and James T. Farrell's novels. Alienated from their families and from the rest of society, these figures are even more the victims of fate and circumstances. The tightly structured family saga is replaced by the peer-group novel and its multifaceted perspective. Yet in contrast to a nightmarish Chicago, there exists also the countermetaphor of Chicago as a place of fascination and even hope, as the poems of Carl Sandburg, the works of city-planners, architects, and painters, and even Dreiser's novels amply testify. Heinrich F. and Renate Plett's "New York: Variationen über das Thema Metropolis im amerikanischen Drama der zwanziger Jahre" (*LiLi* 12:103–33) shares with the foregoing paper the credo that reality is reflected in literature. Focusing on five expressionist plays of the 1920s—Eugene O'Neill's *The Hairy Ape*, John Howard Lawson's *Roger Bloomer*, John Dos Passos' *The Garbage Man*, Francis Edwards Faragoh's *Pinwheel*, and Elmer Rice's *The Subway*—the authors discover a number of common features in the portrayal of New York, among them New York as a background for the protagonist's quest for self-awareness, as a symbol of the modern metropolis, as a place grotesquely distorted in the protagonist's mind, as dramatis persona in its own right, and as a place in sharp contrast to the confinements of a small town. With regard to structure all these New York plays comprise several scenes functioning as stages in the protagonist's search for self-fulfillment. The view of New York, extending from a seemingly realistic depiction to an apocalyptic vision, is overwhelmingly negative. A concept of art, born of a negative vision of an urban, industrial world and its materialism, is also examined in Walter Göbel's "Sherwood Anderson: Das Transzendieren der Wirklichkeit" (*Sprachkunst* 13: 297–308). Göbel interprets Anderson's artistic credo as a call for a retreat from the world of facts, because for this writer the imaginative world is separated from reality. Dream and madness, both forms of the loss of reality, become creative acts, offering access to the world of fancy. The artist becomes, as for Walt Whitman, a seer and a prophet. This conviction makes Anderson a belated romanticist, and in his preference for the ideal instead of the real, also a transcendentalist.

American poetry fared less well than fiction or drama in 1982. Friedel H. Bastein's "Zum Fortleben Catulus in der nordamerikanischen Literatur des 20. Jahrhunderts" (*Haas Festschrift*, pp. 231–51), a substantial, well-documented discussion of Catullus's continuing influence in America, includes poetry, drama, and fiction, ranging from Harriet Monroe, Ezra Pound, and Thornton Wilder to Katherine Mosby. Bernd Engler's essay "Allen Tates and Robert Lowells 'Civil War Odes': Literarische Tradition und modernes Krisenbewußtsein (*LJGG* 23:243–63) is devoted to an inquiry into the clash between traditions and the modern sense of crisis, for which Allen Tate's "Ode to the Confederate Dead" and Robert Lowell's "For the Union Dead" serve as paradigmatic texts. Composed in the tradition of the commemoration ode, both works use the American Civil War as a reference point for the authors' reflections on the present and for questions about transitoriness and the meaning of life. Tate and Lowell, Engler claims, deliberately employed deviant forms and styles in order to turn against a world view of utopian optimism which they rejected. American poetry is also examined in Hans Galinsky's "Amerikas Kolonialgeschichte in seiner Literatur des 20 Jahrhunderts: Ein Überblick und zwei Interpretationsstudien zu William Carlos Williams und Carl Sandburg" (*Kessel Festschrift*, pp. 62–88). This paper, however, is more symptomatic of the newly awakened interest in literary texts dealing with historical themes. Edgar Kleinen's monograph *Amerikanische Geschichte im amerikanischen historischen Drama seit Maxwell Anderson: Forschungsbericht, Werkinterpretation, gattungsgeschichtlicher Wertungsversuch* (Frankfurt: Lang) is another good illustration of this trend. Kleinen's book focuses on a variant of the American drama which gathered momentum in the 1930s, when the need to reinterpret national history was urgently felt in America. Historical fiction is examined in Hans-Joachim Müllenbrock's paper "John Barth's *The Sot-Weed Factor*: Der historische Roman als Instrument satirischer Geschichtsbehandlung" (*Haas Festschrift*, pp. 448–57). Müllenbrock, in contrast to most Barth critics, is not so much interested in *The Sot-Weed Factor* as a parody of Fielding's picaresque novels, but as a parallel to William Makepeace Thackeray's *The History of Henry Esmond* and *The Virginians*, in which he observes "a similar militant or disturbed relationship with Clio." Both *The Sot-Weed Factor* and *The History of Henry Esmond* are bildungsromans of heroes in a process of progressive disillusionment. Both authors are bent on demythologizing history. Thackeray wants to demolish the Victorians' shining image of the Augustan Age, whereas Barth devaluates an epoch equally prestigious as part of America's heroic past. In Barth's satire the American Dream is historically plucked to pieces, but contrary to Thackeray's novels it lacks the foundations of guiding norms. Katherine Anne Porter's controversial satire *Ship of Fools* also attracted a German scholar. In his "Katherine Anne Porters Einladung auf *Das Narrenschiff*" (*Haas Festschrift*, pp. 458–75), H.-J. Lang analyzes the novel's reception in Germany and in the United States, then comments on Porter's relations with Germany, which changed from sympathy for the Germans as individuals to holding everybody responsible for everything which happened after 1933, and points to the fact that verisimilitude is frequently violated. Although the novel is based on Porter's journey from Veracruz to Germany in 1931, Freytag's expulsion from the captain's table because of his having a Jewish wife could not have happened in 1931. But verisimilitude is only of minor importance for a writer working with stereotype, caricature, and parody. *Ship of Fools* is first and foremost a satire. Nightmares of recent history and its mastering in literature are embraced in Kurt Dittmar's essay "Der Holocaust in der jüdisch-amerikanischen Literatur" (*Haas Festschrift*, pp. 392–414). Dittmar contradicts those critics who accuse Jewish-American writers of the 1950s and 1960s of being unable to deal with the most terrible catastrophe in history. The creative reception of the Holocaust, he holds, fostered the emergence of the universal-humanistic Jewish outsider as he appears in the works of Malamud and Bellow. For the latter the Holocaust is not a singular event, but an exemplary manifestation of a radical destructiveness, comparable with Hiroshima and Dresden. This idea seems to be opposed by some of the most recent novelists, e.g., Susan Fromberg Schaeffer's *Anya* (1974) and Leslie Epstein's *King of the Jews* (1979), in which the Holocaust becomes part of the continuity of Jewish history. This tendency, however, competes with a contrary development in gentile literature, in which the Holocaust is turned into an allegory of extreme human suffering. The final step in the appropriation of the Holocaust by the dominant American culture is its commercialization by mass media, as in the case of the *Holocaust* television series.

In addition to Klaus Ensslen's book, two more contributions to research on black literature must be mentioned. In his monograph *Ralph Ellison: The Genesis of an Artist* (Nürnberg: Hans Carl) Rudolf F. Dietze cogently discloses how deeply Ellison's concept of art is rooted in traditions established by T. S. Eliot and André Malraux, the latter providing him with the example of man-as-artist revolting against his fate. The metaphor of invisibility is traced into Western literature, to H. G. Wells and Fyodor Dostoevski. These traditions merge with an art form derived from music, the blues. The most successful part of Dietze's monograph is devoted to an exploration of structure, allusions, and metaphors in *Invisible Man*. Dietze does not take into account much of the ideological context that made Ellison a highly controversial figure in Afro-American letters of the late 1960s and early 1970s. But this is negligible in a study which so comprehensively deals with Ellison's art. In *The Afro-American Novel* the essays provided by German scholars focus on single works, e.g., Karrer in "Multiperspective and the Hazards of Integration: John A. Williams' *Night Song* (1961)" (pp. 75–105) and Klaus Ensslen in "Collective Experience and Individual Responsibilities: Alice Walker's *The Third Life of Grange Copeland* (1970)" (pp. 189–218).

John Updike, the chronicler of white middle-class suburbia, is represented in Klaus P. Hansen's "Psychologie und religiöse Typologie bei John Updike" (*Amst* 27:119–39). Hansen examines three of Updike's short stories, "The Kid's Whistling," "Walter Briggs," "Giving Blood," and, in passing, most of his novels in order to postulate his thesis of the "two different halves" in Updike's oeuvre. The first half circumscribes a correspondence between Updike's work and the current psychology of communication, as outlined by Paul Watzlawick, Janet H. Beavin, Don D. Jackson, and their emphasis on the breakdown of communication between family members. The second half denotes a "mythic superstructure," a transcendence overlying the realistically drawn middle-class milieu. The solutions drawn from religion, mythology, or natural philosophy rarely help Updike's protagonists to overcome their personal problems, but this inadequacy is posited deliberately in order to underline the shortcomings of traditional forms of transcendence.

The 1982 survey should fittingly end with two papers concerned with German-American literary interrelationships. Hans Galinsky's "The Give-and-Take of an American Section: Literary Relations between the American South and Germany in the Early Post-War Period (1945–50)" (*Haas Festschrift*, pp. 363–91) reminds us that southern writers occupied a prominent place when the German postwar reading community discovered American literature. Writers like Edgar Allan Poe, Mark Twain, William Faulkner, Thomas Wolfe, and Margaret Mitchell had already been popular before 1939. They were joined by such newcomers as Marjorie Kinnan Rawlings, Frank Yerby, Eudora Welty, Tennessee Williams, and Truman Capote after 1945. As for the South's reception of German literature, Galinsky finds a wider range than early post-1945 German taste from the fact that translations of eight German authors as divergent as Paracelsus, Goethe, Hölderlin, Novalis, Hebbel, George, and Thomas Mann were published by southern presses between 1945 and 1950. The strong interest in Stefan George's lyrical poetry is attributed to the "southern sympathy with the classic and neoclassicist tradition of the 'poet as seer.'" The influence of Rilke on Randall Jarrell, one of the most prolific southern poets of the immediate postwar era, and of Kafka on a host of southern writers, including Caroline Gordon, Flannery O'Connor, Richard Wright, and Ralph Ellison, is also commented on. Volker Bischoff's essay "Rainer Maria Gerhardt und die amerikanische Lyrik: Eine Episode deutsch-amerikanischer Wechselbeziehungen im Kontext der deutschen Pound-Rezeption" (*Haas Fest-*

*schrift*, pp. 415–36) contains an overview of the slowly growing recognition of Pound's poetry from the 1920s on, but is mainly concerned with the role of the young German poet and critic Rainer Maria Gerhardt (1927–54) as intermediary between Ezra Pound and German poetry after 1945. Of interest also are Bischoff's discussions of German comments on Pound's involvement with fascism and of Gerhardt's position as a European representative of lyrical poetry for his American poet friends, Charles Olson and Robert Creeley.

*Universität Hamburg*

## iv. Japanese Contributions

### Hiroko Sato

The perpetual question concerning the text and its context in studies of American literature was raised again at the beginning of 1982. The February issue of *Eigo-Seinen* (127:672–80) collected articles written by eight noted scholars on American literature under the overall title "Studies of American Literature and American Studies." The ideas expressed in these articles are varied, and naturally there is no definite answer to the question. Kenzaburo Ohashi, who chaired the forum on the same topic at the national convention of the American Literature Society of Japan in the fall of 1981, emphasizes the importance of the interrelationship between the text of a literary work and its cultural context and points out that sometimes the text may serve as a context for other approaches to American culture and society. Koji Oi presents the method used by Leo Marx in *The Machine in the Garden* and "The American Revolution and the American Landscape" as one of the most useful models in forming a methodology to combine these two overlapping fields of study. Some scholars, however, still cling to the textual criticism developed by the New Critics and regard the context as something secondary in understanding the text. The most poignant article is the one by Toshio Watanabe, who raises a very fundamental question: "Why has this topic come up again and again, when everybody knows that there is no definite answer?" Watanabe's seemingly naive question hides a serious concern with the easy-going way of some of the schol-

ars in the field of American literature in this country, who merely
borrow and copy ideas and methods from research and critical works
published abroad. Watanabe thinks that this lack of solid individual
research causes an instability in the scholarship of this country; hence
the anxious search for *the* method of research and criticism. The
accumulation of conscientious research studies will eventually make
such questioning unnecessary, Watanabe thinks. However diverse
the opinions expressed here, or because of them, the feature is, on
the whole, quite instructive to students of American literature and
culture.

Many studies have appeared this year which answer Watanabe's
call for solid, imaginative, and original research. The last (third)
volume of Kenzaburo Ohashi's book on William Faulkner, *Faulkner Kenkyu* [*Faulkner Studies*] (Nan'un-do),[1] has finally been completed this year. As has been mentioned several times (*ALS 1977,
1979, 1980, 1981*), the first volume, subtitled "Shiteki Genso kara
Shosetsu teki Sozo e [From Poetic Illusion to Fictional Creation]"
(1977), deals with Faulkner's work up to *As I Lay Dying*. The second, "Monogatari no Kaitai to Kochiku [Dismembering and Re-
constructing of 'Story-telling']" (1979), analyzes his novels from
*Sanctuary* to *The Hamlet*. The last volume, "Katari no Fukken [Re-
instatement of 'Narrative']" (1982), discusses the works from *Go
Down, Moses* to the last book, *The Reivers*. Ohashi's book, which
equals those by Cleanth Brooks and Joseph Blotner in massiveness,
also rivals these powerful works in its contents.

It seems that Ohashi intends to do mainly two things in this book.
Using practically all the primary and secondary materials available
for Faulkner studies, Ohashi presents Faulkner's novels in the perspective of world literature. The explication of Faulkner's design to
endow Yoknapatawpha County, a small portion of land in Mississippi, with qualities not only of the South but of America and of the
world is consistently developed throughout this 1,200-page book,
so that the reader is indeed convinced of Faulkner's grand design.
The other point Ohashi examines minutely is Faulkner's technique
of "story-telling." Modern novelists can no longer use the technique
of "story-telling" which satisfied their predecessors of the 19th century. Faulkner first broke up "story-telling," using "modernistic" nar-

---

1. Here and below when no place of publication is indicated, one should
assume the place to be Tokyo.—*Ed.*

rative devices flexibly in his search for the fundamental way of communicating "truth," and finally came to establish his unique way of "narrating" in *Go Down, Moses*. Discussing Faulkner's novels, stories, and poems in chronological order, Ohashi's argument is marvelously coherent until the end of the book, which presents his passionate affinity with Faulkner and his work. Yet Faulkner as a creative artist with a deep understanding of his time is vividly presented. Ohashi's study is, without question, the most notable research work on American literature so far published in Japan; it is a monumental landmark that celebrates the coming of age of studies on American literature in this country, which began after World War II.

Shuji Muto's *Amerika Bungaku to Shukusai* [*American Literature and Feasts*] (Kenkyusha) answers the question raised at the beginning of this article from a different angle. While Ohashi's interest is mainly in literature, Muto pays a great deal of attention to the cultural and historical background of American literature. Using Hawthorne's "The Maypole of Merry Mount," Poe's "The Cask of Amontillado," James's *The Wings of the Dove*, and Hemingway's *The Sun Also Rises*, Muto explains how the concept of the "carnival" (or communal festivity) of Western civilization was denied in the puritanical society of America. "Feast" lost its communal meaning and turned into something individualistic and private; hence the death of the idea of "festival." Muto's exact textual reading, combined with his wide cultural perspective, makes this book quite stimulating and suggestive.

*Amerika Bungaku no Jiko Hatten—Nijusseiki no Amerika Bungaku* [*The Self-Development of American Literature—20th-Century American Literature*] (Kyoto: Yamaguchi Shoten), ed. Toshio Ogata, is a sequel to *The Self-Formation of American Writers*, which was published last year (see *ALS 1981*, pp. 508–09). Fifteen scholars discuss 26 writers, poets, and playwrights of the 1930s, such as Fitzgerald, Wolfe, Farrell, O'Neill, and E. L. Masters. The editor, in his introduction, emphasizes the large role this political era played in the maturing of American literature and tries to unify these essays around that idea. The omission of some important writers like Dos Passos, however, weakens the editor's argument, and the various approaches to the literature of the era adopted by the writers of these articles —some political, some social, some aesthetic—reduce the volume to a collection of ambitious and interesting essays.

There have been quite a few book-length studies of individual writers of fiction this year. Two books on Nathaniel Hawthorne— Haruto Fujikawa's *Kyodotai to Hawthorne* [*Community and Hawthorne*] ( Yumi Shobo ) and Masaru Yamamoto's *Hawthorne to Shakai Shimpo Shiso—Shinryo to Shimpo* [*Hawthorne and Social Progressivism—Providence and Progress*] (Shinozaki Shorin)—are worth special mention. Though Fujikawa deals only with "The Gentle Boy," "Young Goodman Brown," and *The Scarlet Letter,* his argument as to why Hawthorne, however sympathetic he is with dark mysterious characters like Pearl, transforms them into "common" members of the Puritan community at the end, is persuasive. Yamamoto spends about one-fourth of his 500-page book in explicating the development of the idea of progressivisim in the West, which shows his erudition; then he tries to explain Hawthorne's work as the expression of two contending concepts of history—one based on the idea that history is made by man's effort to better himself ( progressivism ), and the other that history is made not by man, limited in his powers, but by Providence. Yamamoto presents his case with power and confidence, though some readers might not be satisfied by his too-clear-cut exposition.

Though we have had several good biographies (for example, Toshio Yagi's *Poe*; see *ALS 1978,* pp. 477–78 ) and some studies of Poe from the viewpoint of comparative literature, Noriko Mizuta's *Edgar Allan Poe no Sekai—Tsumi to Yume* [*The World of Edgar Allan Poe —Sin and Dream*] (Nan'un-do) is the first book-length critical study of this versatile man of letters. Mizuta places Poe in the main current of American romanticism, basing her argument on Poe's idea of the "grotesque." Using *Eureka* as an example, Mizuta proves that grotesqueness is Poe's means of restoring a harmony to the world through its destructive effect on the self. Mizuta's coherent discussion of Poe's aesthetics of unity and harmony through destruction, together with her clear prose style, makes this book a major addition to Poe scholarship here and abroad.

It is generally admitted that the humor and laughter of a foreign culture is difficult to understand, and so far very few studies of humor in American literature have been made here. Kenichi Akao's book, *Amerika Bungaku ni okeru Yumoa—Mark Twain o Chushin ni* [*Humor in American Literature—Mainly on Mark Twain*] (Kenkyusha), is thus a pioneering work in this field. After explaining aptly the social conditions of the backwoods and mining camps which generated the rough and sturdy laughter of 19th-century America, Akao proceeds to the discussion of Mark Twain's "Jumping Frog," *Innocents Abroad*, and *Roughing It*, demonstrating the process of how laughter and humor are created in Twain's stories.

Muneyuki Kato's *Hemingway Note—Kyomu no Chokoku* [*Notes on Hemingway—The Transcendence of Nothingness*] (Fukuoka: Univ. of Kyushu Press) surveys the Hemingway novels chronologically to show how the writer reaches a state which transcends nihilism in creating Santiago of *The Old Man and the Sea*. There were two books written in English: Yasuhiro Yoshizaki's *Faulkner's Theme of Nature* (Kyoto: Yamaguchi Shoten) and Noboru Shimomura's *A Study of John Steinbeck: Mysticism in His Novels* (Hokuseido). Yoshizaki argues against Cleanth Brooks's idea of nature in Faulkner's novels and asserts that to Faulkner "nature" represents primitivism, innocence, and goodness and is treated as the source of the virtuousness of human beings. However consistent his contention, Yoshizaki's conception of Faulkner's "nature" seems too naive. Shimomura's book on Steinbeck is dedicated to Warren French. Discussing Steinbeck's novels in the order of publication and minutely examining early scholarship, Shimomura explicates the complex interplay of Christianity and paganism in Steinbeck's novels, showing the depth and the darkness of his world. Shimomura takes advantage of his status as a foreigner living in a non-Christian society, and his example serves as a model of what a foreign student of American literature can contribute to this field of study.

In poetry, after the miraculously productive year of 1981, the yield for 1982 is very scanty. *Emily Dickinson—Ai to Shi no Junkyosha* [*Emily Dickinson—The Martyr of Love and Poetry*] (Sogensha), by Noriko Iwata, is, however, a warm and personal book as well as a scholarly one, based on the writer's own research and field work in Amherst, her thorough examination of previous research, and above all her own passionate sympathy with the poet as a woman. Though feministically inclined, Iwata does not rank Dickinson with such feminists as Charlotte Brontë and George Eliot but rather regards her as unique in her fulfillment of her own expectations in life.

Another book is on another woman poet, Sylvia Plath. Unlike Iwata's book, which is sustained by the writer's personal affinity with the poet, this book on Plath is a collection of essays by five experts.

*Sylvia Plath no Sekai* [*The World of Sylvia Plath*] (Nan'un-do), ed. Akira Minami and Ikuko Atsumi, is a good introductory book on Plath, containing a biography (Ryo Nonaka) and discussions of the poems before *Ariel* (Akira Minami), *Ariel* (Toshiko Oshio), *The Bell Jar* (Fumiko Inoue), the short stories (Toshiko Oshio), and *Three Women* (Sachiko Yoshida). At the end of the book three feminist poets present a forum on Plath entitled "I'm a Woman of the Resurrection."

Among the major periodicals *Eigo-Seinen* apportioned a great deal of space to American literature this year. In the column "The Present Situation of Scholarship and the Prospect of Research," Whitman (January), Mark Twain (March), Hemingway (May), and Dreiser (November) have been surveyed. These articles as a whole are good guidelines for future students of American literature. This magazine has also run three special features on American literature. The first, on studies of American literature, was already mentioned at the beginning of this article. The other two are "New Developments in American Poetry" in the May issue (128:104–14), and "Reading the New Novel by Saul Bellow," in the July issue (128: 209–16). The one on American poetry includes articles on Charles Olson (by Makoto Takashima), John Ashbery (by Hisao Kanaseki), and Robert Bly (by Shunichi Niikura). There is also an article on the versatile artist John Cage by Yukinobu Kagitani, and Junnosuke Sawasaki's general survey of contemporary poetry, entitled "Liberated Party—An Introduction to Post-Modernism Poetry," clearly explains the difference between modern and postmodern poetry. Together, these articles show the direction American poetry is now taking. Four impressions of Bellow's *The Dean's December* are in the special collection of articles on Saul Bellow. Though dealing with only one book by the novelist, references to his other works and other contemporary novelists are abundant. As is to be expected, the reactions of these four specialists are quite diverse. Kenji Inoue expresses his dissatisfaction with the novel, saying that Bellow preaches too much. Iwao Iwamoto notices a change in the characterization of the main character; Corde remains a bystander and does not try to weave his own story as Herzog and Mr. Sammler have done. Koji Oi reviews the novel favorably, regarding Corde as a kind of "poet" who expresses the suffering of human beings in a society which believes in "progress." According to Oi, Corde is trying to liberate Americans

from "a deformed conception of human nature"; he sees the novel as
Bellow's attempt to question American writers' identity in the present
world.

Among the other articles which have appeared in *Eigo-Seinen*,
Konomi Ara's "What Will Become of Uncas?" (127:666–69) is worth
mentioning here. Ara starts with a discussion of how James Fenimore
Cooper treated Indians in his Leather-Stocking Tales and then surveys the various treatments of the race in American literature until
the present day. Ara's personal sympathy with and understanding
of the minority race group in America is manifestly revealed.

Among the academic periodicals with nationwide distribution,
*American Review* (vol. 16) has carried four articles on American
literature. They are Minoru Iida's "H. D. Thoreau and 'the Spirit of
Place'" (pp. 116–34), Hideo Higuchi's "Dreiser on the Jews, or 'Is
Dreiser Anti-Semite?'" (pp. 88–104), Misako Koike's "Lillian Hellman as a Playwright of the 1930s" (pp. 72–87), and Hisao Kawai's
"An Approach to Auschwitz: On William Styron's *Sophie's Choice*"
(pp. 135–53). Iida's article explains how Thoreau and his philosophy
are dominated by his attachment to the small village of Concord.
Higuchi throws light on an aspect of Dreiser which has so far been
ignored—his attitude toward the Jews—and tries to explicate his
ambivalent attitude toward the Communist party. Koike's essay on
Hellman is perhaps the only product in the field of drama this year.
This paper surveys all of Hellman's plays, with summaries and comments on structure, and gives an all-round portrait of the playwright.
Kawai insists that Styron's novel should be placed in wider social
aspects and not criticised solely on its literary merits.

Among the articles which have appeared in *Studies in American
Literature* (vol. 19), two are worth mentioning here. Ikuko Fujihira's "Truth in Uttering: The Speaking Voice in *The Sound and the
Fury*" (pp. 33–50) deals with Faulkner's belief in the magical power
of words, using Quentin Compson as an example. Fujihira thinks this
belief in language is "inevitably associated with his creative impulses." Akira Uesugi's "Narrating I: On Kosinski" (pp. 13–31) is
a pioneering study of this novelist. Uesugi explains how the episodic
structure and the use of the first-person narrator play a decisive role
in the texture of reality in Kosinski's novels.

Two charming attempts have been made in spheres marginal to
American literature. Masao Shimura's article "American Literature

and Movies" appeared in three installments in *Eigo-Seinen* (127: 626–28, 695–97, 726–28). Shimura analyzes the influence of movies on such writers as Barthelme, Kerouac, and Pynchon. Shimura's amazing erudition in the field of films and his precise reading of literary texts combine to make quite significant suggestions for understanding these writers. The other attempt is by Shoichi Saeki, a noted literary critic as well as an outstanding Hemingway scholar. His series of articles in *Eigo-Seinen* is titled "Autobiographies of Literary Critics." This series has continued into 1983 and will be duly mentioned in next year's report. In 1982 eight installments appeared; they refer to such autobiographies as Alfred Kazin's *A Walker in the City, Starting out in the Thirties,* and *New York Jew* and Norman Podhoretz's *Making It* and *Breaking Ranks.* Saeki brilliantly traces the pattern of the success story in those Jewish critics' lives.

The Japanese reading public is as voracious as ever. The ambitious publications of the collected works of Melville (Kokusho Kankokai) and of Lafcadio Hearn (Kobunsha) are continuing. In conclusion, let it suffice to mention also that Alice Walker's *Meridian,* Zora Neale Hurston's *Mules and Men* (both Asahi Shimbun Sha), and John Barth's *Giles Goat Boy* (Kokusho Kankokai) have been translated and welcomed by the public.

*Tokyo Woman's Christian University*

## v. Scandinavian Contributions

### Mona Pers

This year Scandinavian literary scholarship has been richly varied in its choice of both writers and critical approaches. Novelists and short-story writers are most prominently represented, as usual, and the majority of them are women writers and/or southerners. The essayist Susan Sontag, the poet Adrianne Rich, the playwright Edward Albee, and the critic T. S. Eliot have also attracted critical attention. Two lengthy articles discuss specific literary genres, one the modern American war novel, the other diary fiction.

"Diary fiction is best conceived not as a genre but as fiction employing a particular narrative device," says H. Porter Abbott in the introduction to his article "Diary Fiction" (*OL* 37:12–31). The purpose of Abbott's essay is to "demonstrate the flexibility of the device and the rich diversity of ends it has been made to serve." His survey of diary fiction, "organized by the three principal areas—mimetic, thematic, and temporal—" includes a few American works. Updike's *A Month of Sundays* serves to illustrate the thematic function, Nabokov's *Lolita* the mimetic function, Poe's "MS Found in a Bottle" and James's "The Diary of a Man of Fifty" the temporal function.

The 50–50 representation in Abbott's essay of older American writers and contemporary ones does not reflect the pattern of Scandinavian scholarship activities in general in the field of American literature this year. Older writers are scantily represented. One exception is Henry David Thoreau, who has been coupled with Joyce Carol Oates in an article by Monica Loeb suggestively entitled "Walden Revisited by Joyce Carol Oates" (*AmerSS* 14:99–106). It seems Loeb was encouraged to attempt a comparison of these two writers by the fact that Oates had borrowed the title of one of her short stories from *Walden*, chapter 2, "Where I Lived, and What I Lived For." Loeb declares that the twofold aim of her article is "to make a comparison of these two stories" and "to see how and to what extent the contemporary writer has chosen to use the original story by Thoreau." She concedes that "on first glance there are more contrasts than obvious similarities between the two stories." On second glance she still does not manage to detect more than two similarities: both stories are about "two men who are concerned with the quality of life," and the date is the same, July 4. "Aside from these similarities, the dissimilarities dominate," says Loeb.

Joyce Carol Oates is by no means the only woman writer to be subjected to Scandinavian scrutiny this year. Except for Charlotte Perkins Gilman they are all of the same generation, and all but one are prose writers. The only article on poetry is Anita Segerberg's "Drömmen om ett gemensamt språk: Om Adrienne Richs diktning" [The Dream of a Common Language: On Adrienne Rich's Poetry] (*Horisont* 3:42–47). Besides offering an initiated presentation and interpretation of Rich's poetry, seeing it in the context of contemporary American poetry by other women poets, Segerberg makes helpful comparisons with the work of the Scandinavian poet Edith Södergran, a sure touchstone for Scandinavian readers. A carefully argued article by Brian J. W. Morton "The Princess in the Consulate:

Joan Didion's Fiction" (*Edda* [1982]:73–87), could have been appropriately subtitled "In Defense of Joan Didion" because of the persuasive way it demonstrates how and explains why Didion has been unfairly treated or ignored by academic critics. In his seven-part article Morton traces favorite themes and character combinations, stylistic development, and variations in the use of irony in Didion's major works. Morton is convinced that "the inherent unpopularity and unfashionability of her expressed attitudes" will not forever prevent critics from recognizing the artistic excellence of a writer just because "she strives to restore the cognitive basis of fiction to its traditional role, to see the novel as a historical object, a process in history."

Susan Sontag is treated with less leniency by Carl Henrik Svenstedt in his punningly entitled article "Sontag, Montag . . . Den motsägelsefulla essäisten" [The Contradictory Essayist] (*Allt om böcker* 1:10–11). Svenstedt shows Sontag to be both contradictory as a thinker and uneven as a stylist. He argues that she is alternately banal and incisively analytical, boring and stylistically elegant, i.e., a "Sunday and Monday" writer in one. In Svenstedt's opinion Sontag is decidedly European both in her style of writing and in her way of thinking and reacting, a possible explanation for her unswerving popularity in Sweden.

Another woman writer who has a strong critical appeal, especially among feminists, is Charlotte Perkins Gilman. Two enthusiastic articles were written about her in Scandinavia this year. Elsie Wenström's "Våra förmödrar" [Our Ancestral Mothers] (*Kvin* 2:74–76) centers on the writer's life and ideas expressed in her writings, while Drude Daae von der Fehr's "Charlotte Perkins Gilman *The Yellow Wallpaper*: Ansatser til en semiologisk tekstanalyse" [Attempts at a Semiological Text Analysis] (*Edda* [1982]:39–53) focuses on structural and stylistic aspects in one single work. The aim of von der Fehr's essay is to explain Gilman's narrative technique by answering "the question who sees? and the question who speaks?" in *The Yellow Wallpaper*. von der Fehr's analysis is based on Gérard Genette's theories on the fundamental difference between "who is the character whose point of view orients the narrative perspective" and the actual narrator, a point of departure that suits an interpretation of *The Yellow Wallpaper* well. A pertinent comparison with Poe's "The Fall of the House of Usher" concludes this valuable study.

In von der Fehr's hands the semiological method is a sharp tool used to great advantage to reach a deeper understanding of a literary text. In her article, "The Reflection in the Mirror—An Interpretation of Hemingway's Short Story 'Cat in the Rain'" (*MSpr* 76: 329–38), Ingegerd Friberg, too, has chosen for her critical tool a specific approach, Roger Fowler's "linguistic method of interpreting fiction" by integrating "linguistic and literary analysis." In her paper Friberg proposes to demonstrate the validity of Fowler's method "by interpreting Hemingway's short story . . . first intuitively by applying the pattern of a central image [that of the mirror] to the traditional concepts of plot, setting, characters, structure, and theme, and then linguistically by adopting and applying . . . Fowler's categories of 'text,' 'discourse,' and 'content' " to the text. She hopes to "show that the two interpretations support each other in bringing out the theme." Not surprisingly, Friberg manages to prove that they do. It would, of course, have been more remarkable had she found that they did not.

To start with a critical theory and then go in search of a literary text to which to apply it has its pitfalls. The critical mold seldom fits the material altogether, and thus tends to get in the way of rather than facilitate our understanding of the literary text itself. Strict categorization might prove equally fallacious. Richard Shusterman's essay, "Objectivity and Subjectivity in Eliot's Critical Theory" (*OL* 37:217–26) is a case in point. Although Shusterman recognizes that the terms "objective" and "subjective" are "problematic and vague," he deems an attempt to "chart the relations between objective and subjective in Eliot's critical theory" meaningful enough. His aim is to "establish the importance of the subjective in Eliot's critical theory by tracing its role and relationship to critical objectivity with which Eliot's theory is typically identified." Shusterman skillfully reveals and offers plausible explanations for the incongruous elements inherent in Eliot's critical theory and poetic practice. But the stylistic straitjacket Shusterman has imposed on his interesting material makes his study unnecessarily repetitious and at times even tends to obscure his arguments.

Fredrik Chr. Brøgger, in my opinion, falls into the same trap. His essay, "Formal Vacillation in Modern American Drama" (*AmerSS* 14: 1–23) opens with the statement that "one of the most fascinating features of modern American drama is its constant vacillation between the different dramatic modes of realism, expressionism, and (more recently) absurdism, both within one and the same period and within the individual productions of major playwrights." This is the reason why Brøgger decided to "look more closely at the thematic implications of this medley of dramatic modes and to speculate on some of the possible reasons for such a continual vacillation in dramatic form." Brøgger chose Edward Albee's production as the main target for his investigation because he rightly thought it could furnish him with "the most comprehensive illustration."

Brøgger's analysis of Albee's plays is pedagogically clear and offers new insights into Albee's art. The problem is that Brøgger does not seem quite comfortable with his own "basic presumption," the ordering principle or frame of his essay, that "the dramatic modes of realism, expressionism and absurdism express quite different world views." He admits that "this in itself is a problematic contention, not least since these modes are frequently combined in modern plays." As I see it, this fact effectively prevents them from "expressing quite different world views," a complication that Brøgger's somewhat facile conclusion does not satisfactorily resolve: "Certainly the coexistence and combination of these three modes in contemporary drama can be seen to testify to the disharmony, not to say schizophrenia, of contemporary life," a speculation, to use Brøgger's own word, less well grounded than the rest of the ideas and observations in this otherwise sensitive study.

"The categories of World, Body, Fellow Men, and Time, which I shall employ to discuss 'Miss Zilphia Gant' are appropriated from *The Phenomenological Approach to Psychiatry* by Van den Berg," Matti J. Savolainen declares at the outset of his article, "Mrs. Gant and Miss Zilphia Gant: Two Faulknerian Women. A Phenomenological View" (*AmerSS* 14:25–34). Savolainen feels confident that "even though the categories overlap, they provide a viable framework with which to analyze the story." His article, unfortunately, does not prove him right. Faulkner's story does not profit from being treated like a psychological case study.

William Faulkner reappears, albeit merely as background material, in an extensive survey presentation of three other southern writers, "En sakramental syn på livet: Om William Styron, Flannery O'Connor, Walker Percy och den amerikanska Södern" [A Sacramental View of Life: On William Styron, Flannery O'Connor, Walker Percy, and the American South] by Åke Nylinder (*Horisont* 3,xix:

84–98). Nylinder describes and analyzes the works of the three individual writers, establishing what their unique artistic qualities are,
clarifying how they differ, what they have in common, and how
they distinguish themselves collectively from Americans outside the
South. Nylinder concentrates his efforts primarily on Percy and
Styron. The latter is also dealt with separately in the same periodical
by Steve Sem-Sandberg in his short article, "William Styron och
problemet Nat Turner" (*Horisont* 3,xix:96–98). Sandberg defends
Styron against the accusations of black writers that his "account" of
Nat Turner is a distortion and falsification of the "real" Nat Turner's
personality. He also discusses the ethical problems that are introduced when fiction writers use biographical material, and analyzes
the novel's artistic merits and demerits. Such questions are also
latent in another article dealing with a novel in the category of "fictional reporting" or "journalistic fiction," Raoul Granqvist's "Gary Gilmore's Pilgrimage: Mailer's *The Executioner's Song*" (*AmerSS* 14:35–
48), in which Granqvist attempts to analyze the process whereby the
protagonist of *The Executioner's Song* "develops through a murder,
into a mystic and public saint," and at the same time to "rehearse
Mailer's obsession with the oppositions and paradoxes in the American psyche, recall his hatred of unauthentic and anonymous violence. . . ."

"Violence" can be treated in more ways than one, as Arne Axelsson makes clear in his thought-provoking, yet catchingly witty essay,
"Fun as Hell: War and Humor in some Post–World War II American
Novels" (*SN* 54:263–86). In a racy language, spiced with tongue-in-
cheek remarks, Axelsson shows how and explains why so "many
American writers have tried to make use of the humor-war mix as a
major ingredient in their works, in particular during the three decades
following World War II," as well as why Joseph Heller's *Catch-22* has
been such a powerful trendsetter for younger generations of war
novelists.

*University College at Västerås*

## vi. Italian Contributions

### *Gaetano Prampolini*

The year 1982 records a contraction in the scholarly output of Italian Americanists, after two years of intense productivity. As a consequence, I will give account of 40 items—one-third and about one-fifth less than those reviewed in *ALS 1980* and *ALS 1981*, respectively. Eleven of them are books. The usual share of attention continues to be given to the great authors (the most studied of whom are James and Pound, once again, and Eliot), but there also appears to be an expanding tendency to dwell on minor figures and works, to favor novel angles of approach, and to investigate aspects and areas that are (or at least until recently used to be) considered peripheral and secondary. Whether this should be interpreted as a sign of sophistication in the development of our studies or as a symptom of exhaustion of an intensively cultivated field, it is too early to decide. This report consists of two parts: the first reviews general works as well as items clustering around some broader topic or theme; the second reviews contributions of monographic scope.

Two of the items that fall into the first of our groupings are valuable works of reference. *Novecento americano* (Roma: Lucarini), the three-volume guide to the American literature of our century directed by Elémire Zolla (and more extensively described in *ALS 1981*, pp. 486–87), is now complete with the publication of volume 1 (comprising 38 monographs on writers born up to 1896) and volume 2 (comprising 50 monographs on writers born between 1898 and 1917). *Repertorio bibliografico della letteratura americana in Italia (1960–1964)* (Roma: Ed. di Storia e Letteratura), which is compiled under the direction of Biancamaria Tedeschini Lalli and the supervision of Alessandra Pinto Surdi, is volume 4 of a monumental and accurate bibliography listing virtually everything that has been written in Italy on American literature (reviews and brief mentions included) as well as all the American works—creative (middle- and low-brow writers included) and critical—that have been translated into Italian since 1945. Since volumes 1 and 2 came out in 1966 and volume 3 in 1969, the appearance of the present volume can be saluted as a kind of resurrection and, hopefully, a pledge for a more regular continuation and a final bringing up to date of this very useful work.

Another side of Italian-American cultural relationships is scrutinized in Remo Ceserani's "Odisseo e una mappa letteraria d'America" (*Belfagor* 37,ii:125–36). Mainly an overview of American criticism from the "new critical" heyday to the present post-structuralistic stage (with intelligent glosses to René Wellek's 1978 assessment of New Criticism, which appeared in *Critical Inquiry*), this essay begins in an autobiographical mode, and the author's lively account of his year at Yale, where in 1958 he was a student in Wellek's and W. K. Wimsatt's classes, may cause a shock of recognition to more than one Italian reader of Ceserani's generation, whose allegiance to Croce's historicism was similarly tested in America through an exposure to radically different approaches to literature.

The third in a series of volumes of essays by a research team directed by Elémire Zolla (volume 1 was noticed in *ALS 1978*, pp. 466–67, and volume 2 in *ALS 1979*, pp. 512–13), *L'esotismo della letteratura angloamericana* (Roma: Lucarini) opens with Zolla's definition of syncretism as "the specifically American vocation." In his essay (pp. 9–19), however, Zolla chooses to dwell on a case of failed syncretism—Percival Lowell's (1855–1916), whose approach to Korea and Japan reveals the inadequacy of a progress-worshiping, positivism-imbued mind in understanding traditional cultures, but whose *Occult Japan or the Way of the Gods* (1894) with its meticulous and awed description of Shinto liturgies prepares the way for Ernest Fenellosa's more fecund penetration of Japanese esotericism.

While each of the essays in this collection increases or refines our knowledge of its respective topic, there is one of them for which the word "seminal" does not seem wasted. Although centered on Washington Irving's Spanish writings, Cristina Giorcelli's essay (pp. 23–58) does indeed have far-reaching implications. It modifies in fact our ideas on the massive corpus of works Irving wrote after 1826 by intimating that it should be seen as a part, artistically and intellectually significant, of a whole plan—a vital development of that basic concern with history through which Irving kept tracing the roots of "Americanness" and attempted the foundation of a national mythology. Thus, it is not simply fashionable exoticism, Giorcelli convincingly insists, that attracts Irving to Spain. In the his-

torical and biographical works of 1828–31 (where he investigates the
causes, near and far, of the discovery and conquest of the New
World), Spain is presented as the crucible of the strongest and
most intelligent peoples of the Old World and therefore as the European country predestined to expand Western civilization across the
ocean. In *The Alhambra* Spain also emerges as a precious repository of those universal, perennial resources of the human imagination
(myths, symbols, storytelling) on which the writer most counts to
establish a continuity between the past and the present, the Old and
the New World. Teeming with acute insights and stimulating suggestions (e.g., Irving as forerunner of 19th-century artist-historians
such as Prescott and Parkman; Irving as pioneer in that "patchwork,"
dynamic kind of writing, accommodating fact and fiction, narration
and meditation, which was to prove so fortunate in American literature), this essay should encourage the author to develop her line
of study in a more systematic and leisurely form.

   As to the instances of exotic syncretism explored in the other
essays, Caterina Ricciardi (pp. 61–91) demonstrates how the reading
of a little book of Old Egyptian maxims (translated into Italian by
Boris De Rachewiltz in 1954) disclosed to Pound an ethical-political
message tallying with Confucianism and Christianity both in the belief in "man's good nature" and in the celebration of love and justice
as fundamental human values: hence the importance of Egyptian
motives throughout *Rock Drill* and *Thrones* and, in particular, their
interplay with Chinese and Dantean motives in the *panis angelicus*
metaphor that governs Canto 93. Fedora Giordano (pp. 95–117)
shows how Jaime de Angulo's literary writings reflect—in their meanings and forms as well—both the writer's personal quest for sha-
manic powers and the extraordinary understanding of the archaic
mind he gained through his long and intense involvement with Indian tribes of Northern California. Annalisa Goldoni (pp. 121–34)
studies the letters written by Charles Olson to Robert Creeley and
Cid Corman during his 1951 sojourn in Yucatan and indicates how
Olson's observations on Mayan culture relate to some of his most
characteristic theoretical concerns. Andrea Mariana (pp. 137–60)
points out how exotic elements are present throughout James Merrill's poetry and elegantly illustrates the crucial function of Greece
as midpoint in the physical and intellectual journey that leads the
poet away from his native culture, which he feels to be stifling and

one-sided, and then back to it—but with the fuller, more mature
vision of life and the finer poetic awareness he has acquired in "the
exotic place." Finally, Marina Camboni (pp. 163–93) describes the
impact of 19th-century Urdu poet Ghalib on Adrienne Rich. She
shows how Rich saw Ghalib as the interpreter of a turmoil, personal
and historical, similar to the turmoil she and America experienced
in the late 1960s. Camboni also demonstrates how Rich found in the
*ghazal* (which she used in *Leaflets* and *Will to Chance* with increasing autonomy and mastery) a poetic form particularly apt, "like the
pages of a journal," for a moment-to-moment, intimate, and tentative
exploration of the self, as well as being instrumental in the transition
toward her later poetry of "imaginative processes in action."

On a topic related to exoticism—expatriation—there is a reader
edited by Andrea Mariani, *Four American Fugitives* (Napoli: Ligu-
ori). Under a title that is meant to suggest escape from America
and the sense of guilt arising from it, this 210-page volume collects
texts by James, Edith Wharton, Gertrude Stein, and George Santayana, all focusing on these four writers' complex relationship to
America. In his introduction Mariani provides a perceptive commentary on each of the anthologized texts and a worthwhile description of expatriation in its various forms and implications.

The favorable judgment passed on William Boelhower's essay on
Constantine Panunzio's autobiography in *ALS 1981* (p. 489) can be
extended to *Immigrant Autobiography in the United States (Four
Versions of the Italian American Self)* (Verona: Essedue Edizioni),
the book by the same author which now includes that essay. Besides
Panunzio's *Soul of an Immigrant,* Boelhower chooses Pascal D'Angelo's *Son of Italy: The Autobiography of Emanuel Carnevali* and
Jerre Mangione's *Mount Allegro* as his texts and analyzes them as
variants of the "immigrant autobiographical macro-text"—a model
he constructs by isolating three "fabula moments" (dream anticipation of, contact, and contrast with the New World) and three cor-
responding "isotopic systems" ("Old-World Reality vs. New-World
Ideal," "New-World Ideal vs. New-World Reality," "New-World
Reality vs. Old-World Reality"). By a deft deployment of his methodological weaponry, mainly derived from semiotics, he succeeds
both in fully substantiating his overall thesis and bringing out the
specificity of each text. The overall thesis is a very important one on
historical, cultural, and literary accounts: even as mass immigration

of the 1880–1920 period makes obsolete the image of America as a monolithically Anglo-Saxon culture, immigrant autobiography is the genre that deconstructs "the native patterns of American identity" as presented in traditional autobiographies, introducing "a new typology of the self"; but it also "witnesses the birth of the modern condition, the American condition *par excellence*" and helps found the multiethnic paradigm that was clearly to emerge in the 1960s. Each of the texts, read by Boelhower with admirable penetration, illustrates one of the four possible responses of the immigrant autobiographer to the New World dominant culture: *confirmation* (Panunzio), *variation* (D'Angelo), *negation* of its codes (Carnevali), or *substitution* of the codes with a countercultural alternative (Mangione).

On autobiography, a favorite topic in American studies of recent years, there are also two shorter pieces. In her competent introduction to Patrizia Paggio's translation of Benjamin Franklin's *Autobiography* (*Autobiografia*, Roma: Savelli) Paola Ludovici recognizes the importance of Franklin's book as an enlightening document of the change in ethical orientation that took place in 18th-century America and, after noticing that the writer's account of his life goes no further than the year 1757, suggests that Franklin's aim was not so much to write a full-scale, all-inclusive autobiography as to compose an exemplary self-portrait as the perfect self-made man. In " 'A scrapbook of madness': musica, autobiografia e denuncia sociale" (*LetA* 3,xii:69–98) Silvia Albertazzi deals with the autobiographical writings of three musicians: Leonard Cohen's *The Favourite Game*, Charles Mingus' *Beneath the Underdog*, and Billie Holiday's *Lady Sings the Blues*. Her discussion centers on the three authors' attitudes toward sex, death, and their pasts. Although rather diffuse, her essay manages to prove convincingly enough that the interest of these narratives lies in their offering a valuable key to the interpretation of their authors' music but, even more, in their being poignant expressions of their authors' sense of alienation both as artists and members of ethnic minorities.

In *La frontiera proletaria: marxismo, intellettuali e letteratura in America (1926–1936)* (Ravenna: Longo) Giordano De Biasio reexamines a widely studied episode of the literary history of the 1930s —the encroachment of politics on aesthetics ensuing from the fervent if short-lived enthusiasm of large numbers of writers for Marxism and the Soviet-directed Communist party's endeavors to manipulate them. After two introductory chapters on Michael Gold's "Towards a Proletarian Art" manifesto of 1921, and the polarizing effect of the Sacco and Vanzetti case on left-wing intellectuals, the bulk of the book chronicles the debate that developed in *New Masses* and *Partisan Review* over the nature, function, and goals of the kind of literature that was to hasten revolution. The last chapter defines the generic proprieties of the "proletarian novel" and ascribes its failure to a doctrinaire disregard for American values as well as to the poverty of its poetics based on the cult of simplicity and experience. Well-documented and unimpassioned, De Biasio's interpretation does not seem however to be particularly innovative—except, perhaps, in the discussion of the first two years of *Partisan Review*, those generally considered as its "Stalinist" years, where the author detects the signs of a muted and yet unmistakable dissent from party-line orthodoxy in Philip Rahv's, William Phillips', and James T. Farrell's contributions.

The five essays included in this year's Anglo-American issue of *Letteratura d'America* (3,xii) come under the common heading of "Multi Media," by which—a short editorial note explains—"those hybrids, those daring ingraftings" are meant that so often grow out of New World cultures' constant impulse to experimentation. Only two of them, though, appear to fill out the editorial description with a certain precision—Guido Fink's "From Showing to Telling: Off-Screen Narration in the American Cinema" (pp. 5–37), which refers to an alternation of narrative modes common to fiction and film; and Emanuela Dal Fabbro's "*The Heart Is a Lonely Hunter* come forma contrappuntistica" (pp. 38–68), which shows a homological functioning of musical and linguistic-literary codes within the same text. Fink's essay is a well-researched, exhaustive study of the various aspects (speaker's identity, verbal message–visual message relationship, spectator's responses) of offscreen narration as it was widely used in Hollywood movies of the 1940s—and a good reminder of how not even cinema, supposedly the narrative language of pure *showing*, can do without a certain amount of *telling* (which, indeed, it may turn to advantage). Through a systematic, painstaking, and very skillful analysis of characters' relationships, story line, and discourse organization in *The Heart Is a Lonely Hunter*, Dal Fabbro demonstrates how literally must McCullers' statement be taken that "the form [of this novel] is contrapuntal throughout." While vastly improving on Michael C. Smith's article on the same topic (see *ALS 1979*, p. 263), this essay does not sensibly alter the current interpretations of the novel. And yet the author's suggestion that polyphony (its fugue pattern, in particular) offered the writer a perfect embodiment of the plurality-unity opposition (and coexistence) informing her vision may prove of some consequence for the interpretation of the McCullers canon as a whole.

References to American utopian and science fiction and, even more, to American studies, theoretical and critical, of these two subgenres abound throughout *L'utopia e le sue forme* (Bologna: Il Mulino). But this substantial and wide-ranging symposium on utopian thought and literature edited by Nicola Matteucci also contains three essays that fall entirely within our scope. Two significant aspects of contemporary American utopian fiction are indicated by Rosella Mamoli Zorzi in her agile "L'utopia oggi in America" (pp. 309–21). One is the continuing and, indeed, increasing attraction that the world-changing impulse inherent to this kind of writing exerts on women writers, as witnessed by two of the three novels she considers, Marge Piercy's *Woman on the Edge of Time* and Ursula Le Guin's *The Dispossessed*. The other is the disruption of the rigid conventions of the genre, as shown by the new fictional assumptions and techniques adopted by Robert Nichols in his *Daily Lives in Nghsi-Altai*. The first of these points finds corroboration in Liana Borghi's "Utopia e femminismo americano degli anni settanta" (pp. 291–307). With a militant's knowledgeability and scholarly dispassion, Borghi discusses Joanna Russ's *The Female Man*, Suzy McKee Charnas' *Motherlines*, and Sally Gearheart's *The Wanderground* within the ideological frame of the radical feminism of the 1970s and concludes by stressing their importance not only as intransigent indictments of patriarchal oppression but also as strong affirmations of the viability of autonomous communities of women. Finally, in "Dall'utopia alla fantascienza: le metamorfosi di un genere letterario" (pp. 255–69) Vita Fortunati argues, somewhat summarily, that science fiction derives primarily from utopian narratives but also that the subversive potential of the latter is completely absent from the former, since it replaces the political concerns of utopianism with an all but unlimited faith in technological achievements.

Moving on to monographic studies, let us start with those concerning poetry. The first Italian translation of the whole canon of Poe's poems provided by Tommaso Pisanti, *Tutte le poesie* (Roma: Newton Compton), is preceded by an introduction in which Pisanti clearly delineates and judiciously assesses Poe's achievement as a poet.

Besides the essay already mentioned, three more items bear witness to the interest Ezra Pound and his work continue to elicit in what is to be considered the poet's adoptive country. *Una ghirlanda per Ezra Pound* edited by Alfredo Rizzardi (Urbino: Argalia [1981]) is a collection of miscellaneous material, a good share of it heretofore unpublished. Along with the Italian versions of Canto 98 (by Mary De Rachewiltz) and "Indiscretions or une Revue de Deux Mondes" (by Rizzardi), the volume contains novelist Richard Stern's sensitive memoir of his visits to the old poet in Venice in the early 1960s (pp. 29–35) and ten critical pieces. Three of these are evaluations focusing on Pound's interest in Italian literature and his activities while in Italy. Both Carlo Bo (pp. 7–10) and Piero Sanavio (pp. 195–209) sound a warning against letting Pound's on the whole innocuous Fascist sympathies interfere with the appreciation his literary achievement commands. Romance philologist Gianfranco Contini, instead, in another review (pp. 13–26) of Zapponi's book, takes Pound to task for tampering with ancient Italian texts and for his almost absolute disregard for Italian writers more modern than the Stinovists. Contini's acrid but cogent debunking of what he calls Pound's *Halbkultur* is rather ineffectively countered by Mary De Rachewiltz' explanation of Pound's notion of "total translation," but her paper (pp. 213–22) gives some interesting clues to her method as translator of *The Cantos*. Of the other contributions, which are all of an interpretive kind, we will mention only those that have not previously appeared elsewhere. Hugh Kenner (pp. 39–51), after observing how serial publication delayed the recognition of the overall structure of *The Cantos*, indicates shifts and recurrences in themes and tones from section to section of the poem up to *Drafts and Fragments*, where he sees the old poet revert to motives that had been dear to him in youth and his self-imposed Confucianism overcome by a more congenial Taoism. Glauco Cambon (pp. 55–71) closely and perceptively examines Pound's "maieutic" effort on behalf of *The Waste Land*. Sigfried De Rachewiltz (pp. 75–97) ends his useful review of Pound's lifelong intellectual passion for Guido Cavalcanti with the quotation of extended passages from Canto 73, one of the "missing Cantos" that were published in 1945 in Fascist-controlled northern Italy. What the work of Pound has meant for 20th-century poetry is clearly summarized by Italian poet Mario Luzi, one of the participants in a roundtable that was broadcast in 1972 and the proceedings of which complete the volume (pp. 289–99).

"*The Pisan Cantos*: Our Modern Classic" (*SpM* 14[1980]:3–8) is the text of a lecture in which M. L. Rosenthal, arguing finely and forcefully for the claim made in the title, points out the relevance of this sequence to "our daily circumstances" and ascribes its extraordinary power as a work of poetry to Pound's firm control over a copious and even "intractable" matter, felicitous conversion of epic concerns into lyrical tonalities, supple handling of associative materials, and masterful matching of sound patterns and syntax patterns to complex emotional states. In *Hugh Selwyn Mauberley* (Milano: Il Saggiatore), a volume in a current uniform series devoted to significant 20th-century works of poetry, the text of Pound's earlier masterpiece and Giovanni Giudici's excellent version of it are accompanied by exegetic apparatuses written by Massimo Bacigalupo. The interpretation of *Mauberley* offered here (as Bacigalupo himself says in his compact and comprehensive introduction) does not differ in the main from that offered by John Espey in his classic study of 1955. Nonetheless, Bacigalupo's work must be pointed up as a model of philological precision and critical discrimination for what he does in his presentations of the single sections and line-by-line commentary, where every relevant shred from Poundian writings, lore, and scholarship is brought to bear on the elucidation of the poem, and the semantic importance of its musical texture is sensitively highlighted through painstaking analyses of sound figures and prosody.

Scholarly work of a comparable caliber is that done by Alessandro Serpieri with his introduction and annotations to that other pillar of modernism in poetry, *The Waste Land*, in a volume (*La terra desolata*; Milano: Rizzoli) that includes the definitive text of the poem, its original drafts, and Serpieri's versions of both. Lucid and compendious, the introduction reviews the basic questions concerning *The Waste Land*, wholly reflecting the intelligent study of Eliot so fruitfully pursued by Serpieri over the years (see *ALS 1973*, p. 449). Giuseppe Martella's contention in "La coerenza logica di 'Gerontion' nella prospettiva epistemologica di F. L. Bradley" (*SpM* 14[1980]:

98–113) is that the logical looseness found by some critics in the
structure of "Gerontion" can be disproved once Bradleyan epistemology is recognized to be the conceptual model informing the poem.
In the light of Bradley's notions of identity, memory, and reality "as
experience in a finite center," Martella maintains, "Gerontion" will
appear to be a five-movement "epistemological interrogation the
speaker is addressing to himself on the nature of the self and reality."
Densely (if not always perspicuously) reasoned, this essay bears
further testimony to Eliot's familiarity with Bradley's philosophy,
which helped make both his verse and criticism expressions of that
general reorientation in thinking—relativistic and relational—that
took place at the end of the last century. In "The Tradition of Italian
*poesia ermetica* and T. S. Eliot" (*RLMC* 35,i:55–66) Joseph Pivato
charts the influence that Eliot's views on English metaphysical poetry
had on the several scholars who concurred in ascertaining the existence of a continuing tradition of intellectual, "hermetic," poetry
starting from the *Stilnovisti*. While his discussion of Eliot's verse as
part of this tradition is much too hurried, Pivato makes some shrewd,
if summary, distinctions as to the disparate sets of causes that produce obscurity with the medieval (or Renaissance) hermetic poets
and their modern counterparts.

Franca Bacchiega Minuzzo's *Robinson Jeffers: La natura la sci-
enza la poesia* (Firenze: Nuovedizioni Enrico Vallecchi [1980]) and
Daniela M. Ciani Forza's *Poesie di Kenneth Rexroth (1920–1956)*
(Brescia: Paideia) are the first full-length studies written by Italians
on these two poets. Bacchiega Minuzzo's book reads more like the
record of a long-standing intellectual love affair with Jeffers' poetry
than like a scholarly investigation into it. The exposition of the poet's
ideas, themes, and subjects, which takes the greater part of the volume, is accurate enough, even if it too often tends to turn into apolo-
getics. The long chapter devoted to Jeffers' style reveals a certain
uneasiness on the part of the author at tackling poetry from any other
angle than a thematic one. Ciani Forza gives a diligent account of
the evolution of Rexroth's thought and art up to *The Dragon and the
Unicorn* and *In Defense of the Earth*—the first being the work where
the poet's long quest for transcendence reaches its most articulate
stage with the envisaging of an ideal "community of love," the second
being the one containing some of the poems that best fulfill Rexroth's aspiration to a poetry made of strictly denotative language,

visionary purity, and working as an immediate, sacramental "live dialogue" between persons. Other aspects of Rexroth's multiform activity (e.g., his achievements as literary critic and translator) are only tangentially dealt with by Ciani Forza, and the same thing can be said as to the positioning of Rexroth in relation to 20th-century American poetry as a whole. While a more intensive pursuit of these objects might have helped render the tone of the book less unreservedly eulogistic, a more careful editing might have spared the reader many a moment of embarrassment at the author's not infrequent spells of awkward writing.

Two of the essays in *LetA* ( 3,xii) remind us of how often painting has been a source of inspiration for modern poets. Brueghel's presentation of human suffering through the correlative of human indifference and his compositional technique which makes everydayness the organizing principle of his paintings are quite rightly indicated by Renzo S. Crivelli as the main reasons for the Flemish master's appeal to the three poets he deals with in "La parabola dell'artista: Bruegel e la poesia di Auden, Williams e Plath" ( pp. 99–122). What does not appear entirely successful is instead Crivelli's attempt to read his three poets' interpretations of Brueghel's paintings as parables of the predicament of the modern artist: his assertions are not always sufficiently documented nor, at times, clearly warranted by the poems. ( What is there, for instance, in Auden's "Museé des Beaux Arts" to validate the author's interpretation of Icarus as the artist estranged from his times' most pressing concerns?) In "Frank O'Hara: A New Dada Poet in New York" ( pp. 123–51) Carolyn Christov-Bakargiev maintains that the "I do this, I do that" poems O'Hara wrote in the late 1950s are poetic equivalents of contemporary New Dada paintings—Robert Rauschenberg's, in particular. The author brings forth significant analogies in imagery ( New York cityscape and daily life) and in themes as well (the perception-reflection dialectic implying the impossibility of a random, instant-by-instant, neutral registering of reality, doing away with ordering, memory, and emotions), and strengthens her thesis with a closely attentive reading of "A Step Away from Them."

Interest in the most recent developments of American poetry is witnessed by two good bilingual anthologies, *Storie di ordinaria poesia* (Roma: Savelli) and *Poesia americana oggi* (Roma: Newton Compton), edited respectively by Riccardo Duranti and Barbara

Lanati. In a restrained introduction to his own versions of 116 poems by 30 poets born between 1923 and 1951 Duranti enumerates the initiatives and channels that favored a real boom both in the production and fruition of poetry during the 1970s, and finds that the distinguishing features of the verse of this period are the coalescence and hybridization of poetic programs and styles still clearly divergent in the 1960s, the inclination for a narrative mode, and, above all, an "inward drive." Nearly half of the poets represented in each anthology are women; eight poets of Duranti's choice—i.e., John Ashbery, Robert Bly, Robert Creeley, Bill Knott, Maxine Kumin, Denise Levertov, W. S. Merwin, Marge Piercy, and Anne Sexton— also figure in Lanati's anthology. Consisting of 92 poems translated into Italian by Rossella Bernascone and Attilia Lavagno, this includes 36 poets born between 1913 and 1947 whom Lanati sees as writing, during the past two decades, a kind of poetry quite different from that written by both "academic" and "beat" poets. Lanati's description of its distinctive traits, although a little redundant and occasionally lapsing into the oracular style made fashionable by some recent French critics, is remarkably penetrating: low-voiced and colloquial, introverted and self-conscious, this is poetry uttered from the dark and ready to subside into silence, anxious to open up a communication but doubtful of its ability to do it—a poetry questioning its own coming into being and value.

In a brisk, short introduction to a selection of Irving's tales, *Racconti per una sera d'inverno* (Milano: Serra e Riva), Attilo Brilli points up an encyclopedic commixture of styles and genres within a Menippean frame, a metaliterary stance, a ludic exploitation of intertextuality, parody as the traits which make Irving modern and his fictions intensely intriguing for modern readers. The only other contribution to the study of the fiction of the Romantic Period is Giuseppe Lombardo's "Criticism of Herman Melville, 1972–1977: A Preliminary Annotated Checklist" (*The Blue Guitar* [Fac. di Magistero, Univ. di Messina], 3–4[antedated 1977–78]:231–391). This bibliography, which for the year 1972 lists only the items that do not appear in Ricks and Adams' *Herman Melville: A Reference Bibliography*, includes 840 numbered and alphabetically ordered entries, is subdivided into three sections (books and articles, book reviews, and dissertations), and has author and subject indexes. Although I have been unable to check it against Jeanette Boswell's recent compilation

(q. v., *ALS 1981*, pp. 53–54), this checklist looks on the whole accurate and soundly annotated.

The interest of Italian Americanists in the work of James keeps steady, year after year. But "Tra *romance e novel*" (*Il piccolo Hans* 33:84–94), in which Nadia Fusini takes passages from James's *Hawthorne* and "Preface" to *The American* as her texts, neither adds much of importance to what is generally known about the difference between the two narrative modes indicated in the title nor adequately supports the author's conclusive assertion that James is, like Hawthorne, essentially a writer of romances. Two fine items are introductions: Stefania Piccinato's to a reprint of Carlo Linati's classic version of *The American* (*L'Americano*, Milano: Mondadori) and Agostino Lombardo's to his own version of *The Other House* (*L'altra casa*, Roma: Editori Riuniti). Lombardo limpidly pinpoints the importance of this novel as the work that, through the very imperfections of its form, best witnesses a crucial transition in James's intellectual life and literary career. Piccinato avails herself of Jurij Lotman's theory of "space" both to outline Newman's European adventure in terms of two alien, incompatible cultural spaces and to highlight the stage-like organization of space in most of the settings; she concludes her sound reading of *The American* by acutely noticing how ambiguity in style somewhat undermines the certainties conveyed through the clear-cut quality of story, plot, and theme. Lotman plays a primary role also in Giovanna Mochi's *Le "cose cattive" di Henry James* (Parma: Pratiche Editrice), a graciously written and well-argued metacritical essay on *The Turn of the Screw*. Of the never-ending critical *querelle* about the most controversial of James's tales the author discusses two significant moments to prove that, beyond the profound differences in methods and objects, both the readings offered during the Anglo-American debate that went on between "apparitionists" and Freudian "allucinationists" from the mid-1920s to the mid-1960s and the readings offered by *absence*-minded and Lacanian-oriented French critics a little later all share an inquisitive, aggressive, and reductive attitude to the text—the former trying to make it say what it does not say, the latter forbidding it to say what it does say. The Soviet semiotician's pronouncement that "the perception and the creation of a work of art require a particular (artistic) behavior which has a good many traits in common with the ludic one" furnishes for Mochi a key to the nature of the

Jamesian text, which the reader is asked to read-play like a game to
its very end (the ghosts both *exist* and *do not exist*), as well as an
indication of the kind of reading she advocates at the end of her essay
—a reading respectful of both "the said" and "the untellable" *within*
the text.

In "Jack London e la rivoluzione mancante" (*Calibano* 5[1980]:
52–76) Alessandro Portelli calls attention to such aspects of *The
Iron Heel* as the elliptical treatment of the pivotal event in the story
(the revolution), the absence of real working-class characters, the
intrinsic affinity between revolutionists and oligarchs as to social
origins, fighting strategies, and political goals, the almost physio-
logical diversity between Superman-like revolutionary leaders and
animal-like rioting masses. Although its interpretive aims remain
rather nebulous, Portelli's analysis has a number of suggestive points
and is worthwhile reading for the further evidence it offers on the
superficial and contradictory quality of London's socialism. In her
introduction to Giulia Angelini's translation of *Adventure* (*Avven-
tura* [Verona: Essedue Edizioni]) Rosella Mamoli Zorzi justifies
the rescue of this minor work of London's from oblivion by cleverly isolating two topical elements: metafiction—London's allusions,
throughout the novel, to the generic conventions and stock devices
he is exploiting—and feminism—the characterization of the female
protagonist, so very different from that of the traditional heroine of
happy-end adventure cum love romances: enterprising and un-
daunted, bright and independent, she puzzles the male protagonist
with her behavior and forces him to reconsider his assumptions
about male prerogatives. This notwithstanding, Mamoli Zorzi cau-
tions, she bespeaks no conversion of London's to the women's cause,
being rather a further embodiment of the "woman-mate" type so
frequent in his fiction.

Exceptionally little has been written this year on 20th-century
fiction. The alternation of utopian dreams with nightmarish visions,
the voicing of anti-Semitic feelings (especially in works written by
Jewish authors), further illustrations of the theme of initiation in
its typically American pattern, a blurring of reality and fiction under
the overriding influence of filmmaking processes are the main features of the "Hollywood novel" that Guido Fink makes the object
of a brilliant overview in his well-informed "Chi è Victor Milgrim e
perché parliamo tanto male di lui? Note sul romanzo hollywoodiano"

(*Paragone*, 394:75–85). Two items concern writers coming from the South. Mario Corona accompanies his own version of Lillian Hellman's *Maybe* (*Una donna segreta* [Roma: Editori Riuniti]) with a sober, well-paced brief introduction. The "colossal despair" at the impossibility of any certainty, metaphorically signified by Sarah's elusiveness in *Maybe*, appears to Corona as an unexpected turn in a writer of deep-set radical feelings. In "Il Sud speculativo di Walker Percy" (*SpM* 14[1980]:75–96) Daniela Fortezza clearly delineates this writer's aims and achievement, focusing on the phases of his philosophical *iter* and on the Southern components in his culture and writings up to *Lancelot*. Although this essay is unlikely to reveal anything new to the specialist, it must be welcomed as the first extended Italian treatment of an author whose work has so far failed, in Italy, to attract the attention it deserves.

Finally, two books on drama can be recommended. In *Storia del teatro americano* (Milano: Bompiani) Sergio Perosa has revised and updated text and bibliography of his 1966 *Il teatro nord-americano*. The bibliography is selective, shrewd, and accurate; the text offers a streamlined and penetrating, richly informative, and well-balanced 204-page account of the American drama from its 18th-century beginnings to the 1960s. The space allotted to the theater prior to 1800 is ampler than in histories of a comparable size, and this enables Perosa to draw attention to the continuity of American drama, both in themes and characters, from its earlier stages to its 20th-century achievements. Ruggero Bianchi's thick-set, 352-page *Off Off & Away. Percorsi processi spazi del Nuovo Teatro americano* (Torino: Studioforma, 1981) is a detailed study of the New American Theater complementing the same author's *Autobiografia dell'avanguardia* (see *ALS 1980*, p. 574). In the first and most substantial section of the book Bianchi sorts out prominent theater groups according to their different aims (political, ritual, or experimental), the different emphasis placed on director- or actor-role, and the different kind of participation asked of the audience. At the same time he stresses what all these groups share—namely, a concern with creative process rather than end product and with space as the performance-defining element. These issues are further explored in the second section through a step-by-step close analysis of four experiments (*Utopia, Inc.* by the Ridiculous Company, the Children's Workshop of the Wooster Group, *Madness and Tranquillity* by Richard Foreman, and

*Edison* by Robert Wilson) as well as in the "marginalia" that conclude the book. Pictures, drawings, diagrams, and long bibliographical notes support and clarify the author's argument. Although Bianchi's avowed purpose is not so much evaluative as descriptive, this book, if a bit hypertrophic and sprawling, provides a well-grounded and timely assessment of the most recent trends in American drama.

*Università di Firenze*

# 22. General Reference Works

## J. Albert Robbins

The year's reference works range from competent to superb, with an exception or two, and continue to require large sums to acquire. A 177-page bibliography by Hugh Holman on the American novel, published five years ago, costs $13.95—in paper covers. A 258-page, hardcover bibliography on interviews—produced by photo-offset from typed copy—costs $16.00 A distinctly large (965-page) letterpress volume on *Twentieth-Century Western Writers* carries a list price of $80.00. Reference books are rapidly being priced beyond the reach, beyond the pocketbooks of many (or should I say most?) scholars.

The ambitious Gale series, *Dictionary of Literary Biography*, continues to proliferate. *DLB* 11, edited by Stanley Trachtenberg, is on *American Humorists, 1800–1950* (683 pages altogether, bound in two volumes); and *DLB* 12, edited by Donald Pizer and Earl N. Harbert, on *American Realists and Naturalists* (465 pages). *American Humorists* provides biographical-critical essays, with selected bibliographical references. Of the 72 humorists, only six are women, only eight were born before 1800, none is black. *Realists and Naturalists* chronicles this important era with 42 author entries, of whom ten are women.

Last year gave us the first of a *Yearbook* series of *DLB* (see *ALS 1981*, p. 523). This year brings the second, *Yearbook: 1981* (issued 1982), with 25 updated entries—some, summations or tributes for recently deceased authors, such as Caroline Gordon; others, new material and even an occasional interview. The other large section consists of 23 "New Entries" (for example, Paul Blackburn, Jack Conroy, Peter Taylor). These yearbook entries are included in the cumulative index, which each new volume carries. In 1982 yet a new *DLB* satellite series was born: *Documentary Series, An Illustrated Chronicle* in two volumes of over 400 pages each. The editor says that this series has two objectives: to make "significant literary documents" accessible; and to supplement the core *DLB* volumes (something I assumed that the yearbooks were doing). In the first documentary volume, Sinclair Lewis is one of the seven authors included. The 62-page segment on Lewis collects seven letters, 11 reviews of Lewis' books, two interviews, two Nobel Prize documents (a statement to the press and the acceptance speech), a mock obituary and the *Time* magazine obituary, plus, of course, an abundance of photos and other visual documents. In *DS* 2 are seven more 20th-century authors—including Richard Wright, the first black author to get documentary treatment.

The year's *DLB* volumes come to a hefty 2,712 pages, with the very hefty price tag of $416. A hefty drain on the budget of even the most affluent libraries. And what I have been describing is just half of the enterprise. Meanwhile, volumes on British literature are coming out.

Each year, it seems, interviews become increasingly popular and appear in journals as diverse as the *Yale Review* and *Playboy*. Until now there has been no guide to this mass of significant material. Stan A. Vrana has compiled *Interviews and Conversations with 20th-Century Authors Writing in English: An Index* (Scarecrow). It is an admirable undertaking—but obviously the 220-page text, covering British, Australian, American, and other English-speaking countries, cannot be more than superficial in so abbreviated a text. I would have liked to see a volume concentrating upon either British or American writers—and more consequent depth. But the author calls it merely an "introductory list," which indeed it is. The larger bibliographical task must someday be undertaken for American writers, with real effort for thorough coverage and, ideally, with abstracts and a thorough subject index.

This was the year for reference aids on western literature: three solid volumes which total 1,856 pages altogether. Two of them are encyclopedic, with basic facts about lives and careers. *Fifty Western Writers: A Bio-Bibliographical Sourcebook* (Greenwood), edited by Fred Erisman and Richard W. Etulain, covers a select number of western writers and gives biographical facts, major themes, a survey of criticism, and short bibliography (of primary and secondary works). Gale's large *Twentieth-Century Western Writers*, edited by James Vinson and D. L. Kirkpatrick, has used a large staff of contributors to write the entries for 300 authors, covering basic biographical facts, primary and secondary bibliographies, and a compact critical assessment. Location of major manuscript collections is also noted. There is an extensive index of book titles. Finally, Richard W. Etulain's *A Bibliographical Guide to the Study of Western American Literature* (Nebraska) is a guide to books and articles—the first third devoted to general works and special topics (such as local color and regionalism, and the Beats); the remainder to books and articles on 369 individual authors. Although there is attention to "the western" short story and novel as genres, be advised that these works deal with western writers geographically. Thus, in one or more of these three volumes such people as these can be found: Gertrude Atherton, Willa Cather, Allen Ginsberg, Hamlin Garland, James Fenimore Cooper, Stephen Crane, Sinclair Lewis, Richard Brautigan. There is a wealth of data and information in these three works.

In a greatly enlarged second edition (which incorporates the contents of the first edition) Norman Kiell has edited a substantial work of 1,269 pages, *Psychoanalysis, Psychology, and Literature: A Bibliography* (2 vols., Scarecrow). The first (1963) edition had 4,460 items; the second edition, 19,674 numbered items—more than a fourfold increase. The oldest entry, the editor tells us, is an article on *Hamlet* published in 1790. There are three indexes (author, title, and subject). This volume should be a useful bibliographic tool in a large and important area, but a word of caution. One suspects a subject index in which there is only one citation under "Novel, anxiety in"! Apparently subjects are indexed solely from key words in titles—not the best way to compile a subject index.

In a fat (898-page) volume, editor James Vinson and a large staff of contributors have compiled a bibliographical document of popular literature, *Twentieth-Century Romance and Gothic Writers* (Gale), covering the English-speaking world. Entries are arranged by author; each one gives biographical facts, a list of publications, and a short critical commentary. There is a record of pseudonyms, and the author's other works outside the romance-gothic genre are given. The editor has provided a lengthy title index.

In 1960 Jarvis Thurston and others published *Short Fiction Criticism: A Checklist of Interpretation since 1925 of Stories and Novelettes (American, British, Continental), 1800–1958*. Now, focusing upon American fiction only, there is an updated volume by Joe

Weixlmann, *American Short-Fiction Criticism and Scholarship, 1959–1977: A Checklist* (Swallow), compiled by examining about 5,000 books and instructors' manuals, "minority" and other journals. This will be an essential work in locating critical and other material on short fiction. Under authors' names, there are items on "General Studies," "Bibliography," and works on individual stories. To give a sense of quantity in the listings, there are 438 items on Poe, 195 on Stephen Crane, and 394 on Faulkner.

What will be a standard reference work for many years was completed in 1982, *American Women Writers: A Critical Reference Guide from Colonial Times to the Present*, edited by Lina Mainiero (4 vols., Ungar, 1979–82). The brief but authoritative biographical-critical sketches are a good starting point for information on women authors.

In an emerging area of ethnic studies, Julio A. Martínez has prepared *Chicano Scholars and Writers: A Bio-Bibliographical Dictionary* (Scarecrow, 1979), citing over 500 living Chicano scholars and writers writing chiefly in Spanish. Under each author's name Martínez provides information on personal data, education, professional and community affiliations, honors, publications, papers and speeches, and a criticism of the biographee's works. The literary scholar should note that, in the subject index, there are entries under "Chicano fiction," "Chicano poetry," and "Chicano drama."

Another aid in another type of ethnic study is Jack W. Marken's *The American Indian: Language and Literature* (Goldentree Bibliographies; AHM, 1978). It lists collections and anthologies, Indian authors, types of Indian literature and criticism and discussion of it, and, most usefully, studies by tribal regions (both U.S. and Canada).

Murray Blackman's *A Guide to Jewish Themes in American Fiction, 1940–1980* (Scarecrow, 1981) cites 1,615 titles of fiction relating to Jews and Judaism. The arrangement is by author, but there is an index to such themes as adolescence, anti-Semitism, Bathsheba, Christian-Jewish relations, death, family relationships, and suicide.

Normally we do not go back four years to pick up overlooked works, but two more titles in the Goldentree Bibliographies series, I feel, should be noted because they are so useful and intelligently selective. One is Charles F. Altieri's *Modern Poetry* (AHM, 1979), which commences with several sections of general studies, followed by single-author entries, ranging from works and other primary materials to reference materials and critical books and essays. The other is the second edition of C. Hugh Holman's *The American Novel through Henry James* (AHM, 1979)—again, commencing with general studies and concluding with author entries. The first edition has been revised, supplemented, and reset, so this makes the earlier edition obsolete. In coverage it comes down through 1976. Both will be useful works of reference to have on one's bookshelf, within handy reach.

Last year the third and last volume of M. Thomas Inge's *Handbook of Popular Culture* appeared (see *ALS 1981*, pp. 521–22). This year Inge has extracted 50 of the topical essays and published them under the title *Concise Histories of American Popular Culture* (Greenwood). Most of them have been revised and updated, some completely rewritten; two essays are new (on dance and on fashion), plus a new essay on the study of popular culture. Eight essays have to do with writing: best sellers, children's literature, detective and mystery fiction, Gothic novels, historical fiction, romantic fiction, verse and popular poetry, and westerns. The others treat such topics as advertising, automobiles, comic art, death, fashion, jazz, physical fitness (currently popular indeed), television, and women (perennially popular). Here is a perfect starting point for research on a popular culture topic if that topic is one of the fifty.

Randy F. Nelson's *Almanac of American Letters* (Los Altos, Calif.: William Kaufmann, 1981) is an almanac in the sense of being a collection of dates, lists, curiosa, and trivia. Examples: "James Russell Lowell introduced Alfred, Lord Tennyson to Bull Durham tobacco." "William Carlos Williams delivered more than 2,000 babies." "Thomas Hardy stole an entire chapter of Longstreet's *Georgia Scenes* to use in his *Trumpet Major*." (How many of those three did you know? Or care to know?) There are chronologies, lists, anecdotes, sections on "Losers," "Banned Books," "Hoaxes, Forgeries, Frauds, Thefts," "Phenomena." Great for browsing, if you like facts and oddities.

A very specialized compilation is Jeanetta Boswell's *Past Ruined Ilion . . . : A Bibliography of English and American Literature Based on Greco-Roman Mythology* (Scarecrow). It is arranged by author into two alphabets: the first, authors making use of mythology, with citation of the works and an abstract; the second, authors and works cited only by titles. For ease of reference each item has a number. A total of 58 Americans are cited in the principal alphabet, with 113 in the secondary alphabet. It is interesting to browse through both lists, finding the ones we would expect (31 poems of Hilda Doolittle and 18 poems and plays of Robinson Jeffers, for example), and some that surprise us (Willa Cather, Wallace Stevens, and James Dickey, for example).

The title of Herbert S. Donow's *The Sonnet in England and America: A Bibliography of Criticism* (Greenwood) is misleading. It stops at 1900 and thus is silent on the varied course of the sonnet in this century. I have not tested the coverage of British sonneteers but that of American poets is poor. He cites only six nineteenth-century American poets—ignoring Washington Allston, James Russell Lowell, and George Henry Boker (who wrote over 300 sonnets). If the one critical item for Poe is typical, his coverage of published scholarship is equally weak. He cites only one article for Poe, whereas the Esther F. Hyneman bibliography of Poe cites four. I deem this bibliography poor.

*Indiana University*

# Author Index

# Subject Index

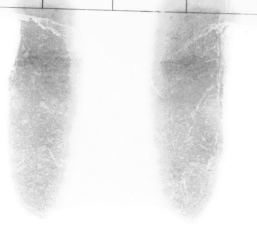

DATE DUE

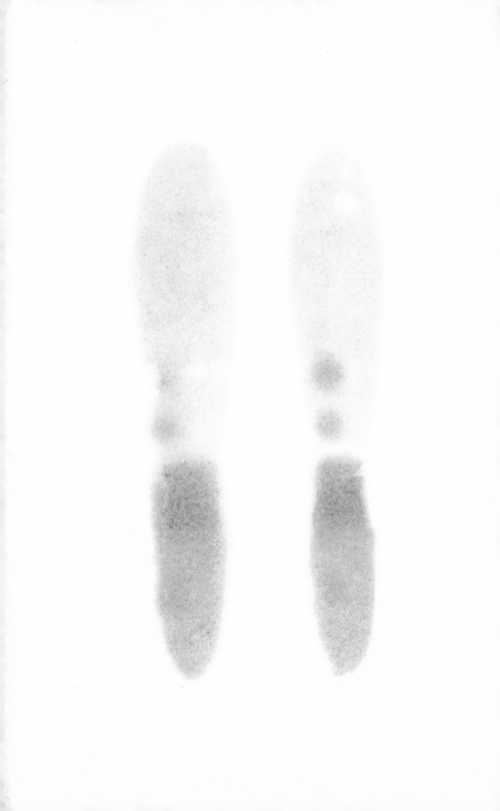